MATERIALS ON THE LAW OF THE EUROPEAN COMMUNITIES

EUROPE INSTITUTE
UNIVERSITY OF AMSTERDAM

MATERIALS ON THE LAW OF THE EUROPEAN COMMUNITIES

FIRST EDITION

Edited by

D.J. Gijlstra and E.L.M. Völker

KLUWER LAW AND TAXATION PUBLISHERS
Deventer/Netherlands
Antwerp · Boston · London · Frankfurt

ISBN 90 6544 069 0

© 1983 Kluwer Law and Taxation Publishers, Deventer/Netherlands

H2781/2/2

INTRODUCTION

The Europa Institute of the University of Amsterdam has for nine years
used as its basic course book in EEC law "Leading Cases and Materials
on the Law of the European Communities".

The expansion of Community law has forced the editors to include more
and more cases at the cost of materials (Regulations, decisions,
resolutions etc.)

Teaching experience suggests that students learn most about European
law when confronted with the original materials read in conjunction
with the cases decided by the Court of Justice of the European Communities.

Therefore we have decided in cooperation with the publishers to produce
two volumes, one containing leading cases and the other basic materials.
The structure of the two volumes is the same. The volume of leading
cases contains cross references to the materials volume.
We have decided not to include any parts of the basic community treaties
since these are widely available.

Selection of materials presents a Hobson's choice. The editors would
therefore welcome critisisms and suggestions for future editions.

The editors are grateful to miss Annelies Kramers, student assistant
at the Europa Institute of the University of Amsterdam, who assisted
with the collection of the materials and to miss Mary Emms,
secretary in the law office Paris, Oldham and Gijlstra, who typed
the manuscript.

Amsterdam, October 1982

D.J. Gijlstra - E.L.M. Völker

V

O.J. (Special Edition 1970) p. 224.

CHAPTER TWO

CHAPTER THREE

Relationship between Community Law and National Law.
Fundamental Rights in the Community.

CHAPTER FOUR

The Foundations of the Community

Second Series, Volume IX), p. 32.

TABLE OF MATERIALS

Chapter One

LANGUAGES, TERRITORIAL APPLICATION AND
INSTITUTIONS OF THE EUROPEAN COMMUNITIES

1. Regulation No. 1

Determining the languages to be used by the
European Economic Community
(JO 1958 No 17 p. 385)

THE COUNCIL OF THE EUROPEAN ECONOMIC COMMUNITY

Having considered Article 217 of the Treaty, pursuant to which the
languages to be used by the institutions of the Community, without prejudice to the rules of procedure of the Court of Justice, shall be
determined by the Council by unanimous vote.

Whereas each of the four languages in which the Treaty is worded is an
official language in one or more of the Member States of the Community,

HAS ADOPTED THE FOLLOWING REGULATION:

Article 1.

The official languages and the working languages of the institutions of
the Community shall be Danish, Dutch, English, French, German, Greek
and Italian.

Article 2.

Documents which a Member State or a person subject to the jurisdiction
of a Member State sends to institutions of the Community may at the
option of the sender be worded in any one of the official languages.
The answer shall be given in the same language.

Article 3.

Documents which an institution of the Community sends to a Member State
or to a person subject to the jurisdiction of a Member State shall be
worded in the language of such State.

Article 4.

Regulations and other documents of general application shall be worded
in the seven official languages.

Article 5.

The Official Journal of the Community shall appear in the seven official
languages.

Article 6.

The institutions of the Community may stipulate in their rules of procedure what languages are to be used in specific cases.

Article 7.

The languages to be used in the proceedings of the Court of Justice shall be laid down in the rules of procedure of the latter.

Article 8.

If a Member State has more than one official language, the language to be used shall at the request of such State be governed by the general rules of its law.

The present regulation is binding in its entirety and is directly enforceable in every Member State

Done at Brussels on 15th April 1958.

By the Council
The President,
V. Larock.

(Amended by the Act of Accession 1972 and Act of Accession 1979)

2. Rules of Procedure of the Court of Justice

Languages

Article 29.

1. The language of a case shall be Danish, Dutch, English, French, German, Greek, Irish or Italian.

2. The language of a case shall be chosen by the applicant, except that:
   (a) where the application is made against a Member State or a natural or legal person having the nationality of a Member State, the language of the case shall be the official language of that State; where that State has more than one official language, the applicant may choose between them;
   (b) at the joined request of the parties the Court may authorize another of the languages mentioned in paragraph 1 of this Article to be used as the language of the case for all or part of the proceedings;
   (c) at the request of one of the parties, and after the opposite party and the Advocate-General have been heard, the Court may, by way of derogation from subparagraphs (a) and (b), authorize another of the languages mentioned in paragraph 1 of this article to be used as the language of the case for all or part of the proceedings;
   such a request may not be submitted by an institution of the European Communities.
   Where Article 103 of these rules applies, the language of the case shall be the language of the national court or tribunal which refers the matter to the Court.

3. The language of the case shall in particular be used not only in parties' written statements and oral addresses to the Court and in supporting documents but also in the minutes and decisions of the Court.
   Supporting documents expressed in any other language must be accompanied by a translation into the language of the case.
   In the case of long documents translations may be confined to extracts. However, the Court or Chamber may, of its own motion or at request of a party, at any time call for a complete or fuller translation.
   Notwithstanding the foregoing provisions, a Member State shall be entitled to use its official language when intervening in a case before the Court or when taking part in any reference of a kind mentioned in Article 103. This provision shall apply both to written statements and to oral addresses. The Registrar shall cause any such statement or address to be translated into the language of the case.

4. Where a witness or expert states that he is unable adequately to express himself in one of the languages referred to in paragraph 1 of this article, the Court or Chamber may authorize him to give his evidence in another language. The Registrar shall arrange for translation into the language of the case.

5. The President of the Court and the President of Chambers in conducting oral proceedings, the Judge Rapporteur both in his preliminary report and in his report at the hearing, Judges and Advocates-General

3

in putting questions and Advocates-General in delivering their opinions may use a language referred to in paragraph 1 of this article
other than the language of the case. The Registrar shall arrange for
translation into the language of the case.

Article 30.

1. The Registrar shall, at the request of any Judge, of the Advocate-
   General or of a party, arrange for anything said or written in the
   course of the proceedings before the Court or a Chamber to be translated into the languages he chooses from those referred to in
   Article 29 (1).

2. Publications of the Court shall be issued in the langauges referred
   to in Article 1 of Council Regulation No 1.

Article 31.

Texts of documents drawn up in the language of the case or in any other
language authorized pursuant to Article 29 of these rules shall be
authentic.
.....

3. Written Question No 489/73

by Lord O'Hagan
to the Commission of the European Communities

(7 November 1973)

(OJ No C 49, 27 April 1974, p. 3)

Subject: North Sea Oil

What is the attitude of the Commission to North Sea Oil? To what extent
does the Commission regard these deposits as a Community resource, and
to what extent as a British resource? In the Commission's thinking on
energy policy, what importance do they attach to North Sea Oil? What
attitude would the Commission adopt if a British Government nationalized existing North Sea oil concessions?

Answer (12 March 1974)

According to present estimates the North Sea oil reserves could in 1980
cover about 15% of Community oil requirements. These reserves clearly
offer very considerable technical and economic advantages to the Member
States who exercise jurisdiction over parts of the North Sea, advantages
which will also accrue through these Member States to the Community as
a whole. In present circumstances there are good reasons why the initial
development of these reserves should be undertaken as quickly as possible. It may be noted in this connection that the Community Regulation
No 3056/73 of 9 November 1973 made possible support for Community projects in the hydrocarbon sector.

More particularly the Commission considers that the provisions of the
Treaty, and the acts of the Community pursuant to the Treaty, clearly
specify the sovereign rights enjoyed by Member States over economic
activities on the Continental Shelf, and in particular over the exploitation and exploration of oil resources. (This view was first stated
by the Commission in its 1970 Memorandum to the Council, in which the
Commission affirmed the applicability of the Treaty as much to the
Continental Shelf as to the mainland territory of Member States.) It
follows that these natural resources belong entirely to the Member
States concerned which may therefore derive the full economic advantages
from them (for example, dues, taxation and balance of payments benefits).
It is of course the case that in the exploitation of these resources,
account must be given to the various provisions of the Treaty which
apply to different aspects of industrial and commercial activity, particularly those governing the principles of freedom of movement of goods
and of establishment, although these rules do not diminish the benefits to the Member States concerned already referred to. The Treaty
does not exclude the possible nationalization by a Member State of any
sector of economic activity, although nationalized industries are of
course also subject to the provisions of the Treaty.

5

4. COUNCIL

Rules of Procedure

adopted by the Council on 24 July 1979 on the basis of Article 5 of the Treaty of 8 April 1965 establishing a single Council and a single Commission of the Eropean Communities

(OJ No L 268, 25 October 1979, p. 1)

Article 1.

1. The Council shall meet when convened by its President on his own initiative or at the request of one of its members or of the Commission.
2. The President shall make known the dates which he envisages for meetings of the Council during his period of office as President, seven months before the beginning thereof.

Article 2.

1. The President shall draw up the provisional agenda for each meeting. The agenda shall be sent to the other members of the Council and to the Commission at least 10 days before the beginning of the meeting.
2. The provisional agenda shall contain the items in respect of which a request for inclusion on the agenda, together with any documents relating thereto, has been received by the General Secretariat from a member of the Council or from the Commission at least 12 days before the beginning of that meeting.
3. Only items in respect of which the documents have been sent to the members of the Council and to the Commission at the latest by the date on which the provisional agenda is sent may be placed on that agenda.
4. The General Secretariat shall transmit to the members of the Council and to the Commission requests for the inclusion of items in the agenda and documents relating thereto in respect of which the time limits specified above were not respected.
5. The agenda shall be adopted by the Council at the beginning of each meeting. The inclusion in the agenda of an item other than those on the provisional agenda shall require unanimity in the Council.
6. The provisional agenda shall be divided into Part A and Part B. Items for which the approval of the Council is possible without discussion shall be included in Part A, but this does not exclude the possibility of any member of the Council or of the Commission expressing an opinion at the time of the approval of these items and having statements included in the minutes.
7. However, an 'A' item shall be withdrawn from the agenda, unless the Council decides otherwise, if a position on an 'A' item might lead to further discussion thereof or if a member of the Council or the Commission so requests.

Article 3.

1. Meetings of the Council shall not be public, unless the Council unanimously decides otherwise.
2. The Commission shall be invited to take part in meetings of the Council. The Council may, however, decide to deliberate without the

6

presence of the Commission.

3. The members of the Council and of the Commission may be accompanied by officials who assist them. The number of such officials may be laid down by the Council.

   Their names and functions shall be notified in advance to the Secretary-General.

4. Admission to meetings of the Council shall be subject to the production of a pass.

Article 4

Subject to the provisions of Article 5 on the delegation of voting rights, a member of the Council who is prevented from attending a meeting may arrange to be represented.

Article 5

1. The members of the Council shall vote in the alphabetical order of the Member States laid down in Article 2 of the Treaty establishing a single Council and a single Commission of the European Communities, beginning with the member who, according to that order, follows the member holding the office of President.

2. Delegation of the right to vote may only be made to another member of the Council.

Article 6

1. Acts of the Council on an urgent matter may be adopted by a written vote where all the members of the Council agree to that procedure in respect of the matter in question.

2. Furthermore, agreement by the Commission to the use of this procedure shall be required where the written vote is on a matter which the Commission has brought before the Council.

3. A summary of acts adopted by the written procedure shall be drawn up every month.

Article 7.

1. Minutes of each meeting shall be drawn up and, when approved, shall be signed by the President-in-office at the time of such approval and by the Secretary-General.

   The minutes shall as a general rule indicate in respect of each item on the agenda:
   - the documents submitted to the Council,
   - the decisions taken or the conclusions reached by the Council,
   - the statements made by the Council and those whose entry has been requested by a member of the Council or the Commission.

2. The draft minutes shall be drawn up by the General Secretariat within 15 days and submitted to the Council for approval.

3. Prior to such approval any member of the Council, or the Commission, may request that more details be inserted in the minutes regarding any item on the agenda.

4. The texts referred to in Article 9 shall be annexed to the minutes.

Article 8.

1. Except as otherwise decided unanimously by the Council on grounds of urgency, the Council shall deliberate and take decisions only on the

basis of documents and drafts drawn up in the languages specified in the rules in force governing languages.

2. Any member of the Council may oppose discussion if the texts of any proposed amendments are not drawn up in such of the said languages as he may specify.

Article 9

The texts of the acts adopted by the Council shall be signed by the President-in-office at the time of their adoption and by the Secretary-General.

Article 10

Regulations of the Council shall include in their title the word 'Regulation', followed by a serial number, by the date of their adoption and by an indication of their subject matter.

Article 11

Council Regulations shall contain the following:

(a) the formula 'The Council of the European Communities';
(b) a reference to the provisions under which the Regulation is adopted, preceded by the words 'Having regard to';
(c) a reference to proposals and opinions obtained and to consultations held;
(d) a statement of the reasons on which the Regulation is based, introduced by the word 'Whereas';
(e) the phrase 'has adopted this Regulation', followed by the body of the regulation.

Article 12

1. Regulations shall be divided into Articles.
2. The last Article shall fix the date of entry into force, where that date is before or after the 20th day following publication. It shall be followed by:
   -'This Regulation shall be binding in its entirety and directly applicable in all Member States.', and
   - 'Done at .....', followed by the date on which the Council adopted the Regulation, and
   - 'For the Council
     The President'
     followed by the name of the President-in-office at the time when the Regulation is adopted.

Article 13

Regulations adopted by the Council shall be published in the Official Journal of the European Communities by the Secretary-General.

Article 14

Directives and Decisions of the Council shall include in their titles the word 'Directive' or 'Decision'.
  The provisions relating to Regulations set out in Article 11 shall also apply to Directives and Decisions.

Article 15

1. The President shall notify Directives, Decisions and recommendations
   of the Council. He may entrust to the Secretary—General the task of
   attending to such notifications on his behalf.
2. The Secretary—General shall send authentic copies of Directives,
   Decisions and recommendations to the Governments of the Member States
   and to the Commission.
3. The Council shall decide unanimously whether Directives, Decisions
   and recommendations should be published for purposes of information
   in the Official Journal of the European Communities.

Article 16

1. The Committee consisting of the Permanent Representatives of the
   Member States referred to in Article 4 of the Treaty establishing
   a single Council and a single Commission of the European Communities
   shall prepare the work of the Council and shall carry out the tasks
   assigned to it by the Council.
2. It may set up working parties and instruct them to carry out such
   preparatory work or studies as it shall define.
3. Unless the Council decides otherwise, the Commission shall be invited
   to be represented in the work of the Committee and of the working
   parties.
4. The Committee shall be presided over by the delegate of that Member
   State whose representative is President of the Council. The same
   shall apply to the working parties, unless the Committee decides
   otherwise.

Article 17

1. The Council shall be assisted by a General Secretariat under the
   direction of a Secretary—General. The Secretary—General shall be
   appointed by the Council acting unanimously.
2. The Council shall determine the organization of the General
   Secretariat.
      Under its authority the Secretary—General shall take all the
   measures necessary to ensure the smooth running of the General
   Secretariat.
3. The Secretary—General shall submit to the Council the draft estimate
   of the expenditure of the Council in sufficient time to ensure the
   respect of the time limits laid down by the financial provisions.
4. In accordance with the provisions of the Financial Regulation referred to in Article 78h of the ECSC Treaty, in Article 209 of the EEC
   Treaty and in Article 183 of the Euratom Treaty, the Secretary-
   General shall administer the funds placed at the disposal of the
   Council.

Article 18

Without prejudice to other applicable provisions, the deliberations
of the Council shall be covered by the obligation of professional
secrecy, except in so far as the Council decides otherwise.
   The Council may authorize the production of a copy or an extract
from its minutes for use in legal proceedings.

Article 19

1. Subject to special procedures, the Council may be represented by its President or by any other of its members before the European Parliament or its Committees.
2. The Council may also present its views to the European Parliament by means of a written statement.

Article 20

Correspondence to the Council shall be sent to the President at the address of the General Secretariat.

Done at Brussels, 24 July 1979.

For the Council

The President

M. O'Kennedy

5. Rules of Procedure of the Commission

(JO No 17, 31 January 1975, p. 81;
OJ Special Edition 1962–1963, p. 9)

THE COMMISSION,

Having regard to the second paragraph of Article 162 of the Treaty,

HAS ADOPTED THESE RULES OF PROCEDURE:

CHAPTER I

THE COMMISSION

Article 1

The Commission shall act collectively in accordance with these Rules.

Section I

Acts of the Commission

Article 2

1. The quorum of members required to be present for the Commission to take valid decisions shall be fixed at eight.
2. In conformity with Article 17, first paragraph, of the Treaty establishing a single Council and a single Commission of the European Communities, the conclusion of the Commission shall be deemed to be adopted when there have been at least eight votes in favour.

Article 3

Meetings of the Commission shall be convened by the President.

The Commission shall, as a general rule, meet at least once a week. It shall hold additional meetings whenever necessary.

Article 4

The President shall prepare the draft agenda for each meeting. Any item put forward by a member of the Commission for inclusion must be placed on the draft agenda.

The draft agenda and the necessary working documents must be circulated to the members of the Commission within the time limit set by the Commission.

Any member of the Commission may request or, in his absence, have a request made for the deferment to a later meeting of the discussion of an item on the draft agenda.

The Commission, having before it the draft agenda and any requests for amendments thereto, shall approve the agenda at its meeting. It may decide unanimously to discuss a question which is not on the draft agenda or in respect of which the necessary working documents have been distributed late.

Article 5

The President of the Commission shall take the chair at meetings.

Article 6

Five members present shall constitute a quorum.

Article 7

In accordance with the first paragraph of Article 163 of the Treaty, acts of the Commission shall require for their adoption at least five votes in favour.

Article 8

Meetings of the Commission shall not be public.

Discussions shall be confidential.

Article 9

Save as otherwise decided by the Commission, the Executive Secretary to the Commission and his deputy shall   attend meetings.

In the absence of a member of the Commission, one of the members of his personal staff may attend the meeting and state the views of the absent member.

The President may, at the request of a member of the Commission, invite certain officials to be present for the whole or part of any meeting and to speak. The Commission may, by way of exception, decide to hear any other person at a meeting.

Article 10

Minutes shall be taken of all meetings of the Commission.

The draft minutes shall be submitted to the Commission for approval at a subsequent meeting. The approved minutes shall be authenticated by the signature of the President and the countersignature of the Executive Secretary.

Article 11

The agreement of the Commission to a proposal by one of its members may be obtained by means of a written procedure.

For this purpose, the text of the proposal shall be circulated in writing to all members of the Commission, with a time limit within which members must notify any reservations or amendments they wish to make.

Any member of the Commission may, in the course of the written procedure, request that the proposal be discussed at a meeting. In such case, the matter shall be placed on the agenda of the next meeting of the Commission.

A proposal on which no member of the Commission has made a reservation and maintained it up to the time limit set for a written procedure shall be deemed to be agreed by the Commission. Such agreement shall be noted in the minutes of the next meeting.

The Commission shall establish detailed rules for giving effect to this Article.

Article 12

Acts adopted by the Commission, at a meeting or by written procedure, shall be authenticated in the language or languages in which they are binding by the signatures of the President and the Executive Secretary.

The texts of such acts shall be annexed to the minutes in which their adoption is recorded.

The President shall, as may be required, notify acts adopted by the Commission to those to whom they are addressed.

Section II

Preparation and implementation of acts of the Commission

Article 13

The Commission may assign to its members responsibility for the preparation and implementation of acts of the Commission in particular fields.

Where a field of responsibility specially assigned to a member of the Commission coincides with that of a Directorate-General or equivalent department, the latter shall take its instructions from that member.

Article 14

The Commission may set up working groups of its members for the preparation of its discussions, in particular on matters within the field of responsibility of a Directorate-General or equivalent department.

Where a working group is concerned with a field of responsibility specially assigned to a member of the Commission under Article 13, that member shall be chairman of the group.

Article 15

The President and members of the Commission may each appoint personal staff to assist them in their work.

Article 16

The Executive Secretary shall assist the President in the preparation of meetings of the Commission, in implementing the written procedures provided for in Article 11, and in ensuring that propoer effect is given to acts of the Commission.

To this end, he shall see that the rules are complied with regarding submission of documents which the Commission is to consider and shall acquaint himself with the manner in which acts of the Commission are being implemented.

He shall take the necessary steps to ensure official notification of acts of the Commission and their publication in the Official Journal of the European Communities.

He shall be responsible for day-to-day liaison with the other institutions of the European Communities, subject to any decision by the Commission to exercise any function itself or to assign it to its members or departments.

CHAPTER II

ADMINISTRATION

Article 17

A number of departments forming a single administrative service shall assist the Commission in the performance of its official functions.

The first paragraph of this Article shall be without prejudice to the provisions of Article 13.

Article 18

The administrative services of the Commission shall consist of Directorates-General and equivalent departments.

Directorates-General shall be divided into Directorates, and Directorates into Divisions.

Article 19

The Commission shall establish a table of duties, in which the functions of each Directorate-General, Directorate and Division are so defined as to minimize overlapping and duplication.

In special cases the allocation of duties within a Directorate-General or equivalent department may be temporarily modified for the duration of the current budget year by the member of the Commission who is responsible for that Directorate-General or department in pursuance of Article 13. Such modification shall at once be brought to the notice of the Commission, which may reverse it.

Article 20

The basic administrative unit shall be a Division.

Related matters should be grouped within a Division; undue fragmentation of responsibilities is to be avoided.

As a general rule, each matter as it arises must be assigned to a Division.

Article 21

The administrative units of the Commission shall work in the closest possible coordination. Before submitting a document to the Commission they must advise all departments which, according to the table of duties or from the nature of the subject, are concerned in the matter, so as to avoid duplication and so that their agreement or comments may be obtained.

The department responsible for the document shall endeavour to reach agreement with the departments consulted on a single proposal. In the event of disagreement, it must mention in its proposal the differing views expressed by the departments consulted.

Article 22

All departmental communications, whether written or oral, must be made through the official channels, save where special instructions are issued.

Unless authorized to take decisions themselves, staff should lay before or refer to their immediate superior all proposals, reports, statements of views, etc.

A superior may amend the form and content of any draft submitted to him; a draft submitted by a subordinate shall, at his request, be placed on the file.

Article 23

All official business must be dispatched as promptly and economically as possible. Expedited action should be requested only in exceptional cases and where really necessary.

If a matter cannot be settled quickly, an interim reply must be sent; this applies especially in dealings with individuals.

All official business requires a decision in writing showing how it has been dealt with or what action is to be taken; such decision may be handwritten on the original document.

CHAPTER III

Deputizing and Delegation of Powers

Article 24

If the President is prevented from exercising his functions, they shall be exercised by one of the Vice-Presidents chosen in the order laid down by the Commission. If the President and the Vice-Presidents are prevented from exercising those functions, they shall be exercised by the longest serving member and, in the event of equal length of service, by the senior member by age.

Article 25

Where the Executive Secretary is prevented from exercising his functions, they shall be exercised by the Deputy Executive Secretary or, where this is not possible, by an official designated by the Commission.

Article 26

Save as otherwise decided by the Commission, where any senior official is prevented from exercising his functions, his place shall be taken by the longest serving subordinate official present and, in the event of equal length of service, by the official who is the senior by age in the highest category and grade.

Article 27

Subject to the principle of collegiate responsibility being respected in full the Commission may empower its members to take, in its name and subject to its control, clearly defined measures of management or administration.

Officials may also be empowered to take such measures if this is indispensable for the Commission properly to be able to fulfil its tasks.

Unless they have been delegated to him personally powers vested in an official shall be valid for his deputy.

Powers conferred in this way may not be sub-delegated except to the extent expressly laid down in the enabling decision.

The provisions of this article shall not affect the rules concerning delegation in respect of financial matters and staff administration.

Article 28

Provisions of these Rules of Procedure relating to members of the Commission shall also apply to the President and Vice-President of the Commission.

Final provision

Article 29

These Rules of Procedure shall be published in the Official Journal of the European Communities.

Done at Brussels, 9 January 1963.

For the Commission

The President

Walter Hallstein

(as amended in 1967, 1975 and 1981; JO No 147, 11-7-1967, p. 1; OJ No L 199, 30-7-1975, p. 43; OJ No L8, 8-1-1981, p. 16).

6. Organization of European Council Meetings

Agreement reached at the meeting of the European
Council in London, 29 and 30 June 1977.
(Bull EC 1-1977, p. 83)

Prior to the European Council meeting in Rome at the end of March, the
Presidency circulated a paper which sought to establish points of agreement which had emerged from the correspondence between Heads of Government about the ways in which the organization of European Council meetings might be improved. In the light of the discussion at that meeting,
which was followed up by Foreign Ministers on 5 April, the following
points are understood to represent a generally acceptable framework for
the organization of future meetings:

(a)   Types of discussion

There is general agreement that the European Council should have both:
(i) informal exchanges of view of a wide-ranging nature held in the
     greatest privacy and not designed to lead to formal decisions or
     public statements;
(ii)discussions which are designed to produce decisions, settle guide-
     lines for future action or lead to the issue of public statements
     expressing the agreed view of the European Council.
It is also recognized that the European Council will sometimes need
to fulfil a third function, namely to settle issues outstanding from
discussions at a lower level. In dealing with matters of Community
competence the European Council will conform to the appropriate procedures laid down in the Community Treaties and other agreements.

(b)   Advance preparation of the agenda

For informal exchanges of view,   it is generally agreed that little
preparation is necessary, although some limited prior clarification of
the questions is not to be excluded if it would facilitate discussion.
Heads of Government should inform each other or the Presidency, a few
days beforehand, of the subjects which they will wish to discuss.
There is general agreement that there should be adequate preparation
of those discussions which are aimed at reaching decisions or issuing
statements. Foreign Ministers should have responsibility for such
preparation, which could take place in the Council or the Political
Cooperation machinery as appropriate, and will wish to meet at an
appropriate time, and if necessary to hold a special meeting before
the European Council, for this purpose.

(c)   The issuing of statements

It is generally agreed that the European Council will wish to make
public its decisions on some subjects or sometimes to issue a statement registering a concerted Community opinion on a topic of international concern.Such statements should not, other than in exceptional
circumstances, be issued without advance preparation. A list of the
subjects on which it is proposed statements should be issued should be
drawn up two to three weeks in advance.

(d)   The recording of conclusions

17

There should be no record of the informal exchanges of view between Heads of Government. For the discussion aimed at reaching decisions or issuing statements there should be a written record of conclusions, which should be issued on the authority of the Presidency.

(e) Attendance of officials

There is general agreement that the exchanges of views should be as intimate as possible and that attendance should be restricted as at present.

----

7. Luxembourg Agreement 1966

(Bull EC 3-1966, p. 8)

At the meeting of 28 and 29 January the Six reached agreement and the following statements were issued:

a) Relations between the Commission and the Council

Close cooperation between the Council and the Commission is essential for the functioning and development of the Community.

In order to improve and strengthen this co-operation at every level, the Council considers that the following practical methods of co-operation should be applied, these methods to be adopted by joint agreement, on the basis of Article 162 of the EEC Treaty, without compromising the respective competences and powers of the two institutions.

1. Before adopting any particularly important proposal, it is desirable that the Commission should take up the appropriate contacts with the Governments of the Member States, through the Permanent Representatives, without this procedure compromising the right of initiative which the Commission derives from the Treaty.
2. Proposals and any other official acts which the Commission submits to the Council and to the Member States are not to be made public until the recipients have had formal notice of them and are in possession of the texts.

   The "Journal Officiel" (official gazette) should be arranged so as to show clearly which acts are of binding force. The methods to be employed for publishing those texts whose publication is required will be adopted in the context of the current work on the re-organization of the "Journal Officiel".
3. The credentials of Heads of Missions of non-member States accredited to the Community will be submitted jointly to the President of the Council and to the President of the Commission, meeting together for this purpose.
4. The Council and the Commission will inform each other rapidly and fully of any approaches relating to fundamental questions made to either institution by the representatives of non-member States.
5. Within the scope of application of Article 162, the Council and the Commission will consult together on the advisability of, the procedure for, and the nature of any links which the Commission might establish with international organizations pursuant to Article 229 of the Treaty.
6. Co-operation between the Council and the Commission on the Community's information policy, which was the subject of the Council's discussions on 24 September 1963, will be strengthened in such a way that the programme of the Joint Information Service will be drawn up and carried out in accordance with procedures which are to be decided upon at a later date, and which may include the establishment of an ad hoc body.
7. Within the framework of the financial regulation relating to the drawing up and execution of the Communities' budgets, the Council and the Commission will decide on means for more effective control over the commitment and expenditure of Community funds.

(b) Majority voting procedure

I. Where, in the case of decisions which may be taken by majority vote
on a proposal of the Commission, very important interests of one or
more partners are at stake, the Members of the Council will endeavour,
within a reasonable time, to reach solutions which can be adopted by
all the Members of the Council while respecting their mutual interests and those of the Community, in accordance with Article 2 of the
Treaty.

II.With regard to the preceding paragraph, the French delegation considers that where very important interests are at stake the discussion must be continued until unanimous agreement is reached.

III The six delegations note that there is a divergence of views on
what whould be done in the event of a failure to reach complete
agreement.

IV.The six delegations nevertheless consider that this divergence does
not prevent the Community's work being resumed in accordance with the
normal procedure.

The members of the Council agreed that decisions on the following should
be by common consent.

a) The financial regulation for agriculture;

b) Extensions to the market organization for fruit and vegetables;

c) The regulation on the organization of sugar markets;

d) The regulation on the organization of markets for oils and fats;

e) The fixing of common prices for milk, beef and veal, rice, sugar,
olive oil and oil seeds.

Finally the Council drew up the following programme of work:

(1) The draft EEC and Euratom budgets will be approved by written procedure before 15 February 1966.

(2) The EEC Council will meet as soon as possible to settle as a matter
of priority the problem of financing the common agricultural policy.
Concurrently, discussions will be resumed on the other questions, particularly the trade negotiations in GATT and the problems of adjusting
national duties on imports from non-member countries.

(3) The Representatives of the Member States' Governments will meet on
the day fixed for the next Council meeting and will begin discussions
on the composition of the new single Commission and on the election
of the President and Vice-Presidents.
    Theywill also agree on the date - in the first half of 1966 - when
instuments of ratification of the Treaty on the merger of the institutions are to be deposited, on condition that the required parliamentary
ratifications have been obtained and agreement has been reached on the
composition and on the presidency and vice-presidency of the Commission.

----

8. Second Report (Copenhagen)
   on European political cooperation
   on Foreign policy
   10 - 11 September 1973
   (Bull EC 6-1973 p. 14)

Part I

The Heads of State or of Government of the Member States of the European Communities approved on 27 October 1970 the Report of the Foreign
Ministers drawn up in implementation of paragraph 15 of the Communiqué
of The Hague Conference of 1 and 2 December 1969. The document reflected
the belief that progress towards concerted action in the field of
foreign policy was likely to promote the development of the Communities
and to help the Europeans to realise more fully their common responsibilities. The objectives of that cooperation are:

(i) to ensure, by means of regular consultations and exchanges of information, improved mutual understanding as regards the main problems
of international relations;

(ii) to strengthen solidarity between governments by promoting the
harmonization of their views and the alignment of their positions and,
wherever it appears possible and desirable, joint action.

The Report also proposed that the Foreign Ministers should submit a
second general report which would, inter alia, contain an assessment
of the results obtained from such consultation. At the time when the
enlargement of the European Communities became a fact, paragraph 14 of
the Summit Declaration in Paris on 21 October 1972 required the Foreign
Ministers to produce by 30 June 1973 a second report on methods of improving political cooperation in accordance with the Luxembourg Report.
   The Heads of State or of Government, meeting in Paris, expressed
their satisfaction at the results obtained since the political cooperation machinery was formally set up on the basis of the texts of 27
October 1970. In several fields, the Member States have been able to
consider and decide matters jointly so as to make common political action possible. This habit has also led to the 'reflex' of coordination
among the Member States which has profoundly affected the relations of
the Member States between each other and with third countries. This
collegiate sense in Europe is becoming a real force in international
relations.
   The Ministers note that the characteristically pragmatic mechanisms
set up by the Luxembourg Report have shown their flexibility and effectiveness. What is involved in fact is a new procedure in international
relations and an original European contribution to the technique of
arriving at concerted action. The experience acquired so far has resulted in a strengthening of the belief in the usefulness of concerted action by means of direct contact between senior officials of Foreign
Ministries and of a very thorough preparation of the matters under consideration as a basis for the decisions by Ministers.
   Such concerted action has also had a positive influence in so far
as it has brought a more conscious collaboration between representatives
of Member States of the Communities in third countries. They have been
encouraged to meet and compare the information available to them. This
habit of working together has enabled the procedure for concerted action to become more widespread wherever common action or common consider-

ation seemed desirable.

In the Luxembourg Report provision was made for the Commission to be invited to make known its views when the work of the Ministers affected the activities of the European Communities. The Foreign Ministers express satisfaction that these contacts have now become a reality and that a constructive and continuing dialogue is in course both at the level of experts and of the Political Committee, and at ministerial meetings.

The colloquy with the Political Commission of the European Parliament and the communication by the President of the Council to the European Parliament have put into effect the desire of the Foreign Ministers to make a contribution to the democratic character of the construction of political union.

The final Declaration of the Conference of Heads of State or of Government held on 19-21 October 1972 expressed, inter alia, the conviction that Europe must be able to make its voice heard in world affairs and to affirm its own views in international relations.

Europe now needs to establish its position in the world as a distinct entity, especially in international negotiations which are likely to have a decisive influence on the international equilibrium and on the future of the European Community.

In the light of this it is essential that, in the spirit of the conclusion of the Paris Summit Conference, cooperation among the Nine on foreign policy should be such as to enable Europe to make an original contribution to the international equilibrium. Europe has the will to do this, in accordance with its traditionally outward-looking mission and its interest in progress, peace and cooperation. It will do so, loyal to its traditional friends and to the alliances of its Member States, in the spirit of good neighbourliness which must exist between all the countries of Europe both to the east and the west, and responding to the expectations of all the developing countries.

The results obtained by the procedure of political consultation since its inception, referred to in the preceeding paragraphs, are the subject of a descriptive Annex attached to this Report.

Part II

In implementation of the task entrusted to them by paragraph 14 of the Paris Summit Declaration, and having regard to the objective which the Heads of State or of Government set themselves, namely to transform, before the end of the present decade, the whole complex of the relations between the Member States of the European Communities into a European Union, the Foreign Ministers propose that the Heads of State or of Government approve the following measures:

1. Ministerial Meetings

Henceforth, the Foreign Ministers will meet four times a year. They may also, whenever they consider it necessary to consult each other on specific subjects between meetings, meet for that purpose when they happen to come together on other occasions.

2. The Political Committee of the Member States of the European
   Communities

The Political Directors of the Member States of the Community will meet in the Political Committee of the Member States of the European Communities with a view to preparing ministerial meetings and carrying out tasks entrusted to them by the Ministers. In order to attain that objective, meetings of the Committee will be held as frequently as the intensification of the work requires.

3. The Group of 'Correspondants'

A group consisting of European 'Correspondants' in the Foreign Ministry (called the Group of Correspondants) will be set up. That Group will be entrusted with the task of following the implementation of political cooperation and of studying problems of organization and problems of a general nature. Furthermore, for certain matters, the Group will prepare the work of the Political Committee on the basis of instructions given by that Committee.

4. Working Parties

(a) In order to ensure more thorough consultation on individual questions, working parties will be set up to bring together senior officials of the Ministries of Foreign Affairs responsible for the subject under consideration. These working parties will cease to meet as soon as they have completed the task entrusted to them. Exceptionally, and especially in order to ensure continuity if the work can be completed in the near future, the chairman of a working party may be required to continue in office beyond the usual period.

(b) The chairman in office may approach the Political Committee about the need to bring together senior officials of the major ministerial departments who have not met during the preceding six month period with a view to keeping them in contact with each other.

5. Medium and Long-Term Studies

In accordance with paragraph 14 of the Declaration of the Paris Summit Conference, which set as an objective of political cooperation the formulation, where possible, of common medium and long term positions, several methods of work can be envisaged. According to circumstances, this will be done either by groups of experts in addition to the current matters which they normally deal with, or by entrusting the preparations of such studies to a special analysis and reasearch group consisting normally of officials.
The Political Committee will propose to the Foreign Ministers specific subjects for study.

6. The rôle of the Embassies of the Nine in the Capitals of the Member countries of the Community

The Embassies of the Nine participate closely in the implementation of political cooperation. In particular, they receive information on a Community basis issued by the Foreign Ministry of their country of residence. Furthermore, they are occasionally entrusted with consultations on specific subjects:

(i) at the seat of the Presidency at the request of the Political Committee, the Presidency or another Member State; or

(ii) in another Capital at the request of the Foreign Ministry.

They will appoint one of their diplomatic staff who will specifically

23

be entrusted with ensuring the necessary contacts with the Foreign
Ministry of their country of residence, within the framework of political cooperation.

7. Rôles of the Embassies in third countries and of the Offices of
   Permanent Representatives to major international organizations

With the introduction of the political cooperation machinery, it proved
useful to associate Embassies and Permanent Representatives' offices
with the work. In the light of the experience gained, better information
on the work in progress in the field of political cooperation should be
provided so as to enable them, where necessary, to put forward in an
appropriate form those aspects which they consider of interest for
this work, including considerations on joint action.

With this in mind, the Political Committee will notify the missions
concerned when it considers it necessary to obtain a contribution on a
specific item of its agenda. Where appropriate, it may require a common
report to be prepared by them on specific questions.

In addition to the provisions contained in the texts in force governing reciprocal information on the occasion of importan visits, the
Ambassador concerned, accredited in the country where the visit takes
place, should first provide information to his colleagues on the spot
so as to enable any appropriate exchange of views. After the visit,
such information as may interest them should be given to them in the
most appropriate manner.

Finally, in application of the provisions governing the rôle of
missions abroad, the permanent representatives of the Member States to
the major international organizations will regularly consider matters
together and, on the basis of instructions received, will seek common
positions in regard to important questions dealt with by those organizations.

8. The Presidency

As regards the internal organization of the work of political cooperation, the Presidency:

(i) sees to it that the conclusions adopted at meetings of Ministers
and of the Political Committee are implemented on a collegiate basis;

(ii) proposes, on its own initiative or on that of another State, consultation at an appropriate level;

(iii) may also, between meetings of the Political Committee, meet the
Ambassadors of the Member States in order to inform them to the progress
of the political cooperation. The meeting may take place at the request
of an Ambassador of a Member State seeking consultation on a specific
subject.

Experience has also shown that the Presidency's task presents a
particularly heavy administrative burden. Administrative assistance
may therefore be provided by other Member States for specific tasks.

9. Improvement of contact between the Nine

The Foreign Ministers have agreed to establish a communications system
with a view to facilitating direct contact between their departments.

10. Relations with the European Parliament

Having regard to the widening scope of the European Communities and the intensification of political cooperation at all levels, four colloquies will be held each year at which the Ministers will meet with members of the Political Committee of the European Parliament. For the purpose of preparing the colloquies, the Political Committee will draw to the attention of Ministers proposals adopted by the European Parliament on foreign policy questions.

In addition the Minister exercising the function of President will continue, as in the past, to submit to the European Parliament, once a year, a communication on progress made in the field of political co-operation.

11. Priorities to be set in respect of the matters to be dealt with within the framework of Political Cooperation

Governments will consult each other on all important foreign policy questions and will work out priorities, observing the following criteria:

(i) the purpose of the consultation is to seek common policies on practical problems;

(ii) the subjects dealt with must concern European interests whether in Europe itself or elsewhere where the adoption of a common position is necessary or desirable.

On these questions each State undertakes as a general rule not to take up final positions without prior consultation with its partners within the framework of the political cooperation machinery.

The Political Committee will submit to the meetings of Foreign Ministers subjects among which the Ministers may select those to be given priority in the course of political cooperation. This is without prejudice to the examination of additional subjects either at the suggestion of a Member State or as a result of recent developments.

12. Relationship between the work of the political cooperation machinery and that carried out within the framework of the European Communities

(a) The political cooperation machinery, which deals on the intergovernmental level with problems of international politics, is distinct from and additional to the activities of the institutions of the Community which are based on the juridical commitments undertaken by the Member States in the Treaty of Rome. Both sets of machinery have the aim of contributing to the development of European unification. The relationship between them is discussed below.

(b) The Political cooperation machinery, which is responsible for dealing with questions of current interest and where possible for formualating common medium and long term positions, must do this keeping in mind, inter alia, the implications for and the effects of, in the field of international politics, Community policies under construction.

For matters which have an incidence on Community activities close contact will be maintained with the institutions of the Community.

(c) The last section of the previous paragraph is implemented in the following way:
(i) the Commission is invited to make known its views in accordance with current practice;
(ii) the Council, through the President of the Committee of Permanent Representatives, is informed by the Presidency of the agreed conclusions

which result from the work of the Political Cooperation machinery, to
the extent that these conclusions have an interest for the work of the
Community;
(iii) the Ministers will similarly be able, if it is so desired, to
construct the political cooperation machinery to prepare studies on
certain political aspects of problems under examination in the framework of the Community. These reports will be transmitted to the Council
through the President of the Committee of Permanent Representatives.

In drawing up this Report, the Ministers have demonstrated their
belief that even more important than the contents of their proposals is
the spirit in which these are put into effect. That spirit is the one
that emerges from the decisions taken at the Paris Summit meeting.
    The Ministers consider that cooperation on foreign policy must be
placed in the perspective of European Union.
    From now on, it is of the greatest importance to seek common posit-
ions on major international problems.

----

9. Extract of the Communiqué after the Conference of Heads of Government in Paris on 9 and 10 December 1974

(Bull EC 12-1974, p. 7)

1. The heads of Government of the nine States of the Community, the Ministers of Foreign Affairs and the President of the Commission, meeting in Paris at the invitation of the French President, examined the various problems confronting Europe. They took note of the reports drawn up by the Ministers of Foreign Affairs and recorded the agreement reached by these Ministers on various points raised in the reports.

2. Recognizing the need for an overall approach to the internal problems involved in achieving European unity and the external problems facing Europe, the Heads of Government consider it essential to ensure progress and overall consistency in the activities of the Communities and in the work on political cooperation.

3. The Heads of Government have therefore decided to meet, accompanied by the Ministers of Foreign Affairs, three times a year and, whenever necessary, in the Council of the Communities and in the context of political cooperation.

The administrative secretariat will be provided for in an appropriate manner with due regard for existing practices and procedures.

In order to ensure consistency in Community activities and continuity of work, the Ministers of Foreign Affairs, meeting in the Council of the Community, will act as initiators and coordinators. They may hold political cooperation meetings at the same time.

These arrangements do not in any way affect the rules and procedures laid down in the Treaties or the provisions on political cooperation in the Luxembourg and Copenhagen Reports. At the various meetings referred to in the preceding paragraphs the Commission will exercise the powers vested in it and play the part assigned to it by the above texts.

4. With a view to progress toward European unity, the Heads of Government reaffirm their determination gradually to adopt common positions and coordinate their diplomatic action in all areas of international affairs which affect the interests of the European Community. The President-in-Office will be spokesman for the Nine and will set out their views in international diplomacy. He will ensure that the necessary concertation always takes place in good time. In view of the increasing role of political cooperation in the construction of Europe, the European Assembly must be more closely associated with the work of the Presidency, for example through replies to questions on political cooperation put to him by its Members.

----

10. Report from the Commission to the Council
    pursuant to the mandate of 30 May 1980

(Bulletin of the European Communities,
supplement 1981/1)

1. At the end of the war the lessons of history led the countries of
Europe to choose interdependence as the basis for reconstruction.
Thus the construction of Europe has come about in a way which means
that a shared inheritance already exists.

   Today the Community's institutions owe it to the people of Europe,
and to history, to defend and develop his inheritance. The Commission
has been given responsibility for directing this development: it has
a constant duty to preserve what has been achieved and act in such a
way that the people of Europe come to regard the Community as the surest
way of shaping and influencing the future.

   It is in this spirit that the Commission submits its replies to the
mandate given by the Council on 30 May 1980.[1)]

2. In a period of world crisis this organized Europe must use its
strength to loosen the external constraints that bind it. Its size
places it in a better position to get to grips with the problems affecting it, whether these be energy, international competition, inflation or unemployment. The degree of integration which has been achieved
but which has yet to be exploited to the full, has increased the means
available for confronting these problems.

3. Aside from the use which can be made of such Community measures, the
scale of the present problems calls for a joint strategy based on a
strengthened internal solidarity and the adoption of a more vigorous
stand towards the outside world. If this were generally accepted, if
the strategy were made sufficiently broad and credible, this potential
force could be harnessed to generating internal change, guaranteeing
the success of the third enlargement and giving renewed confidence
and hope to a young generation concerned about the future.

   The Community, soon to be enlarged to twelve can set an example to
the world by adopting a constructive approach to the problems facing
mankind. This is a formidable task, but the challenge of having to
extend this approach beyond our own frontiers and of fulfilling the
expectations of those who refuse to give in to fear and egotism is an
exciting one.

4. If they are to tackle this ambitious task, the institutions must
resolve without hesitation to fulfil the political alliance entered into by each Member State when it signed the original Treaties or the
Treaties of Accession.

   In this way the Community will finally take its rightful place in
the world and become a catalyst for peace and development as it already
is for its Member States.

5. The Commission is of the firm view that a return to the institutional balance provided for in the Treaties would help to re-establish the
unity of purpose which prevailed when the Community was created. Without a process of decision-making based on a better balance between the
contributions made by all the institutions, the Community will never
regain its dynamism or live up to the expectations of the people of
Europe.

Finally, the Commission considers that there can be no development of Community activities as long as the Community budget remains artificially limited by the current ceiling on its resources. It will take the initiatives required to have this constraint removed.

6. The construction of the Community, founded on solidarity and economic integration, and with the constant improvement of living and working conditions as its declared goal, has developed on a twofold basis:

- a single internal market governed by jointly-devised competition rules which guarantee the free movement of goods and allow Community industry to reap the benefits of an extensive market;

- a common agricultural policy which allows the free movement of agricultural products, this raising the standard of living of Europe's agricultural community - traditionally the less favoured section of the population - and guaranteeing our food supplies.

These two achievements need to be completed by a monetary system, which is essential for balanced economic development and progress towards the free movement of people, services and capital. The common commercial policy and the Community's development policy should enable the Community to fulfil its appropriate role in the world. Additional policies should be established to cope with specific situations which market rules alone cannot regulate satisfactorily.

7. It has to be said that up to now action has not been taken at the same rate in all areas. This is doubtless one of the factors underlying the crisis currently facing the Community and the consequent lack of confidence.

Furthermore, the changes in the world economy over the last ten years and the upheavals that have occurred in internationl relations have shown that existing policies will have to be developed or revised.

8. At present, the budget reflects the imbalance between Community policies, but the Commission considers that the budgetary aspect alone gives only a partial idea of the nature of the Community. In particular, it gives no idea of those policies which have no budgetary dimension, such as competition policy, or which have so far had a virtually negligible impact, such as industrial and energy policy. In any case, Community policies have economic implications that go well beyond the purely budgetary aspect.

This is why the Commission has chosen not to confine itself to a purely budgetary view in implementing its mandate.

9. An effort must be made in all areas to make up for lost time. This is the only way of ensuring that unacceptable situations do not recur and ensuring that consideration is given to the interests of all present or future Member States.

It is unrealistic to talk in terms of large-scale industrial restructuring or more balanced agricultural development if no progress is made towards economic and monetary union, or to talk in terms of full freedom of movement for workers in the absence of an employment policy capable of affording a coherent answer at Community level to the unemployment problem. The increasingly important rule which the Community should be playing in the world will be illusory if it is seen to be at the expense of the weakest regions and sectors of activity.

The Commission believes that if an overall Community strategy were to be evolved, based on a general approach and guiding principles to which all could subscribe without hesitation, then the greater discipline and solidarity that this would entail would open up new prospects for stable, and therefore lasting growth and fuller employment.

10. The Commission accordingly proposes that as regards monetary and economic questions the Community should build on a foundation of genuine - and much tighter - internal coordination between the Member States, coupled with a clearly-defined common stance toward the outside world, so as to enhance the effects of national policies, consolidate the zone of monetary stability which it is endeavouring to construct, and take responsibility for defending European interests vis-a-vis our trading partners.

Expansion of the European Monetary System could be a powerful force in making such a policy succeed, once all the Member States were participating in it and the commitment to place the ECU at the centre of the system had been realized. The needs of the Community's economy and the state of the international monetary system are such that decisive and rapid progress must be made towards a fully institutionalized European Monetary System.

11. Equal priority attaches to systematic exploitation of the opportunities provided by the European market. If we are to develop a modern and dynamic industrial sector in Europe, it is essential that we have a single integrated market as this allows firms to benefit from outlets on a continental scale and to invest with the same degree of security as their American or Japanese competitors. Community firms must fully exploit the stock of confidence which flows from a genuine internal market defined in both economic and legal terms.

The customs union was one of the Community's first real achievements. If it is to be completed, the variety of remaining barriers which are still preventing the completion of the single market must as a priority be eliminated. The Commission will take the specific initiatives in this respect. It is quite legitimate for public authorities - and Community authorities whenever their powers permit - to maintain their contribution to the creation of a better economic environment to promoting and to raising productivity.

12. Nevertheless, the opportunities provided by a genuine internal market are no longer sufficient in themselves to enable the Community to complete the process of economic change, given the crippling uncertainties which beset it. A new dynamism is required, which can transform action and attitudes and thus help to overcome the upheavals provoked by the evergy crisis, as well as to catch up on the growing delays in the research field and to get industrial innovation off the ground at last.

The failure to pursue a number of quite reasonable objectives - such as substituting Community cooperation for fragmented and isolated national policies, choosing the path of initiative rather than accepting the existing situation, combining financial resources rather than dispersing them, reaping the benefits in external relations of positions agreed in advance - has prevented the Community from benefiting from its size. A new strategy must be proposed for facing up to the challenges of the 1980s.

13. Energy production, particularly the new forms of energy and the industries involved in developing them, offers considerable potential in terms of growth and employment. Furthermore, by helping to ease

pressures on the balance of payments, a successful energy policy will create the conditions for an economic upturn.

The Commission intends to propose that precise targets be set, firstly to achieve essential savings and secondly to expand the means of energy production, build the necessary infrastructure, diversify sources of supply and encourage the use of new forms of energy. It will help to finance these activities by coordinating national resources and making greater use of Community instruments. Small and medium-sized enterprises will be closely involved.

Community solidarity should also be expressed through joint machinery for responding to supply crises and through a coherent policy on prices. The Commission will be making proposals on these matters.

On this basis the Community, acting in its own best interests, will be able to develop cooperation with the other industrialized nations, launch a constructive debate with the oil producers and help find a solution to the problems of the developing countries both through the transfer of technology and by assisting them to develop their own energy resources.

14. It is not possible to devise a new model for society, to secure the Community's political and economic autonomy or to guarantee competitiveness without a complete mastery of the most sophisticated technologies. Accumulated delays, rising costs and the fact that the necessary effort is too great for any Member State to make individually are all compromising the Community's ability to compete in science and technology. The need for a proper response is all the more urgent: the Community dimension makes it possible to provide this response efficiently and at minimum cost.

Apart from identifying delays and coordinating new action, the Commission will support priority research programmes in energy, the agri-food industry, environmental protection, nuclear safety and biotechnology. These Community programmes will promote the formation of the multi-disciplinary European research teams without which the quality and integration of research, crucial to success, cannot be attained.

15. The development of these new technologies – particularly regarding data transmission systems – and of the industries launching them is revolutionizing the whole outlook. New goods and services are coming on to the market, and demand for them is expanding. Production conditions are changing and the basic pattern of international competition is shifting accordingly. All this is of particular importance to small firms, for the environment in which they work is in a state of flux and they are not all equipped, financially or technically, to cope with the situation.

Hence the Community is falling behind the other major industrial powers. It can catch up if, realizing that this pattern of development, with all it entails in terms of new forms of industrial and social relationships, is both inevitable and desirable, it then draws the right conclusion and rapidly embarks on a suitably dynamic programme.

By adding to the efforts made by European firms and the Member States, the Community can make and original and probably unique contribution to the development of new techniques and industries. To this end it must not only devise and implement the coherent R&D programme referred to above but also deal with wholly new problems of information and training. Moreover it must set common standards and exploit all the possibilities offered by public procurement in the Member States so as to tap the full potential of this vast market.

31

16. Finally an active competition policy, particularly as applied to State aids, is also essential.

This policy must ensure that competition between Member States is not distorted. It must offer Community industry a positive incentive to adapt and at the same time serve as a source of coordination and economic convergence. For this purpose, regional needs must be better defined and the rules of competition must be applied more coherently to national aids to firms. The application of these rules in the process of industrial adjustment will assist the drive to modernize the production apparatus.

The powers assigned to the Commission by the Treaties give it only partial control over some other policy areas which affect the competitiveness of industry. The Community will have to make a fresh attempt at identifying those areas and taking action, particularly with regard te transport subsidies, differentiated energy prices and certain tax measures.

17. Yet it is hard to see how the Community can hope to advance in a balanced, decisive fashion on these various points unless it puts its budgetary affairs in order.

The Commission's reflections, and its resulting proposals, concern essentially the common agricultural policy, regional policy and social policy, given the proportion of the budget which they represent. The Commission objective has been to see that within a limited budgetary framework, Community financial solidarity should be both more effective and more equally distributed.

The Commission has also taken into account the fact that the Community dimension will be further enhanced as the result of the accession of two new Member States whose economic and social situation will tend to aggravate a number of existing problems.

18. The major effort concerns the common agricultural policy.
Taken as a whole, the result of twenty years of the application of the CAP is positive.

The objectives set by the Treaty of Rome - be it security of food supplies, satisfaction of consumers' requirements, increased productivity or higher farm incomes - have been achieved.

Set against the objectives and the results achieved, the total cost of the common agricultural policy, which corresponds to 0.5% of the Community's GDP, is not excessive. Renationalization would cost Member States more. Every country needs an agricultural policy and it is worth remembering that the policies pursued by the Community's main competitors are just as costly.

19. The Commission considers - indeed this was emphasized in the terms of the mandate - that the three interrelated principles on which the common agricultural policy is based - market unity, Community preference and financial solidarity - remain essential. It is neither possible nor desirable to jettison the mechanisms of the common agricultural policy but on the other hand adjustments are both possible and necessary.

Technological progress and the play of the market organizations mean that the Community is now more than self-sufficient for most major products. The imperatives of sound market management, combined with budgetary constraints, therefore call for improved control of the unwelcome effects of the operation of market organizations.

20. The Commission has accordingly come to the following conclusions:

- farm income considerations, important though they may be, cannot be the
  sole point of reference for fixing guaranteed prices;
- it is neither economically sensible nor financially possible to give
  producers a full guarantee for products in structural surplus;
- given the Community's degree of selfsufficiency for most agricultural
  products and bearing consumers' interests in mind, prices must reflect market realities more than they have in the past.

21. Having considered all the alternatives, the Commission recommends
that future decisions in respect of the common agricultural policy
should be based on the guidelines set out below, which should be combined to achieve the objectives set by the Treaty at as low a cost as
possible:
- a price policy based on a narrowing of the gap between Community prices
  and prices applied by its main competitors in the interests of competitiveness and a hierarchy of prices designed to improve the balance
  of production;
- an active export policy which would honour the Community's international commitments;
- modulation of guarantees in line with Community production targets;
- an active structures policy tailored to the needs of individual agricultural regions;
- the possibility of income support subsidies to certain producers in
  specific circumstances;
- improved quality control at Community level and tighter financial control by the Community in the management of EAGGF expenditure;
- stricter discipline in relation to national aids to avoid undermining
  Community policies.

22. The policy of common prices remains a central instrument of a common
agricultural policy.
    But this policy presupposes the smooth operation of the European
Monetary System and a significant alignment of inflation rates. National
and Community policies promoting this alignment will make it unnecessary
for price decisions to allow for widely differing national situations.
    Price policy must reflect trends on the world market more than it
has in the past. The Commission is well aware that world prices can
develop erratically. This is why the practical implementation of such
a price policy will vary from product to product. The Community's objective should be the gradual alignment of guaranteed prices on prices
ruling on a better organized world market. This would make it possible
to take advantage of increases in productivity and avoid windfall profits.
    To this end the Community should pursue a rigorous policy with regard
to prices within its frontiers and adopt a more active export policy
designed to stabilize world prices by means of cooperation agreements
with other major exporters. These could be supplemented by long-term
export contracts.
    A trade strategy of this kind would encourage the emergence of a
strong, well organized agri-food industry. At the same time it would
not damage the interests of developing countries.
    The Commission should also monitor imports that might cause market
imbalances and see to it that its commercial and agricultural policies
are mutually consistent.

23. Producers must be made more aware of market realities than they have
been in the past. To this end production targets in terms of volume must
be set for every sector at Community level. Once these are reached pro-

ducers would be required to contribute or the intervention guarantee could be reduced.

These targets would, of necessity, integrate projected market trends and the degree of self-sufficiency desired. They would also allow for imports flowing from the Community's international commitments and its concern to take its place as a structural supplier on a world market which is persistently in deficit for a number of essential commodities.

24. Production targets and intervention arrangements would vary from product to product.

For sugar, an effective system is already in operation. For cereals, where the Community's most efficient farms can compete at world level, payment of a lower intervention price for tonnages above a production target, corresponding roughly to domestic consumption, would give a boost to the most competitive farms and cut the cost of intervention.

For milk products, the Commission considers that the objective of controlling production can only be achieved if the principle of co-responsibility is extended. If this is not done, other measures will be inevitable.

25. The Commission considers that these changes should be accompanied by a rigorous quality control policy.

Moreover the Commission should be given its own powers of control in managing the agricultural funds for which it is responsible.

26. The Commission's guidelines on prices and production cannot be applied in a vacuum, ignoring the income problems of certain producers. This is why it is proposing the introduction, in certain specific cases, of direct income subsidies which, given the cost, would be confined to small producers. A decision on the grant of such subsidies would be taken by the Community in line with Community criteria. On this basis a Community contribution to their financing could be envisaged.

27. The problems of producers in regions with a natural handicap must be seen in a different context. The Community has alsready taken action on the problems of mountain and peripheral areas.

But the problems of the Mediterranean area merit special consideration given the importance of agriculture in its economy. The market and structural components of the common agricultural policy should help to improve the situation. But they cannot take the place of other policies or deal alone with a series of questions which reflect a particular economic context.

28. Any solution to current difficulties in Mediterranean agriculture must be based on changes in depth in the attitudes of producers and in production structures. While recognizing that results will take time, the Commission intends to propose that there should be a number of medium-term Community programmes covering an integrated policy for incomes, markets, production and structures.

29. In making its contribution to a solution of the difficulties facing agriculture the Community must keep two principles in mind: equivalence and equity. Equivalence means that, in line with the basic principles of the Treaties, the common agricultural policy must apply without discrimination to Mediterranean products. Equity means that change cannot be allowed to lead to a drop in living standards for those involved.

30. The Community programmes for the Mediterranean to be prepared by the

Commission will involve both the Community's financial and agricultural instruments. They will be devised in close collaboration with the Member States concerned so as to incorporate the objectives of national and regional plans. They will be presented to the Council and Parliament before the end of 1982.

31. The guidelines for reform of the common agricultural policy leave the principles on which it is based intact. They introduce the adjustments which must be made to market management if perverse effects of gains in productivity for consumers and the Community's budget are to be avoided. If the guidelines are agreed, their application will mean that agricultural spending in the years ahead will grow less rapidly than the Community's own resources, making it possible to release additional resources to reinforce Community solidarity in other sectors.

32. The regional and social policies are an expression of this solidarity, which takes on a new urgency in the present economic and social climate.
   All the instruments available to these policies have expanded rapidly in recent years: in 1981 the budget is providing some 3 000 million ECU for regional and social activities. This amount, severely limited in comparison with national budgets, leaves little room for flexibility in attaining the objectives of the Funds. Admittedly, to this should be added around 4 000 million ECU by way of Community borrowing and lending operations.

33. That these instruments have proved their worth is shown by their rate of expansion and the heavy demand within the Community for the facilities which they provide. But there is considerable room for improvement in their efficiency. This need can be met by concentrating efforts on the areas of gravest difficulty, by combining the targets and interventions of the various Community instruments, and finally by coordinating them with national measures to ensure that Community aids are additional to national ones.

34. The regulations and procedures governing the Regional and Social Funds provide for their revision by the end of 1981 and in 1982 respectively. The Commission sets out here a framework for these revisions which will be elaborated in detail at the appropriate time. It also presents some guidelines for the future of the borrowing and lending mechanisms.

35. The reduction of regional imbalances remains a priority Community objective. Responsibility in this field lying largely with national and local authorities, the Community has to base its actions on a wide range of instruments not exclusively of a financial nature. The coordination of national regional policies and regional aid systems with the intervention of the Community's Regional Fund are particularly important, as is the significance attached to regional impact in the definition of other Community policies.

36. As far as the Regional Fund itself is concerned, the Commission believes that major changes should be made to enhance the effectiveness of its interventions and increase its impact. There is a strong case for greater concentration of the Fund's budgetary resources, which are and are likely to remain inadequate to cope with the development problems that will increasingly face the Community as it continues to enlarge.

The section of the Regional Funds at present divided into national quotas should be adjusted to focus even more on regions suffering severely from structural underdevelopment. (Including Greenland and the French overseas departments)

The proportion of the Fund's resources allocated to the section which is not divided into national quotas (the non-quota section) should be substantially expanded. Intervention will be directed more selectively to the regions of the Community currently suffering most from serious problems of industrial decline or from the effects of certain Community policies.

Changes in the working and operating criteria of the Fund should include replacing support for isolated projects by a new system of co-financing with Member States of regional infrastructure programmes and regional investment aid schemes, which would incorporate the individual, Community-aided projects.

37. Community solidarity must also be expressed in the social sphere, in line with economic and social policy objectives. Priority should henceforth be given to job creation. The traditional role of the Social Fund, which is to increase the geographical and occupational mobility of workers, will be of greater importance in the future.

The Community will need to make a special effort in regions where traditional industries are concentrated, with the aim of developing a more imaginative approach to the labour market. Moreover the Social Fund must be given the necessary resources to ensure that the Community's workforce can adapt adequately and in good time to the jobs which will be created by exploiting new areas of growth and local economic potential.

The Social Fund will therefore have to promote integrated training and employment programmes, specifically adapted to local and regional economic conditions. With this in view, the current administratively complex range of interventions should be reviewed. New emphasis should be given to job creation, including aids to essential support services in the field of information, guidance and technical assistance and in preparing young people for working life. In addition, the use of integrated programmes would enable a much closer relationship to be established with other Community funds and with national sources of assistance.

If it is to act as an effective driving force, the Social Fund must be allocated sufficient resources to produce a real increase in employment measures, and particularly in the volume of training. To ensure that the Fund's operations can be concentrated on essentials and its efforts coordinated, it should be freed from the constraints which have hitherto limited its effectiveness. With this in mind, the Commission intends to present proposals for injecting greater flexibility into the funds formal operating procedures.

38. In the Commission's view appropriations for the two Funds will have to grow faster than the general budget as a whole if they are to attain their objectives.

Here, as elsewhere, the Commission excludes the presentation of illusory budgetary balances via the introduction of artificial Community policies.

39. While the Community can continue to increase the volume of its borrowing and lending instruments, the Commission considers that they must be used to greater effect. In particular it recommends

- an increased emphasis on small and medium-sized firms;
- the use of interest subsidies in certain priority regions for major programmes other than those linked to productive investment projects;
- the combined use of borrowing and lending instruments and the structural funds, notably the Regional Fund, which is already in a position to finance some of the interest subsidies mentioned above.

40. The options and guidelines which the Commission has proposed are inevitably dependent on the Community's financial resources. The most effective use of available funds must be seen as a permanent priority. The Commission cannot accept that an artificial ceiling be put on own resources, and will propose that they be increased when this becomes necessary to achieve agreed objectives.

41. The Commission has studied the likely consequences of its recommendations for the development of the Community budget. It is clear that their implementation could not have a significant impact for some time to come. The Commission has therefore proceeded to examine the budgetary position.
   Scrutiny of the structure of expenditure,[2] divided into six main categories, namely:
- administrative expenditure;
- reimbursements;
- support expenditure on certain common projects (industry, energy, research, etc.);
- structural expenditure (ERDF, ESF, EAGGF Guidance Section, etc.);
- aid to non-member countries;
- EAGGF Guarantee Section,
shows that utilization of appropriations in the first five categories presents no particular problem for any Member State.
   By contrast, an analysis of the destination of appropriations from the EAGGF Guarantee Section, which forms the bulk of the budget, shows that under present circumstances, the United Kingdom obtains a much smaller financial benefit from the CAP than the other Member States on account of the special features of its agriculture. Community solidarity demands that a remedy be found to this inequitable situation.

42. The size of the imbalance to be corrected could, in the Commission's view, be assessed by comparing the United Kingdom's share of the Community's gross national product with the proportion it obtains of EAGGF Guarantee Section expenditure. On the basis of this data the amount of compensation could then be established following simple rules, using a reference period extending over several years, and with a view to a fairly high level of compensation.

43. As this compensation would be provided by the Community itself, it should be financed from the budget on the basis of the own resources system.

44. However, should this be rendered impracticable either by a delay in taking the decisions needed to create new own resources (exceeding the 1% limit on VAT) or by the current trend in budget expenditure, the Commission would envisage that consideration be given to a subsidiary measure by which the Member States which benefit more from the CAP than their British partner would demonstrate their solidarity. In practice, the compensation could be financed by Member States other than the United Kingdom via abatements on their receipts from the Community, based on the payments they receive under the EAGGF Guarantee

Section. In establishing the abatement percentages, account should be taken of the proposals put forward by the Commission in this report, to the effect that Community policies must put emphasis on solidarity between the more prosperous Member States and the less prosperous (particularly Ireland, Greece and Italy).

45. The Commission considers that the new measure should apply for a limited period, but long enough for the effects of the new guidelines it proposes to be felt. The position would be reviewed before the compensation system expires, notably when a decision is taken on creating the additional own resources needed to implement common policies.

The Commission could also propose amendments to the system if this was justified by the development of the common agricultural policy or other policies, or if practical difficulties emerged.

46. The funds made available to the United Kingdom should be used to finance activities in that country which accord with Community politics and are designed to increase convergence of the economies.

47. With regard to the existing financial mechanism[3], based on the Council Regulation of May 1976, as adapted by the 1980 Regulation, the Commission will make a report by the end of this year, in order that this mechanism continues in being if it is needed.

48. The guidelines which the Commission has just set out in response to the mandate given to it on 30 May 1980 form a coherent package of measures which both correspond to the framework which was given and can be applied in a relatively short space of time. The impetus given by the adoption of these priority measures will be a key element in relaunching the whole development of the Community.

49. By its very nature, this report cannot hope to cover the complete spectrum of Community activity. Many areas have scarcely been touched upon, such as the Community's external relations, and particularly the effort which the Community is making, and would like to increase, in the field of development aid.

Because of its history, its geography, through its power and its economic needs, the Community faces the world, where the role it plays and the responsibilities it bears are highly regarded as a source of hope and confidence, especially in the developing countries. A fulfilment of the political alliance entered into by each Member State will not only strengthen the Community's internal solidarity but also endow the Community with the means to play more effectively the role its partners expect of it. By strengthening its position on the international economic stage, the Community will be able to make a greater contribution to solving world problems.

50. A political decision is needed if the Community is to be relaunched. This means working together to find solutions which correspond to the general interest. The Treaties have provided a method and procedures for advancing in this way. The Commission has started the process by outlining the way forward. It is now for the other institutions to commit themselves.

----

1) For 1982, the Community is pledged to resolve the problem by means of structural changes (Commission mandate, to be fulfilled by the end of June 1981: the examination will concern the development of

Community policies, without calling into question the common financial responsibility for these policies which are financed from the Community's own resources, or the basic principles of the common agricultural policy. Taking account of the situations and interests of all Member States, this examination will aim to prevent the recurrence of unacceptable situations for any of them). If this is not achieved, the Commission will make proposals along the lines of the 1980 and 1981 solution and the Council will act accordingly.

2) As identified in the reference paper presented by the Commission in 1979 (COM (79) 462 of 12 September 1979).

3) Financial mechanism set up by the Council Regulation of 17 May 1976, adapted by the Regulation of 27 October 1980.

----

11. COUNCIL DECISION

of 21 April 1970

on the Replacement of Financial Contributions from
Member States by the Community's own Resources

(J.O. No L 94, 28 April 1970, p. 19; O.J. (Special
Edition 1970, p. 224)

THE COUNCIL OF THE EUROPEAN COMMUNITIES,

Having regard to the Treaty establishing the European Economic Community, and in particular Article 201 thereof;

Having regard to the Treaty establishing the European Atomic Energy
Community, and in particular Article 173 thereof;

Having regard to the proposal from the Commission;

Having regard to the Opinion of the European Parliament;

Having regard to the Opinion of the Economic and Social Committee;

Whereas complete replacement of the financial contributions from Member States by the Community's own resources can only be achieved progressively;

Whereas Article 2(1) of Regulation No 25 on financing the common agricultural policy stipulates that at the single market stage revenue
from agricultural levies shall be allocated to the Community and
appropriated to Community expenditure;

Whereas Article 201 of the Treaty establishing the European Economic
Community refers explicitly, among the Community's own resources
which could replace financial contributions from Member States, to
revenue acruing from the Common Customs Tariff when the latter has
been finally introduced;

Whereas the effects on the budgets of the Member States of the transfer to the Commmunities of revenue acruing from the Common Customs
Tariff should be mitigated; whereas a system should be provided which
will make it possible to achieve total transfer progressively and
within a definite period of time;

Whereas revenue acruing from agricultural levies and customs duties
is not sufficient to ensure that the budget of the Communities is
in balance; whereas, therefore, it is advisable to allocate to the
Communities, in addition, tax revenue, the most appropriate being
that acruing from the application of a single rate to the basis for

40

assessing the value added tax, determined in a uniform manner for the Member States;

HAS LAID DOWN THESE PROVISIONS, WHICH IT RECOMMENDS TO THE MEMBER STATES FOR ADOPTION:

Article 1

The Communities shall be allocated resources of their own in accordance with the following Articles in order to ensure that their budget is in balance.

Article 2

From 1 January 1971 revenue from:

(a) levies, premiums, additional or compensatory amounts, additional amounts or factors and other duties established or to be established by the institutions of the Communities in respect of trade with non-member countries within the framework of the common agricultural policy, and also contributions and other duties provided for within the framework of the organisation of the markets in sugar (hereinafter called 'agricultural levies');

(b) Common Customs Tariff duties and other duties established or to be established by the institutions of the Communities in respect of trade with non-member countries (hereinafter called 'customs duties');

Shall, in accordance with Article 3, constitute own resources to be entered in the budget of the Communities.

In addition, revenue acruing from other charges introduced within the framework of a common policy in accordance with the provisions of the Treaty establishing the European Economic Community or the Treaty establishing the European Atomic Energy Community shall constitute own resources to be entered in the budget of the Communities, subject to the procedure laid down in Article 201 of the Treaty establishing the European Economic Community or in Article 173 of the Treaty establishing the European Atomic Energy Community having been followed.

Article 3

1. From 1 January 1971 the total revenue from agricultural levies shall be entered in the budget of the Communities.

From the same date, revenue from customs duties shall progressively be entered in the budget of the Communities.

The amount of the customs duties appropriated to the Communities each year by each Member State shall be equal to the difference between a reference amount and the amount of the agricultural levies appropriated to the Communities pursuant to the first subparagraph. Where this difference is negative, there shall be no payment of customs

duties by the Member State concerned nor payment of agricultural
levies by the Communities.

The reference amount referred to in the third subparagraph shall be:

- 50 % in 1971

- 62.5 % in 1972

- 75 % in 1973

- 87.5 % in 1974

- 100 % from 1 January 1975 onwards

of the total amount of the agricultural levies and customs duties
collected by each Member State.

The Communities shall refund to each Member State 10 % of the amounts
paid in accordance with the preceeding subparagraphs in order to
cover expense incurred in collection.

2. During the period 1 January 1971 to 31 December 1974, the financial
contributions from Member States required in order to ensure that the
budget of the Communities is in balance shall be apportioned on the
following scale:

- Belgium   6.8

- Germany   32.9

- France   32.6

- Italy   20.2

- Luxembourg   0.2

- Netherlands   7.3

3. During the same period, however, the variation from year to year
in the share of each Member State in the aggregate of the amounts paid
in accordance with paragraphs 1 and 2 may not exceed 1 % upwards or
1.5 % downwards, where these amounts are taken into consideration
within the framework of the second subparagraph. For 1971, the financial contributions of each Member State to the combined budgets för
1970 shall be taken as reference for the application of this rule,
to the extent that these budgets are taken into consideration within
the framework of the second subparagraph.

In the application of the first subparagraph, the following factors
shall be taken into consideration for each financial year:

(a) Expenditure relating to payment appropriations decided on for the
    financial year in question for the research and investment budget
    of the European Atomic Energy Community, with the exception of
    expenditure relating to supplementary programmes;

(b) Expenditure relating to appropriations to the European Social Fund;

(c) For the European Agricultural Guidance and Guarantee Fund, expenditure relating to appropriations to the Guarantee Section and to the Guidance Section, with the exception of appropriations entered or re-entered for accounting periods preceeding the financial year concerned. For the reference year 1970 such expenditure shall be:

- for the Guarantee section, that referred to in Article 8 of Council Regulation (EEC) No 728/70 of 21 April 1970 laying down additional provisions for financing the common agricultural policy;

- for the Guidance section, an amount of 285 million units of account apportioned on the basis of the scale laid down in Article 7 of that Regulation;

it being understood that, for calculating the share of Germany, a percentage of 31.5 shall be taken as the reference scale;

(d) Other expenditure relating to the appropriations entered in the Community budget.

Should the application of this paragraph to one or more Member States result in a deficit in the budget of the Communities, the amount of that deficit shall be shared for the year in question between the other Member States within the limits laid down in the first subparagraph and according to the contribution scale fixed in paragraph 2. If necessary, the operation shall be repeated.

4. Financing from the Communities' own resources of the expenditure connected with research programmes of the European Atomic Energy Community shall not exclude entry in the budget of the Communities of expenditure relating to supplementary programmes or the financing of such expenditure by means of financial contributions from Member States determined according to a special scale fixed pursuant to a Decision of the Council acting unanimously.

5. By way of derogation from this Article, appropriations entered in a budget preceding that for the financial year 1971 and carried over or re-entered in a later budget shall be financed by financial contributions from Member States according to scales applicable at the time of their first entry.

Appropriations to the Guidance section which, while being entered for the first time in the 1971 budget, refer to accounting periods of the European Guidance and Guarantee Fund preceding 1 January 1971 shall be covered by the scale relating to those periods.

Article 4

1. From 1 January 1975 the budget of the Communities shall, irrespective of other revenue, be financed entirely from the Communities' own resources.

Such resources shall include those referred to in Article 2 and also those acruing from the value added tax and obtained by applying a rate not exceeding 1 % to an assessment basis which is determined in a uniform manner for Member States according to Community rules. The rate shall be fixed within the framework of the budgetary procedure. If at the beginning of a financial year the budget has not yet been adopted, the rate previously fixed shall remain applicable until the entry into force of a new rate.

During the period 1 January 1975 to 31 December 1977, however, the variation from year to year in the share of each Member State in relation to the preceding year may not exceed 2 %. Should this percentage be exceeded, the necessary adjustment shall be made, within that variation limit, by financial compensation between the Member States concerned proportionate to the share borne by each of them in respect of revenue accruing from value added tax or from the financial contributions referred to in paragraphs 2 and 3.

2. By way of derogation from the second subparagraph of paragraph 1, if on 1 January 1975 the rules determining the uniform basis for assessing the value added tax have not yet been applied in all Member States but have been applied in at least three of them, the financial contribution to the budget of the Communities to be made by each Member State not yet applying the uniform basis for assessing the value added tax shall be determined according to the proportion of its gross national product to the sum total of the gross national products of the Member States. The balance of the budget shall be covered by revenue accruing from the value added tax in accordance with the second subparagraph of paragraph 1, collected by the other Member States. This derogation shall cease to effective as soon as the conditions laid down in paragraph 1 are fulfilled.

3. By way of derogation from the second subparagraph of paragraph 1, if on 1 January 1975 the rules determining the uniform basis for assessing the value added tax have not yet been applied in three or more Member States, the financial contribution of each Member State to the budget of the Communities shall be determined according to the proportion of its gross national product to the sum total of the gross national products of the Member States. This derogation shall cease to be effective as soon as the conditions laid down in paragraphs 1 and 2 are fulfilled.

4. For the purpose of paragraphs 2 and 3, 'gross national product' means the gross national product at market prices.

5. From the complete application of the second subparagraph of paragraph 1, any surplus of the Communities' own resources over and above the actual expenditure during a financial year shall be carried over to the following financial year.

6. Financing expenditure connected with research programmes of the European Atomic Energy Community from the Communities' own resources shall not exclude entry in the budget of the Communities of expenditure relating to supplementary programmes nor the financing of such expenditure by means of financial contributions from Member States determined according to a special scale fixed pursuant to a Decision of the Council acting unanimously.

Article 5

The revenue referred to in Article 2, Article 3(1) and (2) and Article 4(1) to (5) shall be used without distinction to finance all expenditure entered in the budget of the Communities in accordance with Article 20 of the Treaty establishing a Single Council and a Single Commission of the European Communities.

Article 6

1. The Community resources referred to in Articles 2, 3 and 4 shall be collected by the Member States in accordance with national provisions imposed by law, regulation or administrative action, which shall, where necessary, be amended for that purpose. Member States shall make these resources available to the Commission.

2. Without prejudice to the auditing of accounts provided for in Article 206 of the Treaty establishing the European Economic Community, or to the inspection arrangements made pursuant to Article 209(c) of that Treaty, the Council shall, acting unanimously on a proposal from the Commission and after consulting the European Parliament, adopt provisions relating to the supervision of collection, the making available to the Commission, and the payment of the revenue referred to in Articles 2, 3 and 4, and also the procedure for application of Article 3(3) and Article 4.

Article 7

Member States shall be notified of this Decision by the Secretary-General of the Council of the European Communities; it shall be published in the *Official Journal of the European Communities*.

Member States shall notify the Secretary-General of the Council of the European Communities without delay of the completion of the procedures for the adoption of this Decision in accordance with their respective constitutional requirements.

This Decision shall enter into force on the first day of the month following receipt of the last of the notifications referred to in the second subparagraph. If, however, the instruments of ratification provided for in Article 12 of the Treaty amending Certain Budgetary Provisions of the Treaties establishing the European Communities and the Treaty establishing a Single Council and a Single Commission of the European Communities, have not been deposited before that date by all the Member States, this Decision shall enter into force on the first day of the month following the deposit of the last of those instruments of ratification.

Done at Luxembourg, 21 April 1970.

For the Council
The President
P. HARMEL

12. JOINT DECLARATION

of the European Parliament, the Council and the Commission

(O.J. No C89, 22 April 1975, p. 1)

THE EUROPEAN PARLIAMENT, THE COUNCIL AND THE COMMISSION,

Whereas from 1 January 1975, the Budget of the Communities will be financed entirely from the Communities' own resources;

Whereas in oredr to implement this system the European Parliament will be given increased budgetary powers;

Whereas the increase in the budgetary powers of the European Parliament must be accompanied by effective participation by the latter in the procedure for preparing and adopting decisions which give rise to important expenditure or revenue to be charged or credited to the budget of the European Communities,

HAVE AGREED AS FOLLOWS:

1. A conciliation procedure between the European Parliament and the Council with the active assistance of the Commission is hereby instituted.

2. This procedure may be followed for Community acts of general application which have appreciable financial implications, and of which the adoption is not required by virtue of acts already in existence.

3. When submitting its proposal the Commission shall indicate whether the act in question is, in its opinion, capable of being the subject of the conciliation procedure. The European Parliament, when giving its Opinion, and the Council may request that this procedure be initiated.

4. The procedure shall be initiated if the criteria laid down in paragraph 2 are met and if the Council intends to depart from the Opinion adopted by the European Parliament.

5. The conciliation shall take place in a 'Conciliation Committee' consisting of the Council and representatives of the European Parliament. The Commission shall participate in the work of the Conciliation Committee.

6. The aim of the procedure shall be to seek an agreement between the European Parliament and the Council.

The procedure should normally take place during a period not exceeding three months, unless the act in question has to be adopted before a specific date or if the matter is urgent, in which case the Council may fix an appropriate time limit.

7. When the position of the two institutions are sufficiently close, the European Parliament may give a new Opinion, after which the Council shall take definitive action.

Done at Brussels, 4 March 1975.

For the European Parliament
C. BERKHOUWER

For the Council
G. FITZGERALD

For the Commission
Francois-Xavier ORTOLI

Chapter Two

THE COURT OF JUSTICE OF THE EUROPEAN COMMUNITIES

EXCERPTS OF THE RULES OF PROCEDURE

1. Organization of the Court

Chapter I

Judges and Advocates-General

Article 2.

The term of office of a Judge shall begin on the date laid down in the instrument of his appointment. In the absence of any provision regarding the date, the term shall begin on the date of the instrument.

Article 3.

(1) Before taking up his duties, a Judge shall at the first public sitting of the Court which he attends after his appointment take the following oath:
"I swear that I will perform my duties impartially and conscientiously; I swear that I will preserve the secrecy of the deliberations of the Court".
.....

Article 6.

Judges and Advocates-General shall rank equally in precedence according to their seniority in office.
Where there is equal seniority in office precedence shall be determined by age.
Retiring Judges and Advocates-General who are reappointed shall retain their former precedence.

Chapter 2

Presidency of the Court and constitution of the Chambers

Article 7.

(1) The Judges shall, immediately after the partial replacement provided for in Article 32b of the ECSC Treaty, Article 167 of the EEC Treaty and Article 139 of the Euratom Treaty, elect one of their number as President of the Court for a term of three years.
.....
Article 8.

The President shall direct the judicial business and the administration of the Court; he shall preside at hearings and at deliberations in the

Deliberation Room.

Article 9.

(1) The Court shall appoint the Registrar. Two weeks before the date fixed for making the appointment, the President shall inform the Members of the Court of the applications which have been made for the post.
. . . . .
(7) If the office of Registrar falls vacant before the normal date of expiry of the term thereof, the Court shall appoint a new Registrar for a term of six years.

Article 13.

The Court may, following the procedure laid down in respect of the Registrar, appoint one or more Assistant Registrars to assist the Registrar and to take his place so far as the Instructions to the Registrar referred to in Article 15 of these rules allow.
. . . . .
Article 16.

(1) There shall be kept in the Registry, under the control of the Registrar, a register initiated by the President, in which all pleadings and supporting documents shall be consecutively entered in the order in which they are lodged.

(2) When a document has been registered, the Registrar shall make a note to that effect on the original and, if a party so requests, on any copy submitted for the purpose.

(3) Entries in the register and the notes provided for in the preceding paragraph shall constitute official records.

(4) Rules for keeping the registrar shall be prescribed by the Instructions to the Registrar referred to in Article 15 of these rules.

(5) Interested persons may consult the register at the Registry and may obtain copies or extracts on payment of a charge on a scale to be fixed by the Court acting on a proposal from the Registrar.
    The parties to a case may on payment of the appropriate charge also obtain copies of pleadings and authenticated copies of judgments and orders.

(6) Notice shall be given in the Official Journal of the European Communities of the date of registration of an application originating proceedings, the names and permanent residences of the parties, the subject-matter of the dispute, the claims made in the application and a summary of the contentions and of the main arguments adduced in support.

(7) Where the Council or the Commission is not a party to a case, the Court shall forward to it copies of the application and of the defence, without the annexes thereto, to enable it to assess whether the inapplicability of one of its acts is being invoked under the third paragraph of Article 36 of the ECSC Treaty, Article 184 of the EEC Treaty or Article 156 of the Euratom Treaty.

Article 17.

(1) The Registrar shall be responsible, under the authority of the President, for the acceptance, transmission and custody of documents and for effecting such service as is provided for by these rules.

(2) The Registrar shall assist the Court, the Chambers, the President and the Judges in all their official functions.

Article 18.

The Registrar shall have custody of the seals. He shall be responsible for the records and be in charge of the publications of the Court.

Article 19.

Subject to Articles 4 and 27 of these rules, the Registrar shall attend the sittings of the Court and of the Chambers.
. . . . .

Chapter 5

The Working of the Court

Article 25.

(1) The dates and times of the sittings of the Court shall be fixed by the President.

(2) The dates and times of the sittings of the Chambers shall be fixed by their respective Presidents.

(3) The Court and the Chambers may choose to hold one or more particular sittings in a place other than that where the Court has its seat.

Article 26.

(1) Where, by reason of a Judge being absent or prevented from attending, there is an even number of Judges, the most junior Judge within the meaning of Article 6 of these rules shall abstain from taking part in the deliberations.

(2) If after the Court has been convened it is found that the quorum of seven Judges has not been attained, the President shall adjourn the sitting until there is a quorum.

(3) If in any Chamber the quorum of three Judges has not been attained, the President of that Chamber shall so inform the President of the Court who shall designate another Judge to complete the Chamber.

Article 27.

(1) Deliberations of the Court and Chambers shall take place in the Deliberation Room.

(2) Only those Judges who were present at the oral proceedings and the Assistant Rapporteur, if any, entrusted with the consideration of the case may take part in the deliberations.

(3) Every Judge taking part in the deliberations shall give his view
and the reasons for it.

(4) Any Judge may require that any question be formulated in the
language of his choice and be communicated in writing to the Court or
Chamber before being put to the vote.

(5) The opinion reached by the majority of the Judges after final
discussion shall determine the decision of the Court. Votes shall be
cast in reverse order to the order of precedence laid down in Article
6 of these rules.

(6) Differences of view on the substance, wording or order of questions,
or on the interpretation of the voting shall be settled by decision of
the Court or Chamber.

(7) Where the deliberations of the Court concern questions of its own
administration, the Advocates-General shall take part and have a vote.
The Registrar shall be present, unless the Court decides to the contrary.

(8) Where the Court sits without the Registrar being present it shall,
if necessary, instruct the most junior Judge within the meaning of
Article 6 of these rules to draw up minutes. The minutes shall be
signed by this Judge and by the President.

Article 28.

(1) Subject to any special decision of the Court, its vacations shall
be as follows:
- from 18 December to 10 January,
- from the Sunday before Easter to the second Sunday after Easter,
- from 15 July to 15 September.
During the vacations, the functions of President shall be exercised
at the place where the Court has its seat either by the President himself, keeping in touch with the Registrar, or by a President of a
Chamber or by such other Judge as he may invite to take his place.

(2) In a case or urgency, the President may convene the Judges and the
Advocates-General during the vacations.

(3) The Court shall observe the official holidays of the place where it
has its seat.

(4) The Court may, in proper circumstances, grant leave of absence to
any Judge or Advocate-General.

Chapter 6

Languages - See Chapter One

Chapter 7

Rights and Obligations of Agents, Advisers and Lawyers

Article 32.

(1) Agents representing a State or an institution, as well as advisers and lawyers, appearing before the Court or before any judicial authority to whom the Court has addressed letters rogatory, shall enjoy immunity in respect of words spoken or written by them concerning the case or the parties.

(2) Agents, advisers and lawyers shall enjoy the following further privileges and facilities:
(a) papers and documents relating to the proceedings shall be exempt from both search and seizure; in the event of a dispute the customs officials or police may seal those papers and documents; they shall then be immediately forwarded to the Court for inspection in the presence of the Registrar and of the person concerned;
(b) agents, advisers and lawyers shall be entitled to such allocation of foreign currency as may be necessary for the performance of their duties;
(c) agents, advisers and lawyers shall be entitled to travel in the course of duty without hindrance.

Article 33.

In order to qualify for the privileges, immunities and facilities specified in Article 32, persons entitled to them shall furnish proof of their status as follows:
(a) agents shall produce an official document issued by the State or institution which they represent; a copy of this document shall be forwarded without delay to the Registrar by the State or institution concerned;
(b) advisers and lawyers shall produce a certificate signed by the Registrar. The validity of this certificate shall be limited to a specified period, which may be extended or curtailed according to the length of the proceedings.

Article 34.

The privileges, immunities and facilities specified in Article 32 of these rules are granted exclusively in the interests of the proper conduct of proceedings.
    The Court may waive the immunity where it considers that the proper conduct of proceedings will not be hindered thereby.

Article 35.

(1) Any adviser or lawyer whose conducts towards the Court, a Chamber, a Judge, ad Advocate-General or the Registrar is incompatible with the dignity of the Court, or who uses his rights for purposes other than those for which they were granted, may at any time be excluded from the proceedings by an order of the Court or Chamber, after the Advocate-General has been heard; the person concerned shall be given an opportunity to defend himself.

The order shall have immediate effect.

(2) Where an adviser or lawyer is excluded from the proceedings, the proceedings shall be suspended for a period fixed by the President in order to allow the party concerned to appoint another adviser or lawyer.

(3) Decisions taken under this Article may be rescinded.

Article 36.

The provisions of this Chapter shall apply to university teachers who
have a right of audience before the Court in accordance with Article 20
of the ECSC Statute and Articles 17 of the EEC and Euratom Statutes.

TITLE 2

PROCEDURE

Chapter 1

Written Procedure

Article 37

(1) The original of every pleading must be signed by the party's agent
or lawyer.
   The original, accompanied by all annexes referred to therein shall be
lodged together with five copies for the Court and a copy for every
other party to the proceedings. Copies shall be certified by the party
lodging them.

(2) Institutions shall in addition produce, within time limits laid
down by the Court, translations of all pleadings into the other languages provided for by Article 1 of Council Regulation No 1. The second
subparagraph of paragraph 1 of this Article shall apply in a corresponding manner.

(3) All pleadings shall bear a date. In the reckoning of time limits for
taking steps in proceedings, the only relevant date shall be that of
lodgment at the Registry.

(4) To every pleading there shall be annexed a file containing the
documents relied on in support of it, together with a schedule listing
them.

(5) Where in view of the length of a document only extracts from it
are annexed to the pleading, the whole document or a full copy of it
shall be lodged at the Registry.

Article 38.

(1) An application of the kind referred to in Article 22 of the ECSC
Statute and Articles 19 of the EEC and Euratom Statutes shall state:
   (a) the name and permanent residence of the applicant;
   (b) the name of the party against whom the application is made;
   (c) the subject-matter of the dispute and the grounds on which the
       application is based;
   (d) the form of order sought by the applicant;
   (e) the nature of any evidence founded upon by him.

   (2) For the purpose of the proceedings, the application shall state
   an address for service in the place where the Court has its seat.
   It shall also give the name of a person who is authorized and has

expressed willingness to accept service.

(3) The lawyer acting for a party must lodge at the Registry a certificate that he is entitled to practice before a Court of a Member State.

(4) The application shall be accompanied, where appropriate, by the documents specified in the second paragraph of Article 22 of the ECSC Statute and in the second paragraph of Articles 19 of the EEC and Euratom Statutes.

(5) An application made by a legal person governed by private law shall be accompanied by:
    (a) the instrument or instruments constituting and regulating that legal person;
    (b) proof that the authority granted to the applicant's lawyer has been properly conferred on him by someone authorized for the purpose.

(6) An application submitted under Articles 42 and 89 of the ECSC Treaty, Articles 181 and 182 of the EEC Treaty and Articles 153 and 154 of the Euratom Treaty shall be accompanied by a copy of the arbitration clause contained in the contract governed by private or public law entered into by the Communities or on their behalf, or, as the case may be, by a copy of the special agreement concluded between the Member States concerned.

(7) If an application does not comply with the requirements set out in paragraphs 2 to 6 of this Article, the Registrar shall prescribe a reasonable period within which the applicant is to comply with them whether by putting the application itself in order or by procuding any of the abovementioned documents. If the applicant fails to put the application in order or to produce the required documents within the time prescribed, the Court shall, after hearing the Advocate-General, decide whether to reject the application on the ground of want of form.

Article 39.

The application shall be served on the defendant. In a case where Article 38 (7) applies, service shall be effected as soon as the application has been put in order or the Court has declared it admissible notwithstanding the failure to observe the formal requirements set out in that Article.

Article 40.

(1) Within one month after service on him of the application, the defendant shall lodge a defence, stating:
    (a) the name and permanent residence of the defendant;
    (b) the points of fact and law relied on;
    (c) the form of order sought;
    (d) the nature of any evidence founded upon by him.

The provisions of Article 38 (2) to (5) of these rules shall apply in a corresponding manner to the defence.

(2) The time limit laid down in paragraph 1 of this Article may be extended by the President on a reasoned application by the defendant.

Article 41.

(1) The application originating the proceedings and the defence may be supplemented by a reply from the applicant and by a rejoinder from the defendant.

(2) The President shall fix the time limits within which these pleadings are to be lodged.

Article 42.

(1) In reply or rejoinder a party may indicate further evidence. The party must, however, give reasons for the delay in indicating it.

(2) No fresh issue may be raised in the course of proceedings unless it is based on matters of law or of fact which come to light in the course of the written procedure.

If in the course of the written procedure one of the parties raises a fresh issue which is so based, the President may, even after the expiry of the normal procedural time limits, acting on a report of the Judge Rapporteur and after hearing the Advocate-General, allow the other party time to answer on that issue.

The decision on the admissibility of the issue shall be reserved for the final judgment.

Article 43.

The Court may, at any time, after hearing the parties and the Advocate-General, order that for the purpose of the written or oral procedure or of its final judgment, a number of related cases concerning the same subject matter shall be dealt with jointly. The decision to join the cases may subsequently be rescinded.

Article 44

(1) After the rejoinder provided for in Article 41 (1) of these rules has been lodged, the President shall fix a date on which the Judge-Rapporteur is to present his preliminary report to the Court. The report shall contain recommendations as to whether a preparatory inquiry or any other preparatory step should be undertaken and whether the case should be referred to the Chamber to which it has been assigned under Article 9 (2).

The Court shall decide, after hearing the Advocate-General, what action to take upon the recommendations of the Judge-Rapporteur.

The same procedure shall apply:
   (a) where no reply or no rejoinder has been lodged within the time limit fixed in accordance with Article 41 (2) of these rules;
   (b) where the party concerned waives his right to lodge a reply or rejoinder.

(2) Where the Court orders a preparatory inquiry and does not undertake it itself, it shall assign the inquiry to the Chamber.

Where the Court decides to open the oral procedure without an inquiry, the President shall fix the opening date.

Chapter 2

Preparatory Inquiries

Section 1 - measures of inquiry

Article 45.

(1) The Court, after hearing the Advocate-General, shall prescribe the measures of inquiry that it considers appropriate by means of an order setting out the issues of fact to be determined. The order shall be served on the parties.

(2) Without prejudice to Articles 24 and 25 of the ECSC Statute, Articles 21 and 22 of the EEC Statute or Articles 22 and 23 of the Euratom Statute, the following measures of inquiry may be adopted:

    (a) the personal appearance of the parties;
    (b) a request for information and production of documents;
    (c) oral testimony;
    (d) expert's reports;
    (e) an inspection of the place or thing in question.

(3) The measures of inquiry which the Court has ordered may be conducted by the Court itself, or be assigned to the Judge Rapporteur.
    The Advocate-General shall take part in the measures of inquiry.

(4) Evidence may be submitted in rebutal and previous evidence may be amplified.

Article 46.

(1) A Chamber to which a preparatory inquiry has been assigned may exercise the power vested in the Court by Articles 45 and 47 to 53 of these rules; the powers vested in the President of the Court may be exercised by the President of the Chamber.

(2) Articles 56 and 57 of these rules shall apply in a corresponding manner to proceedings before the Chamber.

(3) The parties shall be entitled to attend the measures of enquiry.
.....

Section 3 - Closure of the preparatory inquiry

Article 54.

Unless the Court prescribes a period within which the parties may lodge written observations, the President shall fix the date for the opening of the oral procedure after the preparatory inquiry has been completed.
    Where a period had been prescribed for the lodging of written ob-servations, the President shall fix the date for the opening of the oral procedure after that period has expired.

Chapter 3

Oral Procedure

Article 55.

(1) Subject to the priority of decisions provided for in Article 85 of
these rules, the Court shall deal with the cases before it in the order
in which the preparatory inquiries in them have been completed. Where
the preparatory inquiries in several cases are completed simultaneously,
the order in which they are to be dealt with shall be determined by the
dates of entry in the register of the applications originating them
respectively.

The President may in special circumstances order that a case be
given priority over others.

(2) On a joint application by the parties the President may order that
a case in which the preparatory inquiry has been competed be deferred.
In the absence of agreement between the parties the President shall
refer the matter to the Court for a decision.

Article 56.

(1) The proceedings shall be opened and directed by the President, who
shall be responsible for the proper conduct of the hearing.

(2) The oral proceedings in cases which are heard 'in camera' shall not
be published.

Article 57.

The President may in the course of the hearing put questions to the
agents, advisers or lawyers of the parties.

The other Judges and the Advocate-General may do likewise.

Article 58.

A party may address the Court only through his agent, adviser or
lawyer.

Article 59.

(1) The Advocate-General shall deliver his opinion orally at the end
of the oral procedure.

(2) After the Advocate-General has delivered his opinion, the President
shall declare the oral procedure closed.

Article 60.

The Court may at any time, after hearing the Advocate-General, order
any measure of inquiry to be taken or that a precious inquiry be repeated or expanded. The Court may direct the Chamber or the Judge
Rapporteur to carry out the measures so ordered.

Article 61.

The Court may after hearing the Advocate-General order the reopening of
the oral procedure.

Article 62.

(1) The Registrar shall draw up minutes of every hearing. The minutes shall be signed by the President and by the Registrar and shall constitute an official record.

(2) The parties may inspect the minutes at the Registry and obtain copies at their own expense.

Chapter 4

Judgments

Article 63.

The judgments shall contain:

- a statement that it is the judgment of the Court,
- the date of its delivery,
- the names of the President and of the Judges taking part in it,
- the name of the Advocate-General,
- the name of the Registrar,
- the description of the parties,
- the names of the agents, advisers and lawyers of the parties,
- the submissions of the parties,
- a statement that the Advocate-General has been heard,
- a summary of the facts,
- the grounds for the decision,
- the operative part of the judgment, including the decision as to costs.

Article 64.

(1) The judgment shall be delivered in open court; the parties shall be given notice to attend to hear it.

(2) The original of the judgment, signed by the President, by the Judges who took part in the deliberations and by the Registrar, shall be sealed and deposited at the Registry; the parties shall be served with certified copies of the judgment.

(3) The Registrar shall record on the original of the judgment the date on which it was delivered.

Article 65.

The Judgment shall be binding from the date of its delivery.

Article 66.

(1) Without prejudice to the provisions relating to the interpretation of judgments the Court may, of its own motion or on application by a party made within two weeks after the delivery of a judgment, rectify clerical mistakes, errors in calculation and obvious slips in it.

(2) The parties, whom the Registrar shall duly notify, may lodge written observations within a period prescribed by the President.

(3) The Court shall make its decision in de Deliberation Room after hearing the Advocate-General.

(4) The original of the rectification order shall be annexed to the original of the rectified judgment. A note of this order shall be made in the margin of the original of the rectified judgment.

Article 67.

If the Court should omit to give a decision on a particular point at issue or on costs, any party may within a month after service of the judgment apply to the Court to supplement its judgment.
 The application shall be served on the opposite party and the President shall prescribe a period within which that party may lodge written observations.
 After these observations have been lodged, the Court shall, after hearing the Advocate-General, decide both on the admissibility and on the merits of the application.

Article 68.

The Registrar shall arrange for the publication of reports of cases before the Court.

Chapter 5

Costs

Article 69.

(1) The Court shall give a decision as to costs in its final judgment or in the order which closes the proceedings.

(2) The unsuccessful party shall be ordered to pay the costs if they have been asked for in the successful party's pleading.
 Where there are several unsuccessful parties the Court shall decide how the costs are to be shared.

(3) Where each party succeeds on some and fails on other heads, or where the circumstances are exceptional, the Court may order that the parties bear their own costs in whole or in part.
 The Court may order even a successful party to pay costs which the Court considers that party to have unreasonably or vexatiously caused the opposite party to incur.

(4) A party who discontinues or withdraws from proceedings shall be ordered to pay the costs, unless the discontinuance or withdrawal is justified by the conduct of the opposite party.
 If the opposite party has not asked for costs, the parties shall bear their own costs.

(5) Where a case does not proceed to judgment the costs shall be in the discretion of the Court.

Article 70 (1).

Without prejudice to the second subparagraph of Article 69 (3) of these rules, in proceedings under Article 95 (3) of these rules, institutions shall bear their own costs.

Article 71.

Costs necessarily incurred by a party in enforcing a judgment or order of the Court shall be refunded by the opposite party on the scale in force in the State where the enforcement takes place.

Article 72.

Proceedings before the Court shall be free of charge, except that:
(a) where a party has caused the Court to incur avoidable costs the Court may, after hearing the Advocate-General, order that party to refund them;
(b) where copying or translation work is carried out at the request of a party, the cost shall, in so far as the Registrar considers it excessive, be paid for by that party on the scale of charges referred to in Article 16 (5) of these rules.

Article 73.

Without prejudice to the preceding Article, the following shall be regarded as recoverable costs:
(a) sums payable to witnesses and experts under Article 51 of these rules;
(b) expenses necessarily incurred by the parties for the purpose of the proceedings, in particular the travel and subsistence expenses and the remuneration of agents, advisers and lawyers.

Article 74.

If there is a dispute concerning the costs to be recovered the Chamber to which the case has been assigned shall, on application by the party concerned and after hearing the opposite party and the Advocate-General, make an order, from which no appeal shall lie.

(2) The parties may, for the purposes of enforcement, apply for an authenticated copy of the order.

Article 75.

(1) Sums due from the cashier of the Court shall be paid in the currency of the country where the Court has its seat.
    At the request of the person entitled to any sum, it shall be paid in the currency of the country where the expenses to be refunded were incurred or where the steps in respect of which payment is due were taken.

(2) Other debtors shall make payment in the currency of their country of origin.

(3) Conversions of currency shall be made at the official rates of exchange ruling on the day of payment in the country where the Court has its seat.

Chapter 6

Legal aid

Article 76.

(1) A party who is wholly or in part unable to meet the costs of the proceedings may at any time apply for legal aid.

The application shall be accompanied by evidence of the applicant's need of assistance, and in particular by a document from the competent authority certifying his lack of means.

(2) If the application is made prior to proceedings which the applicant wishes to commence, it shall briefly state the subject of such proceedings.

The application need not be made through a lawyer.

(3) The President shall designate a Judge to act as Rapporteur. The Chamber to which the latter belongs shall, after considering the written observations of the opposite party and after hearing the Advocate-General decide whether legal aid should be granted in full or in part, or whether it should be refused. Where there is manifestly no cause of action, legal aid shall be refused.

The Chamber shall make an order without giving reasons and no appeal shall lie therefrom.

(4) The Chamber may at any time, either of its own motion or on application, withdraw legal aid if the circumstances which led to its being granted alter during the proceedings.

(5) Where legal aid is granted, the cashier of the Court shall advance the funds necessary to meet the expenses.

In its decision as to costs the Court may order the payment to the cashier of the Court of the whole or any part of amounts advanced as legal aid.

The Registrar shall take steps to obtain the recovery of these sums from the party ordered to pay them.

Chapter 7

Discontinuance

Article 77.

If, before the Court has given its decision, the parties reach a settlement of their dispute and intimate to the Court the abandonment of their claims, the Court shall order the case to be removed from the register.

This provision shall not apply to proceedings under Articles 33 and 35 of the ECSC Treaty, Articles 173 and 175 of the EEC Treaty or Articles 146 and 148 of the Euratom Treaty.

Article 78.

If the applicant informs the Court in writing that he wishes to discontinue the proceedings, the Court shall order the case to be removed from the register.

Chapter 8

Service

Article 79.

(1) Where these rules require that a document be served on a person,
the Registrar shall ensure that service is effected at that person's
address for service either by the dispatch of a copy of the document
by registered post with a form for acknowledgment of receipt or by
personal delivery of the copy against a receipt.

The Registrar shall prepare and certify the copies of documents to
be served, save where the parties themselves supply the copies in
accordance with Article 37 (1) of these rules.

(2) The official record of dispatch together with the acknowledgment
or the receipt shall be annexed to the original of the document.

Chapter 9

Time Limits

Article 80.

(1) In the reckoning of any period of time prescribed by the ECSC, EEC
or Euratom Treaties, the Statutes of the Court or these rules for the
taking of any procedural step, the day of the event from which the
period is to run shall be excluded.

Time shall continue to run during vacations.

(2) If the period whould otherwise end on a Sunday or on an official
holiday it shall be extended until the end of the first following
working day.

A list of official holidays drawn up by the Court shall be published
in the Official Journal of the European Communities.

Article 81.

(1) The period of time allowed for commencing proceedings against a
measure adopted by an institution shall run from the day following the
receipt by the person concerned of notification of the measure or,
where the measure is published, from the 15th day after publication
thereof in the Official Journal of the European Communities.

(2) The extensions, on account of distance, of prescribed time limits
shall be provided for in a decision of the Court which shall be published in the Official Journal of the European Communities.

Article 82.

Any time limit prescribed pursuant to these rules may be extended by
whoever prescribed it.

TITLE 3

SPECIAL FORMS OF PROCEDURE

Chapter 1

Suspension of operation or enforcement and other interim measures

Article 83.

(1) An application to suspend the operation of any measure adopted
by an institution, made pursuant to the second paragraph of Article 39
of the ECSC Treaty, Article 185 of the EEC Treaty or Article 157 of
the Euratom Treaty, shall be admissible only if the applicant is
challenging that measure in proceedings before the Court.
    An application for the adoption of any other interim measure refer-
ed to in the third paragraph of Article 39 of the ECSC Treaty, Article
186 of the EEC Treaty or Article 158 of the Euratom Treaty shall be
admissible only if it is made by a party to a case before the Court
and relates to that case.

(2) An application of a kind referred to in paragraph 1 of this Article
shall state the subject matter of the dispute, the circumstances giving
rise to urgency and the factual and legal grounds establishing a'prima
facie' case for the interim measures applied for.

(3) The application shall be made by a separate document and in accordance with the provisions of Articles 37 and 38 of these rules.

Article 84.

(1) The application shall be served on the opposite party, and the
President shall prescribe a short period within which that party may
submit written or oral observations.

(2) The President may order a preparatory inquiry.
    The President may grant the application even before the observations
of the opposite party have been submitted. This decision may be varied
or cancelled even without any application being made by any party.

Article 85.

The President shall either decide on the application himself or refer
it to the Court.
    If the President is absent or prevented from attending, Article 11
of these rules shall apply in a corresponding manner.
    Where the application is referred to it, the Court shall postpone
all other cases, and shall give a decision after hearing the Advocate-
General. Article 84 shall apply in a corresponding manner.

Article 86.

(1) The decision on the application shall take the form of a reasoned
order, from which no appeal shall lie. The order shall be served on
the parties forthwith.

(2) The enforcement of the order may be made conditional on the lodging
by the applicant of security, of an amount and nature to be fixed in

the light of the circumstances.

(3) Unless the order fixes the date on which the interim measure is to lapse, the measure shall lapse when final judgment is delivered.

(4) The order shall have only an interim effect, and shall be without prejudice to the decision of the Court on the substance of the case.

Article 87.

On application by a party, the order may at any time be varied or cancelled on account of a change in circumstances.

Article 88.

Rejection of an application for an interim measure shall not bar the party who made it from making a further application on the basis of new facts.

Article 89.

The provisions of this Chapter shall apply in a corresponding manner to applications to suspend the enforcement of a decision of the Court or of any measure adopted by another institution, submitted pursuant to Articles 44 and 92 of the ECSC Treaty, Articles 187 and 192 of the EEC Treaty or Articles 159 and 164 of the Euratom Treaty. The order granting the application shall fix a date on which the interim measure is to lapse.

Article 90.

(1) An application of a kind referred to in the third and fourth paragraphs of Article 81 of the Euratom Treaty shall contain:
(a) the names and addresses of the persons or undertakings to be inspected;
(b) an indication of what is to be inspected and of the purpose of the inspection.

(2) The President shall give his decision in the form of an order. Article 86 of these rules shall apply in a corresponding manner.
    If the President is absent or prevented from attending, Article 11 of these rules shall apply.

Chapter 2

Procedural issues

Article 91.

(1) A party wishing to apply to the Court for a decision on a preliminary objection or on any other procedural issue shall make the application by a separate document.
    The application must tate the grounds of fact and law relied on and the form of order sought by the applicant; any supporting documents must be annexed to it.

(2) As soon as the application has been lodged, the President shall

prescribe a period within which the opposite party is to lodge a document containing that party's submissions and the grounds for them.

(3) Unless the Court decides otherwise, the remainder of the proceedings shall be oral.

(4) The Court shall, after hearing the Advocate-General, decide on the application or reserve its decision for the final judgment.

If the Court refuses the application or reserves its decision, the President shall prescribe new time limits for the further steps in the proceedings.

Article 92

(1) Where it is clear that the Court has no jurisdiction to take cognizance of an application lodged with it in pursuance of Article 38 (1), the Court may by reasoned order declare the application inadmissible. Such a decision may be adopted even before the application has been served on the party against whom it is made.

(2) The Court may at any time of its own motion consider whether there exists any absolute bar to proceedings with a case, and shall give its decision in accordance with Article 91 (3) and (4) of these rules.

Chapter 3

Intervention

Article 93

(1) An application to intervene must be made within three months of the publication of the notice referred to in Article 16 (6) of these rules.

(2) The application shall contain:

(a) a description of the case;
(b) the description of the parties;
(c) the name and permanent residence of the intervener;
(d) the reasons for the intervener's interest in the result of the case, having regard to Article 37 of the EEC Statute and Article 38 of the Euratom Statute;
(e) submissions supporting or opposing the submissions of a party to the original case;
(f) an indication of any evidence founded upon and, in an annex, the supporting documents;
(g) the intervener's address for service at the place where the Court has its seat.

The intervener shall be represented in accordance with the first and second paragraphs of Article 20 of the ECSC Statute and with Article 17 of the EEC and Euratom Statutes.

Articles 37 and 38 of these rules shall apply in a corresponding manner.

(3) The application shall be served on the parties to the original case. The Court shall give the parties an opportunity to submit their

written or oral observations an shall, after hearing the Advocate-
General, give its decision in the form of an order.

(4) If the Court allows the intervention, the intervener shall receive
a copy of every document served on the parties. The Court may, however,
on application by one of the parties, omit secret or confidential
documents.

(5) The intervener must accept the case as he finds it at the time of
his intervention.
    The President shall prescribe a period within which the intervener
is to state in writing the grounds for his submissions.

Chapter 4

Judgments by default and applications to set them aside

Article 94.

(1) If a defendant on whom an application originating proceedings has
been duly served fails to lodge a defence to the application in the
proper form within the time prescribed, the applicant may apply for
judgment by default.
    The application shall be served on the defendant. The President
shall fix a date for the opening of the oral procedure.
. . . . .

Chapter 5

Cases assigned to Chambers

Article 95

(1) The Court may assign to a Chamber any reference for a preliminary
ruling of a kind mentioned in Article 103 of these rules as well as
any action instituted by a natural or legal person under
Article 33 (2), Article 34 (2), Article 35, Article 36 (2), Article 40
(1) and (2), and Article 42 of the ECSC Treaty, Article 172, Article 173
(2), Article 175 (3), Article 178 and Article 181 of the EEC Treaty,
and Article 144, Article 146 (2), Article 148 (3), Article 151 and
Article 153 of the Euratom Treaty, in so far as the difficulty or the
importance of the case or particular circumstances are not such as to
require that the Court decide it in plenary session.

(2) The decision so to assign a case shall be taken by the Court at
the end of the written procedure upon consideration of the preliminary
report presented by the Judge-Rapporteur and after the Advocate-General
has been heard.
    However, a case may not be so assigned if a Member State or an in-
stitution of the Communities, being a party to the proceedings, has
requested that the case be decided in plenary sessions. In this subparagraph the expression 'party to the proceedings' means any Member
State or any institution which is a party to or an intervener in the
 proceedings or which has submitted written observations in any reference of a kind mentioned in Article 103 of these rules.

(3) Proceedings commenced by an official or other servant of an in-

stitution against the institution shall, with the exception of applications for the adoption of interim measures, be tried by a Chamber designated each year by the Court for that purpose. Such allocation shall not preclude the adoption of appropriate measures in cases whose subject-matter is related.

(4) A Chamber may at any stage refer to the Court any case assigned to or devolving upon it.

Article 96

(1) Where an application for the adoption of interim measures is made to the President in the course of proceedings under Article 95 (3) of these rules but the President is absent or prevented from hearing the application, his place shall be taken by the President of the designated Chamber.

(2) Without prejudice to his power or referral under Article 85 of these rules, the President may refer the application to the designated Chamber.
. . . . .

Chapter 8

Interpretation of Judgments

Article 102.

(1) An application for interpretation of a judgment shall be made in accordance with Articles 37 and 38 of these rules. In addition it shall specify:
(a) the judgment in question;
(b) the passages of which interpretation is sought.
The application must be made against all the parties to the case in which the judgment was given.

(2) The Court shall give its decision in the form of a judgment after having given the parties an opportunity to submit their observations and after hearing the Advocate-General.
The original of the interpreting judgment shall be annexed to the original of the judgment interpreted. A note of the interpreting judgment shall be made in the margin of the original of the judgment interpreted.

Chapter 9

Preliminary Rulings and other references for interpretation

Article 103.

(1) In cases governed by Article 20 of the EEC Statute and Article 21 of the Euratom Statute, the provisions of Article 43 et seq. of these rules shall apply after the statements of case or written observations provided for in the said Articles 20 and 21 have been lodged.
The same provisions shall apply even where such documents are not logded within the time prescribed in those Articles 20 and 21, or where the parties to the main action, the Member States, the Commission or,

as the case may be, the Council declare an intention to dispense with
them.

(2) The provisions of paragraph 1 shall apply to the references for a
preliminary ruling provided for in the Protocol concerning the interpretation by the Court of Justice of the Convention of 29 February
1968 on the Mutual Recognition of Companies and Legal Persons and the
Protocol concerning the interpretation by the Court of Justice of the
Convention of 27 September 1968 on jurisdiction and the enforcement of
civil and commercial judgments, signed at Luxembourg on 3 June 1971,
and to the references provided for by Article 4 of the latter Protocol.
    The provisions of paragraph 1 shall apply also to references for
preliminary rulings provided for by other existing or future agreements.

(3) In cases provided for in Article 41 of the ECSC Treaty, the text
of the decision to refer the matter shall be served on the parties in
the case, the Member States, the High Authority and the Special Council
of Ministers.
    These parties, States and institutions may, within two months from
the date of such service, lodge written statements of case or written
observations.
    After these documents have been lodged, or where they have not been
lodged within the time prescribed in the preceding subparagraph, the
provisions of Article 43 et seq. of these rules shall apply.

Article 104

(1) The decisions of national courts or tribunals referred to in Article
103 of these rules shall be communicated to the Member States in the
original version, accompanied by a translation into the official language of the State to which they are addressed.

(2) As regards the representation and attendance of the parties to the
main proceedings in the preliminary ruling procedure the Court shall
take account of the rules of procedure of the national court or tribunal which made the reference.

(3) It shall be for the national court or tribunal to decide as to the
costs of the reference.
    In special circumstances the Court may grant, as legal aid, assist-
ance for the purpose of facilitating the representation or attendance
of a party.
.....

Chapter 11

Opinions

Article 107.

(1) A request by the Council for an Opinion under Article 228 of the
EEC Treaty shall be served on the Commission. Such a request by the
Commission shall be served on the Council and on the Member States.
Such a request by a Member State shall be served on the Council, the
Commission and the other Member States.
    The President shall prescribe a period within which the institutions
and Member States which have been served with a request may submit their

written observations.

(2) The Opinion may deal not only with the question whether the envisaged agreement is compatible with the provisions of the EEC Treaty
but also with the question whether the Community or any Community institution has the power to enter into that agreement.

Article 108.

(1) As soon as the request for an Opinion has been lodged, the President
shall designate a Judge to act as Rapporteur.

(2) The Court sitting in the Deliberation Room shall, after hearing the
Advocate-General, deliver a reasoned Opinion.

(3) The Opinion signed by the President, by the Judges who took part
in the deliberations and by the Registrar shall be served on the Council, the Commission and the Member States.

Article 109.

Requests for the opinion of the Court under the fourth paragraph of
Article 95 of the ECSC Treaty shall be submitted jointly by the High
Authority and the Special Council of Ministers.
  The Opinion shall be delivered in accordance with the provisions of
the preceding Article. It shall be communicated to the High Authority,
the Special Council of Ministers and the European Parliament.
. . . . .

Chapter Three

RELATIONSHIP BETWEEN COMMUNITY LAW AND NATIONAL LAW

FUNDAMENTAL RIGHTS IN THE COMMUNITY

1. Extract of the Commission's special report on the protection of
   fundamental rights of 4 February 1976 submitted to the European
   Parliament and the Council.
   (Supplement to the Bulletin of the European Communities 6/76)

The standard of fundamental rights in the Community

Fundamental rights as an essential part of the Community
legal order

7. There are provisions in the Treaties themselves whose aim, or at
   least effect, is to guarantee and improve the position of the individual in the Community: e.g., Articles 7, 48, 52, 57, 117, 119
   EEC. It is on the basis of some of these articles that the Court
   of Justice has been able to give important judgments as regards the
   protection of fundamental rights.
      At the same time, it must not be forgotten that the creation of
   the Common Market has had the effect of extending beyond national
   frontiers the area over which the freedom of the citizen, especially
   in the economic sector, may be exercised.

8. Turning to fundamental rights, strictly speaking, the Community institutions have, since the beginning of the Community, been faced
   with the question of their existence and with a precise definition
   of their scope under the Community legal order. Today, fundamental
   rights - however they may be defined[1]- undeniably constitute an
   essential part of the Community legal order.
      The individual citizen should not be without protection in the
   face of official power. He must have certain inviolable rights. This
   is one of the fundamental elements in the identity and cohesion of
   the Community.
      In its report on European Union[2] the Commission has already stated
   that it sees democracy as one of the basic conditions for coexistence
   and integration of the Member States within the Community. An essential part of any democracy is protection of and respect for human
   rights and fundamental freedoms which alone enable the individual
   citizen freely to develop his personality. There can be no democracy
   without recognition and protection of human rights and guaranteed
   freedom of the citizen. This is equally true of the Community.
      Even if the basic principles are clear it has nevertheless been
   difficult to secure agreement on the scope and effect of the various
   fundamental rights.

The case law of the Court of Justice

9. The Court of Justice of the European Communities was faced with the
   question of fundamental rights for the first time in 1959. Its case

law is sufficiently well known and may be summarized as follows:

(i) In two judments in 1959 and 1960[3] the Court of Justice initially held that it was not competent to examine the legality of acts of the Community institutions according to the yardstick of national fundamental rights.

(ii) The subsequent cases of Stauder (1969) and Internationale Handelsgesellschaft (1970)[4] reveal a new attitude in the jurisprudence of the Court when it held that 'respect for fundamental rights forms an integral part of the general principles of law of which (it) ensures respect'.

(iii) In 1974, in the Nold case[5] the Court of Justice went one step further. It seemed to have moved towards a sort of optimum standard of fundamental rights by holding that 'in safeguarding these rights, the Court is bound to draw inspiration from the constitutional traditions common to the Member States, and it cannot, therefore, uphold measures which are incompatible with fundamental rights recognized and protected by the Constitutions of those States'. In addition, the Court of Justice draws from international treaties on the protection of human rights in which the Member States have collaborated or of which they are signatories guidelines for determining general legal principles which apply in the Community legal order.

The abovementioned decisions concern the right to human dignity and freedom in general (Stauder) and the principles of the freedom to develop and deal with property from an economic standpoint (in ternationale Handelsgesellschaft). The Nold case concerned rights of ownership in the economic sense and freedom to choose and practice a profession or trade.

The Court of Justice has, however, recognized that fundamental rights are not to be considered as absolute. As in all legal systems, there are no fundamental rights which are not subject to limitations, the extent of which depends on the nature of the right involved.

In this way the Court of Justice has already held in the International Handelsgesellschaft case that 'the protection of (fundamental) rights, while inspired by the constitutional principles common to the Member States, must be ensured within the framework of the Community's structure and objectives'. In the Nold case, the Court decided that even if the fundamental rights at issue in the case were protected, nevertheless these were to be considered 'in the light of the social function of the property and activities protected thereunder' so that it is legitimate 'that these rights should if necessary be subject to certain limits justified by the overall objectives pursued by the Community, on condition that the substance of these rights is left untouched'.

Furthermore, other judgments of the Court have recognized a number of important general principles of law as essential elements of the principle of the rule of law in order to secure an effective protection of fundamental rights. These include the principle of proportionality,[6] the requirement of legal certainty and the protection of confidence thereby,[7] observance of the principle of the right to be heard and to defend one's rights in legal proceedings,[8] the prohibition of conviction of a single offence twice,[9] the general obligation to give reasons[10] and the principle of non-discrimination.[11]

Furthermore the Court of Justice has not only paid attention to the substantive standard as regards the protection of the citizen against public authority: it has also considered the problem of the access of the individual to the Community court.

On the one hand, by developing a more and more favourable jurisprudence on the subject of the direct effect of Community provisions, it has considerably widened access to the national courts and thereby broadened the scope of application of Article 177 EEC. On the other hand, the cases decided by it since 1971 involving Article 215 EEC[12] enable the individual citizen to go before the Court of Justice even where the damages alleged arise out of Community legal acts which cannot be directly attacked.

In this way access to the Court as laid down in Articles 173 and 175 EEC has been substantially extended.

. . . . .

----

1) Point 9.
2) Supplement 5/75 - Bull. EC.
3) CJEC 4.2.1959 - Stork v. High Authority, 1/58, (1958-59) ECR 43; CJEC 15.7.1960 - Ruhrkohlenverkaufsgesellschaften v. High Authority, 36-38, 40/59, (1960) ECR 857.
4) CJEC 12.11.1969, 29/69, (1969) ECR 419; CJEC 17.12.1970, 11/70, (1970) ECR 1125. For a translation in English, see respectively (1970) CMLR 112 and (1972) CMLR 255.
5) CJEC 14.5.1974 - Nold v. Commission, 4/73, (1974) ECR 491; CJEC 28.10.1975 - Rutili v. The French Minister for the Interior, 36/75, (1975) ECR 1219.
6) CJEC 12.6.1958 - Compagnie des Hauts Fourneaux de Chasse v. High Authority, 15/57, (1958) ECR 155.
7) CJEC 4.7.1973 - Westzucker v. Einfuhr- und Vorratstelle für Zucker, 1/73, (1973) ECR 723.
8) CJEC 22.3.1961 - Société Nouvelle des Usines de Pontlieue v. High Authority, 42 and 49/59, (1961) ECR 101.
9) CJEC 14.12.1972 - Boehringer Mannheim GmbH v. Commission, 7/72, (1972) ECR 1281.
10) CJEC 15.3.1967 - SA Cimenteries CBR, Cementbedrijven NV et al. v. Commission, 8-11/66, (1967) ECR 75; CJEC 28.10.1975 - Rutili v. the French Minister for the Interior, 36/75, (1975) ECR 1219.
11) CJEC 24.10.1973 - Merkur-Aussenhandels-GmbH v. Commission, 43/72, (1973) ECR 1055.
12) CJEC 2.12.1971 - Zuckerfabrik Schöppenstedt v. Council. 5/71, (1971) ECR 1975.

2. Joint Declaration

by

the European Parliament, the Council and the Commission

(OJ No C 103, 27 April 1977, p.1)

THE EUROPEAN PARLIAMENT, THE COUNCIL AND THE COMMISSION,

Whereas the Treaties establishing the European Communities are based on the principle of respect for the law;

Whereas, as the Court of Justice has recognized, that law comprises, over and above the rules embodied in the treaties and secondary Community legislation, the general principles of law and in particular the fundamental rights, principles and rights on which the constitutional law of the Member States is based;

Whereas, in particular, all the Member States are Contracting Parties to the European Convention for the Protection of Human Rights and Fundamental Freedoms signed in Rome on 4 November 1950,

HAVE ADOPTED THE FOLLOWING DECLARATION:

1. The European Parliament, the Council and the Commission stress the prime importance they attach to the protection of fundamental rights, as derived in particular from the constitutions of the Member States and the European Convention for the Protection of Human Rights and Fundamental Freedoms.

2. In the exercise of their powers and in pursuance of the aims of the European Communities they respect and will continue to respect these rights.

Done at Luxembourg on the fifth day of April in the year one thousand nine hundred and seventy-seven.

For the European Parliament	For the Council	For the Commission
E. COLOMBO	D. OWEN	R. JENKINS

3. The European Council meeting in Copenhagen on 7 and 8 April 1978
issued the following statement on democracy:

The election of the Members of the Assembly by direct universal suffr-
age is an event of outstanding importance for the future of the European Communities and a vivid demonstration of the ideals of democracy
shared by the people within them.

The creation of the Communities, which is the foundation of ever closer
union among the peoples of Europe called for in the Treaty of Rome,
marked the determination of their founders to strengthen the protection of peace and freedom.

The Heads of State and of Government confirm their will, as expressed
in the Copenhagen Declaration on the European identity, to ensure that
the cherished values of their legal, political and moral order are
respected and to safeguard the principles of representative democracy,
of the rule of law, of social justice and of respect for human rights.

The application of these principles implies a political system of
pluralist democracy which guarantees both the free expression of opinions within the constitutional organization of powers and the procedures
necessary for the protection of human rights.

The Heads of State and of Government associate themselves with the
Joint Declaration by the Assembly, the Council and the Commission
whereby these institutions expressed their determination to respect
fundamental rights in pursuing the aims of the Communities.

They solemnly declare that respect for andmaintanance of representative
democracy and human rights in each Member State are essential elements
of membership of the European Communities.

----

1) O.J. No C 103, 27 April 1977, p. 1.

Chapter Four

THE FOUNDATIONS OF THE COMMUNITY

1. FIRST COUNCIL DIRECTIVE

of 11 April 1967

on the harmonisation of legislation of Member States concerning
turnover taxes

(67/227/EEC)
(J.O. 1967, p. 1301; O.J. (Special Edition 1967) p. 14)

THE COUNCIL OF THE EUROPEAN ECONOMIC COMMUNITY,

Having regard to the Treaty establishing the European Economic
Community, and in particular Articles 99 and 100 thereof;
Having regard to the proposal from the Commission;
Having regard to the Opinion of the European Parliament;
Having regard to the Opinion of the Economic and Social Committee;
Whereas the main objective of the Treaty is to establish, within
the framework of an economic union, a common market within which
there is healthy competition and whose characteristics are similar
to those of a domestic market;
Whereas the attainment of this objective presupposes the prior
application in Member States of legislation concerning turnover taxes
such as will not distort conditions of competition or hinder the free
movement of goods and services within the common market;
Whereas the legislation at present in force does not meet these
requirements; whereas it is therefore in the interest of the common
market to achieve such harmonisation of legislation concerning turnover taxes as will eliminate, as far as possible, factors which may
distort conditions of competition, whether at national or Community
level, and make it possible subsequently to achieve the aim of abolishing the imposition of tax on importation and the remission of tax
on exportation in trade between Member States;
Whereas, in the light of the studies made, it has become clear
that such harmonisation must result in the abolition of cumulative
multi-stage taxes and in the adoption by all Member States of a common system of value added tax;
Whereas a system of value added tax achieves the highest degree of
simplicity and of neutrality when the tax is levied in as general a
manner as possible and when its scope covers all stages of production
and distribution and the provision of services; whereas it is therefore in the interest of the common market and of Member States to
adopt a common system which shall also apply to the retail trade;
Whereas, however, the application of that tax to retail trade
might in some Member States meet with practical and political difficulties; whereas, therefore, Member States should be permitted, subject
to prior consultation, to apply the common system only up to and
including the wholesale trade stage, and to apply, as appropriate, a
separate complementary tax at the retail trade stage, or at the preceeding stage;
Whereas it is necessary to proceed by stages, since the harmonis-

ation of turnover taxes will lead in Member States to substantial alterations in tax structure and will have appreciable consequences in the budgetary, economic and social fields;

Whereas the replacement of the cumulative multi-stage tax systems in force in the majority of Member States by the common system of value added tax is bound, even if the rates and exemptions are not harmonised at the same time, to result in neutrality in competition, in that within each country similar goods bear the same tax burden, whatever the length of the production and distribution chain, and that in international trade the amount of the tax burden borne by goods is known so that an exact equalisation of that amount may be ensured; whereas, therefore, provision should be made, in the first stage, for adoption by all Member States of the common system of value added tax, without an accompanying harmonisation of rates and exemptions;

Whereas it is not possible to foresee at present how and within what period the harmonisation of turnover taxes can achieve the aim of abolishing the imposition of tax on importation and the remission of tax on exportation in trade between Member States; whereas it is therefore preferable that the second stage and the measures to be taken in respect of that stage should be determined later on the basis of proposals made by the Commission to the Council;

HAS ADOPTED THIS DIRECTIVE,

Article 1. Member States shall replace their present system of turn-over taxes by the common system of value added tax defined in Article 2.

In each Member State the legislation to effect this replacement shall be enacted as rapidly as possible, so that it can enter into force on a date to be fixed by the Member State in the light of the conjunctural situation; this date shall not be later than 1 January 1970.

From the entry into force of such legislation, the Member State shall not maintain or introduce any measure providing for flat-rate equalisation of turnover taxes on importation or exportation in trade between Member States.

Article 2. The principle of the common system of value added tax involves the application to goods and services of a general tax on consumption exactly proportional to the price of the goods and serv-ices, whatever the number of transactions which take place in the production and distribution process before the stage at which tax is charged.

On each transaction, value added tax, calculated on the price of the goods or services at the rate applicable to such goods or ser-vices, shall be chargeable after deduction of the amount of value added tax borne directly by the various cost components.

The common system of value added tax shall be applied up to and including the retail trade stage.

However, until the abolition of the imposition of tax on importa-tion and the remission of tax on exportation in trade between Member States, Member States may, subject to the consultation provided for in Article 5, apply this system only up to and including the whole-sale trade stage, and may apply, as appropriate, a separate comple-mentary tax at the retail trade stage or at the preceeding stage.

Article 3. The Council shall issue, on a proposal from the Commission, a second Directive concerning the structure of, and the procedure for applying, the common system of value added tax.

Article 4. In order to enable the Council to discuss this, and if possible to take decisions before the end of the transitional period, the Commission shall submit to the Council, before the end of 1968, proposals as to how and within what period the harmonisation of turnover taxes can achieve the aim of abolishing the imposition of tax on importation and the remission of tax on exportation in trade between Member States, while ensuring the neutrality of those taxes as regards the origin of the goods or services.

In this connection, particular account shall be taken of the relationship between direct and indirect taxes, which differs in the various Member States; of the effects of an alteration in tax systems on the tax and budget policy of Member States; and of the influence which tax systems have on conditions of competition and on social conditions in the Community.

Article 5. Should a Member State intend to exercise the power provided for in the last paragraph of Article 2, it shall so inform the Commission in good time, having regard to Article 102 of the Treaty.

Article 6. This Directive is addressed to the Member States.

Done at Brussels, 11 April 1967.

For the Council

The President

R. VAN ELSLANDE

2. Extract of

SIXTH COUNCIL DIRECTIVE

of 17 May 1977

on the harmonisation of the laws of the Member States relating to turnover taxes – Common system of value added tax: uniform basis of assessment

(77/388/EEC)
(O.J. No L 145, 13 June 1977, p. 1)

THE COUNCIL OF THE EUROPEAN ECONOMIC COMMUNITIES,

Having regard to the Treaty establishing the European Economic Community, and in particular Articles 99 and 100 thereof;
Having regard to the proposal from the Commission,

Having regard to the opinion of the European Parliament,
Having regard to the opinion of the Economic and Social Committee,

Whereas all Member States have adopted a system of value added tax in accordance with the first and second Council Directives of 11 April 1967 on the harmonisation of the laws of the Member States relating to turnover taxes;
Whereas the decision of 21 April 1970 on the replacement of financial contributions from Member States by the Communities' own resources provides that the budget of the Communities shall, irrespective of other revenue, be financed entirely from the Communities' own resources; whereas these resources are to include those accruing from value added tax and obtained by applying a common rate of tax on a basis of assessment determined in a uniform manner according to Community rules;

Whereas further progress should be made in the effective removal of restrictions on the movement of persons, goods, services and capital and the integration of national economies;

Whereas account should be taken of the objective of abolishing the imposition of tax on the importation and the remission of tax on exportation in trade between Member States; whereas it should be insured that the common system of turnover taxes is non-discriminatory as regards the origin of goods and services, so that a common market permitting fair competition and resembling a real internal market may ultimately be achieved;

Whereas, to enhance the non-discriminatory nature of the tax, the term 'taxable person' must be clarified to enable the Member States to extend it to cover persons who occasionally carry out certain transactions;

Whereas the term 'taxable transaction' has led to difficulties, in particular as regards transactions treated as taxable transactions; whereas these concepts must be clarified;

Whereas the determination of the place where taxable transactions are effected has been the subject of conflicts concerning jurisdiction as between Member States, in particular as regards supplies of goods for assembly and the supply of services; whereas although the place where a supply of services is effected should in principle be defined as the place where the person supplying the services has his principal place of business, that place should be defined as being in the country of the person to whom the services are supplied, in particular in the case of certain services supplied between taxable persons where the cost of the services is included in the price of the goods;

Whereas the concepts of chargeable event and of the charge to tax must be harmonised if the introduction and any subsequent alterations of the Community rate are to become operative at the same time in all Member States;

Whereas the taxable base must be harmonised so that the application of the Community rate to taxable transactions leads to comparable results in all the Member States;

Whereas the rates applied by Member States must be such as to allow the normal deduction of the tax applied at the preceeding stage;

Whereas a common list of exemptions should be drawn up so that the Communities' own resources may be collected in a uniform manner in all the Member States;

Whereas the rules governing deductions should be harmonised to the extent that they affect the actual amounts collected; whereas the deductible proportion should be calculated in a similar manner in all the Member States;

Whereas it should be specified which persons are liable to pay tax, in particular as regards services supplied by a person established in another country;

Whereas the obligations of taxpayers must be harmonised as far as possible so as to ensure the necessary safeguards for the collection of taxes in a uniform manner in all the Member States; whereas taxpayers should, in particular, make a periodic aggregate return of their transactions, relating to both inputs and outputs where this appears necessary for establishing and monitoring the basis of assessment of own resources;

Whereas Member States should nevertheless be able to retain their special schemes for small undertakings, in accordance with common provisions, and with a view to closer harmonisation; whereas Member States should remain free to apply a special scheme involving flat rate rebates of input value added tax to farmers not covered by normal schemes; whereas the basic principles of this scheme should be established and a common method adopted for calculating the value added of these farmers for the purposes of collecting own resources;

Whereas the uniform application of the provisions of this Directive should be ensured; whereas to this end a Community procedure for consultation should be laid down; whereas the setting up of a Value Added Tax Committee would enable the Member States and the Commission to cooperate closely;

Whereas Member States should be able, within certain limits and subject to certain conditions, to take or retain special measures derogating from this Directive in order to simplify the levying of tax or to avoid fraud or tax avoidance;

Whereas it might appear appropriate to authorise Member States to conclude with non-member countries or international organisations agreements containing derogations from this Directive;

Whereas it is vital to provide for a transitional period to allow national laws in specified fields to be gradually adapted.
. . . . .

3. REGULATION (EEC) No 1544/69 OF THE COUNCIL

of 23 July 1969

on the tariff applicable to goods contained in travellers'
personal luggage
(J.O. No L 191/69, p. 1; O.J. (Special Edition 1969 11) p. 359)

THE COUNCIL OF THE EUROPEAN COMMUNITIES,

Having regard to the Treaty establishing the European Economic
Community, and in particular Article 28 thereof;

Having regard to the draft Regulation submitted by the Commission;

Whereas, following the entry into force on 1 July 1968 of the
Common Customs Tariff, the rules concerning the tariff applicable to
goods contained in travellers' personal luggage should be reviewed on
a Community basis;

Whereas the assessment of customs duties to which such goods may
be subject raises complex problems for the customs authorities by
reason of the volume of traffic, the speed requirements involved,
and the variety of goods imported which generally, for goods falling
within any one tariff heading, are of little chargeable value;

Whereas Community arrangements for relief from duty covering passenger traffic between third countries and the Community appear therefore to be necessary;

Whereas such relief must be confined to non-commercial importations
of goods by travellers;

HAS ADOPTED THIS REGULATION,

TITLE 1

Exemptions

Article 1. 1. Goods contained in the personal luggage or travellers
coming from third countries shall be exempt from common customs
duties if the imported goods have no commercial character and the
total value of the goods does not exceed 40 European units of account
per person.

For the purposes of this Regulation, "personal luggage" shall mean
the whole of the luggage which a traveller is in a position to submit
to the customs authorities upon his arrival, as well as luggage which
he submits later to the same authorities, subject to proof that such
luggage was registered as accompanied luggage, at the time of his
departure, with the company which has been resposible for conveying
him.

The definition of "personal luggage" shall not cover portable
containers containing fuel. However for each means of motor transport
a quantity of fuel not exceeding 10 litres shall be admitted duty free
in such a container, without prejudice to national provisions governing the possession and transport of fuel.

2. Member States may reduce this exemption to 20 European units of
account for travellers under 15 years of age.

3. Where the total value per person of several items exceeds 40
European units of account or the amount fixed pursuant to paragraph 2,

as the case may be, exemption up to those amounts shall be granted
for such of the items as would, if imported separately, have been
granted exemption, it being understood that the value of an individual
item cannot be split up.

Article 2. 1. The following quantitative limits shall apply to importation of the under-mentioned goods under exemption from common customs
duties:

(a) tobacco products:
  - in the case of travellers residing outside Europe:

    up to 400 cigarettes

    or 200 cigarillos (cigars of a maximum weight of 3 grammes each)

    or 100 cigars

    or 500 grammes of smoking tobacco;

  - in the case of travellers residing in Europe:

    200 cigarettes

    or 100 cigarillos (cigars of a maximum weight of 3 grammes each)

    or 50 cigars

    or 250 grammes of smoking tobacco;

(b) alcoholic beverages:

  - distilled beverages and spirits of an alcoholic strength exceed-
    ing 22°:

    1 standard bottle (0.70 to 1 litre)

    or

  - distilled beverages and spirits and aperitifs with a wine or
    alcoholic base of an alcoholic strength not exceeding 22°;
    sparkling wines, fortified wines: to a total of 2 litres,

    and

  - still wines: to a total of 2 litres;

(c) Perfumes: 50 grammes

    and toilet waters: $\frac{1}{4}$ litre.

  2. Travellers under 17 years of age shall not qualify for any
exemption in respect of the goods referred to in paragraph 1(a) and(b).
  3. Within the quantitative limits set in paragraph 1 and taking
account of the restrictions in paragraph 2,the value of the goods listed in paragraph 1 shall not be taken into consideration in ascertaining the amount of the exemption under Article 1.

Article 3. For purposes of ascertaining the amount of the exemption under Article 1 the value of the following shall not be taken into consideration:

- personal effects temporarily imported, or re-imported after being temporarily exported;

- books, newspapers and periodicals.

Article 4. Member States may set lower limits as to value and/or quantity for the exemption of goods when they are imported:

- in frontier zone travel

- by the crew of the means of transport used in travel between third countries and the Community.

TITLE II

Standard rate of duty

Article 5. 1. Standard *ad valorem* customs duty of 10% shall apply to goods contained in travellers' personal luggage in excess of the exemption limits set in Article 1 and/or Article 2(1), where such imports have no commercial character and the total value of the goods does not exceed eighty-five units of account per person.
2. The total value referred to in paragraph 1 shall be ascertained:

- taking into account the value of goods which qualified for exemption under Article 1, up to the amounts specified in that Article,

- without taking into account the value of goods which qualified for exemption under Article 2(1).

3. The standard rate of customs duty specified in paragraph 1 shall not apply to products listed in Chapter 24 of the Common Customs Tariff.

Article 6. The standard rate of customs duty mentioned in Article 5 shall not apply where, before the goods are charged to duty at that rate, the traveller has applied for them to be assessed to duty in accordance with the appropriate scale. In such case, all the imported goods shall be subject to the appropriate duties, save for, but not exceeding, the amount of the exemptions under Article 1 and/or Article 2(1).

TITLE III

General provisions

Article 7. For the purposes of application of this Regulation, importations shall be treated as having no commercial character if they:

(a) take place occasionally and

(b) consist exclusively of goods for the personal or family use of the travellers, or of goods intended as presents; the nature and quantity of such goods must not be such as might indicate that they are being imported for commercial reasons.

Article 8. 1. Member States may round off the sums resulting from the conversion into national currency of the amounts provided for in Article 1.

2. Member States may maintain unchanged the exchange value of the amounts of 40 and 25 European units of account in national currency if, at the time of the annual adjustment referred to in the first sub-paragraph of Article 2(2) of Council Regulation (EEC) No 2779/78 of 23 November 1978 applying the European unit of account (EUA) to legal acts adopted in the customs sphere, the conversion of these amounts leads, before the rounding off provided for in paragraph 1, to an alteration of less than 5% in the exchange value denominated in national currencies.

Article 9. In Title 11 B of Part 1 of the Annex to Council Regulation (EEC) No 950/68 of 28 June 1968 on the Common Customs Tariff, the following words shall be deleted:

(a) in paragraph 1: 'or contained in the personal luggage of travellers',

(b) in paragraph 3: 'or the traveller'.

Article 10. Each Member State shall inform the Commission of the measures it is taking to implement this Regulation.

The Commission shall communicate this information to the other Member States.

Article 11. As amended by Council Regulation 3061/78 entered into force 1 January 1979.

This Regulation shall be binding in its entirety and directly applicable in all Member States.

Done at Brussels, 23 July 1969.

For the Council

The President

J. M. A. H. LUNS

4. COUNCIL DIRECTIVE

of 28 May 1969

on the harmonisation of provisions laid down by law, regulation
or administrative action relating to exemption from turnover tax
and excise duty on imports in international travel

(69/169/EEC)
(J.O. No L 133, 4 June 1969, p. 6; O.J. (Special Edition 1969 1)p.232)

THE COUNCIL OF THE EUROPEAN COMMUNITIES,

Having regard to the Treaty establishing the European Economic
Community, and in particular Article 99 thereof;

Having regard to the proposal from the Commission;

Whereas, not withstanding the achievement of the customs union, which
involves the abolition of customs duties and the majority of charges
having equivalent effect in trade between Member States, it is necessary, until harmonisation of indirect taxes has reached an advanced
stage, to retain the imposition of tax on importation and the remission of tax on exportation in such trade;

Whereas it is desirable that, even before such harmonisation, the
populations of the Member States should become more strongly conscious
of the reality of the common market and that to this end measures
should be adopted for the greater liberalisation of the system of
taxes on imports in travel between Member States; whereas the need for
such measures has been emphasised repeatedly by members of the Assembly;

Whereas reductions of this kind in respect of travel constitute a
further step in the direction of the reciprocal opening of the markets
of the Member States and the creation of conditions similar to those
of a domestic market;

Whereas such reductions must be limited to non-commercial importations
of goods by travellers; whereas, as a general rule, such goods can
only be obtained in the country from which they come (country of exit)
already taxed, so that if the country of entry forgoes, within the
prescribed limits, charging turnover tax and excise duty on imports,
this avoids double taxation without leading to an absence of taxation;

Whereas a Community system of tax reductions on imports has proved
necessary also in respect of travel between third countries and the
Community;

HAS ADOPTED THIS DIRECTIVE,

Article 1. 1. Exemption from turnover tax and excise duty on imports
shall apply, as regards travel between third countries and the Commun-

84

ity, to goods in travellers' personal luggage, if such imports have no commercial character and the total value of the goods does not exceed 25 units of account per person.

2. Member States may reduce this exemption to 10 units of account for travellers under fifteen years old.

3. Where the total value per person of several items exceeds 25 units of account or the amount fixed pursuant to paragraph 2, as the case may be, exemption up to these amounts shall be granted for such of the items as would, if imported separately, have been granted exemption, it being understood that the value of an individual item cannot be split up.

Article 2. 1. Exemption from turnover tax and excise duty on imports shall apply to goods contained in the personal luggage of travellers coming from Member States of the Community provided that they fulfil the conditions laid down in Articles 9 and 10 of the Treaty, have been acquired subject to the general rules governing taxation on the domestic market of one of the Member States and have no commercial character and that the total value of the goods does not exceed 180 European units of account per person.

2. Member States may reduce this exemption to 50 European units of account for travellers under fifteen years old.

3. Where the total value per person of several items exceeds 180 European units of account or the amount fixed pursuant to paragraph 2, as the case may be, exemption up to these amounts shall be granted for such of the items as would, if imported separately, have been granted exemption, it being understood that the value of an individual item cannot be split up.

4.Where the travel referred to in paragraph 1:

- involves transit through the territory of a third country; overflying without landing shall not, however, be regarded as transit within the meaning of this Directive,

- begins in a part of the territory of another Member State in which turnover tax and/or excise duty is not chargeable on goods consumed within that territory,

the traveller must be able to establish that the goods transported in his luggage have been acquired subject to the general conditions governing taxation on the domestic market of a Member State and do not qualify for any refunding of turnover tax and/or excise duty, failing which Article 1 shall apply.

5. Under no circumstances may the total value of the goods exempted exceed the amount provided for in paragraph 1 or 2.

Article 3. For the purposes of this Directive:

1. The value of personal effects which are imported temporarily or are re-imported following their temporary export shall not be taken into consideration for determining the exemption referred to in Articles 1 and 2.

2. Importations shall be regarded as having no commercial character if they:

(a) take place occasionally, and

(b) consist exclusively of goods for the personal or family use of the travellers, or of goods intended as presents; the nature or quantity of such goods must not be such as might indicate that they are being imported for commercial reasons.

Article 4. 1. Without prejudice to national provisions applicable to travellers whose residence is outside Europe, each Member State shall set the following quantitative limits for exemptions from turnover tax and excise duty of the goods listed below:

	1 *Travel between* *third countries* *and the Community*	11 *Travel between* *Member States*
(a) tobacco products		
cigarettes	200	300
or		
cigarillos (cigars of a maximum weight of 3 grammes each)	100	150
or		
cigars	50	75
or		
smoking tobacco	250g	400g
(b) alcoholic beverages		
– distilled beverages and spirits of an alcoholic strength exceeding 22°	1 standard bottle (0.70 to 1 litre)	to a total of 1.5 litres
or		
distilled beverages and spirits, and aperitifs with a wine or alcoholic base of an alcoholic strength not exceeding 22°; sparkling wines, fortified wines	to a total of 2 litres	to a total of 3 litres
and		
– still wines	to a total of 2 litres	to a total of 4 litres
(c) perfumes	50g	75g
and		
toilet waters	$\frac{1}{4}$ litre	3/8 litre
(d) coffee	500g	750g
or		
coffee extracts and essences	200g	300g
(e) tea	100g	150g
or		
tea extracts and essences	40g	60g

2. Exemption of the goods mentioned in paragraph 1(a) and (b) shall not be granted to travellers under 17 years of age.

Exemption for the goods mentioned in paragraph 1(d) shall not be granted to travellers under 15 years of age.

3. Within the quantitative limits set in paragraph 1 and taking account of the restrictions in paragraph 2, the value of the goods listed in paragraph 1 shall not be taken into consideration in determining the exemption referred to in Articles 1 and 2.

4. Where the travel referred to in Article 2(1):

- involves transit through the territory of a third country; overflying without landing shall not, however, be regarded as transit within the meaning of this Directive,

- begins in the part of a territory of another Member State in which turnover tax and/or excise duty is not chargeable on goods consumed within that territory,

the traveller must be able to establish that the goods transported in his luggage have been acquired subject to the general conditions governing taxation on the domestic market of a Member State and do not qualify for any refunding of turnover tax and/or duty, failing which the quantities set out in paragraph 1, column 1, shall apply.

5. Under no circumstances may the total quantity of goods exempted exceed the quantities provided for in paragraph 1, column 11.

Article 5. 1. Member States may reduce the value and/or quantity of the goods which may be admitted duty free, down to one tenth of the values and/or quantities provided for in Articles 2 and 4(1), column 11, where such goods are imported from another Member State by persons resident in the frontier zone of the importing Member State or in that of the neighbouring Member State, by frontier zone workers, or by the crew of the means of transport used in international travel.

However, duty free entitlement in respect of the goods listed below may be as follows:

(a) Tobacco products:
Cigarettes   40
or
cigarillos
(cigars of a maximum weight
of 3 grammes each)   20
or
cigars   10
or
smoking tobacco   50g

(b) alcoholic beverages:
- distilled beverages and
spirits, of an alcoholic
strength exceeding 22° 0.25 litre
or
- distilled beverages and
spirits, and aperitifs
with a wine or alcoholic
base of an alcoholic strength
not exceeding 22°; sparkling
wines, fortified wines   0.50 litre

and
  - still wines   0.50 litre

2. Member States may set lower limits as to value and/or quantity
for the exemption of goods when they are imported from a third country
by persons resident in the frontier zone, by frontier zone workers
or by the crew of the means of transport used in travel between third
countries and the Community.

3. Member States may set lower limits as to value and/or quantity
for the exemption of goods when they are imported from another Member
State by members of the armed forces of a Member State, including
civilian personnel and spouses and dependent children, stationed in
another Member State.

4. The restrictions in paragraphs 1 and 2 shall not apply where the
persons referred to therein produce evidence to show that they are
going beyond the frontier zone or that they are not returning from
the frontier zone of the neighbouring Member State or third country.

These restrictions shall, however, still apply to frontier zone
workers and to the crew of the means of transport used in international travel where they import goods when travelling in the course of
their work.

5. For the purposes of paragraphs 1, 2 and 4:
  - 'frontier zone' means a zone which, as the crow flies, does not
    extend more than 15 kilometres from the frontier of a Member
    State. Each Member State must however include within its frontier
    zone the local administrative districts part of the territory of
    which lies within the zone;

  - 'frontier zone worker' means any person whose normal activities
    ·require that he should go to the other side of the frontier on
    working days.

6. Member States may exclude from exemption goods falling within
headings Nos 71.07 and 71.08 of the Common Customs Tariff.

7. Member States may reduce the quantities of goods referred to
in Article 4(1)(a) and (d) for travellers coming from a third country
who enter a Member State.

Article 6. 1. Member States shall take appropriate measures to avoid
remission of tax being granted for deliveries to travellers whose
domicile, habitual residence or place of work is situated in a
Member State and who benefit from the arrangements provided for in
this Directive.

2. Without prejudice to rules relating to sales made at airport
shops under customs control and on board aircraft, Member States
shall take the necessary steps with regard to sales at the retail
stage to permit in the cases and under the conditions provided for in
paragraphs 3 and 4 the remission of turnover tax on deliveries of
goods carried in the personal luggage of travellers leaving a Member
State. No remission may be granted in respect of excise duty.

3. Member States may exclude their residents from the benefit of
this tax remission.

As regards travellers whose domicile, habitual residence or place
of work is situated in a Member State, there may be remission of tax
only in respect of items the individual value of which, inclusive of
tax, exceeds the amount specified in Article 2(1).

Member States may increase that amount. They may furthermore exclude their residents from the benefit of this tax remission.

4. Remission of tax shall be subject:

(a) in the cases referred to in the first subparagraph of paragraph 3, to production of a copy of the invoice or other document in lieu thereof, endorsed by the customs of the exporting Member States to certify exportation of the goods;

(b) in the cases referred to in the second subparagraph of paragraph 3, to production of a copy of the invoice or other document in lieu thereof, endorsed by the customs of the Member State where final importation takes place or by another authority of that Member State competent in matters of turnover tax.

5. For the purposes of this Article:

- 'domicile or habitual residence' means the place entered as such in a passport, identity card or, failing those, other identity documents which the exporting Member State recognises as valid;

- 'item' means a thing or a group of things which normally constitutes a whole.

Article 7. 1. For the purposes of this Directive, 'European unit of account' (EUA) shall be as defined in the Financial Regulation of 21 December 1977.

2. The EUA equivalent in national currency which shall apply for the implementation of this Directive shall be fixed once a year. The rates applicable shall be those obtaining on the first working day of October with effect from 1 January of the following year.

3. Member States may round off the amounts in national currency resulting from the conversion of the amounts in EUA provided for in Articles 1 and 2, provided such rounding-off does not exceed 2 EUA.

4. Member States may maintain the amounts of the exemptions in force at the time of the annual adjustment provided for in paragraph 2 if, prior to the rounding-off provided for in paragraph 3, conversion of the amounts of the exemptions expressed in EUA would result in a change of less than 5% in the exemption expressed in national currency.

Article 8. 1. Member States shall bring into force not later than 1 January 1979 the measures necessary to comply with this Directive.

2. Each Member State shall inform the Commission of the measures which it adopts to implement this Directive.

The Commission shall communicate such information to the other Member States.

Article 9. This Directive is addressed to the Member States.

Done at Brussels, 28 May 1969.

For the Council

The President

G. THORN

(As amended by Directive 72/230/EEC, J.O. No L 139, 17 June 1972, p. 28 and 78/1032/EEC, O.J. No L 366, 28 December 1978, p. 28)

By way of derogation from Article 2(1) of Directive 69/169/EEC, as amended by Article 1(a) of this Directive:
- the Kingdom of Denmark may, until 31 December 1981, exclude from tax exemption goods whose unit value is in excess of 135 EUA,
- Ireland may, until 31 December 1983, exclude from tax exemption goods whose unit value is in excess of 77 EUA.

During the period of implementation of the derogations referred to in paragraph 1, the other Member States shall take the necessary steps to permit the remission of tax, in accordance with the procedures referred to in Article 6(4) of Directive 69/169/EEC, on goods imported into the Kingdom of Denmark and into Ireland which are excluded from exemption in those countries.
By way of derogation from Article 4(1)(b) of Directive 69/169/EEC, as amended by Article 2(a) of this Directive, with regard to the import of still wines with exemption from turnover tax and excise duty, the Kingdom of Denmark may maintain, until 31 December 1983, the quantitative limit of three litres.

5. REGULATION (EEC) No 1818/75 OF THE COUNCIL

of 10 July 1975

on the agricultural levies, compensatory amounts and other import charges applicable to agricultural products and to certain goods resulting from their processing, contained in travellers' personal baggage

(O.J. No L 185, 16 July 1975, p. 3)

THE COUNCIL OF THE EUROPEAN COMMUNITIES,

Having regard to the Treaty establishing the European Economic Community, and in particular Articles 43 and 235 thereof;
Having regard to the proposal from the Commission;
Having regard to the Opinion of the European Parliament;
Whereas Council Regulation (EEC) No 1544/69 of 23 July 1969 on the tariff applicable to goods contained in travellers' personal baggage, provides, under certain conditions, for either the admission free of Common Customs Tariff duties of the goods in question or for the charge of a flat-rate; whereas it is necessary to extend these measures to agricultural levies and other import charges provided for under the common agricultural policy or under arrangements laid down under Article 235 of the Treaty and which apply only to certain goods resulting from the processing of agricultural products;
Whereas, in order that the nationals of the Member States should be more aware of the common market, Council Directive No 69/169/EEC

90

of 28 May 1969, on the harmonisation of provisions laid down by law, regulation or administrative action relating to exemption from turnover tax and excise duty on imports in international travel, as amended by Directive No 72/230/EEC, laid down a system of tax relief applicable to goods contained in the personal baggage of persons travelling between Member States; whereas it is necessary to allow relief within the same limits and conditions with regard to compensatory amounts or other import charges under the common agricultural policy or under special arrangements laid down under Article 235 of the Treaty, for agricultural products and certain goods resulting from their processing,

HAS ADOPTED THIS REGULATION:

Article 1. 1. Regulation (EEC) No 1544/69 shall be extended to agricultural levies and other import charges provided for under the common agricultural policy or under arrangements laid down under Article 235 of the Treaty and which apply only to certain goods resulting from the processing of agricultural products when contained in the personal baggage of travellers entering the Community.

2. Where Article 5 of Regulation (EEC) No 1544/69 applies, the flat-rate of 10% laid down in that Article shall also cover all the charges referred to in paragraph 1 of this Article.

Article 2. Relief from compensatory amounts or other import charges made under the common agricultural policy or under the special arrangements laid down under Article 235 of the Treaty shall be allowed for agricultural products and certain goods resulting from their processing, contained in the personal baggage of persons travelling from a Member State.

The limits and the conditions for granting this relief shall be the same as those set out in Council Directive No 69/169/EEC.

Article 3. This Regulation shall enter into force on 1 September 1975.

This Regulation shall be binding in its entirety and directly applicable in all Member States.

Done at Brussels, 10 July 1975.

For the Council

The President

E. COLOMBO

6. COUNCIL REGULATION (EEC) No 3023/77

of 20 December 1977

on certain measures to put an end to abuses resulting from the
sale of agricultural products on board ship

(O.J. No L 358, 31 December 1977, p. 2)

THE COUNCIL OF THE EUROPEAN COMMUNITIES,

Having regard to the Treaty establishing the European Economic
Community,

Having regard to the proposal from the Commission,

Having regard to the Opinion of the European Parliament,

Whereas Council Regulation (EEC) No 1544/69 of 23 July 1969 on the
tariff treatment applicable to goods contained in travellers' personal
luggage provided for Community arrangements for relief from duty
covering passenger traffic between third countries and the Community;
   Whereas this Regulation does not apply to goods imported following
a voyage from a Member State on a ship which has not called at a port
within the customs territory of a third country;
   Whereas Council Regulation (EEC) No 1818/75 of 10 July 1975 on the
agricultural levies, compensatory amounts and other import charges
applicable to agricultural products and to certain goods resulting
from their processing, contained in travellers' personal baggage
extended the scope of Regulation (EEC) No 1544/69 to agricultural
levies and other import charges provided for under the common agricultural policy or under arrangements laid down under Article 235 of
the Treaty and which apply only to certain goods·resulting from the
processing of agricultural products;
   Whereas experience has shown that Community agricultural products
which have benefited from export refunds and agricultural products
coming from third countries have been sold or distributed on board
ships which have left a Community port and are returning to a Community port without calling at a port outside the customs territory of
the Community, with a view to their introduction into the Community
free of levies under Regulations (EEC) No 1544/69 and (EEC) No 1818/75:
   Whereas the legal situation in this connection should be clarified;
whereas to this end Member States should be authorised to grant exemptions for the products listed in Annex 11 to the Treaty sold or distributed on board ships under the above conditions for very limited
quantities beyond which these products may no longer be introduced
into the Community unless the proper import duties are paid,

HAS ADOPTED THIS REGULATION:

Article 1. 1. Member States may authorise exemption from import duties
for products listed in Annex 11 to the Treaty,sold or distributed
on board ships which have left a Community port and are returning to
a Community port without calling at a port outside the customs territory of the Community, where these products,

- were, at the time of their exportation from the Community, the subject of export customs formalities with a view to obtaining refunds or other amounts granted on exportation within the framework of the common agricultural policy, or

- were not, at the time of their delivery on board ship, covered by either of the situations provided for in Article 9(2) of the Treaty.

2. Where Member States make use of the option referred to in paragraph 1, the exemption shall be limited to the following quantities per traveller:

- one kilogram of butter

- one kilogram of cheese

- one kilogram of meat, including prepared or preserved meat and sausages,

- two litres of wine, including sparkling and liqueur wine,

- a total of two kilograms of other products listed in Annex 11 to the Treaty.

3. Paragraph 2 shall apply only to products contained in travellers' personal baggage and provided it can be shown that such imports:
    (a) take place occasionally and

    (b) consist exclusively of products for the personal or family use of the travellers, or of products intended as gifts.

4. Member States making use of the option referred to in paragraph 1 shall inform the Commission thereof.

Article 2. For the purposes of this Regulation 'import duties' means customs duties and charges having equivalent effect as well as agricultural levies and other import charges applied under the common agricultural policy.

Article 3. As necessary, the detailed rules for the implementation of this Regulation shall be adopted in accordance with the procedure laid down in Article 26 of Council Regulation (EEC) No 2727/75 of 29 October 1975 on the common organisation of the market in cereals, as last amended by Regulation (EEC) No 2560/77 or, as the case may be, in the corresponding Articles of the other Regulations on the common organisation of agricultural markets.

Article 4. This Regulation shall enter into force on 1 February 1978.

This Regulation shall be binding in its entirety and directly applicable in all Member States.

Done at Brussels, 20 December 1977.

*For the Council
The President*
J. CHABERT

7. Excerpt of the Commission Report on the scope for convergence of tax systems in the Community of 26 March 1980

(Supplement 1/80 to the Bulletin of the European Communities)

Chapter I

INTRODUCTION

1. The purpose of this report is twofold: to describe the measures the Community should take in the years ahead in order to establish the tax conditions necessary for a genuine economic integration; and to identify the obstacles hampering achievement of this objective and the ways and means of overcoming them.

TAX HARMONIZATION: OBJECTIVES AND LIMITS

2. In all developed countries, taxation has, over many years, come to play a rapidly expanding role as a result of growing public budgets and its own increasing importance as an instrument of economic and social policy. For this reason, taxes, which account for a large proportion of gross domestic product, have become one of the key determinants of economic and social activity.

3. It is only natural, therefore, that taxation should be a focus of attention in the Community. However, there can be no question at the moment of framing a genuine tax policy similar to that applied by the Member States. In the first place, although it is now financed out of own resources, the Community budget is still very modest when compared with the Member States' budgets taken together (2.6% in 1978), with the result that taxation can play only a very limited budgetary role at Community level. Secondly, economic and social policy is still very much a matter for national governments and for this reason the use of taxation as an instrument of this policy cannot be made subject to Community rules. Lastly, even where economic policy objectives such as containment of inflation rates and the programming of economic growth are fixed at Community level, the actual measures to be taken, including those in the tax field, are generally left to the discretion of the Member States.
    And so, in the tax field, fundamental decisions are the prerogative of the Member States and extensive transfers of decisionmaking powers will not be feasible unless substantial progress is made towards integration. Tax harmonization is not intended, therefore, to serve the purpose of instituting a Community tax policy, nor is it an end in itself. It forms part of the means and powers granted to the Community to carry out its responsibilities.

4. The EEC Treaty lays down a number of fundamental objectives, including:

    (i) the establishment of a common market by way of, among other things, the free movement of persons, goods, services and capital and a system that ensures that competition is not distorted;

    (ii) the institution of a number of common policies: the EEC Treaty

94

provides for only three such policies (external trade, agriculture and transport), but other common policies have been decided on, in principle at least, by the Community institutions, notably for energy, regional policy and the environment.

In addition, it was decided as early as 1970 that, under the procedure provided for in Article 201 of the Treaty, the Member States' financial contributions would be replaced by the Community's own resources in order to give the Community greater financial independence.

The tax harmonization measures already or to be introduced by the Community must be seen in the light of these objectives, for, as this Chapter shows, none of them can be achieved without Community action in the field of taxation.

All these objectives have been restated in the context of the economic and monetary union decided on by the Heads of State or Government. With regard to tax matters, the Council Resolution of 22 March 1971 reads as follows:

"In order that effectively free movement of persons, goods, services and capital and progress in interpenetration of economies may be achieved at a faster rate, the Council, acting on a proposal from the Commission and having regard to the need to preserve a balance, shall decide on measures concerning:

(i) Community rules determining the uniform basis for assessing the value added tax within the meaning of the Decision of 21 April 1970 on the replacement of financial contributions from the Member States by the Communities' own resources;

(ii) the harmonization of the scope, basis of assessment and the mode of levying excise duties, in particular those which have an appreciable influence on trade;

(iii) the harmonization of those kinds of tax which are likely to have a direct influence on capital movements within the Community, in particular the taxation of interest from fixed-interest securities and dividends;

(iv) the further harmonization of the taxation of companies and firms;

(v) The progressive extension of duty-free concessions granted to private individuals crossing frontiers within the Community.
Before the end of the first stage the Council shall examine the results of research on the alignment of rates of value added tax and excise duties and the proposals of the Commission in this field."

Although the path towards economic and monetary union has by no means been smooth since that first Council Resolution was adopted, the objective has never been abandoned. Indeed, a renewed drive is now evident — with the recent establishment of the European Monetary System.

5. Bringing Member States' tax systems into closer alignment is not a straightforward matter for a number of reasons:

a) Tax sovereignty is one of the fundamental components of national sovereignty, and at present all the Member States set great store by the inviolability of national sovereignty. It is important here to remember that one of the fundamental prerogatives of national parliaments is the right to vote taxes;

(b) Two equally necessary objectives - the progressive approximation of Member States' economic policies provided for in Article 2 of the EEC Treaty and the harmonization of their tax systems - may come into conflict. This is because Member States may need to manipulate differently the instruments at their disposal for implementing national economic policies in order to remedy the divergences existing between those policies. The instrument of taxation is in this respect very important, not least because it determines to a very large degree public expenditure policy and investment incentives; in any case, its importance is unlikely to decline since, in the European Monetary System, the Member States are unable to use the monetary instrument as freely as before;

(c) The general public is becoming increasingly sensitive to taxation; people think taxes are both too high and too complicated.

(d) It is extremely difficult to remove disparities in the structure of the tax system, the overall burden of taxation and the allocation of revenue between the different taxes, since they are not fortuitous but are a function of deep-rooted causes.

These causes include:

(i) differences in economic and social structures;
(ii) different conceptions of the role of taxation in general or of one tax in particular: for instance, views differ on the volume of investment that the State should finance and on the range of services it should supply as a 'quid pro quo' for taxes paid, on the degree of income and wealth distribution to be aimed at and on the way in which taxation should be used as an economic policy instrument;
(iii) differences in acceptability: a tax that is fairly well tolerated in one country is accepted grudgingly or not at all in another country;

(e) The complexity of present tax systems means that tax harmonization is faced with technical difficulties.
    Lastly, there can be no hiding the fact that further enlargement of the Comm·ni·y to bring it op to twelve Member States, far from simplifying the task, will complicate it even more.

6. All these considerations explain the hesitations by the Member States and the slowness of tax harmonization.
    In spite of these daunting difficulties, tax harmonization has in fact scored some undoubted successes, and this can be put down to the combination of several factors.
    Firstly, agreement was reached on a number of priority objectives (free movement of persons, goods, services and capital; neutrality of taxation in respect of merchandise trade; institution of a system ensuring that competition is not distorted; abolition of tax frontiers; creation of the Community's own resources) and there has emerged a genuine political resolve to achieve some of them, at least in part.
    Secondly, there has been no need for any steps affecting the

personal taxes paid by individuals (income tax and wealth tax), which are the most politically sensitive ones.

Lastly, virtually all the measures so far adopted or merely proposed (concerned for the most part with turnover taxes, excise duties, indirect taxes on the raising of capital and corporation tax) are for the time being confined to structures and bases of assessment. As long as they are at liberty to determine tax rates, Member States can avoid jeopardizing the balance that has been forged between the different taxes, while at the same time remaining free to use the taxes to be harmonized for budgetary or economic purposes. As a result, it has been possible to avoid conflict between tax harmonization and Member States' freedom to determine the budgetary and economic function of taxation.

7. Although, the record in tax harmonization is certainly positive, the successes have been limited, because of the difficulties and long delays that have piled up at Council level as regards excise duties and direct taxes. For instance, in spite of the Commission's efforts, the Council has not as yet been able to act on the long-standing proposals concerning the excise duties on wine, beer spirits and mineral oils, which, however, deal only with tax structures and not tax rates.

Even more serious difficulties are therefore to be expected once the approximation of tax legislation is extended to tax rates. For this reason, such approximation will be possible only at a much more advanced stage of economic integration, Then, however, it will be absolutely necessary, since the harmonization of structures and bases of assessment will no longer be sufficient.

Admittedly, the present uncertainty as to how far the economic integration of the Community should go and how fast progress can be made makes it extremely difficult to determine exactly what tax measures will be needed; and of course, it is even more difficult to draw up a detailed timetable for such measures. In the final analysis, everything will depend on the division of powers between the Member States and the Community and hence on the transfers of sovereignty to the Community. Discussion of this matter has hardly advanced beyond the initial stage.

In spite of this uncertainty, a number of points are worth considering. Economic integration implies a 'single market', that is to say a common market with characteristics similar to those of a domestic market, and at once we have the problems of abolishing tax frontiers (i.e. border adjustments and checks in respect of intra-Community trade) and of harmonizing tax burdens.

As we have said, taxation is one of the major determinants of a country's economic and social life. The level of taxes influences a wide range of factors, including the structure of consumption and hence of production, company profitability, the location of investment projects and, generally speaking, the conditions of competition.

With the prospect before us of a thrust for economic integration, these various factors must not be artificially influenced by differences in tax burdens. Eventually therefore, closer alignment of these burdens will be necessary.

Given the rule of taxation as an instrument of economic and social policy, such a move towards alignment is equally important in the context of increasingly close coordination of national policies and the framing of genuine common policies in the key economic sectors.

8. Before we consider the measures that would have to be taken in this

respect, it may be useful to recapitulate the measures already decided upon or awaiting adoption.

In addition, it is worth emphasizing once again that the closer alignment of tax burdens which must be tackled will be a much more difficult process than the harmonization of structures and bases of assessment, because it will conflict with the principle that countries should have complete latitute in their use of taxation as an instrument of budgetary policy and economic and social policy and will consequently have important repercussions. These are discussed in Chapter V. Clearly, then, progress will have to be very cautious, the Member States must be allowed sufficient room for manoeuvre and the process of tax harmonization and economic integration must keep in step.

----

8. 1979 Multiannual Programme for the Attainment of the Customs Union

(O.J. C 84, 31 March 1979, p.2)

INTRODUCTION

A - General remarks

This programme for the attainment of the customs union is part of the
stated policy of working towards the creation of a single market in all
its aspects. The measures advocated by the Commission under the programme are designed to complete and consolidate the customs union, the
instruments of which do not simply express a common customs policy but
at the same time make it possible to implement other common policies,
thereby helping to eliminate progressively the formalities and controls
in intra-Community trade. The measures which go to make up this programme should, by providing more reliable external protection for the
European economy and streamlining internal trade, put the internal
market on a firm footing. The programme sets out various proposals for
giving practical effect to Community preference and aiding development
of the free movement of goods.
    Such a programme, then, is closely linked with the Community policy
for the establishment of an economic and monetary union as adopted by
the Community institutions, in the form of a multiannual   programme
to be acieved in yearly stages. The link is confirmed by the parallel
nature of the priorities proposed for 1979 and the proposals on customs
union put forward in the 1979 EMU programme.
.....

I. THE MULTIANNUAL   PROGRAMME

A. Basic objectives

1. Article 9 (1) of the Treaty provides that: 'The Community shall be
   based upon a customs union ...'. The ultimate objective of that
   customs union, is to create the conditions on which the fusion of
   the national markets into a single market and the elimination of
   internal frontiers depend. These conditions entail more than the mere
   establishment of a Common Customs Tariff and a number of basic principles governing the application of such a tariff. They must be given
   practical effect via the establishment of a complete, uniform and
   effective body of legislation, designed to ensure the homogeneity
   of trade arrangements between the Community and non-member countries
   and thereby to create the conditions required for goods to be able
   to move within the Community under the same conditions as within
   domestic markets.

2. The liberalization of intra-Community trade, while depending very
   much on the homogeneity of the rules in force at external frontiers
   and their being applied in a uniform manner - which should be facil-
   itated by the introduction of Community procedures - is naturally
   linked to progress achieved in other fields, particularly in matters
   of taxation, currency, transport and statistics.
       The Commission feels, however, that even in the absence of sub-
   stantial progress on these matters, customs measures may contribute
   greatly to the simplification of the formalities and controls applied
   in intra-Community trade, to greater fluidity of trade and to accent-

99

uating Community preference.

3. While it is very important that formalities and controls in intra-Community trade be eliminated, it must not be forgotten that the European citizen judges the progress achieved on integration by the controls and formalities which he sees applied when he travels within the Community or when he sends or receives non-commercial parcels.

The Commission therefore considers that a fresh impetus should be given to deal with all the problems arising in connection with relief from duty on goods carried by travellers or contained in parcels sent to individuals.

4. Full harmonization of the customs rules must be achieved before the barriers between national markets can be fully dismantled and is therefore essential for the development of economic and monetary union. The harmonized rules must be as reliable as each of the old national systems, given the new demands arising from the facts of life in a common market, and would in particular permit greater uniformity as regards establishment of the Community's own resources.

5. The only way to ensure that customs legislation is uniform and reliable is to see that binding measures are enacted which are obligatory and directly applicable within the Member States, and therefore offer legal guarantees for the individual. Particular attention must therefore be paid to the form of the legal act to be adopted for establishing this Community customs legislation.

As a result of past experience, particularly in the field of the 'economic' customs procedures, the Commission is categorically in favour of Regulations. New line Directives certainly confer obligations on Member States, but normally require intermediate national legislation in order to produce legal consequences for individuals. This procedure is time-consuming; moreover, Directives do not adequately provide the legal certainty and uniformity of Community law necessary for the proper functioning of the common market. These aims can be achieved only by the use of Regulations.

6. The establishment of a body of Community customs law inevitably raises the problem of harmonization of penalties and organization of legal protection for those liable to such penalties.

If disparities as regards penalties persist, this may not only give rise to unequal treatment or even deflection of trade, but may also seriously affect the operation of customs arrangements and procedures and jeopardize the effectiveness of common policy measures whose implementation is based on those arrangements and procedures. Similarly, the national systems currently in force should be reconsidered with a view to finding solutions appropriate to the new dimension and specific needs of the Community. Unity of legislation also makes it necessary to introduce the same level of legal protection throughout the Community.

7. Among other qualities which Community legislation must possess are clarity and transparency.

It is necessary to ensure the desire to bring the decision-making process to a successful conclusion does not lead to the adoption of vague or ambiguous formulations, which will be bound to give rise to differences of interpretation, and hence further disparities, between Member States.

The establishment of uniform rules which, by their nature, will

have to undergo frequent amendments, inevitably gives rise to the
problem of their codification, without which it will be difficult
to consult the provisions. The codification must initially take the
form of recasting into a basic Regulation and a single implementing
Regulation the provisions relating to a given sector which are to
be found scattered in different numbers of the Official Journal.
The next step is to undertake codification proper, entailing a basic
text of a general nature (customs code) dealing systematically and
on the basis of uniform formulations and concepts with all customs
arrangements and procedures, this basic text being supplemented
where necessary by implementing provisions.

8. The establishment of the customs union inevitably brings the national customs administrations face to face with the problem of adapting their structures, just as it poses the problem of the Community
machinery needed for such a union to operate properly. While the
national administrations are still giving thought to these matters,
it can be stated here and now that action in the customs field is
no longer motivated solely by national considerations but is increasingly taken with due consideration for the interests of partner
States or Community interests proper.

   Strengthening the Community element in customs matters raises not
only the problem of teaching Community law in the framework of vocational training, but also that of wide-ranging cooperation between
national administrations and the Commission's departments. The development of this cooperation at all levels must be one of the major
concerns in the years ahead.

   While there is already some cooperation between the Member States,
cooperation between the Commission departments and national administrations is still only in its early stages. The experience of the
past few months regarding the measures adopted concerning textile
products and steel, however, shows how much the effectiveness of a
measure and its homogeneous implementation throughout the Community
depends on close cooperation between the Commission and the Member
States' authorities. The regular contacts introduced in this context
between the Commission's departments and national customs experts
have turned out to be extremely fruitful and have already enabled
a fair number of practical problems to be resolved. These encouraging examples undoubtedly deserve to be applied on a wider scale
beyond the strictly sectoral framework to which they are still confined at present.

   With regard to the institutional structure of the customs union,
the cumbersome nature of the procedures is a serious impediment to
the rapid adaptation of existing instruments which is required to
meet unforeseen situations. A solution to these problems can be
found only in making wider use of the delegation of powers, as provided for in Article 155 of the Treaty. The powers which the Commission already has in this respect must be extended to other matters,
including temporary derogations from the application of Common Customs Tariff duties. While the main objective of such tariff measures
is to enable the Community to react to unforeseen shortages, the
procedures for giving effect to such measures generally take more
than six months before final publication in the Official Journal of
the European Communities.

9. It is also necessary to make the most of the Community's weight and
size in order to strengthen its image in international meetings
dealing with customs matters. To this end, Community participation

in international organizations must be improved and common positions
be worked out more rapidly and more efficiently.

B - Commitment procedure

1. The Commission wondered whether it would be possible to draw up in
   advance a detailed timetable for implementing the multiannual programme, but thought it better, on reflection, to reject this idea
   so that it would have some flexibility in selecting its priorities
   - the latter being likely to change with economic developments -
   so that it would be able to adjust periodically the measures aimed
   at unifying internal markets in the light of progress made in the
   meantime in areas other than customs matters.

2. This is why the Commission has chosen to establish by year a coherent
   set of priorities designed to advance the creation for the construction of a true customs union.

3. The Commission proposes to take stock in November of each year of
   the results obtained and efforts made during the previous year as
   regards achievement of the overall objectives and to present the
   priorities for the following year, with specific commitments.

4. The Commission will not, however, confine itself solely to the
   priorities set out under the above procedure, since it will be continuing its activities in those areas where it is competent either
   under the provisions of the Treaty or by virtue of powers delegated
   by the Council, for instance with regard to administration and
   negotiation.
   The bulk of these measures will be incorporated each year in the
   list of priorities to be presented. This also applies to certain
   executive measures which the Commission intends to introduce in conjunction with the national authorities and which are needed in order
   to strengthen the inter cohesion of the customs union and improve
   trading conditions on the basis of increased mutual trust.

5. The priorities for 1979 are set out in Part II of this communication.
   The work of establishing these priorities was done by the Commission
   and the heads of the customs administrations of the Member States in
   close collaboration.
   . . . . .

9. 1981 Programme for the achievement of the Customs Union

(OJ No C 106, 8 May 1981, p. 2)

INTRODUCTION

In its 'Multiannual programme for the attainment of the customs union'
(1979) the Commission undertook to submit each year to the relevant
Community institutions a programme setting out in full both the past
year's achievements and the priorities for the next 12 months.
    In this paper the undertaking is fulfilled for the second time.

The principles of these annual communications has been approved and encouraged by the European Parliament and by the Economic and Social Committee.

. . . . .

The professional associations represented on the Advisory Committee on Customs Matters have reaffirmed their strong interest in respect of the actions featuring in the programme and have renewed their complete support for the achievement of the priorities adopted.

CHAPTER I

Statement of Results for 1980

The support given by Member States for the implementation of the multi-annual programme for the attainment of the customs union which was trans-mitted by the Commission in March 1979 to the Council, the European Parliament and the Economic and Social Committee, seemed to mark a significant turning point in establishing a common wish to achieve pro-gress in the customs union, based on the fact that the proper operation of the internal market of the Community and the opening up of Member State markets to third countries are essential to the economies of the Member States.

The programme put forward ambitious but realistic objectives on which certain hopes were based in view of the very satisfactory results of the first annual programme in 1979.

Nine customs proposals of signal importance were adopted by the Council in 1979; only two of the priority proposals contained in the 1979 programme had to be carried over to 1980.

But this impetus, which had notably featured the determination of any hitherto isolated Member State to rally to the majority position, would appear to have faltered in 1980 in the face of a programme which, while admittedly wide-ranging, was a logical follow-up to the previous achievements. The net result is a return to the situation which obtain-ed before the introduction of the multiannual programme, when the lack of will to compromise led to proposals languishing indefinitely at Council level. In the first six months of 1980 the only major proposal adopted by the Council has been the one revising the definition of value for customs purposes.

In those circumstances (achievements to mid-1980 are set out in Annex I) the backlog of unfinished business is so great that there ap-pears little point in trying to set further priorities for 1981.

It is to be regretted that in the Community's present situation the spirit of cooperation needed to push ahead with one of the least contro-versial common policies and that which is most essential for developing or restructuring other fields is no longer to be found.

It is important to bear in mind that the preservation of an economic-ally strong, competitive common market is closely bound up with unified external frontiers; that is an imperative which ought to be reflected in a constant common will to forge ahead with the harmonization of customs rules on uniform trade arrangements between the Community and non-member countries. Most of the proposals currently being discussed by the Council relate to this aspect of the customs union; and yet little progress is being made with their examination.

It is also worth noting that the Community bodies consider that the internal market should be as far advanced as possible before the ac-cession of Portugal and Spain. (As the Economic and Social Committee stressed in its opinion on the multiannual programme), the major inequalities in economic and administrative structures which will necessarily be made manifest with enlargement will greatly complicate economic transactions with the future Member States and the work outstanding on the harmonization of Community law. Therefore, 'for the sake of the customs union and its continued operation, customs legislation should be extensively harmonized before the new Member States join'.

In the present critical state of the economic climate both worldwide and in the Community, at a time when far-reaching changes in the structure of the Community and the organization of world trade are taking place, the Community can no longer afford to drag its feet over the attainment of a full customs union, the reliability of which is essential to ensure that Community policies will have some chance of effectively coping with today's economic difficulties.

For that to happen, this key component of European integration, a cornerstone of the Community fabric and sine qua non of a true common market and economic and monetary union, must be established in full by harnessing the political will to achieve a true customs union which is enshrined in the Treaty of Rome and revealed its capacity for practical achievement in 1979.

In view of the results for 1980, which are clearly less satisfactory than those for 1979, the Commission will press continually in political debates in the Council for the continued implementation of the multi-annual programme.

When it comes to administrative activities concerning the implementation of such customs law as is already harmonized at Community level, the picture of achievements for 1980 looks more positive.

For instance, 1980 has seen the ad hoc working party responsible for the examination of the practical application of Community customs legislation commence work on a first study of transit arrangements. Having gone through the relevant national regulations and operational rules, the working party is now visiting various customs offices in the Member States to study the application of these regulations in practice. The value of such work must be emphasized; it makes it possible not only to spot the divergence in the Member States' application of Community customs legislation but also more importantly, to suggest ways of ensuring that Community rules are applied in a uniform manner and to propose any improvements that may need to be made to those rules. A report on the results of the study on Community transit will be published before the middle of 1981 so that the Commission and heads of customs administrations can take cognizance of the findings.

In the informatics field important work is being done by another panel of experts, the EDP Working Party, which will be following the progress of two pilot projects on computerization in customs work, one dealing with checks on Community transit operations and the other on the exchange of urgent import and export data between the Member States and the Commission. The working party is also monitoring informatics work being carried out by bodies such as the UN's Economic Commission for Europe, the Customs Cooperation Council and the International Organization for Standardization on the development of standards in national codes and on codes dealing with methods of transport and customs operations.

Completion of the work on Taric, the Integrated Tariff of the European Communities, is also an important milestone on the road towards establishment of the customs union.

In its current form (known as Taric I), the Integrated Tariff is of use mainly for information purposes, making it possible to see at a glance for each tariff heading all the tariff measures (suspensions,

quotas, preferences, anti-dumping duties, surveillance, etc.) relating
to it. Not until 1985, with the introduction of the harmonized system
for the description and codification of goods which is at present being
elaborated by the Customs Cooperation Council will Taric (as Taric II,
adapted and based on the old system) come into effect as an operational
instrument.

Also noteworthy, in conclusion, is the completion of a compendium of
Community customs legislation, though for technical reasons this is
available in only one Community language for the moment. This is a work
which should make it much easier for both users and customs administrations to consult the relevant Community texts.

Community acts adopted by the committees on rules are listed in
Annex II.

CHAPTER II

Priorities for 1981

Given the poor results mentioned already and the need to adopt a realistic attitude, the 1981 programme is bound to be largely a repeat of
the 1980 one.

However, the Commission would like to reiterate that, for the customs
union to make headway, the priority objectives are harmonization of the
customs arrangements for trade between the Community and non-member
countries and further efforts to abolish formalities and controls in
intra-Community trade.

Homogeneity in the Community's customs legislation for external relations is more vital than ever for trade with the rest of the world
at a time when the protectionist urge is strong, particularly on the
part of the other industrial powers. The Community's exporters as well
as its importers must be able to refer to uniform, reliable rules and
be faced with identical circumstances in whichever Member State they
are operating.

The importance of this requirement so often expressed by business
and industrial circles gives ample grounds for overcoming differences
of outlook which have more to do with the defence of traditional practices than promotion of the common interest.

It is impossible to adapt the machinery of customs to the considerable development of the Community's external trade and the new patterns
of world trade without a deliberate measure of upheaval.

The Commission would also point out that, failing substantial progress
with integration in other fields, that achieved in the customs sphere can
do much to improve the flow of intra-Community trade. As the Court
emphasized in its judgment in Case 159/78:

'customs controls properly so-called have lost their raison d'être
as regards such trade. Frontier controls remain justified only in
so far as they are necessary either for the implementation of the exceptions to free movement referred to in Article 36 of the Treaty; or
for the levying of internal taxation within the meaning of Article 95
of the Treaty; or for transit controls; or finally when they are essential in order to obtain reasonably complete and accurate information on
movement of goods within the Community.'

Adoption of the Commission's proposals for simplification along these
lines, coupled with enhanced cooperation between the Member States'
customs administrations to provide an effective counter to fraud could
be a major step toward liberalizing intra-Community trade, particularly
as regards improving the Community transit system.

105

Achieving a uniform level of legal protection in customs matters throughout the Community, thus eliminating a further cause of distortion of
treatment between firms, should also be regarded as a firm goal of the
Member States in the context of their joint endeavours to lay down a consistent and fairer body of rules providing citizens of Europe with a
legitimate feeling of certainty as to the law.

The Commission will continue with its management tasks in 1981 and
keep up its efforts to ensure the effective application of Community
customs legislation.

......

10. 1982 Programme for the Attainment of the Customs Union

(OJ No C 80, 31 March 1982, p. 1)

RESUME

In accordance with the annual commitment procedure laid down in the
'multiannual programme for the attainment of the customs union', forwarded to the Council, the European Parliament and the Economic and
Social Committee in March 1979, the Commission submits this document
to those institutions.

Considering the inadequacy of the results obtained since 1979, the
communication looks into the reasons for this and invites the Council
to accord effective priority to work on the attainment of the Customs
Union and the greater use of the powers of delegation provided for in
Article 155 of the Treaty.

This communication records the achievements in 1981 and the priorities
for 1982 at Council level and Commission level.

1982 PROGRAMME FOR THE ATTAINMENT OF THE CUSTOMS UNION

This communication, which follows those on the 1980 and 1981 programmes,
is part of the series of measures for the attainment of the customs
union inaugurated by the Multiannual Programme which was sent in 1979
to the Council, Parliament and the Economic and Social Committee. This
is the third implementation of the procedure laid down in the Multiannual Programme in 1979 whereby the Commission undertakes to send the
appropriate Community institutions an annual report setting out the
achievements of the past year and priorities for the following year.

The Commission set up this procedure partly in response to the
European Parliament's wish expressed in its 1978 resolution on the
development of the customs union and of the internal market. This called
upon the Commission to draw up regularly up-dated programmes, thereby
creating a new method for making periodic checks on progress, taking
into account also the rule of the customs union in the implementation
of other policies.

2. The Commission feels that the programmes should not merely list the
proposals sent to the Council, with details of action taken, if any.
Given the small number of proposals adopted by the Council, such a
course of action would mean that the priorities to be adopted would
remain largely unchanged from year to year.

The Commission wishes above all to emphasize by this new method its own resolve to work towards attainment of the customs union and thus to highlight the political factors which have governed the implementation of the programme.

It expects moreover that this commitment will lead the other Community institutions to make similar political commitments in which the Member States' governments, together with the customs administrations and other relevant departments and their officials, and all who have a part to play in the attainment of the customs union, will be called upon to participate.

While on this subject, the Commission thinks it worth recalling the fundamental role which has fallen to the customs union in the task building an internal market. Thus the declaration made by the European Council which met at Luxembourg on 29 and 30 June 1981, following the Commission's communication to the Council on the state of the internal market of 17 June 1981, and according to which a special effort should be made to reinforce and develop the internal market, makes the strengthening of the customs union on issue of immediate importance.

3. Twenty-four years after the creation of the European Community, it must be admitted that full customs union is still a long way off. Such a union should have the following features:

- externally: a Community customs policy based on a comprehensive, uniform and effective set of customs rules applied at the Community's frontier; these homogeneous arrangements applicable to foreign trade are not only an expression of the Community's customs policy but also the essential platform on which the internal market is built and the success of other policies, such as those in the commercial, agricultural, development and monetary spheres, depends.

  Community customs legislation now covers a substantial part of customs law, even though in come cases only the most important aspects of arrangements and procedures have been harmonized. This structure needs to be extended by harmonization in the sectors as yet untouched and by consolidation of provisions in other sectors, notably those in which harmonization was carried out on the basis of Directives. Once the harmonization of basic principles is complete, a customs code binding the legislation by sector into a structural whole can then be drawn up.

- internally: the achievement of free trade in Community goods which, aided by the execution of common external laws, must flow from the abolition of formalities connected with checking goods at internal frontiers. Some of the formalities which must at present be carried out at internal frontiers are customs requirements - the new customs entity and its structures being as yet incomplete - but for the most part they are justified by other requirements, for example of a statistical or fiscal kind.

  On account of this situation, and well aware that only an overall action taking in all the fields concerned could succeed in achieving a substantial simplification of formalities and checks at internal frontiers, the Commission forwarded a proposal for a resolution to the Council in October 1981 on the strengthening of the internal market, setting out all the various measures deemed necessary to attain this goal. In the same context one should also draw attention to the programme for the simplification of administrative procedures and formalities applicable for the purposes of levying value-added tax in intra-Community trade, which also forms part of the move to complete   the internal market.

4. The Commission cannot remain indifferent in the face of the marked slackening-off, after the initial enthusiasm in 1979, in the process of examination and adoption of its customs proposals. This slackening-off means that it would be foolhardy now to predict at what date the objectives, as realistic as they are precise, set out in the Multi-annual Programme will be attained.

The root causes of this slackening-off must therefore be examined in the light of an awareness of the positive impact that the customs achievements would be bound to have on the working of the internal market and on the productivity and competitiveness of the Community's industries, particularly in these times of economic crisis and the fight against unemployment.

5. The Community's foundation obviously cannot be secured by mere declarations of intent: a genuine political commitment is called for, involving the daily participation of all Community bodies. These bodies must endeavour to succeed despite all the technical difficulties, on the basis of the intention clearly stated in the Treaty by its authors to give the Community a customs policy which would be the cornerstone of the European endeavour in the context of the harmonious development of world trade.

The record of achievements since 1979, consisting in the adoption of a substantial number of customs proposals (3) may be regarded as being relatively satisfactory.

However, it should be recalled that most of those proposals - and the most important among them - were adopted in 1979, that some of them had been before the Council for years, that several of them were of limited scope or did no more than implement international provis-ons already negotiated and above all that other important proposals have not het been adopted by the Council within the set time limits.

6. While considerable progress has been made toward the attainment of the customs union since the unveiling of the Multiannual Programme in 1979, an analysis of the record overall shows that unless there is evidence of clear political will, further progress will be all the harder to achieve as it depends on the Member States agreeing to changes in some of their legal and administrative arrangements.

This is one of the main reasons for the slackening-off already mentioned.

7. It is the Commission's view that the slow progress made in meetings at Council level is due to the fact that the relevant working group is called upon to devote too much of its energy to the technical details of harmonization proposals which have to be put into their final version. In order for the examination of these proposals to be carried out with the best possible effectiveness and speed, the group should be able to direct its discussions essentially towards their economic and political implications.

To that end, the Commission considers that an expression of real political will on the part of the Council should logically result in that body making greater use of the scope available under Article 155 of the Treaty to delegate the necessary powers to the Commission. A judicious distribution of work, leaving to the Commission the task of settling the implementing details of acts adopted by the Council, would make it possible to reduce the highly technical nature of most of the proposals and enable the Council to concentrate its duscussions on the main aspects of customs policy. Past experience in this respect has proved very positive, as demonstrated by the numerous acts passed by the Commission within the procedural framework of the committee on rules, for example, those which have been adopted on the subject of customs value. Such an approach would be fully in line with the statement by the Heads of State and Government in Paris in December 1974, drawing attention to the advantage of implementing the provisions of the Treaty for devolving on the Commission the powers of implementation and administration under Community regulations.

8. The Commission welcomes Parliament's recent resolution of 17 September on the 1981 programme for the attainment of the customs union. It hopes moreover that the interest shown once again by Parliament will not be thwarted by the difficulties encountered in certain national parliaments which sometimes oppose the adoption of customs proposals. In this context, the Commission would recall the resolution on relations between the European Parliament and the national parliaments adopted by the former on 9 July 1981(4). The Commission also hopes that Parliament will issue its opinions as soon as possible in accordance with its past practice. Indeed, most of the customs proposals require immediate examination and a quick decision.

9. The Commission also notes with satisfaction the praiseworthy efforts of the Economic and Social Committee, which has shown time and again its desire to see full customs union attained, and the cooperation of the professional organisations in the Advisory Committee on Customs Matters, which have emphasised the importance which they attach to the attainment of the customs union. The Commission is following with great interest the initiatives taken by certain members of the Committee to encourage the relevant Community and national bodies to give full support to the implementation of the customs programmes. The fact that such enthusiasm for attainment of the customs union emanates from the Advisory Committee on Customs Matters, which comprises representatives of Community-wide professional organisations covering industry, commerce, chambers of commerce, agriculture, transport, consumers and forwarding customs agents, shows clearly the impact of this policy in the current economic climate.

In conclusion, the Commission confirming its political will to bring about the attainment of the customs union, invites the Council to accord effective priority to work on attainment of the customs union and to confer on the Commission wider powers for implementing the rules adopted by the Council.

. . . . .

(1) COM(81) 313 of 17.6.1981.
(2) EC Bulletin No 6 of 1981, p. 8.
(3) Nine in 1979, seven in 1980 and five in 1981 (situation at November 1981), not to mention purely administrative proposals.
(4) O.J. No C 234, 14.9.1981, p. 58.

ANNEX I

PRIORITIES FOR THE COUNCIL FOR 1982 AND STATEMENT OF
RESULTS FOR 1981

1. Priorities

Given the considerable backlog which accumulated in 1980 and 1981, the proposals which should be adopted as a matter of priority in 1982 are essentially those already included under A and B in the previous programmes.

These proposals are listed below.

Following the practice adopted since the March 1979 communication, priority proposals are divided into three separate categories:

A. proposals to be sent to the Council in 1982;

B. proposals not yet examined at all by the Council or only in the early stages of examination, but which should be adopted before 1 January 1983,

C. proposals already examined by the Council or in the final stages of examination, which could therefore be adopted in the first half of 1982.

These three categories contain only the most important proposals for the attainment of the customs union. They do not include the proposals being considered by the Council which were submitted by the Commission in order to ensure the day-to-day management of customs legislation of the Common Customs Tariff, either by unilateral measures or in implementation of international obligations already entered into by the Community under agreements with certain non-member countries.

A.   Proposals to be sent to the Council in 1982

A1. *Proposals relating to implementation of the programme to simplify formalities in intra-Community trade*

A2. *Proposal for a Regulation defining the persons liable for payment of a customs debt and the period after which an action in respect of such debt is barred.*

A3. *Proposal for a Regulation on temporary importation of means of transport in the Community.*

A4. *Proposal for a Directive laying down the conditions governing release for free circulation of goods sold by customs.*

A5. *Proposal for a Council Regulation on the security to be provided to ensure payment of a customs debt.*

A6. *Proposal for a Regulation on outward processing arrangements.*

A7. *Proposal for a Regulation on standard exchange arrangements.*

A8. *Proposal for a Regulation on free zones.*

A9. *Proposal for a Regulation on customs warehousing arrangements*

A10. *Proposal for a Regulation on the introduction of an import declaration form*

A11. *Proposal on the extension of the scope of Community transit arrangements*

A12. *Proposals relating to activities in the field of customs data processing*

B.   Proposals not yet examined at all by the Council or only in the early stages of examination but which should be adopted in 1982

B1. *Proposal for a Council Regulation on the definition of the customs territory of the Community*

B2. *Proposal for a Council Regulation simplifying the adoption of temporary measures derogating from the application of Common Customs Tariff duties*

B3. *Proposal for a Council Directive on the harmonisation of provisions laid down by law, regulation or administrative action concerning the exercise of the right of appeal in respect of customs matters*

B4. *Proposal for a Council Regulation introducing arrangements for movement within the Community of goods sent from one Member State for temporary use in one or more other Member States*

B5. *Proposal for a Council Regulation on the information provided by the customs authorities of the Member States concerning the classification of goods in the customs nomenclature*

B6. *Proposal for a Council Regulation amending Council Regulation (EEC) No 97/69 on the nomenclature of the Common Customs Tariff*

B7. *Proposals connected with the negotiation and acceptance of international customs conventions by the Community*

B8. *Proposal for a Council Directive establishing a list of compensating products and intermediate products referred to in Article 18 of Council Directive 69/73/EEC of 4 March 1969 on the harmonisation of provisions laid down by law, regulation or administrative action in respect of inward processing*

B9. *Proposal for a Council Regulation on the application of a decision of the EEC-Israel Cooperation Council*

B10. *Proposal for a Regulation amending Council Regulation (EEC) No 1908/73 of 4 July 1973 on the procedure to facilitate the issue of movement certificates under the provisions governing trade between the European Economic Community and certain non-member countries*

B11. *Proposal for a Council Regulation amending for the third time Regulation (EEC) No 222/77 on Community transit*

C. Proposals already examined by the Council or in the final stages of examination which could therefore be adopted in the first half of 1982

C1. *Proposal for a Council Regulation on processing prior to customs clearance*

C2. *Proposal for a Council Regulation laying down the customs procedure applicable to the stores of vessels, aircraft and international trains*

C3. *Proposal for a Council Regulation on temporary admission procedure*

C4. *Proposals on the rationalisation of preferential rules of origin (EFTA)*

C5. *Proposal for a Council Regulation defining the conditions under which natural or legal persons may be allowed to enter goods for customs purposes*

C6. *Proposal for a Council Regulation setting up a Community system of reliefs from customs duty*

C7. *Proposal for a Council Regulation amending for the second time Regulation (EEC) No 222/77 on Community transit*

C8. *Proposal for a Council Regulation on inward processing arrangements*

C9. *Proposals establishing economic outward processing arrangements applicable to certain textile and clothing products reimported into the Community after working or processing in certain third countries*

II. Proposals adopted by the Council in 1981

The following texts adopted by the Council in 1981 are sufficiently important to merit mention in this communication.

1. Council Decision of 24 February 1981 authorising the Commission to participate in the negotiation of an international convention on the harmonisation of border controls.

2. Council Directive 81/177/EEC on the harmonisation of procedures for the export of Community goods.

   (O.J. No L 83, 30.3.1981, p. 40)

The aim of this Directive is:

   (a) to ensure uniform application of the common rules applied to goods exported to non-member countries, particularly measures adopted in connection with the common agricultural policy;

(b) to eliminate distortions of treatment which currently arise between Community commercial operators because application of the rules varies depending on the Member State in which operators carry out export formalities for their goods.

3. Council Regulation (EEC) Nos 1013/81 and 1014/81 of 17 February 1981 implementing Decisions of the EEC-Switzerland and EEC-Austria Joint Committees - Community transit.

   (OJ No L 107 and OJ No L 108, 18 April 1981, p. 1)

4. Council Regulation (EEC) No 1468/81 on mutual assistance between the administrative authorities of the Member States and cooperation between the latter and the Commission to ensure the correct application of the Community Regulations on customs or agricultural matters.

   (O.J. No L 144, 2.6.1981, p. 1).

5. Council Regulation (EEC) No 1681/81 of 11 June 1981 amending Regulation (EEC) No 616/78 on proof of origin for certain textile products falling within Chapter 51 or Chapters 53 to 62 of the Common Customs Tariff and imported into the Community, and on the conditions for the acceptance of such proof.

   (O.J. No L 169, 26.6.1981).

11. Proposal for a Council Regulation on the definition of the customs
territory of the Community

(Submitted by the Commission to the Council on 7 November 1980)

(OJ No C 305, 22 November 1980, p. 4)

THE COUNCIL OF THE EUROPEAN COMMUNITIES,

Having regard to the Treaty, establishing the European Economic Community and in particular Article 235 thereof;

Having regard to the proposal from the Commission;

Having regard to the opinion of the European Parliament;

Having regard to the opinion of the Economic and Social Committee;

Whereas the customs territory of the Community is defined by Council Regulation (EEC) No 1496/68, last amended by the Act of Accession of Greece; whereas Article 4 of the above Regulation provides that it shall not affect the customs system applicable to the continental shelf or that applicable to the waters and foreshores situated between the coast or shore and the limit of territorial waters, or the provisions applicable in accordance with Community rules to be adopted with regard to free zones;

Whereas Council Regulation (EEC) No 802/68 of 27 June 1968 on the common definition of the concept of the origin of goods defined the customs system appliable to products taken from the continental shelf; whereas there is no justification for integration the continental shelf adjacent to the Member States into the customs territory of the Community;

Whereas Council Directive 69/75/EEC of 4 March 1969 on provisions relating to free zones established the Community rules applicable in those zones;

Whereas, in accordance with the Community's consistent interpretation, particularly when laying down the terms of agreements governing trade arrangements with its associated countries, the territorial waters of the Member States must be considered an integral part of their territory and, consequently, of the customs territory of the Community;

Whereas Article 4 of Regulation (EEC) No 1496/68 has consequently lost all meaning and whereas maintaining it can only have the effect of creating consfusion;

Whereas it should be specified that the air space above the sea and land of the customs territory of the Community is also an integral part of it;

Whereas the definition of the common customs territory is designed to establish the geographical space in which all Community customs rules must be applied uniformly, except in the case of specific provisions to the contrary; whereas this should be stated expressly;

114

Whereas, for the sake of clarity, it is desirable to collect all the provisions henceforth applicable with regard to the definition of the customs territory of the Community in a new regulation, and therefore to repeal Regulation (EEC) No 1496/68;

HAS ADOPTED THIS REGULATION:

Article 1

The customs territory of the Community shall comprise the territories listed below, including, where appropriate, their inland and archipelagic waters, together with the adjacent territorial sea and the air space above all of these;

- the territory of the Kingdom of Belgium;

- the territory of the Kingdom of Denmark, except the Faroe Islands;

- the German territories to which the Treaty establishing the European Economic Community applies, except the Island of Heligoland and the territory of Büsingen (Treaty of 23 November 1964 between the Federal Republic of Germany and the Swiss Confederation);

- the territory of the Hellenic Republic;

- the territory of the French Republic, except the overseas territories;

- the territory of Ireland;

- the territory of the Italian Republic, excepting the communes Livigno and Campione d'Italia and the national waters of Lake Lugano which are between the bank and the political frontier of the area between Ponte Tresa and Porto Ceresio;

- the territory of the Grand Duchy of Luxembourg;

- the territory of the Kingdom of the Netherlands in Europe;

- the territory of the United Kingdom of Great Britain and Northern Ireland together with the Channel Islands and the Isle of Man.

Article 2

The territories situated outside the territory of Member States and covered by the Annex to this Regulation shall, in accordance with the convention and treaties applicable to them, be considered part of the customs territory of the Community.

Article 3

Except where there are specific provisions to the contrary, particularly those arising from the application of international conventions, the customs rules of the Community shall apply uniformly throughout the whole of the customs territory of the Community.

Article 3

Except where there are specific provisions to the contrary, particularly those arising from the application of international conventions, the
application of international conventions, the customs rules of the
Community shall apply uniformly throughout the whole of the customs
territory of the Community.

Article 4

The provisions of this Regulation shall apply without prejudice to the
arrangements set out in the Protocol to the Treaty on German internal
trade and connected problems, particularly to German rules regarding
the German customs territory.

Article 5

1. Regulation (EEC) No 1496/68 is hereby repealed.

2. In all Community acts referring to Council Regulation (EEC) No 1496/
68, such reference shall be considered as applying to this Regulation.

Article 6

This Regulation shall enter into force on 1 July 1981.

This Regulation shall be binding in its entirety and directly applicable in all Member States.

-----

12. Commission Directive

of 22 December 1969

Based on the provisions of Article 33 (7), on the abolition of measures
which have an effect equivalent to quantitative restrictions on imports
and are not covered by other provisions adopted in pursuance of the
EEC Treaty

(70/50/EEC)

(OJ No L 13, 19 January 1970, p. 29; OJ Special Edition 1970 I, p.17)

THE COMMISSION OF THE EUROPEAN COMMUNITIES,

Having regard to the provisions of the Treaty establishing the European
Economic Community, and in particular Article 33 (7) thereof;

Whereas for the purpose of Article 30 et seq. 'measures' means laws,
regulations, administrative provisions, administrative practices, and
all instruments issuing from a public authority, including recommendations;

Whereas for the purposes of this Directive 'administrative practices' means any standard and regularly followed procedure of a public author-ty; whereas 'recommendations' means any instruments issuing from a public authority which, while not legally binding on the addressees thereof, cause them to pursue a certain conduct;

Whereas the formalities to which imports are subject do not as general rule have an effect equivalent to that of quantitative restrictions and, consequently, are not covered by this Directive;

Whereas certain measures adopted by Member States, other than those applicable equally to domestic and imported products, which were operat-ive at the date of entry into force of the Treaty and are not covered by other provisions adopted in pursuance of the Treaty, either preclude importation or make it more difficult or costly than the disposal of domestic production;

Whereas such measures must be considered to include those which make access of imported products to the domestic market, at any marketing stage, subject to a condition which is not laid down for domestic products or to a condition differing from that laid down for domestic products, and more difficult to satisfy, so that a burden is thus placed on imported products only;

Whereas such measures must also be considered to include those which, at any marketing stage, grant to domestic products a preference, other than an aid, to which conditions may or may not be attached, and where such measures totally or partially preclude the disposals of imported products;

Whereas such measures hinder imports which could otherwise take place, and thus have an effect equivalent to quantitative restrictions on imports;

Whereas effects on the free movement of goods of measures which relate to the marketing of products and which apply equally to domestic and imported products are not as a general rule equivalent to those of quantitative restrictions, since such effects are normally inherent in the disparities between rules applied by Member States in this respect;

Whereas, however, such measures may have a restrictive effect on the free movement of goods over and above that which is intrinsic to such rules;

Whereas such is the case where imports are either precluded or made more difficult or costly than the disposal of domestic production and where such effect is not necessary for the attainment of an objective within the scope of the powers for the regulation of trade left to Member States by the Treaty; whereas such is in particular the case where the said objective can be attained just as effectively by other means which are less of a hindrance to trade; whereas such is also the case where the restrictive effect of these provisions on the free move-ment of goods is out of proportion to their purpose;

Whereas these measures accordingly have an effect equivalent to that of quantitative restrictions on imports;

Whereas the customs union cannot be achieved without the abolition of such measures having an equivalent effect to quantitative restrictions on imports;

Whereas Member States must abolish all measures having equivalent effect by the end of the transitional period at the latest, even if no Commission Directive expressly requires them to do so;

Whereas the provisions concerning the abolition of quantitative restrictions and measures having equivalent effect between Member States apply both to products originating in third countries and put into free circulation in the other Member States;

Whereas Article 33 (7) does not apply to measures of the kind referred to which fall under other provisions of the Treaty, and in particular those which fall under Articles 37(1) and 44 of the Treaty or form an integral part of a national organization of an agricultural market;

Whereas Article 33 (7) does not apply to the charges and taxation referred to in Article 12 et seq. and Article 95 et seq. or to the aids mentioned in Article 92;

Whereas the provisions of Article 33 (7) do not prevent the application, in particular, of Articles 36 and 223;

HAS ADOPTED THIS DIRECTIVE:

Article 1

The purpose of this Directive is to abolish the measures referred to in Articles 2 and 3, which were operative at the date of entry into force of the EEC Treaty.

Article 2

1. This Directive covers measures, other than those applicable equally to domestic or imported products, which hinder imports which could otherwise take place, including measures which make importation more difficult or costly than the disposal of domestic production.

2. In particular, it covers measures which make imports or the disposal, at any marketing stage, of imported products subject to a condition – other than a formality – which is required in respect of imported products only, or a condition differing from that required for domestic products and more difficult to satisfy. Equally, it covers, in particular, measures which favour domestic products or grant them a preference, other than an aid, to which conditions may or may not be attached.

3. The measures referred to must be taken to include those measures which:

(a) lay down, for imported products only, minimum or maximum prices below or above which imports are prohibited, reduced or made subject to conditions liable to hinder importation;

(b) lay down less favourable prices for imported products than for domestic products;

(c) fix profit margins or any other price components for imported products only or fix these differently for domestic products and for
imported products, to the detriment of the latter;

(d) preclude any increase in the price of the imported products cor-
respondending to the supplementary costs and charges inherent in
importation;

(e) Fix the prices of procucts solely on the basis of the cost price
or the quality of domestic products at such level as to create a
hindrance to importation;

(f) lower the value of an imported product, in particular by causing a
reduction in its intrinsic value, or increase its costs;

(g) make access of imported products to the domestic market conditional
upon having an agent or representative in the territory of the importing Member State;

(h) lay down conditions of payment in respect of imported products
only, or subject imported products to conditions which are different from those laid down for domestic products and more difficult
to satisfy;

(i) require, for imports only the giving of guarantees or making of
payments on account;

(j) subject imported products only to conditions, in respect, in particular of shape, size, weight, composition, presentation, identification or putting up, or subject imported products to conditions
which are different from those for domestic products and more
difficult to satisfy;

(k) hinder the purchase by private individuals of imported products
only, or encourange, require or give preference to the purchase
of domestic products only;

(l) totally or partially preclude the use of national facilities or
equipment in respect of imported products only, or totally or
partially confine the use of such facilities or equipment to
domestic products only;

(m) prohibit or limit publicity in respect of imported products only,
or totally or partially confine publicity to domestic products
only;

(n) prohibit, limit or require stocking in respect of imported products
only; totally or partially confine the use of stocking facilities
to domestic products only, or make the stocking of imported products subject to conditions which are different from those required
for domestic products and more difficult to satisfy;

(o) make importation subject to the granting of reciprocity by one or
more Member States;

(p) prescribe that imported products are to conform, totally or partially, to rules other than those of the importing country;

(q) specify time limits for imported products which are insufficient or excessive in relation to the normal course of the various transactions to which these time limits apply;

(r) subject imported products to controls or, other than those inherent in the customs clearance procedure, to which domestic products are not subject or which are stricter in respect of imported products than they are in respect of domestic products, without this being necessary in order to ensure equivalent protection;

(s) confine names which are not indicative of origin or source to domestic products only.

Article 3

This Directive also covers measures governing the marketing of products which deal, in particular, with shape, weight, composition, presentation, identification or putting up and which are equally applicable to domestic and imported products, where the restrictive effect of such measures on the free movement of goods exceeds the effects intrinsic to trade rules.
    This is the case, in particular, where:

- the restrictive effects on the free movement of goods are out of proportion to their purpose;

- the same objective can be attained by other means which are less of a hindrance to trade.

Article 4

1. Member States shall take all necessary steps in respect of products which m st be allowed to enjoy free movement pursuant to Articles 9 and 10 of the Treaty to abolish measures having an effect equivalent to quantitative restrictions on imports and covered by this Directive.

2. Member States shall inform the Commission of measures taken pursuant to this Directive.

Article 5

1. This Directive does not apply to measures:

(a) which fall under Article 37 (1) of the EEC Treaty;

(b) which are referred to in Article 44 of the EEC Treaty or form integral part of a national organization of an agricultural market not yet replaced by a common organization.

2. This Directive shall apply without prejudice to the application, in particular, of Articles 36 and 223 of the EEC Treaty.

Article 6

This Directive is addressed to the Member States.

Done at Brussels, 22 December 1969.   For the Commission, The President,
Jean REY.

13. Communication from the Commission concerning the consequences of
the judgment given by the Court of Justice on 20 February 1979 in
Case 120/78 ('Cassis de Dijon')

(OJ No C 256, 3 October 1980, p. 2)

The following is the text of a letter which has been sent to the
Member States; the European Parliament and the Council have also been
notified of it.

In the Commission's Communication of 6 November 1978 on 'Safeguarding
free trade within the Community', it was emphasized that the free
movement of goods is being affected by a growing number of restrictive
measures.

The Judgment delivered by the Court of Justice on 20 February 1979 in
Case 120/78 (the 'Cassis de Dijon' case), and recently reaffirmed in
the judgment of 26 June 1980 in Case 788/79, has given the Commission
some interpretative guidance enabling it to monitor more strictly the
application of the Treaty rules on the free movement of goods, particularly Articles 30 to 36 of the EEC Treaty.

The Court gives a very general definition of the barriers to free trade
which are prohibited by the provisions of Article 30 et seq. of the
EEC Treaty. These are taken to include 'any national measure capable
of hindering, directly or indirectly, actually or potentially, intra-
Community trade'.

In its judgment of 20 February 1979 the Court indicates the scope of
this definition as it applies to technical and commercial rules.

Any product lawfully produced and marketed in one Member State must,
in principle, be admitted to the market of any other Member State.

Technical and commercial rules, even those equally applicable to national and imported products, may create barriers to trade only where those
rules are necessary to satisfy mandatory requirements and to serve a
purpose which is in the general interest and for which they are an
essential guarantee. This purpose must be such as to take precedence
over the requirements of the free movement of goods which constitutes
one of the fundamental rules of the Community.

The conclusions in terms of policy which the Commission draws from
this new guidance are set out below.

- Whereas Member States may, with respect to domestic products and in
  the absence of relevant Community provisions, regulate the terms on
  which such products are marketed, the case is different for products
  imported from other Member States.

  Any product imported from another Member State must in principle be
  admitted to the territory of the importing Member State if it has
  been lawfully produced, that is, conforms to rules and processes of
  manufacture that are customarily and traditionally accepted in the
  exporting Country, and is marketed in the territory of the latter.

This principle implies that Member States, when drawing up commercial or technical rules liable to affect the free movement of goods, may not take an exclusively national viewpoint and take account only of requirements confined to domestic products. The proper functioning of the common market demands that each Member State also give consideration to the legitimate requirements of the other Member States.

- Only under very strict conditions does the Court accept exceptions to this principle; barriers to trade resulting from differences between commercial and technical rules are only admissible:

  - if the rules are necessary, that is appropriate and not excessive, in order to satisfy mandatory requirements (public health, protection of consumers or the environment, the fairness of commercial transactions, etc.);
  - if the rules serve a purpose in the general interest which is compelling enough to justify an exception to a fundamental rule of the Treaty such as the free movement of goods;
  - if the rules are essential for such a purpose to be attained, i.e. are the means which are the most appropriate and at the same time least hinder trade.

The Court's interpretation has induced the Commission to set out a number of guidelines.

- The principles deduced by the Court imply that a Member State may not in principle prohibit the sale in its territory of a products lawfully produced and marketed in another Member State even if the product is produced according to technical or quality requirements which differ from those imposed on its domestic products. Where a product 'suitably and satisfactorily' fulfils the legitimate objective of a Member State's own rules (public safety, protection of the consumer or the environment, etc.) the importing country cannot justify prohibiting its sale in its territory by claiming that the way it fulfils the objective is different from that imposed on domestic products.

  In such case, an absolute prohibition of sale could not be considered 'necessary' to satisfy a 'mandatory requirement' because it would not be an 'essential guarantee' in the sense defined in the Court's judgment.

  The Commission will therefore have to tackle a whole body of commercial rules which lay down that products manufactured and marketed in one Member State must fulfil technical or qualitative conditions in order to be admitted to the market of another and specifically in all cases where the trade barriers occasioned by such rules are inadmissible according to the very strict criteria set out by the Court.

  The Commission is referring in particular to rules covering the composition, designation, presentation and packaging of products as well as rules requiring compliance with certain technical standards.

- The Commission's work of harmonization will henceforth have to be directed mainly at national laws having an impact on the functioning of the common market where barriers to trade to be removed arise from national provisions which are admissible under the criteria set by the Court.

The Commission will be concentrating on sectors deserving priority because of their economic relevance to the creation of a single internal market.

To forestall later difficulties, the Commission will be informing Member States of potential objections, under the terms of Community law, to provisions they may be considering introducing which come to the attention of the Commission.

It will be producing suggestions soon on the procedures to be followed in such cases.

The Commission is confident that this approach will secure greater freedom of trade for the Community's manufacturers, so strengthening the industrial base of the Community, while meeting the expectations of consumers.

----

14. Agreement

of the Representatives of the Governments of the Member States meeting in the Council of 28 May 1969

providing for standstill and notification to the Commission

(JO No C 76, 17 June 1979, p. 1; OJ Special Edition, Second Series IV, p. 32)

The Representatives of the Governments of the Member States, meeting in the Council,

Whereas the elimination of technical barriers to trade resulting from disparities between the provisions laid down by law, Regulation or administrative action in Member States requires the approximation of those provisions; whereas a General Programme, which includes inter alia a programme for industrial products and a programme for foodstuffs has to that end been adopted by the Council; whereas steps should be taken to prevent the implementation of that General Programme from being prejudiced by new action on the part of Governments of Member States;

Whereas the Governments of Member States should not therefore act without taking account of work initiated at Community level;

Whereas it is therefore necessary to establish a procedure for coordinating national activities with activities carried out at Community level for the elimination of technical barriers, and to provide for standstill arrangements;

Whereas the standstill must be observed for the minimum period necessary for the Community bodies concerned to initiate or complete a measure providing for approximation, this period being the longest during which the Governments are to refrain from adopting provisions

or from presenting legislation on the subject;
Whereas as regards products not covered by the General Programme any new action by an individual Member State such as to change existing laws, Regulations or administrative provisions is liable to render more diffucult any subsequent approximation in the field in question; whereas a procedure should therefore be introduced whereby the Commission is made aware of that action before any measure is adopted so that it may make an examination.

Whereas the Governments of the Member States must however retain the right to resort to immediate action at national level where reasons of safety or health so require;

Have agreed[1]:

1. To act in such manner as to facilitate implementation of the General Programme, in particular by refraining, in accordance with the detailed provisions set out below, from taking measures by way of law, Regulation or administrative action in relation to products covered by the General Programme.

    (a) In the case of products in respect of which the Commission has already presented to the Council a proposal for a Directive, a Government faced with the need to take action with a view to the adoption or amendment of any law, Regulation or administrative provision relating to matters covered by that proposal may not adopt the measure envisaged until the expiry of six months after it has informed the Council of its intention and only then on condition that the Council shall not within that period have adopted the Directive;

    (b) In the case of products in respect of which the Commission has not yet presented to the Council a proposal for a Directive, a Government faced with the need to take action with a view to the adoption or amendment of any law, Regulation or administrative provision may not adopt the measure envisaged until the expiry of five months after it has informed the Commission of its intention and only then on condition that the Commission shall not within that period have submitted to the Council a proposal for a Directive on the subject covered by the measures envisaged.

    If, however, within one month from being so informed, the Commission does not inform the Government concerned of its intention to present a proposal for a Directive, that Government may adopt immediately the measure envisaged.

    If, within the aforesaid five-month period, the Commission presents to the Council a proposal for a Directive, the Government concerned must postpone adoption of the measure envisaged for a further period of six months from the presentation of the proposal;

    (c) Where the implementation of provisions by way of law, Regulation or administrative action relating to products not covered by the General Programme could give rise to barriers to trade, the Governments of Member States shall, for information purposes, supply the Commission, with the texts of such provisions before they are adopted, stating the reasons therefor. This information must be supplied at least two months prior to the intended date of entry into force of the provisions in question;

(d) Notwithstanding the foregoing, Governments of Member States
may adopt such provisions by way of law, Regulation or administrative
action as are urgently required on grounds of safety or of health.

They shall forthwith supply the texts of such provisions to the Commission, which shall inform the Governments of the other Member States
thereof.

2. That the Governments of the Member States will also apply the
arrangements herein agreed for standstill and notification to the
Commission in cases where they take part, within the framework of
international organizations such as FAO or WHO, in work aimed at
the approximation of provisions laid down by law, Regulation or
administrative action relating to foodstuffs.

----

1) The Representatives of the Governments of the Member States meeting
in Council take note that this Agreement is a gentlemen's agreement.

15. Council Resolution

of 28 May 1969

(JO No C 76, 17 June 1969,p.1; OJ(Special Edition, second series IX)p.32)

drawing up a programme for the elimination of technical barriers to
trade in foodstuffs which result from disparities between the provisions
laid down by law, regulation or administrative action in Member States.

THE COUNCIL OF THE EUROPEAN COMMUNITIES,

Whereas, despite the abolition as between the Member States of customs
duties and quantitative restrictions and charges and measures having
equivalent effect, trade in foodstuffs is still hindered by the existence of disparities between the provisions laid down by law, Regulation
or administrative action in Member States; whereas, in order to speed
up the approximation of such provisions laid down by law, Regulation
or administrative action, a programme must be adopted which takes into
account both the extent of the barriers and the stage which has been
reached in the work to eliminate them; whereas, however, it should be
possible to make admendments to that programme,

Has adopted the following programme for the elimination of technical
barriers to trade in foodstuffs which result from disparities between

the provisions laid down by law, Regulation or administrative action in Member States. The programme may be amended on a proposal from the Commission.

FIRST STAGE

Decision by the Council before 1 July 1969.

Antioxidants
Meat products
Cocoa and chocolate
Jams, marmalades, fruit jellies, chestnut purée
Sucrose
Butter
Food extracts, bouillons, soups and meat-based sauces
Pasta
Margarine

SECOND STAGE

Presentation of proposals to the Council before 1 April 1969

Decision by the Council before 1 October 1969

Emulsifier/stabilizers, thickeners and gelling agents
Materials and objects which come into contact with foodstuffs
Dietary foods
Fruit juices and 'nectars'
Emulsified sauces
Edible ices
Sugar confectionery
Wines

THIRD STAGE

Presentation of proposals to the Council before 1 July 1969

Decision by the Council before 1 January 1970

Labelling foodstuffs
Sugars
Preserved milks
Soft drinks
Chocolate confectionery
Ordinary bakers' wares
Biscuits, cakes and other fine bakers' wares
Casein
Honey

FOURTH STAGE

Presentation of proposals to the Council before 1 January 1970

Decision by the Council before 1 July 1970

Flavourings and essences
Sampling procedures
Starches

Fish and fishproducts
Products of the milling industry
Vinegar
Beer
Natural mineral waters
Spices and condiments, including prepared condiments (other than emulsified sauces)

FIFTH STAGE

Presentation of proposals to the Council before 1 July 1970

Decision by the Council before 1 January 1971

Oils and fats
Cheeses
Spirits
Aromatized wines
Extracts, essences and concentrates of coffee or tea
Malt extract
Tapioca
Yeasts

----

16. COUNCIL

CONVENTION

FOR THE EUROPEAN PATENT FOR THE COMMON MARKET

(Community Patent Convention)

(76/76/EEC)
(O.J. No L 17, 26 January 1976, p. 1)

PREAMBLE

THE HIGH CONTRACTING PARTIES to the Treaty establishing the European Economic Community,

DESIRING to give unitary and autonomous effect to European patents granted in respect of their territories under the Convention on the grant of European patents of 5 October 1973,

ANXIOUS to establish a Community patent system which contributes to the attainment of the objectives of the Treaty establishing the European Economic Community, and in particular to the elimination within the Community of the distortion of competition which may result from the territorial aspect of national protection rights,

CONSIDERING that one of the fundamental objectives of the Treaty establishing the European Economic Community is the abolition of obstacles to the free movement of goods,

CONSIDERING that one of the most suitable means of ensuring that this objective will be achieved, as regards the free movement of goods protected by patents, is the creation of a Community patent system,

CONSIDERING that the creation of such a Community patent system is therefore inseparable from the attainment of the objectives of the Treaty and thus linked with the Community legal order,

CONSIDERING that it is necessary for these purposes for the High Contracting Parties to conclude a Convention which constitutes a special agreement within the meaning of Article 142 of the Convention on the grant of European patents, a Regional Patent Treaty within the meaning of Article 45(1) of the Patent Cooperation Treaty of 19 June 1970, and a special agreement within the meaning of Article 19 of the Convention for the protection of industrial property, signed in Paris on 20 March 1883 and last revised on 14 July 1967,

CONSIDERING that it is essential that this Convention be interpreted in a uniform manner so that the rights and obligations flowing from a Community patent be identical throughout the Community and that therefore jurisdiction be conferred on the Court of Justice of the European

Communities,

PART 1

GENERAL AND INSTITUTIONAL PROVISIONS

CHAPTER 1

GENERAL PROVISIONS

Article 1

Common system of law for patents

1. A system of law, common to the Contracting States, concerning patents for invention is hereby established.

2. The common system of law shall govern the European patents granted for the Contracting States in accordance with the Convention on the grant of European patents, hereinafter referred to as 'the European Patent Convention', and the European patent applications in which such States are designated.

Article 2

Community Patent

1. European patents granted for the Contracting States shall be called Community patents.

2. Community patents shall have a unitary character. They shall have equal effect throughout the territories to which this Convention applies and may only be granted, transferred, revoked or allowed to lapse in respect of the whole of such territories. The same shall apply *mutatis mutandis* to applications for European patents in which the Contracting States are designated.

3. Community patents shall have an autonomous character. They shall be subject only to the provisions of this Convention and those provisions of the European Patent Convention which are binding upon every European patent and which shall consequently be deemed to be provisions of this Convention.

. . . . .

Article 5

Jurisdiction of the Court of Justice of the European Communities

1. The Court of Justice of the European Communities shall in respect of this Convention have the jurisdiction conferred on it by this Convention. The Protocol on the Statute of the Court of Justice of the European Economic Community and the Rules of Procedure of the Court of Justice shall apply.

2. The Rules of Procedure shall be adapted and supplemented, as necessary, in conformity with Article 188 of the Treaty establishing the European Economic Community.

Article 6

National patents

This Convention shall be without prejudice to the right of the Contracting States to grant national patents.

. . . . .

PART 11

. . . . .

CHAPTER 11

EFFECTS OF THE COMMUNITY PATENT AND THE EUROPEAN PATENT APPLICATION

Article 29

Prohibition of direct use of the invention

A Community patent shall confer on its proprietor the right to prevent all third parties not having his consent:

(a) from making, offering, putting on the market or using a product which is the subject-matter of the patent, or importing or stocking the product for those purposes;

(b) from using a process which is the subject-matter of the patent or, when the third party knows, or it is obvious in the circumstances, that the use of the process is prohibited without the consent of the proprietor of the patent, from offering the process for use within the territories of the Contracting States;

(c) from offering, putting on the market, using, or importing or stocking for these purposes the product obtained directly by a process which is the subject-matter of the patent.

Article 30

Prohibition of indirect use of the invention

1. A Community patent shall also confer on its proprietor the right to prevent all third parties not having his consent from supplying or offering to supply within the territories of the Contracting States a person, other than a party entitled to exploit the patented invention, with means, relating to an essential element of that invention, for putting it into effect therein, when the third party knows, or it is obvious in the circumstances, that these means are suitable and intended for putting that invention into effect.

2. Paragraph 1 shall not apply when the means are staple commercial products, except when the third party induces the person supplied to commit acts prohibited by Article 29.

3. Persons performing the acts referred to in Article 31(a) to (c) shall not be considered to be parties entitled to exploit the invention within the meaning of paragraph 1.

Article 31

Limitation of the effects of the Community patent

The rights conferred by a Community patent shall not extend to:

(a) acts done privately and for non-commercial purposes;

(b) acts done for experimental purposes relating to the subject-matter of the patented invention;

(c) the extemporaneous preparation for individual cases in a pharmacy of a medicine in accordance with a medical prescription or acts concerning the medicine so prepared;

(d) the use on board vessels of the countries of the Union of Paris for the Protection of Industrial Property, other than the Contracting States, of the patented invention, in the body of the vessel, in the machinery, tackle, gear and other accessories, when such vessels temporarily or accidentally enter the waters of Contracting States, provided that the invention is used there exclusively for the needs of the vessel;

(e) the use of the patented invention in the construction or operation of aircraft or land vehicles of countries of the Union of Paris for the Protection of Industrial Property, other than the Contracting States, or of accessories to such aircraft or land vehicles, when these temporarily or accidentally enter the territory of Contracting States;

(f) the acts specified in Article 27 of the Convention on international civil aviation of 7 December 1944, where these acts concern the aircraft of a State, other than the Contracting States, benefiting from the provisions of that Article.

Article 32

Exhaustion of the rights conferred by the Community patent

The rights conferred by a Community patent shall not extend to acts concerning a product covered by that patent which are done within the territories of the Contracting States after that product has been put on the market in one of these States by the proprietor of the patent or with his express consent, unless there are grounds which, under Community law, would justify the extension to such acts of the rights conferred by the patent.
. . . . .

Article 35

Effect of revocation of the Community patent

1. A European patent application in which the Contracting States are designated and the resulting Community patent shall be deemed not to have had, as from the outset, the effects specified in this chapter, to the extent that the patent has been revoked.

2. Subject to the national provisions relating either to claims for compensation for damage caused by negligence or lack of good faith on the part of the proprietor of the patent, or to unjust enrichment, the retroactive effect of the revocation of the patent as a result of opposition or revocation proceedings shall not affect:

(a) any decision on infringement which has acquired the authority of a final decision and been enforced prior to the revocation decision;

(b) any contract concluded prior to the revocation decision, in so far as it has been performed before that decision; however, repayment, to an extent justified by the circumstances, of sums paid under the relevant contract, may be claimed on grounds of equity.

Article 36

Complementary application of national law regarding infringement

1. The effects of a Community patent shall be governed solely by the provisions of this Convention. In other respects, infringement of a Community patent shall be governed by the national law relating to infringement of a national patent in the Contracting State where the court hearing the action is located, in so far as the private international law of that State does not require application of the national law of another Contracting State.

2. The Rules of Procedure applicable are those specified in Article 74.

3. Paragraphs 1 and 2 shall apply *mutatis mutandis* to a European patent application in which the Contracting States are designated.

CHAPTER III

NATIONAL RIGHTS

Article 37

National prior right

1. With regard to a Community patent having a date of filing or, where priority has been claimed, a date of priority later than that of a national patent application or national patent made public in a Contracting State on or after that date, the national patent application or patent shall, for that Contracting State, have the same prior

right effect as a published European patent application designating that Contracting State.

2. If, in a Contracting State, a national patent application or patent, which is unpublished by reason of the national law of that State concerning the secrecy of inventions, has a prior right effect with regard to a national patent in that State having a later date of filing, or where priority has been claimed a later date of priority, the same shall apply in that State with regard to a Community patent.

Article 38

Right based on prior use and right of personal possession

1. Any person who, if a national patent had been granted in respect of an invention, would have had, in one of the Contracting States, a right based on prior use of that invention or a right of personal possession of that invention, shall enjoy, in that State, the same rights in respect of a Community patent for the same invention.

2. The rights conferred by a Community patent shall not extend to acts concerning a product covered by that patent which are done within the territory of the State concerned after that product has been put on the market in that State by the person referred to in paragraph 1, in so far as the national law of that State makes provision to the same effect in respect of national patents.

CHAPTER IV

THE COMMUNITY PATENT AS AN OBJECT OF PROPERTY

Article 39

Dealing with the Community patent as a national patent

1. Unless otherwise specified in this Convention, a Community patent as an object of property shall be dealt with in its entirety, and for the whole of the territories in which it is effective, as a national patent of the Contracting State in which, according to the Register of European Patents provided for in the European Patent Convention:

(a) the applicant for the patent had his residence or principal place of business on the date of filing of the European patent application,

(b) where subparagraph (a) does not apply, the applicant had a place of business on that date, or

(c) where neither subparagraph (a) nor subparagraph (b) applies, the applicant's representative whose name is entered first in the Register of European Patents had his place of business on the date of that entry.

2. Where subparagraphs (a), (b) and (c) of paragraph 1 do not apply, the Contracting State referred to in that paragraph shall be the Federal Republic of Germany.

3. If two or more persons are mentioned in the Register of European Patents as joint applicants, paragraph 1 shall apply to the joint applicant first mentioned; if this is not possible it shall apply to the joint applicant next mentioned in respect of whom it is applicable. Where paragraph 1 does not apply to any of the joint applicants, paragraph 2 shall apply.

4. If in a Contracting State as determined by the preceeding paragraphs a right in respect of a national patent is effective only after entry in the national patent register, such a right in respect of a Community patent shall be effective only after entry in the Registry of Community Patents.

. . . . .

Article 43

Contractual licensing

1. A Community patent may be licensed in whole or in part for the whole or part of the territories in which it is effective. A licence may be exclusive or non-exclusive.

2. The rights conferred by the Community patent may be invoked against a licensee who contravenes any restriction in his licence which is covered by paragraph 1.

3. Article 40(2) and (3) shall apply *mutatis mutandis* to the grant or transfer of a licence in respect of a Community patent.

Article 44

Licences of right

1. Where the proprietor of a Community patent files a written statement with the European Patent Office that he is prepared to allow any person to use the invention as a licensee in return for appropriate compensation, the renewal fees for the Community patent which fall due after receipt of the statement shall be reduced; the amount of the reduction shall be fixed in the rules relating to fees. Where there is a complete change of proprietorship of the patent as a result of legal proceedings under Article 27, the statement shall be deemed withdrawn upon the entry of the name of the person entitled to the patent in the Register of Community Patents.

2. The statement may be withdrawn at any time upon written notification to this effect to the European Patent Office, provided that no-one has informed the proprietor of the patent of his intention to use the invention. Such withdrawal shall take effect from the date of its notification. The amount by which the renewal fees were reduced shall be paid within one month after withdrawal; Article 49(2) shall apply, but the six-month period shall start upon expiry of the above period.

3. The statement may not be filed while an exclusive licence is recorded in the Register of Community Patents or a request for the recording of such a licence is before the European Patent Office.

4. On the basis of the statement, any person shall be entitled to use the invention as a licensee under the conditions laid down in the implementing regulations. A licence so obtained shall, for the purposes of this Convention, be treated as a contractual licence.

5. On written request by one of the parties, a Revocation Division shall determine the appropriate compensation or review it if circumstances have arisen or become known which render the compensation determined obviously inappropriate. The provisions governing revocation proceedings shall apply *mutatis mutandis*, unless they are inapplicable as a result of the particular nature of revocation proceedings. The request shall not be deemed to have been made until such time as an administrative fee has been paid.

6. No request for recording an exclusive licence in the Register of Community Patents shall be admissable after the statement has been filed, unless it is withdrawn or deemed withdrawn.

Article 45

The European patent application as an object of property

1. Articles 39 to 43 shall apply *mutatis mutandis* to a European patent application in which the Contracting States are designated, the references to the Register of Community Patents being understood as referring to the Register of European Patents provided for in the European Patent Convention.

2. The rights acquired by third parties in respect of a European patent application referred to in paragraph 1 shall continue to be effective with regard to the Community patent granted upon that application.

CHAPTER V

COMPULSORY LICENCES IN RESPECT OF A COMMUNITY PATENT

Article 46

Compulsory licences

1. Any provision in the law of a Contracting State for the grant of compulsory licences in respect of national patents shall be applicable to Community patents. The extent and effect of compulsory licences granted in respect of Community patents shall be restricted to the territory of the State concerned. Article 32 shall not apply.

. . . . .

PART VI

JURISDICTION AND PROCEDURE IN ACTIONS RELATING TO COMMUNITY
PATENTS

CHAPTER 1

JURISDICTION AND ENFORCEMENT

Article 68

General provisions

Unless otherwise specified in this Convention, the Convention on
jurisdiction and enforcement of judgments in civil and commercial
matters, signed at Brussels on 27 September 1968, hereinafter referred
to as 'the Convention on jurisdiction and enforcement', shall apply
to actions relating to Community patents and to decisions given in
respect of such actions.

Article 69

Jurisdiction of national courts concerning actions relating
to Community patents

1. Actions for infringement of a Community patent may be heard before
the courts of the Contracting State in which the defendant has his
residence or, if he is not so resident, an establishment. If the
defendant has neither his residence nor an establishment in one of
the Contracting States, such actions may, by way of derogation from
Article 4 of the Convention on jurisdiction and enforcement, be heard
before the courts of the Contracting State in which the plaintiff has
his residence or, if he is not so resident, an establishment. If
neither the defendant nor the plaintiff is so resident or has such an
establishment, such actions may be brought before the courts of the
Federal Republic of Germany. The court hearing the action shall have
jurisdiction in respect of acts of infringement committed within the
territory of any of the Contracting States.

2. Actions for infringement of a Community patent may also be heard
before the courts of the Contracting State in which an act of
infringement was committed. The court hearing the action shall have
jurisdiction only in respect of acts of infringement committed
within the territory of that State.

3. Article 5(3) and (4) of the Convention on jurisdiction and enforcement shall not apply to actions for infringement of a Community
patent.

4. The following courts shall have exclusive jurisdiction, regardless
of residence:

(a) in actions relating to compulsory licences in respect of a
Community patent, the courts of the Contracting State the national

law of which is applicable to the licence;

(b) in actions relating to the right to a patent in which an employer and an employee are in dispute, the courts of the Contracting State under whose law the right to a European patent is determined in accordance with the second sentence of Article 60(1) of the European Patent Convention. Any agreement conferring jurisdiction shall be valid only in so far as the national law governing the contract of employment allows the agreement in question.

5. For the purposes of this Article, the residence of a party shall be determined by applying Articles 52 and 53 of the Convention on jurisdiction and enforcement.

Article 70

Supplementary provisions on jurisdiction

1. Within the Contracting State whose courts have jurisdiction under Articles 68 and 69, those courts shall have jurisdiction which would have jurisdiction *ratione loci* and *ratione materiae* in the case of actions relating to a national patent granted in that State.

2. Articles 68 and 69 shall apply to actions relating to a European patent application in which the Contracting States are designated, except in so far as the right to the grant of a European patent is claimed.

3. Actions relating to a Community patent for which no court has jurisdiction under Articles 68 and 69(1) and (2) may be heard before the courts of the Federal Republic of Germany.

Article 71

Supplementary provisions on recognition and enforcement

1. Article 27(3) and (4) of the Convention on jurisdiction and enforcement shall not apply to decisions relating to the right to the Community patent.

2. In the case of irreconcilable decisions relating to the right to a Community patent given in proceedings between the same parties, only the decision of the court first seised of the matter shall be recognised. Neither party may invoke any other decision even in the Contracting State in which it was given.

Article 72

National authorities

For actions relating to the right to a Community patent or to compulsory licences in respect of a Community patent the term 'courts' in this Convention and the Convention on jurisdiction and enforcement shall include authorities which, under the national law of a Contracting State, have jurisdiction to decide such actions relating to a national patent granted in that State. Any Contracting State shall notify the European Patent Office of any authority on which such jurisdiction is conferred and the European Patent Office shall inform the other Contracting States accordingly.

Article 73

Preliminary ruling by the Court of Justice of the European Communities

1. In proceedings relating to a Community patent which are brought before a national court or tribunal, the Court of Justice of the European Communities shall have jurisdiction to give preliminary rulings concerning:

(a) the interpretation of this Convention and of the provisions of the European Patent Convention which are binding upon every Community patent in accordance with Article 2(3);

(b) the validity and interpretation of provisions enacted in implementation of this Convention, to the extent that they are not national provisions.

2. Where such a question is raised before a national court or tribunal, that court or tribunal may, if it considers that a decision on the question is necessary to enable it to give judgment, request the Court of Justice of the European Communities to give a ruling thereon.

3. Where any such question is raised in a case pending before a national court or tribunal, against whose decisions there is no judicial remedy under national law, that court or tribunal shall bring the matter before the Court of Justice of the European Communities.

PART VII

IMPACT ON NATIONAL LAW

Article 80

Prohibition of simultaneous protection

1. Where a national patent granted in a Contracting State relates to an invention for which a Community patent has been granted to the same inventor or to his successor in title with the same date of filing, or, if priority has been claimed, with the same date of priority, that national patent shall be ineffective to the extent that it covers the same invention as the Community patent, from the date on which:

(a) the period for filing an opposition to the Community patent has expired without any opposition being filed;

(b) the opposition proceedings are concluded with a decision to maintain the Community patent; or

(c) the national patent is granted, where this date is subsequent to the date referred to in subparagraph (a) or (b), as the case may be.

2. The subsequent lapse or revocation of the Community patent shall not affect the provisions of paragraph 1.

3. Each Contracting State may prescribe the procedure whereby the loss of effect of the national patent is determined and, where appropriate, the extent of that loss. It may also prescribe that the loss of effect shall apply from the outset.

4. Prior to the date applicable under paragraph 1, simultaneous protection by a Community patent or a European patent application and a national patent or a national patent application shall exist unless any Contracting State provides otherwise.

Article 81

Exhaustion of the rights conferred by a national patent

1. The rights conferred by a national patent in a Contracting State shall not extend to acts concerning a product covered by that patent which are done within the territory of that Contracting State after that product has been put on the market in any Contracting State by the proprietor of the patent or with his express consent, unless there are grounds which, under Community law, would justify the extension to such acts of the rights conferred by the patent.

2. Paragraph 1 shall also apply with regard to a product put on the market by the proprietor of a national patent, granted for the same invention in another Contracting State, who has economic connections with the proprietor of the patent referred to in paragraph 1. For the purpose of this paragraph, two persons shall be deemed to have economic connections where one of them is in a position to exert a decisive influence on the other, directly or indirectly, with regard to the exploitation of a patent, or where a third party is in a position to exercise such an influence on both persons.

3. The preceeding paragraphs shall not apply in the case of a product put on the market under a compulsory licence.

Article 82

Compulsory licences in respect of national patents

Article 47 shall apply *mutatis mutandis* to the grant of compulsory licences for lack or insufficiency of exploitation of a national patent.

Article 83

Effect of unpublished national applications or patents

1. Where Article 37(2) applies, the Community patent shall be ineffective in the Contracting State concerned to the extent that it covers the same invention as the national patent application or patent.

2. The procedure confirming that, pursuant to paragraph 1, the Community patent is ineffective in the Contracting State shall, in that State, be that according to which, if the Community patent had been a national patent, it could have been revoked or made ineffective.

17. COMMISSION

Proposal for a first Council Directive to approximate the laws of the Member States relating to trade marks

(Submitted by the Commission to the Council on 25 November 1980)
(O.J. No L 351, 31 December 1980, p. 1)

THE COUNCIL OF THE EUROPEAN COMMUNITIES,

Having regard to the Treaty establishing the European Economic Community, and in particular Article 100 thereof,

Having regard to the proposal from the Commission,

Having regard to the opinion of the European Parliament,

Having regard to the opinion of the Economic and Social Committee,

Whereas:

the trade marks laws at present applicable in the Member States contain disparities which may impede the free movement of goods and freedom to provide services, may distort competition within the common market and may therefore directly affect the establishment and functioning of that market;

it does not appear to be necessary at present to undertake full-scale harmonisation of the trade marks laws of the Member States. It will be sufficient if approximation is limited to those national provisions of law which most directly affect free movement of goods and services. It follows that this Directive does not deprive Member States of the right to continue to protect trade marks acquired through use but takes them into account only in regard to the relationship between them and trade marks acquired by registration, the only mark which it covers. It is, further, important not to disregard the solutions and advantages which the Community trade mark system affords to undertakings wishing to acquire trade marks. Under this system there is no point in requiring the Member States, *inter alia*, to authorise the registration of additional categories of signs or to recognise service marks. For the same reason, there is no justification for increasing the protection of marks which enjoy a particular reputation;

this Directive excludes the application to trade marks of other rules of law of the Member States, such as the provisions relating to fair competition. Moreover, as it only partially approximates the laws of the Member States, Article 36 of the Treaty continues to apply;

attainment of the objectives at which this approximation of laws is aiming requires that the conditions for obtaining and continuing to hold a trade mark are, in general, identical in all Member States;

in order to reduce the total number of trade marks registered and protected in the Community and, consequently, the number of conflicts which arise between them, it is essential that the trade marks be actually used;

the principal purpose of the directive is to ensure that henceforth trade marks enjoy uniform protection under the legal systems of all the Member States;

the protection afforded by the trade marks is bound up with the concept of similarity of signs, similarity of goods and services and the possibility of confusion arising therefrom. The purpose of protection is to guarantee the trade mark's function as an indicator of origin. It is essential to give strict interpretation to the abovementioned concepts so as not to impede the free movement of goods and the freedom to provide services beyond the limits required for the protection of trade marks. The current case-law in several of the Member States affords to trade marks a degree of protection which is to some extent inconsistent with the specific purpose of trade marks law. The directive therefore requires that the case-law be examined. It is necessary, in particular, that by simultaneous comparison of signs, goods and services it be certain in each case that customers are likely to be confused as to the goods or services which are identified by the signs. Where a trade mark consists of several elements it must be considered in its entirety in determining whether the sign which is alleged to infringe it is so similar to it that the sign may be confused with the trade mark. It is no longer possible, in determining whether, in a particular Member State, two verbal signs are homophones or are, at any rate, phonetically similar, to disregard the existence of the Community and the fact that the public is increasingly aware of the correct pronunciation of words in the languages which are spoken therein;

the function of indicating origin which is fulfilled by a trade mark implies that it is not, in principle, possible to prohibit its use by a third party in respect of goods marketed within or outside the Community under the trade mark by the proprietor or with his consent, or to prohibit its use, for reasons based on trade mark law, by a licensee supplying goods or providing services under the trade mark outside the territory covered by the licence.

Whereas it is necessary for the functioning of the common market to approximate national procedural rules only insofar as this will contribute to the settlement of disputes between the proprietors of

trade marks or between the latter and holders of other private
rights; whereas, for the present, provision is made for an amicable
settlement procedure only; whereas it may, however, be proper at
some later stage, depending in particular on the degree of integration
then achieved by the Community, to contemplate new measures which
would enable such conflicts to be resolved more easily.

HAS ADOPTED THIS DIRECTIVE:

Article 1

This Directive applies to every trade mark in respect of goods or
services which is the subject of an application in a Member State for
registration as an individual trade mark, a collective mark or a
guarantee mark, or which is the subject of an international registration having effect in a Member State.

Article 2

1. Trade marks shall be refused registration or shall be invalidated
if, on the date of application therefor, they consist of signs which,
under the law of the Member State concerned, cannot constitute a trade
mark or be held as such by the applicant, or if, on that date, are
devoid of distinctive character in a Member State, and in particular:

(a) those which consist solely of signs or indications which in trade
may be requisite for the purpose of showing the kind, quality, quantity, intended purpose, value, geographical origin, the time of production of the goods or of rendering of the service or other characteristics of the goods or service, unless those marks have acquired
distinctive character in consequence of the use made of them;

(b) those which consist solely of signs or indications which are
customarily used to designate the goods or service in the current
language of the trade or in the bona fide and established practices
thereof.

2. Trade marks shall also be refused registration or shall be invalidated if, on the date of application therefor,

(a) they consist of a shape which is determined by the nature of the
goods or which has some technical consequence, or they consist of the
shape of the goods and this affects their intrinsic value, to the
extent that, in the Member State concerned, a shape may constitute a
trade mark;

(b) they include signs or indications liable to mislead the public,
particularly as to the nature, quality or geographical origin of the
goods or services;

(c) they are contrary to public order or to accepted principles of
morality or are covered by Article 6 ter of the Paris Convention for
the Protection of Industrial Property, hereinafter referred to as the
'Paris Convention'.

3. A trade mark shall also be invalidated where the goods for which
it is registered in the Member State concerned has been marketed in
another Member State under another trade mark by the proprietor or

with his consent, unless there are legitimate grounds which justify the use of different marks for those goods in those Member States; but this provision shall not apply if the proprietor decides to surrender, in respect of the goods in question, the trade mark that exists in the other Member State and furnishes proof, within the period laid down by the authority to which the application for invalidation is submitted, that the trade mark has been properly surrendered.

4. Trade marks for which application has been made prior to the date laid down in Article 18(1) or which are registered before that date shall be invalidated if any of the grounds specified in paragraph 1 to 3 apply to them.

Article 3

1. The trade mark confers on the proprietor thereof an exclusive right. That right entitles him to prohibit any third party from using, without his consent, and in the course of trade a sign which is identical with or similar to the trade mark in relation to goods or services identical with or similar to those in respect of which application was made, where such use creates a serious likelihood of confusion on the part of the public;

2. Where the conditions specified in paragraph 1 are satisfied, the following types of use, in particular may be prohibited:

(a) affixing the sign to the goods or to the packaging thereof;

(b) putting the goods on the market under that sign, or supplying services thereunder;

(c) using the sign on business correspondence or invoices.

3. The Member States shall determine under what conditions compensation may be obtained for loss or damage caused by the acts mentioned in paragraph 1, and the rules of procedure which are to apply.

. . . . .

Article 11

1. A trade mark shall be put to serious use in the Member State concerned, consistently with the terms of this Directive, in connection with the goods or services in respect of which it is registered, unless there exist legitimate reasons for not doing so.

2. Circumstances arising independently of the will of the proprietor of a trade mark are alone sufficient to constitute legitimate reasons for not using it.

3. Use of a trade mark by a licensee, by a person who is associated economically with the proprietor or by a person who is entitled to use a collective mark or guarantee mark shall be deemed to constitute use by the proprietor.

4. In relation to trade marks for which application was made in the Member State concerned before the date laid down in Article 18(1),

143

the provisions of this Article shall apply with effect from that date
only.

.....

Proposal for a Council Regulation on Community trade marks

(Submitted by the Commission to the Council on 25 November 1980)

THE COUNCIL OF THE EUROPEAN COMMUNITIES

Having regard to the Treaty establishing the European Economic
Community, and in particular Article 235 thereof,

Having regard to the proposal from the Commission,

Having regard to the opinion of the European Parliament,

Having regard to the opinion of the Economic and Social Committee,

Whereas:

it is desirable to promote throughout the Community a harmonious
development of economic activities and a continuous and balanced
expansion by establishing a common market which functions properly
and offers conditions which are similar to those obtaining in a
national market. In order to create a market of this kind and make it
increasingly a single market, not only must the barriers to free
movement of goods and services be removed and arrangements be instituted which ensure that competition is not distorted, but, in addition,
legal conditions must be created which enable undertakings to adapt
their activities to the scale of the Community, whether in manufac-
turing and distributing goods or in providing services. For those
purposes, trade marks enabling the products and services of undertakings to be distinguished by identical means throughout the entire
community, regardless of frontiers, should feature amongst the legal
instruments which undertakings have at their disposal;

action by the Community would appear to be necessary for the purpose
of attaining the Community's said objectives. Such action involves
the creation of Community arrangements for trade marks whereby
undertakings can by means of one system of procedure obtain Community
trade marks to which uniform protection is given and which produce
their effects throughout the entire area of the Community;

the Treaty does not provide the requisite powers to create a legal
instrument such as a Community trade mark. The barrier of territorial-
ity of the rights conferred on proprietors of trade marks by the laws
of the Member States cannot be removed by approximation of laws. In
these circumstances the only appropriate way of opening up unrestricted
economic activity in the whole of the common market for the benefit
of undertakings is to create trade marks which are governed solely by
a law of the Community, that law being directly applicable in all

144

Member States;

the Community law relating to trade marks nevertheless does not replace the laws of the Member States on trade marks, for at the stage to which the establishment of the common market has now advanced it would not appear to be proper to require undertakings to apply for registration of their trade marks as Community trade marks. National trade marks do in fact continue to be necessary for those undertakings whose activities are such that protection of their trade marks at Community level is of no use to them;

in order not to detract from the unity of the system of Community trade marks and from the primacy of the Community law which governs them, such trade marks must not be subject to the laws of the Member States, save insofar as this Regulation expressly provides;

the rights in a Community trade mark are not to be capable of being obtained otherwise than by registration, and registration is to be refused if the trade mark is not distinctive, is unlawful or is not available. In the latter case the Office should not withhold registration unless the prior right which conflicts with the trade mark is a trade mark which is registered and used in the common market, if the proprietor of the prior right has entered opposition to registration of the trade mark as a Community trade mark and all efforts to produce an amicable settlement between the parties have failed;

the interests of proprietors of prior private rights which have not been registered will also be protected, whatever those rights may be, for any proprietor of a prior right, whether registered or not, is entitled to claim that a Community trade mark, once registered, is invalid. It may in due time be appropriate, depending particularly on the degree of integration then achieved by the Community, to contemplate new measures for the purpose of settling conflicts between Community trade marks and prior rights existing at national level;

the protection conferred by a Community trade mark is bound up with the concept of similarity of signs, similarity of goods and services and the possibility of confusion arising therefrom. The purpose of protection is to guarantee the trade mark's function as an indicator of origin. It is essential that the said concepts be interpreted strictly so that the freedom of action of persons who are in competition with each other is not needlessly restricted. It is necessary, in particular, that by simultaneous comparison of signs, goods and services it be certain in each case that customers are in reality likely to confuse products and services which are identified by those signs. For the purpose of determining whether a sign which is alleged to infringe a trade mark which consists of a number of elements is so similar to it that confusion may arise between them, the trade mark must be viewed as a whole. In order to determine whether a Community trade mark and a sign consisting of words sound the same or are at any rate phonetically similar, it is not possible to disregard the fact that the Community exists and that the public is increasingly aware of the correct pronunciation of words in the languages which are spoken therein;

in view of the fact that the function of a Community trade mark is to indicate origin, the proprietor must not be entitled to prohibit its use by a third party in relation to goods which have been put into circulation in the Community or outside it, under the trade mark, by him or with his consent, nor to prohibit its use, for reasons based on trade marks law, by a licensee who supplies the goods or services under the trade mark outside the territory covered by the licence;

there is no justification for protecting Community trade marks or, as against them, any trade mark which has been registered before them, except where the trade marks are actually used;

a Community trade mark is to be regarded as an object of property which exists separately from the undertaking whose products or services are designated by it. Accordingly, a Community trade mark must be capable of being, *inter alia*, transferred to, or charged as security in favour of, a third party and of being the subject-matter of licences. The conditions applicable for revocation and invalidity of trade marks must also be regulated in a uniform manner;

decisions regarding the validity of Community trade marks must have absolute effect and cover the entire area of the common market, for this is the only way of preventing inconsistent decisions on the part of the courts and the Office and of ensuring that the unitary character of Community trade marks is not undermined. The rules contained in the Convention on jurisdiction and enforcement of judgments in civil and commercial matters apply to all actions at law relating to Community trade marks, save where this Regulation derogates from those rules;

administrative measures are necessary at Community level for implementing in relation to every trade mark the trade marks law created by this Regulation. It is therefore essential, while retaining the Community's existing institutional structure and balance of powers, to establish a Community Trade Marks Office which is independent in relation to technical matters and has legal, administrative and financial autonomy. To this end it is necessary and appropriate that it should be a body of the Commission having legal personality and exercising the precisely delimited implementing powers which are conferred on it by this Regulation, and that it should operate within the framework of Community law without detracting from the competences exercised by the Community's Institutions;

in order to ensure that in interpreting and applying this Regulation the law is observed, the decisions made by the boards of appeal must be open to appeal to the Court of Justice. This judicial control must be available even in cases where none of the parties appeals against an erroneous decision made by a board of appeal. The Commission must in such cases be enabled to enter an appeal in the Court of Justice in the interest of the law;

the institutional structure of the Community, the balance of powers and the democratic control of the Office's budget can be maintained only if the Assembly and the Council adopt the Office's budget in conformity with the provisions contained in the Treaty which relate to the adoption of the budget of the European Communities, and utilise, in relation to the Office's revenue and expenditure, together with the Audit Board, the powers of control which are conferred by the Treaty

. . . . .

18. COMMISSION RECOMMENDATION

of 22 December 1969

to the Italian Republic on the adjustment of the State monopoly
of a commercial character in matches

(Only the Italian text is authentic)

(70/119/EEC)
(J.O.No L 31/1, 9 February 1970; O.J. (Special Edition. Second
Series, Volume VI) p. 10)

I

1. The Italian Government, by letter of 24 March 1959, informed the
Commission of the European Economic Community that matches are in
Italy subject to a State monopoly of a commercial character within
the meaning of Article 37 of the EEC Treaty.

Under that provision Member States are required progressively to adjust State monopolies of a commercial character so as to ensure that,
when the transitional period has ended, no discrimination regarding
the conditions under which goods are procured and marketed exists
between nationals of Member States,

2. Royal Decree No 560 of 11 March 1923, and the convention annexed
to it, abolished the State monopoly in the sale of matches which had
been in existence since 1916 and introduced instead a tax on manufacture. At the same time a consortium was set up, known as the *Consorzio
industrie fiammiferi* (CIF), to which all Italian undertakings which
produced matches were required to belong; the State concluded the
abovementioned convention with the consortium, granted it the monopoly
in the manufacture and sale of matches in Italy and entrusted it
with the task of ensuring that the tax on the manufacture of matches
was paid to the State.

The right to import is reserved to the State, which may grant import
permits to individuals.

The State undertook for the duration of the convention not to authorise the setting up of new factories for the manufacture of matches
or substitutes therefor. On the occasion of one of the renewals of
the convention, it was decided that that obligation should also apply
to the opening of factories whose production would be exclusively
for export (Article 12 of the implementing provisions of Legislative
Decree No 525 of 17 April 1948 on the renewal of the convention
between the State and the CIF).

The convention, due to expire on 31 May 1932, was several times renewed. The latest renewal of it, by Ministerial Decree of 29 April 1965, provides for its expiry on 31 December 1974.

As regards manufacture, the CIF is empowered to allocate the volume of production needed for the domestic market among the different undertakings which are members of the consortium. Matches are then sold by producers to the CIF, which distributes them through the network of the *Amministrazione autonoma dei monopoli di Stato* (AAMS)(since Royal Decree No 396 of 5 April 1925 matches have in fact been assimilated to other monopoly products).

The selling prices of matches are fixed by a Decree of the Ministry of Finance on a proposal from a committee on which the CIF is represented(Article 6 of the Decree of 11 March 1923). These are maximum prices and the CIF has the right to sell at lower prices(Article 6 of the Convention).

3. For several years the needs of the Italian market have been almost entirely covered by domestic production(in 1965, 1 metric ton was imported from Member States, total imports from all countries amounting to 3 metric tons); in 1966 there were no imports(total imports: 1 metric ton); in 1967, 4 metric tons were imported(total imports: 4 metric tons), and in 1968, 3 metric tons(total imports: 4 metric tons).

The Commission considered that this situation gave rise to discrimination against suppliers in other Member States in respect of marketing conditions and, on 11 April 1962, recommended the Italian Republic, in pursuance of Article 37(6):

- to allow the importation and marketing of matches from other Member States, either by permitting suppliers of these products to supply the distribution network of the AAMS or by adopting any other suitable means to that end, within the limit, for the year 1962, of 5% of the domestic production for 1960, and to increase that amount by at least 15% each year;

- to fix selling prices to consumers so that, apart from customs duty, the same margin between the delivery price and the selling price is applied to goods imported from other Member States as to domestic goods with the same delivery price;

- to permit advertising of matches from other Member States under the same conditions as those permitted in respect of domestic products.

The Italian Government has not taken any measures to comply with that recommendation. By letter of 13 May 1963 the Italian Government expressed its readiness to consider solutions such as those recommended by the Commission on condition, however, that the question of import restrictions in existence in France and Germany were resolved at the same time.

As it has already had occasion to point out to the Italian Government in answer to the letter of 13 May 1963, the Commission, while aware of the importance of the problems raised by the Italian Government, considers that the difficulties which are liable to arise with regard to the establishment of the common market can only be solved in a balanced manner if all Member States apply the provisions of the Treaty. As has been mentioned above, Article 37 requires the Italian Republic to ensure that from 1 January 1970 no discrimination regarding conditions under which goods are procured and marketed exists between nationals of Member States; the same obligation applies to the French Republic to which the Commission is addressing, at the same time as to the Italian Republic, a recommendation concerning the adjustment of its match monopoly. As to the Federal Republic of Germany, it may invoke Article 37(5), whereby the obligations on Member States are binding only in so far as they are consistent with existing international agreement. The Commission is prepared, if the failure to adjust the German monopoly gives rise to difficulties for Italy, to discuss the problem with the Italian authorities on a practical basis. The Commission points out in this connection that under the second subparagraph of Article 37(3) it may, where a product is subject to a State monopoly of a commercial character in only one or some Member States, authorise the other Member States to apply protective measures until the adjustment provided for in paragraph 1 of that Article has been effected; the conditions and details of such measures would be determined by the Commission.

In the light of the foregoing the obligation to effect the adjustment laid down in Article 37 cannot be made conditional on the solution of the questions referred to by the Italian Government.

Since the end of the transitional period is approaching, measures should now be adopted to bring to an end all discrimination between nationals of Member States regarding the conditions under which goods are procured and marketed.

Article 37, which comes under the Title relating to the free movement of goods and, more particularly, under the Chapter concerning the elimination of quantitative restrictions between Member States, aims at achieving by the end of the transitional period in respect of products subject to a State monopoly of a commercial character(or a like system) the same result as that achieved for other products by the application of Articles 30 to 34, that is to say the free movement of goods.

However, a different procedure was provided in order to achieve that result in the sectors covered by State monopolies. Their progressive adjustment was provided for partly in order to take account of the fact that in the view of the Member States concerned the products subject to a monopoly presented special problems and partly so that the elimination of quantitative restrictions and of measures having an equivalent effect in those sectors should not be without practical result. There were indeed grounds for fearing that the liberalisation of trade in respect of the products subject to a monopoly would not take place if the monopolies, by virtue of their exclusive right to import, export and market certain products, were to remain free to decide to what extent and under what conditions products from other Member States could be allowed on the domestic market(or, conversely, to what extent domestic products could be exported to other Member States).

It is for that reason that Article 37 contains the provision designed 'to ensure that when the transitional period has ended no discrimination regarding the conditions under which goods are procured and marketed exists between nationals of Member States'.

It should be stressed that the ending of discrimination resulting directly from provisions applicable to products subject to a monopoly is not the only requirement laid down in Article 37; that objective could be attained, in the absence of an Article governing State monopolies, by means of other provisions of the Treaty, in particular those prohibiting charges having an equivalent effect to customs duties and measures having an equivalent effect to quantitative restrictions. It follows from what has been said above in relation to the special characteristics of State monopolies and of the restrictions to which they can give rise that the objective of the 'adjustment', i.e. of ensuring that 'no discrimination exists', is to eliminate the possibility that the particular powers vested in the monopolies in respect of the importing and domestic marketing, or the exporting, of certain products might at the end of the transitional period still give rise to discrimination.

Since these are the objectives laid down in Article 37, it is incumbent upon Italy to adjust the monopoly in matches before the end of the transitional period in order that the objectives may be attained. On the other hand, it is for the Commission, in addition to its general duty to see that the Treaty is implemented, to make recommendations in accordance with Article 37(6), as to the manner in which the adjustment provided for in that Article shall be carried out.

4. As explained in paragraph 3, the restriction of the Italian market to domestic products constitutes discrimination against suppliers from other Member States. It should be stressed in this connection that the introduction on to the Italian market of a given quantity of matches from other Member States and the gradual increase of that quantity will not be sufficient to attain the objective of Article 37 so long as the State is able, by refusing import permits, to decide to what extent and in respect of which qualities the needs of the Italian market may be met by suppliers in other Member States and so long as the CIF, being the sole agent authorised to sell matches on the Italian market, is able to prevent those suppliers from entering that market.

For these reasons it seems to the Commission that the best solution for attaining the objective laid down in Article 37, because there is no doubt it will be effective, is to abolish the State's exclusive right to import as well as the CIF'S exclusive right to market matches, in so far as those rights concern trade between Member States.

5. Pursuant to Article 90(2), undertakings having the character of a revenue-producing monopoly are subject to the rules contained in the Treaty in so far as the application of such rules does not obstruct the performance of the particular tasks assigned to them. Furthermore, the development of trade must not be affected to such an extent as would be contrary to the interests of the Community.

The tax to which matches are subject in Italy is a tax on manufacture; the CIF cannot therefore be regarded as a revenue-producing monopoly. It is true that the CIF performs a revenue function: as a distributor of revenue stamps and on account of the fact that it makes advance payment of taxes to the State, it simplifies the collection of tax revenue. However, there is no necessary and direct link between the tax and the exclusive right of the CIF to market matches.

Moreover, in view of the small number of match manufacturers, the Commission feels that the performance of the CIF's revenue collecting role would not be jeopardised by the introduction of a straight-forward tax on manufacture, such as indeed exists both in Italy and other countries for products which are, from the point of view of tax revenue, much more important than matches and yet in respect of which no monopoly has been set up.

II

On these grounds the Commission of the European Communities recommends the Italian Republic to take the following measures, in accordance with Article 37 of the EEC Treaty:

1. To allow matches to be imported from Member States without any restriction. To that end, all formalities necessary for the introduction of these products on to the Italian market must be such as can be carried out directly by the buyers or persons appointed by them, so that those concerned may immediately dispose of the products.

2. To allow all operations necessary for the marketing of matches from other Member States to be freely carried out on the Italian market. To that end, in particular:

- to allow suppliers from other Member States to set up their own wholesale trade network in Italy and to hold stocks there;

- to allow prices for products from other Member States to be established on the basis of agreement between buyers and sellers at the different stages of marketing;

- to allow suppliers from other Member States to advertise their products freely;

- to take all measures necessary to ensure that retailers are commercially independent of the public authorities.

Done at Brussels, 22 December 1969

For the Commission

The President

Jean REY

19. COMMISSION RECOMMENDATION

of 22 December 1969

to the Federal Republic of Germany on the adjustment of the State monopoly of a commercial character in alcohol

(Only the German text is authentic)

(70/126/EEC)

(J.O. No L 31/70, 9 February 1970; O.J. (Special Edition; Second Series) Volume VI, p. 30)

I

1. The Government of the Federal Republic of Germany, by letter of 29 January 1959, informed the Commission of the European Economic Community that ethyl alcohol, spirits and spirituous beverages, with the exception of rum, arrack, cognac and liqueurs are in the Federal Republic of Germany subject to a State monopoly of a commercial character within the meaning of Article 37 of the EEC Treaty.

In pursuance of Council Regulation No 7a of 18 December 1959, ethyl alcohol derived from agricultural products, excluding spirits and spirituous beverages, was added to Annex 11 to the Treaty. Articles 38 *et seq* of the Treaty are therefore applicable to ethyl alcohol derived from agricultural products.

Under Article 37(1) of the EEC Treaty Member States are required progressively to adjust State monopolies of a commercial character so as to ensure that, when the transitional period has ended, no discrimination regarding the conditions under which goods are pro-cured and marketed exists between nationals of Member States.

2. Since the entry into force of the EEC Treaty the Government of the Federal Republic of Germany has to an increasing extent granted import permits in respect of spirits and spirituous beverages from other Member States. Such measures are not, however, sufficient to ensure the free movement of spirits and spirituous beverages within the Community by the end of the transitional period. For that reason, on 26 November 1963, the Commission recommended the Federal Republic of Germany to grant all requests for import permits within certain quotas and to increase these quotas by 15% each year. The Federal Republic of Germany has complied with that Recommendation.

In order to achieve the final abolition of those quantitative restr-ictions by progressive steps by the end of 1969, the Commission by letter of 27 June 1969, recommended a greater increase in import quotas, referring in this connection to Article 37(3) in conjunction with Article 33(3) of the EEC Treaty. The Government of the Federal Republic of Germany has not yet taken the measures proposed.

The Federal Republic of Germany has progressively reduced the differential treatment of German and imported spirits with regard to the deferment of tax payments *(Monopolausgleich* and *Branntweinaufschlag)*. Certain differences however still remain: deferred payment is allowed on the whole of the *Branntweinaufschlag*, levied on domestic products, but deferment of the *Monopolausgleich* is allowed only for an amount corresponding to the duty on the alcohol.

Apart from these measures the Federal Republic of Germany has so far taken no steps to harmonise the *Monopolausgleich* on imported spirits with the Branntweinaufschlag on corresponding German products.

3. As in the case of ethyl alcohol derived from agricultural products, ethyl alcohol not derived from agricultural products may be imported, as before, only by the monopoly. Trade in such products is also reserved exclusively to the monopoly.

Since the two kinds of ethyl alcohol cannot be distinguished in the pure form, and since, in Germany, there is a national organisation of the market in ethyl alcohol derived from agricultural products, the effectiveness of which depends on regulations concerning the production and importation of, and trade in, ethyl alcohol not derived from agricultural products, the Commission has refrained until now from recommending the Federal Republic of Germany to take certain measures with regard to the latter product. Moreover, consideration is being given to the substitution of a common organisation of the market in ethyl alcohol derived from agricultural products for the national organisation of that market.

4. Although the steps taken so far by the Government of the Federal Republic of Germany concerning spirits and spirituous beverages are in accordance with the requirement progressively to adjust the monopoly, they are not sufficient to ensure that, as laid down in Article 37 of the EEC Treaty, no discrimination regarding the conditions under which goods are procured and marketed exists between nationals of Member States.

Since the end of the transitional period provided for by the EEC Treaty is approaching, all measures must be taken, not only in respect of spirits and spirituous beverages but also in respect of ethyl alcohol not derived from agricultural products, to ensure that by 31 December 1969 at the latest no discrimination regarding the conditions under which goods are procured and marketed exists between nationals of Member States.

Article 37, which comes under the Title relating to the free movement of goods and, more particularly, under the Chapter concerning the elimination of quantitative restrictions between Member States, aims at achieving by the end of the transitional period in respect of products subject to a State monopoly of a commercial character (or a like system) the same result as that achieved for other products by the application of Articles 30 to 34, that is to say the free movement of goods.

However, a different procedure was provided in order to achieve that result in the sectors covered by State monopolies. Their progressive adjustment was provided for partly in order to take account of the fact that in the view of the Member States concerned the products subject to a monopoly presented special problems and partly so that the elimination of quantitative restrictions and of measures having an equivalent effect in those sectors should not be without practical result. There were indeed grounds for fearing that the liberalisation of trade in respect of the products subject to a monopoly would not take place if the monopolies, by virtue of their exclusive right to import, export and market certain products, were to remain free to decide to what extent and under what conditions products coming from other Member States could be allowed on the domestic market (or, conversely, to what extent domestic products could be exported to other Member States).

It is for that reason that Article 37 contains the provision designed to ensure that when the transitional period has ended no discrimination regarding the conditions under which goods are procured and marketed exists between nationals of Member States'.

It should be stressed that the ending of discrimination resulting directly from the provisions applicable to products subject to a monopoly is not the only requirement laid down in Article 37; that objective could be achieved, in the absence of an Article governing State monopolies, by means of other provisions of the Treaty, in particular those prohibiting charges having an equivalent effect to customs duties and measures having an equivalent effect to quantitative restrictions. It follows from what has been said above in relation to the special characteristics of State monopolies and of the restrictions to which they may give rise that the objective of the 'adjustment', i.e. of ensuring that 'no discrimination exists', is to eliminate the possibility that the particular powers vested in the monopolies in respect of the importing and domestic marketing, or the exporting, of certain products might at the end of the transitional period still give rise to discrimination.

Since these are the objectives laid down in Article 37, it is incumbent upon the Federal Republic of Germany to adjust the alcohol monopoly before the end of the transitional period in order that the objectives may be attained. On the other hand, it is for the Commission, in addition to its general duty to see that the Treaty is implemented, to make recommendations in accordance with Article 37(6) as to the manner in which the adjustment provided for in that Article shall be carried out.

The Commission considers that the objective of Article 37 of the EEC Treaty will not be attained so long as the German alcohol monopoly is in a position to decide whether, to what extent and in respect of what quantities products from other Member States may be imported and marketed and so long as taxation differences remain between imported and domestic products. The Commission considers that, apart from the abolition of such discrimination in taxation, the best solution for attaining the objective laid down in Article 37 - because there is no doubt that it will be effective - is to abolish the exclusive rights to import, export and market which the German monopoly in respect of alcohol still has, in so far as these rights concern trade between Member States.

5. The Commission considers, however, that, since there is no common

organisation of the market in ethyl alcohol derived from agricultural products, since there is an interdependence between such alcohol and ethyl alcohol not derived from agricultural products, and since spirits may often be a substitute for ethyl alcohol, thus adversely affecting its saleability, it might prove necessary to take special measures until the entry into force of a common organisation of the market.

Under Article 37(4) of the EEC Treaty, if a State monopoly of a commercial character has rules which are designed to make it easier to dispose of agricultural products or obtain for them the best return, steps should be taken in applying the rules contained in Article 37 to ensure equivalent safeguards for the employment and standard of living of the producers concerned, account being taken of the adjustments that will be possible and the specialisation that will be needed with the passage of time. That provision is applicable to the German alcohol monopoly.

The German alcohol monopoly does in fact constitute a national market organisation. It influences the production of ethyl alcohol, in particular by means of quotas and the fixing of purchase prices and thereby ensures that the producers concerned receive an adequate income. Moreover, the production of spirits is guided, as to both quantity and price, so as to favour the production and sale of ethyl alcohol derived from agricultural products and in this way account is taken of the interests of producers of certain agricultural raw materials. The unrestricted opening of the German market to products from other Member States before the entry into force of a common organisation of the market could thus adversely affect the sale of German ethyl alcohol derived from agricultural products as well as the competitive position of German spirits and, in consequence, the employment and standard of living of producers of certain agricultural raw materials.

The Commission considers that these facts set out above must be taken into account in connection with the adjustment of the German alcohol monopoly.

II

On these grounds the Commission recommends the German Federal Republic to take the following measures, in accordance with Article 37 of the EEC Treaty:

1. As regards spirits and spirituous beverages:

(a) - from 1 January 1970 at the latest, to grant import permits applied for in respect of spirits and spirituous beverages from other Member States without restriction and without delay;

- to impose on spirits and spirituous beverages from other Member States a duty to that levied on corresponding domestic products;

- to allow the payment of the duty to be deferred for the same period as in the case of corresponding domestic products.

(b) The Commission considers that, until the entry into force of regulations establishing a common organisation of the market in ethyl alcohol derived from agricultural products, the interests of German producers of agricultural raw materials processed into alcohol and spirits could be adequately protected by the following measures:

- in principle to regard imported spirits, so far as taxation is concerned, as having been manufactured in distilleries producing 10 000 hectolitres of pure alcohol per annum;

- to maintain the basic obligation to bottle spirits before importation;

- where necessary, and until Community provisions are adopted, to apply non-discriminatory quality standards, in particular in respect of rum, corn spirit, molasses, and sugar cane, and to adopt non-discriminatory provisions regarding the alcoholic strength of spirits;

- to levy a special charge on spirituous beverages imported from another Member State, provided that the selling price of ethyl alcohol derived from agricultural products which is intended for the manufacture in Germany of spirituous beverages is higher than the lowest price at which producers of spirituous beverages in the exporting Member State may obtain ethyl alcohol, whether on their own market or on the market of another Member State. The amount of the charge may in no circumstances exceed the difference between those prices. Where the spirituous beverage has come from a Member State other than the exporting Member State it may be treated as if it had been imported directly from the Member State whence it comes.

2. With regard to ethyl alcohol not derived from agricultural products:

(a) - it should allow nationals of all Member States freely and directly to import from other Member States ethyl alcohol not derived from agricultural products;

- it should allow suppliers from all Member States to set up their own distribution network in the Federal Republic of Germany, to hold stocks there and to fix their selling price freely;

- it should allow suppliers from all Member States to supply German consumers freely and directly;

- it should allow direct exports to the other Member States without restriction.

(b) Until the entry into force of regulations establishing a common organisation of the market in ethyl alcohol derived from agricultural products, the Federal Republic of Germany may, in order to safeguard the market for ethyl alcohol derived from agricultural products, decide:

- that ethyl alcohol not derived from agricultural products may be used only in certain sectors of industry, no distinction being permitted however between German products and those from other Member States;

- that a special charge, equal to the difference between the purchase price for German ethyl alcohol not derived from agricultural products and the price at which the German monopoly sells to the industry concerned, may, where necessary, be levied on imports from other Member States of ethyl alcohol not derived from agricultural products.

Done at Brussels, 22 December 1969.

For the Commission

The President

Jean REY

20. COUNCIL DIRECTIVE

of 25 February 1964

on the co-ordination of special measures concerning the movement and residence of foreign nationals which are justified on grounds of public policy, public security or public health

(64/221/EEC)

(J.O. 1964, p. 850; O.J. (Special Edition 1963-1964) p. 117)

THE COUNCIL OF THE EUROPEAN ECONOMIC COMMUNITY,

Having regard to the Treaty establishing the European Economic Community, and in particular Article 56(2) thereof;

Having regard to Council Regulation No 15 of 16 August 1961 on initial measures to bring about free movement of workers within the Community, and in particular Article 47 thereof;

Having regard to Council Directive of 16 August 1961 on administrative procedures and practices governing the entry into and employment and residence in a Member State of workers and their families from other Member States of the Community;

Having regard to the General Programmes for the abolition of restrictions on freedom of establishment and on freedom to provide services, and in particular Title II of each such programme;

Having regard to the Council Directive of 25 February 1964 on the abolition of restrictions on movement and residence within the Community for nationals of Member States with regard to establishment and the provision of services;

Having regard to the proposal from the Commission;

Having regard to the Opinion of the European Parliament;

Having regard to the Opinion of the Economic and Social Committee;

Whereas co-ordination of provisions laid down by law, regulation or administrative action which provide for special treatment for foreign nationals on grounds of public policy, public security or public health should in the first place deal with the conditions for entry and residence of nationals of Member States moving within the Community either in order to pursue activities as employed or self-employed persons, or as recipients of services;

Whereas such co-ordination presupposes in particular an approximation of the procedures followed in each Member State when invoking grounds of public policy, public security or public health in matters connected with the movement or residence of foreign nationals;

Whereas, in each Member State, nationals of other Member States should have adequate legal remedies available to them in respect of the decisions of the administration in such matters;

Whereas it would be of little practical use to compile a list of diseases and disabilities which might endanger public health, public policy or public security and it would be difficult to make such a list exhaustive; whereas it is sufficient to classify such diseases and disabilities in groups;

HAS ADOPTED THIS DIRECTIVE:

Article 1

1. The provisions of this Directive shall apply to any national of a Member State who resides in or travels to another Member State of the Community, either in order to pursue an activity as an employed or self-employed person, or as a recipient of services.

2. These provisions shall apply also to the spouse and to members of the family who come within the provisions of the regulations and directives adopted in this field in pursuance of the Treaty.

Article 2

1. This Directive relates to all measures concerning entry into their territory, issue or renewal of residence permits, or expulsion from their territory, taken by Member States on grounds of public policy, public security or public health.

2. Such grounds shall not be invoked to service economic ends.

Article 3

1. Measures taken on grounds of public policy or of public security shall be based exclusively on the personal conduct of the individual concerned.

2. Previous criminal convictions shall not in themselves constitute

grounds for the taking of such measures.

3. Expiry of the identity card or passport used by the person concerned to enter the host country and to obtain a residence permit
shall not justify expulsion from the territory.

4. The State which issued the identity card or passport shall allow
the holder of such document to re-enter its territory without any
formality even if the document is no longer valid or the nationality
of the holder is in dispute.

Article 4

1. The only diseases or disabilities justifying refusal of entry into
a territory or refusal to issue a first residence permit shall be
those listed in the Annex to this Directive.

2. Diseases or disabilities occurring after a first residence permit
has been issued shall not justify refusal to renew the residence
permit or expulsion from the territory.

3. Member States shall not introduce new provisions or practices
which are more restrictive than those in force at the date of notification of this Directive.

Article 5

1. A decision to grant or to refuse a first residence permit shall
be taken as soon as possible and in any event not later than six
months from the date of application for the permit.

The person concerned shall be allowed to remain temporarily in the
territory pending a decision either to grant or to refuse a residence
permit.

2.The host country may, in cases where this is considered essential,
request the Member State of origin of the applicant, and if need be
other Member States, to provide information concerning any previous
police record. Such enquiries shall not be made as a matter of routine.
The Member State consulted shall give its reply within two months.

Article 6

The person concerned shall be informed of the grounds of public
policy, public security, or public health upon which the decision
taken in his case is based, unless this is contrary to the interests
of the security of the State involved.

Article 7

The person concerned shall be officially notified of any decision to
refuse the issue or renewal of a residence permit or to expel him
from the territory. The period allowed for leaving the territory
shall be stated in this notification. Save in cases of urgency, this
period shall be not less than fifteen days if the person concerned
has not yet been granted a residence permit and not less than one
month in all other cases.

Article 8

The person concerned shall have the same legal remedies in respect of
any decision concerning entry, or refusing the issue or renewal of a
residence permit, or ordering expulsion from the territory, as are
available to nationals of the State concerned in respect of acts of
administration.

Article 9

1. Where there is no right of appeal to a court of law, or where
such appeal may be only in respect of the legal validity of the
decision, or where the appeal cannot have suspensory effect, a decision refusing renewal of a residence permit or ordering the expulsion
of the holder of a residence permit from the territory shall not be
taken by the administrative authority, save in cases of urgency, until
an opinion has been obtained from a competent authority of the host
country before which the person concerned enjoys such rights of
defence and of assistance or representation as the domestic law of
that country provides for.

This authority shall not be the same as that empowered to take the
decision refusing renewal of the residence permit or ordering
expulsion.

2. Any decision refusing the issue of a first residence permit
or ordering expulsion of the person concerned before the issue of the
permit shall, where that person so requests, be referred for consideration to the authority whose prior opinion is required under paragraph
1. The person concerned shall then be entitled to submit his defence
in person, except where this would be contrary to the interests of
national security.

Article 10

1. Member States shall within six months of notification of this
Directive put into force the measures necessary to comply with its
provisions and shall forthwith inform the Commission thereof.

2. Member States shall ensure that the texts of the main provisions
of national law which they adopt in the field governed by this
Directive are communicated to the Commission.

Article 11

This Directive is addressed to the Member States.

Done at Brussels, 25 February 1964

For the Council

The President

H. FAYAT

. . . . .

20 A. COUNCIL DIRECTIVE

of 17 December 1974

extending the scope of Directive No 64/221/EEC on the coordination of special measures concerning the movement and residence of foreign nationals which are justified on grounds of public policy, public security or public health to include nationals of a Member State who exercise the right to remain in the territory of another Member State after having pursued therein an activity in a self-employed capacity

(75/35/EEC)
(O.J. No L 14, 20 January 1975, p. 14)

THE COUNCIL OF THE EUROPEAN COMMUNITIES,

Having regard to the Treaty establishing the European Economic Community, and in particular Article 56(2) and Article 235 thereof;

Having regard to the proposal from the Commission;

Having regard to the Opinion of the European Parliament;

Having regard to the Opinion of the Economic and Social Committee;

Whereas Directive No 64/221/EEC coordinated special measures concerning the movement and residence of foreign nationals which are justified on grounds of public policy, public security or public health and whereas Directive No 75/34/EEC laid down conditions for the exercise of the right of nationals of a Member State to remain in the territory of another Member State after having pursued therein an activity in a self-employed capacity;

Whereas Directive No 64/221/EEC should therefore apply to persons to whom Directive No 75/34/EEC applies,

HAS ADOPTED THIS DIRECTIVE,

Article 1

Directive No 64/221/EEC shall apply to nationals of Member States and members of their families who have the right to remain in the territory of a Member State pursuant to Directive No 75/34/EEC.

Article 2

Member States shall, within twelve months of notification of this Directive, bring into force the measures necessary to comply with its provisions and shall forthwith inform the Commission thereof.

Article 3

This Directive is addressed to the Member States.

Done at Brussels, 17 December 1974.

For the Council

The President

M. DURAFOUR

21. REGULATION (EEC) No 1612/68 OF THE COUNCIL

of 15 October 1968

on freedom of movement for workers within the Community

(J.O. No L 257/2, 19 October 1968; O.J. (Special Edition
1968 II) p. 475)

THE COUNCIL OF THE EUROPEAN COMMUNITIES,

Having regard to the Treaty establishing the European Economic
Community, and in particular Article 49 thereof;

Having regard to the proposal from the Commission;

Having regard to the Opinion of the European Parliament;

Having regard to the Opinion of the Economic and Social Committee;

Whereas freedom of movement for workers should be secured within the
Community by the end of the transitional period at the latest; whereas the attainment of this objective entails the abolition of any
discrimination based on nationality between workers of the Member
States as regards employment, remuneration and other conditions of
work and employment, as well as the right of such workers to move
freely within the Community in order to pursue activities as employed
persons subject to any limitations justified on grounds of public
policy, public security or public health;

Whereas by reason in particular of the early establishment of the
customs union and in order to ensure the simultaneous completion of
the principal foundations of the Community, provisions should be
adopted to enable the objectives laid down in Articles 48 and 49 of
the Treaty in the field of freedom of movement to be achieved and to
perfect measures adopted successively under Regulation No 15 on the
first steps for attainment of freedom of movement and under Council
Regulation No 38/54/EEC of 25 March 1964 on freedom of movement for
workers within the Community;

Whereas freedom of movement constitutes a fundamental right of workers
and their families; whereas mobility of labour within the Community
must be one of the means by which the worker is guaranteed the possibility of improving his living and working conditions and promoting

his social advancement, while helping to satisfy the requirements of
the economies of the Member States; whereas the right of all workers
in the Member States to pursue the activity of their choice within
the Community should be affirmed;

Whereas such right must be enjoyed without discrimination by permanent,
seasonal and frontier workers and by those who pursue their activities
for the purpose of providing services;

Whereas the right of freedom of movement, in order that it may be
exercised, by objective standards, in freedom and dignity, requires
that equality of treatment shall be ensured in fact and in law in respect of all matters relating to the actual pursuit of activities as
employed persons and to eligibility for housing, and also that obstacles to the mobility of workers shall be eliminated, in particular
as regards the worker's right to be joined by his family and the
conditions for the integration of that family into the host country;

Whereas the principle of non-discrimination between Community workers
entails that all nationals of Member States have the same priority as
regards employment as is enjoyed by national workers;

Whereas it is necessary to strengthen the machinery for vacancy clearance, in particular by developing direct co-operation between the
central employment services and also between the regional services,
as well as by increasing and co-ordinating the exchange of information
in order to ensure in a general way a clearer picture of the labour
market; whereas workers wishing to move should also be regularly
informed of living and working conditions; whereas, furthermore,
measures should be provided for the case where a Member State under-
goes or foresees disturbances on its labour market which may seriously
threaten the standard of living and level of employment in a region
or an industry; whereas for this purpose the exchange of information,
aimed at discouraging workers from moving to such a region or industry,
constitutes the method to be applied in the first place but, where
necessary, it should be possible to strengthen the results of such
exchange of information by temporarily suspending the abovementioned
machinery, any such decision to be taken at Community level;

Whereas close links exist between freedom of movement for workers,
employment and vocational training, particularly where the latter
aims at putting workers in a position to take up offers of employment
from other regions of the Community; whereas such links make it
necessary that the problems arising in this connection should no
longer be studied in isolation but viewed as inter-dependent, account
also being taken of the problems of employment at the regional level;
and whereas it is therefore necessary to direct the efforts of Member
States toward coordinating their employment policies at Community
level;

Whereas the Council, by its Decision of 15 October 1968 made Articles
48 and 49 of the Treaty and also the measures taken in implementation
thereof applicable to the French overseas departments;

HAS ADOPTED THIS REGULATION:

PART I

EMPLOYMENT AND WORKERS' FAMILIES

TITLE I

Eligibility for employment

Article 1

1. Any national of a Member State, shall, irrespective of his place
of residence, have the right to take up an activity as an employed
person, and to pursue such activity, within the territory of another
Member State in accordance with the provisions laid down by law,
regulation or administrative action governing the employment of
nationals of that State.

2. He shall, in particular, have the right to take up available
employment in the territory of another Member State with the same
priority as nationals of that State.

Article 2

Any national of a Member State and any employer pursuing an activity
in the territory of a Member State may exchange their applications
for and offers of employment, and may conclude and perform contracts
of employment in accordance with the provisions in force laid down
by law, regulation or administrative action, without any discrimination resulting therefrom.

Article 3

1. Under this Regulation, provisions laid down by law, regulation or
administrative action or administrative practices of a Member State
shall not apply:

- where they limit application for and offers of employment, or
  the right of foreign nationals to take up and pursue employment
  or subject these to conditions not applicable in respect of their
  own nationals; or

- where, though applicable irrespective of nationality, their
  exclusive or principal aim or effect is to keep nationals of
  other Member States away from the employment offered.

This provision shall not apply to conditions relating to linguistic
knowledge required by reason of the nature of the post to be filled.

2. There shall be included in particular among the provisions or
practices of a Member State referred to in the first subparagraph of
paragraph 1 those which:

(a) prescribe a special recruitment procedure for foreign nationals;

(b) limit or restrict the advertising of vacancies in the press or
through any other medium or subject it to conditions other than those
applicable in respect of employers pursuing their activities in

164

the territory of that Member State;

(c) subject eligibility for employment to conditions of registration with employment offices or impede recruitment of individual workers, where persons who do not reside in the territory of that State are concerned.

Article 4

1 Provisions laid down by law, regulation or administrative action of the Member States which restrict by number or percentage the employment of foreign nationals in any undertaking, branch of activity or region, or at a national level, shall not apply to nationals of the other Member States.

2. When in a Member State the granting of any benefit to undertakings is subject to a minimum percentage of national workers being employed, nationals of the other Member States shall be counted as national workers, subject to the provisions of the Council Directive of 15 October 1963.

Article 5

A national of a Member State who seeks employment in the territory of another Member State shall receive the same assistance there as that afforded by the employment offices in that State to their own nationals seeking employment.

Article 6

1. The engagement and recruitment of a national of one Member State for a post in another Member State shall not depend on medical, vocational or other criteria which are discriminatory on grounds of nationality by comparison with those applied to nationals of the other Member State who wish to pursue the same activity.

2. Nevertheless, a national who holds an offer in his name from an employer in a Member State other than that of which he is a national may have to undergo a vocational test, if the employer expressly requests this when making his offer of employment.

TITLE II

Employment and equality of treatment

Article 7

1. A worker who is a national of a Member State may not, in the territory of another Member State, be treated differently from national workers by reason of his nationality in respect of any conditions of employment and work, in particular as regards remuneration, dismissal, and should he become unemployed, reinstatement or re-employment;

2. He shall enjoy the same social and tax advantages as national workers.

3. He shall also, by virtue of the same right and under the same

165

conditions as national workers, have access to training in vocational schools and retraining centres.

4. Any clause of a collective or individual agreement or of any other collective regulation concerning eligibility for employment, employment remuneration and other conditions of work or dismissal shall be null and void in so far as it lays down or authorises discriminatory conditions in respect of workers who are nationals of the other Member States.

Article 8

1. A worker who is a national of a Member State and who is employed in the territory of another Member State shall enjoy equality of treatment as regards membership of trade unions and the exercise of rights attaching thereto, including the right to vote, Amendment by Council Regulation No 312/76, and to be eligible for the administration or management posts of a trade union; he may be excluded from taking part in the management of bodies governed by public law and from holding an office governed by public law. Furthermore, he shall have the right of eligibility for workers' representative bodies in the undertaking. The provisions of this Article shall not affect laws or regulations in certain Member States which grant more extensive rights to workers coming from the other Member States.

Article 9

1. A worker who is a national of a Member State and who is employed in the territory of another Member State shall enjoy all the rights and benefits accorded to national workers in matters of housing, including ownership of the housing he needs.

2. Such worker may, with the same right as nationals, put his name down on the housing lists in the region in which he is employed, where such lists exist; he shall enjoy the resultant benefits and priorities.

If his family has remained in the country whence he came, they shall be considered for this purpose as residing in the said region, where national workers benefit from a similar presumption.

TITLE III

Workers' families

Article 10

1. The following shall, irrespective of their nationality, have the right to install themselves with a worker who is a national of one Member State and who is employed in the territory of another Member State:

(a) his spouse and their descendants who are under the age of 21 years or are dependants;

(b) dependent relatives in the ascending line of the worker and his spouse.

2. Member States shall facilitate the admission of any member of the family not coming within the provisions of paragraph 1 if dependent on the worker referred to above or living under his roof in the country whence he comes.

3. For the purposes of paragraphs 1 and 2, the worker must have available for his family housing considered as normal for national workers in the region where he is employed; this provision, however, must not give rise to discrimination between national workers and workers from the other Member States.

Article 11

Where a national of a Member State is pursuing an activity as an employed or self-employed person in the territory of another Member State, his spouse and those of the children who are under the age of 21 years or dependent on him shall have the right to take up any activity as an employed person throughout the territory of that same State, even if they are not nationals of any Member State.

Article 12

The children of a national of a Member State who is or has been employed in the territory of another Member State shall be admitted to that State's general educational, apprenticeship and vocational training courses under the same conditions as the nationals of that State, if such children are residing in its territory.

Member States shall encourage all efforts to enable such children to attend these courses under the best possible conditions.

PART III

CLEARANCE OF VACANCIES
AND APPLICATIONS FOR EMPLOYMENT

TITLE I

Co-operation between the Member States
and with the Commission

Article 13

1. The Member States or the Commission shall instigate or together undertake any study of employment or unemployment which they consider necessary for securing freedom of movement for workers within the Community.

The central employment services of the Member States shall co-operate closely with each other and with the Commission with a view to acting jointly as regards the clearing of vacancies and applications for employment within the Community and the resultant placing of workers in employment.

2. To this end the Member States shall designate specialist services which shall be entrusted with organising work in the fields referred to above and co-operating with each other and with the departments of the Commission.

The Member States shall notify the Commission of any change in the designation of such services; the Commission shall publish details thereof for information in the *Official Journal of the European Communities*.

Article 14

1. The Member States shall send to the Commission information on problems arising in connection with the freedom of movement and employment of workers and particulars of the state and development of employment by region and by branch of activity.

2. In co-operation with the Technical Committee, the Commission shall determine the manner in which the information referred to in paragraph 1 shall be drawn up and the intervals at which it shall be communicated. To assess the state of their labour markets, the Member States shall use uniform criteria established by the Commission in accordance with the results of the work of the Technical Committee carried out in pursuance of Article 33(d), after having obtained the Opinion of the Advisory Committee.

3. In accordance with the procedure laid down by the Commission in agreement with the Technical Committee, the specialist service of each Member State shall send to the specialist services of the other Member States and to the European Co-ordination Office such information concerning living and working conditions and the state of the labour market as is likely to be of guidance to workers from the other Member States. Such information shall be brought up to date regularly.

The specialist services of the other Member States shall ensure that wide publicity is given to such information, in particular by circulating it among the appropriate employment services and by all suitable means of communication for informing the workers concerned.

TITLE II

Machinery for vacancy clearance

Article 15

1. At least once a month the specialist service of each Member State shall send to the specialist services of the other Member States and to the European Co-ordination Office a return showing by occupation and by region:

(a) vacancies unfilled or unlikely to be filled by manpower from the national labour market;

(b) applicants for employment who have declared themselves actually ready and able to accept employment in another country.

The specialist service of each Member State shall forward such information to the appropriate employment services and agencies.

2.The returns referred to in paragraph 1 shall be circulated according to a uniform system to be established by the European Co-ordination Office in collaboration with the Technical Committee, within eighteen months following the entry into force of this Regulation.

Article 16

1. Any vacancy communicated to the employment services of a Member State which cannot be filled from the national labour market and which, on the basis of the returns referred to in Article 15, can be cleared within the Community, shall be notified to the competent employment services of the Member State which has indicated that it has manpower available in the same occupation.

2. Such services shall forward to the services of the first Member State the details of suitable applications. For a period of 18 days from receipt of the communication of the vacancy to the services of the second Member State, such applications shall be submitted to employers with the same priority as that granted to national workers over nationals of non-Member States. During the above-mentioned period, vacancies shall be notified to non-Member States only if the Member State having such vacancies considers that for the occupations corresponding to such vacancies there are insufficient workers available who are nationals of the Member States.

3. The provisions of paragraph 1 shall not apply to vacancies offered to workers who are nationals of non-Member States where:

(a) such an offer is made to a named worker and is of a special nature in view of:

  (i) the requirement of specialist qualifications or the confidential nature of the post offered or previous occupational ties;

  (ii) the existence of family ties either between the employer and the worker asked for, or between the latter and a worker who has been employed regularly for at least a year in the undertaking.

  Items (i) and (ii) shall be applied in accordance with the provisions set out in the Annex;

(b) such vacancies are for the recruitment of homogeneous groups of seasonal workers of whom at least one named member has been offered a vacancy;

(c) such vacancies are offered by employers to workers resident in regions adjacent to either side of the frontier between a Member State and a non-Member State;

(d) vacancies are offered expressly to workers from non-Member States by the employer for reasons connected with the smooth running of the undertaking, where the employment services, having intervened for the purposes of securing the employment of national workers

169

or workers from the other Member States of the Community, are of the opinion that such reasons are justified.

Article 17

1. The provisions of Article 16 shall be implemented by the specialist services. However, in so far as they have been authorised by the central services and in so far as the organisation of the employment services of a Member State and the placing techniques employed make it possible:

(a) the regional employment services of the Member States shall:

  (i) on the basis of the returns referred to in Article 15, on which appropriate action will be taken, directly bring together and clear vacancies and applications for employment;

  (ii) establish direct relations for clearance:

    - of vacancies offered to a named worker;

    - of individual applications for employment sent either to a specific employment service or to an employer pursuing his activity within the area covered by such a service;

    - where the clearing operations concern seasonal workers who must be recruited as quickly as possible;

(b) the services territorially responsible for the border regions of two or more Member States shall regularly exchange data relating to vacancies and applications for employment outstanding in their area and, acting in accordance with their arrangements with the other employment services of their countries, shall directly bring together and clear vacancies and applications for employment;

(c) official employment services which specialise in certain occupations or specific categories of persons shall cooperate directly with each other.

2. The Member States concerned shall forward to the Commission the list, drawn up by common accord, of services referred to in paragraph 1; the Commission shall publish such list, and any amendment thereto, in the *Official Journal of the European Communities.*

Article 18

Adoption of recruiting procedures as applied by the implementing bodies provided for under agreements concluded between two or more Member States shall not be obligatory.

. . . . .

(As amended by Regulation No 312/76; O.J. No L 39/2 of 14 February 1976)

22. COUNCIL DIRECTIVE

of 15 October 1968

on the abolition of restrictions on movement and residence within
the Community for workers of Member States and their families

(68/360/EEC)
(J.O. No L 257/13, 19 October 1968; O.J. (Special Edition 1968 II)

THE COUNCIL OF THE EUROPEAN COMMUNITIES,

Having regard to the Treaty establishing the European Economic
Community, and in particular Article 49 thereof;

Having regard to the proposal from the Commission;

Having regard to the Opinion of the European Parliament;

Having regard to the Opinion of the Economic and Social Committee;

Whereas Council Regulation (EEC) No 1612/68 fixed the provisions
governing freedom of movement for workers within the Community;
whereas, consequently, measures should be adopted for the abolition
of restrictions which still exist concerning movement and residence
within the Community, which conform to the rights and privileges
accorded by the said Regulation to nationals of any Member State who
move in order to pursue activities as employed persons and to members
of their families;

Whereas the rules applicable to residence should, as far as possible,
bring the position of workers from other Member States and members of
their families into line with that of nationals;

Whereas the co-ordination of special measures relating to the movement
and residence of foreign nationals, justified on grounds of public
policy, public security or public health, is the subject of the
Council Directive of 25 February 1964, adopted in application of
Article 56(2) of the Treaty;

HAS ADOPTED THIS DIRECTIVE:

Article 1

Member States shall, acting as provided in this Directive, abolish
restrictions on the movement and residence of nationals of the said
States and of members of their families to whom Regulation (EEC) No
1612/68 applies.

Article 2

1. Member States shall grant the nationals referred to in Article 1 the right to leave their territory in order to take up activities as employed persons and to pursue such activities in the territory of another Member State. Such right shall be exercised simply on production of a valid identity card or passport. Members of the family shall enjoy the same right as the national on whom they are dependent.

2. Member States shall, acting in accordance with their laws, issue to such nationals, or renew, an identity card or passport, which shall state in particular the holder's nationality.

3. The passport must be valid at least for all Member States and for countries through which the holder must pass when travelling between Member States. Where a passport is the only document on which the holder may lawfully leave the country, its period of validity shall be not less than five years.

4. Member States may not demand from the nationals referred to in Article 1 any exit visa or any equivalent document.

Article 3

1. Member States shall allow the persons referred to in Article 1 to enter their territory simply on production of a valid identity card or passport.

2. No entry visa or equivalent document may be demanded save from the members of the family who are not nationals of a Member State. Member States shall accord to such persons every facility for obtaining any necessary visas.

Article 4

1. Member States shall grant the right of residence in their territory to the persons referred to in Article 1 who are able to produce the documents listed in paragraph 3.

2. As proof of the right of residence, a document entitled 'Residence Permit for a National of a Member State of the EEC' shall be issued. This document must include a statement that it has been issued pursuant to Regulation (EEC) No 1612/68 and to the measures taken by the Member States for the implementation of the present Directive. The text of such statement is given in the Annex to this Directive.

3. For the issue of a Residence Permit for a National of a Member State of the EEC, Member States may require only the production of the following documents;

- by the worker:

    (a) the document with which he entered their territory;

    (b) a confirmation of engagement from the employer or a certificate of employment;

172

- by the members of the worker's family:

  (c) the document with which they entered the territory;

  (d) a document issued by the competent authority of the State of origin or the State whence they came, proving their relationship;

  (e) in the cases referred to in Article 10(1) and (2) of Regulation (EEC) No 1612/68, a document issued by the competent authority of the State of origin or the State whence they came, testifying that they are dependent on the worker or that they live under his roof in such country.

4. A member of the family who is not a national of a Member State shall be issued with a residence document which shall have the same validity as that issued to the worker on whom he is dependent.

Article 5

Completion of the formalities for obtaining a residence permit shall not hinder the immediate beginning of employment under a contract concluded by the applicants.

Article 6

1. The residence permit:

(a) must be valid throughout the territory of the Member State which issued it;

(b) must be valid for at least five years from the date of issue and be automatically renewable.

2. Breaks in residence not exceeding six consecutive months and absence on military service shall not affect the validity of a residence permit.

3. Where a worker is employed for a period exceeding three months but not exceeding a year in the service of an employer in the host State or in the employ of a person providing services, the host Member State shall issue him a temporary residence permit, the validity of which may be limited to the expected period of the employment.

Subject to the provisions of Article 8(1)(c), a temporary residence permit shall be issued also to a seasonal worker employed for a period of more than three months. The period of employment must be shown in the documents referred to in paragraph 4(3)(b).

Article 7

1. A valid residence permit may not be withdrawn from a worker solely on the grounds that he is no longer in employment, either because he is temporarily incapable of work as a result of illness or accident, or because he is involuntarily unemployed, this being duly confirmed by the competent employment office.

2. When the residence permit is renewed for the first time, the period of residence may be restricted, but not to less than twelve months, where the worker has been involuntarily unemployed in the Member State for more than twelve consecutive months.

Article 8

1. Member States shall, without issuing a residence permit, recognise the right of residence in their territory of:

(a) a worker pursuing an activity as an employed person, where the activity is not expected to last for more than three months. The document with which the person concerned entered the territory and a statement by the employer on the expected duration of the employment shall be sufficient to cover his stay; a statement by the employer shall not, however, be required in the case of workers coming within the provisions of the Council Directive of 25 February 1964 on the attainment of freedom of establishment and freedom to provide services in respect of the activities of intermediaries in commerce, industry and small craft industries;

(b) a worker who, while having his residence in the territory of a Member State to which he returns as a rule, each day or at least once a week, is employed in the territory of another Member State. The competent authority of the State where he is employed may issue such worker with a special permit valid for five years and automatically renewable;

(c) a seasonal worker who holds a contract of employment stamped by the competent authority of the Member State on whose territory he has come to pursue his activity.

2. In all cases referred to in paragraph 1, the competent authorities of the host Member State may require the worker to report his presence in the territory.

Article 9

1. The residence documents granted to nationals of a Member State of the EEC referred to in this Directive shall be issued and renewed free of charge or on payment of an amount not exceeding the dues and taxes charged for the issue of identity cards to nationals.

2. The visa referred to in Article 3(2) and the stamp referred to in Article 8(1)(c) shall be free of charge.

3. Member States shall take the necessary steps to simplify as much as possible the formalities and procedure for obtaining the documents mentioned in paragraph 1.

Article 10

Member States shall not derogate from the provisions of this Directive save on grounds of public policy, public security or public health.

Article 11

1. This Directive shall not affect the provisions of the Treaty establishing the European Coal and Steel Community which relate to workers with recognised skills in coal mining and steel making, or the provisions of the Treaty establishing the European Atomic Energy Community which deal with the right to take up skilled employment in the field of nuclear energy, or any measures taken in implementation of those Treaties.

2. Nevertheless, this Directive shall apply to the categories of workers referred to in paragraph 1, and to members of their families, in so far as their legal position is not governed by the above-mentioned Treaties or measures.

Article 12

1. Member States shall, within nine months of notification of this Directive, bring into force the measures necessary to comply with its provisions and shall forthwith inform the Commission thereof.

2, They shall notify the Commission of amendments made to provisions imposed by law, regulation or administrative action for the simplification of the formalities and procedure for issuing such documents as are still necessary for the entry, exit and residence of workers and members of their families.

Article 13

1. The Council Directive of 25 March 1964 on the abolition of restrictions on movement and on residence within the Community of workers and their families shall continue to have effect until this Directive is implemented by the Member States.

2. Residence permits issued pursuant to the Directive referred to in Paragraph 1 shall remain valid until the date on which they next expire.

Article 14

This Directive is addressed to the Member States.

Done at Luxembourg, 15 October 1968

For the Council

The President

G. SEDATI

. . . . .

23. REGULATION (EEC) No 1251/70 OF THE COMMISSION

of 29 June 1970

on the right of workers to remain in the territory of a Member
State after having been employed in that State
(J.O. No L 142, 30 June 1970, p. 24; O.J. (Special Edition
1970 II) p. 402)

THE COMMISSION OF THE EUROPEAN COMMUNITIES,

Having regard to the Treaty establishing the European Economic
Community, and in particular Article 48(3)(d) thereof, and Article 2
of the Protocol on the Grand Duchy of Luxembourg;

Having regard to the Opinion of the Europian Parliament,

Whereas Council Regulation (EEC) No 1612/68 of 15 October 1968 and
Council Directive No 68/360/EEC of 15 October 1968 enabled freedom of
movement for workers to be secured at the end of a series of measures
to be achieved progressively; whereas the right of residence acquired
by workers in active employment has as a corollary the right, granted
by the Treaty to such workers, to remain in the territory of a Member
State after having been employed in that State; whereas it is important to lay down the conditions for the exercise of such right;

Whereas the said Council Regulation and Council Directive contain the
appropriate provisions concerning the right of workers to reside in
the territory of a Member State for the purposes of employment;
whereas the right to remain, referred to in Article 48(3)(d) of the
Treaty, is interpreted therefore as the right of the worker to maintain his residence in the territory of a Member State when he ceases
to be employed there;

Whereas the mobility of labour in the Community requires that workers
may be employed successively in several Member States without thereby
being placed at a disadvantage;

Whereas it is important, in the first place, to guarantee to the worker residing in the territory of a Member State the right to remain
in that territory when he ceases to be employed in that State because
he has reached retirement age or by reason of permanent incapacity to
work; whereas, however, it is equally important to ensure that right
for the worker who, after a period of employment and residence in the
territory of a Member State, works as an employed person in the territory of another Member State, while still retaining his residence in
the territory of the first State;

Whereas, to determine the conditions under which the right to remain
arises, account should be taken of the reasons which have led to the
termination of employment in the territory of the Member State con-

176

cerned and, in particular, of the difference between retirement, the normal and foreseeable end of working life, and incapacity to work which leads to a premature and unforeseeable termination of activity; whereas special conditions must be laid down where termination of activity is the result of an accident at work or occupational disease, or where the worker's spouse is or was a national of the Member State concerned;

Whereas the worker who has reached the end of his working life should have sufficient time in which to decide where he wishes to establish his final residence;

Whereas the exercise by the worker of the right to remain entails that such right shall be extended to members of his family; whereas in the case of the death of the worker during his working life, maintenance of the right of residence of the members of his family must also be recognised and be the subject of special conditions;

Whereas persons to whom the right to remain applies must enjoy equality of treatment with national workers who have ceased their working lives;

HAS ADOPTED THIS REGULATION:

Article 1

The provisions of this Regulation shall apply to nationals of a Member State who have worked as employed persons in the territory of another Member State and to members of their families, as defined in Article 10 of Council Regulation (EEC) No 1612/68 on freedom of movement for workers within the Community.

Article 2

1. The following shall have the right to remain permanently in the territory of a Member State:

(a) a worker who, at the time of termination of his activity, has reached the age laid down by the law of that Member State for entitlement to an old-age pension and who has been employed in that State for at least the last twelve months and has resided there continuously for more than three years;

(b) a worker who, having resided continuously in the territory of that State for more than two years, ceases to work there as an employed person as a result of permanent incapacity to work. If such incapacity is the result of an accident at work or an occupational disease entitling him to a pension for which an institution of that State is entirely or partially responsible, no condition shall be imposed as to length of residence;

(c) a worker who, after three years' continuous employment and residence in the territory of that State, works as an employed person in the territory of another Member State, while retaining his residence in the territory of the first State, to which he returns, as a rule, each day or at least once a week.

177

Periods of employment completed in this way in the territory of the other Member State shall, for the purposes of entitlement to the rights referred to in subparagraphs (a) and (b), be considered as having been completed in the territory of the State of residence.

2. The conditions as to length of residence and employment laid down in paragraph 1(a) and the condition as to length of residence laid down in paragraph 1(b) shall not apply if the worker's spouse is a national of the Member State concerned or has lost the nationality of that State by marriage to that worker.

Article 3

1. The members of a worker's family referred to in Article 1 of this Regulation who are residing with him in the territory of a Member State shall be entitled to remain there permanently if the worker has acquired the right to remain in the territory of that State in accordance with Article 2, and to do so even after his death.

2. If, however, the worker dies during his working life and before having acquired the right to remain in the territory of the State concerned, members of his family shall be entitled to remain there permanently on condition that:

- the worker, on the date of his decease, had resided continuously in the territory of that Member State for at least 2 years; or

- his death resulted from an accident at work or an occupational disease; or

- the surviving spouse is a national of the State of residence or lost the nationality of that State by marriage to that worker.

Article 4

1. Continuity of residence as provided for in Articles 2(1) and 3(2) may be attested by any means of proof in use in the country of residence. It shall not be affected by temporary absences not exceeding a total of three months per year, nor by longer absences due to compliance with the obligations of military service.

2. Periods of involuntary unemployment, duly recorded by the competent employment office, and absences due to illness or accident shall be considered as periods of employment within the meaning of Article 2(1).

Article 5

1. The person entitled to the right to remain shall be allowed to exercise it within two years from the time of becoming entitled to such right pursuant to Article 2(1)(a) and (b) and Article 3. During such period he may leave the territory of the Member State without adversely affecting such right.

2. No formality shall be required on the part of the person concerned in respect of the exercise of the right to remain.

Article 6

1. Persons coming under the provisions of this Regulation shall be entitled to a residence permit which:

(a) shall be issued and renewed free of charge or on payment of a sum not exceeding the dues and taxes payable by nationals for the issue or renewal of identity documents;

(b) must be valid throughout the territory of the Member State issuing it;

(c) must be valid for at least five years and be renewable automatically.

2. Periods of non-residence not exceeding six consecutive months shall not affect the validity of the residence permit.

Article 7

The right to equality of treatment, established by Council Regulation (EEC) No 1612/68, shall apply also to persons coming under the provisions of this Regulation.

Article 8

1. This Regulation shall not affect any provisions laid down by law, regulation or administrative action of one Member State which would be more favourable to nationals of other Member States.

2. Member States shall facilitate re-admission to their territories of workers who have left those territories after having resided there permanently for a long period and having been employed there and who wish to return there when they have reached retirement age or are permanently incapacitated for work.

Article 9

1. The Commission may, taking account of developments in the demographic situation of the Grand Duchy of Luxembourg, lay down, at the request of that State, different conditions from those provided for in this Regulation, in respect of the exercise of the right to remain in Luxembourg territory.

2. Within two months after the request supplying all appropriate details has been put before it, the Commission shall take a decision, stating the reasons on which is based.

It shall notify the Grand Duchy of Luxembourg of such decision and inform the other Member States thereof;

This Regulation shall be binding in its entirety and directly applicable in all Member States.

Done at Brussels, 29 June 1970.

24. COUNCIL RESOLUTION

of 9 February 1976

on an action programme for migrant workers and members
of their families

(O.J. L 34, 14 February 1976, p. 2)

THE COUNCIL OF THE EUROPEAN COMMUNITIES,

Having regard to the Treaties establishing the European Economic
Communities,

Whereas the Council resolution of 21 January 1974 concerning a social
action programme provides, among the measures to be adopted during a
first stage covering the period from 1974 to 1976, for the establishment of an action programme for migrant workers and members of their
families;

Whereas following the Council resolution of 21 January 1974, the
Commission submitted to the Council a communication on an action programme for migrant workers and their families on which the European
Parliament and the Economic and Social Committee have given their
opinions;

Whereas the prime objective, already stated in the Council resolution
of 21 January 1974, is to enable workers who are nationals of Member
States to find employment in their own region; whereas, however,
pending the economic and social development of the regions from which
they come it is necessary to improve the conditions of freedom of
movement for such workers and for members of their families and to
seek appropriate solutions with a view to eliminating progressively
such unwarranted restrictions on their rights as may still exist under
Community Regulations in force;

Whereas it is also necessary to strengthen the measures designed to
humanise further freedom of movement for workers who are nationals
of Member States, which, although it constitutes a basic right, can
nevertheless involve serious difficulties when they and members of
their families find themselves confronted,lacking adequate assistance,
with the problems arising in the various stages of migration;

Whereas it is also necessary to improve the circumstances of workers who are nationals of third countries and members of their families who are allowed into the Member States, by aiming at equality between their living and working conditions, wages and economic rights and those of workers who are nationals of the Member States and members of their families;

Whereas it is necessary to promote consultation on migration policies *vis à vis* third countries and to examine, where appropriate, problems facing workers who are nationals of the Member States residing in third countries;

Whereas the actions to be taken in favour of migrant workers and members of their families must accord with activities concerning consultation on the employment and social protection policies of Member States;

Whereas it is necessary to implement this resolution in accordance with the guidelines laid down in the Council resolution of 21 January 1974;

Whereas, when the actions provided for in this resolution are implemented, account should be taken of the policies and conditions peculiar to each Member State and, in particular, of the differing extent and the differing characteristics of the migratory movements and of the numbers and density of the migrant populations,

1. Takes note of the Commission communication on an action programme for migrant workers and their families,

2. Considers that in the Community's present economic and social situation action in favour of migrant workers and members of their families should concentrate on the improvement of the circumstances of migrant workers and members of their families within the Member States, and in particular on measures which will:

(a) continue and enhance the humanisation of freedom of movement for workers provided for in Articles 48 to 51 of the Treaty establishing the European Economic Community by means of appropriate measures designed to promote, in accordance with the rights deriving from Community acts in force, genuine equality of treatment with national workers and taking into account all the requirements arising in the various stages of migration.

These shall include, in particular:

(i) taking whatever organisational steps are appropriate to, and strenghthening cooperation between, national employment services, particularly as regards official machinery for vacancy clearance, in order to encourage as many migrant workers as possible to use these services,

(ii) offering appropriate assistance to migrant workers and members of their families to facilitate their integration in the host country, particularly by improving the social infrastructure and making more information available, and by encouraging them to take advantage of the official services available to nationals.

      (iii) providing, during the stages of return to and reintegra-
           tion into the country of origin, as part of the collabor-
           ation between the host country and the country of origin,
           appropriate assistance to those migrant workers and members
           of their families wishing to resettle in their country
           of origin;

  (b) seek appropriate solutions with a view to eliminating progress-
     ively such unwarranted restrictions on the rights of workers
     who are nationals of other Member States and members of their
     families as may still exist under Community Regulations in
     force;

  (c) encourage the achievement of equality for workers who are nat-
     ionals of third countries and members of their families who
     are legally resident in the Member States, with regard to liv-
     ing and working conditions, wages and economic rights;

3. Considers that with a view to promoting the social and occupational
advancement of migrant workers and members of their families, particular importance should be attached to measures concerning vocational
training, housing, social services, medical and social care schemes
including preventive medicine, schooling of children, information, and
the creation of a better understanding among the general public of
the host country of the problems of migrant workers and members of
their families;

4. Expresses the wish that the work being carried out to implement
point 11 to the communiqué of the Conference of Heads of Government
held in Paris on 9 and 10 December 1974, concerning the grant of
special rights to citizens of the Member States, will be expedited;

5. Considers that it is important to:

  (a) undertake appropriate consultation on migrant policies *vis à
     vis* third countries,

  (b) strengthen cooperation between Member States in the campaign
     against illegal immigration of workers who are nationals of
     third countries and ensure that appropriate sanctions are laid
     down to repress trafficking and abuses linked with illegal
     immegration and that the obligations of employers are fulfilled
     and the rights of workers relating to the work they have carri-
     ed out safeguarded without prejudice to other consequences of
     the unlawful nature of their residence and employment;

6. Considers that the social problems arising for workers who are
nationals of the Member States and resident in certain third countries
and for members of their families should be examined as necessary;

7. Expresses the political resolve that the measures referred to in
this Resolution be implemented, with account being taken of the competence of the Community institutions on the one hand and that of
the Member States on the other;

8. Considers that future developments of this resolution should be
examined in the framework of the implementation of the Council Resol-

ution of 21 January 1974.

25. DECISION OF THE ASSOCIATION COUNCIL No 2/76

on the implementation of Article 12 of
the Ankara Agreement

(Collected Acts - EEC - Turkey Associations)
INST I 24

THE ASSOCIATION COUNCIL,

Having regard to the Agreement establishing an Association between
the European Economic Community and Turkey,

Having regard to the Additional Protocol referred to in Article 1(1)
of the Provisional Protocol annexed to the said Agreement, and in
particular Article 36 thereof,

Whereas the Contracting Parties agreed pursuant to Article 12 of the
Ankara Agreement to be guided by Articles 48, 49 and 50 of the Treaty
establishing the European Economic Community in gradually introducing
freedom of movement for workers betweentheir countries; whereas Article 36 of the Additional Protocol provides that this freedom of
movement shall be secured by progressive stages between the end of
the twelfth and of the twenty-second year after entry into force of
the Association Agreement;

Whereas the Articles referred to above imply that the Member States
of the Community and Turkey shall accord each other priority as regards access by their workers to their respective employment markets;
whereas this principle must be given effect under conditions that exclude any serious danger to the standard of living and the level of
employment in the various regions and branches of activity in the
Member States of the Community and Turkey, and without prejudice to
the application between Member States of the Community of Community
provisions governing the freedom of movement of workers or to any
international undertakings by either Party on the subject under consideration;

Whereas the content of a first stage should be laid down, the Association Council having to decide on the content of the subsequent stages
at a later date,

HAS DECIDED AS FOLLOWS:

Article 1

1. This decision establishes for a first stage the detailed rules for
the implementation of Article 36 of the Additional Protocol.

2. This first stage shall last four years, as from 1 December 1976.

Article 2

1(a) After three years of legal employment in a Member State of the
Community, a Turkish worker shall be entitled, subject to the
priority to be given to workers of Member States of the Community,
to respond to an offer of employment, made under normal conditions and registered with the employment services of that State,
for the same occupation, branch of activity and region.

(b) After five years of legal employment in a Member State of the
Community, a Turkish worker shall enjoy free access in that
country to any paid employment of his choice.

(c) Annual holidays and short absences for reasons of sickness, maternity or an accident at work shall be treated as periods of
legal employment. Periods of involuntary unemployment duly certified by the relevant authorities and long absences on account
of sickness shall not be treated as periods of legal employment,
but shall not affect rights acquired as the result of the preceding period of employment.

2. The procedures for applying paragraph 1 shall be those established
under national rules.

Article 3

Turkish children who are residing legally with their parents in a
Member State of the Community shall be granted access in that country
to courses of general education.

They may also be entitled to enjoy in that country the advantages
provided for in this connection under national laws.

Article 4

Nationals of the Member States who are in paid employment in Turkey,
and their children, shall enjoy in that country the rights and advantages referred to in Articles 2 and 3 if they meet the conditions
laid down in these Articles.

Article 5

Should it not be possible in the Community to meet an offer of employment by calling on the labour available on the employment market of
the Member States and should the Member States, within the framework
of their provisions laid down by law, regulation or administrative
action, decide to authorise a call on workers who are not nationals of
a Member State of the Community in order to meet the offer of employment, they shall endeavour in so doing to accord priority to Turkish
workers.

Article 6

Where a Member State of the Community or Turkey experiences or is
threatened with disturbances on its employment market which might seriously jeopardise the standard of living or level of employment in a

particular region, branch of activity or occupation, the State concerned may refrain from automatically applying Article 2(1)(a) and (b).

The State concerned shall inform the Association Council of any such temporary restriction.

Article 7

The Member States of the Community and Turkey may not introduce new restrictions on the conditions of access to employment applicable to workers legally resident and employed in their terriory.

Article 8

This decision shall not affect any rights or obligations arising from national laws or bilateral agreements existing between Turkey and the Member States of the Community where these provide for more favourable treatment for their nationals.

Article 9

The provisions of this Decision shall be applied subject to limitations justified on grounds of public policy, public security or public health.

Article 10

So as to be in a position to ensure the harmonious application of the provisions of this Decision and determine that they are applied in such a way as to exclude the danger of disturbance of the employment markets, the Association Council shall be informed of the employment situation in the Member States of the Community and Turkey.

Article 11

One year before the end of the first stage and in the light of the results achieved during it, the Association Council shall commence discussions to determine the content of the subsequent stage and to ensure that the Decision on that stage is enforced as from the date of expiry of the first stage. The provisions of this Decision shall continue to apply until the beginning of the subsequent stage.

Article 12

The Contracting Parties shall each take the measures necessary to implement this Decision.

Article 13

This Decision shall enter into force on 20 December 1976.

Done at Brussels, 20 December 1976.

For the Association Council

The President

M. van der STOEL

26. EXTRACTS OF REGULATION No 1408/71 OF THE COUNCIL

of 14 June 1971

on the application of social security schemes to employed
persons and their families moving within the Community

(O.J. No L 149, 5 July 1971, p. 2; Codified Version
O.J. No C 138, 9 June 1980, p. 1)

TITLE 1

GENERAL PROVISIONS

Article 1

Definitions

For the purpose of this Regulation:

(a) 'worker' means:

(i) subject to the restrictions set out in Annex V, any person
who is insured, compulsorily or on an optional continued basis, for one or more of the contingencies covered by the
branches of a social security scheme for employed persons;

(ii) any person who is compulsorily insured for one or more of
the contingencies covered by the branches of social security
dealt with in this Regulation, under a social security
scheme for all residents or for the whole working population
if such person:

- can be identified as an employed person by virtue of the
manner in which such scheme is administered or financed, or

- failing such criteria, is insured for some other contingency specified in Annex V under a scheme for employed persons, either compulsorily or on an optional continued
basis;

(iii) any person who is voluntarily insured for one or more of
the contingencies covered by the branches dealt with in this
Regulation, under a social security scheme of a Member State
for employed persons or for all residents or for certain
categories of residents if such person has previously been
compulsorily insured for the same contingency under a scheme
for employed persons of the same Member State;

(b) 'frontier worker' means any worker employed in the territory of a

Member State and residing in the territory of another Member State to which he returns as a rule daily or at least once a week; however, a frontier worker who is posted elsewhere in the territory of the same or another Member State by the undertaking to which he is normally attached shall retain the status of frontier worker for a period not exceeding four months, even if he is prevented during the course of such posting from returning daily or at least once a week to the place where he resides;

(c) 'seasonal worker' means any worker who goes to the territory of a Member State other than the one in which he is resident to do work there of a seasonal nature for an undertaking or an employer of that State for a period which may on no account exceed eight months, and who stays in the territory of the said State for the duration of his work; work of a seasonal nature shall be taken to mean work which, being dependent on the succession of the seasons, automatically recurs each year;

(d) 'refugee' shall have the meaning assigned to it in Article 1 of the Convention on the Status of Refugees, signed at Geneva on 28 July 1951;

(e) 'stateless person' shall have the meaning assigned to it in Article 1 of the Convention on the Status of Stateless Persons, signed in New York on 28 September 1954;

(f) 'member of the family' means any person defined or recognised as a member of the family or designated as a member of the household by the legislation under which benefits are provided or, in the cases referred to in Article 22(1)(a) and Article 31, by the legislation of the Member State in whose territory such person resides; where, however, the said legislations regard as a member of the family or a member of the household only a person living under the same roof as the worker, this condition shall be considered satisfied if the person in question is mainly dependent on that worker;

(g) 'survivor' means any person defined or recognised as such by the legislation under which the benefits are granted; where, however, the said legislation regards as a survivor only a person who was living under the same roof as the deceased worker, this condition shall be considered satisfied if such person was mainly dependent on the deceased worker;

(h) 'residence' means habitual residence;

(i) 'stay' means temporary residence;

(j) 'legislation' means in respect of each Member State statutes, regulations and other provisions and all other implementing measures, present or future, relating to the branches and schemes of social security covered by Article 4(1) and (2).

The term excludes provisions of existing or future industrial agreements, whether or not they have been the subject of a decision by the authorities rendering them compulsory or extending their scope. However, in so far as such provisions:

(i) serve to put into effect compulsory insurance imposed by the laws and regulations referred to in the preceding subparagraph; or

(ii) set up a scheme administered by the same institution as that which administers the schemes set up by the laws and regulations referred to in the preceding subparagraph,

the limitation on the term may at any time be lifted by a declaration of the Member State concerned specifying the schemes of such a kind to which this Regulation applies. Such a declaration shall be notified and published in accordance with the provisions of Article 96.

The provisions of the preceding subparagraph shall not have the effect of exempting from the application of this Regulation the schemes to which Regulation No 3 applied;

(k) 'social security convention' means any bilateral or multilateral instrument which binds or will bind two or more Member States exclusively, and any other multilateral instrument which binds or will bind at least two Member States and one or more other States in the field of social security, for all or part of the branches and schemes set out in Article 4(1) and (2), together with agreements, of whatever kind, concluded pursuant to the said instruments;

(1) 'competent authority' means, in respect of each Member State, the Minister, Ministers or other equivalent authority responsible for social security schemes throughout or in any part of the territory of the State in question;

(m) 'Administrative Commission' means the Commission referred to in Article 80;

(n) 'institution' means, in respect of each Member State, the body or authority responsible for administering all or part of the legislation;

(o) 'competent institution' means:

(i) the institution with which the person concerned is insured at the time of application for benefit; or

(ii) the institution from which the person concerned is entitled or would be entitled to benefits if he or a member or members of his family were resident in the territory of the Member State in which the institution is situated; or

(iii) the institution designated by the competent authority of the Member State concerned; or

(iv) in the case of a scheme relating to an employer's liability in respect of the benefits set out in Article 4(1), either the employer or the insurer involved or, in default thereof,

188

a body or authority designated by the competent authority of the Member State concerned;

(p) 'institution of the place of residence' and 'institution of the place of stay' mean respectively the institution which is competent to provide benefits in the place where the person concerned resides and the institution which is competent to provide benefits in the place where the person concerned is staying, under the legislation administered by that institution or, where no such institution exists, the institution designated by the competent authority of the Member State in question;

(q) 'competent State' means the Member State in whose territory the competent institution is situated;

(r) 'periods of insurance' means periods of contribution or periods of employment as defined or recognised as periods of insurance by the legislation under which they were completed or considered as completed, and all periods treated as such, where they are regarded by the said legislation as equivalent to periods of insurance;

(s) 'periods of employment' means periods defined or recognised as such by the legislation under which they were completed, and all periods treated as such, where they are regarded by the said legislation as equivalent to periods of employment;

(s) (a): 'periods of residence' means periods of residence as defined or recognised as such by the legislation under which they were completed or considered as completed;

(t) 'benefits' and 'pensions' mean all benefits and pensions, including all elements thereof payable out of public funds, revalorisation increases and supplementary allowances, subject to the provisions of Title III, as also lump-sum benefits which may be paid in lieu of pensions, and payments made by way of reimbursement of contributions;

(u) (i) 'family benefits' means all benefits in kind or in cash intended to meet family expenses under the legislation provided for in Article 4(1)(h), excluding the special childbirth allowances mentioned in Annex 1;

(ii) 'family allowances' means periodical cash benefits granted exclusively by reference to the number and, where appropriate, the age of members of the family;

(v) 'death grants' means any once-for-all payment in, the event of death, exclusive of the lump-sum benefits referred to in subparagraph (t).

Article 2

Persons covered

1. This Regulation shall apply to workers who are or have been subject to the legislation of one or more Member States and who are nationals

of one of the Member States or who are stateless persons or refugees residing within the territory of one of the Member States, as well as to the members of their families and their survivors.

2. In addition, this Regulation shall apply to the survivors of workers who have been subject to the legislation of one or more Member States, irrespective of the nationality of such workers, where their survivors are nationals of one of the Member States, or stateless persons or refugees residing within the territory of one of the Member States.

3. This Regulation shall apply to civil servants and to persons who, in accordance with the legislation applicable, are treated as such, where they are or have been subject to the legislation of a Member State to which this Regulation applies.

Article 3

Equality of treatment

1. Subject to the special provisions of this Regulation, persons resident in the territory of one of the Member States to whom this Regulation applies shall be subject to the same obligations and enjoy the same benefits under the legislation of any Member State as the nationals of that State.

2. The provisions of paragraph 1 shall apply to the right to elect members of the organs of social security institutions or to partici- pate in their nomination, but shall not affect the legislative provis- ions of any Member State relating to eligibility or methods of nomin- ation of persons concerned to those organs.

3. Save as provided in Annex II, the provisions of social security conventions which remain in force pursuant to Article 7(2)(c) and the provisions of conventions concluded pursuant to Article 8(1), shall apply to all persons to whom this Regulation applies.

Article 4

Matters covered

1. This Regulation shall apply to all legislation concerning the following branches of social security:

(a) sickness and maternity benefits;

(b) invalidity benefits, including those intended for the maintenance or improvement of earning capacity;

(c) old-age benefits;

(d) survivors' benefits;

(e) benefits in respect of accidents at work and occupational diseases;

(f) death grants;

(g) unemployment benefits;

(h) family benefits.

2. This Regulation shall apply to all general and special social security schemes, whether contributory or non-contributory, and to schemes concerning the liability of an employer or ship owner in respect of the benefits referred to in paragraph 1.

3. The provisions of Title III of this Regulation shall not, however, affect the legislative provisions of any Member State concerning a ship owner's liability.

4. This Regulation shall not apply to social and medical assistance, to benefit schemes for victims of war or its consequences, or to special schemes for civil servants and persons treated as such.

Article 5

Declarations of Member States on the scope of this Regulation

The Member States shall specify the legislation and schemes referred to in Article 4(1) and (2), the minimum benefits referred to in Article 50 and the benefits referred to in Articles 77 and 78 in declarations to be notified and published in accordance with Article 96.

Article 6

Social security conventions replaced by this Regulation

Subject to the provisions of Articles 7, 8 and 46(4) this Regulation shall, as regards persons and matters which it covers, replace the provisions of any social security convention binding either:

(a) two or more Member States exclusively; or

(b) at least two Member States and one or more other States, where settlement of the cases concerned does not involve any institution of one of the latter States.

Article 7

International provisions not affected by this Regulation

1. This Regulation shall not affect obligations arising from:

(a) any convention adopted by the International Labour Conference which,after ratification by one or more Member States, has entered into force;

(b) the European Interim Agreements on Social Security of 11 December 1953 concluded between the Member States of the Council of Europe.

2. The provisions of Article 6 notwithstanding, the following shall continue to apply:

(a) the provisions of the Agreement of 27 July 1950 concerning social security for Rhine boatmen, revised on 13 February 1961;

(b) the provisions of the European Convention of 9 July 1956 concerning social security for workers in international transport;

(c) the provisions of the social security conventions listed in Annex II.

Article 8

Conclusion of conventions between Member States

1. Two or more Member States may, as need arises, conclude conventions with each other based on the principles and in the spirit of this Regulation.

2. Each Member State shall notify, in accordance with the provisions of Article 96(1), any convention concluded with another Member State under the provisions of paragraph 1.

Article 9

Admission to voluntary or optional continued insurance

1. The provisions of the legislation of any Member State which make admission to voluntary or optional continued insurance conditional upon residence in the territory of that State shall not apply to workers to whom this Regulation applies and who are resident in the territory of another Member State, provided that at some time in their past working life they were subject to the legislation of the first State.

2. Where, under the legislation of a Member State, admission to voluntary or optional continued insurance is conditional upon completion of periods of insurance, the periods of insurance or residence completed under the legislation of another Member State shall be taken into account, to the extent required, as if they were completed under the legislation of the first State.

Article 10

Waiving of residence clauses – Effect of compulsory insurance on reimbursement of contributions

1. Save as otherwise provided in this Regulation, invalidity, old-age or survivors' cash benefits, pensions for accidents at work or occupational diseases and death grants acquired under the legislation of one or more Member States shall not be subject to any reduction, modification, suspension, withdrawal or confiscation by reason of the fact that the recipient resides in the territory of a Member State

other than that in which the institution responsible for payment is situated.

The preceding subparagraph shall also apply to lump-sum benefits granted in cases of remarriage of a surviving spouse who was entitled to a survivor's pension.

2. Where under the legislation of a Member State reimbursement of contributions is conditional upon the person having ceased to be subject to compulsory insurance, this condition shall not be considered satisfied as long as the person concerned is subject to compulsory insurance as a worker under the legislation of another Member State.

Article 11

Revalorisation of benefits

Rules for revalorisation provided by the legislation of a Member State shall apply to benefits due under that legislation taking into account the provisions of this Regulation.

Article 12

Prevention of overlapping of benefits

1. This Regulation can neither confer nor maintain the right to several benefits of the same kind for one and the same period of compulsory insurance. However, this provision shall not apply to benefits in respect of invalidity, old age, death (pensions) or occupational disease which are awarded by the institutions of two or more Member States, in accordance with the provisions of Article 41, Article 43(2) and (3), Articles 46, 50 and 51 or Article 60 (1) (b).

2. The provisions of the legislation of a Member State for reduction, suspension or withdrawal of benefit in cases of overlapping with other social security benefits or other income may be invoked even though the right to such benefits was acquired under the legislation of another Member State or such income arises in the territory of another Member State. However, this provision shall not apply when the person concerned receives benefits of the same kind in respect of invalidity, old age, death (pensions) or occupational disease which are awarded by the institutions of two or more Member States in accordance with the provisions of Articles 46, 50, 51 or Article 60(1) (b).

3. The provisions of the legislation of a Member State for reduction, suspension or withdrawal of benefit in the case of a person in receipt of invalidity benefits or anticipatory old-age benefits pursuing a professional or trade activity may be invoked against such person even though he is pursuing his activity in the territory of another Member State.

4. An invalidity pension payable under Netherlands legislation shall, in a case where the Netherlands institution is bound under the provisions of Article 57(3) (c) or Article 60(2) (a) to contribute also

to the cost of benefits for occupational disease granted under the
legislation of another Member State, be reduced by the amount payable
to the institution of the other Member State which is responsible
for granting the benefits for occupational disease.

TITLE II

DETERMINATION OF THE LEGISLATION APPLICABLE

Article 13

General rules

1. A worker to whom this Regulation applies shall be subject to the
legislation of a single Member State only. That legislation shall be
determined in accordance with the provisions of this Title.

2. Subject to the provisions of Articles 14 to 17:

(a) a worker employed in the territory of one Member State shall be
   subject to the legislation of that State even if he resides in the
   territory of another Member State or if the registered office or
   place of business of the undertaking or individual employing him
   is situated in the territory of another Member State;

(b) a worker employed on board a vessel flying the flag of a Member
   State shall be subject to the legislation of that State;

(c) civil servants and persons treated as such shall be subject to
   the legislation of the Member State to which the administration
   employing them is subject;

(d) a worker called up or recalled for service in the armed forces,
   or for civilian service, of a Member State shall retain the status
   of a worker and shall be subject to the legislation of that State.
   If entitlement under that legislation is subject to the completion
   of periods of insurance before entry into or after release from
   such military or civilian service, periods of insurance completed
   under the legislation of any other Member State shall be taken
   into account, to the extent necessary, as if they were periods
   of insurance completed under the legislation of the first State.

Article 14

Special rules

1. Article 13 (2) (a) shall apply subject to the following exceptions
or circumstances:

(a) (i) a worker employed in the territory of a Member State by an
        undertaking to which he is normally attached who is posted
        by that undertaking to the territory of another Member State
        to perform work there for that undertaking shall continue to
        be subject to the legislation of the first Member State,

provided that the anticipated duration of that work does not exceed 12 months and that he is not sent to replace another worker who has completed his term of posting;

(ii) if the duration of the work to be done extends beyond the duration originally anticipated, owing to unforeseeable circumstances, and exceeds 12 months, the legislation of the first State shall continue to apply until the completion of such work, provided that the competent authority of the State in whose territory the worker is posted or the body designated by that authority gives its consent; such consent must be requested before the end of the initial 12 month period. Such consent cannot, however, be given for a period exceeding 12 months;

(b) a worker employed in international transport in the territory of two or more Member States as a member of travelling or flying personnel and who is working for an undertaking which, for hire or reward on its own account, operates transport services for passengers or goods by rail, road, air or inland waterway and has its registered office or place of business in the territory of a Member State, shall be subject to the legislation of the latter State, with the following restrictions:

(i) where the said undertaking has a branch or a permanent representation in the territory of a Member State other than that in which it has its registered office or place of business, a worker employed by such branch or permanent representation shall be subject to the legislation of the Member State in whose territory such branch or permanent representation is situated;

(ii) where a worker is employed principally in the territory of the Member State in which he resides, he shall be subject to the legislation of that State, even if the undertaking which employs him has no registered office or place of business or branch or permanent representation in that territory;

(c) a worker, other than one employed in international transport, who normally pursues his activity in the territory of two or more Member States shall be subject:

(i) to the legislation of the Member State in whose territory he resides, if he pursues his activity partly in that territory or if he is attached to several undertakings or several employers who have their registered offices or places of business in the territory of different Member States;

(ii) to the legislation of the Member State in whose territory is situated the registered office or place of business of the undertaking or individual employing him, if he does not reside in the territory of any of the Member States where he is pursuing his activity;

(d) a worker who is employed in the territory of one Member State by an undertaking which has its registered office or place of business in the territory of another Member State and which straddles the common frontier of these States shall be subject to the legislation of the Member State in whose territory the undertaking has its registered office or place of business.

2. Article 13(2) (b) shall apply subject to the following exceptions and circumstances:

(a) a worker employed by an undertaking to which he is normally attached, either in the territory of a Member State or on board a vessel flying the flag of a Member State, who is posted by that undertaking on board a vessel flying the flag of another Member State to perform work there for that undertaking shall, subject to the conditions provided in paragraph 1(a), continue to be subject to the legislation of the first Member State;

(b) a worker who, while not being habitually employed at sea, is employed in the territorial waters or in a port of a Member State on a vessel flying the flag of another Member State, but is not a member of the crew, shall be subject to the legislation of the first State;

(c) a worker employed on board a vessel flying the flag of a Member State and remunerated for such employment by an undertaking or a person whose registered office or place of business is in the territory of another Member State shall be subject to the legislation of the latter State if he is resident in the territory of that State; the undertaking or person paying the remuneration shall be considered as the employer for the purposes of the said legislation.

3. The provisions of the legislation of a Member State under which a pensioner who is pursuing a professional or trade activity is not subject to compulsory insurance in respect of such activity shall also apply to a pensioner whose pension was acquired under the legislation of another Member State, unless the person concerned expressly asks to be so subject by applying to the institution designated by the competent authority of the first Member State and listed in Annex 10 to the Implementing Regulation.

Article 15

Rules concerning voluntary insurance or optional continued insurance

1. The provisions of Articles 13 and 14 shall not apply to voluntary insurance or to optional continued insurance unless in respect of one of the branches referred to in Article 4 there exists in any Member State only a voluntary scheme of insurance.

2. Where application of the legislations of two or more Member States entails overlapping of insurance:

- under a compulsory insurance scheme and one or more voluntary or optional continued insurance schemes, the person concerned shall be subject exclusively to the compulsory insurance scheme,

- under two or more voluntary or optional continued insurance schemes, the person concerned may join only the voluntary or optional continued insurance scheme for which he has opted.

3. However, in respect of invalidity, old age and death (pensions), the person concerned may join the voluntary or optional continued insurance scheme of a Member State, even if he is compulsorily subject to the legislation of another Member State, to the extent that such overlapping is explicitly or implicitly admitted in the first Member State.

(Second subparagraph:deleted)

Article 16

Special rules regarding persons employed by diplomatic missions and consular posts, and auxiliary staff of the European Communities

1. The provisions of Article 13(2) (a) shall apply to persons employed by diplomatic missions and consular posts and to the private domestic staff of agents of such missions or posts.

2. However, workers covered by paragraph 1 who are nationals of the Member State which is the accrediting or sending State may opt to be subject to the legislation of that State. Such right of option may be renewed at the end of each calendar year and shall not have retrospective effect.

3. Auxiliary staff of the European Communities may opt to be subject to the legislation of the Member State in whose territory they are employed, to the legislation of the Member State to which they were last subject or to the legislation of the Member State whose nationals they are, in respect of provisions other than those relating to family allowances, the granting of which is governed by the conditions of employment applicable to such staff. This right of option, which may be exercised once only, shall take effect from the date of entry into employment.

Article 17

Exceptions to the provisions of Articles 13 to 16

Two or more Member States, the competent authorities of those States or the bodies designated by those authorities may, by common agreement, provide for exceptions to the provisions of Articles 13 to 16 in the interest of certain workers or categories of workers.

TITLE III

SPECIAL PROVISIONS RELATING TO THE VARIOUS CATEGORIES OF BENEFITS

.....

CHAPTER 2

INVALIDITY

Section 1

Workers subject only to legislations under which the
amount of invalidity benefits is independent of the
duration of periods of insurance

Article 37

General provisions

1. A worker who has been successively or alternately subject to the
legislations of two or more Member States and who has completed periods of insurance exclusively under legislations according to which
the amount of invalidity benefits is independent of the duration of
periods of insurance shall receive benefits in accordance with the
provisions of Article 39. This Article shall not affect pension
increases or supplements in respect of children, granted in accordance with the provisions of Chapter 8.

2. Annex III lists legislations of the kind mentioned in paragraph 1
which are in force in the territory of each of the Member States
concerned.

Article 38

Aggregation of periods of insurance

1. The competent institution of a Member State whose legislation makes
the acquisition, retention or recovery of the right to benefit conditional upon the completion of periods of insurance shall take
account, to the extent necessary, of periods of insurance completed
under the legislation of any other Member States, as if they were
periods completed under the legislation which it administers.

2. Where the legislation of a Member State makes the granting of
certain benefits conditional upon the periods of insurance having been
completed in an occupation which is subject to a special scheme or,
where appropriate, in a specific employment, periods of insurance completed under the legislations of other Member States shall be taken
into account for the granting of these benefits only if completed
under a corresponding scheme or, failing this, in the same occupation
or, where appropriate, in the same employment. If, account having
been taken of the periods thus completed, the person concerned does
not satisfy the conditions for receipt of these benefits, these
periods shall be taken into account for the granting of the benefits
under the general scheme or, failing this, under the scheme applicable
to manual or clerical workers, as appropriate.

198

Article 39

Award of benefits

1. The institution of the Member State, whose legislation was applicable at the time when incapacity for work followed by invalidity occurred, shall determine, in accordance with that legislation, whether the person concerned satisfies the conditions for entitlement to benefits, taking account where appropriate of the provisions of Article 38.

2. A person who satisfies the conditions referred to in paragraph 1 shall obtain the benefits exclusively from the said institution, in accordance with the provisions of the legislation which it administers.

3. A person who does not satisfy the conditions referred to in paragraph 1 shall receive the benefits to which he is still entitled under the legislation of another Member State, taking account where appropriate of the provisions of Article 38.

4. If the legislation applicable under paragraph 2 or 3 provides that the amount of the benefits shall be determined taking into account the existence of members of the family other than the children, the competent institution shall also take into consideration those members of the family of the person concerned who are residing in the territory of another Member State, as if they were residing in the territory of the competent State.

Section 2

Workers subject either only to legislations under which the amount of invalidity benefit depends on the duration of periods of insurance or residence or to legislations of this type and of the type referred to in Section 1

Article 40

General provisions

1. A worker who has been successively or alternately subject to the legislations of two or more Member States, of which at least one is not of the type referred to in Article 37(1), shall receive benefits under the provisions of Chapter 3, which shall apply by analogy, taking into account the provisions of paragraph 4.

2. However, a worker who suffers incapacity for work followed by invalidity while subject to a legislation listed in Annex III, shall receive benefits in accordance with the provisions of Article 37(1) on two conditions:

- that he satisfies the conditions of that legislation or other legislations of the same type, taking account where appropriate of the provisions of Article 38, but without having recourse to periods of insurance completed under legislations not listed in Annex III, and

- that he does not satisfy the conditions for entitlement to benefits under a legislation not listed in Annex III.

3. (a) For the purpose of determining the right to benefits under the legislation of a Member State, listed in Annex III, which makes the granting of invalidity benefits conditional upon the person concerned during a specified period having received cash sickness benefit or having been incapable of work, where a worker has been subject to that legislation suffers incapacity for work followed by invalidity while subject to the legislation of another Member State, account shall, without prejudice to Article 37(1), be taken of:

(i) any period during which, in respect of that incapacity for work, he has, under the legislation of the second Member State, received cash sickness benefits or, in lieu thereof, continued to receive his wage or salary;

(ii) any period during which, in respect of the invalidity which followed that incapacity for work, he has received invalidity benefits under the legislation of the second Member State,

as if it were a period during which cash sickness benefits were paid to him under the legislation of the first Member State or during which he was incapable of work within the meaning of that legislation.

(b) The right to invalidity benefits under the legislation of the first Member State shall be acquired either upon expiry of the preliminary period of compensation for sickness as required by that legislation or upon expiry of the preliminary period of incapacity for work as required by that legislation, and at the earliest:

(i) on the day on which the right to invalidity benefits is acquired under the legislation of the second Member State, or

(ii) on the day following the last day on which the person concerned is entitled to cash sickness benefits under the legislation of the second Member State.

4. A decision taken by an institution of a Member State concerning the degree of invalidity of a claimant shall be binding on the institution of any other Member State concerned, provided that the concordance between the legislations of these States on conditions relating to the degree of invalidity is acknowledged in Annex IV.

Section 3

Aggravation of invalidity

Article 41

1. In the case of aggravation of an invalidity for which a worker is receiving benefits under the legislation of a single Member State, the following provisions shall apply:

(a) if the person concerned has not been subject to the legislation of another Member State since receiving benefits, the competent institution of the first State shall grant the benefits, taking the aggravation into account, in accordance with the provisions of the legislation which it administers;

(b) if the person concerned has been subject to the legislation of one or more other Member States since receiving benefits, the benefits shall be granted to him, taking the aggravation into account, in accordance with the provisions of Article 37(1) or Article 40(1) or (2) as appropriate;

(c) if the total amount of the benefit or benefits payable under the provisions of subparagraph (b) is lower than the amount of the benefit which the person concerned was receiving at the expense of the institution previously liable for payment, such institution shall pay him a supplement equal to the difference between the two amounts;

(d) if, in the case referred to in subparagraph (b), the institution responsible for the initial incapacity is a Netherlands institution, and if:

  (i) the illness which caused the aggravation is the same as the one which gave rise to the granting of benefits under Netherlands legislation;

  (ii) this illness is an occupational disease within the meaning of the legislation of the Member State to which the person concerned was last subject and entitles him to payment of the supplement referred to in Article 60(1) (b); and

  (iii) the legislation or legislations to which the person concerned has been subject since receiving benefits is a legislation, or are legislations, listed in Annex III,

  the Netherlands institution shall continue to provide the initial benefit after the aggravation occurs, and the benefit due under the legislation of the last Member State to which the person concerned was subject shall be reduced by the amount of the Netherlands benefit;

(e) if, in the case referred to in subparagraph (b), the person concerned is not entitled to benefits at the expense of an institution of another Member State, the competent institution of the first State shall grant the benefits, according to the provisions of the legislation of that State, taking into account the aggravation and, where appropriate, the provisions of Article 38.

2. In the case of aggravation of an invalidity for which a worker is receiving benefits under the legislations of two or more Member States, the benefits shall be granted to him, taking the aggravation into account, in accordance with the provisions of Article 40(1).

Section 4

Resumption of provision of benefits after suspension or withdrawal - Conversion of invalidity benefits in - to old age benefits

Article 42

Determination of the institution responsible for the provision of benefits where provision of invalidity benefits is resumed

1. If provision of benefits is to be resumed after their suspension such provision shall, without prejudice to the provisions of Article 43, be the responsibility of the institution or institutions which were responsible for provision of the benefits at the time of their suspension.

2. If, after withdrawal of benefits, the condition of the person concerned warrants the granting of further benefits, they shall be granted in accordance with the provisions of Article 37(1) or Article 40(1) or (2), as appropriate.

Article 43

Conversion of invalidity benefits into old age benefits

1. Invalidity benefits shall be converted into old age benefits, where appropriate, under the conditions laid down by the legislation or legislations under which they were granted, and in accordance with the provisions of Chapter 3.

2. Any institution of a Member State which is responsible for providing invalidity benefits shall, where a person receiving invalidity benefits can, by virtue of the provisions of Article 49, establish a claim to old age benefits under the legislation of other Member States, continue to provide such person with the invalidity benefits to which he is entitled under the legislation which it administers until the provisions of paragraph 1 become applicable as regards that institution.

3. However, if in the case referred to in paragraph 2 the invalidity benefits have been granted pursuant to the provisions of Article 39, the institution remaining responsible for providing those benefits may apply the provisions of Article 49(1) (a) as if the recipient of the said benefits satisfied the conditions of the Member State concerned for entitlement to old age benefits, by substituting for the theoretical amount referred to in Article 46(2) (a) the amount of the invalidity benefits due from the said institution.

CHAPTER 3

OLD AGE AND DEATH (PENSIONS)

Article 44

General provisions for the award of benefits when a worker
has been subject to the legislation of two or more Member
States

1. The rights to benefits of a worker who has been subject to the
legislation of two or more Member States, or of his survivors, shall
be determined in accordance with the provisions of this chapter.

2. Subject to the provisions of Article 49, when a claim for the
award of a benefit is lodged, such award must be made having regard
to all the legislations to which the worker has been subject. Exception shall be made to this rule if the person concerned expressly
asks for postponement of the award of old-age benefits to which he
would be entitled under the legislation of one or more Member States.

3. This chapter shall not apply to increases in or supplements to pensions in respect of children or to orphans' pensions granted in accor-
ance with the provisions of Chapter 8.

Article 45

Consideration of periods of insurance or residence completed
under the legislations to which a worker has been subject, for
the acquisition, retention or recovery of the right to benefits

1. The competent institution of a Member State whose legislation makes
the acquisition, retention or recovery of the right to benefits conditional upon the completion of periods of insurance or residence
shall take into account, to the extent necessary, periods of insurance
or residence completed under the legislation of any Member State as
if they were periods completed under the legislation which it administers.

2. Where the legislation of a Member State makes the granting of
certain benefits conditional upon the periods of insurance having
been completed in an occupation subject to a special scheme or, where
appropriate, in a specific employment, periods completed under the
legislations of other Member States shall be taken into account for
the granting of such benefits only if completed under a corresponding
scheme or, failing this, in the same occupation or, where appropriate,
in the same employment. If, taking into account periods thus completed, the person concerned does not satisfy the conditions for receipt
of these benefits, those periods shall be taken into account for the
granting of benefits under the general scheme or, failing this,
under the scheme applicable to manual or clerical workers, as appropriate.

3. Where the legislation of a Member State which makes the granting

203

of benefits conditional upon a worker being subject to its legislation at the time when the risk materialises has no conditions as to the length of periods of insurance either for entitlement to or calculation of benefits, any worker who is no longer subject to that legislation shall for the purposes of implementing the provisions of this Chapter, be deemed to be still so subject at the time when the risk materialises, if at that time he is subject to the legislation of another Member State or, failing this, can establish a claim to benefits under the legislation of another Member State. However, this latter condition shall be deemed to be satisfied in the case referred to in Article 48(1).

Article 46

Award of benefits

1. Where a worker has been subject to the legislation of a Member State and where the conditions for entitlement to benefit have been satisfied, without application of the provisions of Article 45 being necessary, the competent institution of that Member State shall, in accordance with the provisions of the legislation which it administers determine the amount of benefit corresponding to the total length of the periods of insurance or residence to be taken into account in pursuance of such legislation.

This institution shall also calculate the amount of benefit which would be obtained by applying the rules laid down in paragraph 2(a) and (b). Only the higher of these two amounts shall be taken into consideration.

2. Where a worker has been subject to the legislation of a Member State and where the conditions for entitlement to benefits are not satisfied unless account is taken of the provisions of Article 45 and/or Article 40(3), the competent institution of that Member State shall apply the following rules:

(a) the institution shall calculate the theoretical amount of benefit that the person concerned could claim if all the periods of insurance or residence completed under the legislation of the Member States to which the worker has been subject had been completed in the Member State in question and under the legislation administered by it on the date the benefit is awarded. If, under that legislation, the amount of the benefit does not depend on the length of the periods completed then that amount shall be taken as the theoretical amount referred to in this subparagraph;

(b) the institution shall then establish the actual amount of the benefit on the basis of the theoretical amount referred to in the preceding subparagraph, and in the ratio which the length of the periods of insurance or residence completed before the risk materialises under the legislation administered by that institution bears to the total length of the periods of insurance and residence completed under the legislations of all the Member States concerned before the risk materialised;

(c) if the total length of the periods of insurance and residence completed before the risk materialises under the legislations of all the Member States concerned is longer than the maximum period required by the legislation of one of these States for receipt of full benefit, the competent institution of that State shall, when applying the provisions of this paragraph, take into consideration this maximum period instead of the total length of the periods completed; this method of calculation must not result in the imposition on that institution of the cost of a benefit greater than the full benefit provided for by the legislation which it administers;

(d) the procedure for taking into account overlapping periods, when applying the rules of calculation laid down in this paragraph, shall be laid down in the implementing Regulation referred to in Article 97.

3. The person concerned shall be entitled to the total sum of the benefits calculated in accordance with the provisions of paragraphs 1 and 2, within the limit of the highest theoretical amount of benefits calculated according to paragraph 2(a).

Where the amount referred to in the preceding subparagraph is exceeded, any institution applying paragraph 1 shall adjust its benefit by an amount corresponding to the proportion which the amount of the benefit concerned bears to the total of the benefits determined in accordance with the provisions of paragraph 1.

4. When in a case of invalidity, old age or survivors' pensions, the total of the benefits due from two or more Member States, under the provisions of a multilateral social security convention referred to in Article 6(b), is lower than the total which would be due from such Member States under paragraphs 1 and 3, the person concerned shall benefit from the provisions of this Chapter.

Article 47

Additional provisions for the calculation of benefits

1. For the calculation of the theoretical amount referred to in Article 46(2) (a), the following rules shall apply:

(a) where, under the legislation of a Member State, benefits are calculated on the basis of an average wage or salary, an average contribution, an average increase or on the ratio which existed, during the periods of insurance, between the claimant's gross wage or salary and the average gross wage or salary of all insured persons other than apprentices, such average figures or ratios shall be determined by the competent institution of that State solely on the basis of the periods of insurance completed under the legislation of the said State, or the gross wage or salary received by the person concerned during those periods only;

(b) where, under the legislation of a Member State, benefits are calculated on the basis of the amount of wages or salaries, contributions or increases, the competent institution of that State shall determine the wages or salaries, contributions and increases to be taken into account in respect of the periods of insurance or residence completed under the legislation of other Member States on the basis of the average wages or salaries, contributions or increases recorded in respect of the periods of insurance completed under the legislation which it administers;

(c) where, under the legislation of a Member State, benefits are calculated on the basis of a standard wage or salary or a fixed amount, the competent institution of that State shall consider the standard wage or salary or the fixed amount to be taken into account by it in respect of periods of insurance or residence completed under the legislations of other Member States as being equal to the standard wage or salary or the fixed amount or, where appropriate, to the average of the standard wages or salaries or the fixed amount corresponding to the periods of insurance completed under its own legislation;

(d) where, under the legislation of a Member State, benefits are calculated for some periods on the basis of the amount of wages or salaries, and, for other periods, on the basis of a standard wage or salary or a fixed amount, the competent institution of that State shall, in respect of periods of insurance or residence completed under the legislations of other Member States, take into account the wage, salary or fixed amount determined in accordance with the provisions of (b) or (c) above or, as appropriate, the average of these wages, salaries or fixed amounts; where benefits are calculated on the basis of a standard wage or salary or fixed amount for all the periods completed under the legislation which it administers, the competent institution shall consider the wage or salary to be taken into account in respect of the periods of insurance or residence completed under the legislations of other Member States as being equal to the notional wage or salary corresponding to the standard wage, salary or fixed amount.

2. The provisions of the legislation of a Member State concerning the revalorisation of the factors taken into account for the calculation of benefits shall apply, as appropriate, to the factors to be taken into account by the competent institution of that State, in accordance with the provisions of paragraph 1, in respect of the periods of insurance or residence completed under the legislation of other Member States.

3. If, under the legislation of a Member State, the amount of benefits is determined taking into account the existence of members of the family other than children, the competent institution of that State shall also take into consideration those members of the family of the person concerned who are residing in the terrory of another Member State as if they were residing in the territory of the competent State.

Article 48

Periods of insurance or residence of less than one year

1. Notwithstanding the provisions of Article 46(2), if the total

length of the periods of insurance or residence completed under the legislation of a Member State does not amount to one year and if under that legislation no right to benefit is acquired by virtue only of those periods, the institution of that State shall not be bound to award benefits in respect of such periods.

2. The competent institution of each of the other Member States concerned shall take into account the periods referred to in paragraph 1, for the purposes of applying the provisions of Article 46(2) excepting those of subparagraph (b).

3. If the effect of applying the provisions of paragraph 1 would be to relieve of their obligations all the institutions of the Member States concerned benefits shall be awarded exclusively under the legislation of the last of those States whose conditions are satisfied, as if all the periods of insurance and residence completed and taken into account in accordance with the provisions of Article 45(1) and (2) had been completed under the legislation of that State.

Article 49

Calculation of benefits when the person concerned does not simultaneously satisfy the conditions laid down by all the legislations under which periods of insurance or of residence have been completed

1. If, at a given time, the person concerned does not satisfy the conditions laid down for the provision of benefits by all the legislations of the Member States to which he has been subject, taking into account where appropriate the provisions of Article 45, but satisfies the conditions of one or more of them only, the following provisions shall apply:

(a) each of the competent institutions administering a legislation whose conditions are satisfied shall calculate the amount of the benefit due, in accordance with the provisions of Article 46;

(b) however,

    (i) if the person concerned satisfies the conditions of at least two legislations without having recourse to periods of insurance or residence completed under the legislations whose conditions are not satisfied, these periods shall not be taken into account for the purposes of the provisions of Article 46(2);

    (ii) if the person concerned satisfies the conditions of only one legislation without having recourse to periods of insurance or residence completed under the legislations whose conditions are not satisfied, the amount of the benefit payable shall be calculated in accordance with the provisions only of that legislation whose conditions are satisfied, taking account of the periods completed under that legislation only.

2. The benefit or benefits awarded under one or more of the legislations in question, in the case referred to in paragraph 1, shall be recalculated automatically in accordance with the provisions of

Article 46, as and when the conditions required by one or more of the other legislations to which the person concerned had been subject are satisfied, taking into account as appropriate the provisions of Article 45.

3. A recalculation shall automatically be made in accordance with the provisions of paragraph 1, and without prejudice to the provisions of Article 40(2), when the conditions required by one or more of the legislations concerned are no longer satisfied.

Article 50

Award of a supplement when the total of benefits payable under the legislations of the various Member States does not amount to the minimum laid down by the legislation of the State in whose territory the recipient resides

A recipient of benefits to whom this Chapter applies may not, in the State in whose territory he resides and under whose legislation a benefit is payable to him, be awarded a benefit which is less than the minimum benefit fixed by that legislation for a period of insurance or residence equal to all the periods of insurance taken into account for the payment in accordance with the provisions of the preceding Articles. The competent institution of that State shall, if necessary, pay him throughout the period of his residence in its territory a supplement equal to the difference between the total of the benefits payable under this Chapter and the amount of the minimum benefit.

Article 51

Revalorisation and recalculation of benefits

1. If, by reason of an increase in the cost of living or changes in the level of wages or salaries or other reasons for adjustment, the benefits of the States concerned are altered by a fixed percentage or amount, such percentage or amount must be applied directly to the benefits determined under the provisions of Article 46, without the need for a recalculation in accordance with the provisions of that Article.

2. On the other hand, if the method of determining, or the rules for calculating benefits should be altered, a recalculation shall be carried out in accordance with the provisions of Article 46.

CHAPTER 4

ACCIDENTS AT WORK AND OCCUPATIONAL
DISEASES

Section 1

Right to benefits

Article 52

Residence in a Member State other than the competent State

- General rules

A worker who sustains an accident at work or contracts an occupational disease, and who is residing in the territory of a Member State other than the competent State, shall receive in the State in which he is residing:

(a) benefits in kind, provided on behalf of the competent institution by the institution of his place of residence in accordance with the provisions of the legislation which it administers as if he were insured with it;

(b) cash benefits provided by the competent institution in accordance with the provisions of the legislation which it administers. However, by agreement between the competent institution and the institution of the place of residence, these benefits may be provided by the latter institution on behalf of the former in accordance with the legislation of the competent State.

Article 53

Frontier workers - Special rule

A frontier worker may also obtain benefits in the territory of the competent State. Such benefits shall be provided by the competent institution in accordance with the provisions of the legislation of that State, as if the worker were residing there.

Article 54

Stay in or transfer of residence to the competent State

1. A worker covered by Article 52 who is staying in the territory of the competent State shall receive benefits in accordance with the provisions of the legislation of that State, even if he has already received benefits before his stay. This provision shall not, however, apply to frontier workers.

2. A worker covered by Article 52 who transfers his place of residence to the territory of the competent State shall receive benefits in accordance with the provisions of the legislation of that State, even if he has already received benefits before transferring his residence.

Article 55

Stay outside the competent State - Return to or transfer of residence to another Member State after sustaining an accident or contracting an occupational disease - Need to go to another Member State in order to receive appropriate treatment

1. A worker who sustains an accident at work or contracts an occupational disease and:

(a) who is staying in the territory of a Member State other than the competent State; or

(b) who, after having become entitled to benefits chargeable to the competent institution, is authorised by that institution to return to the territory of the Member State where he is resident, or to transfer his place of residence to the territory of another Member State; or

(c) who is authorised by the competent institution to go to the territory of another Member State in order to receive there the treatment appropriate to his condition,

shall be entitled:

(i) to benefits in kind provided on behalf of the competent institution by the institution of the place of stay or residence in accordance with the provisions of the legislation administered by that institution as though he were insured with it, the period during which benefits are provided shall, however, be governed by the legislation of the competent State;

(ii) to cash benefits provided by the competent institution in accordance with the legislation which it administers. However, by agreement between the competent institution and the institution of the place of stay or residence, those benefits may be provided by the latter institution on behalf of the former institution, in accordance with the legislation of the competent State.

27. EXTRACT OF REGULATION No 574/72 OF THE COUNCIL

of 21 March 1972

laying down the procedure for implementing Regulation No 1408/71 on the application of social security schemes to employed persons and their families moving within the Community

(O.J. No L 74, 27 March 1972, p. 1; Codified Version O.J. C 138, 9 June 1980, p. 65)

TITLE 1

GENERAL PROVISIONS

Article 1

Definitions

For the purposes of this Regulation:

(a) 'Regulation' means Regulation (EEC) No 1408/71;

(b) 'Implementing Regulation' means this Regulation;

(c) the definitions in Article 1 of the Regulation have the meaning assigned to them in the said Article.

Article 2

Printed model forms – Information on legislations – Guides

1. Models of certificates, certified statements, declarations, applications and other documents necessary for the application of the Regulation and of the Implementing Regulation shall be drawn up by the Administrative Commission.

Two Member States or their competent authorities may, by mutual agreement and having received the opinion of the Administrative Commission, adopt simplified forms for use between them.

2. For the benefit of the competent authorities of each Member State, the Administrative Commission may assemble information on the provisions of national legislations which come within the scope of the Regulation.

3. The Administrative Commission shall prepare guides for the purpose of advising persons concerned of their rights and of the administrative formalities to be completed for the exercise of those rights.

The Advisory Committee shall be consulted before such guides are drawn up.

Article 3

Liaison bodies – Communications between institutions and between beneficiaries and institutions

1. The competent authorities may designate liaison bodies which may communicate directly with each other.

2. Any institution of a Member State, and any person residing or staying in the territory of a Member State, may make application to the institution of another Member State, either directly or through the liaison bodies.

Article 4

Annexes

1. The competent authority or authorities of each Member State are listed in Annex I.

2. The competent institutions of each Member State are listed in Annex 2.

3. The institutions of the place of residence and the institutions of the place of stay of each Member State are listed in Annex 3.

4. The liaison bodies designated pursuant to Article 3(1) of the Implementing Regulation are listed in Annex 4.

5. The provisions referred to in Articles 5, 53(3), 104, 105(2), 116 and 120 of the Implementing Regulation are listed in Annex 5.

6. The procedure for the payment of benefits chosen by the institutions responsible for payment in each Member State, in accordance with Article 53(1) of the Implementing Regulation, is listed in Annex 6.

7. The names and registered offices or places of business of the banks referred to in Article 55(1) of the Implementing Regulation are listed in Annex 7.

8. The Member States to which the provisions of Article 10(2) (d) of the Implementing Regulation apply in their dealings with each other are listed in Annex 8.

9. The schemes to be taken into consideration when calculating the average annual cost of benefits in kind, in accordance with Article 94(3) (a) of the Implementing Regulation, are listed in Annex 9.

10. Annex 10 lists the institutions or bodies designated by the competent authorities pursuant, in particular, to the following provisions:

(a) Regulation: Article 14(3), Article 17;

(b) Implementing Regulation: Article 6(1), Article 11(1), Article 12a, Article 13(2) and (3), Article 14(1), (2) and (3), Article 38(1), Article 70(1), Article 80(2), Article 81, Article 82(2), Article 85(2), Article 86(2), Article 89(1), Article 91(2), Article 102(2), Article 110, Article 113(2).

TITLE II

IMPLEMENTATION OF THE GENERAL PROVISIONS OF THE REGULATION

Implementation of Articles 6 and 7 of the Regulation

Article 5

Replacement by the Implementing Regulation of arrangements for implementing conventions

The provisions of the Implementing Regulation shall replace those of the arrangements for implementing the conventions referred to in Article 6 of the Regulation; they shall also replace the provisions relating to the implementation of the provisions of the conventions referred to in Article 7(2) (c) in so far as they are not listed in Annex 5.

Implementation of Article 9 of the Regulation

Article 6

Admission to voluntary or optional continued insurance

1. If, by virtue of Articles 9 and 15(3) of the Regulation, a person satisfies the conditions for admission to a voluntary or optional continued insurance in respect of invalidity, old age and death (pensions) in several schemes under the legislation of one Member State, and if he has not been subject to compulsory insurance under one of those schemes by virtue of his last employment he may, under the said Articles, join the voluntary or optional continued insurance scheme specified by the legislation of that Member State or, failing that, the scheme of his choice.

2. In order to invoke the provisions of Article 9(2) of the Regulation, a person shall submit to the institution of the Member State in question a certified statement relating to the insurance periods or periods of residence completed under the legislation of any other Member State. Such certified statement shall be issued, at the request of the person concerned, by the institution or institutions who administer the legislations under which he has completed those periods.

Implementation of Article 12 of the Regulation

Article 7 (C 40)

General rules for the implementation of provisions dealing with the prevention of overlapping of benefits - Application of those provisions to benefits in respect of invalidity, old age and death (pensions)

1. Where a person entitled to a benefit due under the legislation of one Member State is also entitled to benefits under the legislation of one or more of the other Member States, the following rules shall apply:

(a) if the application of Article 12(2) or (3) of the Regulation entails the reduction or the concurrent suspension of those benefits, none of them may be reduced or suspended by an amount greater than the amount obtained by dividing the sum which is subject to reduction or suspension under the legislation by virtue of which the benefit is due by the number of benefits subject to reduction or suspension to which the person concerned is entitled;

(b) as regards benefits in respect of invalidity, old age or death (pensions) awarded under Article 46(2) of the Regulation by the institution of a Member State, that institution shall take into account any benefits of a different kind and any income or remuneration likely to entail the reduction or suspension of the benefit due from that institution, not for the calculation of the theoretical amount referred to in Article 46(2) (a) of the Regulation but exclusively for the reduction or suspension of the amount referred to in Article 46(2) (b) of the Regulation. However, only a fraction of the total amount of such benefit, income or remuneration shall be taken into account, and that fraction shall be determined in proportion to the duration of the periods of insurance completed, in accordance with Article 46(2) (b) of the Regulation;

(c) as regards benefits in respect of invalidity, old age or death
(pensions) awarded under the first subparagraph of Article 46(1)
of the Regulation by the institution of a Member State, that institution shall, where the provisions of Article 46(3) of the Regulation apply, take into account any benefits of a different kind
and any income or remuneration likely to entail the reduction or
suspension of the benefit due from that institution, not for the
calculation of the amount referred to in Article 46(1) of the
Regulation, but exclusively for the reduction or suspension of
the amount resulting from the application of Article 46(3) of the
Regulation. However, only a fraction of the amount of those benefits, income or remuneration shall be taken into account; such
fraction shall be obtained by applying to that amount a coeffici-
ent equal to the ratio between the amount of benefit resulting
from the application of Article 46(3) of the Regulation and the
amount resulting from the application of the first subparagraph
of Article 46(1) of the Regulation.

2. For the purposes of Article 12(2), (3) and (4) of the Regulation,
the competent institutions concerned shall, on request, exchange all
requisite information.

Article 8

Rules applicable in the case of overlapping of rights to sickness
or maternity benefits under the legislation of several Member States

If a worker or a member of his family is entitled to claim maternity
benefits under the legislations of two or more Member States, those
benefits shall be granted exclusively under the legislation of the
Member State in whose territory the confinement took place or, if
the confinemnt did not take place in the territory of one of these
Member States, exclusively under the legislation of the Member State
to which the worker was last subject.

If a worker is entitled to claim sickness benefits under the legislations of Ireland and the United Kingdom for the same period of incapacity for work, those benefits shall be granted exclusively under the
legislation of the Member State to which the worker was last subject.

Article 9

Rules applicable in the case of overlapping of rights to death
grants under the legislations of several Member States

1. Where the death occurs in the territory of a Member State, the
right to a death grant acquired under the legislation of that Member
State only shall be maintained, whilst the right acquired under the
legislation of any other Member State shall lapse.

2. Where the death occurs in the territory of one Member State when
the right to a death grant has been acquired under the legislation
of two or more other Member States, or where the death occurs outside

the territory of the Member States and the said right has been acquired under the legislation of two or more Member States, only the right acquired under the legislation of the Member State to which the deceased person was last subject shall be maintained, whilst the right acquired under the legislation of any other Member State shall lapse.

Article 10

Rules applicable in the case of overlapping of rights to family benefits or family allowances or when, during the same period or part of a period, the worker is successively subject to the legislation of several Member States

1. Entitlement to family benefits or family allowances due under the legislation of a Member State, according to which acquisition of the right to those benefits or allowances is not subject to conditions of insurance or employment, shall be suspended when, during the same period and for the same member of the family:

(a) benefits are due in pursuance of Article 73 or Article 74 of the Regulation. If, however, the spouse of the worker or unemployed worker referred to in those Articles exercises a professional or trade activity in the territory of the said Member State, the right to family benefits or family allowances due in pursuance of the said Articles shall be suspended; and only those family benefits or family allowances of the Member State in whose territory the member of the family is residing shall be paid, the cost to be borne by that Member State;

(b) benefits are due in pursuance of Article 77 or Article 78 of the Regulation. If, however, a pensioner who is entitled to benefits under Article 77 of the Regulation, his spouse or the person looking after the orphans to whom benefits are due under Article 78 of the Regulation, exercises a professional or trade activity in the territory of the said Member State, entitlement to family allowances due in pursuance of Article 77 or Article 78 of the Regulation under the legislation of another Member State shall be suspended; where this is the case, the person concerned shall be entitled to the family benefits or family allowances of the Member State in whose territory the children reside, the cost to be borne by that Member State, and, where appropriate, to benefits other than the family allowances referred to in Article 77 or Article 78 of the Regulation, the cost to be borne by the competent State as defined by those Articles.

2. If a worker has been subject successively to the legislation of two Member States during the period separating two dates for the payment of family benefits or family allowances as provided for by the legislation of one or both of the Member States concerned, the following rules shall apply:

(a) the family benefits or family allowances which such worker may claim by virtue of being subject to the legislation of each one of these States shall correspond to the number of daily benefits or allowances due under the relevant legislation. Where these

215

legislations do not provide for daily benefits or allowances, the family benefits or family allowances shall be granted in proportion to the length of time during which such worker has been subject to the legislation of each one of the Member States in relation to the period fixed by the legislation concerned;

(b) where the family benefits or family allowances have been provided by an institution during a period when they should have been provided by another institution, there shall be an adjustment of accounts between the said institutions;

(c) for the purposes of subparagraphs (a) and (b) where periods of employment completed under the legislation of one Member State are expressed in units different from those which are used in the calculation of family benefits or family allowances under the legislation of another Member State to which the worker has also been subject during the same period, the conversion shall be carried out in accordance with the provisions of Article 15(3) of the Implementing Regulation;

(d) notwithstanding the provisions of subparagraph (a), in respect of dealings between the Member States listed in Annex 8 to the Implementing Regulation, the institution bearing the costs of the family benefits or family allowances by reason of the first employment during the period concerned, shall bear their cost throughout the whole of the current period.

3. If the members of the family of a worker subject to French legislation, or of an unemployment person in receipt of unemplyment benefits under French legislation, transfer their residence from the territory of one Member State during the same calendar month, the institution responsible for providing the family allowances at the beginning of that month shall continue to provide them throughout the whole of the current month.

TITLE III

IMPLEMENTATION OF THE PROVISIONS OF THE REGULATIONS
FOR DETERMINING THE LEGISLATION APPLICABLE

Implementation of Articles 13 to 17 of the Regulation

Article 11

Formalities in the case of posting elsewhere pursuant to Article 14 (1) (a) and 2(a) and in the case of Agreements concluded under Article 17 of the Regulation

1. The institution designated by the competent authority of the Member State whose legislation is to remain applicable shall issue a certificate stating that a worker shall remain subject to that legislation up to a specified date,

(a) at the request of the worker or his employer in cases referred to in Article 14(1) (a) and 2(a) of the Regulation;

(b) in cases where Article 17 of the Regulation applies.

2. The consent provided for in Article 14(1) (a) (ii) of the Regulation shall be requested by the employer.

Article 12

Special provisions concerning insurance under the German social security scheme

Where, under the terms of Article 13(2) (a), Article 14(1) (a), (b) and (c) or 2(a) of the Regulation, or under an agreement concluded pursuant to Article 17 of the Regulation, German legislation applies to a worker employed by an undertaking or employer whose registered office or place of business is not situated on German territory, and the worker has no fixed job on German territory, this legislation shall apply as if the worker were employed in his place of residence on German territory.

If the worker has no residence on German territory, German legislation shall apply as if he were employed in a place for which the Allgemeine Ortskrankenkasse Bonn (General Sickness Fund of Bonn), Bonn is competent.

Article 12a

Rules applicable in respect of a worker, other than one employed in international transport, who normally pursues his activity in the territory of two or more Member States

1. For the purposes of Article 14(1) (c) (i) of the Regulation a worker who normally pursues his activity in the territory of two or more Member States shall notify this fact to the institution designated by the competent authority of the Member State in the territory of which he resides.

That institution shall issue to him a certificate stating that he is subject to the legislation of that Member State and shall send a copy thereof to the institution designated by the competent authority of any other Member State:

(a) in the territory of which the said worker pursues a part of his activity; and/or

(b) in the territory of which an undertaking or an employer by whom he is employed has its registered office or place of business. This latter institution shall, where necessary, send to the institution designated by the competent authority of the Member State whose legislation is applicable the information necessary to assess the contributions for which the employer or employers and/or the worker are liable by virtue of that legislation.

2. For the purposes of Article 14(1) (c) (ii) of the Regulation a

worker who normally pursues his activity in the territory of two or
more Member States shall notify this fact to the institution designated by the competent authority of the Member State in the territory
of which the undertaking or employer employing the said worker has
its registered office or place of business.

The provisions of paragraph 1, second subparagraph (a) shall apply by
analogy. However, the said worker may obtain the certificate in
question through the institution designated by the competent authority
of the Member State in the territory of which he resides.

Article 13

Exercise of the right of option by persons employed by diplomatic
missions and consular posts

1. The right of option provided for in Article 16 (2) of the Regulation must be exercised in the first instance within the three months
following the date on which the worker was engaged by the diplomatic
mission or consular post concerned, or on which he entered into the
personal service of agents of such mission or post. The option shall
take effect on the date of entry into employment.

When a worker renews his right of option at the end of a calendar
year, the option shall take effect on the first day of the following
calendar year.

2. A worker who exercises his right of option shall inform the institution designated by the competent authority of the Member State for
whose legislation he has opted, at the same time notifying his
employer thereof. The said institution shall, where necessary, forward such information to all other institutions of the same Member
State, in accordance with directives issued by the competent authority
of that Member State.

3. The institution designated by the competent authority of the Member
State for whose legislation a worker has opted, shall issue to him a
certificate testifying that he is subject to the legislation of that
Member State while he is employed by the diplomatic mission or consular post in question or in the personal service of agents of such
mission or post.

4. Where a worker has opted for German legislation to be applied the
provisions of such legislation shall be applied as though that worker
were employed in the place where the German Government has its seat.
The competent authority shall designate the competent sickness
insurance institution.

Article 14

Exercise of the right of option by auxiliary staff of the European
Communities

1. The right of option provided for in Article 16 (3) of the Regulation must be exercised at the time when the contract of employment is

concluded. The authority empowered to conclude such contract shall inform the institution designated by the competent authority of the Member State for whose legislation the auxiliary staff member has opted. The said institution shall, where necessary, forward such information to all institutions of the same Member State.

TITLE IV

IMPLEMENTATION OF THE SPECIAL PROVISIONS
OF THE REGULATION RELATING TO THE VARIOUS CATEGORIES OF
BENEFITS

CHAPTER 1

GENERAL RULES FOR THE AGGREGATION OF PERIODS

Article 15

1. In the cases referred to in Article 18(1), Article 38, Article 45 (1) and (2), Article 64, and Article 67(1) and (2) of the Regulation, aggregation of periods shall be effected in accordance with the following rules:

(a) to periods of insurance or residence completed under the legislation of one Member State shall be added periods of insurance or residence completed under the legislation of any other Member State, to the extent that it is necessary to have recourse thereto in order to supplement periods of insurance or residence completed under the legislation of the first Member State for the purpose of acquiring, retaining, or recovering the rights to benefits, provided that such periods of insurance or residence do not overlap. Where benefits in respect of invalidity, old age or death (pensions) are to be awarded by the institutions of two or more Member States in accordance with the provisions of Article 46(2) of the Regulation, each of the institutions concerned shall effect a separate aggregation, by taking into account the whole of the periods of insurance or residence completed by the worker under the legislations of all the Member States to which he has been subject, without prejudice, where appropriate, to the provisions of Article 45(2) and Article 46(2) (c) of the Regulation;

(b) when a period of insurance or residence completed under compulsory insurance under the legislation of one Member State coincides with a period of insurance completed under voluntary or optional continued insurance under the legislation of another Member State, only the period completed under compulsory insurance shall be taken into account;

(c) when a period of insurance or residence, other than a period treated as such, completed under the legislation of one Member State coincides with a period treated as such under the legislation of another Member State, only the period other than a period treated as such shall be taken into account;

(d) any period treated as such under the legislations of two or more Member States, shall be taken into account only by the institution of the Member State under whose legislation the insured person was last compulsorily insured prior to the said period; where the insured person has not been compulsorily insured under the legislation of a Member State before the said period, the latter shall be taken into account by the institution of the Member State under whose legislation he was compulsorily insured for the first time after the said period;

(e) where it is not possible to determine accurately the period of time in which certain periods of insurance or residence were completed under the legislation of one Member State, such periods shall be presumed not to overlap with periods of insurance or residence completed under the legislation of another Member State and shall, where advantageous, be taken into account;

(f) where under the legislation of one Member State, certain periods of insurance or residence are taken into account only if they have been completed within a specified time limit, the institution which administers such legislation shall:

    (i) only take into account periods of insurance or residence completed under the legislation of another Member State if they were completed within the said time limit; or

    (ii) extend such time limit for the duration of periods of insurance or residence completed wholly or partly within the said time limit under the legislation of another Member State, where the periods of insurance or residence involved under the legislation of the second Member State give rise only to the suspension of the time limit within which the periods of insurance or residence must be completed.

2. Periods of insurance or residence completed under the legislation of a Member State to which the Regulation does not apply, but which are taken into account under the legislation of that Member State to which the Regulation does apply, shall be considered as periods of insurance or residence to be taken into account for the purposes of aggregation.

3. When periods of insurance completed under the legislation of one Member State are expressed in units different from those used by the legislation of another Member State, the conversion necessary for the purposes of aggregation shall be carried out according to the following rules:

(a) where the worker has been subject to a six-day week:

    (i) one day shall be equivalent to eight hours and vice versa;

    (ii) six days shall be equivalent to one week and vice versa;

    (iii) 26 days shall be equivalent to one month and vice versa;

    (iv) three months or 13 weeks or 78 days shall be equivalent to one quarter and vice versa;

(v) for the conversion of weeks into months and vice versa the weeks and months shall be converted into days;

(vi) the application of the preceding rules shall not have the effect of producing, for the sum total of the periods of insurance completed during one calendar year, a total exceeding 312 days or 52 weeks or 12 months or four quarters;

(b) where the worker has been subject to a five-day week:

(i) one day shall be equivalent to nine hours and vice versa;

(ii) five days shall be equivalent to one week and vice versa;

(iii) 22 days shall be equivalent to one month and vice versa;

(iv) three months or 13 weeks or 66 days shall be equivalent to one quarter and vice versa;

(v) for the conversion of weeks into months and vice versa, the weeks and the months shall be converted into days;

(vi) the application of the preceding rules shall not have the effect of producing, for the sum total of the periods of insurance completed during one calendar year, a total exceeding 264 days or 52 weeks or 12 months or four quarters.

. . . . .

28. General Programme

for the abolition of restrictions on freedom of establishment
(JO 15 January 1962, p. 36; OJ Special Edition, Second Series p.3)

THE COUNCIL OF THE EUROPEAN ECONOMIC COMMUNITY,

Having regard to the provisions of the Treaty, and in particular
Articles 43 and 132 (5) thereof;

Having regard to the proposal from the Commission;

Having regard to the Opinion of the Economic and Social Committee;

Having regard to the Opinion of the European Parliament;

Has adopted this General Programme for the abolition of restrictions
on freedom of establishment within the European Economic Community.

Title I: Beneficiaries

Subject to any decisions taken by the Council under the second subparagraph of Article 227 (2) of the Treaty and without prejudice to subsequent provisions laying down association arrangements between the
European Economic Community and the overseas countries and territories
having attained independence after the entry into force of the Treaty,
the persons entitled to benefit from the abolition of restrictions on
freedom of establishment as set out in this General Programme are:

- nationals of Member States or of the overseas countries and territories, and
- companies and firms formed under the law of a Member State or of an
  overseas country or territory and having either the seat prescribed
  by their statutes, or their centre of administration, or their main
  establishment situated within the Community or in an overseas country
  or territory,

who wish to establish themselves in order to pursue activities as self-
employed persons in a Member State; and

- nationals of Member States or of the overseas countries and territories who are established in a Member State or in an overseas country
  or territory, and
- companies and firms as above, provided that, where only the seat
  prescribed by their statutes is situated within the Community or in
  an overseas country or territory, their activity shows a real and
  continuous link with the economy of a Member State or of an overseas
  country or territory; such link shall not be one of nationality,
  whether of the members of the company or firm, or of the persons
  holding managerial or supervisory posts therein, or of the holders
  of the capital,

who wish to set up agencies, branches or subsidiaries in a Member
State.

Title II: Entry and residence

The following steps are to be taken before the end of the second year
of the second stage of the transitional period:

A. The provisions laid down by law, Regulation or administrative action
which in any Member State govern the entry and residence of nationals
of other Member States will, where such provisions are not justified
on grounds of public policy, public security or public health, and are
liable to hinder those nationals in taking up or pursuing activities
as self-employed persons, be so amended, in particular by the abrogation of those having an economic purpose, as to eliminate this source
of hindrance;

B. The abolition of provisions laid down by law, Regulation or administrative action which in a Member State prohibit nationals of other
Member States working in paid employment in that State from staying
on and taking up an activity there in a self-employed capacity even
though such nationals satisfy the requirements which they would have to
meet if they were entering the Member State in question at the time when
they wished to take up the activity concerned.

Title III: Restrictions

Subject to the exceptions or special provisions laid down in the Treaty
and in particular to:
- Article 55 concerning activities which are connected with the exercise of official authority in a Member State; and
- Article 56 concerning provisions on special treatment for foreign
  nationals on grounds of public policy, public security or public
  health,
the following restrictions are to be eliminated in accordance with the
timetable laid down under Title IV:

A. Any measure which, pursuant to any provision laid down by law,
   Regulation or administrative action in a Member State or as the
   result of the application of such a provision or of administrative
   practices prohibits or hinders nationals of other Member States in
   their pursuit of an activity as a self-employed person by treating
   nationals of other Member States differently from nationals of the
   country concerned.
      Such restrictive provisions and practices are in particular
   those which, in respect of foreign nationals only:
   (a) Prohibit the taking up or pursuit of an activity as a self-
       employed person;
   (b) make the taking up or pursuit of an activity as a self-employed
       person subject to an authorization or to the issue of a document
       such as a foreign trader's permit;
   (c) impose additional conditions in respect of the granting of any
       authorization required for the taking up or pursuit of an act-
       ivity as a self-employed person;
   (d) make the taking up or pursuit of an activity as a self-employed
       person subject to a period of prior residence or training in
       the host country;
   (e) make the taking up or pursuit of an activity as a self-employed
       person more costly by through taxation or other financiel burd-
       ens, such as a requirement that the person concerned shall

lodge a deposit or provide security in the host country;

(f) limit or hinder, by making it more costly or more difficult access to sources of supply or to distribution outlets;

(g) prohibit or hinder access to any vocational training which is necessary or useful for the pursuit of an activity as a self-employed person;

(h) prohibit foreign nationals from becoming members of companies or firms, or restrict their rights as members, in particular as regards the functions which they may perform within the company or firm;

(i) deny or restrict the right to participate in social security schemes, in particular sickness, accident, invalidity or old age insurance schemes, or the right to receive family allowances;

(j) grant less favourable treatment in the event of nationalization, expropriation or requisition.

The like shall apply to provisions and practices which, in respect of foreign nationals only, exclude, limit or impose conditions on the power to exercise rights normally attaching to an activity as a self-employed person, and in particular the power:

(a) to enter into contracts, in particular contracts for work, business or agricultural tenancies, and contracts of employment, and to enjoy all rights arising under such contracts;

(b) to submit tenders for or to act directly as a party or as a sub-contractor in contracts with the State or with any other legal person governed by public law;

(c) to obtain licences or authorizations issued by the State or by any other legal person governed by public law;

(d) to acquire, use or dispose of movable or immovable property or rights therein;

(e) to acquire, use or dispose of intellectual property and all rights deriving therefrom;

(f) to borrow, and in particular to have access to the various forms of credit;

(g) to receive aids granted by the State, whether direct or indirect;

(h) to be a party to legal or administrative proceedings;

(i) to join professional or trade organizations;

where the professional or trade activities of the person concerned necessarily involve the exercise of such power.

Furthermore, included among the abovementioned provisions and practices are those which limit or impair the freedom of personnel belonging to the main establishment in one Member State to take up managerial or supervisory posts in agencies, branches or subsidiaries in another Member State.

B. Any requirements imposed, pursuant to any provision laid down by law, Regulation or administrative action or in consequence of any administrative practice, in respect of the taking up or pursuit of an activity as a self-employed person where, although applicable irrespective of nationality, their effect is exclusively or principally, to hinder the taking up or pursuit of such activity by foreign nationals.

Title IV: timetable

The effective abolition of restrictions in respect of freedom of establishment shall take place according to the following timetable:

A. For activities listed in Annex I it shall, save where paragraph B otherwise provides, take place before the end of the second year of the second stage of the transitional period.

B. For activities falling within Annex I, group 400 – 'Construction', carried out under public works contracts it shall take place by 31 December 1963.

   However, in view of the particular nature and requirements of this sector and in order to ensure that restrictions are lifted in a progressive and balanced manner and that the removal of restrictions is accompanied by appropriate measures for the coordination of procedures:

   1. When the value of the public works contracts awarded in one Member State to nationals or companies or firms of other Member States by that State or by its regional or local authorities, such as Länder, regions, provinces, departments, communes, or other legal persons governed by public law still to be determined exceeds the quota referred to in Title VC (e) 1 (a) of the General Programme on the Provision of Services, then that State shall be entitled to order that no further public works contracts may be awarded until the end of the year in question to nationals or companies or firms of other Member States acting through their agencies or branches established in that State.

   2. As regards legal persons governed by public law which as at 31 December 1963 have not been included among those referred to in the first subparagraph, before the end of the transitional period. Restrictions on the award of public works contracts by the aforesaid legal persons to such agencies or branches are to be abolished.

C. For the following activities it shall take place between the date specified in paragraph A and the end of the second stage of the transitional period that is to say for:
   - activities listed in Annex II;
   - activities of undertakings providing direct insurance other than life insurance. However, the lifting restrictions as regards the setting up of agencies or branches shall be dependent on coordination of the conditions for the taking up and pursuit of the aforesaid activities.

D. For the following activities it shall take place between the beginning of the third stage and the end of the second year of the third stage, that is to say for:
   - activities listed in Annex III,
   - activities of undertakings providing life assurance. However, the lifting of restrictions as regards the setting up of agencies or branches shall be dependent on coordination of the conditions for the taking up and pursuit of the aforesaid activities. Nevertheless, pending such coordination, before the end of the second stage a limit shall be fixed on the conditions in this respect which may be imposed on such agencies or branches.

E. For activities listed in Annex IV it shall take place between the last date specified in paragraph D and the end of the transitional period.

E. For agriculture, in respect of activities listed in Annex V, the abolition of restrictions on freedom of establishment shall take place as follows:

1. Restrictions relating to establishment on agricultural holdings abandoned or left uncultivated for more than two years shall be abolished as soon as the General Programme is adopted; establishment will not, however, entail the right to transfer from one such holding to another;

2. Restrictions on establishment in agriculture for nationals of other Member States who have been employed as paid agricultural workers in the host country for a continuous period of two years shall be abolished at the end of the first stage;

3. At the beginning of the third year of the second stage each Member State will so amend its legislation relating to agricultural tenancies as to ensure that such legislation applies to tenant farmers who are nationals of other Member States in like manner as it applies to nationals of the Member State concerned. At the same time each Member State shall grant to nationals of other Member States who have farmed in the Member States in question for more than two years the right to transfer from one holding to another.

4. Each Member State will, at the beginning of the third stage, take the necessary steps to ensure that farmers who are nationals of other Member States enjoy the same rights as its own nationals with regard to access to the various forms of credit and membership of cooperatives.

5. Each Member State will, at the beginning of the third year of the third stage, take the necessary steps to ensure that farmers who are nationals of other Member States enjoy the same rights as its own nationals with regard to access to the various forms of aid.

6. All other existing restrictions in respect of the taking up and pursuit of the abovementioned activities will be abolished at the end of the transitional period.

G. 1. As regards transport by rail, road and inland waterway, the abolition of restrictions will take place in accordance with the timetable laid down in the General Programme and will be accompanied by such measures for the coordination of provisions laid down by law, Regulation or administrative action of Member States in respect of the rights to take up and pursue the various activities concerned as are necessary for the avoidance of distortions arising from the abolition of restrictions. Such coordination will be carried out under the common transport policy.

2. A General Programme for sea and air transport will be decided on by unanimous vote of the Council.

Title V: Mutual recognition of diplomas and other evidence
        of formal qualifications - Coordination

Subject to Article 57 (3) of the Treaty and to Title IV of this General
Programme, when Directives implementing the General Programme for each
activity as a self-employed person are being drawn up, it shall at the
same time be examined whether lifting of restrictions on freedom of
establishment should be proceeded, accompanied or followed by the
mutual recognistion of diplomas, certificates and other evidence of
formal qualifications, or by the coordination of provisions laid down
by law, Regulation or administrative action in respect of the taking
up and pursuit of these activities.
    Pending such mutual recognition of diplomas, or such coordination,
and in order to facilitate the taking up and pursuit of activities
as self-employed persons and to avoid distortions, a transitional system may be applied; such a system may where appropriate include provision for the production of a certificate establishing that the activity in question was actually and lawfully carried on in the country
of origin.
    The duration and details of this transitional system shall be settl-
ed when the Directives are drawn up.

Title VI: Coordination of safeguards required of companies
         and firms

It is intended that the safeguards required by Member States of companies and firms for the protection of the interests of members and
others should, to the extent necessary and with a view to making such
safeguards equivalent, be coordinated before the end of the second
year of the second stage of the transitional period.

Title VII: Aids

It is intended that, without prejudice to Article 92 et seq. of the
Treaty, the granting by Member States of aids liable to distort the
conditions of establishment should in each case be prohibited on or
before the removal of restrictions on freedom of establishment in the
activity where the distortion occurs.

Done at Brussels, 18 December 1961

                              For the Council

                              The President

                              Ludwig ERHARD

29. General Programme

for the abolition of restrictions on
freedom to provide services
(JO, No 32/62, 15 January 1962; OJ Special Edition, Second Series p.7)

THE COUNCIL OF THE EUROPEAN ECONOMIC COMMUNITY,

Having regard to the provisions of the Treaty, and in particular
Articles 63, 106 and 227(2) thereof;

Having regard to the proposal from the Commission;

Having regard to the Opinion of the Economic and Social Committee;

Having regard to the Opinion of the European Parliament,

Has adopted this General Programme for the Abolition of Restrictions
on Freedom to Provide Services within the European Economic Community.

Title I: Beneficiaries

The persons entitled to benefit from the abolition of restrictions on
freedom to provide services as set out in this General Programme are:

- nationals of Member States who are established within the Community;

- companies or firms formed under the law of a Member State and having
the seat prescribed by their statutes, or their centre of administration, or their main establishment situated within the Community, provided that where only that seat is situated within the Community their
activity shows a real and continuous link with the economy of a Member
State; such link shall not be one of nationality, whether of the
members of the company or firm, or of the persons holding managerial
or supervisory posts therein, or of the holders of the capital;

subject to the condition that the service is carried out either person-
nally by the person contracting to provide it or by one of his agencies
or branches established in the Community.

Title II: Entry, exit and residence

Before the end of the second year of the second stage of the transitional period provisions laid down by law, Regulation or administrative
action which in any Member State govern the entry, exit and residence
of nationals of other Member States are to be amended, in particular
by the abrogation of provisions having an economic purpose, where
such provisions are not justified on grounds of public policy, public
security or public health and are liable to hinder the provisions of
services by such nationals, or by staff possessing special skills or
holding positions of responsibility accompanying the person providing
the services or carrying out the services on his behalf.

Title III: Restrictions

Subject to the exceptions or special provisions laid down in the Treaty, and in particular to:

- Article 55 concerning activities which are connected with the exercise of official authority in a Member State;
- Article 56 concerning provisions on special treatment for foreign nationals on grounds of public policy, public security or public health;
- Article 61, which provides that freedom to provide services in the field of transport is to be governed by the provisions of the Title relating to transport; and to
- the provisions concerning the free movement of goods, capital and persons, and those concerning taxation systems;

the following restrictions are to be eliminated in accordance with the timetable laid down under Title V, whether they affect the person providing the services directly, or indirectly through the recipient of the service or through the service itself;

A. Any measures which, pursuant to any provision laid down by law, Regulation or administrative action in a Member State, or as a result of the application of such a provision, or of administrative practices, prohibits or hinders the person providing services in his pursuit of an activity as a self-employed person by treating him differently from nationals of the State concerned.

Such restrictive provisions and practices are in particular those which, in respect of foreign nationals only:

(a) prohibit the provision of services;

(b) make the provision of services subject to an authorization or to the issue of a document such as a foreign trader's permit;

(c) impose additional conditions in respect of the granting of any authorization required for the provision of services;

(d) make the provision of services subject to a period of prior residence or training in the host country;

(e) make the provision of services more costly through taxation or other financial burdens, such as a requirement that the person concerned must lodge a deposit or provide security in the host country;

(f) limit or hinder, by making it more costly or more difficult, access to sources of supply or to distribution outlets;

(g) deny or restrict the right to participate in social security schemes, in particular, in sickness, accident, invalidity or old age insurance schemes, or the right to receive family allowances;

(h) grant less favourable treatment in the event of nationalization, expropriation or requisition.

The like shall apply to provisions and practices which, in respect of foreign nationals only, exclude, limit or impose conditions on the power to exercise rights normally attaching to the provision of serv-

229

ices and in particular the power:

(a) to enter into contracts, in particular contracts for work, contracts of hire and contracts of employment, and to enjoy all rights arising under such contracts;

(b) to submit tenders for or to act directly as a party or a subcontractor in contracts with the State or with any other legal person governed by public law;

(c) to obtain licences or authorizations issued by the State or by any other legal person governed by public law;

(d) to acquire, use or dispose of movable or immovable property or rights therein;

(e) to acquire, use or dispose of intellectual property and all rights deriving therefrom;

(f) to borrow, and in particular to have access to the various forms of credit;

(g) to receive aids granted by the State, whether direct or indirect;

(h) to be a party to legal or administrative proceedings;

where the professional or trade activities of the person concerned necessarily involve the exercise of such power.

Furthermore, any requirements imposed, pursuant to any provision laid down by law, Regulation or administrative action or in consequence of any administrative practice, in respect of the provision of services are also to be regarded as restrictions where, although applicable irrespective of nationality, their effect is exclusively or principally, to hinder the provision of services by foreign nationals.

B. Any prohibition of, or hindrance to, the movement of the item to the supplied in the course of the service or of the materials comprising such item or of the tools, machinery equipment and other means to be employed in the provision of the service.

C. Any prohibition of, or impediment to, the transfer of the funds needed to perform the service.

D. Any prohibition of, or hindrance to, payments for services, where the provision of such services between the Member States is limited only by restrictions in respect of the payments therefor.

However, in respect of the provisions referred to in paragraphs C and D, Member States shall retain the right to verify the nature and genuineness of transfer of funds and of payments and to take all necessary measures in order to prevent contravention of their laws and regulations, in particular as regards the issue of foreign currency to tourists.

Title IV: Equality of treatment between nationals of
Member States

Until restrictions have been abolished, each Member State shall apply them in such a way as to accord to all beneficiaries falling within Title I, without distinction on grounds of nationality or residence, the most favourable treatment accorded under existing practices and bilateral or multilateral agreements, other than those establishing regional unions between Belgium, Luxembourg and the Netherlands.

Title V: Timetable

The effective abolition of restrictions in respect of freedom to provide services shall take place according to the following timetable:

A. ITEM TO BE SUPPLIED, MATERIALS COMPRISING THAT ITEM AND MEANS TO BE EMPLOYED IN THE PROVISION OF THE SERVICE

The restrictions specified in Title III (B) shall be abolished before the end of the first stage.

B. TRANSFER OF FUNDS, PAYMENT

The restrictions specified in Title III(C) and (D) shall be abolished before the end of the first stage.

However, limits on foreign currency allowances for tourists may be maintained in force during the transitional period, but they are to be progressively raised from the end of the first stage.

C. OTHER RESTRICTIONS

The remaining restrictions specified in Title III on freedom to provide services are to be abolished at the latest during the operation of the timetable for freedom of establishment. However, as regards the activities therein specified, the following timetable shall apply:

(a) Direct insurance

    1. As regards insurance undertakings, restrictions shall be abolished, subject to the condition that freedom of establishment shall have been attained in the branch of insurance concerned, that the legal or administrative provisions governing insurance contracts shall have been coordinated — in so far as the disparity between such provisions is detrimental to the insured or to third persons — and that formalities for the recognition and reciprocal enforcement of judgments shall have been simplified, by the following dates:

        – for direct insurance other than life insurance, the end of the second year of the third stage;
        – for life assurance, the end of the third stage;

    2. As regards self-employed intermediaries in the abovementioned branches of insurance, restrictions shall be abolished:

        – at the same time as freedom to provide services is granted to insurance undertakings;

(b) Banking

    1. As regards services other than those connected with movements

of capital, restrictions shall be abolished before the end of the second year of the second stage;

2. As regards services connected with capital movements, restricttions shall be abolished concurrently with the liberalization of such movements;

(c) The film industry

Restrictions shall be abolished before the end of the third stage.
However, in States where existing rules restrict the importation of exposed and developed films, the bilateral quotas existing between Member States at the time of the entry into force of the Treaty shall, before the end of the first stage, be increased by one third;

(d) Agricultural and horticultural services

1. Restrictions shall be abolished before the end of the second year of the second stage in respect of:
- technical assistance;
- spraying, weed killing and pest control; pruning; picking, packing and presentation; the operation of irrigation systems and the letting out for hire of agricultural machinery;

2. As regards soil cultivation and tillage, reaping and harvesting, threshing, baling and collecting, whether by mechanical or non-mechanical means, restrictions shall be abolished before the end of the second stage;

3. As regards service other than those specified above, abolition of restrictions shall take place before the end of the third stage;

(e) Public works contracts

1. In the case of services provided by a national or company or firm of a Member State under a public works contract awarded by another State, or by its regional or local authorities such as Länder, regions, provinces, departments, communes or other legal persons governed by public law still to be determined, the date for the abolition of restrictions shall be 31 December 1963, subject, however, to the provisions set out below, which take into account the particular nature and requirements of this sector and are intended to ensure that restrictions are lifted in a progressive and balanced manner and that the removal of restrictions is accompanied by appropriate measures for the coordination of procedures:

a) When the value of the public works contracts awarded in one Member State to nationals or companies or firms of other Member States by that State, by its regional or local authorities or by other legal persons governed by public law, determined as above, exceeds a specified quota, that State shall be intitled to order that no further contracts may be awarded to such nationals or companies or firms until the end of the year in question.

This quota shall correspond to a specific percentage of the average total annual value of the public works contracts awarded during the preceding two years, the percentage to be in principle the same for all Member States and to rise every two years from 31 December 1963 to 31 December 1969,

Furthermore, the value of public works contracts which nationals and companies or firms of one Member States, established in that State, obtain in other Member States shall, save where there is good reason to the contrary, also be taken into account.

b) 'Public works contracts awarded in one Member State to nationals or companies or firms of other Member States' means:
- contracts awarded directly to such nationals and companies or firms established in other Member States; and
- contracts awarded to such nationals and companies or firms through their agencies or branches established in the Member State concerned.

Each Member State shall take all measures necessary to enable it to determine and periodically to make known the value of public works contracts awarded to nationals and companies or firms of other Member States.

2. Restrictions on the provision of services under public works contracts awarded by legal persons governed by public law which as at 31 December 1963 have not been included among those referred to in the first subparagraph of paragraph 1 are to be abolished before the end of the transitional period.

Title VI: Mutual recognition of diplomas and other evidence of formal qualifications - coordination

Subject to Article 57 (3) of the Treaty and to Title V of this General Programme, when Directives implementing the General Programme for each kind of provision of services are being drawn up, it shall at the same time be examined whether the lifting of restrictions on freedom to provide services should be preceded, accompanied or followed by the mutual recognition of diplomas, certificates and other evidence of formal qualifications, or by the coordination of provisions laid down by law, Regulation or administrative action in respect of the provision of such services.

Pending such mutual recognition of diplomas, or such coordination, and in order to facilitate the provision of services and to avoid distortions, a transitional system may be applied; such system may where appropriate include provision for the production of a certificate establishing that the activity in question was actually and lawfully carried on in the country of origin.

The duration and details of this transitional system shall be settled when the Directives are drawn up.

Done at Brussels, 18 December 1961.

For the Council

The President

Ludwig ERHARD

30. Council Directive

of 21 May 1973

on the abolition of restrictions on movement and residence within the
Community for nationals of Member States with regard to establishment
and the provision of services
(73/148/EEC)

(OJ No L 172, 28 June 1973, p.14)

THE COUNCIL OF THE EUROPEAN COMMUNITIES

Having regard to the Treaty establishing the European Economic Community, and in particular Article 54(2) and Article 63(2) thereof;

Having regard to the General Programme for the abolition of restrictions
on freedom of establishment and freedom to provide services, and in
particular Title II thereof;

Having regard to the proposal from the Commission;

Having regard to the Opinion of the European Parliament;

Having regard to the Opinion of the Economic and Social Committee;

Whereas freedom of movement of persons as provided for in the Treaty
and the General Programmes for the abolition of restrictions on freedom of establishment and on freedom to provide services entails the
abolition of restrictions on movement and residence within the Community for nationals of Member States wishing to establish themselves or
to provide services within the territory of another Member State;

Whereas freedom of establishment can be fully attained only if a
right of permanent residence is granted to the persons who are to enjoy freedom of establishment; whereas freedom to provide services
entails that persons providing and receiving services should have the
right of residence for the time during which the services are being
provided;

Whereas the Council Directive of 25 February 1964 on the abolition of
restrictions on movement and residence within the Community for nationals of Member States with regard to establishment and the provision
of services laid down the rules applicable in this area to activities
as self-employed persons;

Whereas Council Directive of 15 October 1968 on the abolition of restrictions on movement and residence within the Community for workers
of Member States and their families, which replaced the Directive of
25 March 1964 bearing the same title, has in the meantime amended the
rules applicable to employed persons;

Whereas the provisions concerning movement and residence within the
Community of self-employed persons and their families should likewise
be improved;

234

Whereas the coordination of special measures concerning the movement and residence of foreign nationals, justified on grounds of public policy, public security or public health, is already the subject of the Council Directive of 25 February 1964;

HAS ADOPTED THIS DIRECTIVE:

Article 1

1. The Member States shall, acting as provided in this Directive, abolish restrictions on the movement and residence of:
(a) nationals of a Member States who are established or who wish to establish themselves in another Member State in order to pursue activities as self-employed persons, or who wish to provide services in that State;

(b) nationals of Member States wishing to go to another Member State as recipients of services;

(c) the spouse and the children under twenty-one years of age of such nationals, irrespective of their nationality;

(d) the relatives in the ascending and descending lines of such nationals and of the spouse of such nationals, which relatives are dependent on them, irrespective of their nationality;

2. Member States shall favour the admission of any other member of the family of a national referred to in paragraph 1 (a) or (b) or of the spouse of that national, which member is dependent on that national or spouse of that national or who in the country of origin was living under the same roof.

Article 2

1. Member States shall grant the persons referred to in Article 1 the right to leave their territory. Such right shall be exercised simply on production of a valid identity card or passport. Members of the family shall enjoy the same right as the national on whom they are dependent.

2. Member States shall, acting in accordance with their laws, issue to their nationals, or renew, an identity card or passport, which shall state in particular the holder's nationality.

3. The passport must be valid at least for all Member States and for countries through which the holder must pass when travelling between Member States. Where a passport is the only document on which the holder may lawfully leave the country its period of validity shall be not less than five years.

4. Member States may not demand from the persons referred to in Article 1 any exit visa or any equivalent requirement.

Article 3

1. Member States shall grant to the persons referred to in Article 1 right to enter their territory merely on production of a valid identity

235

card or passport.

2. No entry visa or equivalent requirements may be demanded save in respect of members of the family who do have the nationality of a Member State. Member States shall afford to such persons every facility for obtaining any necessary visas.

Article 4.

1. Each Member State shall grant the right of permanent residence to nationals of other Member States who establish themselves within its territory in order to pursue activities as self-employed persons, when the restrictions on these activities have been abolished pursuant to the Treaty.

As proof of the right of residence, a document entitled 'Residence Permit for a National of a Member State of the European Communities' shall be issued. This document shall be valid for not less than five years from the date of issue and shall be automatically renewable.

Breaks in residence not exceeding six consecutive months and absence on military service shall not affect the validity of a residence permit.

A valid residence permit may not be withdrawn from a national referred to in Article 1 (1)(a) solely on the grounds that he is no longer in employment because he is temporarily incapable of work as a result of illness or accident.

Any national of a Member State who is not specified in the first subparagraph but who is authorized under the laws of another Member State to pursue an activity within its territory shall be granted a right of abode for a period not less than that of the authorization granted for the pursuit of the activity in question.

However, any national referred to in subparagraph 1 and to whom the provisions of the preceding subparagraph apply as a result of a change of employment shall retain his residence permit until the date on which it expires.

2. The right of residence for persons providing and receiving services shall be of equal duration with the period during which the services are provided.

Where such period exceeds three months, the Member State in the territory of which the services are performed shall issue a right of abode as proof of the right of residence.

Where the period does not exceed three months, the identity card or passport with which the person concerned entered the territory shall be sufficient to cover his stay. The Member State may, however, require the person concerned to report his presence in the territory.

3. A member of the family who is not a national of a Member State shall be issued with a residence document which shall have the same validity as that issued to the national on whom he is dependent.

Article 5

The right of residence shall be effective throughout the territory of the Member State concerned.

Article 6

An applicant for a residence permit or right of abode shall not be required by a Member State to produce anything other than the following,

namely:
(a) the identity card or passport with which he or she entered its territory;
(b) proof that he or she comes within one of the classes of person referred to in Articles 1 and 4.

Article 7

1. The residence documents granted to nationals of a Member State shall be issued and renewed free of charge or on payment of an amount not exceeding the dues and taxes charged for the issue of identity cards to nationals. These provisions shall also apply to documents and certificates required for the issue and renewal of such residence documents.

2. The visas referred to in Article 3 (2) shall be free of charge.

Article 8

Member States shall not derogate from the provisions of this Directive save on grounds of public policy, public security or public health.

Article 9

1. Member States shall, within six months of notification of this Directive, bring into force the measures necessary to comply with its provisions and shall forthwith inform the Commission thereof.

2. They shall notify the Commission of amendments made to provisions imposed by law, regulation or administrative action for the simplification with regard to establishment and the provision of services of the formalities and procedure for issuing such documents as are still necessary for the movement and residence of persons referred to in Article 1.

Article 10

1. The Council Directive of 25 February 1964 on the abolition of restrictions on movement and residence within the Community for nationals of Member States with regard to establishment and the provision of services shall remain applicable until this Directive is implemented by the Member States.

2. Residence documents issued pursuant to the Directive referred to in paragraph 1 shall remain valid until the date on which they next expire.

Article 11

This Directive is addressed to the Member States.

Done at Brussels, 21 May 1973.

For the Council

The President

E. GLINNE

237

to facilitate the effective exercise by lawyers of freedom to provide
services

(77/249/EEC)

(OJ No 278, 26 March 1977, p 17)

THE COUNCIL OF THE EUROPEAN COMMUNITIES

Having regard to the Treaty establishing the European Economic Community, and in particular Articles 57 and 66 thereof,

Having regard to the proposal from the Commission,

Having regard to the opinion of the European Parliament,

Having regard to the opinion of the Economic and Social Committee,

Whereas, pursuant to the Treaty, any restriction on the provision of
services which is based on nationality or on conditions of residence has
been prohibited since the end of the transitional period;
　Whereas this Directive deals only with measures to facilitate the
effective pursuit of the activities of lawyers by way of provision of
services; whereas more detailed measures will be necessary to facilitate
the effective exercise of the right of establishment;
　Whereas if lawyers are to exercise effectively the freedom to provide services host Member States must recognize as lawyers those persons
practising the profession in the various Member States;
　Whereas, since this Directive solely concerns provision of services
and does not contain provisions on the mutual recognition of diplomas,
a person to whom the Directive applies must adopt the professional
title used in the Member State in which he is established, hereinafter
referred to as 'the Member State from which he comes',

HAS ADOPTED THIS DIRECTIVE:

Article 1

1. This Directive shall apply, within the limits and under the conditions laid down herein, to the activities of lawyers pursued by way
of provision of services.
　Notwithstanding anything contained in this Directive, Member States
may reserve to prescribed categories of lawyers the preparation of
formal documents for obtaining title to administer estates of deceased
persons, and the drafting of formal documents creating or transferring
interests in land.

2. 'Lawyer' means any person entitled to pursue his professional activities under one of the following designations:

Belgium	– Avocat – Advocaat
Denmark	– Advokat
Germany	– Rechtsanwalt
France	– Avocat

Ireland	– Barrister
	– Solicitor
Italy	– Avvocado
Luxembourg	– Avocat-avoué
Netherlands	– Advocaat
United Kingdom	– Advocate
	– Barrister
	– Solicitor

Article 2

Each Member State shall recognize as a lawyer for the purpose of pursuing the activities specified in Article 1 (1) any person listed in
paragraph 2 of that Article.

Article 3

A person referred to in Article 1 shall adopt the professional title
used in the Member State from which he comes, expressed in the language
or one of the languages of that State, with an indication of the professional organization by which he is authorized to practise or the
court of law before which he is entitled to practise pursuant to the
laws of that State.

Article 4

1. Activities relating to the representation of a client in legal proceedings or before public authorities shall be pursued in each host
Member State under the conditions laid down for lawyers established in
that State, with the exception of any conditions requiring residence,
or registration with a professional organization, in that State.

2. A lawyer pursuing these activities shall observe the rules of professional conduct of the host Member State, without prejudice to his
obligations in the Member State from which he comes.

3. When these activities are pursued in the United Kingdom, 'rules of
professional conduct of the host Member State' means the rules of professional conduct applicable to solicitors, where such activities are
not reserved for barristers and advocates. Otherwise the rules of professional conduct applicable to the latter shall apply. However,
barristers from Ireland shall always be subject to the rules of professional conduct applicable in the United Kingdom to barristers and
advocates.
    When these activities are pursued in Ireland 'rules of professional
conduct of the host Member State' means, in so far as they govern the
oral presentation of a case in court, the rules of professional conduct applicable to barristers. In all other cases the rules of professional conduct applicable to solicitors shall apply. However,
barristers and advocates from the United Kingdom shall alway be subject
to the rules of professional conduct applicable in Ireland to barristers.

4. A lawyer pursuing activities other than those referred to in paragraph 1 shall remain subject to the conditions and rules of professional conduct of the Member State from which he comes without prejudice
to respect for the rules, whatever their source, which govern the
profession in the host Member State, especially those concerning the
incompatibility of the exercise of the activities of a lawyer with the

239

exercise of other activities in that State, professional secrecy, relations with other lawyers, the prohibition on the same lawyer acting
for parties with mutually conflicting interests, and publicity. The
latter rules are applicable only if they are capable of being observed
by a lawyer who is not established in the host Member State and to the
extent to which their observance is objectively justified to ensure
in that State the proper exercise of a lawyer's activities, the standing
of the profession and respect for the rules concerning incompatibility.

Article 5.

For the pursuit of activities relating to the representation of a client
in legal proceedings, a Member State may require lawyers to whom Article 1 applies:

- to be introduced, in accordance with local rules or customs, to the
  presiding judge and, where appropriate, to the President of the
  relevant Bar in the host Member State;

- to work in conjunction with a lawyer who practices before the judicial authority in question and who would, where necessary, be answer-
  able to that authority, or with an 'avoué' or 'procuratore' practising
  before it.

Article 6

Any Member State may exclude lawyers who are in the salaried employment of a public or private undertaking from pursuing activities relating to the representation of that undertaking in legal proceedings
in so far as lawyers established in that State are not permitted to
pursue those activities.

Article 7

1. The competent authority of the host Member State may request the
person providing the services to establish his qualifications as a
lawyer.

2. In the event of non-compliance with the obligations referred to in
Article 4 and in force in the host Member State, the competent authority of the latter shall determine in accordance with its own rules and
procedures the consequences of such non-compliance, and to this end
may obtain any appropriate professional information concerning the
person providing services. It shall notify the competent authority of
the Member State from which the person comes of any decision taken.
Such exchanges shall not affect the confidential nature of the information supplied.

Article 8

1. Member States shall bring into force the measures necessary to comply with this Directive within two years of its notification and shall
forthwith inform the Commission thereof.

2. Member States shall communicate to the Commission the texts of the
main provisions of national law which they adopt in the field covered
by this Directive.

Article 9

This Directive is addressed to the Member States.

Done at Brussels, 22 March 1977.

For the Council

The President

Judith HART

32. First Directive

for the implementation of Article 67 of the
Treaty

(JO No 921/60, 12 July 1960; OJ (Special Edition 1959-1962) p. 49)

THE COUNCIL OF THE EUROPEAN ECONOMIC COMMUNITY,

Having regard to the Treaty and in particular Articles 5, 67 (1), 69, 105 (2) and 106 (2) thereof;

Having regard to the proposal from the Commission, which consulted the Monetary Committee for this purpose;

Having regard to the Decision of 11 May 1960 on the application to Algeria and to the French overseas departments of the provisions of the Treaty concerning capital movements;

Whereas the attainment of the objectives of the Treaty establishing the European Economic Community requires the greatest possible freedom of movement of capital between Member States and therefore the widest and most speedy liberalisation of capital movements;

HAS ADOPTED THIS DIRECTIVE:

Article 1

1. Member States shall grant all foreign exchange authorizations required for the conclusion or performance of transactions or for transfers between residents of Member States in respect of the capital movements set out in List A of Annex I to this Directive.

2. Member States shall enable such transfers of capital to be made on the basis of the exchange rate ruling for payments relating to current transactions.
   Where such transfers are made on a foreign exchange market on which the fluctuations of exchange rates are not officially restricted, this

obligation shall be taken to mean that the exchange rates applied must not show any appreciable and lasting differences from those ruling for payments relating to current transactions.

The monetary Committee shall watch closely the trend of exchange rates applied to such transfers of capital, and shall report thereon to the Commission. If the Commission finds that these rates show appreciable and lasting differences from those ruling for payments relating to current transactions, it shall initiate the procedure provided for in Article 169 of the Treaty.

Article 2

1. Member States shall grant general permission for the conclusion or performance of transactions and for transfers between residents of Member States in respect of the capital movements set out in List B of Annex I to this Directive.

2. Where such transfers of capital are made on a foreign exchange market on which the fluctuations of exchange rates are not officially restricted, Member States shall endeavour to ensure that transfers are made at rates which do not show appreciable and lasting differences from those ruling for payments relating to current transactions.

The Commission may, after consulting the Monetary Committee, make recommendations in this connection to the Member States.
.....

Article 3

1. Subject to paragraph 2 of this Article, Member States shall grant all foreign exchange authorizations required for the conclusion or performance of transactions and for transfers between residents of Member States in respect of the capital movements set out in List C of Annex I to this Directive.

2. Where such free movement of capital might form an obstacle to the achievement of the economic policy objectives of a Member State, the latter may maintain or reintroduce the exchange restrictions on capital movements which were operative on the date of entry into force of this Directive. (in the case of new Member States, the date of accession)(Amended by Directive 63/21/EEC and the First and Second Accession Treaties). It shall consult the Commission on the matter.

The Commission shall examine the measures for co-ordinating the economic policies of Member States which will enable these difficulties to be overcome and, after consulting the Monetary Committee, shall recommend their adoption by the Member States.

3. The Commission may recommend that the State in question abolishes the exchange restrictions which are maintained or reintroduced.

Article 4

The Monetary Committee shall examine at least once a year the restrictions which are applied to the capital movements set out in the lists contained in Annex I to this Directive; it shall report to the Commission regarding restrictions which could be abolished.

Article 5

1. The provisions of this Directive shall not restrict the right of Member States to verify the nature and genuineness of transactions or transfers, or to take all requisite measures to prevent infringements of their laws and regulations.

2. Member States shall simplify as far as possible the authorization and control formalities applicable to the conclusion or performance of transactions and transfers and shall where necessary consult one another with a view to such simplifications.

3. The restrictions on capital movements under the rules for establishment in a Member State shall be abolished pursuant to this Directive only in so far as it is incumbent upon the Member States to grant freedom of establishment in implementation of Articles 52 and 58 of the Treaty.

Article 6

Member States shall endeavour not to introduce within the Community any new exchange restrictions affecting the capital movements that were liberalized at the date of entry into force of this Directive (in the case of new Member States, the date of Accession nor to make existing provisions more restrictive.

Article 7

Member States shall make known to the Commission, not later than three months after the entry into force of this Directive (in the case of new Member States, the date of Accession):

(a) the provisions governing capital movements at the date of entry into force of this Directive which are laid down by law, regulation and administrative action;

(b) the provisions adopted in pursuance of the Directive;

(c) the procedures for implementing those provisions.

They shall also make known, not later than the time of entry into force thereof, any new measures going beyond the obligations of this Directive, and any amendment of the provisions governing the capital movements set out in List D of Annex I to this Directive.

Article 8

Deleted

Article 9

This Directive shall apply without prejudice to the provisions of Articles 67 (2), 68 (3) and 221 of the Treaty.

Article 10

Lists A, B, C and D contained in Annex I, together with the Nomenclature of Capital Movements and the Explanatory Notes in Annex II, form an

243

integral part of this Directive.

Done at Luxembourg, 11 May 1960.

For the Council

The Secretary-General   The President

CALMES   Eugène SCHAUS

(Amended by Directive 63/21/EEC and the Fist and Second Accession
Treaties)

ANNEX II

NOMENCLATURE OF CAPITAL MOVEMENTS

I. Direct investments

A. Direct investments on national territory by non-residents

1. Establishment and extension of branches or new undertakings belonging solely to the person providing the capital, and the acquisition in
full of existing undertakings

2. Participation in new or existing undertakings with a view to establishing or maintaining lasting economic links

3. Long-term loans with a view to establishing or maintaining lasting
economic links

4. Reinvestments of profits with a view to maintaining lasting economic
links

B. Direct investments abroad by residents

1. Establishment and extension of branches or new undertakings belonging solely to the person providing the capital, and the acquisition
in full of existing undertakings

2. Participation in new or existing undertakings with a view to
establishing or maintaining lasting economic links

3. Long-term loans with a view to establishing or maintaining lasting
economic links

4. Reinvestment of profits with a view to maintaining lasting economic
links.

II. Liquidation of direct investments

A. Repatriation of the proceeds of liquidation of direct investments on national territory by non-residents

1. Principal

2. Capital appreciation

B. Use of the proceeds of liquidation of direct investments abroad by residents

1. Principal

2. Capital appreciation

III. Admission of securities to the capital market

A. Admission of securities of a domestic undertaking to a foreign capital market

1. Introduction on a foreign stock exchange:
   (a) of shares and other securities of a participating nature;
   (b) of bonds:
       (i) denominated in national currency;
       (ii) denominated in foreign currency.

2. Issue and placing on a foreign capital market:
   (a) of shares and other securities of a participating nature;
   (b) of bonds:
       (i) denominated in national currency;
       (ii) denominated in foreign currency.

B. Admission of securities of a foreign undertaking to a domestic capital market

1. Introduction on a domestic stock exchange:
   (a) of shares and other securities of a participating nature;
   (b) of bonds:
       (i) denominated in national currency;
       (ii) denominated in foreign currency.

2. Issue and placing on a domestic capital market:
   (a) of shares and other securities of a participating nature;
   (b) of bonds:
       (i) denominated in national currency;
       (ii) denominated in foreign currency.

C. Admission of domestic securities of the public sector to a foreign capital market pursuant to Article 68 (3) of the Treaty

1. Introduction of securities on a foreign stock exchange:
   (a) denominated in national currency;
   (b) denominated in foreign currency.

2. Issue and placing of securities on a foreign capital market:

(a) denominated in national currency;
(b) denominated in foreign currency.

D. Admission of foreign securities of the public sector to a domestic capital market pursuant to Article 68 (3) of the Treaty

1. Introduction of securities on a domestic stock exchange:
(i) denominated in national currency;
(ii) denominated in foreign currency.

2. Issue and placing of securities on a domestic capital market:
(i) denominated in national currency;
(ii) denominated in foreign currency.

IV. Operations in securities (not included under I, II or III)

A. Acquisition by non-residents of domestic securities dealt in on a stock exchange and repatriation of the proceeds of liquidation thereof

(a) quoted;
(b) unquoted.

1. Acquisition of shares and other securities of a participating nature.

2. Repatriation of the proceeds of liquidation of shares and other securities of a participating nature.

3. Acquisition of bonds:
(i) denominated in national currency;
(ii) denominated in foreign currency.

4. Repatriation of the proceeds of liquidation of bonds.

B. Acquisition by residents of foreign securities dealt in on a stock exchange and use of the proceeds of liquidation thereof

(a) quoted;
(b) unquoted.

1. Acquisition of shares and other securities of a participating nature.

2. Use of the proceeds of liquidation of shares and other securities of a participating nature.

3. Acquisition of bonds:
(i) denominated in national currency;
(ii) denominated in foreign currency.

4. Use of the proceeds of liquidation of bonds.

C. Acquistion by non-residents of domestic securities not dealt in on a stock exchange and repatriation of the proceeds of liquidation thereof

1. Acquisition of shares and other securities of a participating nature.

2. Repatriation of the proceeds of liquidation of shares and other securities of a participating nature.

3. Acquisition of bonds:
   (i) denominated in national currency;
   (ii) denominated in foreign currency.

4. Repatriation of the proceeds of liquidation of bonds.

D. Acquisition by residents of foreign securities not dealt in on a stock exchange and use of the proceeds of liquidation thereof

1. Acquisition of shares and other securities of a participating nature.

2. Use of the proceeds of liquidation of shares and other securities of a participating nature.

3. Acquisition of bonds:
   (i) denominated in national currency;
   (ii) denominated in foreign currency.

4. Use of the proceeds of liquidation of bonds.

E. Physical movements of securities

1. Belonging to non-residents:
   (a) import;
   (b) export.

2. Belonging to residents:
   (a) import;
   (b) export.

V. Investments in real estate (not included under I and II)

A. Investments in real estate on national territory by non-residents and repatriation of the proceeds of liquidation thereof

1. Acquistiom of real estate.
2. Repatriation of the proceeds of liquidation of real estate.

B. Investments in real estate abroad by residents and use of the proceeds of liquidation thereof

1. Acquisition of real estate.

2. Use of the proceeds of liquidation of real estate.

VI. Short-term investments in Treasury bills and other
    securities normally dealt in on the money market

1. denominated in national currency.

2. denominated in foreign currency.

A. Short-term investments by non-residents on a domestic money market
   and repatriation of the proceeds of liquidation thereof.

(a) by natural persons   )
(b) by legal persons   ) other than financial institutions

(c) by financial institutions

B. Short-term investments by residents on a foreign money market and use
   of the proceeds of liquidation thereof

(a) by natural persons   )
(b) by legal perons   ) other than financial institutions

(c) by financial institutions

VII. Granting and repayment of credits related to commercial
     transactions or to provision of services

1. In which a resident is participating.

2. In which no resident is participating.

A. Credits granted by non-residents to residents:
   (i) short-term (less than one year);
   (ii) medium-term (from one to five years);
   (iii) long-term (five years or more);

(a) by natural persons   )
(b) by financial institutions) other than financial institutions

(c) by financial institutions.

B. Credits granted by residents to non-residents:
   (i) short-term (less than one year)
   (ii) medium-term (from one to five years);
   (iii) long-term (five years or more);

(a) by natural persons)
(b) by legal persons   ) other than financial institutions

(c) by financial institutions.

VIII. Granting and repayment of loans and credits not re-
      lated to commercial transactions or to provision of
      services

      (not included under I and X)

248

A. Loans and credits granted by non-residents to residents;

    (i) short-term (less than one year);
    (ii) medium-term (from one to five years);
    (iii) long-term (five years or more);

(a) by natural persons)
(b) by legal persons   ) other than financial institutions

(c) by financial institutions.

B. Loans and credits granted by residents to non-residents:

    (i) short-term (less than one year);
    (ii) medium-term (from one to five years);
    (iii) long-term (five years or more);

(a) by natural persons)
(b) by legal persons   ) other than financial institutions

(c) by financial institutions.

IX. Opening and placing of funds on current or deposit accounts, repatriation or use of balances on current or deposit accounts with credit institutions

A. By non-residents with domestic credit institutions

1. Accounts and balances in national currency.

(2) Accounts and balances in foreign currency:

    (a) by natural persons)
    (b) by legal persons   ) other than financial institutions

    (c) by financial institutions.

B. By residents with foreign credit institutions

1. Accounts and balances in national currency.

2. Accounts and balances in foreign currency:

    (a) by natural persons)
    (b) by legal persons   ) other than financial institutions

    (c) by financial institutions

X. Personal capital movements
(not covered by the other sections)

A. Loans

1. Loans granted by non-residents to residents.

2. Loans granted by residents to non-residents.

B. Gifts and endowments

C. Dowries

D. Inheritances

E. Settlement of debts in their country of origin by immigrants

F. Transfers of capital belonging to residents who emigrate and are

    1. Nationals of the country in question
    2. Nationals of other countries.

G. Transfers of capital belonging to emigrants returning to their country of origin

H. Transfers of workers' savings during their period of stay

I. Transfers by instalment of blocked funds belonging to non-residents by the holders of such funds in the case of special hardship

L. Annual transfers of blocked funds to another Member State by a non-resident account-holder, up to an amount or a percentage of the total assets, fixed uniformly by the Member State concerned for all applicants

M. Transfers of minor amounts abroad.

XI. Transfers in performance of insurance contracts

A. Premiums and payments in respect of life insurance

    1. Contracts concluded between domestic life assurance companies and non-residents.
    2. Contracts concluded between foreign life assurance companies and residents.

B. Premiums and payments in respect of credit insurance

    1. Contracts concluded between domestic credit insurance companies and non-residents.
    2. Contracts concluded between foreign credit insurance companies and residents.

C. Other capital transfers in respect of insurance contracts

XII. Sureties, other guarantees and pledges and transfers connected with them

A. Granted by non-residents to residents

B. Granted by residents to non-residents

XIII. Import and export of financial assets

A. Securities (not included under IV) and means of payment of all kinds.

B. Gold

XIV. Other capital movements

A. Death duties

B. Damages (where these can be considered as capital)

C. Refunds in the case of cancellation of contracts and refunds of uncalled-for payments (where these can be considered as capital)

D. Author's royalties.
   Patents, designs, trade marks and inventions (assignments and trans- fers arising out of such assignments)

E. Transfers of the moneys required for the provision of services (not included in Category IX)

F. Miscellaneous.

Explanatory notes

For the purpose of this Nomenclature the following expressions have the meanings assigned to them respectively:

Direct investments

Investments of all kinds by natural persons or commercial, industrial or financial undertakings, and which serve to establish or to maintain lasting and direct links between the person providing the capital and the entrepreneur to whom or the undertaking to which the capital is made available in order to carry on an economic activity. This concept must therefore be understood in its widest sense.
   The undertakings mentioned under 1 include legally independent un- dertakings (wholly owned subsidiaries) and branches.
   As regards those undertakings mentioned under 2 which have the status of companies limited by shares, there is participation in the nature of direct investment where the block of shares held by a natural person or another undertaking or any other holder, enables the share- holder, either pursuant to the provisions of national laws relating to companies limited by shares or otherwise, to participate effectively in the management of the company or in its control.
   Long-term loans of a participating nature, mentioned under 3, means loans for a period of more than five years which are made for the pur- pose of establishing or maintaining lasting economic links. The main examples which may be cited are loans granted by a company to its subsidiaries or to companies in which it has a share and loans linked with a profit-sharing arrangement. Loans granted by financial institut- ions with a view to establishing or maintaining lasting economic links are also included under this heading.

Residents or non-residents

Natural and legal persons according to the definitions laid down in the exchange control regulations in force in each Member State.

Proceeds of liquidation (of investments, securities, etc.)

Proceeds of sales, amount of repayments, proceeds of execution of judgments, etc.

Introcution on a stock exchange

The admission of securities in accordance with a specified procedure to dealings on a stock exchange, whether controlled officially or unofficially, and their admission to public sale.

Securities dealt in on a stock exchange (quoted or unquoted)

Securities the dealing in which are controlled by regulations, and prices for which are regularly published, either by official stock exchanges (quoted securities) or by other bodies attacked to a stock exchange, e.g. committees of banks (unquoted securities).

Placing of securities

The direct sale of securities by the issue, or sale thereof by the consortium which the issuer has instructed to sell them.

Operations in securities

Any dealings in securities, including the initial sale of units by unit trusts.

Domestic or foreign securities

Securities according to the country in which the issuer has his principal place of business.

Shares

Include rights to subscribe for new issues of shares.

Bonds (under IV of the Nomenclature)

Bonds issued by public or private bodies.

Investments in real estate

Purchases of buildings and land and the contruction of buildings by private persons for gain or personal use. This category does not include loans secured by mortgages but it does include rights of usufruct, easement and building rights.

Natural or legal person

As defined by the national rules.

Financial institutions

Banks, savings banks and institutions specialising in the provision of

252

short- medium- and long-term credit, and insurance companies, building societies, investment companies and other institutions of like character.

Credit institutions

Banks, savings banks and institutions specialising in the provision of short- medium- and long-term credit.

Chapter Five

POLICY OF THE COMMUNITY

1. Regulation No 17/62/EEC[1] of the Council

of 6 February 1962

First Regulation implementing Articles 85 and 86 of the Treaty modified and completed by Regulation 59/62/EEC[2], by Regulation 118/63/EEC[3], by Regulation 2822/71/EEC[4] and amended by the Act of Accession[5] and the Act of Accession of the Hellenic Republic[6].

THE COUNCIL OF THE EUROPEAN ECONOMIC COMMUNITY,

Having regard to the Treaty establishing the European Economic Community, and in particular Article 87 thereof;
    Having regard to the proposal from the Commission;
    Having regard to the Opinion of the Economic and Social Committee;
    Having regard to the Opinion of the European Parliament;
    Whereas, in order to establish a system ensuring that competition shall not be distorted in the common market, it is necessary to provide for balanced application of Articles 85 and 86 in a uniform manner in the Member States;
    Whereas in establishing the rules for applying Article 85 (3) account must be taken of the need to ensure effective supervision and to simplify administration to the gratest possible extent;
    Whereas it is accordingly necessary to make it obligatory, as a general principle, for undertakings which seek application of Article 85 (3) to notify to the Commission their agreements, decisions and concerted practices;
    Whereas, on the one hand, such agreements, decisions and concerted practices are probably very numerous and cannot therefore all be examined at the same time and, on the other hand, some of them have special features which may make them less prejudicial to the development of the common market;
    Whereas there is consequently a need to make more flexible arrangements for the time being in respect of certain categories of agreement, decision and concerted practice without prejudging their validity under Article 85;
    Whereas it may be in the interest of undertakings to know whether any agreements, decisions or practices to which they are party, or propose to become party, may lead to action on the part of the Commission pursuant to Article 85 (1) or Article 86;
    Whereas in order to secure uniform application of Articles 85 and 86 in the common market, rules must be made under which the Commission acting in close and constant liaison with the competent authorities of the Member States, may take the requisite measures for applying those Articles;
    Whereas for this purpose the Commission must have the co-operation of the competent authorities of the Member States and be empowered, throughout the common market, to require such information to be supplied and to undertake such investigations as are necessary to bring to light any agreement, decision or concerted practice prohibited by Article 85(1) or any abuse of a dominant position prohibited by Article 86;
    Whereas, in order to carry out its duty of ensuring that the pro-

254

visions of the Treaty are applied, the Commission must be empowered to address to undertakings or associations of undertakings recommendations and decisions for the purpose of bringing to an end infringements of Articles 85 and 86;

Whereas compliance with Articles 85 and 86 and the fulfilment of obligations imposed on undertakings and associations of under- takings under this Regulation must be enforceable by means of fines and periodic penalty payments;

Whereas undertakings concerned must be accorded the right to be heard by the Commission, third parties whose interests may be affected by a decision must be given the opportunity of submitting their comments beforehand, and it must be ensured that wide publicity is given to decisions taken;

Whereas all decisions taken by the Commission under this Regulation are subject to review by the Court of Justice under the conditions specified in the Treaty; whereas, it is moreover desirable to confer upon the Court of Justice, pursuant to Article 172, unlimited juris- diction in respect of decisions under which the Commission imposes fines or periodic penalty payments;

Whereas this Regulation may enter into force without prejudice to any other provisions that may hereafter be adopted pursuant to Article 87;

HAS ADOPTED THIS REGULATION:

Art.1. *Basic provision.* Without prejudice to Articles 6, 7 and 23 of this Regulation, decisions and concerted practices of the kind described in Article 85(1) of the Treaty and the abuse of a dominant position in the market, within the meaning of Article 86 of the Treaty, shall be prohibited, no prior decision to that effect being required.

Art.2. *Negative clearance.* Upon application by the undertakings or associations of undertakings concerned, the Commission may certify that, on the basis of the facts in its possession, there are no grounds under Article 85(1) or Article 86 of the Treaty for action on its part in respect of an agreement, decision or practice.

Art.3. *Termination of Infringements.* 1. Where the Commission, upon application or upon its own initiative, finds that there is infringe- ment of Article 85 or Article 86 of the Treaty, it may by decision require the undertakings or associations of undertakings concerned to bring such an infringement to an end.

2. Those entitled to make application are:
   (a) Member States;
   (b) natural or legal persons who claim a legitimate interest.

3. Without prejudice to the other provisions of this Regulation, the Commission may, before taking a decision under paragraph 1, address to the undertakings or associations of undertakings concerned recommendations for termination of the infringement.

Art. 4. *Notification of new agreements, decisions and practices.*

1. Agreements, decisions and concerted practices of the kind described in Article 85 (1) of the Treaty which come into existence after the entry into force of this Regulation and in respect of which the parties seek application of Article 85(3) must be notified to the Commission. Until they have been notified, no decision in application of Article 85(3) may be taken.

2. Paragraph 1 shall not apply to agreements, decisions and[7] concerted practices where:

(1) the only parties thereto are undertakings from one Member State and the agreements, decisions or practices do not relate either to imports or to exports between Member States;

(2) not more than two undertakings are party thereto, and the agreements only:

(a) restrict the freedom of one party to the contract in determining the prices or conditions of business upon which the goods which he has obtained from the other party to the contract may be resold; or

(b) impose restrictions on the exercise of the rights of the assignee or user of industrial property rights - in particular patents, utility models, designs or trade marks - or of the person entitled under a contract to the assignment, or grant, of the right to use a method of manufacture or knowledge relating to the use and to the application of industrial processes;

(3) they have as their sole object:

(a) the development or uniform application of standards or types; or

(b) joint research and development[8],

(c) specialisation in the manufacture of products, including agreements necessary for achieving this,

- where the products which are the subject of specialisation do not, in a substantial part of the Common Market, represent more than 15% of the volume of business done in identical products or those considered by consumers to be similar by reason of their characteristics, price and use, and

- where the total annual turnover of the participating under-takings does not exceed 200 million units of account.

These agreements, decisions and practices may be notified to the Commission.[9]

Art. 5. *Notification of existing agreements, decisions and practices.*

1. Agreements, decisions and concerted practices of the kind described in Article 85(1) of the Treaty which are in existence at the date of entry into force of this Regulation and in respect of which the parties seek application of Article 85(3) shall be notified to the Commission before 1 November 1962. However notwithstanding the foregoing provisions any agreements, decisions and concerted practices to which not more than two undertakings are party shall be notified before 1 February 1963[10].

2. Paragraph 1 shall not apply to agreements, decisions or con-certed practices falling within Article 4(2); these may be notified to the Commission.

Art. 6. *Decisions pursuant to Article 85(3).* 1. Whenever the Commission takes a decision pursuant to Article 85(3) of the Treaty, it shall specify therein the date from which the decision shall take effect. Such date shall not be earlier than the date of notification.

2. The second sentence of paragraph 1 shall not apply to agreements, decisions or concerted practices falling within Article 4(2) and Article 5 (2), nor to those falling within Article 5(1) which have been notified within the time limit specified in Article 5(1).

Art. 7. *Special provisions for existing agreements, decisions and practices.* 1. Where agreements, decisions and concerted practices in existence at the date of entry into force of this Regulation and notified within the time limits specified in Article 5(1) do not satisfy the requirements of Article 85(3) of the Treaty and the under-takings or associations of undertakings concerned cease to give effect to them or modify them in such manner that they no longer fall within the prohibition contained in Article 85(1) or that they satisfy the requirements of Article 83(3), the prohibition contained in Article 85(1) shall apply only for a period fixed by the Commission. A decision by the Commission pursuant to the foregoing sentence shall not apply as against undertakings and associations of undertakings which did not expressly consent to the notification.

2. Paragraph 1 shall apply to agreements, decisions and concerted practices falling within Article 4(2) which are in existence at the date of entry into force of this Regulation if they are notified before 1 January 1967.[11]

Art. 8. *Duration and revocation of decisions under Article 85(3).*

1. A decision in application of Article 85(3) of the Treaty shall be issued for a specified period and conditions and obligations may be attached thereto.

2. A decision may on application be renewed if the requirements of Article 85(3) of the Treaty continue to be satisfied.

3. The Commission may revoke or amend its decision or prohibit specified acts by the parties:

(a) where there had been a change in any of the facts which were basic to the making of the decision;

(b) where the parties commit a breach of any obligation attached to the decision;

(c) where the decision is based on incorrect information or was induced by deceit;

(d) where the parties abuse the exemption from the provisions of the Treaty granted to them by the decision.

In cases to which subparagraphs (b), (c) or (d) apply, the decision may be revoked with retroactive effect.

Art. 9. *Powers.* 1. Subject to review of its decisions by the Court of Justice, the Commission shall have sole power to declare Article 85(1) inapplicable pursuant to Article 85(3) of the Treaty.

2. The Commission shall have power to apply Article 85(1) and Article 86 of the Treaty; this power may be exercised notwithstanding that the time limits specified in Article 5(1) and in Article 7(2) relating to notification have not expired.

3. As long as the Commission has not initiated any procedure under Articles 2, 3 or 6, the authorities of the Member States shall remain competent to apply Article 85(1) and Article 86 in accordance with Article 88 of the Treaty; they shall remain competent in this respect notwithstanding that the time limits specified in Article 5(1) and in Article 7(2) relating to notification have not expired.

Art. 10. *Liaison with the authorities of the Member States.*

1. The Commission shall forthwith transmit to the competent authorities of the Member States a copy of the applications and notifications together with copies of the most important documents lodged with the Commission for the purpose of establishing the exis-tence of infringements of Articles 85 or 86 of the Treaty or of obtaining negative clearance or a decision in application of Article 85(3).

2. The Commission shall carry out the procedure set out in para-graph 1 in close and constant liaison with the competent authorities of the Member States; such authorities shall have the right to

express their views upon that procedure.

3. An Advisory Committee on Restrictive Practices and Monopolies shall be consulted prior to the taking of any decision following upon a procedure under paragraph 1, and of any decision concerning the renewal, amendment or revocation of a decision pursuant to Article 85(3) of the Treaty.

4. The Advisory Committee shall be composed of officials competent in the matter of restrictive practices and monopolies. Each Member State shall appoint an official to represent it who, if prevented from attending, may be replaced by another official.

5. The consultation shall take place at a joint meeting convened by the Commission; such meeting shall be held not earlier than fourteen days after dispatch of the notice convening it. The notice shall, in respect of each case to be examined, be accompanied by a summary of the case together with an indication of the most important documents, and a preliminary draft decision.

6. The Advisory Committee may deliver an opinion notwithstanding that some of its members or their alternates are not present. A report of the outcome of the consultative proceedings shall be annexed to the draft decision. It shall not be made public.

Art. 11. *Requests for information.* 1. In carrying out the duties assigned to it by Article 89 and by provisions adopted under Article 87 of the Treaty, the Commission may obtain all necessary information from the Governments and competent authorities of the Member States and from undertakings and associations of undertakings.

2. When sending a request for information to an undertaking or association of undertakings, the Commission shall at the same time forward a copy of the request to the competent authority of the Member State in whose territory the seat of the undertaking or association of undertakings is situated.

3. In its request the Commission shall state the legal basis and the purpose of the request and also the penalties provided for in Article 15(1)(b) for supplying incorrect information.

4. The owners of the undertakings or their representatives and, in the case of legal persons, companies or firms, or of associations having no legal personality, the persons authorised to represent them by law or by their constitution shall supply the information requested.

5. Where an undertaking or association of undertakings does not supply the information requested within the time limit fixed by the Commission, or supplies incomplete information, the Commission shall by decision require the information to be supplied. The decision shall specify what information is required, fix an appropriate time limit within which it is to be supplied and indicate the penalties provided for in Article 15(1)(b) and Article 16(1)(c) and the right to have the decision reviewed by the Court of Justice.

6. The Commission shall at the same time forward a copy of its decision to the competent authority of the Member State in whose territory the seat of the undertaking or association of undertakings is situated.

Art. 12. *Inquiry into sectors of the economy.* 1. If in any sector of the economy the trend of trade between Member States, price movements, inflexibility of prices or other circumstances suggest that in the economic sector concerned competition is being restricted or distorted within the common market, the Commission may decide to conduct a general inquiry into that economic sector and in the course thereof may request undertakings in the sector concerned to supply

the information necessary for giving effect to the principles
formulated in Articles 85 and 86 of the Treaty and for
carrying out the duties entrusted to the Commission.

2. The Commission may in particular request every undertaking or
association of undertakings in the economic sector concerned to
communicate to it all agreements, decisions and concerted practices
which are exempt from notification by virtue of Article 4(2) and
Article 5(2).

3. When making inquiries pursuant to paragraph 2, the Commission
shall also request undertakings or groups of undertakings whose size
suggests that they occupy a dominant position within the common
market or a substantial part thereof to supply to the Commission such
particulars of the structure of the undertakings and of their behaviour as are requisite to an appraisal of their position in the light
of Article 86 of the Treaty.

4. Article 10(3) to (6) and Articles 11, 13 and 14 shall apply
correspondingly.

Art. 13. *Investigations by the authorities of the Member States.*
1. At the request of the Commission, the competent authorities of
the Member States shall undertake the investigations which the
Commission considers to be necessary under Article 14(1), or which
it has ordered by decision pursuant to Article 14(3). The officials
of the competent authorities of the Member States responsible for
conducting these investigations shall exercise their powers upon
production of an authorisation in writing issued by the competent
authority of the Member State in whose territory the investigation is
to be made. Such authorisation shall specify the subject matter and
purpose of the investigation.

2. If so requested by the Commission or by the competent
authority of the Member State in whose territory the investigation
is to be made, the officials of the Commission may assist the
officials of such authorities in carrying out their duties.

Art. 14. *Investigating powers of the Commission.* 1. In carrying
out the duties assigned to it in Article 89 and by provisions
adopted under Article 87 of the Treaty, the Commission may undertake
all necessary investigations into undertakings and associations
of undertakings. To this end the officials authorised by the
Commission are empowered:

  (a) to examine the books and other business records;
  (b) to take copies of or extracts from the books and business
records;
  (c) to ask for oral explanations on the spot;
  (d) to enter any premises, land and means of transport of undertakings.

2. The officials of the Commission authorised for the purpose
of these investigations shall exercise their powers on production
of an authorisation in writing specifying the subject matter and
purpose of the investigation and the penalties provided for in
Article 15(1)(c) in cases where production of the required books
or other business records is incomplete. In good time before the
investigation, the Commission shall inform the competent authority
of the Member State in whose territory the same is to be made of
the investigation and of the identity of the authorised officials.

3. Undertakings and associations of undertakings shall submit to
investigations ordered by decision of the Commission. The decision
shall specify the subject matter and purpose of the investigation,
appoint the date on which it is to begin and indicate the penalties

provided for in Article 15(1)(c) and Article 16(1)(d) and the right to have the decision reviewed by the Court of Justice.

4. The Commission shall take decisions referred to in paragraph 3 after consultation with the competent authority of the Member State in whose territory the investigation is to be made.

5. Officials of the competent authority of the Member State in whose territory the investigation is to be made may, at the request of such authority or of the Commission, assist the officials of the Commission in carrying out their duties.

6. Where an undertaking opposes an investigation ordered pursuant to this Article, the Member State concerned shall afford the necessary assistance to the officials authorised by the Commission to enable them to make their investigation. Member States shall, after consultation with the Commission, take the necessary measures to this end before 1 October 1962.

Art. 15. *Fines*. 1. The Commission may by decision impose on undertakings or associations of undertakings fines of from 100 to 5 000 units of account where, intentionally or negligently:

(a) they supply incorrect or misleading information in an application pursuant to Article 2 or in a notification pursuant to Article 4 or 5; or

(b) they supply incorrect information in response to a request made pursuant to Article 11(3) or (5) or to Article 12, or do not supply information within the time limit fixed by a decision taken under Article 11(5); or

(c) they produce the required books or other business records in incomplete form during investigations under Article 13 or 14, or refuse to submit to an investigation ordered by decision issued in implementation of Article 14(3).

2. The Commission may by decision impose on undertakings or associations of undertakings fines of from 1 000 to 1 000 000 units of account, or a sum in excess thereof but not exceeding 10% of the turnover in the preceding business year of each of the undertakings participating in the infringement where, either intentionally or negligently:

(a) they infringe Article 85(1) or Article 86 of the Treaty; or

(b) they commit a breach of any obligation imposed pursuant to Article 8(1).

In fixing the amount of the fine, regard shall be had both to the gravity and to the duration of the infringement.

3. Article 10(3) to (6) shall apply.

4. Decisions taken pursuant to paragraphs 1 and 2 shall not be of a criminal law nature.

5. The fines provided for in paragraph 2(a) shall not be imposed in respect of acts taking place:

(a) after notification to the Commission and before its decision in application of Article 85(3) of the Treaty, provided they fall within the limits of the activity described in the notificacion;

(b) before notification and in the course of agreements, decisions or concerted practices in existence at the date of entry into force of this Regulation, provided that notification was effected within the time limits specified in Article 5(1) and Article 7(2).

6. Paragraph 5 shall not have effect where the Commission has informed the undertakings concerned that after preliminary examination it is of opinion that Article 85(1) of the Treaty applies and that application of Article 85(3) is not justified.

Art. 16. *Periodic penalty payments.* 1. The Commission may by
decision impose on undertakings or associations of undertakings
periodic penalty payments of from 50 to 1 000 units of account per
day, calculated from the date appointed by the decision, in order
to compel them:

(a) to put an end to an infringement of Article 85 or 86 of the
Treaty, in accordance with a decision taken pursuant to Article 3 of
this Regulation;

(b) to refrain from any act prohibited under Article 8(3);

(c) to supply complete and correct information which it has
requested by decision taken pursuant to Article 11(5);

(d) to submit to an investigation which it has ordered by
decision taken pursuant to Article 14(3).

2. Where the undertakings or associations of undertakings have
satisfied the obligation which it was the purpose of the periodic
penalty payment to enforce, the Commission may fix the total amount
of the periodic penalty payment at a lower figure than that which
would arise under the original decision.

3. Article 10(3) to (6) shall apply.

Art. 17. *Review by the Court of Justice.* The Court of Justice shall
have unlimited jurisdiction within the meaning of Article 172 of the
Treaty to review decisions whereby the Commission has fixed a fine
or periodic penalty payment; it may cancel, reduce or increase the
fine or periodic penalty payment imposed.

Art. 18. *Unit of account.* For the purposes of applying Articles 15 to
17 the unit of account shall be that adopted in drawing up the
budget of the Community in accordance with Articles 207 and 209 of
the Treaty.

Art. 19. *Hearing of the parties and of third persons.* 1. Before taking
decisions as provided for in Articles 2, 3, 6, 7, 8, 15 and 16, the
Commission shall give the undertakings or associations of undertakings
concerned the opportunity of being heard on the matters to which
the Commission has taken objection.

2. If the Commission or the competent authorities of the Member
States consider it necessary, they may also hear other natural or
legal persons. Applications to be heard on the part of such persons
shall, where they show a sufficient interest, be granted.

3. Where the Commission intends to give negative clearance
pursuant to Article 2 or take a decision in application of Article
85(3) of the Treaty, it shall publish a summary of the relevant application or notification and invite all interested third parties to
submit their observations within a time limit which it shall fix being
not less than one month. Publication shall have regard to the
legitimate interest of undertakings in the protection of their
business secrets.

Art. 20. *Professional secrecy.* 1. Information acquired as a result
of the application of Articles 11, 12, 13 and 14 shall be used
only for the purpose of the relevant request or investigation.

2. Without prejudice to the provisions of Articles 19 and 21, the
Commission and the competent authorities of the Member States, their
officials and other servants shall not disclose information acquired
by them as a result of the application of this Regulation and of the
kind covered by the obligation of professional secrecy.

3. The provisions of paragraphs 1 and 2 shall not prevent publication of general information or surveys which do not contain

information relating to particular undertakings or associations of undertakings.

Art. 21. *Publication of decisions*. 1. The Commission shall publish the decisions which it takes pursuant to Articles 2, 3, 6, 7, and 8.

2. The publication shall state the names of the parties and the main content of the decision; it shall have regard to the legitimate interest of undertakings in the protection of their business secrets

Art. 22. *Special provisions*. 1. The Commission shall submit to the Council proposals for making certain categories of agreement, decision and concerted practice falling within Article 4(2) or Article 5(2) compulsorily notifiable under Article 4 or 5.

2. Within one year from the date of entry into force of this Regulation, the Council shall examine, on a proposal from the Commission, what special provisions might be made for exempting from the provisions of this Regulation agreements, decisions and concerted practices falling within Article 4(2) or Article 5(2).

Art. 23. *Transitional provisions applicable to decisions of authorities of the Member States*. 1. Agreements, decisions and concerted practices of the kind described in Article 85(1) of the Treaty to which, before the entry into force of this Regulation, the competent authority of a Member State has declared Article 85(1) to be inapplicable pursuant to Article 85(3) shall not be subject to compulsory notification under Article 5. The decision of the competent authority of the Member State shall be deemed to be a decision within the meaning of Article 6; it shall cease to be valid upon expiration of the period fixed by such authority but in any event not more than three years after the entry into force of this Regulation. Article 8(3) shall apply.

2. Applications for renewal of decisions of the kind described in paragraph 1 shall be decided upon by the Commission in accordance with Article 8(2).

Art. 24. *Implementing provisions*. The Commission shall have power to adopt implementing provisions concerning the form, content and other details of applications pursuant to Articles 2 and 3 and of notifications pursuant to Articles 4 and 5, and concerning hearings pursuant to Article 19(1) and (2).

Art. 25. 1. As regards agreements, decisions and concerted practices to which Article 85 of the Treaty applies by virtue of accession, the date of accession shall be substituted for the date of entry into force of this Regulation in every place where reference is made in this Regulation to this latter date.

2. Agreements, decisions and concerted practices existing at the date of accession to which Article 85 of the Treaty applies by virtue of accession shall be notified pursuant to Article 5(1) or Article 7(1) en (2) within six months from the date of accession.

3. Fines under Article 15(2)(a) shall not be imposed in respect of any act prior to notification of the agreements, decisions and practices to which paragraph 2 applies and which have been notified within the period therein specified.

4. New Member States shall take the measures referred to in Article 14(6) within six months from the date of accession after consulting the Commission.

the provisions of paragraphs 1 to 4 above still apply in the same way in the case of the accession of the Hellenic Republic.[13]

This Regulation shall be binding in its entirety and directly applicable in all Member States.

Done at Brussels, 6 February 1962.

For the Council

The President

M. COUVE de MURVILLE

1. J.O. No 13, 21 February 1962, p. 204; O.J. (Special Edition 1959-1962) p. 87.
2. J.O. No 58, 10 July 1962, p. 1655; O.J. (Special Edition 1959-1962) p. 249.
3. J.O. No 162, 7 November 1963, p. 2696.
4. J.O. No L 285, 20 December 1971, p. 49; O.J. (Special Edition 1971 111) p. 1035.
5. Annex 1. v. 1 of the Act of Accession, signed at Brussels 22 January 1972.
6. Act concerning the conditions of accession of the Hellenic Republic, signed at Athens 28 May 1979, O.J. No L 291, 19 November 1979.
7. Amended by Regulation 2822/71/EEC.
8. Previous text applying till 18 January 1972 'joint research for improvement of techniques, provided the results are accessible to all the parties thereto and may be used by each of them'.
9. Supplemented by Regulation 2822/71/EEC.
10. Amended by Regulation 59/62/EEC.
11. Amended by Regulation 118/63/EEC.
12. Supplemented by the Act of Accession.
13. Supplement by the Act of Accession of the Hellenic Republic.

THE EUROPEAN ECONOMIC COMMUNITY

Regulation No. 26/62

2. REGULATION No 26/62/EEC[1] OF THE COUNCIL

of 4 April 1962

applying certain rules of competition to production of and trade in agricultural products as amended by Council Regulation 49/62/EEC of 29 June 1962[2]

THE COUNCIL OF THE EUROPEAN ECONOMIC COMMUNITY,

Having regard to the Treaty establishing the European Economic
Community, and in particular Articles 42 and 43 thereof;
    Having regard to the proposal from the Commission;
    Having regard to the Opinion of the European Parliament;
    Whereas by virtue of Article 42 of the Treaty one of the matters
to be decided under the common agricultural policy is whether the
rules on competition laid down in the Treaty are to apply to production of and trade in agricultural products, and accordingly the
provisions hereinafter contained will have to be supplemented in the
light of developments in that policy;
    Whereas the proposals submitted by the Commission for the formula-
tion and implementation of the common agricultural policy show that
certain rules on competition must forthwith be made applicable to
production of and trade in agricultural products in order to eliminate
practices contrary to the principles of the common market and prejudicial to attainment of the objectives set out in Article 39 of the
Treaty and in order to provide a basis for the future establishment
of a system of competition adapted to the development of the common
agricultural policy;
    Whereas the rules on competition relating to the agreements, decis-
ions and practices referred to in Article 85 of the Treaty and to the
abuse of dominant positions must be applied to production of and trade
in agricultural products, in so far as their application does not
impede the functioning of national organisations of agricultural
markets or jeopardise attainment of the objectives of the common
agricultural policy;
    Whereas special attention is warranted in the case of farmers'
organisations which are particularly concerned with the joint production or marketing of agricultural products or the use of joint facilities, unless such joint action excludes competition or jeopardises
attainment of the objectives of Article 39 of the Treaty;
    Whereas, in order both to avoid compromising the development of
a common agricultural policy and to ensure certainty in the law and
non-discriminatory treatment of the undertakings concerned, the
Commission must have sole power, subject to review by the Court of
Justice, to determine whether the conditions provided for in the two
preceding recitals are fulfilled as regards the agreements, decisions
and practices referred to in Article 85 of the Treaty;
    Whereas, in order to enable the specific provisions of the Treaty
regarding agriculture, and in particular those of Article 39 thereof,
to be taken into consideration, the Commission must, in questions of
dumping, assess all the causes of the practices complained of and in
particular the price level at which products from other sources are
imported into the market in question; whereas it must, in the light
of its assessment, make recommendations and authorise protective
measures as provided in Article 91(1) of the Treaty;
    Whereas, in order to implement, as part of the development of the
common agricultural policy, the rules on aids for production of or
trade in agricultural products, the Commission should be in a position
to draw up a list of existing, new or proposed aids, to make appro-

priate observations to the Member States and to propose suitable measures to them;

HAS ADOPTED THIS REGULATION:

Art. 1. From the entry into force of this Regulation, Articles 85 to 90 of the Treaty and provisions made in implementation thereof shall, subject to Article 2 below, apply to all agreements, decisions and practices referred to in Articles 85(1) and 86 of the Treaty which relate to production of or trade in the products listed in Annex 11 to the Treaty;

Art. 2. 1. Article 85(1) of the Treaty shall not apply to such of the agreements, decisions and practices referred to in the preceding Article as form an integral part of a national market organisation or are necessary for the attainment of the objectives set out in Article 39 of the Treaty. In particular, it shall not apply to agreements, decisions and practices of farmers, farmers' associations, or associations of such associations belonging to a single Member State which concern the production or sale of agricultural products or the use of joint facilities for the storage, treatment or processing of agricultural products, and under which there is no obligation to charge identical prices, unless the Commission finds that competition is thereby excluded or that the objectives of Article 39 of the Treaty are jeopardised.

2. After consulting the Member States and hearing the undertakings or associations of undertakings concerned and any other natural or legal person that it considers appropriate, the Commission shall have sole power, subject to review by the Court of Justice, to determine, by decision which shall be published, which agreements, decisions and practices fulfil the conditions specified in paragraph 1.

3. The Commission shall undertake such determination either on its own initiative or at the request of a competent authority of a Member State or of an interested undertaking or association of undertakings.

4. The publication shall state the names of the parties and the main content of the decision; it shall have regard to the legitimate interest of undertakings in the protection of their business secrets.

Art. 3. 1. Without prejudice to Article 46 of the Treaty, Article 91(1) thereof shall apply to trade in the products listed in Annex 11 to the Treaty.

2. With due regard for the provisions of the Treaty relating to agriculture, and in particular those of Article 39, the Commission shall assess all the causes of the practices complained of, in particular the price level at which products from other sources are imported into the market in question.

In the light of its assessment, it shall make recommendations and authorise protective measures as provided in Article 91(1) of the Treaty.

Art. 4. The provisions of Article 93(1) and of the first sentence of Article 93(3) of the Treaty shall apply to aids granted for production of or trade in the products listed in Annex 11 to the Treaty.

Art. 5. This Regulation shall enter into force on the day following its publication in the *Official Journal of the European Communities*, with the exception of Articles 1 to 3, which shall enter into force on 1 July 1962.

This Regulation shall be binding in its entirety and directly applicable in all Member States.

Done at Brussels, 4 April 1962.

For the Council

The President

M. COUVE de MURVILLE

1. J.O. No 30, 20 April 1962, p. 993; O.J. (Special Edition 1959-1962, p. 129).
2. J.O. No 53, p. 129, 1 July 1962, p. 1571. (Rec. D.O. No 65, 27 July 1962, p. 1855).

_____

THE EUROPEAN ECONOMIC COMMUNITY

Regulation 99/63

3. REGULATION No 99/63/EEC[1] OF THE COMMISSION

of 25 July 1963

on the hearings provided for in Article 19(1) and (2) of Council Regulation No 17[2]

THE COMMISSION OF THE EUROPEAN ECONOMIC COMMUNITY,

Having regard to the Treaty establishing the European Economic Community, and in particular Articles 87 and 155 thereof;
   Having regard to Article 24 of Council Regulation No 17[2] of 6 February 1962 (First Regulation implementing Articles 85 and 86 of the Treaty);
   Whereas the Commission has power under Article 24 of Council Regulation No 17 to lay down implementing provisions concerning the hearings provided for in Article 19(1) and (2) of that Regulation;
   Whereas in most cases the Commission will in the course of its inquiries already be in close touch with the undertakings or associa-

tions of undertakings which are the subject thereof and they will accordingly have the opportunity of making known their views regarding the objections raised against them;

Whereas, however, in accordance with Article 19(1) of Regulation No 17 and with the rights of defence, the undertakings and associations of undertakings concerned must have the right on conclusion of the inquiry to submit their comments on the whole of the objections raised against them which the Commission proposes to deal with in its decisions;

Whereas persons other than the undertakings or associations of undertakings which are the subject of inquiry may have an interest in being heard; whereas, by the second sentence of Article 19(2) of Regulation No 17, such persons must have the opportunity of being heard if they apply and show that they have a sufficient interest;

Whereas it is desirable to enable persons who, pursuant to Article 3(2) of Regulation No 17, have applied for an infringement to be terminated to submit their comments where the Commission considers that on the basis of the information in its possession there are insufficient grounds for granting the application;

Whereas the various persons entitled to submit comments must do so in writing, both in their own interest and in the interests of good administration, without prejudice to oral procedure where appropriate to supplement the written evidence;

Whereas it is necessary to define the rights of persons who are to be heard, and in particular the conditions upon which they may be represented or assisted and the setting and calculation of time limits;

Whereas the Advisory Committee on Restrictive Practices and Monopolies delivers its Opinion on the basis of a preliminary draft decision; whereas it must therefore be consulted concerning a case after the inquiry in respect thereof has been completed; whereas such consultation does not prevent the Commission from re-opening an inquiry if need be;

HAS ADOPTED THIS REGULATION:

Art. 1. Before consulting the Advisory Committee on Restrictive Practices and Monopolies, the Commission shall hold a hearing pursuant to Article 19(1) of Regulation No 17.

Art. 2. 1. The Commission shall inform undertakings and associations of undertakings in writing of the objections raised against them. The communication shall be addressed to each of them or to a joint agent appointed by them.

2. The Commission may inform the parties by giving notice in the *Official Journal of the European Communities*, if from the circumstances of the case this appears appropriate, in particular where notice is to be given to a number of undertakings but no agent has been appointed. The notice shall have regard to the legitimate interest of the undertakings in the protection of their business secrets.

3. A fine or a periodic penalty payment may be imposed on an undertaking or association of undertakings only if the objections were notified in the manner provided for in paragraph 1.

4. The Commission shall when giving notice of objections fix a time limit up to which the undertakings and associations of undertakings may inform the Commission of their views.

Art. 3. 1. Undertakings and associations of undertakings shall, within the appointed time limit, make known in writing their views concerning the objections raised against them.

2. They may in their written comments set out all matters relevant to their defence.

3. They may attach any relevant documents in proof of the facts set out. They may also propose that the Commission hear persons who may corroborate those facts.

Art. 4. The Commission shall in its decisions deal only with those objections raised against undertakings and associations of undertakings in respect of which they have been afforded the opportunity of making known their views.

Art. 5. If natural or legal persons showing a sufficient interest apply to be heard pursuant to Article 19(2) of Regulation No 17, the Commission shall afford them the opportunity of making known their views in writing within such time limit as it shall fix.

Art. 6. Where the Commission, having received an application pursuant to Article 3(2) of Regulation No 17, considers that on the basis of the information in its possession there are insufficient grounds for granting the application, it shall inform the applicants of its reasons and fix a time limit for them to submit any further comments in writing.

Art. 7. 1. The Commission shall afford to persons who have so requested in their written comments the opportunity to put forward their arguments orally, if those persons show a sufficient interest or if the Commission proposes to impose on them a fine or periodic penalty payment.

2. The Commission may likewise afford to any other person the opportunity of orally expressing his views.

Art. 8. 1. The Commission shall summon the persons to be heard to attend on such date as it shall appoint.

2. It shall forthwith transmit a copy of the summons to the competent authorities of the Member States, who may appoint an official to take part in the hearing.

Art. 9. 1. Hearings shall be conducted by the persons appointed by the Commission for that purpose.

2. Persons summoned to attend shall appear either in person or be represented by legal representatives or by representatives authorised by their constitution. Undertakings and associations of undertakings may moreover be represented by a duly authorised agent appointed from among their permanent staff.

Persons heard by the Commission may be assisted by lawyers or university teachers who are entitled to plead before the Court of Justice of the European Communities in accordance with Article 17 of the Protocol on the Statute of the Court, or by other qualified persons.

3. Hearings shall not be public. Persons shall be heard seperately or in the presence of other persons summoned to attend. In the latter case, regard shall be had to the legitimate interest of the undertakings in the protection of their business secrets.

4. The essential content of the statements made by each person

268

heard shall be recorded in minutes which shall be read and approved by him.

Art. 10. Without prejudice to Article 2(2), information and summonses from the Commission shall be sent to the addressees by registered letter with acknowledgment of receipt, or shall be delivered by hand against receipt.

Art. 11. 1. In fixing the time limits provided for in Articles 2, 5 and 6, the Commission shall have regard both to the time required for preparation of comments and to the urgency of the case. The time limit shall be not less than two weeks; it may be extended.

2. Time limits shall run from the day following receipt of a communication or delivery thereof by hand.

3. Written comments must reach the Commission or be dispatched by registered letter before expiry of the time limit. Where the time limit would expire on a Sunday or public holiday, it shall be extended up to the end of the next following working day. For the purpose of calculating this extension, public holidays shall, in cases where the relevant date is the date of receipt of written comments, be those set out in the Annex to this Regulation, and in cases where the relevant date is the date of dispatch, those appointed by law in the country of dispatch.

This Regulation shall be binding in its entirety and directly applicable in all Member States.

Done at Brussels, 25 July 1963.

For the Commission

The President

Walter HALLSTEIN

1. J.O. No 127, 20 August 1962, p. 2268; O.J. (Special Edition 1963–1964) p. 47.
2. J.O.No 13, 21 February 1962, p. 204; O.J. (Special Edition 1959–1962) p. 87.

ANNEX

referred to in the third sentence of Article 11(3)

(List of public holidays)

New Year	1 Jan
Good Friday	
Easter Saturday	
Easter Monday	
Labour Monday	1 May
Schuman Plan Day	9 May
Ascension Day	
Whit Monday	
Belgian National Day	21 July
Assumption	15 Aug
All Saints	1 Nov
All Souls	2 Nov
Christmas Eve	24 Dec
Christmas Day	25 Dec
The day following Christmas Day	26 Dec
New Year's Eve	31 Dec

4. REGULATION No 67/67/EEC[1] OF THE COMMISSION

of 22 March 1967

on the application of Article 85(3) of the Treaty to certain
categories of exclusive dealing agreements as amended by
Regulation 2591/72/EEC[2] and amended by the Act of Accession[3]
and the Act of Accession of the Hellenic Republic[4]

THE COMMISSION OF THE EUROPEAN ECONOMIC COMMUNITY,

Having regard to the Treaty establishing the European Economic Community, and in particular Articles 87 and 155 thereof;

Having regard to Article 24 of Regulation No 17 of 6 February 1962[5];

Having regard to Regulation No 19/65/EEC of 2 March 1965[6] on the application of Article 85(3) of the Treaty to certain categories of agreements and concerted practices;

Having regard to the Opinions delivered by the Advisory Committee on
Restrictive Practices and Monopolies in accordance with Article 6 of
Regulation No 19/65/EEC;

Whereas under Regulation No 19/65/EEC the Commission has power to apply
Article 85(3) of the Treaty by regulation to certain categories of bilateral exclusive dealing agreements and concerted practices coming
within Article 85;

Whereas the experience gained up to now, on the basis of individual
decisions, makes it possible to define a first category of agreements
and concerted practices which can be accepted as normally satisfying
the conditions laid down in Article 85(3);

Whereas, since adoption of such a regulation would not conflict with
the application of Regulation No 17, the right of undertakings to
request the Commission, on an individual basis, for a declaration under
Article 85(3) of the Treaty would not be affected;

Whereas exclusive dealing agreements of the category defined in Article
1 of this Regulation may fall within the prohibition contained in Article 85(1) of the Treaty; whereas since it is only in exceptional
cases that exclusive dealing agreements concluded within a Member
State affect trade between Member States, there is no need to include
them in this Regulation;

Whereas it is not necessary expressly to exclude from the category as
defined those agreements which do not fulfil the conditions of Article
85(1) of the Treaty;

Whereas in the present state of trade exclusive dealing agreements
relating to international trade lead in general to an improvement in

271

distribution because the entrepreneur is able to consolidate his trade
activities; whereas he is not obliged to maintain numerous business
contacts with a large number of dealers, and whereas the fact of maintaining contacts with only one dealer makes it easier to overcome sales
difficulties resulting from linguistic, legal, and other differences;
whereas exclusive dealing agreements facilitate the promotion of the
sale of a product and make it possible to carry out more intensive
marketing and to ensure continuity of supplies, while at the same time
rationalising distribution; whereas, moreover the appointment of an
exclusive distributor or of an exclusive purchaser who will take over,
in place of the manufacturer, sales promotion, after-sales service
and carrying of stocks, is often the sole means whereby small and medi-
um-size undertakings can compete in the market; whereas it should be
left to the contracting parties to decide whether and to what extent
they consider it desirable to incorporate in the agreements terms designed to promote sales; whereas there can only be an improvement in
distribution if dealing is not entrusted to a competitor;

Whereas as a rule such exclusive dealing agreements also help to give
consumers a proper share of the resulting benefit as they gain directly
from the improvement in distribution, and their economic or supply
position is thereby improved as they can obtain products manufactured
in other countries more quickly and more easily;

Whereas this Regulation must determine the obligations restricting
competition which may be included in an exclusive dealing agreement;
whereas it may be left to the contracting parties to decide which of
those obligations they include in exclusive dealing agreements in order
to draw the maximum advantages from exclusive dealing;

Whereas any exemption must be subject to certain conditions; whereas
it is in particular advisable to ensure through the possibility of parallel imports that consumers obtain a proper share of the advantages
resulting from exclusive dealing; whereas it is therefore not possible
to allow industrial property rights and other rights to be exercised
in an abusive manner in order to create absolute territorial protection; whereas these considerations do not prejudice the relationship
between the law of competition and industrial property rights, since
the sole object here is to determine the conditions for exemption of
certain categories of agreements under this Regulation;

Whereas competition at the distribution stage is ensured by the possibility of parallel imports, whereas, therefore, the exclusive dealing
agreements covered by this Regulation will not normally afford any
possibility of preventing competition in respect of a substantial part
of the products in question;

Whereas it is desirable to allow contracting parties a limited period
of time within which they may, in accordance with Article 4 of Regulation No 19/65/EEC, modify their agreements and practices so as to satisfy the conditions laid down in this Regulation, without it being
possible, under Article 4(3) of Regulation No 19/65/EEC, to rely thereon in actions which are pending at the time of entry into force of
this Regulation, or as grounds for claims for damages against third
parties;

Whereas agreements and concerted practices which satisfy the conditions set out in this Regulation need no longer be notified; whereas Article 4(2)(a) of Regulation No 27[7], as amended by Regulation No 153[8], can be repealed, since agreements which it was possible to notify on Form B1 would normally come within the scope of the exemption;

Whereas agreements notified on Form B 1 and not amended so as to satisfy the conditions of this Regulation should be made subject to the normal notification procedure, in order that they may be examined individually;

HAS ADOPTED THIS REGULATION:

Art. 1. 1. Pursuant to Article 85(3) of the Treaty and subject to the provisions of this Regulation it is hereby declared that until 31 December 1982[9] Article 85(1) of the Treaty shall not apply to agreements to which only two undertakings are party and whereby:

(a) one party agrees with the other to supply only to that other certain goods for resale within a defined area of the common market; or

(b) one party agrees with the other to purchase only from that other certain goods for resale; or

(c) the two undertakings have entered into obligations, as in (a) and (b) above, with each other in respect of exclusive supply and purchase for resale.

2. Paragraph 1 shall not apply to agreements to which undertakings from one Member State only are party and which concern the resale of goods within that Member State.

Art. 2. 1. Apart from an obligation falling within Article 1, no restriction on competition shall be imposed on the exclusive dealer other than:

(a) the obligation not to manufacture or distribute, during the duration of the contract or until one year after its expiration, goods which compete with the goods to which the contract relates;

(b) the obligation to refrain, outside the territory covered by the contract, from seeking customers for the goods to which the contract relates, from establishing any branch, or from maintaining any distribution depot.

2. Article 1(1) shall apply notwithstanding that the exclusive dealer undertakes all or any of the following obligations:

(a) to purchase complete ranges of goods or minimum quantities;

(b) to sell the goods to which the contract relates under trade marks or packed and presented as specified by the manufacturer;

(c) to take measures for promotion of sales, in particular:

- to advertise;

- to maintain a sales network or stock of goods;

- to provide after-sale and guarantee services;

- to employ staff having specialised or technical training.

Art. 3. Article 1(1) of this Regulation shall not apply where:

(a) manufacturers of competing goods entrust each other with exclusive dealing in those goods;

(b) the contracting parties make it difficult for intermediaries or consumers to obtain the goods to which the contract relates from other dealers within the common market, in particular where the contracting parties:

    (1) exercise industrial property rights to prevent dealers or consumers from obtaining from other parts of the common market or from selling in the territory covered by the contract goods to which the contract relates which are properly marked or otherwise properly placed on the market;

    (2) exercise other rights or take other measures to prevent dealers or consumers from obtaining from elsewhere goods to which the contract relates or from selling them in the territory covered by the contract.

Art. 4. 1. As regards agreements which were in existence on 13 March 1962 and were notified before 1 February 1963, the declaration contained in Article 1(1) of inapplicability of Article 85(1) of the Treaty shall have retroactive effect from the time when the conditions of application of this Regulation were fulfilled.

2. As regards all other agreements notified before the entry into force of this Regulation, the declaration contained in Article 1(1) of inapplicability of Article 85(1) of the Treaty shall have retroactive effect from the time when the conditions of application of this Regulation were fulfilled, but not earlier than the day of notification.

Art. 5. As regards agreements which were in existence on 13 March 1962, notified before 1 February 1963 and amended before 2 August 1967 so as to fulfil the conditions of application of this Regulation, the prohibition in Article 85(1) of the Treaty shall not apply in respect of the period prior to the amendment, where such amendment is notified to the Commission before 3 October 1967. As regards agreements, decisions or concerted practices for exclusive dealing already in existence at the date of accession to which Article 85(1) applies by virtue of accession, the prohibition in Article 85(1) of the Treaty shall not apply where they are modified within six months from the date of accession so as to fulfil the conditions contained in this Regulation[10]. The notification shall take effect from the time of receipt thereof by the Commission. Where the notification is sent by registered post, it shall take effect from the date on the postmark of the place of dispatch. This provision shall apply in the same way in the case of the accession of the Hellenic Republic[11].

Art. 6. The Commission shall examine whether Article 7 of Regulation

No 19/65/EEC applies in individual cases, in particular when there are grounds for believing that:

(a) the goods to which the contract relates are not subject, in the territory covered by the contract, to competition from goods considered by the consumer as similar goods in view of their properties, price and intended use;

(b) it is not possible for other manufacturers to sell, in the territory covered by the contract, similar goods at the same stage of distribution as that of the exclusive dealer;

(c) the exclusive dealer had abused the exemption:

    (1) by refusing, without objectively valid reasons, to supply in the territory covered by the contract categories of purchasers who cannot obtain supplies elsewhere, on suitable terms, of the goods to which the contract relates;

    (2) by selling the goods to which the contract relates at excessive prices.

Art. 7. 1. Article 4(2) (a) of Regulation No 27 of 3 May 1962, as amended by Regulation No 153, is hereby repealed.

2. Notification, on Form B 1, on an exclusive dealing agreement which does not fulfil the conditions contained in Articles 1 to 3 of this Regulation shall, if such agreement is not amended so as to satisfy those conditions, be effected before 3 October 1967, by submission of Form B, with annexes, in accordance with the provisions of Regulation No 27.

Art. 8. Articles 1 to 7 of this Regulation shall apply by analogy to the category of concerted practices defined in Article 1(1).

Art. 9. This Regulation shall enter into force on 1 May 1967.

This Regulation shall be binding in its entirety and directly applicable in all Member States.

Done at Brussels, 16 June 1967.

For the Commission

The President

Walter HALLSTEIN

1. J.O. No 57, 25 March 1967, p. 849; O.J. (Special Edition 1967) p. 10.
2. J.O. No L 276, 9 December 1972, p. 15; O.J. (Special Edition 1972, 9-28 December) p. 7.
3. Annex I. V. 4 of the Act of Accession, signed at Brussels 22 January 1972.

4. Act concerning the conditions of accession of the Hellenic Republic,

signed at Athens 28 May 1979. O.J. No L 291, 19 November 1979.
5. J.O. No 13, 21 February 1962, p. 204; O.J. (Special Edition 1959–1962) p. 87.
6. J.O. No 36, 6 March 1965, p. 533; O.J. (Special Edition 1965–1966) p. 35.
7. J.O. No 35, 10 May 1962, p. 1118; O.J. (Special Edition 1959–1962) p. 132.
8. J.O. No 139, 24 December 1962, p. 2918.
9. Amended by Regulation 2951/72/EEC.
10. Supplemented by the Act of Accession.
11. Supplemented by the Act of Accession of the Hellenic Republic.

5. COMMISSION NOTICE
of 19 December
1977

concerning agreements of minor importance which do not fall under Article 85 (1) of the Treaty establishing the European Economic Community.

(JO No C 313, 29 December 1977, p.3)

I. On several occasions the Commission has made clear that it considers it important to promote cooperation between undertakings where such cooperation is economically desirable without presenting difficulties from the point of view of competition policy; in particular, it wishes to facilitate cooperation between small- and medium-sized undertakings. To this end it published the 'Notice concerning agreements, decisions and concerted practices in the field of cooperation between undertakings' (hereinafter referred to as 'agreements') listing a number of agreements that by their nature cannot be regarded as being restraints of competition. By issuing the present notice, the Commission is taking a further step towards defining the field of application of Article 85 (1) of the Treaty establishing the European Economic Community, in order to promote cooperation between small- and medium-sized undertakings.

In the Commission's opinion, agreements,whose effects on trade between Member States and on competition are negligible, do not fall within the prohibition on restrictive agreements in Article 85 (1) of the EEC Treaty. Only those agreements are prohibited which have an appreciable impact on market conditions, in that they appreciably alter the market position, i.e. the sales outlets and supply possibilities, of non-participating undertakings and of consumers.

In the present Notice the Commission has given a sufficiently concrete meaning to the term 'appreciable' for undertakings to be able to judge for themselves whether the agreements they have concluded with other undertakings, being of minor importance, do not fall under Article 85 (1). The quantitative definition of 'appreciable' given by the Commission is, however, no absolute yardstick; in fact, it is quite possible that, in individual cases, even agreements between undertakings which exceed the limits mentioned below may well have only a negligible effect on trade between Member States on on competition and are therefore not caught by Article 85 (1).

As a result of this notice, there should no longer be any point in undertakings obtaining negative clearance, as defined by Article 2 of Regulation No 17, for the agreements covered, nor should it be necessary to have the legal position established through Commission decisions on individual cases; notification for this purpose will therefore no longer be necessary for agreements of this type. However, where it is doubtful whether in an individual case an agreement appreciably restricts trade between Member States or competition, undertakings are free to apply for negative clearance or to notify the agreement.

This notice is without prejudice to any interpretation which may be given by the Court of Justice of the European Communities.

II. The Commission holds view that agreements between undertakings engaged in the production or distribution of goods do not fall under the prohibition of Article 85 (1) of the EEC Treaty if:

the products which are the subject of the agreement and other products
of the participating undertakings considered by consumers to be similar
by reason of their characteristics, price or use do not represent in a
substantial part of the common market more than 5% of the total market
for such products, and
- the aggregate annual turnover of the participating undertakings
  does not exceed 50 million units of account.

The Commission also holds the view that the said agreements do not
fall within the prohibition of Article 85 (1) even if the abovementioned market share and turnover are exceeded by up to 10% within two successive financial years.
   For the purposes of this notice the participating undertakings are:
1. The undertakings which are parties to the agreement.
2. Undertakings in which the undertakings which are parties to the
   agreement hold
   - at least 25% of the capital or of the working capital whether di-
     rectly or indirectly, or
   - at least half of the voting rights, or
   - the power to appoint at least half of the members of the super-
     visory board, the board of management or the bodies legally re-
     presenting the undertaking party to the agreement, or
   - the right to manage the affairs of the undertaking.
The aggregate turnover shall include the turnover in all goods and
services achieved during the last financial year by the participating
undertakings. The aggregate turnover shall not include dealings
between undertakings which are parties to the agreement.

----

6. PROPOSAL FOR A REGULATION

OF THE COUNCIL

on the control of concentrations between
undertakings

(OJ No C 92, 31 October 1973, p. 1)

(submitted to the Council by the Commission
on 20 July 1973)

THE COUNCIL OF THE EUROPEAN COMMUNITIES,

Having regard to the Treaty establishing the European Economic Community and in particular to Articles 87 and 235 thereof;

Having regard to the proposal from the Commission;

Having regard to the Opinion of the European Parliament;

Having regard to the Opinion of the Economic and Social Committee;

Whereas, for the achievement of the objectives of the Treaty establishing the European Economic Community, Article 3 (f) requires the Community to institute 'a system ensuring that competition in the common market is not distorted';

Whereas analysis of the market structures in the Community shows that the concentration process is becoming faster and that the degree of concentration is growing in such manner that the preservation of effective competition in the common market and the objective set out in Article 3 (f) could be jeopardized;

Whereas concentration must thereforebe made subject to a systematic control arrangement;

Whereas the Treaty already provides some powers of action of the Community to this end;

Whereas Article 86 applies to concentrations effected by undertakings holding a dominant position in the common market or in a substantial part of it which strengthen such position to such an extent that the resulting degree of dominance would substantially restrict competition;

Whereas the power of action aforesaid extends only to such concentrations, as would result in only undertakings remaining in the market whose conduct depended on the undertaking which had effected the concentration; whereas it does not extend to the prevention of such concentrations;

Whereas additional powers of action must be provided for to make it possible to act against other concentrations which may distort competition in the common market and to establish arrangements for controlling them before they are effected;

Whereas under Article 235 of the Treaty the Community may give itself the powers of action necessary for the attainment of its objectives;

Whereas, to institute a system ensuring that competition in the common market is not distorted, it is necessary, in so far as trade between Member States may be affected, to submit to control arrangements such concentrations which give undertakings the power to prevent effective competition in the common market or in a substantial part of it, or which strengthen such a power;

Whereas the power to prevent effective competition must be appraised by reference, in particular, to the scope for choice available to suppliers and consumers, the economic and financial power of the undertakings concerned, the structure of the market affected and supply and demand trends for the relevant goods or services;

Whereas concentrations which, by reason of the small significance of turnover and market share of the undertakings concerned, are not likely to impede the preservation of effective competition in the common market may be excluded from this Regulation;

Whereas it may be found necessary, for the purpose of reconciling objectives to be attained in the common interest of the Community, especially within the frame of common policies, to exempt certain concentrations from incompatibility, under conditions and obligations to be determined case by case;

Whereas the Commission should be enititled to take decisions to prevent or terminate concentrations which are incompatible with the common market, decisions designed to re-establish conditions of effective competition and decisions declaring that a particular concentration may be considered to be compatible with the common market; whereas the Commission should be given exclusive jurisdiction in this matter, subject to review by the Court of Justice;

Whereas, to ensure effective supervision, prior notification of major concentrations and the suspension of concentrations by undertakings should be made obligatory;

Whereas a time limit within which the Commission must commence proceedings in respect of concentration notified to it and a time-limit within thich it must give a final decision on the incompatibility of a concentration with the common market should be laid down;

Whereas undertakings concerned must be accorded the right to be heard by the Commission as soon as proceedings have commenced, and third parties showing a sufficient interest must be given the opportunity of submitting their comments;

Whereas the Commission must have the assistance of the Member States and must also be empowered to require information to be given and to carry out the necessary investigations in order to examine concentrations in the light of provisions of this Regulation;

Whereas compliance with this Regulation must be enforceable by means of fines and periodic penalty payments; whereas it is desirable to confer upon the Court of Justice, pursuant to Article 172, unlimited jurisdiction to that extent;

Whereas this Regulation should extend both to concentrations which constitute abuses of dominant positions and to concentrations which give the undertakings concerned the power to prevent effective competition in the common market; whereas it should therefore be stipulated that Regulations (EEC) Nos 17 and 1017/68 no longer apply to concentrations from the date of entry into force of the present Regulation,

HAS ADOPTED THIS REGULATION:

Article 1

Basic provisions.

1. Any transaction which has the direct or indirect effect of bringing about a concentration between undertakings or groups of undertakings, at least one of which is established in the common market, whereby they acquire or enhance the power to hinder effective competition in the common market in so far as the concentration may affect trade between Member States.

The power to hinder effective competition shall be appraised by reference in particular to the extent to which suppliers and consumers have a possibility of choice, to the economic and financial power of the undertakings concerned, to the structure of the markets affected, and to supply and demand trends for the relevant goods or services.

2. Paragraph 1 shall not apply where:
- the aggregate turnover of the undertakings participating in the concentration is less than 200 million units of account and
- the goods or services concerned by the concentration do not account in any Member State for more than 25% of the turnover in identical goods or services or in goods or services which, by reason of their characteristics, their price and the use for which they are intended, may be regarded as similar by the consumer.

3. Paragraph 1 may, however, be declared inapplicable to concentrations which are indispensable to the attainment of an objective which is given priority treatment in the common interest of the Community.

Article 2

Definition of concentration

1. The concentrations referred to in Article 1 are those whereby a person or an undertaking or a group of persons or undertakings, acquires control of one or several undertakings.

2. Control is constituted by rights or contracts which, either separately or jointly, and having regard to the considerations of fact or law involved, make it possible to determine how an undertaking shall operate, and particularly by:
   (1) Ownership or the right to use all or part of the assets of an undertaking;
   (2) Rights or contracts which confer power to influence the composition, voting or decisions of the organs of an undertaking;
   (3) Rights or contracts which make it possible to manage the business of an undertaking;
   (4) Contracts made with an undertaking concerning the computation or appropriation of its profits;
   (5) Contracts made with an undertaking concerning the whole or an important part of supplies or outlets, where the duration of these contracts or the quantities to which they relate exceed what is usual in commercial contracts dealing with those matters.

3. Control is acquired by persons, undertakings or groups of persons or undertakings who:
   (1) Are holders of the rights or entitled to rights under the contracts concerned;
   (2) While not being holders of such rights or entitled to rights under such contracts, have power to exercise the rights deriving therefrom;
   (3) In a fiduciary capacity own assets of an undertaking or shares in an undertaking, and have power to exercise the rights attaching thereto.

4. Control of an undertaking is not constituted where, upon formation of an undertaking or increase of its capital, banks or financial institutions acquire shares in that undertaking with a view to selling them on the market, provided that they do not exercise voting rights in respect of those shares.

Article 3

Powers of decision of the Commission

1.1 When the Commission finds that a concentration is caught by Article 1 (1) and that the conditions laid down in Article 1 (3) are not satisfied, it shall issue a decision declaring the concentration to be incompatible with the common market.

2. The decision by which the Commission declares a concentration to be incompatible within the meaning of paragraph 1 shall not automatically render null and void the legal transactions relating to such operation.

3. Where a concentration has already been put into effect, the Commission may require, by decision taken under paragraph 1 or by a separate decision, the undertakings, or assets acquired or concentrated to be separated or the cessation of common control or any other action that may be appropriate in order to restore conditions of effective competition.

4. When the Commission finds that a concentration is caught by Article 1 (1) and that the conditions laid down in Article 1 (3) are satisfied, it shall issue a decision declaring Article 1 (1) to be inapplicable; conditions and obligations may be attached thereto.

5. Subject to review by the Court of Justice, the Commission shall have sole power to take the decisions provided for in this Article.

Article 4

Prior notifications of concentrations

1. Concentrations shall be notified to the Commission before they are put into effect, where the aggregate turnover of the undertakings concerned is not less than one thousand million units of account.

2. Where concentrations proposed by an undertaking or a group of undertakings have already reached or exceeded the amounts referred to in paragraph 1, they shall be exempted from the obligation of prior notification, if the turnover of the undertaking, the control of which they propose to acquire is less than 30 million units of account.

3. The obligation to notify shall be discharged by the person or undertaking or the group of persons or undertakings which proposes to acquire control within the meaning of Article 2.

4. Concentrations which are not caught by paragraph 1 may nevertheless be notified to the Commission before they are put into effect.

Article 5

Detailed rules for calculating turnover and market shares.

1. (a) The aggregate turnover specified in Articles 1 (2) and 4 (1) shall be obtained by adding together the turnover for the last financial year for all goods and services of:
(i) the undertakings participating in the concentration;
(ii) the undertakings and groups of undertakings which control

the undertakings participating in the concentration within the meaning of Article 2;

(iii) the undertakings or groups of undertakings controlled within the meaning of Article 2 by the undertakings participating in the concentration.

(b) The market shares referred to in Article 1 (2) near those held in the last financial year by all the undertakings listed in sub-paragraph (a) above.

2. In place of turnover as specified in Articles 1 (2) and 4 (1) and in paragraph 1 of this Article, the following shall be used:
   - for banking and financial institutions: one tenth of their assets;
   - for insurance companies: the value of the premiums received by them.

Article 6

Commencement of proceedings

1. Where the Commission considers that a concentration is likely to become the subject of a decision under Article 1 (1) or (3), it shall commence proceedings and so inform the undertakings in question and the competent authorities in the Member States.

2. As regards concentrations notified to it, the Commission shall commence proceedings within a period not exceeding 3 months unless the relevant undertakings agree to extend that period. The period of 3 months shall commence on the day following receipt of the notification, or if the information to be supplied with the notification is incomplete, on the day following the receipt of the complete information.

3. The Commission may commence proceedings after the expiry of the 3 months period where the information supplied by the undertakings in the notification is false or misleading.

4. Without prejudice to paragraph 3 a concentration notified to the Commission shall be presumed to be compatible with the common market if the Commission does not commence proceedings before expiration of the period specified in paragraph 2.

Article 7

Suspension of the effecting of the concentration.

1. Undertakings shall not put up into effect a concentration notified to the Commission before the end of the time limit provided for in Article 6 (2) unless the Commission informs them before the end of the time limit that it is not necessary to commence proceedings.

2. Where the Commission commences proceedings it may by decision require the undertakings to suspend the concentration until it has decided whether the concentration is compatible with the common market or has closed the proceedings.

Article 8

Communications of objections and hearings

1. Before taking decisions as provided for in Articles 3, 7, 13 and 14,

the Commission shall give the undertakings concerned the opportunity
of being heard on the matters to which the Commission has taken objection. The same opportunity shall be given to associations of undertakings concerned before decisions being taken as provided for in
Articles 13 and 14.

2. If the Commission or the competent authorities of the Member States
consider it necessary, the Commission may also hear other natural or
legal persons. Applications to be heard on the part of such persons
shall, where they show a sufficient interest, be granted.

3. Articles 2, 3, 4, 7, 8, 9, 10 and 11 of Regulation No 99/63/EEC
shall be applied.

Article 9

Closure of proceedings.

If, after having commenced proceedings, the Commission considers that
there are no grounds for action against a concentration, it shall
close the proceedings and so inform the undertakings concerned and
the competent authorities of the Member States.

Article 10

Requests for information

1. In carrying out the duties assigned to it by this Regulation, the
Commission may obtain all necessary information from the governments
and competent authorities of the Member States and from undertakings
and associations of undertakings.

2. When sending a request for information to an undertaking or association of undertakings, the Commission shall at the same time forward a
copy of the request to the competent authority of the Member State in
whose territory the seat of the undertaking or association of undertakings is situated.

3. In its request the Commission shall state the legal basis and the
purpose of the request and also the penalties provided for in Article
13 (1)(b) for supplying incorrect information.

4. The owners of the undertakings or their representatives and, in the
case of legal persons, companies or forms, or of associations having
no legal personality, the persons authorized to represent them by law
or by their constitution, shall supply the information requested.

5. Where an undertaking or association of undertakings does not supply
the information requested within the time limit fixed by the Commission,
or supplies incomplete information, the Commission shall by decision
require the information to be supplied. The decision shall specify
what information is required, fix an appropriate time limit within
which it is to be supplied and mention the penalties provided for in
Article 13 (1)(b) and Article 14 (1)(a) and the right to have the
decision reviewed by the Court of Justice.

6. The Commission shall at the same time forward a copy of its
decision to the competent authority of the Member State in whose

territory the seat of the undertaking or association of undertakings is situated.

Article 11

Investigations by the authorities of the Member States

1. At the request of the Commission, the competent authorities of the Member States shall undertake the investigations which the Commission considers to be necessary under Article 12 (1), or which it has ordered by decision pursuant to Article 12 (3). The officials of the competent authorities of the Member States responsible for conducting these investigations shall exercise their powers upon production of an authorization in writing issued by the competent authority of the Member State in whose territory the investigation is to be made. Such authorization shall specify the subject matter and purpose of the investigation.

2. If so requested by the Commission or by the competent authority of the Member State in whose territory the investigation is to be made, officials of the Commission may assist the officials of such authority in carrying out their duties.

Article 12

Investigating powers of the Commission

1. In carrying out the duties assigned to it by this Regulation, the Commission may undertake all necessary investigations into undertakings and associations of undertakings.
  To this end the officials authorized by the Commission are empowered:
  (a) to examine the books and other business records;
  (b) to take or demand copies of or extracts from the books and business records;
  (c) to ask for oral explanations on the spot;
  (c) to enter any premises, land and means of transport of undertakings.

2. The officials of the Commission authorized to carry out these investigations shall exercise their powers upon production of an authorization in writing specifying the subject matter and purpose of the investigation and the penalties provided for in Article 13 (1)(c) in caseswhere production of the required books or other business records is incomplete. In good time before the investigation, the Commission shall inform the competent authority of the Member State in whose territory the investigation is to be made of the investigation and of the identity of the authorized officials.

3. Undertakings and associations of undertakings shall submit to investigations ordered by decision of the Commission. The decision shall specify the subject matter and purpose of the investigation, appoint the date on which it is to begin and indicate the penalties provided for in Article 13 (1)(c) and Article 14 (1)(b) and the right to have the decision reviewed by the Court of Justice.

4. The Commission shall take decisions referred to in paragraph 3 after consultation with the competent authority of the Member State in whose territory the investigation is to be made.

5. Officials of the competent authority of the Member State in whose territory the investigation is to be made may, at the request of such authority or of the Commission, assist the officials of the Commission in carrying out their duties.

6. Where an undertaking opposes an investigation ordered pursuant to this Article, the Member State concerned shall afford the necessary assistance to the officials authorized by the Commission to enable them to make their investigation. Member States shall, after consultation with the Commission, take the necessary measures to this end before .....

Article 13

Fines

1. The Commission may by decision impose on undertakings and associations of undertakings fines of from 1 000 to 50 000 units of account where intentionally or negligently:
   (a) they supply incorrect or misleading information in a notification pursuant to Article 4;
   (b) they supply incorrect information in response to a request made pursuant to Article 10 or fail to supply information within the time limit fixed by a decision taken pursuant to Article 10;
   (c) theyproduce the required books or other business records in incomplete form during investigations under Article 11 or 12, or refuse to submit to an investigation ordered by decision taken pursuant to Article 12.

2. The Commission may by decision impose on natural or legal persons fines of from 1 000 to 1 000 000 units of account where, either intentionally or negligently, they commit a breach of the obligation to notify under Article 4.

3. The Commission may by decision impose fines not exceeding 10% of the value of the reorganized assets where undertakings either intentionally or negligently, conclude an unlawful concentration before the end of the time limit provided for in Article 6 (2) or in spite of a decision taken by the Commission under Articles 3 (1) or 7 (2).

Article 14

Periodic penalty payments

1. The Commission may by decision impose on undertakings or associations of undertakings periodic penalty payments up to 25 000 units of account for each day of the delay calculated from the date appointed by the decision, in order to compel them:
   (a) to supply complete and correct information which it has requested by decision taken pursuant to Article 10;
   (b) to submit to an investigation which it has ordered by decision taken pursuant to Article 12.

2. The Commission may by decision impose on such undertakings periodic penalty payments up to 50 000 units of account for each day of the delay, calculated from the day appointed by the decision, in order to compel them to apply the measures resulting from a decision taken pursuant to Article 3 (3).

Article 15

Review by the Court of Justice

The Court of Justice shall have unlimited jurisdiction within the meaning of Article 17 of the Treaty to review decisions whereby the Commission has fixed a fine or periodic penalty payment; it may cancel, reduce or increase the fine or periodic penalty payment imposed.

Article 16

Professional secrecy

1. Information acquired as a result of the application of Articles 10, 11 and 12 shall be used only for the purpose of the relevant request or investigation.

2. The Commission and the competent authorities of the Member States, their officials and other servants shall not disclose information acquired by them as a result of the application of this Regulation and of the kind covered by the obligation of professional secrecy.

3. The provisions of paragraphs 1 and 2 shall not prevent publication of general information or surveys which do not contain information relating to particular undertakings or associations of undertakings.

Article 17

Time limits and publication of decisions

1. (a) Decisions under Article 3 (1) and (4) shall be taken within 9 months following the date of commencement of proceedings, save where there is agreement with the relevant undertakings to extend that period.
   (b) The period of 9 months shall not apply where the Commission is obliged to request information by decision taken pursuant to Article 10 or require an investigation by decision taken pursuant to Article 12.

2. The Commission shall publish the decisions which it takes pursuant to Article 3.

3. The publication shall state the names of the parties and the main content of the decision; it shall have regard to the legitimate interest of undertakings in the protection of their business secrets.

Article 18

Unit of account

For the purpose of this Regulation the unit of account shall be that used in drawing up the budget of the Community in accordance with Articles 207 and 209 of the Treaty.

Article 19

Liaison with the authorities of the Member States

1. The Commission shall forthwith transmit to the competent authorities of the Member States a copy of the notifications together with the most important documents lodged with the Commission pursuant to this Regulation.

2. The Commission shall carry out the procedure set out in this Regulation in close and constant cooperation with the competent authorities of the Member States; such authorities shall have the right to express their views upon that procedure, and in particular to request the Commission to commence proceedings under Article 6.

3. The Advisory Committee on Restrictive Practices and Monopolies shall be consulted prior to the taking of any decisions under Articles 3, 13 and 14.

4. The Advisory Committee shall consist of officials having responsibility for restrictive practices and monopolies. Each Member State shall appoint an official to represent it; he may be replaced by another official where he is unable te act.

5. Consultation shall take place, at a meeting convened at the invitation of the Commission, not earlier than fourteen days following dispatch of the invitation. A summary of the facts together with the most important documents and a preliminary draft of the decision to be taken, shall be set with the invitation.

6. The Committee may deliver an opinion even if certain members are absent and unrepresented. The outcome of the consultation shall be annexed to the draft decision. The minutes shall not be published.

Article 20

Exclusive application of this Regulation

Regulations (EEC) No 17 and 1017/68 shall not apply to the concentrations covered by this Regulation.

Article 21

Implementing provisions

The Commission shall have power to adopt implementing provisions concerning the form, content and other details of notifications pursuant to Article 4 of this Regulation.

Article 22

This Regulation shall enter into force ......

This Regulation shall be binding in its entirety and directly applicable in all Member States.

AMENDED DRAFT REGULATION CONCENTRATION

Amended proposal for a Council Regulation on the control of concentrations between undertakings (merger control Regulation.

(OJ No C 36, 12 February 1982, p.3)

(Submitted by the Commission ot the Council, pursuant to the second
paragraph of Article 149 of the EEC Treaty, on 16 December 1981)

I. BACKGROUND

On 20 July 1973 the Commission submitted to the Council a proposal for
a Council Regulation on the control of concentrations between under--
takings (merger control Regulation).
  The European Parliament and the Economic and Social Committee were
consulted by the Council, and both approved the Commission proposal
by large majorities.
  Discussions in the Council revealed significant differences of
opinion, relating mainly to the scope of the Retulation and to the
division of decision-making power between the Commission and the Council.
  In its resolution on the ninth report on competition policy, Parliament deplored the fact that the Council had still not adopted the merger
control Regulation, which would give the Commission the means to take
effective action at Community level against any irreversible structural
evolution which could seriously jeopardize competition.
  A policy designed to strengthen effective competition plays a significant role in achieving more flexible structural adjustment and
maintaining the competitiveness of our industries and, in so doing,
also contributes to overcoming the current crisis.
  It goes without saying that in applying the merger control rules,
account must be taken of the differences in economic situations (particularly how open markets are) and, where appropriate, of exigencies
stemming from other Community policies.
  The amended proposal attempts to confine the control measures to
mergers with a Community dimension and to involve the Member States
more in the decision-making process.

II PROPOSALS ON THE ASSESSMENT CRITERIA

(Article 1 (1))

(a) Taking into account of the international competitive situation

(Second subparagraph of Article 1 (1))

This subparagraph has been added in response to a request made by
Parliament. Its purpose if to make it clear that account must be taken
of the competitive situation and the development of trade at inter-

289

national level.

(b) Reference to the Community dimension of the merger

(Second subparagraph of Article 1 (1))

Such reference is intended to make it clearer that, as was the intention with the original Commission proposal, the Regulation is to apply to mergers which are of a scale that transcend the national context and produce effects at Community level.

(c) Introduction of a market share criterion

(Third subparagraph of Article 1 (1) - new)

In its original proposal, the Commission applied a market share criterion, in addition to turnover, as a quantitative threshold below which the Community merger control would not apply, It set the threshold at 25% of the relevant market in a member country.

Should it be envisaged, in view of the unity of the common market, to relate this criterion to the common market as a whole, the Commission must underline that it would be difficult to apply and be inappropriate for determining the scope of the Regulation.

The reason is that, if it is difficult to determine a market share with precision at national level, as is shown by experience in the Federal Republic of Germany and the United Kingdom, the difficulty is even greater at common market level, both for the undertakings concerned and for the Commission, creating legal uncertainty for undertakings.

However, market share, used as an indicator of market structure, is without any doubt an important element in assessing whether a merger threatens to eliminate effective competition. It is therefore proposed that the market share criterion be retained as an assessment criterion.

As regards the definition of the geographical market to be taken into account, it is proposed that, in order to make it clear that the Community control applies only to mergers with effects on competition at common market level, reference be made to the market share in the common market as a whole.

As far as the threshold is concerned, it is proposed that this be fixed at 20%: taking the common market as a whole, a market share of 20% may represent a critical threshold for the working of competition, regardless of the market shares held by competitions. This is because, in a market with a low level of concentration, acquiring a 20% market share may result in the creation of a dominant position. On the other hand, if the market already has a high level of concentration, there is a danger of strengthening an oligopolistic structure. Economic research findings have suggested that this is the case. It is not possible to envisage a higher market share threshold if the creation or strengthening of regional monopolies is to be avoided.

However, market share is only one assessment factor among others, though the others cannot be quantified (see the second subparagraph of Article 1 (1)).

Market share may nevertheless be used to make it clear to undertakings and the appropriate authorities that, except in specific cases, the Commission considers that, below the critical threshold envisaged, mergers are not normally likely to have significant repercussions on the maintenance of effective competition.

However, the Commission will still be able to determine that, below the critical threshold, a merger does nevertheless have repercussions that would be harmful to the maintenance of effective competition because of other assessment factors; for example, in the event of a conglomerate merger, because of the size and the financial resources of the undertakings concerned.

It goes without saying that, even if a merger gives the undertakings concerned a market share that is equal to or above the critical threshold, it will always be up to the Commission, in the light of the other assessment criteria (second subparagraph of Article 1 (1)), to determine that the merger gives the undertaking concerned the power to hinder effective competition.

III. PROPOSALS ON THE THRESHOLDS FOR DETERMINING APPLICABILITY OF THE REGULATION

(Article 1 (2))

So as to ensure that mergers of lesser significance were not subject to Community merger control, the Commission's original proposal provided for market share and turnover thresholds, to be used on an alternative basis.

(a) Market share

For the reasons set out at II (c), it is proposed that market share should now be used as one of the criteria allowing the effects of a merger on the working of effective competition to be assessed (assessment criterion), and not as a criterion indicating the limits below which the Regulation would not apply (applicability criterion).

(b) Turnover

As a criterion for defining the scope of the Regulation, turnover has the advantage of being easier to determine and to verify; it also reflects the economic and financial strength of the undertakings concerned, particularly in view of the thresholds envisaged. However, the level originally proposed (200 million ECU) must be raised (500 million ECU) to take account of economic developments that have taken place.

IV. PROPOSAL ON DECISION-MAKING PROCEDURES

The underlying idea is that in the fields where common policies do not exist, Member States may be concerned by the effects which the prohibition of a given merger might have on the implementation of their national policies. Account should be taken of such circumstances, provided that the attainment of a priority objective of the Community is not thereby endangered. The proposed solution is based on Article 17 of Council Regulation (EEC) No 1017/68 which gives the Member States a right to convene the Council.

----

7. PUBLIC UNDERTAKINGS

Extract of the sixth report on
competition policy April 1977

Public undertakings

272. The Commission has been trying for many years, in pursuance of
the Treaty, to eliminate distortions of competition resulting from
Member States' intervention in the economy. Among the provisions conferring powers on the Commission in this field, and indeed imposing
obligations on it, are those of Article 90.

In the Commission's view the fact that a public sector, which in
some cases is very large, exists in the economies of Member States
means that the consequences for the States of their responsibility
for the behaviour of those undertakings covered by Article 90 must be
made as clear as possible. The undertakings in question are public
undertakings, undertakings to which Member States grant special or
exclusive rights, and those which they entrust with the operation
of services of general economic interest or which have the character
of a revenue-producing monopoly. These undertakings may belong to the
private or to the public sector.[1]

After contacts with various interested circles, the Commission has in
the last year begun a process of study and clarification with a view
to defining the obligations set out in Article 90 more precisely.

273. In the eyes of the Commission Article 90 does not of course limit
in any way the principle comtained in Article 222, which states that
the Treaty shall in no way prejudice the rules in Member States governing the system of property ownership. The Member States remain completely free to determine the extent, composition and internal organisation of their public sector, and to introduce whatever reforms
they believe necessary in their rules governing property ownership.

Article 90 states:

(a) first,
    in paragraph 1, that Member States may not use their 'public
    undertakings' to escape from their own obligations under the
    Treaty, nor cause undertakings to violate theirs; and

(b) second,
    in paragraph 2, that 'public undertakings' must respect the rules
    of the Treaty in the same way as other undertakings, except in
    so far as this might obstruct them in performing the particular
    tasks assigned to them.

The Treaty's purpose here is to ensure that the market conduct of these undertakings does not impede the proper application of the rules of the Treaty, either as regards competition or as regards the unity of the market.

This objective is both fair and logical. 'Public undertakings'benefit from the common market as much as other undertakings, and they should comply with the rules in the same way as the others must.

That 'public undertakings' and the Member States should respect the basic principles of the Treaty is particularly important to 'the institution of a system ensuring that competition in the common market is not distorted' (Article 3(f)). For where 'public undertakings' buy or sell goods or services on the market, they are liable to be in direct competition with other firms and their behaviour may affect trade within the Community.

As to the exception provided in Article 90(2) concerning the proper performance by 'public undertakings' of the particular tasks assigned them, the Commission believes that full application of the provisions of the Treaty implies full application of the exceptions expressly provided. On this point it will keep to the administrative practice it follows in the case of other express exceptions, such as those arising directly from Article 6 or those allowed by the Commission under Article 115. This practice is founded on the principle of strict interpretation of these exceptions, a principle upheld by the Court of Justice on many occasions.

This approach, while strict, is in no way restrictive. It allows the Commission to recognise constructively and realistically the legitimate wish of Member States to safeguard the effectiveness of public undertakings assigned particular tasks while at the same time ensuring that the common market functions smoothly. It is in this light that the Commission intends to assess both what is necessary for the performance of any particular task referred to by a Member State and the interest of the Community.[2]

274. The Treaty provides the Commission with various ways of applying the principles stated in Article 90.

Articles 85 and 86 allow it to act where an undertaking, whether or not falling within the scope of Article 90, appears to have taken part in an unlawful agreement or to have abused a dominant position of its own accord. If, however, any such behaviour affecting freedom of movement between Member States was ordered or instigated by the State, it will depend on the nature of the State measure involved whether Article 90(3) or the procedure laid down in Article 169 will be used. An example of this would be where a 'public undertaking' is constrained or encouraged systematically to favour domestic suppliers in breach of the provisions of Article 30. Article 92 *et seq* cover State aids granted to public undertakings.

Article 90(3) allows the Commission to act where a Member State, while possessing the necessary authority, fails to cause a 'public undertaking' to put an end to objectionable practices, i.e. practices which, had they been engaged in by the State itself, would have constituted an infringement of the Treaty.

This does not rule out the possibility of injured parties themselves invoking against 'public undertakings' certain directly applicable provisions of the Treaty or instruments giving effect to the Treaty.

Where a Member State has not got the necessary authority to correct objectionable behaviour on the part of a 'public undertaking', the Commission may invoke Article 90 to call on the Member State to fill the gap in its relationship with the undertaking in question. The Member State must then take the necessary powers and use them to end behaviour incompatible with the common market.

This would be the case, to use the example already given, if a 'public undertaking', acting independently in this instance, systematically favoured national suppliers and the Member State did not possess the powers necessary to make the undertaking act in accordance with the principle of the common market.

275. In order to avoid as far as possible situations like those outlined above, the Commission may, under Article 90(3), take preventive steps. It may call on Member States to take such general or specific preventive measures concerning their 'public undertakings' as are needed to ensure that the Treaty is complied with. This means that the Commission can have procedures and approaches initiated which are not necessarily linked to specific departures from the Treaty but which will serve generally to prevent them happening.

In this way it can overcome the difficulties involved in applying the provisions of Article 90 caused by the lack of transparency in the accounts of some 'public undertakings', in particular as regards commercially unjustified costs[3] and any offsetting of them. The Commission must be able to distinguish between legitimate offsetting of such costs and the granting by a Member State of competitive advantages which are incompatible with the common market.

In the same way the Commission may, where necessary, address appropriate directives, decisions or recommendations to Member States calling upon them to make 'public undertakings', by sector or separately, take the necessary measures as regards the award of contracts.

276. There can be no doubt whatever that 'public undertakings' may be a particularly useful instrument for securing a country's economic or social policy objectives.

If therefore the importance of the tasks which 'public undertakings' may be called upon to carry out should not be underestimated, it is nevertheless indispensable that the Member States should ensure that the behaviour of these undertakings is consistent with the Treaty. The free movement of goods and services and the unity of the common market would be endangered if the behaviour of certain categories of undertakings could evade the provisions of the Treaty. This applies both to provisions applicable to undertakings and to the rules imposing obligations on the Member States.

The Commission is concerned to do two things: on the one hand, to ensure that 'public undertakings' benefit from an enlarged market in the same way as private undertakings, by buying on the best terms, reducing the burden on the public finances and, where appropriate, also

the cost of the services provided and on the other hand, to ensure
that productive industries benefit fully from the common market and
also consolidate their competitive position *vis-à-vis* non-member
countries.

1. For ease of reference, the term 'public undertaking' is employed
   throughout this text to denote any undertaking covered by Article
   90.

2. Judgment of the Court of Justice of 14 July 1971 in Case 10/71
   (Port of Mertert):(1971) ECR.

3. This expression denotes the costs resulting from burdens imposed
   by the State on certain undertakings in order to secure its economic and social aims, and which have as their effect a diminution
   in the profits, or an increase in the losses which would result
   from purely commercial management of the undertaking.

8. COMMISSION DIRECTIVE

of 25 June 1980

on the transparency of financial relations between Member States
and public undertakings

(80/723/EEC)
(O.J. No L 195, 20 July 1980, p. 35)

THE COMMISSION OF THE EUROPEAN COMMUNITIES,

Having regard to the Treaty establishing the European Economic Community, and in particular Article 90(3) thereof;
    Whereas public undertakings play a substantial role in the natio-
nal economy of the Member States;
    Whereas the Treaty in no way prejudices the rules governing the
system of property ownership in Member States and equal treatment of
private and public undertakings must therefore be ensured;
    Whereas the Treaty requires the Commission to ensure that Member
States do not grant undertakings, public or private, aids incompatible
with the common market.
    Whereas, however, the complexity of the financial relations between
national public authorities and public undertakings tends to hinder
the performance of this duty;
    Whereas a fair and effective application of the aid rules in the
Treaty to both public and private undertakings will be possible only
if these financial relations are made transparent;
    Whereas such transparency applied to public undertakings should

enable a clear distinction to be made between the role of the State as public authority and its role as proprietor;

Whereas Article 90(1) confers certain obligations on the Member States in respect of public undertakings;

Whereas Article 90(3) requires the Commission to ensure that these obligations are respected, and provides it with the requisite means to this end; whereas this entails defining the conditions for achieving transparency;

Whereas it should be made clear what is to be understood by the terms 'public authorities' and 'public undertakings';

Whereas public authorities may exercise a dominant influence on the behaviour of public undertakings not only where they are the proprietor or have a majority participation but also by virtue of powers they hold in management or supervisory bodies as a result either of the rules governing the undertaking or of the manner in which the shareholdings are distributed;

Whereas the provision of public funds to public undertakings may take place either directly or indirectly; whereas transparency must be achieved irrespective of the manner in which such provision of public funds is made; whereas it may also be necessary to ensure that adequate information is made available as regards the reasons for such provision of public funds and their actual use;

Whereas Member States may through their public undertakings seek ends other than commercial ones; whereas in some cases public undertakings are compensated by the State for financial burdens assumed by them as a result; whereas transparency should also be ensured in the case of such compensation;

Whereas certain undertakings should be excluded from the application of this Directive by virtue either of the nature of their activities or of the size of their turnover; whereas this applies to certain activities which stand outside the sphere of competition or which are already covered by specific Community measures which ensure adequate transparency, to public undertakings belonging to sectors of activity for which distinct provision should be made, and to those whose business is not conducted on such a scale as to justify the administration burden of ensuring transparency;

Whereas this Directive is without prejudice to other provisions of the Treaty, notably Articles 90(2), 93 and 223;

Whereas, the undertakings in question being in competition with other undertakings, information acquired should be covered by the obligation of professional secrecy;

Whereas this Directive must be applied in close cooperation with the Member States, and where necessary be revised in the light of experience,

HAS ADOPTED THIS DIRECTIVE:

Art. 1. The Member States shall ensure that financial relations between public authorities and public undertakings are transparent as provided in this Directive, so that the following emerge clearly:

    (a) public funds made available directly by public authorities to the public undertakings concerned;

    (b) public funds made available by public authorities through the intermediary of public undertakings or financial institutions;

    (c) the use to which these public funds are actually put.

Art. 2. For the purpose of this Directive:
- 'public authorities' means:
the State and regional or local authorities,
- 'public undertakings' means: any undertaking over which the
public authorities may exercise directly or indirectly a dominant
influence by virtue of their ownership of it, their financial participation therein, or the rules which govern it.
A dominant influence on the part of the public authorities shall be
presumed when these authorities, directly or indirectly in relation
to an undertaking:
(a) hold the major part of the undertaking's subscribed capital; or
(b) control the majority of the votes attaching to shares issued
by the undertakings; or
(c) can appoint more than half of the members of the undertaking's
administrative, managerial or supervisory body.

Art. 3. The transparency referred to in Article 1 shall apply in particular to the following aspects of financial relations between public
authorities and public undertakings:
(a) the setting-off of operating losses;
(b) the provision of capital;
(c) non-refundable grants, or loans on privileged terms;
(d) the granting of financial advantages by forgoing profits or
the recovery of sums due;
(e) the forgoing of a normal return on public funds used;
(f) compensation for financial burdens imposed by the public authorities.

Art. 4. This Directive shall not apply to financial relations between
the public authorities and:
(a) public undertakings, as regards services the supply of which
is not liable to affect trade between Member States to an appreciable
extent;
(b) public undertakings, as regards activities carried on in any
of the following areas:
- water and energy, including in the case of nuclear energy the
production and enrichment of uranium, the re-processing of irradiated
fuels and the preparation of materials containing plutonium,
- posts and telecommunications,
- transport;
(c) public credit institutions;
(d) public undertakings whose turnover excluding taxes has not
reached a total of 40 million EUA during the two financial years preceding that in which the funds referred to in Article 1 are made
available or used.

Art. 5. 1. Member States shall ensure that information concerning the
financial relations referred to in Article 1 be kept at the disposal
of the Commission for five years from the end of the financial year in
which the public funds were made available to the public undertakings
concerned. However, where the same funds are used during a later
financial year, the five-year time limit shall run from the end of
that financial year.
2. Member States shall, where the Commission considers it necessary
so to request, supply to it the information referred to in paragraph
1, together with any necessary background information, notably the
objectives pursued.

Art. 6. 1. The Commission shall not disclose such information supplied to it pursuant to Article 5(2) as is of a kind covered by the obligation of professional secrecy.

2. Paragraph 1 shall not prevent publication of general information or surveys which do not contain information relating to particular public undertakings to which this Directive applies.

Art. 7. The Commission shall regularly inform the Member States of the results of the operation of this Directive.

Art. 8. Member States shall take the measures necessary to comply with the Directive by 31 December 1981. They shall inform the Commission thereof.

Art. 9. This Directive is addressed to the Member States.

Done at Brussels, 25 June 1980.

For the Commission

RAYMOND VOUEL

Member of the Commission

9. COUNCIL DECISION

of 19 December 1960

on the system of aid in existence in France for
certain types of paper pulp
(J.O. 1972/60: O.J. (Special Edition: Second Series, Volume VI)p. 39)

THE COUNCIL OF THE EUROPEAN ECONOMIC COMMUNITY,

Having regard to the Treaty establishing the European Economic Community, and in particular the third subparagraph of Article 93(2) thereof;

Whereas the French Government has introduced a parafiscal charge of one per cent on paper and paper-board whether manufactured in France or imported, the proceeds of which would go towards paying subsidies to the French paper pulp industry and for research and afforestation work by the *Fonds forestier national;*

Whereas the French Government has requested the Council to decide, pursuant to the third paragraph of Article 93(2) of the Treaty, that such aid should be considered compatible with the common market;

Whereas, during intergovernmental negotiations concerning the adoption of the Common Customs Tariff relating to the products in List G annexed to the Treaty, the Representatives of the Member States noted the statement by the French Representative that his Government could agree to the tariff treatment agreed upon in respect of paper pulp, in view of the existence in France of a system of aid to the paper pulp industry;

Whereas, therefore, exceptional circumstances justify the temporary extension of this existing system of aid;

Whereas the operation of the system must be subject to review since it is in the common interest that the aid should be degressive and granted with due regard for the development of the common market;

Having received a favourable Opinion from the Commission,

HAS DECIDED AS FOLLOWS:

Article 1

The French Government is hereby authorised to pay the subsidies provided for under the system of aid to the paper pulp industry introduced by *Ordonnance No* 58.881 and *Decret No* 58.883 of 24 September 1958 *(Journal officiel de la République Française* of 26 September 1958). The authorisation shall expire on 31 December 1966.

Article 2

1. The French Government shall, once a year beginning in 1961, forward to the Commission for examination draft implementing orders relating to that aid.

2. If, after examining those drafts with the Member States concerned, the Commission finds that they might alter the conditions of trade within the Community to an extent contrary to the common interest, the Commission shall refer the matter to the Council for decision as provided in the third and fourth subparagraphs of Article 93(2) of the Treaty.

Article 3

This Decision is addressed to the French Republic.

Done at Brussels, 19 December 1960.

For the Council

The President

J.A.M.H.LUNS

10. COMMISSION DECISION

of 18 July 1969

on the French system of aid for research and the reorganisation
of production and distribution in the textile industry

(69/266/EEC)

(J.O. No L 220, 1 September 1969, p. 1; O.J. (Special Edition:
Second Series,Volume VI) p. 47)

THE COMMISSION OF THE EUROPEAN COMMUNITIES,

Having regard to the Treaty establishing the European Economic Community, and in particular the first subparagraph of Article 93(2)
and Article 93(3) thereof;

Whereas by Decree No 65-1163 of 24 December 1965 (Official Journal
of the French Republic of 31 December 1965) the French Republic introduced, with effect from 1 January 1966, a parafiscal charge for the
purpose of encouraging research and the reorganisation of production
and distribution in the textile industry;

Whereas this charge the rate of which was fixed at 0.2% by Order of
24 December 1965 (Official Journal of the French Republic of 31 December 1965), affects textile products sold in France or imported into
France, export sales being exempt;

Whereas by Orders of 29 March 1966 (Official Journal of the French
Republic of 2 April 1966) and 21 April 1966 (Official Journal of the
French Republic of 3 May 1966) 40% of the proceeds of this charge
have been allocated to the French Textiles Institute (*Institut textile
de France*) for research, and 60% to the trade association called the
Union of the Textile Industries (*Union des industries textiles* - UIT)
to implement 'programmes for the reorganisation of production and
distribution methods of textile undertakings and, by way of exception
in limited fields, for modernisation or collective trade promotion';
whereas the administrative boards of the two bodies, which take all
decisions on the use of these funds, subject to the French Government's right of veto, include members nominated by the industry;

Whereas the French Government informed the Commission of these provisions by letter of 4 May 1966; whereas a preliminary study was
made of them during a multilateral meeting with representatives of
the Member States on 20 June 1966; whereas, in accordance with the
second sentence of Article 93(3) of the Treaty, the Commission then
initiated the procedure provided for in paragraph 2 of that Article
and by letter of 30 May 1967 addressed to all Member States gave the
interested parties notice to submit their comments;

Whereas by Decree No 68-383 of 27 April 1968 (Official Journal of the French Republic of 30 April 1968), the French Republic, with effect from 1 May 1968, modified the system introduced by Decree No 65-1163 of 24 December 1965 and revoked that Decree; whereas the rate of the charge was fixed at 0.35% by an Order adopted the same day (Official Journal of the French Republic of 30 April 1968); whereas by that Order two-sevenths of the proceeds of the charge are allocated to the French Textile Institute for research and five-sevenths to the Union of the Textile Industries for reorganisation; whereas the other provisions of the Order of 21 April 1966 remain in force for the time being;

Whereas the proceeds of the parafiscal charge in question constitute State resources and are allocated in their entirety to the Institute and trade association concerned by way of assistance to French textile undertakings; whereas, by the abovementioned Decrees, the French Government has, therefore, introduced a system of aid;

Whereas the part of the proceeds of the charge which is applied to research by the French Textile Institute is to be used, in particular, to promote technical advances which can improve output and quality in the textile industry, thus relieving that industry, and particularly undertakings which are not in a position to undertake research on their own account, of part of the expenditure connected therewith; whereas the provisions which the French Government has brought to the attention of the Commission do not suggest that textile undertakings of the other Member States would be able, under the same conditions as apply to French undertakings, to take advantage of the results of all the research financed by the proceeds of the charge; whereas, therefore, the aid to the French Textile Institute threatens to distort competition by favouring French textile undertakings;

Whereas the same is true of the other part of the proceeds of the charge which is allocated to the Union of the Textile Industries to provide textile undertakings in France with financial aid for the reorganisation of production and distribution methods and, by way of exception in certain branches of the industry, for modernisation and collective trade promotion.

Whereas by thus strengthening the competitive position of French undertakings receiving aid, to the detriment of those established in other Member States, the aid is liable to disturb trade in textile products between the Member States;

Whereas the effect which the system of aid is likely to have on competition and trade between Member States will be all the more serious in that the textile industry is experiencing difficulties in several Member States and that the aid is financed from a special charge on the products of the sector benefiting from the charge, which is also levied on textile products imported from other Member States;

Whereas by the Decree of 24 December 1965 the French Government has thus introduced a system of aid which falls under Article 92(1) of the Treaty;

Whereas the information supplied by the French Government and the other information available to the Commission give no grounds for

301

applying any of the derogations provided for in Article 92(2) and (3) (a) and (b) of the Treaty, which provisions the French Government has not in fact invoked; whereas, in particular, the aid in question has no specific regional purpose within the meaning of Article 92(3)(a) and is not intended to remedy a serious disturbance in the French economy within the meaning of Article 92(3)(b);

Whereas as regards the derogation provided for in Article 92(3)(c) of the Treaty, the difficulties which the textile industry is at present experiencing in France, as in several other Member States, may justify the introduction of aid to stimulate that industry; whereas in this particular case the granting of aid to the French Textile Institute for research is likely to provide such stimulus; whereas the same applies in respect of aid for the Union of the Textile Industries for the reorganisation of production and distribution, particularly in the light of the explanations as to the manner of its application given by the French delegation during the multilateral meetings held in Brussels on 20 June 1966 and 18 June 1969;

Whereas it is advisable to ensure that the derogations from Article 92(1) are reserved for systems of aid which, although they distort competition and disturb trade between Member States, do so to an extent which does not go beyond what is indispensable for the attainment of their legitimate objectives;

Whereas in this case the aid is financed from a parafiscal charge levied on the products of the industry; whereas the proceeds of that charge are allocated entirely and directly to the French Textile Institute and to the Union of the Textile Industries to finance measures for the benefit of textile undertakings in France; whereas the parafiscal charge is thus an integral part of the system of aid;

Whereas the levying of this charge is likely to lead to a reduction of foreign producers' profit margins and, to the extent to which the charge is passed on to consumers, to a reduction of their markets; whereas, therefore, this levy is liable to aggravate the effect of the aid on competition and on intra-Community trade;

Whereas it is not apparent - nor has the French Government made such a claim - that the parafiscal charge, and in particular its application to products imported from other Member States, is indispensable for the attainment of the legitimate objectives of the aid; whereas it is in fact open to the French authorities to replace the proceeds of the parafiscal charge, either entirely or to the extent of the incidence of the charge on products from other Member States, by funds from other sources, for example by contributions from French textile undertakings;

Whereas, furthermore, even assuming that the abolition of all special taxation on imported textile products would prevent the aid from fully attaining its legitimate objectives, such abolition would nevertheless be necessary, because by aggravating the already difficult situation of the textile industry of other Member States, the taxation of imported products in any case affects trading conditions to an extent contrary to the common interest;

Whereas, consequently, the system of aid instituted by the Decree of

24 December 1965, and amended by the Decree of 27 April 1968, also does not qualify for the derogation provided for in Article 92(3)(c) of the Treaty; whereas it is therefore incompatible with the common market;

Whereas, finally, according to the first subparagraph of Article 93(2) and Article 93(3), the French Republic may not apply the system of aid instituted by the Decree of 24 December 1965 and amended by the Decree of 27 April 1968 and by the implementing Orders of 29 March 1966, 21 April 1966 and 27 April 1968 mentioned above, so long as the granting of the aid is linked with the application to textile products imported from other Member States of the parafiscal charge or any other special taxation on textile products;

Whereas, however, reasonable time should be allowed for the method of financing of the aid referred to in this Decision to be modified,

HAS ADOPTED THIS DECISION:

Article 1

From 1 April 1970 the French Republic shall not grant any aid under the system instituted by Decree No 65-1163 of 24 December 1965, as amended by Decree No 68-383 of 27 April 1968, which introduced a parafiscal charge for the purpose of encouraging research in the textile industry and the reorganisation of production and distribution, unless it first revises that system in such a way that products imported from other Member States are no longer liable to the parafiscal charge introduced by that system or to any other special taxation on textile products.

Article 2

This Decision is addressed to the French Republic.

Done at Brussels, 18 July 1969.

For the Commission

The President

Jean REY

11. COMMISSION DECISION

of 26 April 1972

concerning aid granted pursuant to the Belgian Law of
30 December 1970 on economic expansion

(72/173/EEC)

(J.O. No L 105, 4 May 1972, p. 13; O.J. (Special Edition:
Second Series, Volume VI) p. 60)

THE COMMISSION OF THE EUROPEAN COMMUNITIES,

Having regard to the Treaty establishing the European Economic Community, and in particular the first subparagraph of Article 93(2)
thereof;

Having regard to the written and oral comments made by the Member
States and other interested parties;

I

Whereas by letters of 25 November 1969 and 11 May 1970, the Belgian
Government, in accordance with Article 93(3) of the Treaty, communicated to the Commssion a draft law on economic expansion designed to
establish, in place of the laws on regional aid of 18 July 1959 and
14 July 1966, a new system of regional and sectoral aid;

Whereas the Commission initiated in respect of that draft law the procedure provided for in the first subparagraph of Article 93(2) of
the Treaty by reason of the nature and manner of implementation of
certain aid and because of the too general and too imprecise character of the system as a whole, inasmuch as the scope of the proposed
measures could not be judged from the implementing regulations and
in particular from the definition of the geographical areas of application;

II

Whereas, following the vote of the Belgian Parliament, the draft law
became the Law on economic expansion promulgated on 30 December 1970
and entering into force on 1 January 1971;

Whereas, furthermore a Royal Order of 6 January was published in the
Moniteur belge of 13 January 1971 laying down certain provisional
measures for the inplementation of the Law of 30 December 1970 on
economic expansion;

Whereas these measures constitute an infringement by Belgium of

of Article 93(3) of the Treaty and application of the aid provided
for in the Law of 30 December 1970 on economic expansion is therefore
irregular;

III

Whereas the effect of the Royal Order of 6 January 1971 is that the
implementing regulations in respect of the repealed laws for regional
aid of 18 July 1959 and 14 July 1966, remain in force, and in particular:

- the Royal Order of 27 November 1959 defining the development areas;
  and

- the Royal Order of 17 February 1967 defining the economic areas in
  which the Law of 14 July 1966 is applicable;

Whereas the Belgian authorities are therefore able to grant aid under
the Law in geographical areas defined for purposes of application of
the repealed laws;

Whereas the Belgian Government, by making provision in the Law of
30 December 1970 for a definition of the new areas of application of
regional aid, recognised that not all the areas covered by the repealed laws still corresponded as such to the requirements of regional
development in Belgium and that therefore some areas formerly qualifying no longer needed aid;

Whereas the situation is that, in view of the aid already granted, in
view of the investments made, the changed employment and unemployment position, the development of earnings, economic growth, increased communication and transport facilities and, in some areas, the
proximity of an economic growth point, there are large areas in
certain regions where regional aids are not warranted;

Whereas consequently some of the regional aid granted pursuant to
the Law of 30 December 1970 is incompatible with the common market;
whereas indeed aid to investment projects in developed areas which
do not require such aid affects competition and trade in a manner
contrary to the common interest, since it aggravates the disequilibrium between regions of the Community and is contrary to the fundamental objectives of the Treaty;

IV

Whereas the Belgian Government, upon being informed of the irregular
character of the aid and the incompatibility of some of the aid with
the common market, attempted to define new development areas in
Belgium and has meanwhile, for several months past, suspended the
granting of regional aid;

Whereas, by letter of 24 September 1971, the Belgian Government, in
accordance with Article 93(3) of the Treaty, communicated to the Commission a draft law amending Article 11 of the Law on economic
expansion together with a draft Royal Order listing new development
areas; whereas, by letter of 11 October 1971, the Belgian Government
informed the Commission of the criteria and reasons for the selection

305

of those development areas;

Whereas it may be seen from the list of proposed new areas that they are to be found in practically every region of the country; whereas all 9 of the country's provinces and 41 out of 43 arrondissements would qualify for aid; whereas what is in question is not the size or the shape of the areas but conditions in the regions where these areas are located;

Whereas what is involved is therefore a system of regional aid which would cover practically the whole of the national territory;

Whereas such lack of regional specificity would lead to the aid being granted in regions where it would not be warranted, thereby making it incompatible with the common market; whereas the lack of regional specificity is confirmed, moreover, by the fact that the areas are not grouped into two categories permitting the intensity of aid to be varied according to the gravity of the problems, as was in fact laid down in Article 21 of the Law of 30 December 1970;

Whereas the localisation of the areas in the Belgian regions is to be based on a set of quantitative criteria in place of the four qualitative criteria laid down in Article 11 of the Law, namely present and foreseeable structural under-employment, actual or imminent decline of major economic activities, an abnormally low standard of living and slow economic growth; whereas the choice and application of the quantitative criteria involve an excessive weighting of certain criteria and a method of classification of areas in which the points attributed to an area for each of the criteria are aggregated in such a way that the nature and the gravity of the problems to be solved do not emerge and the principle of regional specificity cannot be properly applied.

Whereas, moreover, the method used to identify the socio-economic problems of the regions is based on an excessive subdivision of the country, with no correlation of the problems thus identified and no adequate consideration of them in their regional context.

Whereas certain situations are defined by means of out-of-date or irrelevant statistics; whereas in respect of none of the quantitative criteria employed or devised have thresholds been determined that would make clear the meaning of the qualitative descriptions used in Article 1 of the Law, such as 'abnormally low' or 'major'; in effect, conditions in each area are expressed, for all the criteria, in terms of the variation from national averages calculated by the same methods the least variation being taken into account;

Whereas on the basis of insufficiently justified exceptions to that classification it is proposed to determine development areas in 41 out of 43 arrondissements of the country thereby covering the whole country with growth points;

V

Whereas there are in Belgium regions where regional aid is warranted, and whereas the rejection of all the new areas, involving the prohibition of aid until new areas have been determined on proper grounds,

306

would unduly penalise those regions;

Whereas regions which need aid cannot be determined accurately and consistently until technical problems affecting the statistics, quantitative criteria and methods have been resolved; whereas, therefore, any decision will have to be of a temporary nature;

Whereas, generally speaking, an examination of the socio-economic situation at the regional level does not always enable all important problems to be recognised; whereas most Member States therefore use statistics collected for smaller administrative units; whereas in this particular case the Belgian Government used as a basis for the selection of areas to be aided statistics collected for arrondissements which it declared to be the smallest administrative units for which the necessary statistics are available for the whole country;

Whereas consequently the Commission, also, had to assess the situation on the basis of arrondissement statistics, while, however, taking into account correlations between neighbouring situations and relating problems to the wider regional context in order to gauge their regional significance;

Whereas by applying so far as possible all the qualitative criteria of the Law of 30 December 1970 on the basis of the various studies made by the Commission, and by making suitably cautious use of the incomplete information supplied by the Belgian Government (present and foreseeable unemployment, decline of certain activities, average income per head and rate of growth), it may be seen that certain problems exist and consequently that certain regions require aid; whereas by cross checking and the use of certain thresholds to distinguish the main factors while avoiding a rigid and mechanical application of criteria yet observing quantitative and qualitative correlations between those criteria, by grouping areas in various ways so that intraregional relations are not neglected, it is possible to ascertain, on the basis of the coherence and correlation of situations, whether the problems which emerge have adequate regional significance;

Whereas, finally, to assess these situations, the Commission also took into account the situation in other Community regions; whereas it found in this connection that the two least well placed Belgian regions have a gross domestic product which is 76% of the 1969 Community average and that the lowest percentage in the Community is 33%; whereas it also took into account the situation in frontier regions;

Whereas the Commission, in the light of those considerations, reached the conclusion that in present circumstances aid within the following regions could be considered as compatible with the common market; in the province of Antwerp, the arrondissement of Turnhout; in the province of West-Vlaanderen, the arrondissements of Diksmuide, Ieper, Tielt and Veurne; in the province of Oost-Vlaanderen, the arondissements of Eeklo and Oudenaerde; in the province of Hainaut, the arrondissements of Ath,Charleroi, Mons, Mouscron, Soignies and Thuin; in the province of Liège, Verviers and Waremme; in the province of Limburg,the arrondissements of Hasselt, Maaseik and Tongeren; in the province of Luxembourg,the arrondissements of Arlon, Bastogne, Marche,

Neufchâteau and Virton; in the province of Namur, the arrondissements of Dinant, Namur and Philippeville;

Whereas it is for the Belgian Government to determine within those regions the localisation and the extent of the areas to be aided in the light of regional development requirements;

VI

Whereas additional information supplied by the Belgian Government in its letters of 10, 13 and 20 March 1972 enable the Commission to ascertain that certain socio-economic situations are not confined within the limits of administrative units but extend into neighbouring arondissements, a circumstance which warrants the granting of regional aid also in the following areas envisaged by the Belgian Government:

- by way of extension to the arrondissement of Turnhout, the area covering the communes of Oostmalle and Westmalle;

- by way of extension to the arrondissement of Turnhout and the province of Limburg, the area covering the communes of Aarschot, Averbode, Begijnendijk, Betekom, Booischot, Diest, Heist-op-den-Berg, Langdorp, Messelbroek, Molenstede, Rillaar, Scherpenheuvel, Testelt, Webbekom, Wiekevorst, Zichem;

- by way of extension to the arrondissement of Oudenaerde, the area covering the communes of Appelterre-Eichem, Denderhoutem, Denderleeuw, Geraardsbergen, Grimmingen, Idegem, Iddergem, Moerbeke, Nederboelare, Nederhasselt, Ninove, Okegem, Onkerzeel, Outer, Schendelbeke, Viane, Zandbergen;

- by way of connection between the two parts of the arrondissement of Mouscron, the area covering the communes of Aalbeke, Lauwe, Menen, Rekkem;

VII

Whereas, independently of the regular review to which all systems of aid are subject, this conclusion can only be provisional until the studies undertaken with experts of the Belgian administration have succeeded in clarifying the technical questions affecting the determination of development areas in Belgium; whereas in the light of these studies and of the effect of the regional aid which will have been granted in the meantime, a fresh development areas plan should be put before the Commission for consideration;

Whereas, owing to the complexity of the questions to be studied and the importance of the end in view, a two year period should be allowed before a further decision is taken;

Whereas the principle of regional specificity requires that areas located in regions where aid will be granted should be differentiated according to the gravity of the regional problem and that maximum aid intensity should also be differentiated; whereas the proposals for differentiation, to be prepared by the Kingdom of Belgium, should be communicated to the Commission in order that it may express its views on the matter;

Whereas, in addition to regional aid, Article 5 of the Law of 30 December 1970 contains outline provisions allowing sectoral aid to be granted outside the development areas; whereas, in accordance with the Law, a prerequisite for application of those provisions is a Royal Order defining the criteria and mode of application of such sectoral aid; whereas the criteria and mode of application must be communicated to the Commission beforehand in order that it may express its views thereon;

Whereas, in order to assess the effects of sectoral aid on competition and trade it is essential to know the sector to which it will be applied; whereas it is practically impossible for a regulation implementing those outline provisions to set out in advance the sectors qualifying for aid even though it may define general criteria for selection;

Whereas, therefore, the Commission must be enabled to express its views beforehand on cases to which the provisions will be applied; whereas it is necessary to distinguish between sectoral aid granted to a sector as a whole and sectoral aid granted to a limited number of undertakings;

Whereas, where such aid is granted to a sector as a whole, it is sufficient that the Commission be provided, in the same way as when a special system of aid is instituted, with the required information on the characteristic features of the sector, the problems requiring attention, the ends in view, and the mode of application and intensity of the aid;

Whereas, on the other hand, where sectoral aid is granted to a limited number of undertakings, the Commission must be provided with details of significant cases so that it may express its views thereon;

Whereas the granting of sectoral aid should to that extent be made subject to appropriate conditions;

Whereas, since investments vary in size according to the nature of sectors and their activities and to the size of the aid, which for a given figure is relatively greater the smaller is the investment, a double criterion is needed (size of the investment and relative size of the aid) to define significant cases; whereas a threshold of 100 million Belgian francs may be taken in respect of the size of the investment and an intensity of 15% in net subsidy equivalent (according to the Community method of assessing regional aid) in respect of the relative size of the aid;

Whereas the examination of the effect of the Law in question on sectors concerned with Annex II products comes within the scope of agricultural aid policy treated in item Vl of the Council Resolution of 25 May 1971 on new guidelines for the common agricultural policy (O.J. No C 52 of 27 May 1971), and whereas, furthermore, aid granted to those sectors is governed by the Council Directive of 17 April 1972 on agricultural reform; whereas, therefore, this Decision could not apply to aid granted in respect of Annex II products,

HAS ADOPTED THIS DECISION:

Article 1

The Kingdom of Belgium shall forthwith take the measures required to modify the system of regional aid provided for in the Law of 30 December 1970 on economic expansion so that aid is granted only:

- to the following regions, within areas to be determined nationally: in the province of Antwerpen, the arrondissement of Turnhout; in the province of West-Vlaanderen, the arrondissements of Diksmuide, Ieper, Tielt and Veurne; in the province of Oost-Vlaanderen, the arrondissements of Eeklo and Oudenaerde; in the province of Hainaut, the arrondissements of Ath, Charleroi, Mons, Mouscron, Soignies and Thuin; in the province of Liège, the arrondissements of Huy, Liège, Verviers and Waremme; in the province of Limburg, the arrondissements of Hasselt, Maaseik and Tongeren; in the province of Luxembourg, the arrondissements of Arlon, Bastogne, Marche, Neufchâteau and Virton; in the province of Namur, the arrondissements of Dinant, Namur and Philippeville;

- to the following areas:

  - by way of extension to the arrondissement of Turnhout, the area covering the communes of Oostmalle and Westmalle;

  - by way of extension to the district of Turnhout and the province of Limburg, the area covering the communes of Aarschot, Averbode, Begijnendijk, Betekom, Booischot, Diest, Heist-op-den-Berg, Langdorp, Messelbroek, Molenstede, Rillaar, Scherpenheuvel, Testelt, Webbekom, Wiekevorst, Zichem;

  - by way of extension to the arrondissement of Oudenaerde, the area covering the communes of Appelterre-Eichem, Denderhoutem, Denderleeuw, Geraardsbergen, Grimmingen, Idegem, Iddergem, Moerbeke, Nederboelare, Nederhasselt, Ninove, Okegem, Onkerzeel, Outer, Schendelbeke, Viane, Zandbergen;

  - by way of connection between the two parts of the district Mouscron, the area covering the communes of Aalbeke, Lauwe, Menen, Rekkem;

Regional aid may no longer be granted for new investments in the areas covered by the Laws on regional aid of 18 July 1959 and 14 July 1966 which do not coincide with the regions and areas listed above, nor in the other areas envisaged by the Kingdom of Belgium.

Article 2

Without prejudice to the review laid down in Article 93(1) of the Treaty, the Kingdom of Belgium shall communicate to the Commission a fresh development areas plan to which all regional aid, whether abolished or not, covered by the Law of 30 December 1970 on economic expansion would apply, so that a further decision may be taken on this matter within two years.

The Kingdom of Belgium shall, as soon as possible, take measures necessary to group development areas into two categories according to the gravity of the regional problems and to make a similar differentiation in respect of maximum aid intensity. Such measures shall be communicated to the Commission in the form of proposals so that it may express its views on the matter.

Article 3

The granting of sectoral aid provided for in Article 5 of the Belgian Law of 30 December 1970 on economic expansion shall be subject to the following conditions:

- the criteria and mode of application, which in accordance with the said Article 5 are to be the subject of an implementing regulation, must be communicated to the Commission beforehand so that it may express its views thereon;

- where sectoral aids are to be granted to a sector as a whole, the information concerning the establishment of a system of specific aid (the characteristic features of the sector, the problems requiring attention, the ends in view, and the mode of application and intensity of the aid) shall be communicated to the Commission beforehand so that it may express its view thereon;

- where sectoral aids are to be granted to part of a sector or to a limited number of undertakings, significant cases as defined in Article 4 shall be notified to the Commission beforehand so that it may express its views thereon.

Article 4

Cases in respect of which investment reaches or exceeds 100 million Belgian francs, irrespective of the size of the aid, and cases in respect of which the size of the aid equals or exceeds, in net subsidy-equivalent, 15% of the amount of the investment, irrespective of the size of the investment, shall be regarded as significant cases of application of sectoral aid under the Belgian Law of 30 December 1970 on economic expansion.

Aid intensity shall be calculated according to the Community method of assessing aid as established for the purpose of applying regional aid coordination principles[1].

Article 5

This Decision is addressed to the Kingdom of Belgium.

Done at Brussels, 26 April 1972

For the Commission

The President

S.L. MANSHOLT

1. Cf. Communication of the Commission to the Council concerning general systems of regional aid, Annex.

   Procedure for the application of the principles of coordination of general systems of regional aid (O.J. No C 111, 4.11.1971, p.10).

12. Aid Schemes for specific industries

Extract Eighth Report on Competition Policy April 1979

General Commission policy

172. Following a request by the Council President for an exchange of views between the two institutions on industry aid policy, in May 1978 the Commission sent the Council a Communication on its industry and schemes policy.

173. The document was of particular significance on account of prevailing circumstances. The grant of State aids has, quite naturally, become increasingly important following the economic crisis, the subsequent period of slow growth and resultant high level of unemployment.

Structural problems were coming to light in all Member States before the economic crisis, but the consequences of increased petroleum prices, persistent inflation, unstable exchange rates and the growth of certain industries in developing countries have accentuated the need for structural changes within the Community.

All Member States are going through a transitional period, characterised by the need to adapt their industries to the consequences of these changes.

The European Council was aware of the situation and at its meeting in Copenhagen on 7 and 8 April 1978 underlined the need to restore the competitiveness of industries in distress; this remained the main objective of the Member States' policy. In this connection the European Council emphasised the need to overcome the serious problems of structural overcapacity in several industries and to promote an industrial structure which can face up to worldwide competition.

While State aids have a role to play in securing an orderly transition to new economic structures enjoying long-term prospects for survival in the context of the modern world, using them to preserve the *status quo* will only serve to hinder the adjustments that the Community's industries must make if they are to secure the economic and social future of the Community. It must be recognised that the granting of State assistance could cause a permanent drift towards protectionism within the Community, both as between the Member States and in relations with the rest of the world. In both serious risks

312

are involved, for protectionism would endanger Community solidarity and provoke retaliation by non-Community countries.

174. The Commission Communication describes the general principles on industry aids and then outlines the specific criteria used in the scrutiny of national schemes and in policy on specific industries. It also points to the sectoral effects of other types of aids.

General principles

175. The Commission's policy on industry aids is based on the rules of the Treaty which aim to ensure that competition within the common market is not distorted. It considers that this basis still holds good in present circumstances for three main reasons:

(i)   the customs union would founder if Member States could unilaterally invalidate it by granting aid;

(ii) the common market makes little sense unless businesses tackle the the market on the strength of their own resources without any aid to distort competition between them;

(iii) lastly, and as a corollary, a system which leaves the field open to competition provides for optimum distribution of production factors and ensures the most rapid economic and social progress possible.

However in many cases aid is justified because it contributes to the achievement of the Community's economic and social aims. This occurs when market forces would:

(i)   obstruct progress towards these aims;

(ii) permit them to be attained only within unacceptable time limits or at unacceptable social cost;

(iii) intensify competition to such an extent that it could destroy itself.

The Commission considers that aid should be authorised when it is needed to correct serious regional imbalance, to encourage or speed up certain essential changes or developments in certain industries, to permit smooth cutbacks in certain activities where this is desirable for social reasons or to neutralise, at least temporarily, certain distortions of competition due to action outside the Community.

The aims, forms and conditions relating to such aids, justifiable in that they facilitate the orderly development of Community structures, must not conflict with the Community's general objectives and must be designed in such a way as to entail a minimum distortion of competition.

Criteria for appraising individual aid plans

176. On the basis of these general principles the Commission has

developed a number of criteria against which it examines the sectoral
aid proposals notified to it. The main criteria are the following:

(i) sectoral aid should be limited to cases where it is justified by
circumstances in the industry concerned;

(ii) aid should lead to a restoration of long-term viability by resolving problems rather than preserve the *status quo* and put off
decisions and changes which are inevitable;

(iii) nevertheless, since adjustment takes time, a limited use of resources to reduce the social and economic costs of change is admissible in certain circumstances and subject to strict conditions;

(iv) unless granted over relatively short periods, aids should be
progressively reduced and clearly linked to the restructuring of
the sector concerned;

(v) the intensity of aid should be proportionate to the problem it is
designed to resolve so that distortions of competition are kept
to a minimum; and

(vi) industrial problems and unemployment should not be transferred
from one Member State to another.

The role assigned by the Treaty to the Commission in handling State
aid cases is principally one of reaction to the proposals of the
Member States. The Commission does not consider it advisable to define
systematically the types of aid to which it is favourably and unfav-
ourably disposed in the case of each industrial sector. To elaborate
such guidelines for aids would risk encouraging a more general recourse to aid by Member States even where it is not strictly necessary.
It would, moreover, result in some inflexibility since such frame-
works could not take into account the specific situation of the
industry concerned in each Member State. However, in cases where it
has become evident that an industry faces a situation of particular
difficulty throughout the Community, or is likely to face such difficulty, it is appropriate to develop guidelines which indicate the
Commission's policy on aids to this industry.

Policy on aids to certain sectors

177. Guidelines have been developed in particular in cases where
industries are in crisis or where the Community industry is insufficiently competitive to take advantage of rapid growth in world demand.
The former group has concerned shipbuilding (four successive Council
Directives on aid[1]), textiles (general principles on aid first elaborated in 1971 and refined and extended in 1976[2]), manmade fibres
(proposal of appropriate measures to the Member States[3]) and steel
(general principles adopted in 1977[4] and draft of a decision under
Article 95 of the ECSC Treaty[5]).

The Commission's approach in the case of each of these industries
has been based on certain common principles. It has recognised that
the crisis that they have met has threatened either a disorderly
rundown of their activities with serious adverse consequences or

for employment in general or a series of interventions by Member States designed to protect their industries. In the latter eventuality aid levels would be fruitlessly bid up and difficulties transferred from one Member State to another at substantial cost to the Community as a whole. The purpose of the Commission's initiatives in defining guidelines has been to avoid both eventualities and at the same time to encourage the restoration of the industries' competitiveness. To these ends it has accepted the justification for aids to enable orderly adjustment to market conditions. Such adjustment requires both a restoration of competitiveness and either an avoidance of undesirable increases or in some cases an actual reduction in productive capacity.

In more concrete terms, this has led to the specification of the following principles:

(i)   aids should not be given where their sole effect would be to maintain the *status quo*. Production aids as such are therefore in principle inadmissible unless they are granted for a limited period and are conditional on action by the recipient which will facilitate adjustment;

(ii)   similarly, while rescue measures may be needed in order to provide a breathing space during which longer-term solutions to a company's difficulties can be worked out, they should not frustrate any necessary reductions in capacity and should therefore be limited to cases where they are required to cope with acute social problems; and

(iii) since it is a common feature of the industries concerned that capacity is excessive, aids should not be given to investment projects which would result in capacity being increased. As discussed below this criterion has in some cases been applied not only to sectoral but also to regional aids.

For other industries the Commission's action has been much more limited, and has been confined to those, such as computers,[6] certain areas of electronics[7] and aerospace,[8] in which, because of the strength of competition from producers in third countries, the Community industry has proved unable to take full advantage of a rapid growth in demand. In these cases the Commission has laid particular stress on the need to avoid a duplication of efforts and has accordingly argued for collaboration between Member States on some projects and more generally for a coordination of national measures. It has in general been favourably disposed to aids which are granted within a coordinated framework of this kind and particularly to those for research and development.

It is also worth mentioning in this context that the Commission has been favourably inclined to Member States' proposals to promote the availability of finance for the creation of new undertakings and for the development of small- and medium-sized enterprises.[9] In many of the fast growing industries these enterprises are among the most innovative and dynamic but their development is often impeded by difficulties in obtaining finance on reasonable terms. The presence of a dynamic small firms sector can, moreover, act as an important competitive stimulus on larger companies.

315

178. Because it makes little sense to exercise control over sectoral aids if other types of aid can nevertheless be granted without being subject to such control and can have similar effects on competition in the sector concerned, the Commission has in the case of certain industries, particularly those which are in difficulties, sought to ensure either that these other types of aid respect the same criteria or that they are only granted on certain conditions. Thus, where employment aids are given to maintain existing jobs, the Commission has considered that if they are concentrated on industrial sectors which face acute difficulties in all Member States and if they are not associated with appropriate adjustment measures designed to restore a company's viability, the grant of these aids will not resolve the social and industrial difficulties but will rather transfer them to other Member States. For those reasons it required the United Kingdom substantially to modify the Temporary Employment Subsidy.[10]

Similarly, in sectors suffering from extreme overcapacity the Commission has required Member States to agree in principle not to grant regional aids for investment projects that would result in increased capacity. Such action was taken by the Commission in the respect of the synthetic fibres industry[11] and of shipbuilding.[12]

179. The discussions of the Commission's memorandum by the Council of Ministers indicated that the latter was in broad agreement with the policy that the Commission follows in this area.

. . . . .

1. Point 182 of this Report
2. First Report on Competition Policy, point 171 and Sixth Report on Competition Policy, point 223.
3. Seventh Report on Competition Policy, point 204.
4. Seventh Report on Competition Policy, point 261.
5. Point 197 of this Report.
6. Second Report on Competition Policy, points 104 and 105; Sixth Report on Competition Policy, point 236.
7. Fifth Report on Competition Policy, point 119; Seventh Report on Competition Policy, point 213.
8. First Report on Competition Policy, points 176 to 178; Second Report on Competition Policy, points 100 to 103.
9. Sixth Report on Competition Policy, points 253 to 256.
10. Points 232 to 234 of this Report.
11. Seventh Report on Competition Policy, points 203 and 204.
12. Point 182 of this Report.

13. Communication of the Commission on Regional Aid Systems

(OJ No C 31, 3 February 1979, p. 9)

On 21 December 1978 the Commission informed the Member States of the
principles which, in accordance with the powers vested in the Commission by Articles 92 et seq. of the EEC Treaty, it will apply to regional aid systems already in force or to be established in the regions of
the Community. The principles were set out in the form of a Communication the text of which is published hereunder.

The Commission has proposed to the Member States under Article 93 (1)
of that Treaty that their Governments take the measures necessary to
give effect to these principles within the time limits provided for in
the Communication.

In its Communication of 26 February 1975 the Commission informed the
Council of the principles of coordination, valid for all regions of
the Community, which it would apply from 1 January 1975.

The Commission undertook at that time to pursue with experts from the
Member States technical studies with a view to finding standards of
measurement capable of making comparable all forms of regional aids in
force in the Community. The common method of evaluation had hitherto
fixed investment as the sole denominator in considering the transparency of aids and aid systems. The employment situation in the various
regions of the Community and the emphasis which some Member States wish
to give the creation of jobs in their regional aid scheme were, however, borne in mind in carrying out the studies on measurability.
In view of this, an alternative denominator expressed in European
units of account per job created by the investment is being introduced
into the principles of coordination. The standard of measurement will
thus be broadened. In addition the methods for measuring aids are
being supplemented as a result of the studies on measurability. All
aids which have maximum intensities which can be expressed in terms of
investment or jobs created can now be coordinated.

Some existing regional aids are not, however, conditional on investment, in the sense envisaged in the principles of coordination, or on
job creation and have the character of operation aids. The Commission
has reservations in principle as to the compatibility of operating
aids with the common market. The Commission will specify the circumstances, if any, in which it might consider operating aids to be compatible. Until then there should be no increase in the level of the
existing aids and no further aids of this type should be introduced.

Finally, a method of coordinating aids given on the transfer of an
establishment is introduced.

These principles of coordination, as set out in this Communication,
do not apply to the products mentioned in Annex II to the EEC Treaty.

To give effect to the above and having regard to the views expressed
in previous Communications, including in particular the preambles to
the Communications of 23 June 1971 and 26 February 1975, the principles
of coordination have been partly redefined and the methods for their
implementation, including the common method of evaluation, have been

317

amended and supplemented.

The Commission, in accordance with the powers vested in it by Articles 92 et seq. of the EEC Treaty, will from 1 January 1979, apply the principles set out hereunder to regional aid systems already in force or to be established in the regions of the Community.

Principles of coordination of regional aid systems

1. The coordination has five principal aspects which form one whole: ceilings of aid intensity differentiated according to the nature and gravity of the regional problems, transparency, regional specificity, the sectoral repercussions of regional aids and a system of supervision.

The differentiated ceilings of aid intensity

2. The differentiated ceilings are fixed in net grant equivalents expressed either as a percentage of initial investment or in European units of account (EUA)[1] per job created by the initial investment. No ceilings are fixed for Greenland. The alternative ceilings for the various categories of region are set out hereunder:

(i) for Ireland, the 'Mezzogiorno', Norhtern Ireland, Berlin (West) and the French Overseas Departments - a ceiling of 75% net grant equivalent of initial investment will apply to aids linked and fixed directly in relation to initial investment or jobs created, the alternative ceiling being a net grant equivalent of 13 000 EUA per job created by the initial investment. In addition, as from 1 January 1981, for projects with an initial investment exceeding three million EUA not more than a further 25% net grant equivalent of initial investment or a net grant equivalent of 4 500 EUA per job created by the initial investment can be paid in other aids and must be spread over a minimum of five years;

(ii) for the part of French territory which receives the regional development premium (as listed in Annex I of decree No 76/325 of 14.4.1976 - J.O.R.F. No 90 of 14.4.1976), the aided areas in the Italian regions of Friuli-Venezia Giulia, Trentino-Alto Adige, Val d'Aosta, Lazio, Marche, Toscana, Umbria and Veneto in so far as these regions are not included in the 'Mezzogiorno', and the parts of the United Kingdom other than Northern Ireland which were defined as Assisted Areas on 1 January 1978 under Section 7 (7) of the Industry Act 1972, with the exception of areas classified as Intermediate Areas at that date, the alternative ceilings will be 30% net grant equivalent of initial investment or a net grant equivalent of initial investment or a net grant equivalent of 5 500 EUA per job created by the initial investment, but the latter may not exceed 40% net grant equivalent of initial investment;

(iii) for the 'Zonenrandgebiet' and the special development area in the North of Denmark and the Islands of Bornholm, Aerø, Samsø and Langeland the alternative ceilings will be 25% net grant equivalent of initial investment or 4 500 EUA per job created by the initial investment, but the latter may not exceed 30% net grant equivalent of initial investment;

(iv) for the other regions of the Community the alternative ceilings

318

will be 20% net grant equivalent of initial investment or a net grant equivalent of 3 500 EUA per job created by the initial investment, but the latter may not exceed 25% net grant equivalent of initial investment; for these regions the trend must be towards a reduction in the level of aids as far as possible.

3. One of the appropriate alternative ceilings must be respected by the total regional aids accorded to a given initial investment or on the creation of jobs. The absolute ceilings fixed above the ceilings expressed in EUA per job created by the initial investment do not apply in the case of the tertiary sector.

Aids not conditional on initial investment or job creation

4. There are some regional aids in use in the Community at present which are not conditional on initial investment or job creation and which have the character of operating aids. The Commission has reservations in principle as to the compatibility of operating aids with the common market.

Application of these aids may however continue until final decisions on their compatibility have been taken in the course of the Commission's review of existing aid systems under Article 93 (1) of the EEC Treaty. Before the end of a three-year period, the Commission will, in the light of these decisions, specify the circumstances, if any, in which the Commission, notwithstanding its reservations in principle, might consider operating aids to be compatible with the common market. Until then the level, duration and geographic scope of application of the existing aids should not be increased and further aids of this type should not be introduced unless a derogation from this principle has been granted under point 7 hereunder.

5. In order to place all Member States in the same position with regard to the ceilings, particularly in the context of outbidding, the Member States concerned will have to ensure that the ceilings fixed at points 2 and 3 above are not exceeded when the above aids are awarded.

Aids to the transfer of an establishment

6. In the case of transfer of an establishment to an aided region, the ceilings will be 100% of the cost of transfer of capital equipment or the appropriate ceiling from point 2 above applied to the value of the capital equipment, or to the number of workers transferred. The absolute ceilings fixed above the ceilings expressed in EUA per job created by the initial investment at point 2 will not apply in the case of transfers.

Derogations

7. Derogations from the intensity ceilings or from the principle at point 4 above regarding increases in, or the introduction of, certain aids may be granted by the Commission provided that the necessary justification is communicated in advance in accordance

with the procedure provided for at Article 93 of the EEC Treaty. The Commission will periodically supply the Member States with a list of any such derogations.

Review of ceilings

8. The level of all ceilings will be revised at the end of a three-year period having regard in particular to experience gained, the evolution of the regional situation in the Community (especially with regard to the evolution of unemployment), the number of jobs created or maintained and changes in aid systems. Before 31 December 1979, however, the Commission will examine with experts from the Member States the problems of the cumulation of regional and other aids beyond that discussed in point 12. Before the same date it will also examine how absolute ceilings expressed in EUA per job created by the initial investment, above the percentage of initial investment ceiling, might be introduced and the levels at which such ceilings might be fixed. The question as to whether an absolute ceiling expressed as a percentage of initial investment should be introduced above the ceiling expressed in EUA per job created by the initial investment for the regions listed at point 2 (i) of these principles will also be examined.

Regional specificity

9. Regional specificity will be implemented in the light of the following principles:

    (i) that regional aids do not cover the whole national territory, i.e. general aids may not be granted under the heading of regional aids;[2]

    (ii) that aid regimes clearly specify, either in geographical terms or by quantitative criteria, the limits of aided regions or, within these, the limits of aided areas;

    (iii) that, except in the case of growth points, regional aids are not granted in a pin-point manner, i.e. to isolated geographical points having virtually no influence on the development of a region;

    (iv) that, where problems which are different in kind, intensity or urgency occur, the aid intensity must be adapted accordingly;

    (v) that the graduation and variation of rates of aid across different areas and regions are clearly indicated;

    (vi) that the regional aids awarded in the regions benefiting from the European Regional Development Fund should in principle form part of a regional development programme within the meaning of Article 6 of Regulation (EEC) No 724/75 establishing that Fund.

Sectorial repercussions

10. The lack of sectorial specificity in regional aid systems makes

their assessment difficult because of the problems that the sectoral repercussions of these aids may pose at Community level.

11. In the absence of a general solution for dealing with these sectoral repercussions, the Commission, following consultation with the Member States, will examine to what extent appropriate restrictions should be applied when awarding regional aids where such restrictions are justified by the situation in a sector.

12. When an investment benefits both from regional aids and from other types of aid on a regionally differentiated basis, the regional aid may be given only in so far as when the regional aid and the regional component of the other types of aid are cumulated, the ceilings mentioned in points 2 and 3 above are not exceeded.

System of supervision

13. The Commission shall supervise the application of the coordination principles by means of a notification system which will ensure business secrecy.

Methods for implementation

14. The methods for implementing the principles of coordination, which include the common method of evaluation, defined in the Annex to the Communication of the Commission of 23 June 1971 supplemented by the Communication of the Commission of 27 June 1973, will continue to apply. They are, however, amended and supplemented in accordance with the Annex to this Communication.

Date of effect

15. The principles of coordination set out in this Communication will be applied by the Commission from 1 January 1979 in all regions of the Community for an initial period of three years. In so far as a transitional period for changes is deemed necessary by a Member State, the Commission may fix such a period.

----

1) As defined by Council Decision 76/250/EEC of 21 April 1975 (OJ No L 104, 24.4.1975).

2) With the exception of Ireland and the Grand Duchy of Luxembourg, which are considered each as one region.

14. COUNCIL DIRECTIVE

of 24 April 1972 :

on the approximation of the laws of the Member States relating to insurance against civil liability in respect of the use of motor vehicles and to the enforcement of the obligation to insure against such liability

(72/166/EEC)

(JO No L 103, 2 May 1972, p. 1; OJ (Special Edition 1972 II) p. 360)

THE COUNCIL OF THE EUROPEAN COMMUNITIES,

Having regard to the Treaty establishing the European Economic Community, and in particular Article 100 thereof;

Having regard to the proposal from the Commission;

Having regard to the Opinion of the European Parliament;

Having regard to the Opinion of the Economic and Social Committee;

Whereas the objective of the Treaty is to create a common market which is basically similar to a domestic market, and whereas one of the essential conditions for achieving this is to bring about the free movement of goods and persons;

Whereas the only purpose of frontier controls of compulsory insurance cover against civil liability in respect of the use of motor vehicles is to safeguard the interests of persons who may be victims of accidents caused by such vehicles; whereas the existence of such frontier controls results from disparities between national requirements in this field;

Whereas these disparities are such as may impede the free movement of motor vehicles and persons within the Community; whereas, consequently, they have a direct effect on the establishment and functioning of the common market;

Whereas the Commission Recommendation of 21 June 1968 on control by customs of travellers crossing intra-Community frontiers calls upon Member States to carry out controls on travellers and their motor vehicles only under exceptional circumstances and to remove the physical barriers at customs posts;

Whereas it is desirable that the inhabitants of the Member States should become more fully aware of the reality of the common market and that to this end measures should be taken further to liberalize the rules regarding the movement of persons and motor vehicles travelling between Member States; whereas the need for such measures has been repeatedly emphasized by members of the European Parliament;

Whereas such relaxation of the rules relating to the movement of travellers constitutes another step towards the mutual opening of their markets by Member States and the creation of conditions similar to those of a domestic market;

Whereas the abolition of checks on green cards for vehicles normally based in a Member State entering the territory of another Member State can be effected by means of an agreement between the six national insurers' bureaux, whereby each national bureau would guarantee compensation in accordance with the provisions of national law in respect of any loss or injury giving entitlement to compensation caused in its territory by one of those vehicles, whether or not insured.

Whereas such a guarantee agreement presupposes that all Community motor vehicles travelling in Community territory are covered by insurance; whereas the national law of each Member State should, therefore, provide for the compulsory insurance of vehicles against civil liability, the insurance to be valid throughout Community territory; whereas such national law may nevertheless provide for exemptions for certain persons and for certain types of vehicles;

Whereas the system provided for in this Directive could be extended to vehicles normally based in the territory of any third country in respect of which the national bureaux of the six Member States have concluded a similar agreement;

HAS ADOPTED THIS DIRECTIVE:

Article 1

For the purposes of this Directive:

1. 'vehicle' means any motor vehicle intended for travel on land and propelled by mechanical power, but not running on rails, and any trailer, whether or not coupled;

2. 'injured party' means any person entitled to compensation in respect of any loss or injury caused by vehicles;

3. 'national insurers' bureau' means a professional organization which is constituted in accordance with Recommendation No 5 adopted on 25 January 1949 by the Road Transport Sub-committee of the Inland Transport Committee of the United Nations Economic Commission for Europe and which groups together insurance undertakings which, in a State, are authorized to conduct the business of motor vehicle insurance against civil liability;

4. 'territory in which the vehicle is normally based' means

   - the territory of the State in which the vehicle is registered; or

   - in cases where no registration is required for a type of vehicle but the vehicle bears an insurance plate, or a distinguishing sign analogous to the registration plate, the territory of the State in which the insurance plate or the sign is issued; or

   - in cases where neither registration plate nor insurance plate nor distinguishing sign is required for certain types of vehicle, the territory of the State in which the person who has custody of the vehicle is permanently resident;

5. 'green card' means an international certificate of insurance issued on behalf of a national bureau in accordance with Recommendation No 5 adopted on 25 January 1949 by the Road Transport Sub-committee of the Inland Transport Committee of the United Nations Economic Commission for Europe.

Article 2

1. Member States shall refrain from making checks on insurance against civil liability in respect of vehicles normally based in the territory of another Member State.

Likewise, Member States shall refrain from making such insurance checks on vehicles normally based in the territory of a third country entering their territory from the territory of another Member State. Member States may, however carry out random checks.

2. As regards vehicles normally based in the territory of a Member State, the provisions of this Directive, with the exception of Articles 3 and 4, shall take effect:

- after an agreement has been concluded between the six national insurers' bureaux under the terms of which each national bureau guarantees the settlement, in accordance with the provisions of its own national law on compulsory insurance, of claims in respect of accidents occurring in its territory caused by vehicles normally based in the territory of another Member State, whether or not such vehicles are insured;

- from the date fixed by the Commission, upon its having ascertained in close cooperation with the Member States that such an agreement has been concluded;

- for the duration of that agreement.

Article 3

1. Each Member State shall, subject to Article 4, take all appropriate measures to ensure that civil liability in respect of the use of vehicles normally based in its territory is covered by insurance. The extent of the liability covered and the terms and conditions of the cover shall be determined on the basis of these measures.

2. Each Member State shall take all appropriate measures to ensure that the contract of insurance also covers:

- according to the law in force in other Member States, any loss or injury which is caused in the territory of those States;

- any loss or injury suffered by nationals of Member States during a direct journey between two territories in which the Treaty establishing the European Economic Community is in force, if there is no national insurers' bureau responsible for the territory which is being crossed; in that case, the loss or injury shall be covered in accordance with the internal laws on compulsory insurance in force in the Member State in whose territory the vehicle is normally based.

Article 4

A Member State may act in derogation of Article 3 in respect of:

(a) certain natural or legal persons, public or private; the list of such persons shall be drawn up by the State concerned and communicated to the other Member States and to the Commission.

A Member State so derogating shall take the appropriate measures to ensure that compensation is paid in respect of any loss or injury caused in the territory of other Member States by vehicles belonging to such persons. It shall in particular designate an authority or body in the country where the loss or injury occurs responsible for compensating injured parties in accordance with the laws of that State in cases where the procedure provided for in the first indent of Article 2 (2) is not applicable. It shall notify the other Member States and the Commission of the measures taken;

(b) certain types of vehicle or certain vehicles having a special plate; the list of such types or of such vehicles shall be drawn up by the State concerned and communicated to the other Member States and to the Commission.

In that case, the other Member States shall retain the right to require, on entry into their territory of such a vehicle, that the person having custody thereof be in possession of a valid green card or that he conclude a frontier insurance contract complying with the requirements of the Member State concerned.

Article 5

Each Member State shall ensure that, where an accident is caused in its territory by a vehicle normally based in the territory of another Member State, the national insurers' bureau shall, without prejudice to the obligation referred to in the first indent of Article 2 (2), obtain information:

- as to the territory in which the vehicle is normally based, and as to its registration mark, if any;

- in so far as is possible, as to the details of the insurance of the vehicle, as they normally appear on the green card, which are in the possession of the person having custody of the vehicle, to the extent that these details are required by the Member State in whose territory the vehicle is normally based.

Each Member State shall also ensure that the bureau communicates this information to the national insurers' bureau of the State in whose territory the vehicle is normally based.

Article 6

Each Member State shall take all appropriate measures to ensure that vehicles normally based in the territory of a third country or in the non-European territory of a Member State entering the territory in which the Treaty establishing the European Economic Community is in force shall not be used in its territory unless any loss or injury caused by those vehicles is covered, in accordance with the requirements of the laws of the various Member States on compulsory insurance against civil liability in respect of the use of vehicles, throughout the territory in which the Treaty establishing the European Economic Community is in force.

Article 7

1. Every vehicle normally based in the territory of a third country or in the non-European territory of a Member State must, before entering the territory in which the Treaty establishing the European Economic Community is in force, be provided either with a valid green card or with a certificate of frontier insurance establishing that the vehicle is insured in accordance with Article 6.

2. However, vehicles normally based in a third country shall be treated as vehicles normally based in the Community if the national bureaux of all the Member States severally guarantee, each in accordance with the provisions of its own national law on compulsory insurance, settlement of claims in respect of accidents occurring in their territory caused by such vehicles.

3. Upon having ascertained, in close cooperation with the Member States, that the obligations referred to in the preceding paragraph have been assumed, the Commission shall fix the date from which and the types of vehicles for which Member States shall no longer require production of the documents referred to in paragraph 1.

Article 8

Member States shall, not later than 31 December 1973, bring into force the measures necessary to comply with this Directive and shall forthwith inform the Commission thereof.

Article 9

This Directive is addressed to the Member States.

Done at Brussels, 24 April 1972

For the Council

The President

G. THORN

15. WRITTEN QUESTION No 614/79

By Lord O'Hagan

to the Commission of the European Communities

(1 October 1979)

(OJ No C 328, 31 December 1979, p. 11)

Subject: Harmonization

The Commission may be aware that the benefits of harmonization are not always self-evident to those outside the Berlaymont.

1. Could the Commission not restate the legitimate purposes which, under the Treaties, harmonization serves?

2. Will the Commission seek to harmonize the attendance records of Commissioners at the plenary sessions and the committees of the European Parliament?

Answer

(30 November 1979)

1. The harmonization of laws within the Community is an instrument for achieving European integration. Article 3 of the Treaty states that the Community's activities shall include the approximation of laws of Member States to the extent required for the proper functioning of the common market. This objective covers the removal of obstacles to the free movement of goods, persons, services and capital within the Community; the establishment of undistorted competition, the adoption of common policies on agriculture, transport and external trade and a social policy and, in general, all areas which are expressly referred to in the Treaty.

Harmonization work has extended also to social legislation and common policies have been initiated in particular on transport, employment and the protection of the environment and consumers.

However, the Commission believes it necessary to apply strict criteria to the need for harmonzation proposals and to consider these case by case. Furthermore, each proposal should be considered not only necessary, but something that is clearly appropriate for the Commission to undertake. The Commission's position on the harmonization of laws was explained in some detail in the reply given to Oral Question No 67/78[1], and was confirmed by Mr Davignon in his recent statement to the Legal Affairs Committee on 9 October.

2. The Commission does not accept the relevance of the Honourable

Member's question. As the Honourable Member will be aware, Members of the Commission make every effort to attend plenary sessions and committee meetings of the new European Parliament.

----

1) Debates of the European Parliament, No 234 (October 1978)

16. REGULATION No 129

OF THE COUNCIL

on the value of the unit of account and the exchange rates to be applied for the purposes of the common agricultural policy.

(JO No 62/2553 of 30 October 1962;OJ Special Edition 1959-1962, p. 274)

THE COUNCIL OF THE EUROPEAN ECONOMIC COMMUNITY,

Having regard to the Treaty establishing the European Economic Community, and in particular Article 43 thereof;

Having regard to the proposal from the Commission;

Having regard to the Opinion of the European Parliament;

Having regard to the Opinion of the Monetary Committee;

Whereas sums should be expressed in a standard unit of account in a number of instruments on the common agricultural policy; whereas the unit of account to be used should be that already applied within the Community under Article 18 of the Financial Regulation on the establishment and implementation of the budget of the European Communities and on the responsibility of authorising and accounting officers;

Whereas it is necessary to fix the rate of exchange to be used for measures taken in pursuance of the common agricultural policy which require sums given in one currency to be expressed in another currency; whereas all Member States and a large number of third countries have communicated par values for their currencies to the International Monetary Fund and whereas the latter has recognised these par values; whereas, under the rules of the Fund, exchange rates which apply to current transactions and are recorded on foreign exchange markets supervised by the monetary authorities of countries the par values of whose currencies have been recognised by the Fund may differ from parity only within narrow limits; whereas, therefore, the use of the exchange rate corresponding to parity normally makes it possible to avoid monetary difficulties which might hinder the implementation of the common agricultural policy;

Whereas, since the unit of account is defined solely as a weigh of gold, either the gold parity or the US dollar parity of national currencies as communicated to and recognised by the International

328

Monetary Fund must of necessity be used to express in national currencies sums given in units of account and vice versa;

Whereas provision should nevertheless be made, in respect of countries
which have communicated a par value for their currency to the International Monetary Fund, for cases where fluctuations in the operative
exchange rate in relation to the par value communicated, although within the limits laid down under the rules of that body, might jeopardise
the implementation of the common agricultural policy;

Whereas, in such cases, the exchange rate on the most representative
foreign exchange market or markets should be used;

Whereas the rate on the most representative foreign exchange market
or markets must be chosen also for the currencies of countries which
have not communicated par values to the International Monetary Fund
or whose par values have not been recognised by the Fund;

Whereas, finally, provision should be made for derogations where
monetary circumstances are likely to hinder the satisfactory implementation of the common agricultural policy;

HAS ADOPTED THIS REGULATION:

Article 1

Where, in instruments concerning the common agricultural policy or
the special trade systems for certain goods resulting from the processing of agricultural products, sums are expressed in units of
account, the value of that unit of account shall be 0.88867088 grammes
of fine gold. This value may be changed only in the cases and in accordance with the procedures laid down in Articles 2 and 3 of Regulation (EEC) No 653/68 of the Council of 30 May 1968 on conditions for
alterations to the value of the unit of account used for the common
agricultural policy.

The provisions of this Article shall apply without prejudice to
Article 18 of the Financial Regulation on the establishment and implementation of the EEC budget and on the responsibility of authorising
officers and accounting officers (Article 209 (a) and (c) of the
Treaty) .

Article 2

1. Where measures taken in pursuance of the instruments or provisions
referred to in Article 1 require sums given in one currency to be
expressed in another currency, the exchange rate to be applied shall
be that which corresponds to the par value communicated to and recognised by the International Monetary Fund.

2. However, where in one or more countries the exchange rate operative
on the foreign exchange market supervised by the monetary authorities
fluctuates in relation to the rate which corresponds to the par value
communicated to and recognised by the International Monetary Fund,
and where in exceptional circumstances such fluctuation, although within the limits set by the rules of the Fund, might jeopardise the

implementation of the instruments or provisions referred to in Article 1, the Council or the Commission, acting within their powers under those instruments or provisions and in accordance with the procedures laid down therein for each individual case, may decide that the exchange rates for the currencies in question on the most representative foreign exchange market or markets, as provided by paragraph 4, must be applied temporarily in measures taken in pursuance of those instruments or provisions.

3. The exchange rate to be applied in respect of the currencies of countries which have not communicated par values to the International Monetary Fund or whose par values are not recognised by that body but whose currencies are quoted on the official foreign exchange markets shall be that recorded on the most representative market or markets, as provided by paragraph 4.

4. For the purposes of paragraphs 2 and 3, the exchange rates on the most representative market or markets shall be those in force on the last working day of the market(s) preceding the date on which the measures referred to in this Article are taken.

Article 3

Where monetary practices of an exceptional nature are likely to jeopardise the implementation of the instruments or provisions referred to in Article 1, the Council, acting by a qualified majority on a proposal from the Commission, or the Commission, acting within its powers under those instruments or provisions and in accordance with the procedures laid down therein for each individual case, may, after consulting the Monetary Committee, make derogations from this Regulation, in particular in the following cases:

(a) when a member country of the International Monetary Fund, having communicated a par value and had it recognised by the Fund, allows the value of its currency to fluctuate beyond the limits laid down under the rules of the Fund;

(b) when a country resorts to abnormal exchange techniques such as floating or multiple exchange rates or applies a barter agreement;

(c) in the case of countries whose currency is not quoted on official foreign exchange markets.

2. However, in an emergency the measures provided for in the preceding paragraph may be taken without prior consultation with the Monetary Committee but provided that at the same time a request for an Opinion is addressed to that body. In such cases these exceptional measures shall apply provisionally; definitive measures shall be taken only after an Opinion has been received from the Monetary Committee.

Article 4

This Regulation shall enter into force on 1 November 1962.

This Regulation shall be binding in its entirety and directly applicable in all Member States.

Done at Brussels, 23 October 1962.

For the Council

The President

E. COLOMBO

(as amended by Regulation 653/68 and Regulation 2543/73)

----

17. REGULATION (EEC) No 974/71 OF THE COUNCIL

of 12 May 1971

on certain measures of conjunctural policy to be taken in agriculture following the temporary widening of the margins of fluctuation for the currencies of certain Member States.

(JO No L 106, 12 May 1971, p. 1; OJ(Special Edition 1971 I) p. 257)

THE COUNCIL OF THE EUROPEAN COMMUNITIES,

Having regard to the Treaty establishing the European Economic Community, and in particular Article 103 thereof;

Having regard to the proposal from the Commission;

Whereas in the course of the last few weeks certain foreign exchange markets within the Community have been disturbed by speculative movements involving an abnormal influx of short-term capital; whereas this influx was such as to provoke an excessive increase in the volume of money in the economies concerned and, consequently, dangerous inflatory effects for economic development;

Whereas, in order to put an end to the abnormal movements of capital, the Council was prepared to envisage that in certain circumstances Member States may, for a limited period, widen the margins of fluctuation for the exchange rates or their currencies in relation to their present parities;

Whereas if, in one Member State, the current rate of exchange deviates from the official parity by more than a specified margin, serious difficulties may arise as regards the proper functioning of the common market; whereas trade to which the current rate of exchange applies may then be effected at a price, in national currency, lower than the intervention or buying-in price laid down by Community rules on the basis of the official parity;

Whereas in the Member State concerned this may entail a disruption of the intervention system laid down by Community rules and abnormal movements of prices jeopardising a normal trend of business in agriculture;

Whereas it would seem justifiable to forestall these difficulties by providing that the Member State concerned may, within the framework of Community rules, apply a system of compensatory amounts in trade with other Member States and third countries;

Whereas the compensatory amounts should be limited to the amounts strictly necessary to compensate the incidence of the monetary measures on the prices of basic products covered by intervention arrangements and whereas it is appropriate to apply them only in cases where this incidence would lead to difficulties;

HAS ADOPTED THIS REGULATION:

Article 1

1. If, for the purposes of commercial transactions, a Member State allows the exchange rate of its currency to fluctuate by a margin wider than the one permitted by international rules, it shall be authorised to:

(a) charge on imports from Member States and third countries,

(b) grant on exports to Member States and third countries,

compensatory amounts for the products referred to below under the conditions determined hereinafter.

2. Paragraph 1 shall apply:

(a) to products covered by intervention arrangements under the common organisation of agricultural markets;

(b) to products whose price depends on the price of the products referred to under (a) and which are governed by the common organisation of market or are the subject of a specific arrangement under Article 235 of the Treaty.

This option shall be exercised only where application of the monetary measures referred to in paragraph 1 would lead to disturbances in trade in agricultural products.

Article 2.

1. The compensatory amounts for the products covered by intervention arrangements shall be equal to the amounts obtained by applying to the prices the percentage difference between:

- the parity of the currency of the Member State concerned declared to and recognised by the International Monetary Fund, on the one hand, and

- the arithmetic mean of the spot market rates of this currency against
  the US dollar during a period to be determined.

  2. For the other products referred to in Article 1, the compensatory
  amounts shall be equal to the incidence, on the prices of the product concerned, of the application of the compensatory amount to the
  prices of the product referred to in paragraph 1, on which they
  depend.

3. However, with regard to trade between one Member State referred to
   in Article 1 and another Member State referred to in that Article,
   the compensatory amount applicable to a specified product shall be
   reduced by the compensatory amount applied to that product in the
   latter Member State.

Article 3

If the difference referred to in Article 2 (1) changes by at least
1 point from the percentage taken as a basis for the preceding determination, the compensatory amount shall be altered by the Commission in
line with the change in the difference.

Article 4

1. No compensatory amount shall be fixed where, in any Member State,
the percentage referred to in Article 2 (1) does not exceed 2.5%.

2. No compensatory amount shall be fixed for products for which the
amount calculated in accordance with Article 2 is negligible in relation to their average value.

Article 5

Until the Member States concerned are in a position to charge compensatory amounts on imports, they may make imports of the products referred to in Article 1 dependent on the lodging of a deposit intended
to guarantee payment of these amounts.

Article 6.

1. Detailed rules for the application of this Regulation, which may
include other derogations from the regulations on the common agricultural policy, shall be adopted in accordance with the procedure laid
down in Article 26 of Council Regulation No 120/67/EEC of 13 June 1967
on the common organization of the market in cereals, as last amended
by Regulation (EEC) No 2434/70, or, if appropriate, the corresponding
article of the other regulations on the common organization of agricultural markets.

2. Subject to the provisions of Article 3, the detailed rules for
application shall cover in particular the fixing of the compensatory
amounts.

Article 7

Partial or temporary use may not be made of the authorisation provided
for in this Regulation.

Article 8

1. This Regulation shall be applicable with effect from 12 May 1971.

2. It shall cease to be applicable as soon as all the Member States
concerned again apply the international rules on margins of exchange
rate fluctuation around official parity.

3. The Commission shall submit a monthly report to the Council on the
way this Regulation is being applied.

This Regulation shall be binding in its entirety and directly applicable in all Member States.

Done at Brussels, 12 May 1971

> For the Council
>
> The President
>
> M. SCHUMANN

(This Regulation has been amended several times after 12 May 1971;
amendments not included here)

18. COUNCIL DECISION

of 18 February
1974

on the attainment of a high degree of convergence of the economic
policies of the Member States of the European Economic Community

(74/120/EEC)

(JO No L 63, 5 March 1974, p. 16)

THE COUNCIL OF THE EUROPEAN COMMUNITIES,

Having regard to the Treaty establishing the European Economic Community, and in particular Articles 103 and 145 thereof;

Having regard to the proposal from the Commission;

Having regard to the Opinion of the European Parliament;

Having regard to the Opinion of the Economic and Social Committee;

Whereas there can be no gradual attainment of economic and monetary union unless the economic policies pursued by the Member States henceforth converge and unless a high degree of convergence is maintained;

Whereas, for this purpose, the coordination procedures at present used must be substantially strengthened and improved; whereas, in particular, permanent consultation machinery must be instituted, covering both general economic policy and those policies for which the central banks are responsible in monetary matters;

Whereas such permanent consultation machinery must be supported by economic policy guidelines established at Community level; whereas such guidelines cannot be confined only to short-term policy, but must also cover medium-term policy; whereas no short-term action can suitably be implemented reconciling the development processes of nine national economies if it is not guided by and towards common objectives established over a longer period; whereas, consequently, medium-term guidelines are an indispensable instrument of a coherent short-term economic policy and thus a measure appropriate to such a policy;

Whereas monitoring of the implementation and effects of the national economic policies is necessary for the maintenance of consistency between these policies, so that any deviation from the guidelines adopted at Community level can be promptly corrected;

Whereas, in respect of currency exchange relations within the Community, the greater convergence of economic policies must be accompanied by specific and effective prior consultation machinery for any decision by a Member State relating to the conditions under which its currency is exchanged for the currencies of other Member States and of third countries,

HAS ADOPTED THIS DECISION:

Article 1

The Council shall set aside each month a specific day, chosen in advance, for meetings on economic and monetary matters. Within this framework, the Council shall hold three meetings yearly to examine the economic situation in the Community. On the basis of a communication from the Commission accompanied, where appropriate, by proposals for decisions, directives or recommendations, the Council shall adopt guidelines on economic policy which the Community and each Member State are to follow in order to achieve harmonious economic development.

Article 2.

The first examination shall take place as soon as possible during the first quarter.

On this occasion, on a proposal from the Commission, the Council shall adjust the economic policy guidelines for the current year as required by economic developments.

The proposals from the Commission shall be accompanied by a summary account of the economic policy pursued in the preceding year and by five-year forecasts covering the main macro-economic variables.

Article 3

A second examination shall take place during the second quarter. On that occasion the Council shall lay down appropriate guidelines for the main elements of the preliminary economic budgets. Within this framework, quantitative guidelines for the draft public budgets for the following year shall be fixed before these budgets are finally adopted and shall cover developments in government expenditure and revenue, the nature and extent of budget surpluses and deficits and the way the latter are to be financed or used. The guideline figures for the draft public budgets shall not be published at this juncture.

Article 4

A third examination shall take place towards the end of the third quarter.At this stage, the Council shall, acting on a proposal from the Commission and after consulting the European Parliament and the Economic and Social Committee, adopt an annual report on the economic situation in the Community and shall establish the guidelines to be followed by each Member State in its economic policy for the following year.

Article 4a

At two-and-a-half year intervals, coinciding every other time with the examination of medium-term economic policy programmes and starting in 1980 on the occasion of the third annual examination referred to in Article 4, the Council, after consulting the European Parliament and the Economic and Social Committee, shall examine a periodic report on the situation and socio-economic developments in the regions of the Community drawn up by the Commission in close collaboration with the Regional Policy Committee.

On the basis of this report, the Council shall discuss the priorities and guidelines proposed by the Commission.

Article 5

As soon as this annual report has been adopted by the Council, Governments shall bring it to the attention of their national parliaments so that it can be taken into account during the debate on the budget.

Article 6

On the basis of the preliminary draft prepared by the Economic Policy Committee, the Commission shall at regular intervals and at least once every five years establish a draft medium-term economic policy programme, whose purpose shall be, in the context of economic and monetary union, to facilitate and guide structural changes - sectoral, regional and social - and to ensure the convergence of overall economic policies.

The draft shall indicate those points on which it departs from the preliminary draft of the Economic Policy Committee.

The Commission shall forward the draft programme to the Council, which shall forthwith place it before the European Parliament and the Economic and Social Committee, for consultation.

The programme shall be adopted by the Council and by the Governments of the Member States.

By adopting the programme, the Council and the Governments of the Member States shall express their intention of acting, in the field covered by the programme, in accordance with the guidelines laid down therein.

Parallel to the adoption of the programme, the Council shall, where appropriate and on a proposal from the Commission, unanimously adopt any decisions, directives or recommendations necessary to achieve the objectives set out in the programme and to implement the measures for which it provides.

Article 7

Any Member State intending de jure or de facto, to change, discontinue or re-establish the parity, central rate or intervention points of its currency shall initiate a prior consultation.

The consultation procedures, which shall be secret and urgent, shall take place in accordance with practical rules adopted by the Council after receiving an Opinion from the Monetary Committee.

Article 8

In addition to the consultations which are held by the Monetary Committee and by the Coordinating Committee on Short-Term Economic and Financial Policies, the Central Banks shall be invited to promote by means of regular and frequent consultations, within the framework of the Council Decision of 22 March 1971 on the strengthening of cooperation between the central banks of the Member States of the European Economic Community, the continual coordination of their monetary policies especially as regards the development of the money supply and bank liquidity, the conditions for granting credit and the level of interest rates.

Article 9

Standing consultations on the general economic policy measures envisaged by the Member States and on their conformity with the economic policy guidelines laid down by the Council according to the procedure laid down in Articles 1 to 5 shall take place within the coordinating group referred to in Title 1, paragraph 2, of the Resolution of the Council

and the Representatives of the Governments of the Member States of
21 March 1972 on the application of the Resolution of 22 March 1971 on
the attainment by stages of economic monetary union in the Community.

The Chairmen of the Economic Policy Committee, of the Monetary Committee and of the Committee of the Governors of the Central Banks shall,
as appropriate, attend the meetings of the Group.

These meetings must involve prior consultation and cover the most
significant measures being taken with a view to the convergence of
economic policy within the Community.

The Group shall meet often enough to ensure the standing nature of the
consultations, and in any event, at least once a month.

Article 10

Any Member State or the Commission may request consultations within
the Council:

- if, in the course of the consultations referred to in Articles 8 and
  9, it appears that any measure or decision contemplated by one or
  more Member States is the subject of serious reservations;

- or if economic developments in a Member State constitute a considerable danger for other Member States or the Community as a whole.

The Council shall meet within eight days.

Article 11

Where a Member State is pursuing economic, monetary and budgetary
policies departing from the guidelines laid down by the Counil or entailing economic risks for the Community as a whole, the Commission
may send a recommendation to the State concerned. Within 15 days of
receipt of this recommendation, the Member State concerned shall provide the Commission with all the appropriate information.

The Commission or a Member State may request an emergency meeting of
the Coordinating Committee on Short-Term Economic and Financial Policies
and possibly an examination within the Council. The latter shall take
a decision on the basis of proposals which the Commission shall submit
to it, where appropriate.

Article 12

On the basis of a report submitted by the Commission, the Council
shall examine once a year, at its meeting held in the first quarter,
as provided for in Article 2 above, the application of
this Decision and the conformity of the policies pursued with the objectives set. The Commission's report shall also be laid before the
European Parliament.

Article 13

The following decisions are hereby repealed:

- the Council Decision of 17 July 1969 on the coordination of short-term economic policies of the Member States;

- the Council Decision of 16 February 1970 on the appropriate procedures for the consultation arrangements provided for in the Council Decision of 17 July 1969;

- the Council Decision of 22 March 1971 on the strengthening of the coordination of short-term economic policies of the Member States of the European Economic Community.

Article 14

This Decision is addressed to the Member States.

Done at Brussels, 18 February 1974.

For the Council

The President

H. SCHMIDT

(As amended by Council Decision of 6 February 1979, OJ No L 35, 9 February 1979, p. 8)

19. COUNCIL DECISION

of 18 February 1974

setting up an Ecnomic Policy Committee

(74/122/EEC)

(OJ No L 63, 5 March 1974, p. 21)

THE COUNCIL OF THE EUROPEAN COMMUNITIES,

Having regard to the Treaty establishing the European Economic Community, and in particular Article 145 thereof;

Having regard to the draft by the Commission;

Having regard to the Opinion of the European Parliament;

Having regard to the Opinion of the Economic and Social Committee;

Whereas coordination of short-term economic policies must take account of the jointly defined medium-term economic objectives;

Whereas budgetary policy must fit into the context of general economic policy;

Whereas the existence of three separate Committees operating in the field of general economic policy is therefore prejudicial to the efficient coordination of economic policies and has often led to over-lapping of responsibilities and duplication of work;

Whereas it is therefore necessary to merge the activities of the Short-term Economic Policy Committee, the Budgetary Policy Committee and the Medium-term Economic Policy Committee into a single Economic Policy Committee,

HAS DECIDED AS FOLLOWS:

Article 1

An Economic Policy Committee (hereinafter called the 'Committee') is set up to promote coordination of Member States' short and medium-term economic policies.

Article 2

The Committee shall exercise all the functions hitherto assigned to te Short-term Economic Policy Committee set up by the Council Decision of 9 March 1960 on coordination of the conjunctural policies of the Member States, the Budgetary Policy Committee set up by the Council Decision of 8 May 1964 on cooperation between the competent government departments of Member States in the field of budgetary policy, and the Medium-term Economic Policy Committee set up by the Council Decision of 15 April 1864 setting up a Medium-term Economic Policy Committee. The Committee shall, in particular:

- assist in coordinating general economic policies;

- examine and compare Member States' budgetary policies and the way they are being implemented;

- prepare, in the light of all available information, the preliminary draft of the medium-term economic policy programme provided for under Article 6 of the Council Decision of 18 February 1974 on the achievement of a high degree of convergence of the economic policies of the Member States of the European Community;

- keep under review the medium-term economic policies of the Member States and examine whether they are compatible with the above pro-gramme;

- analyse the development of the economies in order to discover the reasons for any divergence from the programme.

Article 3

The Committee shall consist of four representatives of the Commission and four representatives of each Member State. The members of the Committee appointed by the Member States shall be selected from among persons who in their countries participate in the formulation of short- and medium-term economic poliy.

Article 4

The opinion of the Committee may be requested by the Council or by the Commission. Moreover, the Committee may, on its own initiative, deliver opinions or present reports whenever it considers this necessary for the proper fulfilment of its task.

Article 5

The Committee may meet with a reduced composition for the purpose of dealing with specific problems in the fields of short-term economic policy, budgetary policy and medium-term economic policy.

Article 6

Proceedings of the Committee shall be valid only if at least one member per delegation is present.

Article 7

The Committee shall elect its officers, consisting of one chairman and three vice-chairmen, for a non-renewable term of two years beginning on 1 March 1974. It shall adopt its rules of procedure.

The Secretariat of the Committee shall be provided by the Commission.

Article 8

The following are hereby repealed:

- the Council Decision of 9 March 1960 on coordination of the conjunctural policies of the Member States;

- Council Decision of 15 April 1964 setting up a Medium-term Economic Policy Committee;

- Council decision of 8 May 1964 on cooperation between the competent government departments of Member States in the field of budgetary policy.

Done at Brussels, 18 February 1974.

For the Council

The President

H. SCHMIDT

----

20.   EXTRACT OF REPORT ON EUROPEAN UNION

Commission of the European Communities

(Supplement 5/75 to the Bulletin of the European
Communities)

II. The Fields of Competence of the Union

The Construction of an Integrated Economic and Social Unit

26. Article 2 of the Treaty of Rome lays down clearly the task of the
Community, which is'to promote throughout the Community a harmonious
development of economic activities, a continuous and balanced expansion, an increase in stability, an accelerated raising of the standard
of living and closer relations between the States belonging to it'.

27. Althought this was a very general objective, the powers and the
instruments and resources allocated to the institutions to carry it
out concerned only some of the factors that determine economic and
social development. For the rest, it was not thought necessary to go
beyond coordination of national policies.

The Community has the powers and instruments needed to make the common
market operate, to implement a common commercial policy and to enforce
the rules on competition.

The Community also has a common agricultural policy. The Treaty contains the necessary basis for the introduction of a common transport
policy. In the social field, it has inter alia the powers needed to
ensure freedom of movement for workers. Further, the Social Fund has
gradually expanded its rule, placing more and more emphasis on structural objectives; it has thus become a first instrument in a European
employment policy. In the regional field, too, the recently created
Fund should have a significant effect on the employment situation of
the Community through the improvement of economic structures. Similarly a number of common instruments are available to the Community in
the area of research, though these are largely confined to the nuclear
field at present.

The Community has also developed a cooperation and development aid
policy based on association agreements and on other instruments such
as its generalized preferences scheme.

342

28. The gradual implementation of the Treaty's objectives in all these fields has resulted in a greater integration and closer interpenetration of the economies concerned and, by creating a large market, has helped to improve welfare and promote economic growth in the original member countries. Once the initial period of adjustment is over, the new Member States will assuredly feel the same beneficial effects as well.

The integration of the member countries' economies and economic developments at international level have, however, brought to light a number of problems that had been tackled only indirectly by the authors of the Treaty, who did not provide any specific instruments for dealing with and resolving such problems. However developments in the economic and social fields have made in essential that these problems be resolved if other objectives laid down in the Treaty are to be attained and if the Community is to be in a position to respond to new needs.

The Community has therefore attached more and more importance to achievinv the convergence of national economic policies, the narrowing of differences in economic structures, and industrial policy, an energy policy, an environment policy, a research policy, etc.

29. The results of these attempts to give economic integration more substance have, however, been meagre. Several factors, such as changes in the world economic situation, the temptation to seek national solutions in times of crisis, structural disparities and the divergent trends of the Member States' economies, but also the inadequacy of the Community's decisionmaking process, the weakness of its institutional structure and the Community's lack of comprehensive and extensive means of intervention and powers, account for the slow pace of progress in this area. Furthermore the extent - probably excessive - to which Community policies have been viewed in isolation has made it difficult to deal effectively with their implications in other areas (for instance, the effects of the agricultural policy on certain regions).

In particular, experience has shown how fruitless it is to attempt to coordinate national policies without the support of effective means of action at community level.

While past setbacks are an indication of the scale of the difficulties to be overcome, they do not invalidate the objective of economic and monetary union, which was reasserted by the Heads of Government in Paris on 9 and 10 December 1974, but call for a better definition of this objective backed up by the creation of the necessary facilities.

30. Both internal and external economic developments mean that the public authorities are having to intervene more - not only in matters of a general nature but also in specific fields. If they are not conceived as part of a European approach, their actions may often prove mutually damaging and shift difficulties onto each other's economies.

The difficulties resulting in several instances from the incomplete nature of the common policies must first be resolved by an overall policy.

If the economic interests of the Union and its Member States are to be protected, the interpenetration of the economies concerned must be strengthened and the structural problems with which the States cannot cope individually and which now hamper a harmonious development of the

Community must be tackled and resolved jointly.

The need for Community responses to a number of fresh problems, such as the protection of the environment and the promotion of research, is also making itself increasingly felt.

Finally, the economies of the member countries are by their very nature open economies; they cannot hope to find refuge in isolation to solve their internal problems. None of them is big enough to cope alone with an international economic situation marked by uncertainty, change and ever-increasing competition. On the contrary, experience has shown that by strengthening their internal solidarity and joint action the member countries are better able to defend their interests, make internal structural adjustments and participate more effectively in the field of international cooperation.

31. The Union should therefore continue to aim for the main Community objective: economic and monetary union. This entails giving it competence, powers, and means of action in five main fields:

(i) monetary policy;
(ii) budgetary expenditure;
(iii) budgetary revenue;
(iv) improving economic structures so as to help reduce imbalances;
(v) social affairs.

Before these fields are dealt with, consideration should be given to general scope for economic and social action.

General features of means of action in the economic field

32. In the effort to confer greater substance on the process of Community intergation, an endeavour has been made to develop the possibilities implicit in the Treaties, particularly in the EEC Treaty, although it should also not be forgotten that adaptations to the EEC Treaty are allowed under Article 236 [2].

For instance, increasing use has been made of certain articles of general application, such as Article 103 for countercyclical measures, Article 100 in connection with the harmonization of national legislation and Article 235 in connection with structural measures. There are, however, legal limits to what can be done in this way, and they can add a further obstacle to the difficulties inherent in the decisions to be taken.

While it is inevitable and even desirable that during an intermediate period efforts to make good use of the possibilities implicit in the Treaties should continue, the conclusion to be drawn from what has been said above is that the creation of European Union should also make it possible to go beyond the present limits by explicitly vesting new powers and new fields of competence in the European institutions.

33. How is this extension of the Union's powers to be defined?

Two lines of apprach are possible. The first - typical mainly of the ECSC and Euratom Treaties but in some respects of the EEC Treaty too - is the treaty-law, which would lay down in detail the areas covered by

the Union and the ways and means by which it could act in each of
these areas. The other line of approach, that of the outline treaty,
would give certain general powers to the Union while at the same time
setting limits to action by the Union and stating certain fundamental
objectives. The experience of the Communities, particularly the
difficulties encountered in implementing a treaty-law such as the
ECSC Treaty, has shown that this second approach is more in line with
requirements. This will be even truer than before as the Union will
have to deal with a multitude of matters no longer merely to ensure
the free movement of the factors of production, but to render coherent
the economic development of the Community as a whole.

34. Intervention by the Union in those fields should always be con-
sonant with the 'principe de subsidiarité' already mentioned. The
Union's aim, therefore, would be to assume direct responsibility for
problems for the solution of which the range of efficient action
available to the Member States is insufficient. At the same time, it
would endeavour to avoid divergent responses from the Member States
which would threaten the cohesion of the Union.

To this end, it is necessary:

(a) to provide an overall framework for national policies by intro-
    ducing common rules; and
(b) to give the institutions of the Union their own instruments and
    facilities for exerting direct influence on certain structures or
    certain factors of economic development.

35. So far the Community has tended to rely more on the implementation
of action of the first type, but there is a good case for assigning
growing importance, in the European Union, to direct action.

Simply to coordinate national policies closely could create constant
tension between the need to obey the common rules and the political
responsibility of national governments which have to face up to very
rapidly changing economic situations, political balances which differ
from country to country and social pressures which are sometimes con-
tradictory. In addition, the mere establishment of rules and general
machinery would not enable the Union to act on economic realities
with the necessary degree of freedom and selectivity. On the other
hand, attaching greater weight to the instruments of direct intervention would have a more important advantage: it would allow greater
flexibility in coordinating national policies and would, therefore,
leave the Member States with the freedom of action they require.

This should not, however, be interpreted as undermining the disciplines
which are still necessary, particularly with regard to the free movement of goods, persons, services and capital and to compliance with
the rules on competition. On the contrary, as recent experience has
shown, providing a greater scope for direct action of a selective
nature would facilitate compliance with the common rules.

The powers of the Union and the instruments of intervention with which
it will be provided concern only a number of well-defined components
of economic and social policy. The authorities in the Member States,
whether national or regional, will still, of course, be free to act
autonomously in a large number of fields (for instance, in a great
many matters concerning tax policy).

Powers in monetary matters

36. The achievement in due course of Monetary Union is a precondition for economic integration within the Union and its cohesion in the world at large.

In an economic union, whatever its institutional structure:

(i) interaction between the Member States in the monetary field is direct and rapid;
(ii) Money, being the vehicle for all economic transactions, determines not only the development of private transactions, but also the possibility of administering at Union level a whole range of policies such as agriculture policy, external policy, competition policy, the free movement of capital and so on.

The European Union will thus have to possess centralised decision-making power in the monetary field. In other words, the ultimate objective should be for monetary resources to be an exclusive field **of** competence of the Union, just as the common customs tariff is already.

37. For this purpose the Union will have to have its own central bank - probably of a federal type - or a common system of central banks (the choice will be determined mainly by political considerations), which will have to manage:

(i) at home, the liquidity of the banking system and of the economy in general, and
(ii) policy on exchange rates with countries outside the Union, which means the pooling of reserves.

One of the institutional problems this raises is that of the relations between the central bank (or the Community system of central banks) and the political authorities of the Union. At present, thinking on this problem varies quite considerably from one Member State to another, as does the degree of independence which each central bank enjoys vis-à-vis the government; for instance, in the Federal Republic of Germany the central bank enjoys a relatively high degree of autonomy, whereas in France it is much more dependent on the government. In the Union, various forms of organization are still possible, but it none the less seems desirable to aim at a fairly high degree of independence.

38. Once the ultimate objective of exclusive competence for the Union in the monetary field is accepted, the next question to be settled is how this is to be achieved.

In the texts adopted by the Council in 1971, progress towards economic and monetary union was to be achieved mainly by putting the following principles into practice:

(a) an increasingly more marked and binding coordination of the short-term and medium-term economic policies of the member countries;

(b) the extension and strengthening of monetary and financial solidarity between member countries;

(c) the development of a Community exchange system designed first to
limit and then to narrow gradually the margins of fluctuation
between member countries' currencies. In a final stage, the
national currencies could be incorporated into a common currency
or could continue to circulate, in which case, however, they would
be convertible at fixed and irreversible exchange rates.

39. This method has not enabled us to make the progress hoped for.

However, without going into the reasons for the setbacks which have
beset the coordination of economic policies, it should not be forgotten
that a core of monetary stability has been maintained in the Community
and that this core, namely the Community 'snake', holds an unquestion-
able attraction even for non-Community currencies.

Alternative methods do not, therefore, have to be sought: it is more
a matter of deciding which new measures could be added to those already adopted so as to ensure that the process of integration is pursued in a flexible and gradual manner.

40. One method which has already been dealt with in numerous studies
would consist of gradually developing a new monetary instrument
peculiar to the Community.

This new instrument would be issued by the Union's monetary authority
and would initially be used solely for transactions between central
banks. At a later stage it could be given a role enabling it:

(i) to serve as a means of settlement for financial operations between
the public institutions of the Union;

(ii) to circulate among banking institutions in connection with certain
types of private operations.

In this way, the common instrument could progressively acquire a
wider monetary role. An important stage in this process would be
reached when the central banks began using the Community instrument
to intervene on the exchanges.

The member countries would then have a common currency which, subject
to certain conditions, would circulate side by side with the national
currencies, just as nowadays foreign currencies are used in the Community side by side with any member country's currency. The national
currencies could retain, in relation to each other and to the common
currency, the degree of flexibility deemed necessary in view of the
differing rates of inflation.

41. If chosen, this method would in no way render obsolete the Community 'snake', and the ultimate objective of stable exchange relationships within the community would be retained. However, the scope
for exchange rate adjustments could be narrowed at a slower rate than
that initially envisaged as the Community's monetary cohesion would
be sustained and stimulated by the existence of a common moneraty
instrument.

Consequently, intra-Community exchange relationships could retain a
certain degree of flexibility even after the creation of the Union
and the establishment of its insitutions.

347

42. The choice of the method to be used to get the movement towards monetary union under way again is already a matter of urgency in the Community. The choice should therefore be made in the near future without waiting for the establishment of the Union itself. To this end, the responsibility for introducing the new monetary instrument could be entrusted to the European Monetary Cooperation Fund, a forerunner of the future monetary authority, with the necessary political control being exercised by the institutions of the present Community.

When the Union is established, the monetary authority would be given its definitive structure and its full range of powers. The institutions of the Union would then be responsible for the further development of the monetary instrument.

The decision must be framed in the light of the essential features of the Union. In this respect, the common-currency method, rather than an unduly rapid freezing of intra-Community exchange relationships, seems to be more in line with the future requirements of a European Union having major powers of its own but allowing for the greatest possible flexibility for national policies.

Experience in the Community has shown the interdependence of monetary problems and problems relating to the Community's economic structures. The common-currency approach would provide more scope for adjusting the rate of advance towards monetary union to the progress made in bringing economic, industrial and regional structures closer into line.

The budget of the Union

43. The budget has many functions to perform, affecting many fields such as structural policy, social policy, regional policy and short-term economic policy.

Hitherto, efforts to direct the Member States' economic policies towards the common objective of gradually establishing economic and monetary union have concentrated, as regards budgetary policy, on providing an agreed framework for national decisions. The sums earmarked in the Community budget have been relatively small, and their actual utilization is largely determined by built-in mechanisms.

These efforts, which, as we have seen, should be pursued within the Union, have, however, come up against serious limitations, for ultimate responsibility for and the democratic control of expenditure are still in the hands of the individual States while the decisions that could bring about convergence of policies must be taken at Community level. Clearly, for decision-making and ultimate responsibility to be out of line in this way is a constant source of conflict.

44. A more rational idea would be to provide the Union with a larger budget which was sufficiently flexible to allow of prompter responses to changes in the needs of the Union as a whole, but in respect of structures (the energy crisis is a good example of this requirement) and in relation to overall demand management. The budget could be used to influence economic trends in this way either by direct intervention measures, or by the Union granting Member States loans or subsidies linked to respect for the objectives of the Union's policies.

348

The Union's budget would thus play an important role in transferring resources between the economies and in redistributing them between the social groups so as to eliminate imbalances.

45. The Union budget will probably continue to be primarily an instrument of structural policy, and its rule in current economic activity will at first be extremely limited, for the total expenditure of national and local authorities will, for a very long time to come, remain far higher than any expenditure that could be decided on and administered at European level. Overall demand management will therefore remain a very complex process, its key features being the increasing use of common budgetary and monetary instruments and the provision of an agreed framework for national policies in clearly defined areas.

The role of the Union budget as an instrument of general economic policy would of course be strengthened if at a later stage in the development of the Union, quite new categories of expenditure could be included (e.g. infrastructure programmes, certain social security expenditure, unemployment benefit, etc.).

46. The increase in expenditure from the Union's budget ought not in itself to speed up the rate at which public spending as a whole is growing. Frequently it will make possible economies in national budgets, and a more rational utilization of resources.

Financing the budget of the Union

47. Transferring the rule of the Union budget in this way will also mean refining the system of 'own resources' by creating a European tax system which would be activated by a decision of the institutions of the Union.

As the measures of financial intervention by the Union are expanded, so too will the present range of sources for financing its budget have to be broadened. The aim ought to be a system of own resources which should be as simple as possible and weigh equitably on the several economies, However, the development of the political aspects of the Union will inevitably bring up the problem of a European tax system which took account of the need to ensure a balanced treatment of different social categories. Consequently, there is a case for increasing use not only of indirect taxes but also of certain kinds of direct taxation (for example, corporation tax). The Union should also be able to choose to create specific Union taxes by a special procedure probably entailing action by the national parliaments.

A European tax system with a more varied range of instruments could also become an additional means of achieving redistribution so as to assist the most needy regions and social groups.

48. As regards other revenue, the Union will have to be able to raise loans on the capital markets (particularly for investment and infrastructure expenditure of common interest).

Hence the Union budget would constitute an instrument which, when combined with the instruments of monetary policy, would enable action to be taken not only to improve structures but also, to some extent at

least, to influence short-term economic trends.
.....

----

1) In the Community of Six, internal trade as a proportion of total
   trade rose from less than 30% to more than 50% between 1958 and
   1972. During the same period trade between the Six rose by 840%;
   nor did this appear to slow down the expansion of the Community's
   external trade which grew at the same dynamic rate as world trade
   overall (350%).
   The gross domestic product of the Member States of the Community
   of Six rose at an annual rate of 5% etween 1958 and 1974, compared
   with 3.9% in the United States.

2) Resolution of the Council and of the Representatives of the Governments
   of the Member States of 22 March 1971 on the attainment by stages
   of economic and monetary union in the Community; OJ C 28 of
   27.3.1971.

----

21. RESOLUTION OF THE EUROPEAN COUNCIL

of 5 December 1978

on the establishment of the European Monetary System (EMS) and related
matters
(Bulletin of the EEC 12-1978)

The European Monetary System

1. Introduction

1.1 In Bremen we discussed a "scheme for the creation of closer monetary cooperation leading to a zone of monetary stability in Europe".
We regarded such a zone "as a highly desirable objective" and envisaged "a durable and effective scheme".

1.2 Today, after careful examination of the preparatory work done by
the Council and other Community bodies, we are agreed as follows:

A European Monetary System (EMS) will be set up on
1 January 1979

1.3 We are firmly resolved to ensure the lasting success of the EMS
by policies conducive to greater stability at home and abroad for
both deficit and surplus countries.

1.4 The following chapters deal primarily with the initial phase of
the EMS.
We remain firmly resolved to consolidate, not later than two years
after the start of the scheme, into a final system the provisions and
procedures thus created. This system will entail the creation

of the European Monetary Fund as announced in the conclusions of the
European Council meeting at Bremen on 6 and 7 July 1978, as well as
the full utilization of the ECU as a reserve asset and a means of
settlement. It will be based on adequate legislation at the Community
as well as the national level.

2. The ECU and its functions

2.1 A European Currency (ECU) will be at the centre of the EMS. The
value and the composition of the ECU will be identical with the value
of the EUA at the outset of the system.

2.2 The ECU will be used

(a) as the denominator (numéraire) for the exchange rate mechanism
(b) as the basis for a divergence indicator
(c) as the denominator for operations in both the intervention and the
   credit mechanism
(d) as a means of settlement between monetary authorities of the EC.

2.3 The weights of currencies in the ECU will be reexamined and if
necessary revised within six months of the entry into force of the
system and thereafter every five years or, on request, if the weight
of any currency has changed by 25%.
Revisions have to be mutually accepted; they will, by themselves, not
modify the external value of the ECU. They will be made in line with
underlying economic criteria.

3. The exchange rate and the intervention mechanism

3.1 Each currency will have an ECU-related central rate. These central
rates will be used to establish a grid of bilateral exchange rates.

Around these exchange rates fluctuation margins of $\pm$ 2.25% will be
established. EC countries with presently floating currencies may opt
for wider margins up to $\pm$ 6% at the outset of EMS; these margins should
be gradually reduced as soon as economic conditions permit to do so.

A Member State which does not participate in the exchange rate mechanism at the outset may participate at a later date.

3.2 Adjustments of central rates will be subject to mutual agreement
by a common procedure which will comprise all countries participating
in the exchange rate mechanism and the Commission. There will be reciprocal consultation in the Community framework about important decisions concerning exchange rate policy between countries participating
and any country not participating in the system.

3.3 In principle, interventions will be made in participating currencies.

3.4 Intervention in participating currencies is compulsory when the
intervention points defined by the fluctuation margins are reached.

3.5 An ECU basket formula will be used as an indicator to detect divergences between Community currencies. A "threshold of divergence"
will be fixed at 75% of the maximum spread of divergence for each
currency. It will be calculated in such a way as to eliminate the

influence of weight on the probability to reach the threshold.

3.6 When a currency crosses its "threshold of divergence" this results in a presumption that the authorities concerned will correct this situation by adequate measures, namely:

(a) Diversified intervention;
(d) Measures of domestic monetary policy;
(c) Changes in central rates;
(d) Other measures of economic policy.

In case such measures, on account of special circumstances, are not taken, the reasons for this shall be given to the other authorities, especially in the "concertation between Central Banks".

Consultations will, if necessary, then take place in the appropriate Community bodies, including the Council of Ministers.

After six months these provisions shall be reviewed in the light of experience. At that date the questions regarding imbalances accumulated by divergent creditor or debtor countries will be studied as well.

3.7 A Very Short-Term Facility of an unlimited amount will be established. Settlements will be made 45 days after the end of the month of intervention with the possibility of prolongation for another 3 months for amounts limited to the size of debtor quotas in the Short-Term Monetary Support.

3.8 To serve as a means of settlement, an initial supply of ECU will be provided by FECOM against the deposit of 20% of gold and 20% of dollar reserves currently held by Central Banks.

This operation will take the form of specified, revolving swap arrangements. By periodical review and by an appropriate procedure it will be ensured that each Central Bank will maintain a deposit of at least 20% of these reserves with FECOM. A Member State not participating in the exchange rate mechanism may participate in this initial operation on the basis described above.

4. The credit mechanisms

4.1 The existing credit mechanisms with their present rules of application will be maintained for the initial phase of the EMS. They will be consolidated into a single fund in the final phase of the EMS.

4.2 The credit mechanisms will be extended to an amount of 25,000 million ECU of effectively available credit. The distribution of this amount will be as follows:

Short-term monetary support   = 14 000 million ECU
Medium-term financial assistance = 11 000 million ECU

4.3 The duration of the Short-Term Monetary Support will be extended for another 3 months on the same conditions as the first extension.

4.4 The increase of the Medium-Term Financial Assistance will be completed by 30 June 1979. In the meantime, countries which still need

352

national legislation are expected to make their extended medium-term quotas available by an interim financing agreement of the Central Banks concerned.

5. Third countries and international organizations

5.1 The durability of EMS and its international implications require cooperation of exchange rate policies vis-à-vis third countries and, as far as possible, a concertation with the monetary authorities of those countries.

5.2 European countries with particularly close economic and financial ties with the European Communities may participate in the exchange rate and intervention mechanism.

Participation will be based upon agreements between Central Banks; these agreements will be communicated to the Council and the Commission of the EC.

5.3 EMS is and will remain fully compatible with the relevant articles of the IMF agreement.

6. Further procedure

6.1 To implement the decisions taken under A, the European Council requests the Council to consider and to take a decision on 18 December 1978 on the following proposals of the Commission:

(a) Council Regulation modifying the unit of account used by the European Fund of Monetary Cooperation, which introduces the ECU in the operations of the EMCF and defines its composition;

(b) Council Regulation permitting the EMCF to receive monetary reserves and to issue ECUs to the monetary authorities of the Member States which may use them as a means of settlement;

(c) Council Regulation on the impact of the European Monetary System on the common agricultural policy. The European Council considers that the introduction of the EMS should not of itself result in any change in the situation obtaining prior to 1 January 1979 regarding the expression in national currencies of agricultural prices, monetary compensatory amounts and all other amounts fixed for the purposes of the common agricultural policy.

The European Council stresses the importance of henceforth avoiding the creation of permanent MCAs and progressively reducing present MCAs in order to re-establish the unity of prices of the common agricultural policy, giving also due consideration to price policy.

6.2 It requires the Commission to submit in good time a proposal to amend the Council Decision of 22 March 1971 on the introduction of a mechanism for the medium-term financial support to enable the Council of Economics and Finance Ministers to take a decision on such proposal at their session of 18 December 1978.

6.3 It requests the Central Banks of Member States to modify their Agreement of 10 April 1972 on the reduction of margins of fluctuation between the currencies of Member States in accordance with the rules

353

set forth above (see paragraph 3).

6.4 It requests the Central Banks of Member States to modify as follows the rules on short-term monetary support by 1 January 1979 at the latest:

(a) The total of debtor quotas available for drawings by the Central Banks of Member States shall be increased to an aggregate amount of 7.9 billion ECU.

(b) The total of creditor quotas made available by the Central Banks of Member States for financing the debtor quotas shall be increased to an aggregate amount of 15.8 billion ECU.

(c) The total of the additional creditor amount as well as the total of the additional debtor amount may not exceed 8.8 billion ECU.

(d) The duration of credit under the extended Short-Term Monetary Support may be prolonged twice for a period of 3 months.

B

Measures designed to strengthen the economies of the less prosperous Member States of the European Monetary System

1. We stress that, within the context of a broadly based strategy aimed at improving the prospects of economic development and based on symmetrical rights and obligations of all participants, the most important concern should be to enhance the convergence of economic policies towards greater stability. We request the Council (Economic and Finance Ministers) to strengthen its procedures for coordination in order to improve that convergence.

2. We are aware that the convergence of economic policies and of economic performance will not be easy to achieve. Therefore, steps must be taken to strengthen the economic potential of the less prosperous countries of the Community. This is primarily the responsibility of the Member States concerned. Community measures can and should serve a supporting role.

3. The European Council agrees that in the context of the European Monetary System, the following measures in favour of the less prosperous Member States effectively and fully participating in the Exchange Rate and Intervention Mechanisms will be taken.

3.1 The European Council requests the Community institutions by the utilization of the new financial instrument and the European Investment Bank to make available for a period of 5 years loans of up to 1 000 million EUA per year to these countries on special conditions.

3.2 The European Council requests the Commission to submit a proposal to provide interest rate subsidies of 3% for these loans, with the following elements:

The total cost of this measure, divided into annual tranches of 200 million EUA each over a period of 5 years shall not exceed 1 000 million

EUA.

3.3 Any less prosperous member country which subsequently effectively and fully participates in the mechanisms would have the right of access to this facility within the financial limits mentioned above. Member States not participating effectively and fully in the mechanisms will not contribute to the financing of the scheme.

3.4 The funds thus provided are to be concentrated on the financing of selected infrastructure projects and programmes, with the understanding that any direct or indirect distortion of the competitive position of specific industries within Member States will have to be avoided.

3.5 The European Council requests the Council (Economics and Finance Ministers) to take a decision on the abovementioned proposals in time so that the relevant measures can become effective on 1 April 1979 at the latest. There should be a review at the end of the initial phase of the EMS.

4. The European Council requests the Commission to study the relationship between greater convergence in economic performance of the Member States and the utilization of Community instruments, in particular the funds which aim at reducing structural imbalances. The results of these studies will be discussed at the next European Council'.

----

22. COUNCIL DECISION

of 1 February
1971

on the reform of the European Social Fund

(71/66/EEC)

(JO No L 28, 4 February 1971, p. 15; OJ (Special Edition 1971 I)p.52)

THE COUNCIL OF THE EUROPEAN COMMUNITIES,

Having regard to the Treaty establishing the European Economic Community, and in particular Article 126 thereof;

Having regard to the Opinion of the Commission;

Having regard to the Opinion of the European Parliament;

Having regard to the Opinion of the Economic and Social Committee;

Whereas Article 123 of the Treaty assigns to the European Social Fund (hereinafter called the 'Fund') the task of rendering the employment of workers easier and of increasing their geographical and occupational mobility within the Community, and whereas the measures now in force have proved to be inadequate to permit the Fund to accomplish this task effectively;

Whereas, in pursuing this task, account must be taken of the demands of social progress in the face of technical development;

Whereas an interdependence exists between social policy and economic policy;

Whereas it is important to continue efforts to remedy the structural unemployment and underemployment still existing in various areas of the Community;

Whereas for this purpose there is also need to intensify preventive action against unemployment and underemployment;

Whereas the Fund must likewise contribute to the furtherance of existing measures for securing for all workers employment that best corresponds to their abilities, and to ensure continuity of employment and of income;

Whereas it is therefore necessary that the Fund should be able to intervene to meet situations arising from Community Decisions or requiring action at Community level and to meet also situations arising indirectly from the functioning of the common market or impeding the harmonious development of the Community;

Whereas the Decision of 21 April 1970 provided for the replacement of financial contributions from Member States by the Communities' own resources;

HAS ADOPTED THIS DECISION:

I. ABOLITION OF THE ASSISTANCE PROVIDED FOR IN ARTICLE 125 OF THE TREATY

Article 1

Subject to the provisions of Article 10 of this Decision, the assistance provided for in Article 125 of the Treaty shall no longer be granted.

II. DEFINITION OF THE NEW TASKS OF THE FUND

Article 2

The new tasks of the Fund, which are in accordance with the objectives laid down in Article 124 of the Treaty, are set out in Articles 3, 4 and 5.

A. Scope as regards persons

Article 3

1. The Fund may grant assistance for members of the labour force who, having benefited from a measure taken under the powers of the Fund,

are to pursue activities as employed persons.

2. The Fund may also grant, in special cases to be determined by the Council, assistance for persons who are to pursue activities as self-employed persons.

B. Areas of intervention

Article 4

1. The Fund can take action when the employment situation:

- is affected or in danger of being affected either by special measures adopted by the Council in the framework of Community policies, or by jointly agreed operations to further the objectives of the Community; or
- calls for specific joint action to improve the balance between supply of and demand for manpower within the Community.

The Fund shall be authorized to intervene by a specific Decision taken by the Council, acting by a qualified majority on a proposal from the Commission, the latter acting either on its own initiative or at the request of the Council or of one or more Member States.

2. The Council in taking specific Decisions of the type referred to in paragraph I, shall state as one of the grounds of such Decisions the fact that the existing or foreseeable imbalance in the field of employment:

- is on a scale justifying Community intervention;
- is such that it leads, or may lead, to the necessity for a considerable number of workers to change employment, to acquire new qualifications, or to move their homes within the Community.

In such Decisions, the Council:

(a) shall determine the areas in which the Fund may intervene;
(b) shall state which of the types of aid defined in provisions laid down pursuant to Article 127 may qualify for assistance from the Fund;
(c) shall determine, where appropriate, the categories of persons who are to pursue activities as self-employed persons to whom assistance may be granted from the Fund.

Article 5

1. The Fund can also take action where the employment situation in certain regions, in certain branches of the economy or in certain groups of undertakings is affected by difficulties which do not arise from any particular measure taken by the Council within the framework of a Community policy, but which result indirectly from the working of the common market or impede the harmonious development of the Community.

In any such cases, assistance shall be granted to eliminate long-term structural unemployment and underemployment, to train a highly skilled labour force and, furthermore, for measures for the absorption and reabsorption into active employment of the disabled, and of older workers, women and young workers.

2. The provisions required to implement this Decision, to be adopted in accordance with Article 127 of the Treaty, shall:

- define the assistance referred to in paragraph 1 which shall be granted forthwith to meet already existing situations or needs that require immediate long-term action; and

- determine the precise criteria which an operation must satisfy to be eligible for assistance from the Fund.

Assistance thus defined shall be granted without further action by the Council, subject only to the approval provided for in Article 7.

C. Submission by Member States of schemes or of applications for assistance and their approval by the Commission

Article 6

The Member State or States concerned shall submit to the Commission their schemes for meeting the situations referred to in Article 4, and any applications made in advance for assistance to meet the situations referred to in Article 5; each scheme or application shall propose a set of specific measures, and shall also give details of their methods, scope and duration.

Article 7

The Commission shall submit the schemes and applications referred to in Article 6 for consideration by the Economic and Social Committee, as provided for in Article 124 of the Treaty, and shall approve them up to the amount of the credits available if they comply with the conditions laid down in the Regulation implementing the provisions of Article 127 of the Treaty and the Decisions taken by the Council under that Regulation.

D. Rate of contribution

Article 8

1. Assistance from the Fund shall be granted at the rate of 50% of eligible expenditure in support of operations by public authorities, bodies governed by public law and joint social institutions entrusted with tasks in the public interest.

2. Assistance shall also be granted in respect of operations by bodies or other entities governed by private law, on condition that the public authorities of the Member State or States concerned guarantee the completion of such operations. In such case, the Fund shall contribute an amount equal to any expenditure taken over by the public authorities.

E. Budgetary procedure

Article 9

1. Each year, on the basis of the preliminary draft budget drawn up by the Commission, credits authorized for the functioning of the Fund during the current financial year shall be included in the budget of the European Communities.

The financial regulations adopted in pursuance of Article 209 of the Treaty shall determine the methods whereby the expenditure may be authorized for a further two-year period after the end of the current financial year.

2. Credits for action by the Fund under Article 4 shall be separate from those for action under Article 5.

Credits for action under Article 5 shall not in any year be less than 50% of the total credits available. This apportionment of credits shall be reviewed by the Council within the time limit laid down in Article 11, it being understood that in the long tern the greater part of the available credits must be reserved for action under Article 4.

III. TRANSITIONAL AND FINAL PROVISIONS

Article 10

1. The provisions of this Decision shall apply from the date of entry into force of the provisions required to implement this Decision, which shall be adopted in accordance with Article 127 of the Treaty.

2. Assistance from the Fund, as provided for in Article 125 of the Treaty, shall be granted in support of operations completed at latest on a date to be fixed by the provisions referred to in paragraph 1.

The periods within which the Member States must submit their applications for reimbursement in respect of these operations shall also be determined by those provisions.

Article 11

The Council shall review this Decision not later than five years after the date of its entry into force as provided in Article 10 (1). If necessary, this Decision shall be amended on the basis of a further Opinion of the Commission based on Article 126 of the Treaty.

Article 12

This Decision shall enter into force on the fifth day following its publication in the Official Journal of the European Communities.

Done at Brussels, 1 February 1971.

For the Council
The President

M. SCHUMANN

359

23. COUNCIL RESOLUTION

of 21 January 1974

concerning a social action programme

THE COUNCIL OF THE EUROPEAN COMMUNITIES,

Having regard to the Treaties establishing the European Communities;

Having regard to the draft from the Commission;

Having regard to the Opinion of the European Parliament;

Having regard to the Opinion of the Economic and Social Committee;

Whereas the Treaties establishing the European Communities assigned
to them tasks with relevance to social objectives;

Whereas, pursuant to Article 2 of the Treaty establishing the European
Economic Community, the European Economic Community shall have as a
particular task to promote throughout the Community a harmonious development of economic activities, a continuous and balanced expansion,
an increase in stability and an accelerated raising of the standard
of living;

Whereas the Heads of State or of Government affirmed at their conference held in Paris in October 1972 that economic expansion is not an
end in itself but should result in an improvement of the quality of
life as well as of the standard of living;

Whereas the Heads of State or Government emphasised as one of the conclusions adopted at the abovementioned conference that they attach as
much importance to vigorous action in the social field as to the achievement of Economic and Monetary Union and invited the Community institutions to draw up a social action programme providing for concrete
measures and the corresponding resources particularly in the framework of the European Social Fund on the basis of suggestions put forward by the Heads of State or of Government and the Commission at the
said Conference;

Whereas such a programme involves actions designed to achieve full and
better employment, the improvement of living and working conditions
and increased involvement of management and labour in the economic and
social decisions of the Community, and of workers in the life of undertakings;

Whereas actions described in the above programme should be implemented
in accordance with the provisions laid down in the Treaties, including

those of Article 235 of the Treaty establishing the European Economic Community;

Having regard to the wishes expressed by management and labour;

Whereas, irrespective of serious threats to employment which may arise from the situation obtaining at the time of adoption of this Resolution, and without prejudice to the results of any future studies or measures, the Community should decide on the objectives and priorities to be given to its action in the social field over the coming years;

Takes note of the Social Action Programme from the Commission,

Considers that vigorous action must be undertaken in successive stages with a view to realising the social aims of European union, in order to attain the following broad objectives: full and better employment at Community, national and regional levels, which is an essential condition for an effective social policy; improvement of living and working conditions so as to make possible their harmonisation while the improvement is being maintained; increased involvement of management and labour in the economic and social decisions of the Community, and of workers in the life of undertakings;

Considers that the Community social policy has an individual role to play and should make an essential contribution to achieving the aforementioned objectives by means of Community measures or the definition by the Community of objectives for national social policies, without however seeking a standard solution to all social problems or attempting to transfer to Community level any responsibilities which are assumed more effectively at other levels;

Considers that social objectives should be a constant concern of all Community policies;

Considers that it is essential to ensure the consistency of social and other Community policies so that measures taken will achieve the objectives of social and other policies simultaneously;

Considers that, to achieve the proposed actions successfully, and particularly in view of the structural changes and imbalances in the Community, the necessary resources should be provided, in particular by strengthening the role of the European Social Fund;

Expresses the political will to adopt the measures necessary to achieve the following objectives during a first stage covering the period from 1974 to 1976, in addition to measures adopted in the context of other Community policies:

Attainment of full and better employment in the Community

- to establish appropriate consultation between Member States on their employment policies, guided by the need to achieve a policy of full and better employment in the Community as a whole and in the regions;

- to promote better cooperation by national employment services;

- to implement a common vocational training policy, with a view to

attaining progressively the principal objectives thereof, especially
approximation of training standards, in particular by setting up a
European Vocational Training Centre;

- to undertake action for the purpose of achieving equality between
  men and women as regards access to employment and vocational training
  and advancement and as regards working conditions, including pay,
  taking into account the important role of management and labour in
  this field;

- to ensure that the family responsibilities of all concerned may be
  reconciled with their job aspirations;

- to establish an action programme for migrant workers and members of
  their families which shall aim in particular:

  - to improve the conditions of free movement within the Community of
    workers from Member States, including social security, and the
    social infrastructure of the Member States, the latter being an
    indispensable condition for solving the specific problems of migr-
    ant workers and members of their families, especially problems
    of reception, housing, social services, training and education of
    children;

  - to humanise the free movement of Community workers and members of
    their families by providing effective assistance during the vari-
    ous phases, it being understood that the prime objective is still
    to enable workers to find employment in their own regions;

  - to achieve equality of treatment for Community and non-Community
    workers and members of their families in respect of living and
    working conditions, wages and economic rights, taking into account
    the Community provisions in force;

  - to promote consultation on immigration policies *vis-à-vis* third
    countries;

- to initiate a programme for the vocational and social integration of
  handicapped persons, in particular making provisions for the promotion of pilot experiments for the purpose of rehabilitating them in
  vocational life, or where appropriate, of placing them in sheltered
  industries, and to undertake a comparative study of the legal provisions and the arrangements made for rehabilitation at national
  level;

- to seek solutions to the employment problems confronting certain
  more vulnerable categories of persons (the young and the aged);

- to protect workers hired through temporary employment agencies and
  to regulate the activities of such firms with a view to eliminating
  abuses therein;

- to continue the implementation of the Council's conclusions on employment policy in the Community and particularly those concerning the
  progressive integration of the labour markets including those relating to employment statistics and estimates;

Improvement of living and working conditions so as to make possible
their harmonisation while the improvement is being maintained

- to establish appropriate consultations between Member States on their
  social protection policies with the particular aim of their approximation on the way of progress;

- to establish an action programme for workers aimed at the humanisation
  of their living and working conditions, with particular reference to:

  - improvement in safety and health conditions at work;

  - the gradual elimination of physical and psychological stress which
    exists in the place of work and on the job, especially through
    improving the environment and seeking ways of increasing job satis-
    faction;

  - a reform of the organisation of work giving workers wider oppor-
    tunities, especially those of having their own responsibilities
    and duties of obtaining higher qualifications;

- to persevere with and expedite the implementation of the European
  Social Budget;

- gradually to extend social protection, particularly within the framework of social security schemes, to categories of persons not covered or inadequately provided for under existing schemes;

- to invite the Commission to submit a report on the problems arising
  in connection with coordination of supplementary schemes for employed persons moving within the Community;

- progressively to introduce machinery for adapting social security
  benefits to increased prosperity in the various Member States;

- to protect workers' interests, in particular with regard to the retention of rights and advantages in the case of mergers, concentrations
  or rationalisation operations;

- to implement, in cooperation with the Member States, specific measures to combat poverty by drawing up pilot schemes;

Increased involvement of management and labour in the economic
and social decisions of the Community, and of workers in the
life of undertakings

- to refer more extensively to the Standing Committee on Employment
  for the discussion of all questions with a fundamental influence
  on employment;

- to help trade union organisations taking part in Community work to
  establish training and information services for European affairs and
  to set up a European Trade Institute;

- progressively to involve workers or their representatives in the
  life of undertakings in the Community;

- to facilitate, depending on the situation in the different countries, the conclusion of collective agreements at European level in appropriate fields;

- to develop the involvement of management and labour in the economic and social decisions of the Community;

Lays down the following priorities among the actions referred to in this Resolution:

Attainment of full and better employment in the Community

1. The establishment of appropriate consultation between Member States on their employment policies and the promotion of better cooperation by national employment services.

2. The establishment of an action programme for migrant workers who are nationals of Member States or third countries.

3. The implementation of a common vocational training policy and the setting up of a European Vocational Training Centre.

4. The undertaking of action to achieve equality between men and women as regards access to employment and vocational training and advancement and as regards working conditions, including pay.

Improvement of living and working conditions so as to make possible their harmonisation while the improvement is being maintained

5. The establishment of appropriate consultations between Member States on their social protection policies.

6. The establishment of an initial action programme, relating in particular to health and safety at work, the health of workers and improved organisation of tasks, beginning in those economic sectors where working conditions appear to be the most difficult.

7. The implementation, in cooperation with the Member States, of specific measures to combat poverty by drawing up pilot schemes.

Increased involvement of management and labour in the economic and social decisions of the Community, and of workers in the life of undertakings

8. The progressive involvement of workers or their representatives in the life of undertakings in the Community.

9. The promotion of the involvement of management and labour in the economic and social decisions of the Community.

Takes note of the Commission's undertaking to submit to it, during 1974, the necessary proposals concerning the priorities laid down above;

Takes note of the Commission's undertaking to submit to it, before 1 April 1974, proposals relating to:

- an initial action programme with regard to migrant workers;

- the setting up of a European Vocational Training Centre;

- a directive on the harmonisation of laws with regard to the retention of rights and advantages in the event of changes in the ownership of undertakings, in particular in the event of mergers;

Notes that the Commission has already submitted to it proposals relating to:

- assistance from the European Social Fund for migrant workers and for handicapped workers;

- an action programme for handicapped workers in an open market econonmy;

- the setting-up of a European General Industrial Safety Committee and the extension of the competence of the Mines Safety and Health Commission;

- a Directive providing for the approximation of legislation of Member States concerning the application of the principle of equal pay for men and women;

- the designation of an immediate objective of the overall application of the principle of the standard 40-hour working week by 1975, and the principle of four weeks annual paid holiday by 1976;

- the setting up of a European Foundation for the improvement of the environment and of living and working conditions;

- a Directive on the approximation of the Member States' legislation on collective dismissals.

Undertakes to act, at the latest five months after the Commission has informed the Council of the results of its deliberations arising from the opinions given by the European Parliament and the Economic and Social Committee, if such consultations have taken place, or, if such consultations have not taken place, at the latest nine months from the date of the transmission of the proposals to the Council by the Commission;

Takes note of the Commission's undertaking to submit to it before 31 December 1976 a series of measures to be taken during a further phase.

24. COUNCIL DIRECTIVE

of 17 February 1975

on the approximation of the laws of the Member States relating to
collective redundancies

(75/129/EEC)

(O.J. No L 48, 22 February 1975, p. 29)

THE COUNCIL OF THE EUROPEAN COMMUNITIES,

Having regard to the Treaty establishing the European Economic Community, and in particular Article 100 thereof;

Having regard to the proposal from the Commission;

Having regard to the Opinion of the European Parliament;

Having regard to the Opinion of the Economic and Social Committee;

Whereas it is important that greater protection should be afforded to
workers in the event of collective redundancies while taking into
account the need for balanced economic and social development within
the Community;

Whereas, despite increasing convergence, differences still remain
between the provisions in force in the Member States of the Community
concerning the practical arrangements and procedures for such redundancies and the measures designed to alleviate the consequences of
redundancy for workers;

Whereas these differences can have a direct effect on the functioning
of the common market;

Whereas the Council resolution of 21 January 1974 concerning a social
action programme makes provision for a Directive on the approximation
of Member States' legislation on collective redundancies;

Whereas this approximation must therefore be promoted while the improvement is being maintained within the meaning of Article 117 of
the Treaty,

HAS ADOPTED THIS DIRECTIVE:

SECTION I

Definitions and scope

Article 1

1. For the purposes of this Directive:

(a) 'collective redundancies' means dismissals effected by an employer
    for one or more reasons not related to the individual workers
    concerned where, according to the choice of the Member States,
    the number of redundancies is:

    - either over a period of thirty days:

        (1) at least 10 in establishments normally employing more than
            20 and less than 100 workers;

        (2) at least 10 % of the number of workers in establishments
            normally employing at least 100 but less than 300 workers;

        (3) at least 30 in establishments normally employing 300 workers
            or more;

    - or, over a period of 90 days, at least 20, whatever the number
      of workers normally employed in the establishments in question;

(b) 'workers' representatives' means the workers' representatives pro-
    vided for by the laws or practices of the Member States.

2. This Directive shall not apply to:

(a) collective redundancies effective under contracts of employment
    concluded for limited periods of time or for specific tasks except
    where such redundancies take place prior to the date of expiry or
    the completion of such contracts;

(b) workers employed by public administrative bodies or by establish-
    ments governed by public law (or, in Member States where this
    concept is unknown, by equivalent bodies);

(c) the crews of sea-going vessels;

(d) workers affected by the termination of an establishment's activi-
    ties where that is the result of a judicial decision.

SECTION II

Consultation procedure

Article 2

1. Where an employer is contemplating collective redundancies, he
shall begin consultations with the workers' representatives with a
view to reaching an agreement.

2. These consultations shall, at least, cover ways and means of avoiding collective redundancies or reducing the number of workers affected, and mitigating the consequences.

3. To enable the workers' representatives to make constructive proposals the employer shall supply them with all relevant information and shall in any event give in writing the reasons for the redundancies, the number of workers to be made redundant, the number of workers normally employed and the period over which the redundancies are to be effected.

The employer shall forward to the competent public authority a copy of all the written communications referred to in the preceding subparagraph.

SECTION III

Procedure for collective redundancies

Article 3

1. Employers shall notify the competent public authority in writing of any projected collective redundancies.

This notification shall contain all relevant information concerning the projected collective redundancies and the consultations with workers' representatives provided for in Article 2, and particularly the reasons for the redundancies, the number of workers to be made redundant, the number of workers normally employed and the period over which the redundancies are to be effected.

2. Employers shall forward to the workers' representatives a copy of the notification provided for in paragraph 1.

The workers' representatives may send any comments they may have to the competent public authority.

Article 4

1. Projected collective redundancies notified to the competent public authority shall take effect not earlier than 30 days after the notification referred to in Article 3(1) without prejudice to any provisions governing individual rights with regard to notice of dismissal.

Member States may grant the competent public authority the power to reduce the period provided for in the preceding paragraph.

2. The period provided for in paragraph 1 shall be used by the competent public authority to seek solutions in the problems raised by the projected collective redundancies.

3. Where the initial period provided for in paragraph 1 is shorter than 60 days, Member States may grant the competent public authority the power to extend the initial period to 60 days following notification where the problems raised by the projected collective redundancies are not likely to be solved within the initial period.

Member States may grant the competent public authority wider powers of extension.

368

The employer must be informed of the extension and the grounds for it before expiry of the initial period provided for in paragraph 1.

SECTION IV

Final provisions

Article 5

This Directive shall not affect the right of Member States to apply or to introduce laws, regulations or administrative provisions which are more favourable to workers.

Article 6

1. Member States shall bring into force the laws, regulations and administrative provisions needed in order to comply with this Directive within two years following its notification and shall forthwith inform the Commission thereof.

2. Member States shall communicate to the Commission the texts of the laws, regulations and administrative provisions which they adopt in the field covered by this Directive.

Article 7

Within two years following expiry of the two year period laid down in Article 6, Member States shall forward all relevant information to the Commission to enable it to draw up a report for submission to the Council on the application of this Directive.

Article 8

This Directive is addressed to the Member States.

Done at Brussels, 17 February 1975.

For the Council

The President

R. RYAN

25. COUNCIL DIRECTIVE

of 10 February 1975

on the approximation of the laws of the Member States relating to
the application of the principle of equal pay for men and women

(75/117/EEC)

(O.J. No L 45, 19 February 1975, p. 19)

THE COUNCIL OF THE EUROPEAN COMMUNITIES,

Having regard to the Treaty establishing the European Economic Community, and in particular Article 100 thereof;

Having regard to the proposal from the Commission;

Having regard to the Opinion of the European Parliament;

Having regard to the Opinion of the Economic and Social Committee;

Whereas implementation of the principle that men and women should receive equal pay contained in Article 119 of the Treaty is an integral part of the establishment and functioning of the common market;

Whereas it is primarily the responsibility of the Member States to ensure the application of this principle by means of appropriate laws, regulations and administrative provisions;

Whereas the Council resolution of 21 January 1974 concerning a social action programme, aimed at making it possible to harmonise living and working conditions while the improvement is being maintained and at achieving a balanced social and economic development of the Community, recognised that priority should be given to action taken on behalf of women as regards access to employment and vocational training and advancement, and as regards working conditions, including pay;

Whereas it is desirable to reinforce the basic laws by standards aimed at facilitating the practical application of the principle of equality in such a way that all employees in the Community can be protected in these matters;

Whereas differences continue to exist in the various Member States despite the efforts made to apply the resolution of the conference of the Member States of 30 December 1961 on equal pay for men and women and whereas, therefore, the national provisions should be approximated as regards the principle of equal pay,

HAS ADOPTED THIS DIRECTIVE:

Article 1

The principle of equal pay for men and women outlined in Article 119 of the Treaty, hereinafter called 'principle of equal pay', means, for the same work or for work to which equal value is attributed, the elimination of all discrimination on grounds of sex with regard to all aspects and conditions of remuneration.

In particular, where a job classification scheme is used for determining pay, it must be based on the same criteria for both men and women and so drawn up as to exclude any discrimination on grounds of sex.

Article 2

Member States shall introduce into their national legal systems such measures as are necessary to enable all employees who consider themselves wronged by failure to apply the principle of equal pay to pursue their claims by judicial process after possible recourse to other competent authorities.

Article 3

Member States shall abolish all discrimination between men and women arising from laws, regulations or administrative provisions which is contrary to the principle of equal pay.

Article 4

Member States shall take the necessary measures to ensure that provisions appearing in collective agreements, wage scales, wage agreements or individual contracts of employment which are contrary to the principle of equal pay shall be, or may be declared, null and void or may be amended.

Article 5

Member States shall take the necessary measures to protect employees against dismissal by the employer as a reaction to a complaint within the underatking or to any legal proceedings aimed at enforcing compliance with the principle of equal pay.

Article 6

Member States shall, in accordance with their national circumstances and legal systems, take the measures necessary to ensure that the principle of equal pay is applied. They shall see that effective means are available to take care that this principle is observed.

Article 7

Member States shall take care that the provisions adopted pursuant to this Directive, together with the relevant provisions already in force, are brought to the attention of employees by all appropriate means, for example at their place of employment.

Article 8

1. Member States shall put into force the laws, regulations and administrative provisions necessary in order to comply with this Directive within one year of its notification and shall immediately inform the Commission thereof.

2. Member States shall communicate to the Commission the texts of the laws, regulations and administrative provisions which they adopt in the field covered by this Directive.

Article 9

Within two years of expiry of the one-year period referred to in Article 8, Member States shall forward all necessary information to the Commission to enable it to draw up a report on the application of this Directive for submission to the Council.

Article 10

This Directive is addressed to the Member States.

Done at Brussels, 10 February 1975.

For the Council

The President

G. FITZGERALD

26. COUNCIL DIRECTIVE

of 9 February 1976

on the implementation of the principle of equal treatment for men and women as regards access to employment, vocational training and promotion, and working conditions

(76/207/EEC)

(O.J. No L 39, 14 February 1976, p. 40)

THE COUNCIL OF THE EUROPEAN COMMUNITIES,

Having regard to the Treaty establishing the European Economic Community, and in particular Article 235 thereof,

Having regard to the proposal from the Commission,

Having regard to the opinion of the European Parliament,

Having regard to the opinion of the Economic and Social Committee,

Whereas the Council, in its resolution of 21 January 1974 concerning a social action programme, included among the priorities action for the purpose of achieving equality between men and women as regards access to employment and vocational training and promotion and as regards working conditions, including pay;

Whereas, with regard to pay, the Council adopted on 10 February 1975 Directive 75/117/EEC on the approximation of the laws of the Member States relating to the application of the principle of equal pay for men and women;

Whereas Community action to achieve the principle of equal treatment for men and women in respect of access to employment and vocational training and promotion and in respect of other working conditions also appears to be necessary; whereas, equal treatment for male and female workers constitutes one of the objectives of the Community, in so far as the harmonisation of living and working conditions while maintaining their improvement are *inter alia* to be furthered; whereas the Treaty does not confer the necessary specific powers for this purpose;

Whereas the definition and progressive implementation of the principle of equal treatment in matters of social security should be ensured by means of subsequent instruments,

HAS ADOPTED THIS DIRECTIVE:

Article 1

1.The purpose of this Directive is to put into effect in the Member States the principle of equal treatment for men and women as regards access to employment, including promotion, and to vocational training and as regards working conditions and, on the conditions referred to in paragraph 2, social security. This principle is hereinafter referred to as 'the principle of equal treatment'.

2. With a view to ensuring the progressive implementation of the principle of equal treatment in matters of social security, the Council, acting on a proposal from the Commission, will adopt provisions defining its substance, its scope and the arrangements for its application.

Article 2

1. For the purposes of the following provisions, the principle of equal treatment shall mean that there shall be no discrimination whatsoever on grounds of sex either directly or indirectly by reference in particular to marital or family status.

2. This Directive shall be without prejudice to the right of Member States to exclude from its field of application those occupational activities and, where appropriate, the training leading thereto, for which, by reason of their nature or the context in which they are carried out, the sex of the worker constitutes a determining factor.

3. This Directive shall be without prejudice to provisions concerning the protection of women, particularly as regards pregnancy and maternity.

4. This Directive shall be without prejudice to measures to promote equal opportunity for men and women, in particular by removing existing inequalities which affect women's opportunities in the areas referred to in Article 1(1).

Article 3

1. Application of the principle of equal treatment means that there shall be no discrimination whatsoever on grounds of sex in the conditions, including selection criteria, for access to all jobs or posts, whatever the sector or branch of activity, and to all levels of the occupational hierarchy.

2. To this end, Member States shall take the measures necessary to ensure that:

(a) any laws, regulations and administrative provisions contrary to the principle of equal treatment shall be abolished;

(b) any provisions contrary to the principle of equal treatment which are included in collective agreements, individual contracts of employment, internal rules of undertakings or in rules governing the independent occupations and professions shall be, or may be declared, null and void or may be amended;

(c) those laws, regulations and administrative provisions contrary to the principle of equal treatment when the concern for protection which originally inspired them is no longer well founded shall be revised; and that where similar provisions are included in collective agreements labour and management shall be requested to take the desired revision.

Article 4

Application of the principle of equal treatment with regard to access to all types and to all levels, of vocational guidance, advanced vocational training and retraining, means that Member States shall take all necessary measures to ensure that:

(a) any laws, regulations and administrative provisions contrary to the principle of equal treatment shall be abolished;

(b) any provisions contrary to the principle of equal treatment which are included in collective agreements, individual contracts of employment, internal rules of undertakings or in rules governing the independent occupations and professions shall be, or may be declared, null and void or may be amended;

(c) without prejudice to the freedom granted in certain Member States to certain private training establishments, vocational guidance, vocational training, advanced vocational training and retraining shall be accessible on the basis of the same criteria and at the same levels without any discrimination on grounds of sex.

Article 5

1. Application of the principle of equal treatment with regard to working conditions, including the conditions governing dismissal, means that men and women shall be guaranteed the same conditions without discrimination on grounds of sex.

2. To this end Member States shall take the measures necessary to ensure that:

(a) any laws, regulations and administrative provisions contrary to the principle of equal treatment shall be abolished;

(b) any provisions contrary to the principle of equal treatment which are included in collective agreements, individual contracts of employment, internal rules of undertakings or in rules governing the independent occupations and professions shall be, or may be declared, null and void or may be amended;

(c) those laws, regulations and administrative provisions contrary to the principle of equal treatment when the concern for protection which originally inspired them is no longer well founded shall be revised; and that where similar provisions are included in collective agreements labour and management shall be requested to undertake the desired revision.

Article 6

Member States shall introduce into their national legal systems such measures as are necessary to enable all persons who consider themselves wronged by failure to apply to them the principle of equal treatment within the meaning of Articles 3, 4 and 5 to pursue their claims by judicial process after possible recourse to other competent authorities.

Article 7

Member States shall take the necessary measures to protect employees against dismissal by the employer as a reaction to a complaint within the undertaking or to any legal proceedings aimed at enforcing compliance with the principle of equal treatment.

Article 8

Member States shall take care that the provisions adopted pursuant to this Directive, together with the relevant provisions already in force, are brought to the attention of employees by all appropriate means, for example at their place of employment.

Article 9

1. Member States shall put into force the laws, regulations and administrative provisions necessary in order to comply with this Directive within 30 months of its notification and shall immediately inform the Commission thereof.

However, as regards the first part of Article 3(2) (c) and the first part of Article 5(2) (c), Member States shall carry out a first examination and if necessary a first revision of the laws, regulations and administrative provisions referred to therein within four years of notification of this Directive.

2. Member States shall periodically assess the occupational activities referred to in Article 2(2) in order to decide, in the light of social developments, whether there is justification for maintaining the exclusions concerned. They shall notify the Commission of the results of this assessment.

3. Member States shall also communicate to the Commission the texts of laws, regulations and administrative provisions which they adopt in the field covered by this Directive.

Article 10

Within two years following expiry of the thirty-month period laid down in the first subparagraph of Article 9(1), Member States shall forward all necessary information to the Commission to enable it to draw up a report on the application of this Directive for submission to the Council.

Article 11

This Directive is addressed to the Member States.

Done at Brussels, 9 February 1976.

For the Council

The President

G. THORN

27. COMMISSION DECISION

of 8 May 1974

authorising the Italian Republic to take certain protective
measures under Article 108 (3) of the Treaty

(74/287/EEC)

(O.J. No L 152, 8 June 1974, p. 18)

THE COMMISSION OF THE EUROPEAN COMMUNITIES,

Having regard to the Treaty establishing the European Economic Community, and in particular Article 108(3) thereof;

Whereas in recent months the Italian economy has been experiencing a
high growth rate and a substantial expansion of consumption; whereas
overall demand has developed in such a way as to spark off a major
acceleration of the inflationary process, a sharp deterioration in
the balance of payments and, consequently, a marked depreciation of
the lira;

Whereas the situation has lately been growing steadily worse, so that
the Italian economy is now facing exceptional circumstances both
internally and externally, with the balance of payments moving unac-
ceptably further into disequilibrium;

Whereas the growing interpenetration of the economies of the Member
States means that the effect of these difficulties will be felt in
all the countries of the Community;

Whereas by letter dated 29 April 1974 Italy informed the Commission
that it had taken a number of measures to reduce its balance of payments disequilibrium;

Whereas these measures include a provision designed to restrict the
money supply by requiring an interest-free six-month deposit to be
lodged in cash with the Bank of Italy; whereas Article 109 of the
Treaty of Rome was relied upon as grounds for the deposit, which
represents 50 % of the value of all imported goods, other than raw
materials, energy products and most capital goods;

Whereas on 6 May 1974 the Commission, having examined, pursuant to
Article 108(1), the state of the Italian economy and the measures
taken by Italy, addressed a Recommendation to Italy under Article
108(1);

Whereas the Council has not decided to provide the mutual assistance
recommended by the Commission;

Whereas, however, the state of the Italian economy is so serious and

377

measures to remedy it ought to be taken so urgently that the measures recommended to Italy under Article 108(1) of the Treaty will not be sufficient for they are not on their own capable of immediately rectifying the Italian balance of payments;

Whereas, however, measures whose effect is to hinder the free movement of goods would strike at the very foundations of the Community, even if their object is to overcome exceptional economic and monetary difficulties; whereas recourse should therefore be had solely to measures which, while likely to achieve the desired result, will nevertheless disturb the operation of the common market as little as possible; whereas the application of such measures should be strictly limited in scope and in duration;

Whereas Italy should therefore be authorised temporarily to require an interest-free bank deposit to be lodged when certain goods are imported;

Whereas it is necessary to ensure that these measures will be applied flexibly and speedily so as to restrict Community trade as little as possible; whereas Italy and the Commission should therefore work together and find appropriate solutions to any difficulties which may arise in the application of these measures;

Whereas in view of the need to redress the external financial situation, Italy should be authorised to continue temporarily, the measures taken in July 1973 by way of derogation from Community obligations in respect of the free movement of capital;

Whereas the development of the economic situation in Italy should be kept under close review so that the measures authorised may be amended or repealed should the circumstances underlying them no longer obtain either with respect to the products covered by them or to the amount or duration of the deposit;

Whereas the overall situation and the practical effects of the Italian measures should be reviewed periodically;

Whereas, for agricultural products subject to a common organisation of the market involving strict price support mechanisms and for products processed therefrom, the measures authorised run counter to the very principles of the common organisation; whereas an expiry date for these measures should therefore be fixed without delay;

Whereas in the meantime alternative solutions will be sought with Italy and the other Member States, it being understood that this joint search cannot be allowed to prejudice the Commission's right to take the decisions which are its responsibility at the appropriate time,

HAS ADOPTED THIS DECISION:

Article 1

The Italian Republic is authorised to require, upon importation of goods listed in the Annex hereto, a certificate from a competent financial institution attesting that an interest-free six-month deposit has been lodged in cash with the bank of Italy; the amount of the deposit shall not exceed 50% of the cif value of the goods.

The Italian Republic shall publish a list of the financial institutions empowered to issue such certificates.

Article 2

The Italian Republic shall ensure that the bank deposit certificates provided for in Article 1 are issued automatically and without delay.

Article 3

The Italian Republic shall ensure that the Bank of Italy releases the deposit without formality as soon as:

(a) the six-month period expires;

(b) the goods in respect of which the deposit was lodged are re-exported as they are or after processing.

Article 4

Should any difficulties arise in implementing the measures hereby authorised, the Italian Republic and the Commission shall examine them together.

Article 5

The Italian Republic is temporarily authorised to require its residents to lodge an interest-free bank deposit not exceeding 50% of the value of their investment transactions in other Member States covered by Articles 1 and 2 of the Council Directive of 11 May 1960 (First Directive for the implementation of Article 67 of the EEC Treaty), as amended by Directive No 63/21/EEC of 18 December 1962: direct investments, investments in real estate, transfer of the financial resources required for the provision of services, operations in securities.

Article 6

The Commission shall ensure that the provisions of this Decision are observed.

Article 7

1. The Commission shall keep the economic situation in Italy under close review.

2. It reserves the right to amend or repeal this Decision if it finds that the circumstances underlying its adoption change or that its

effects are more restrictive than necessary for the attainment of its aims or seriously harm all or part of the Community.

3. It shall, in particular, review the overall situation and the effects of the measures authorised by this Decision before 31 July 1974.

4. It shall, if necessary, proceed to a second review not later than 31 October 1974.

5. The Commission shall without delay set a time limit on the authorisation contained on Article 1 in respect of agricultural products subject to a common organisation of the market involving strict price support mechanisms and for products processed therefrom.

Article 8

This Decision is addressed to the Italian Republic.

Done at Brussels, 8 May 1974.

For the Commission

The President

Francois-Xavier ORTOLI

28. DECISION OF THE COUNCIL
AND OF THE REPRESENTATIVES OF THE GOVERMENTS OF THE
MEMBER STATES MEETING WITHIN THE COUNCIL

of 28 July 1982

adopting the fifth medium-term economic policy programme

(82/534/EEC)

(O.J. No L 236, 11 August 1982, p. 10)

THE COUNCIL OF THE EUROPEAN COMMUNITIES AND THE REPRESENTATIVES OF THE GOVERNMENTS OF THE MEMBER STATES, MEETING WITHIN THE COUNCIL,

Having regard to the Treaty establishing the European Economic Community, and in particular the preamble thereto and Articles 6, 105 and 145 thereof,

Having regard to Council Decision 74/120/EEC of 18 February 1974 on the attainment of a high degree of convergence of the economic policies of the Member States of the European Economic Community, and in particular Article 6 thereof,

Having regard to the comminication from the Commission concerning the draft of the fifth medium-term economic policy programme,

Having regard to the opinion of the European Parliament,

Whereas the Economic and Social Committee, consulted on the Commission proposal, has not submitted its opinion within the time limit set by the Council under Article 198 of the EEC Treaty; whereas the absence of an opinion should not prevent further action;

Whereas the economic policies pursued by the Member States must meet the objectives set out in Article 104 of the Treaty,

HAVE DECIDED AS FOLLOWS:

Sole Article

1. The fifth medium-term economic policy programme set out in the Annex is hereby adopted. The Member States express their intention of acting in accordance with the guidelines contained therein.

2. The programme will be kept under constant review during its period of application.

Done at Brussels, 28 July 1982.

The President
O. MOLLER

ANNEX

FIFTH MEDIUM-TERM ECONOMIC POLICY PROGRAMME

1. The Fifth Programme develops and defines a medium-term strategy for achieving a number of economic policy objectives. This Programme is not a quantified plan, but a kind of framework which lays down guidelines for national policies and policy at Community level. It defines the various elements of a strategy. Concrete measures to realise the strategy would depend on the very different economic situations and structures in the Member States.

2. There is still broad agreement as to the chief medium-term objectives contained in the Economic Policy Committee's preliminary draft of 21 May 1981: the achievement of sustained and balanced growth and improved employment, in particular through higher investment and the promotion of structural change, and further progress in fighting inflation, paralleled by an improvement in the competitiveness of the economies of the Member States.

3. Opinions differed, however, as to the priority objectives and the

timing of measures to achieve improved employment and stability. Some Member States felt that in the medium-term the employment situation would be improved by consistant stabilisation policies (monetary, budgetary and incomes policy) and that, in the given circumstances, measures to stimulate global demand with a view to improving the employment situation in the short-term could make the achievement of medium-term objectives more difficult. Other Member States, however, took the view that, while the ambition of re-establishing in time a broad equilibrium in the course of implementing the medium-term strategy should not be abandoned, a selective support of domestic demand was advisable in order to achieve a more rapid improvement in the employment situation and as a condition in itself for a recovery in investment. For these Member States, it is essential that the adjustment effort be accompanied by resolute structural action, affecting notably industrial structures, and by a better trade-off between income and employment through work-sharing measures.

4. In the year which has elapsed since the submission of the draft Programme, the economic environment has further deteriorated and the cyclical upturn has been slow in starting. Economic trends in the Community remain largely unsatisfactory, notably as regards growth and investment and, more particularly, employment and unemployment. The employment position is a matter of increasing concern to Member States. Nevertheless, since the draft programme was prepared:

- some progress has been achieved in reducing inflation rates but, at the same time, divergences in price and cost developments between Member States have widened. If these divergences are not narrowed, lasting monetary stability within the Community cannot be achieved. In order to prevent frequent central rate adjustments, which undermine the credibility of the European monetary system, the implementation of stabilisation measures is important in those countries where price and cost increases remain high.

- It has been possible to reduce dependence on energy: petroleum imports have fallen partly as a result of the decline in economic activity, but also partly because of real energy savings due to structural adjustment and, in some countries, to dynamic policies of domestic energy supply. However, the Community must not be deflected from its efforts to achieve further progress in reducing petroleum consumption by the developments in crude oil prices.

- The Community's balance of payments deficit has been smaller than expected, partly because of the reduction in oil imports. Nevertheless, given the very different evolution as between Member States, problems for convergence might arise.

5. The actual direction of economic policy in the Member States since mid-1981 has for the most part remained within the broad framework of guidelines set out in the draft Programme. The following points deserve particular mention:

- the measures decided on to promote investment activity and employment,

- the efforts made to moderate pay rises, and

- in countries where budget deficits were particularly large, the efforts made to limit them and to reduce the growth of public expenditure. However, in some cases, the restructuring of public budgets is still insufficient.

6.As regards the present economic outlook, there are signs of a cyclical recovery, but the process is slow in starting and the upturn is endangered by high interest rates and excessive structural budget deficits. There is particular concern over the further rise in unemployment, which could be reduced only in the course of a sustained economic recovery, and over the persistently high inflation rates in some countries.

7. In this situation the first requirement is to strengthen the forces of recovery and to create greater employment opportunities. Policies are required which take account of the developing situation and of the differing positions of the Member States, while emphasising common aims and seeking to achieve greater convergence. Coordination of national policies at Community level and individual Community policies should contribute to structural adjustment and help to reduce divergence between Member States' economies. Particular attention should be given to creating a socio-economic climate which would promote and revive investment activity and improve the competitiveness of the European economies. Specific employment policy measures are also urgent, in particular measures to promote vocational training for young people. The Commission is shortly to put forward a first report on the practical measures or appropriate initiatives to promote investment, which the Economic Policy Committee will examine in due time.

8. The essential elements of this strategy should be the foundation of a medium-term approach. Under present circumstances, the Member States attach different priorities to the individual economic policy objectives. However, even if the stance of economic policy differs, sufficient regard should be paid to the chief common medium-term objectives. It would also be necessary to strengthen the forces underlying growth as the basis of further progress towards stability and to create better conditions for a sustained economic recovery and the requirement of closer convergence. The Economic Policy Committee intends to discuss medium-term developments and problems at regular intervals and to present the results to the Council. It will in particular carefully examine the appropriate mix of the proposed strategy as the necessary progress is made in the fields of inflation and of public finance and balance of payments equilibrium.

I

29. COUNCIL REGULATION (EEC) No 3180/78

of 18 December 1978

changing the value of the unit of account used by the European Monetary Cooperation Fund

(O.J. No L 379, 30 December 1978, p. 1)

THE COUNCIL OF THE EUROPEAN COMMUNITIES,

Having regard to the Treaty establishing the European Economic Community,

Having regard to Council Regulation (EEC) No 907/73 of 3 April 1973 establishing a European Monetary Cooperation Fund, and in particular the last paragraph of Article 5 of the Statutes of the Fund,

Having regard to the proposal from the Commission,

Having regard to the opinion of the Monetary Committee,

Having regard to the opinion of the Board of Governors of the European Monetary Cooperation Fund,

Whereas Regulation (EEC) No 907/73, in Article 5 of the Statutes of the Fund, requires the latter's operations in the currencies of the Member States to be expressed in a European monetary unit of account of a value of 0.88867088 gramme of fine gold;

Whereas this definition no longer conforms with the rules in force in the international monetary system;

Whereas, apart from in cases in which the value of the European monetary unit of account is changed automatically, the last paragraph of the said Article 5 provides that any other changes shall be decided on by the Council, acting unanimously on a proposal from the Commission, after consulting the Monetary Committee and the Board of Governors of the Fund;

Whereas the establishment of a new European monetary system, which was the subject of the resolution of the European Council meeting in Brussels on 4 and 5 December 1978, provides for the use of an 'ECU' defined as a basket of Member States' currencies,

HAS ADOPTED THIS REGULATION:

Article 1

With effect from 1 January 1979, the Fund's operations shall be expressed in a unit of account known as the ECU which is defined as the sum of the following amounts of the currencies of the Member States;

0.828	German mark,
0.0885	pound sterling,
1.15	French francs,
109	Italian lira,
0.286	Dutch guilder,
3.66	Belgian francs,
0.14	Luxembourg franc,
0.217	Danish krone,

0.00759   Irish pound.

Article 2

The Council, acting unanimously on a proposal from the Commission, after consulting the Monetary Committee and the Board of Governors of the Fund, shall determine the conditions under which the composition of the ECU may be changed.

Article 3

This Regulation shall enter into force on 1 January 1979.

This Regulation shall be binding in its entirety and directly applicable in all Member States.

Done at Brussels, 18 December 1978.

For the Council

The President

H. MATTHÖFER

I

30. COUNCIL REGULATION (EEC, EURATOM) No 3308/80

of 16 December 1980

on the replacement of the European unit of account by the ECU in Community legal instruments

(O.J. No L 345, 20 December 1980, p. 1)

THE COUNCIL OF THE EUROPEAN COMMUNITIES,

Having regard to the Treaty establishing the European Economic Community, and in particular Article 235 thereof,

Having reagrd to the Treaty establishing the European Atomic Energy Community, and in particular Article 203 thereof,

Having regard to the proposal from the Commission,

Having regard to the opinion of the European Parliament,

Whereas Regulation (EEC) No 3180/78 defined a new unit of account, known as the ECU;

Whereas steps should be taken to standardise the units of account used by the Communities; whereas the European unit of account (EUA) should, therefore, be replaced by the ECU in all Community legal instruments;

Whereas a provision should be included in order, when the EUA is replaced by the ECU, to safeguard rights and obligations contracted in European units of account,

HAS ADOPTED THIS DECISION:

Article 1

In all Community legal instruments applying at the time of entry into force of this Regulation, 'European unit of account' shall be replaced by 'ECU'.

Article 2

The definition of the European unit of account in force before the entry into force of this Regulation shall continue to apply to rights and obligations arising before the entry into force of this Regulation which were determined in European units of account.

Article 3

This Regulation shall enter into force on 1 January 1981.

This Regulation shall be binding in its entirety and directly applicable in all Member States.

Done at Brussels, 16 December 1980.

For the Council
The President
Colette FLESCH

31. REGULATION No 136/66/EEC OF THE COUNCIL

of 22 September 1966

on the establishment of a common organisation of the market
in oils and fats

(O.J. No 172, 30 September 1966, p. 3025)

THE COUNCIL OF THE EUROPEAN ECONOMIC COMMUNITY,

HAVING REGARD to the Tretay establishing the European Economic Community, and in particular Articles 42 and 43 thereof;

HAVING REGARD to the proposal from the Commission;

HAVING REGARD to the Opinion of the European Parliament;

WHEREAS the situation on the Community market in oils and fats of vegetable or marine origin is characterised by high demand and low overall production; whereas Member States therefore depend to a large extent on the world market for supplies; whereas this situation generally justifies the removal of the various import barriers and their replacement, except where certain olive oil products are concerned, by the Common Customs Tariff which makes it easier for industries to obtain supplies by allowing raw materials to enter the Community duty free while duties on finished products serve to protect these industries and secure consumers supplies at reasonable prices;

WHEREAS, however, the removal of import barriers would leave the Community market in oil seeds, oleaginous fruit and their oils without defence against disturbances caused either by certain imports from third countries or by disparities, resulting from action by third countries, between prices for products derived from oil seeds and oleaginous fruit and prices for these seeds and fruit; whereas these disturbances are seriously prejudicial to the interests of producers and processing industries; whereas provisions must therefore be made for appropriate measures to remedy this situation, inter-

387

national commitments being taken into account;

WHEREAS, because of the situation on the world market, certain sectors of agricultural and industrial production in the Community would be adversely affected if the effects of the removal of import barriers were not offset by other measures; whereas olive oil consumption might decline if there was a substantial fall in the price of competing oils; whereas, furthermore, other oils and oil seeds are in direct competition with oils and oil seeds imported from third countries at a reduced rate of duty or duty free;

WHEREAS olive growing and olive oil production are of special economic importance in certain regions of the Community where they often constitute the most important source of income for a large proportion of the population; whereas olive oil is the most important source of oil and fats for large categories of consumers; whereas the growing of oil seeds, in particular colza, rape and sunflower seeds, contributes to the viability of farms by making it possible to improve technical and financial equilibrium; whereas it is therefore necessary to support these activities by appropriate measures;

WHEREAS to this end the marketing of Community harvests of these products must ensure producers a fair income, the level of which may be determined by a production target price in the case of olive oil and by a target price in the case of oil seeds; whereas the difference between these prices and prices acceptable to the consumer represents the subsidy which should be granted to attain the desired objective;

WHEREAS consumer preferences make it possible to sell olive oil at a higher price than other products of a similar kind; whereas it is therefore possible, prices for competing products being taken into account, to determine a market target price that will, as a general rule, provide the producer with a large proportion of the requisite income in the form of receipts from sales;

WHEREAS the market target price for olive oil cannot attain its objective unless the price actually ruling on the market is as close as possible to the market target price; whereas stabilising machinery should therefore be provided in producer Member States and at the Community frontier;

WHEREAS the desired stability may be obtained within the Community by making it possible in production areas for olive oil to be offered to competent agencies of the Member States; whereas, because of the geographical concentration of production and consumption, the intervention price to be paid for oil by intervention agencies can be the same in all intervention centres; whereas, moreover, in order to ensure that there is a constant balance between supply and demand and to counteract the effects of fluctuation in production, provision should be made for the possibility of entrusting intervention agencies with the task of forming a buffer stocks;

WHEREAS, in order to stabilise the Community market at the desired level, notably by ensuring that fluctuations in world market prices do not affect prices within the Community, provision should be made for charging an import levy corresponding to the difference between the threshold price derived from the market target price and prices ruling on the world market; whereas if protection is to be complete and consistent, a system which would have the same effect must be applied to oil-cake, other residues resulting from the extraction of olive oil and olives for oil production;

WHEREAS, in the case of olive oil used in the manufacture of preserved fish and vegetables, the levy must be suspended or a refund granted to enable manufacturers to meet competition from similar products manufactured with oil bought at world market prices;

WHEREAS supplies of olive oil to the consumer might be jeopardised if the ratio of world prices to Community prices were likely to lead to substantial exports of olive oil; whereas, furthermore, imports or exports of this product might in certain circumstances lead to market disturbances; whereas provision should therefore be made for dealing with such a situation;

WHEREAS, as far as oil seeds are concerned, farmers can be protected against any risks which may arise, despite the proposed system of subsidies, from the unsettled state of the market by intervention machinery involving the buying-in of quantities offered to the competent agencies at intervention prices which must, because the area of production is extensive and processing centres few, be fixed in the light of natural conditions of price formation;

WHEREAS the list of seeds to be covered by the system described above must be drawn up in such a way as to include the species which are most widely grown at the present time; whereas provision should however be made for the possibility of extending this system to other seeds in the light of experience;

WHEREAS the abolition of measures encouraging the production of grape-pip oil in certain Member States calls for the adoption of special measures to enable the industry concerned to adapt to new market conditions;

WHEREAS the consistency of the provisions governing the common organisation of the market in oils and fats would be impaired if their effect were to be combined with those of subsidies incompatible with the Treaty; whereas, until such time as a common agricultural policy for flax is put into effect, an exception must be made in respect of subsidies on the production of linseed for oil extraction;

WHEREAS the common organisation of the market in oils and fats must take appropriate account, at the same time, of the objectives set out in Articles 39 and 110 of the Treaty;

WHEREAS, in order to facilitate implementation of the proposed measures, a procedure should be provided for establishing close cooperation between Member States and the Commission within a Management Committee;

HAS ADOPTED THIS REGULATION:

Article 1

1. A common organisation of the market in oil seeds, oleaginous fruit, vegetable oils and fats, and oils and fats of fish or marine mammals shall be established.

2. This Regulation shall cover the following products:

Common Customs
Tariff heading
No

Description of goods

(a)	12.01	Oil seeds and oleaginous fruit, whole or broken
(b)	.12.02	Flours or meals of oil seeds or oleaginous fruit, non-defatted, (excluding mustard flour)
	15.04	Fats and oils, of fish and marine mammals, whether or not refined
	ex 15.07	Fixed vegetable oils, fluid or solid, crude, refined or purified, excluding olive oil
	15.12	Animal or vegetable oils and fats, wholly or partly hydrogenated, or solidified or hardened by any other process, whether or not refined, but not further prepared
	15.13	Margarine, imitation lard and other prepared edible fats
	ex 15.17	Residues resulting from the treatment of fatty substances or animal or vegetable waxes, excluding those containing oil having the characteristics of olive oil
	ex 23.04	Oil-cake and other residues (except dregs) resulting from the extraction of vegetable oils, excluding oil-cake and other residues resulting from the extraction of olive oil
(c)	ex 15.07	Olive oil, crude, refined or purified
(d)	ex 07.01 N	Olives, fresh or chilled
	ex 07.02	Olives (whether or not cooked), preserved by freezing
	ex 07.03 A	Olives provisionally preserved in brine, in sulphur water or in other preservative solutions, but not specially prepared for immediate consumption
	ex 07.04 B	Dried, dehydrated or evaporated olives, whole, cut, sliced, broken or in powder, but not further prepared
(e)	ex 15.17	Residues resulting from the treatment of fatty substances or animal or vegetable waxes, containing oil having the characteristics of olive oil
	ex 23.04	Oil-cake and other residues resulting from the extraction of olive oil

TITLE I

Trade

Article 2

1. The Common Customs Tariff shall be applied to the products listed in Article 1(2) (a), (b) and (d).

2. A system of levies shall be applied to imports from third countries of the products listed in Article 1(2) (c) and (e) and of those referred to in Article 15(1).

Article 3

1. Subject to the provisions of Article 2, the following shall be incompatible with the provisions of this Regulation in intra-Community trade:

- the levying of any customs duty or charge having equivalent effect;

- the application of any quantitative restriction or measure having equivalent effect;

- recourse to Article 44 of the Treaty.

2. In trade with third countries the following shall be incompatible with the provisions of this Regulation:

- the levying of any customs duty or charge having equivalent effect, other than those provided for by this Regulation;

- the application of any quantitative restriction or measure having equivalent effect, save where derogation therefrom is decided by the Council acting in accordance with the voting procedure laid down in Article 43(2) of the Treaty on a proposal from the Commission.

3. The restriction of the import or export licences provided for in Article 17 to a specified category of those entitled to receive them shall be one of the measures considered as having effect equivalent to a quantitative restriction.

4. Intra-Community trade in the goods listed in Article 1(2) shall be incompatible with the provisions of this Regulation where any products not in free circulation are used in their manufacture.

5. Until such time as national arrangements governing suspension or drawback of customs duties, levies or charges on products for re-export to third countries have been harmonised, and without prejudice to the provisions to be adopted in connection with such harmonisation, the Council, acting in accordance with the voting procedure laid down in Article 43(2) of the Treaty on a proposal from the Commission, shall take the necessary steps to counteract any disturbances on the olive oil market resulting from disparities between these national arrangements.

6. Where the products listed in Article 1(2) (a) and (b) are imported from third countries in such quantities and under such conditions as might seriously prejudice or threaten to prejudice the interests of Community producers of the products listed in Article 1(2), a compensatory amount may be charged on imports.

A compensatory amount may also be charged on imports of the products listed in Article 1(2) where, as a result of direct or indirect subsidies or premiums granted in respect of these products by one or more third countries, or as a result of equivalent measures, actual offers of these products do not correspond to the prices which would prevail in the absence of such measures or practices and where such a situation is causing or is threatening to cause serious prejudice to Community production of the products listed in Article 1(2).

The introduction of such compensatory amounts shall respect the international commitments undertaken by the Member States and the Community. The amounts shall be fixed in accordance with rules to be adopted by the Council acting in accordance with the voting procedure laid down in Article 43(2) of the Treaty on a proposal from the Commission.

TITLE II

Olive Oil

Article 4

Before 1 October of each year the Council, acting in accordance with the voting procedure laid down in Article 43(2) of the Treaty on a proposal from the Commission, shall fix a single production target price, a single market target price, a single intervention price and a single threshold price for olive oil for the Community.

Subject to the provisions of Article 9, these prices shall remain in force throughout the following marketing year. The marketing year shall run from 1 November to 31 October.

These prices shall relate to a standard quality for oil corresponding to one of the definitions in the Annex referred to in Article 35. This standard quality shall be determined by the Council in accordance with the procedure referred to in the first paragraph of this Article.

They shall be fixed at the wholesale marketing stage exclusive of taxes.

Article 5

The production target price shall be fixed at a level which is fair to producers, account being taken of the need to keep Community production at the required level.

Article 6

The market target price shall be fixed at a level which will permit

normal marketing of olive oil produced, account being taken of prices
for competing products and in particular of the probable trend of
these prices during the marketing year and the incidence of the monthly increases referred to in Article 9 on prices for olive oil.

Article 7

The intervention price, which guarantees that producers will be able
to sell their produce at a price which, allowing for market fluctuations, is as close as possible to the market target price, shall be
equal to the market target price reduced by an amount large enough
to allow for these fluctuations and for the transport of olive oil
from production areas to consumption areas.

Article 8

The threshold price shall be fixed in such a way that the selling
price for the imported product at the frontier crossing point referred
to in Article 13(2) shall be the same as the market target price.

Article 9

To enable sales to be staggered, the market target price, the intervention price and the threshold price shall be increased each month,
for a period of ten months beginning 1 January, by an amount which
shall be the same for all three prices.

The monthly increases, which shall be the same for each month, shall
be fixed each year by the Council acting in accordance with the voting
procedure laid down in Article 43(2) of the Treaty on a proposal
from the Commission, account being taken of average storage costs and
interest charges in the Community.

Article 10

1. Where the production target price is higher than the market target
price ruling at the beginning of the marketing year, a subsidy equal
to the difference between these two prices shall be granted to producers of olive oil extracted within the Community from olives harvested
within the Community. Only oil to which the provisions of this paragraph have not already been applied shall be eligible for this subsidy.

2. The principles governing the grant of the subsidy provided for in
paragraph 1 shall be defined by the Council acting in accordance with
the voting procedure laid down in Article 43(2) of the Treaty on a
proposal from the Commission. Acting in accordance with the same procedure, the Council shall adopt measures to ensure that olive oil
producers receive this subsidy only in respect of oils which meet the
conditions set out in paragraph 1.

3. Detailed rules for the application of this Article shall be adopted in accordance with the procedure laid down in Article 38.

393

Article 11

1. In each producer Member State an intervention agency shall, under conditions to be laid down in accordance with the provisions of paragraph 5, buy in olive oil of Community origin offered to it at intervention centres in production areas. The intervention agency shall buy at the intervention price and at that price only.

If, however, the description or quality of the oil offered to the intervention agency does not correspond to that for which the intervention price was fixed, the buying-in price shall be adjusted by means of a scale of price increases and reductions.

Furthermore, if at the request of the intervention agency oil is delivered to a place other than the centre indicated by the seller when the offer is made, the resulting change in transport costs to the seller shall be taken into account when payment is being effected.

2. With a view to stabilising the market during the marketing year, intervention agencies may conclude storage contracts for Community olive oil pursuant to provisions adopted by the Council acting in accordance with the voting procedure laid down in Article 43(2) of the Treaty on a proposal from the Commission.

3. Olive oil bought in by intervention agencies shall not be sold by them on the Community market in terms which might impede price formation at the level of the market target price.

4. The Council, acting in accordance with the voting procedure laid down in Article 43(2) of the Treaty on a proposal from the Commission, shall determine the main intervention centres and lay down criteria to be applied when other centres are being determined; the latter shall be determined in accordance with the procedure laid down in Article 38 after consultation with the Member States concerned.

5. Detailed rules for the application of this Article, and in particular those concerning the quality and size of the consignments offered under paragraph 1, shall be adopted in accordance with the procedure laid down in Article 38.

Article 12

To mitigate the effects of harvest fluctuations on the balance between supply and demand and in this way to stabilise consumer prices, the Council, acting in accordance with the voting procedure laid down in Article 43(2) of the Treaty on a proposal from the Commission, may require intervention agencies to form a buffer stock of olive oil. It shall, in accordance with the same procedure, lay down the conditions governing the formation, management and disposal of the buffer stock.

Article 13

1. If the threshold price is higher than the cif price, a levy equal to the difference between these two prices shall be charged on imports of unrefined olive oil from third countries.

2. The cif price, calculated for a Community frontier crossing point, shall be determined on the basis of the most favourable purchasing opportunities on the world market.

The frontier crossing point shall be fixed by the Council acting in accordance with the voting procedure laid down in Article 43(2) of the Treaty on a proposal from the Commission, account being taken of the extent to which this point is representative for imports.

When the most favourable purchasing opportunities are being determined, only those offers which correspond to actual purchasing opportunities for quantities which are representative of the market shall be taken into account.

Prices shall be adjusted to allow for any deviations from the description or quality for which the threshold price was fixed.

3. Where free quotations on the world market are not a determining factor for the offer price and where this price is lower than world market prices, a price determined on the basis of the offer price shall be substituted for the cif price in respect of these imports and these imports only.

4. The levy shall be fixed by the Commission. The criteria for determining the cif price and the price referred to in paragraph 3 shall be laid down and detailed rules for the application of this Article shall be adopted in accordance with the procedure laid down in Article 38.

Article 14

1. A levy shall be charged on imports of refined olive oil from third countries. This levy shall be composed of a variable component corresponding to the levy applicable to the quantity of olive oil needed for its production (which may be fixed at a standard rate) and a fixed component to protect the processing industry.

2. Detailed rules for the application of this Article shall be adopted by the Council in accordance with the voting procedure laid down in Article 43(2) of the Treaty on a proposal from the Commission.

Article 15

1. On imports from third countries of olives falling within headings Nos 07.01 N and 07.03 A excluding those for purposes other than the production of oil a levy derived from the levy applicable to olive oil pursuant to Article 13 and based on the oil content of the imported product shall be charged in addition to the rate of duty in the Common Customs Tariff. The levy shall be reduced by the amount resulting from application of the customs duty to the value of the imported product. This amount may be fixed at a standard rate.

2. On imports from third countries of the products listed in Article 1(2) (e) a levy derived from the levy applicable to olive oil and based on the oil content of the imported product shall be charged.

However, the levy shall only be charged if commitments undertaken within GATT are respected.

3. Detailed rules for the application of this Article, and in particular those concerning the determination of oil content which may be fixed at a standard rate, shall be adopted by the Council acting in accordance with the voting procedure laid down in Article 43(2) of the Treaty on a proposal from the Commission.

Article 16

The levy applicable to an import shall be that in force on the day of importation.

Article 17

1. Imports from third countries of any of the products listed in Article 1(2) (c), (d) and (e) shall be conditional on the submission of an import licence. Exports of olive oil to third countries shall be conditional on the submission of an export licence.

These licences shall be issued on application by the party concerned under rules to be adopted by the Council acting in accordance with the voting procedure laid down in Article 43(2) of the Treaty on a proposal from the Commission. These rules may require the lodging of a deposit.

2. Import and export licences shall be valid from the date of issue until the end of the third month following the month of issue.

3. Detailed rules for the application of this Article shall be adopted in accordance with the procedure laid down in Article 38.

Article 18

1. When olive oil is exported to third countries:

- the difference between prices within the Community and prices on the world market may be covered by a refund where the former are higher than the latter;

- a levy equal at most to the difference between prices on the world market and prices within the Community may be charged where the former are higher than the latter.

2. Provisions for the application of this Article shall be adopted by the Council acting in accordance with the voting procedure laid down in Article 43(2) of the Treaty on a proposal from the Commission.

Article 19

Olive oil used in the manufacture of preserved fish and vegetables shall benefit from a system of production refunds or from full or partial suspension of the import levy.

Provisions for the application of this Article shall be adopted by the Council acting in accordance with the voting procedure laid down in Article 43(2) of the Treaty on a proposal from the Commission.

Article 20

1. If the olive oil market in the Community experiences or is threatened with serious disturbances by reason of:

- imports from third countries of the products listed in Article 1(2) (c), (d) and (e), in particular where the intervention agencies have been led to buy in substantial quantities of olive oil under Article 11(1); or

- exports of olive oil to third countries, in particular where the market price for olive oil might substantially exceed or threaten to exceed the level of the market target price, or where it has been decided to dispose of the buffer stock,

appropriate measures may be applied until such disturbance or threat of disturbance has ceased.

2. The Council, acting in accordance with the voting procedure laid down in Article 43(2) of the Treaty on a proposal from the Commission, shall determine the nature of the measures which may be applied and shall adopt provisions for the application of this Article.

TITLE III

Other vegetable oils and oil seeds produced in the Community

Article 21

The oil seeds to which the provisions of Articles 22 to 29 shall apply are:

- colza and rape seed,

- sunflower seed.

The Council, acting in accordance with the voting procedure laid down in Article 43(2) of the Treaty on a proposal from the Commission, may decide to extend these provisions to other oil seeds.

Article 22

1. Each year in time to allow farmers to plan their production, and for the first time in 1966, the Council, acting in accordance with the voting procedure laid down in Article 43(2) of the Treaty on a proposal from the Commission, shall fix a single target price for each species of oil seed for the Community and a basic intervention price calculated for an intervention centre to be determined in accordance

with the same procedure.

Subject to the provisions of Article 25, these prices shall remain in force throughout the marketing year beginning in the following calendar year. They shall relate to a standard quality and shall be fixed at the wholesale marketing stage exclusive of taxes.

The dates on which each marketing year begins and ends, the date before which the target prices and basic intervention prices must be fixed, and the standard quality for each species of seed shall be determined by the Council acting in accordance with the procedure referred to in the first subparagraph.

2. In good time before the beginning of each marketing year, the Council, acting in accordance with the procedure referred to in paragraph 1, shall determine the main intervention centres and fix the derived intervention prices applicable in these centres.

Acting in accordance with the same procedure, the Council shall lay down criteria for determining other centres and fixing other derived intervention prices. These centres shall be determined and these prices shall be fixed in accordance with the procedure laid down in Article 38 after consultation with the Member States concerned.

Article 23

Target prices shall be fixed at a level which is fair to producers, account being taken of the need to keep Community production at the required level.

Article 24

The basic intervention price, which guarantees that producers will be able to sell their produce at a price which, allowing for market fluctuations, is as close as possible to the target price, shall be equal to the target price reduced by an amount large enough to allow for these fluctuations.

The derived intervention prices shall be fixed at a level which will allow seeds to move freely within the Community under natural conditions of price formation and in accordance with the needs of the market.

Article 25

To enable sales to be staggered, the target price and the intervention price shall be increased each month, for a period of at least five months beginning with the third month of the marketing year, by an amount which shall be the same for both prices.

The monthly increases, which shall be the same for each month, shall be fixed each year by the Council acting in accordance with the voting procedure laid down in Article 43(2) of the Treaty on a proposal from the Commission, account being taken of average storage costs and interest charges in the Community.

Article 26

1. In each Member State an intervention agency shall, under conditions to be laid down in accordance with the provisions of paragraphs 2 and 3, buy in seeds of Community origin offered to it at intervention centres. The intervention agency shall buy at the intervention price and at that price only.

If, however, the quality of the seeds offered to the intervention agency does not correspond to that for which the intervention price was fixed, the buying-in price shall be adjusted by means of a scale of price increases and reductions.

Furthermore, if at the request of the intervention agency the seeds are delivered to a place other than the centre indicated by the seller when the offer is made, the resulting change in transport costs to the seller shall be taken into account when payment is being effected.

2. The Council, acting in accordance with the voting procedure laid down in Article 43(2) of the Treaty on a proposal from the Commission, shall lay down:

(a) the conditions under which intervention shall take place during the last two months of the marketing year;

(b) the principles governing the disposal by intervention agencies of seeds bought in by them.

3. Detailed rules for the application of this Article, and in particular those concerning the quality and size of the consignments offered, shall be adopted in accordance with the procedure laid down in Article 38.

Article 27

1. Where the target price in force for a species of seed is higher than the world market price for that seed determined in accordance with the provisions of Article 29, a subsidy shall be granted for seed of that species harvested and processed within the Community. Subject to exceptions made pursuant to paragraph 3, this subsidy shall be equal to the difference between these prices.

2. Where entitlement to the subsidy provided for in paragraph 1 is acquired during the first two months of the marketing year, a further allowance for early marketing may be granted.

3. The Council, acting in accordance with the voting procedure laid down in Article 43(2) of the Treaty on a proposal from the Commission, shall lay down:

(a) theprinciples governing the grant of the subsidy provided in paragraph 1;

(b) the principles governing the fixing of the amount of the subsidy under abnormal conditions;

(c) rules for checking entitlement to the subsidy;
these may cover seeds of Community origin and seeds imported
from third countries; in the case of the latter provision may be
made for a system of import licences accompanied by a deposit;

(d) the conditions under which advance fixing of the amount of the
subsidy may be allowed;

(e) provisions for the application of paragraph 2.

4. The amount of the subsidy shall be fixed by the Commission.

5. Detailed rules for the application of this Article shall be adopted
in accordance with the procedure laid down in Article 38.

Article 28

1. A refund may be granted on exports to third countries of oil seeds
harvested within the Community; the amount of this refund may not
exceed the difference between prices within the Community and on the
world market where the former are higher than the latter.

2. Provisions for fixing and, where appropriate, for the advance fix-
ing of the refund referred to in paragraph 1 shall be adopted by the
Council acting in accordance with the voting procedure laid down in
Article 43(2) of the Treaty on a proposal from the Commission.

Article 29

The world market price, calculated for a Community frontier crossing
point, shall be determined on the basis of the most favourable purchasing opportunities, prices being adjusted where appropriate to
take the prices of competing products into account. The criteria for
such determination shall be laid down and the frontier crossing point
to be fixed for each species of seed shall be specified by the Council
acting in accordance with the voting procedure laid down in Article
43(2) of the Treaty on a proposal from the Commission.

Article 30

For a period of five years from the date on which it abolishes national measures having the effect of increasing prices for vegetable oils
other than olive oil, each Member State may grant subsidies for the
extraction of oil from the pips of grapes harvested within the Community.

Article 31

Until such time as a common agricultural policy for flax is put into
effect, Member States may grant subsidies on the production of linseed for oil extraction.

Article 32

The subsidies provided for in Articles 30 and 31 may be granted only in respect of products which have benefited from direct or indirect price support in the Member State concerned during the marketing year preceding the date on which this Regulation begins to apply.

The subsidies must be granted from the first marketing year in which this Regulation is applied and only to the extent necessary to maintain this price support.

Member States shall communicate to the Commission any information concerning the introduction, calculation and granting of these subsidies before they become operative.

TITLE IV

General provisions

Article 33

Save as otherwise provided in this Regulation, Articles 92, 93 and 94 of the Treaty shall apply to the production of and trade in the products listed in Article 1.

Article 34

Measures taken by Member States to increase the price for other vegetable oils in relation to that for olive oil so as to ensure an outlet for nationally produced olive oil shall be incompatible with the application of this Regulation to the products listed in Article 1(2) (c).

Article 35

Without prejudice to the harmonisation of legislation on olive oil for human consumption, Member States shall, for the purposes of intra-Community trade and trade with third countries, except in respect of exports to third countries, adopt the descriptions and definitions of olive oil set out in the Annex to this Regulation.

Article 36

The Council, acting in accordance with the voting procedure laid down in Article 43(2) of the Treaty on a proposal from the Commission, may alter the list of products set out in Article 1 or adopt in respect of them any measures derogating from this Regulation to take account of special conditions which may affect these products.

Article 37

1. A Management Committee for Oils and Fats (hereinafter called the

'Committee') shall be established, consisting of representatives of Member States and presided over by a representative of the Commission.

2. Within the Committee the votes of Member States shall be weighted in accordance with Article 148(2) of the Treaty. The chairman shall not vote.

Article 38

1. Where the procedure laid down in this Article is to be followed, the Chairman shall refer the matter to the Committee either on his own initiative or at the request of the representative of a Member State.

2. The representative of the Commission shall submit a draft of measures to be taken. The Committee shall deliver its Opinion on such measures within a time-limit to be set by the Chairman according to the urgency of the questions under consideration. An Opinion shall be adopted by a majority of 12 votes.

3. The Commission shall adopt measures which shall apply immediately. However, if these measures are not in accordance with the Opinion of the Committee, they shall forthwith be communicated by the Commission to the Council. In that event the Commission may defer application of the measures which it has adopted for not more than one month from the date of such communication.

The Council, acting in accordance with the voting procedure laid down in Article 43(2) of the Treaty, may take a different decision within one month.

Article 39

The Committee may consider any other question referred to it by its Chairman either on his own initiative or at the request of the representative of a Member State.

Article 40

At the end of the transitional period, the Council, acting in accordance with the voting procedure laid down in Article 43(2) of the Treaty on a proposal from the Commission, shall decide in the light of experience whether to retain or amend the provisions of Article 38.

Article 41

1. Council Regulation No 25 on the financing of the common agricultural policy and the provisions adopted in implementation thereof shall apply to the market in the products listed in Article 1 from the date on which this Regulation begins to apply.

2. The compensatory amounts provided for in Article 3(6) shall be considered as levies in relation to third countries within the meaning

of Article 11(4) of Council Regulation No 130/66/EEC on the financing of the common agricultural policy.

Article 42

This Regulation shall be so applied that appropriate account is taken, at the same time, of the objectives set out in Article 39 and 110 of the Treaty.

Article 43

This Regulation shall enter into force on the day following its publication in the *Official Journal of the European Communities*.

It shall apply to the products listed in Article 1(2) (c), (d) and (e) from 1 November 1966 and to the other products listed in Article 1 from 1 July 1967.

Should transitional measures be necessary to facilitate the transition from the system in force in the Member States to that established by this Regulation, in particular if the introduction of this system on the dates provided for would give rise to substantial difficulties in respect of certain products, such measures shall be adopted in accordance with the procedure laid down in Article 38.

Their validity shall be limited to the first year of application of this Regulation to each product.

This Regulation shall be binding in its entirety and directly applicable in all Member States.

Done at Brussels, 22 September 1966.

For the Council
The President
B.W. BIESHEUVEL

ANNEX

Descriptions and definitions referred to in Article 35

1. Virgin olive oil (the expression 'pure virgin olive oil' may also be used): olive oil produced by mechanical processes and free from any admixtures of other types of oil or of olive oil extracted in a different manner.

Virgin olive oil is classified as follows:

(a) Extra: olive oil of absolutely perfect flavour, with a free fatty acid content expressed as oleic acid of not more than 1g per 100g;

(b) Fine: olive oil with the same characteristics as Extra, but with a free fatty acid content expressed as oleic acid of not more than 1.5 g per 100 g;

(c) Ordinary: (the expression 'semi-fine' may also be used): olive oil of good flavour with a free fatty acid content expressed as oleic acid of not more than 3.3 g per 100 g;

(d) Lampante: (lamp oil): off-flavour olive oil or olive oil with a free fatty acid content expressed as oleic acid of more than 3.3 g per 100 g.

2. Refined olive oil (the expression 'pure refined olive oil' may also be used): olive oil obtained by refining virgin olive oil.

3. Pure olive oil: oil consisting of a blend of virgin olive oil and refined olive oil.

4. Olive-residue oil: oil obtained by treating with solvents the products falling within heading No ex 23.04 listed in Article 1(2) (e).

5. Refined olive-residue oil: oil obtained by refining the oil specified in 4, intended for human consumption.

6. Refined olive-residue oil and olive oil: oil consisting of a blend of refined olive-residue oil and virgin olive oil.

7. Olive-residue oil for technical use: any oil extracted from the products falling within heading No ex 23.04 listed in Article 1(2) (e) other than those specified in 1 to 6.

Note: It has been agreed that when the European Communities are enlarged an institutional adaptation will be made to the text of Article 37(2) of this Regulation, substituting the words 'Article ( ) of the Treaty of Accession' for the words 'Article 148(2) of the Treaty', and to the text of Article 38(2) substituting the word 'forty-three' for 'twelve'.

Note: This instrument is subject to institutional adaptations to Articles 37(2) and 38(2) to provide for an appropriate weighting of votes and size of majority required in the Committee on the enlargement of the Community.

32. REGULATION (EEC) No 234/68 OF THE COUNCIL

of 27 February 1968

on the establishment of a common organisation of the market in live
trees and other plants, bulbs, roots, and the like, cut flowers and
ornamental foliage

(J.O. No L 55, 2 February 1968, p. 1; O.J. (Special Edition 1968)p26)

THE COUNCIL OF THE EUROPEAN COMMUNITIES,

Having regard to the Treaty establishing the European Economic Community, and in particular Articles 42 and 43 thereof;

Having regard to the proposal from the Commission;

Having regard to the Opinion of the European Parliament;

Whereas the operation and development of the common market in agricultural products must be accompanied by the establishment of a common
agricultural policy to include in particular a common organisation of
agricultural markets which may take various forms depending on the
product;

Whereas the production of live trees and other plants, bulbs, roots
and the like, cut flowers and ornamental foliage (hereinafter where
appropriate called 'live plants') is of particular importance to the
agricultural economy of certain regions of the Community; whereas
for growers in these regions the proceeds of such production represent
a major part of their income; whereas therefore efforts should be made,
through appropriate measures, to promote the rational marketing of
such production and to ensure stable market conditions;

Whereas one of the measures to be taken with a view to the establishment of the common organisation of the market is the application of
common quality standards to the products in question; whereas the
application of these standards should have the effect of eliminating
from the market products of unsatisfactory quality and of promoting
commercial relations on the basis of genuine competition, thus contributing to an improvement in the profitability of production;

Whereas the application of these standards makes some form of inspection of quality necessary for the products which are subject to standardisation; whereas therefore provision should be made to ensure such
inspection;

Whereas exports of flowering bulbs to third countries are of considerable economic importance to the Community; whereas the continuation
and development of such exports may be ensured by stabilising prices
in this trade; whereas provision should therefore be made for mini-

mum export prices for the products in question;

Whereas the common organisation of the market in live plants justifies the application of the Common Customs Tariff; whereas, moreover, the regulations on imports from third countries should be coordinated and unified without delay;

Whereas, so as not to leave the Community market without defence against exceptional disturbances which may arise by reason of imports and exports, the Community should be enabled to take all necessary measures without delay;

Whereas the common organisation of the market involves the removal at the internal frontiers of the Community of all obstacles to the free movement of the goods in question;

Whereas the provisions of the Treaty which allow the assessment of aids granted by Member States and the prohibition of those which are incompatible with the common market should be made to apply to live plants;

Whereas, in order to facilitate implementation of the proposed measures, a procedure should be provided for establishing close co-operation between Member States and the Commission within a Management Committee;

Whereas the common organisation of the market in live plants must take appropriate account, at the same time, of the objectives set out in Articles 39 and 110 of the Treaty;

HAS ADOPTED THIS REGULATION:

Article 1

A common organisation of the market in live trees and other plants, bulbs, roots and the like, cut flowers and ornamental foliage shall be established in respect of the products falling within Chapter 6 of the Common Customs Tariff; it shall comprise common quality standards and a trading system.

Article 2

In order to encourage action by trade and joint trade organisations, the following Community measures may be taken in respect of the products referred to in Article 1:

- measures to improve quality and stimulate demand;

- measures to promote better organisation of production and marketing;

- measures to facilitate the recording of market price trends.

General rules concerning measures shall be adopted in accordance with the procedure laid down in Article 43(2) of the Treaty.

Article 3

Standards of quality,sizing and packaging, and the scope of these standards, may be determined for the products referred to in Article 1, or for groups of such products; the standards may relate in particular to quality grading, to wrapping, to presentation and to marking.

When standards have been adopted, the products to which they apply may not be displayed for sale, offered for sale, sold, delivered or otherwise marketed except in accordance with the said standards.

Standards and the general rules for their application shall be adopted by the Council, acting in accordance with the voting procedure laid down in Article 43(2) of the Treaty on a proposal from the Commission.

Article 4

Adjustments to quality standards to take account of the requirements of production and marketing techniques shall be decided in accordance with the procedure laid down in Article 14.

Article 5

1. Member States shall subject to quality inspection products for which quality standards have been determined. They shall notify other Member States and the Commission, not later than one month after the entry into force of each quality standard, of the name and address of the bodies entrusted with the inspection of each product or group of products for which the standard is laid down.

2. Detailed rules for the application of paragraph 1 shall be adopted as necessary in accordance with the procedure laid down in Article 14, account being taken in particular of the need to ensure coordination of the work of the inspection bodies and uniformity of interpretation and application of quality standards.

Article 6

When standards have been determined, all offers made to the public by way of advertisements, catalogues or price lists must include, if the price is quoted, mention of the nature of the product and of its size and grading.

Article 7

1. For each of the products falling within heading No 06.01 A of the Common Customs Tariff, one or more minimum prices for exports to third countries may be fixed each year in good time before the marketing season, beginning in 1968, in accordance with the procedure laid down in Article 14.

Exportation of such products shall be permitted only at a price equal to or above the minimum price fixed for the product in question.

2. Detailed rules for the application of paragraph 1 shall be adopted in accordance with the procedure laid down in Article 14.

Article 8

1. The Common Customs Tariff shall be applied from 1 July 1968 to the products referred to in Article 1; from that date no other customs duties shall be levied.

2. The necessary provisions for the co-ordination and unification of the import systems applied by each of the Member States with regard to third countries shall be adopted before 1 July 1968 by the Council, acting in accordance with the voting procedure laid down in Article 43(2) of the Treaty on a proposal from the Commission. These measures shall be put into effect at the latest on 1 January 1969.

Article 9

1. If by reason of imports or exports the Community market in one or more of the products referred to in Article 1 experiences or is threatened with serious disturbances which may endanger the objectives set out in Article 39 of the Treaty, appropriate measures may be applied in trade with third countries until such disturbance or threat of disturbance has ceased.

The Council, acting in accordance with the voting procedure laid down in Article 43(2) of the Treaty on a proposal from the Commission, shall adopt detailed rules for the application of this paragraph and define the cases in which and the limits within which the Member States may take protective measures.

2. If the situation mentioned in paragraph 1 arises, the Commission shall, at the request of a Member State or on its own initiative, decide upon the necessary measures; the measures shall be communicated to the Member States and shall be immediately applicable. If the Commission receives a request from a Member State, it shall take a decision thereon within twenty-four hours following receipt of the request.

3. The measures decided upon by the Commission may be referred to the Council by any Member State within three working days following the day on which they were communicated. The Council shall meet without delay. It may amend or repeal the measures in question in accordance with the voting procedure laid down in Article 43(2) of the Treaty.

Article 10

1. The following shall be prohibited in the internal trade of the Community:

- the levying of any customs duty or charge having equivalent effect;

- any quantitative restriction or measure having equivalent effect;

- recourse to Article 44 of the Treaty.

2. By way of derogation from the provisions of the second and third indents of paragraph 1, the maintenance of quantitative restrictions or measures having equivalent effect and recourse to Article 44 of the Treaty shall continue to be authorised:

- for unrooted cuttings and slips of vines (Common Custons Tariff heading No 06.02 A I) and vine slips, grafted or rooted (Common Customs Tariff heading No 06.02 B) until the date fixed for the application in all Member States of the provisions to be adopted by the Council on the marketing of materials for the vegetative propagation of the vine;

- for potted plants and sapling fruit trees and bushes (Common Customs Tariff heading No 06.02 C II) until 31 December 1968.

As regards potted plants and sapling fruit trees and bushes (Common Customs Tariff heading No 06.02 C II) the Council shall adopt such measures as may be required in pursuance of Articles 3, 12 or 18 of this Regulation.

Article 11

Save as otherwise provided in this Regulation, Articles 92 to 94 of the Treaty shall apply to the production of and trade in the products referred to in Article 1.

Article 12

The Council, acting in accordance with the procedure laid down in Article 43(2) of the Treaty, shall add to this Regulation such further provisions as may be required in the light of experience.

Article 13

1. A Management Committee for Live Plants (hereinafter called the 'Committee') shall be established, consisting of representatives of Member States and presided over by a representative of the Commission.

2. Within the Committee the votes of the Member States shall be weighted in accordance with Article 148(2) of the Treaty. The Chairman shall not vote.

Article 14

1. Where the procedure laid down in this Article is to be followed, the Chairman shall refer the matter to the Committee either on his own initiative or at the request of the representative of a Member State.

2. The representative of the Commission shall submit a draft of the measures to be taken. The Committee shall deliver its Opinion on such measures within a time-limit to be set by the Chairman according to the urgency of the questions under consideration. An Opinion shall be

adopted by a majority twelve votes.

3. The Commission shall adopt measures which shall apply immediately. However, if these measures are not in accordance with the Opinion of the Committee they shall forthwith be communicated by the Commission to the Council. In that event the Commission may defer application of the measures which it has adopted for not more than one month from the date of such communication.

The Council, acting in accordance with the voting procedure laid down in Article 43(2) of the Treaty, may take a different decision within one month.

Article 15

The Committee may consider any other question referred to it by its Chairman either on his own initiative or at the request of the representative of a Member State.

Article 16

At the end of the transitional period the Council, acting in accordance with the voting procedure laid down in Article 43(2) of the Treaty on a proposal from the Commission, shall decide in the light of experience whether to retain or amend the provisions of Article 14.

Article 17

This Regulation shall be so applied that appropriate account is taken, at the same time, of the objectives set out in Articles 39 and 110 of the Treaty.

Article 18

This Regulation shall be applied without prejudice to the provisions adopted or to be adopted with a view to approximating the provisions which have been laid down by law, regulation or administrative action in Member States and which are designed to maintain or improve the technical or genetic level of production of certain products covered by Article 1 and intended specifically for reproduction.

Article 19

This Regulation shall enter into force on the third day following its publication in the *Official Journal of the European Communities*.

It shall apply from 1 July 1968.

This Regulation shall be binding in its entirety and directly applicable in all Member States.

410

Done at Brussels, 27 February 1968.

For the Council
The President
E. FAURE

33. REGULATION (EEC) No 2727/75 OF THE COUNCIL

of 29 October 1975

on the common organisation of the market in cereals

THE COUNCIL OF THE EUROPEAN COMMUNITIES,

Having regard to the Treaty establishing the European Economic Community, and in particular Articles 42 and 43 thereof;

Having regard to the proposal from the Commission;

Having regard to the Opinion of the European Parliament ;

Whereas since their adoption the basic provisions concerning the organisation of the market in cereals have been amended a number of times; whereas, by reason of their number, their complexity and their dispersal among various Official Journals, these texts are difficult to use and thus lack the clarity which should be an essential feature of all legislation; whereas they should, therefore, be consolidated in a single text;

Whereas the operation and development of the common market in agricultural products must be accompanied by the establishment of a common agricultural policy to include in particular a common organisation of agricultural markets which may take various forms depending on the product;

Whereas the common organisation of the market in cereals must include a single price system for cereals in the Community; whereas such a system entails fixing annually for the principal products a target price valid for the whole Community, a single intervention price or a basic intervention price from which are obtained various derived intervention prices at which the relevant agencies must buy in the cereals offered to them and a threshold price to which the price of imported products must be equated by means of a variable import levy;

Whereas the aim of the common agricultural policy is to attain the objectives set out in Article 39 of the Treaty; whereas in the cereals sector, in order to stabilise markets and to ensure a fair standard

411

of living for the agricultural community concerned, intervention agencies should be able to take intervention measures on the market;

Whereas free movement of cereals within the Community should enable shortages in deficit areas to be covered by surpluses in production areas; whereas, so as not to impede this in the case of common wheat, intervention prices derived from the basic price should be fixed in such a way that the differences between them reflect the disparities which, given a normal harvest, arise under natural conditions of price formation on the market, and that the forces of supply and demandmay have free play; whereas, as regards the other basic products, shortages in deficit areas could be covered by surpluses in production areas if a single intervention price is fixed corresponding to the lowest intervention prices which would have been fixed in the Community had the system provided for in respect of common wheat been applied to those products;

Whereas, the intervention agencies must be able, in special circumstances, to take intervention measures suited to those circumstances; whereas, however, so that the required uniformity of intervention systems may be maintained, those special circumstances should be assessed and the appropriate measures determined at Community level;

Whereas, the target prices, intervention prices and threshold prices should, in the course of the marketing year, be subject to a certain number of monthly increases in order to take account, among other things, of storage costs and interest charges for storing cereals in the Community and of the need to ensure that the disposal of stocks conforms to market requirements;

Whereas it may prove impossible to give producers of durum wheat sufficient guarantees by fixing a price which takes into account the ratio existing normally on the world market between durum and common wheat prices; whereas this ratio should be respected so far as possible in the Community because of the interchangeability of these two products; whereas provision must therefore be made for the possibility of granting aid to producers of durum wheat;

Whereas in view of the special market situation for cereal starch, potato starch and glucose produced by the 'direct hydrolysis' process it may prove necessary to provide for a production refund of such a nature that the basic products used by this industry can be made available to it at a lower price than that resulting from the application of the system of levies and common prices;

Whereas the creation of a single Community market for cereals involves, apart from a single price system, the introduction of a single trading system at the external frontiers of the Community; whereas a trading system including levies and export refunds, combined with intervention measures, also serves to stabilise the Community market, in particular by preventing price fluctuations on the world market from affecting prices ruling within the Community; whereas, therefore, provision should be made for charging a levy on imports from third countries and for the payment of a refund on exports to these countries, both being designed to cover the difference between prices ruling outside and within the Community; whereas, moreover, in respect of products processed from cereals to which this Regulation applies, account

should be taken of the need to ensure a measure of protection for
the Community processing industry;

Whereas, in addition to the system described above, and to the extent
necessary for its proper working, provision should be made for regu-
lating or, when the situation on the market so requires, prohibiting
totally or partially the use of 'inward processing arrangements';
whereas, moreover, the refund should be fixed in such a way that operations under inward processing arrangements do not lead the Community
processing industry to use, with a view to export, basic products
imported from third countries in preference to Community basic products;

Whereas the competent authorities must be in a position constantly to
follow trade movements in order to assess market trends and to apply
the measures laid down in this Regulation as necessary; whereas, to
that end, provision should be made for the issue of import and export
licences accompanied by the provision of security guaranteeing that
the transactions for which such licences are requested are effected;

Whereas the levy system makes it possible to dispense with all other
protective measures at the external frontiers of the Community; whereas, however, the common price and levy machinery may in exceptional
circumstances prove defective; whereas, in such cases, so as not to
leave the Community market without defence against disturbances, the
Community should be enabled to take all necessary measures without
delay;

Whereas, in a situation of high prices on the world market, provision
should be made for appropriate measures to be taken in order to safeguard Community supplies and to stabilise prices on Community markets;

Whereas the establishment of a single market based on a common price
system would be jeopardised by the granting of certain aids; whereas,
therefore, the provisions of the Treaty which allow the assessment
of aids granted by Member States and the prohibition of those which
are incompatible with the common market should be made to apply to
cereals;

Whereas Italy should be authorised for some years to take measures
to reduce the impact of the new system on the level of prices for feed
grain in that Member State in order to facilitate the adjustment of
the Italian market to that new system;

Whereas the common organisation of the market in cereals must include
the products of primary processing which contain cereals or certain
products which do not contain cereals but which are directly inter-
changeable in their use with cereals or with products obtained from
cereals;

Whereas the Community is required under international obligations
concerning cereals, to furnish certain information about the trends
on its market; whereas, therefore, provision should be made for Member States to furnish the Commission with the necessary particulars;

Whereas, in order to facilitate implementation of the proposed measures, a procedure should be provided for establishing close coopera-

413

tion between Member States and the Commission within a Management
Committee;

Whereas the European Economic Community is a party to the International Wheat Agreement; whereas provisions for mobilising food aid
should be adopted; whereas it should be provided that, save in exceptional circumstances, products intended as food aid should be obtained
on the Community market; whereas such products are to be purchased
on that market, taken from cereal stocks held by intervention agencies
or manufactured from such cereals;

Whereas the common orgaisation of the market in cereals must take
appropriate account, at the same time, of the objectives set out in
Articles 39 and 110 of the Treaty;

Whereas the expenditure incurred by the Member States as a result of
the obligations arising out of the application of this Regulation fall
on the Community in accordance with the provisions of Articles 2 and
3 of Council Regulation (EEC) No 729/70 of 21 April 1970 on the financing of the common agricultural policy, as amended by Regulation
(EEC) No 1566/72,

HAS ADOPTED THIS REGULATION:

Article 1

The common organisation of the market in cereals shall comprise a
price and trading system and cover the following products:

CCT heading No	Description of goods
a) 10.01 A	Common wheat and meslin
10.02	Rye
10.03	Barley
10.04	Oats
10.05 B	Maize, other than hybrid maize for sowing
10.07	Buckwheat, millet, canary seed and grain sorghum; other cereals
b) 10.01 B	Durum wheat
c) 11.01 A	Wheat or meslin flour
11.01 B	Rye flour
ex 11.02 A	Wheat groats and meal (common wheat and durum wheat)

d) the products listed in Annex A to this Regulation

TITLE I

Prices

· · · · ·

Article 2

The marketing year for all the products listed in Article 1 shall
begin on 1 August and end on 31 July of the following year.

Article 3

1. Before 1 August of each year the following prices shall be fixed
for the Community for the marketing year beginning the following year:

- a common single intervention price for common wheat, barley and
  maize, and a single intervention price for rye and durum wheat,

- a reference price for common wheat of breadmaking quality,

- a target price for common wheat, durum wheat and rye and a common
  target price for barley and maize.

2. These prices shall be fixed for a standard quality to be determined
for each of the above cereals.

3. The single intervention prices shall be fixed for the Ormes intervention centre, which is the centre of the Community area having the
greatest surplus for all cereals, at the wholesale stage, goods delivered at warehouse, before unloading. They shall be valid for all
Community intervention centres designated for each cereal.

The single intervention prices shall be valid from 1 August to 31 May
of the following year. From 1 June to 31 July, the intervention prices
valid for August of the marketing year in progress shall apply.

4. The reference price for common wheat of breadmaking quality shall
be calculated by adding to the common single intervention price for
this product an amount reflecting the difference in return between the
production of common wheat of breadmaking quality and that of common
wheat of non-breadmaking quality.

5. The target prices shall be fixed for Duisburg, which is the centre
of the Community area having the greatest deficit for all cereals, at
the wholesale stage, goods delivered at warehouse, before unloading.

They shall be calculated by adding a market element and an element
reflecting the cost of transport between the Ormes area and the Duisburg area:

- to the reference price, for common wheat,

- to the respective single intervention price for rye and durum wheat,

- to the common single intervention price, for barley and maize.

For rye, durum wheat and common wheat respectively, the market element
shall reflect the difference which should exist between:

(a) the single intervention price for rye, the single intervention
price for durum wheat and the reference price for common wheat of

415

breadmaking quality on the one hand, and

(b) the level of the market prices for rye, durum wheat and common
wheat of breadmaking quality respectively to be expected, in a
normal harvest and under natural conditions of price formation
on the Community market, in the area having the greatest surplus,
on the other.

The market element for barley and maize shall reflect the difference
which should exist between the market price for barley and the common
single intervention price, plus the difference in market prices reflecting the ratio between the average relative values of the two cereals
concerned for use in animal feed. The market prices to be taken into
consideration are those to be expected, in a normal harvest and under
natural conditions of price formation on the Community market, in the
production area having the greatest surplus.

The element reflecting the cost of transport shall be determined on
the basis of the most favourable means of transport or combination
of means of transport and on existing tariffs.

6. The prices referred to in paragraph 1 and the standard qualities
referred to in paragraph 2 shall be determined in accordance with the
procedure laid down in Article 43(2) of the Treaty.

7. The Council, acting by a qualified majority on a proposal from
the Commission, shall lay down the rules for determining the intervention centres to which the single intervention prices apply.

8. The intervention centres referred to in paragraph 7 shall be determined, after consultation with the Member States concerned, before 1
May each year for the following marketing year, in accordance with
the procedure laid down in Article 26.

Article 4

1. To facilitate the transition from the arrangements applied during
the 1975/76 marketing year to those laid down in Article 3 and in
particular the price structure normally established thereby, the
single intervention prices for common wheat, barley and maize may,
by way of derogation from paragraph 1 of that Article, be fixed at
different levels for the 1976/77 marketing year. In that case, the
common single intervention price used to establish the common target
price for barley and maize shall be the single intervention price
for barley.

2. When, in application of the derogation referred to in paragraph 1,
the single intervention price for common wheat is fixed with respect
to its breadmaking quality, the price shall, by way of derogation
from Article 3(2), be fixed in respect of a standard breadmaking
quality.

Such standard quality shall be that defined pursuant to Article 3(6),
with the addition of certain criteria concerning the minimum requirements for breadmaking. Common wheat which does not meet these requirements shall only receive at intervention a price corresponding to

the common single intervention price which for the marketing year in
question shall be that applicable to barley.

In the case covered by this paragraph the reference price referred to
in Article 3(1) shall not be fixed and the target price for common
wheat shall be established according to Article 3(5), by substituting
the single intervention price for that cereal for its reference price.

3. The Council, acting by a qualified majority on a proposal from the
Commission, shall lay down the minimum requirements for breadmaking.

The method to be followed for determining whether common wheat meets
such requirements and the detailed rules for the application of this
Article shall be adopted in accordance with the procedure laid down
in Article 26.

Article 5

1. In respect of common wheat, durum wheat, barley, maize and rye a
threshold price shall be fixed for the Community in such a way that
the selling price for the imported product on the Duisburg market
shall be the same as the target price, differences in quality being
taken into account.

The threshold price shall be fixed for the same standard quality as
the target price.

2. For a standard quality for each of the products listed in Article
1(a) which are not mentioned in paragraph 1 above, a threshold price
shall be fixed for the Community in such a way that the price for those
cereals mentioned in paragraph 1 which are in competition with these
products shall reach the target price on the Duisburg market.

3. For a standard quality for each of the products listed in Article
1(c) a threshold price shall be fixed for the Community, account being
taken of the objective stated in paragraph 2 and of the need to protect the processing industry.

4. The threshold prices shall be calculated for Rotterdam.

5. The Council, acting by a qualified majority on a proposal from the
Commisison, shall determine:

(a) the rules for fixing threshold prices for products referred to in
    paragraph 3 and the standard quality for products referred to in
    paragraphs 2 and 3;

(b) before 15 March of each year, for the following marketing year,
    the threshold prices for products referred to in paragraphs 1 and
    2.

6. Threshold prices for products referred to in paragraph 3 shall be
fixed before 15 March of each year for the following marketing year
in accordance with the procedure laid down in Article 26.

Article 6

1. The intervention prices, the reference price for common wheat of breadmaking quality, the target prices and the threshold prices shall be the subject of monthly increases phased over all or part of the marketing year.

2. The Council, acting by a qualified majority on a proposal from the Commission, shall determine before 15 March of each year, for the following marketing year, the number and amount of the monthly increases and in what month they are to apply.

Article 7

1. Throughout the marketing year, the intervention agencies designated by the Member States shall be obliged to buy in cereals mentioned in Article 3 which have been harvested in the Community and offered to them, provided that the offers comply with conditions, in particular in respect of quality and quantity, to be determined in accordance with paragraph 5.

2. The intervention agencies shall buy in at the single intervention price regardless of the centre at which the cereal is offered, under conditions determined in accordance with paragraphs 4 and 5. If the quality of the cereal is different from the standard quality for which the intervention price has been fixed, the intervention price shall be adjusted in accordance with scales of price increases and reductions. These scales may also include a special price increase for breadmaking rye with certain quality characteristics.

3. Under conditions laid down in accordance with paragraphs 4 and 5, the intervention agencies shall offer for sale:

- for export to third countries,

- or for supply to the internal market,

the product bought in under paragraph 1.

4. The Council, acting by a qualified majority on a proposal from the Commission, shall adopt general rules governing intervention.

5. Detailed rules for the application of this Article shall be adopted in accordance with the procedure laid down in Article 26, in particular as regards:

- the minimum quality and quantity required of each cereal and, in respect of durum wheat, the technical qualities required of it,

- the scales of price increases and reductions applicable for the purposes of intervention,

- the proceduresand conditions for taking over by the intervention agencies,

- the procedures and conditions for disposal of produce by the intervention agencies.

Article 8

1. To avoid substantial purchases having to be made in certain regions
of the Community under Article 7(1), it may be decided that the intervention agencies take particular intervention measures.

2. Where necessitated by the situation on the Community market in
common wheat of breadmaking quality, special intervention measures may
be adopted in respect of this cereal with a view to supporting the
development of the market therein in relation to the reference price
referred to in Article 3(1).

3. The Council, acting by a qualified majority on a proposal from the
Commission, shall adopt general rules for the application of this
Article.

4. The nature and application of particular or special intervention
measures and the conditions and procedures for the sale or for any
other means of disposal of the products subject to these measures
shall be determined in accordance with the procedure laid down in
Article 26.

Detailed rules for the application of this Article shall, where appropriate, be adopted in accordance with the same procedure.

Article 9

1. A carry-over payment may be granted in respect of stocks remaining
at the end of the marketing year of common wheat, durum wheat, rye,
barley and maize harvested in the Community, and of malt.

However, for Member States in which the new harvest is usually available before the beginning of the new marketing year, it may be decided in accordance with the procedure referred to in paragraph 6, that
the stock qualifying for the payment at the end of the marketing year
may not be greater than that declared at an earlier date, to be determined in each year.

Before 15 March of each year the Council, acting by a qualified majority on a proposal from the Commisison, shall decide whether a carry-
over payment should be granted in respect of one or more of the abovementioned products, and, if so, to what extent.

2. Any carry-over payment for maize shall be granted only in respect
of quantities in stock in areas of surplus production.

3. The carry-over payment for each cereal shall not exceed the difference between the target price valid for the last month of the
marketing year and that valid for the first month of the next marketing year.

4. The carry-over payment shall be granted only in respect of stocks
which reach a minimum quantity.

419

5. The amount of the carry-over payment shall be fixed in accordance with the procedure referred to in the third subparagraph of paragraph 1.

6. Detailed rules for the application of this Article, in particular the minimum quantity mentioned in paragraph 4 and the categories of those entitled to it, shall be adopted in accordance with the procedure laid down in Article 26.

Article 10

1. Aid shall be granted for the production of durum wheat in the Community.

2. The amount of such aid shall be fixed per hectare of land sown and harvested and shall be equal throughout the marketing year. However, aid may be differentiated according to the region concerned and confined to certain production regions.

Aid shall be granted for durum wheat only for qualitative and technical characteristics to be determined.

3. The amount of aid shall be fixed before 1 August for the marketing year beginning the following year in accordance with the procedure laid down in Article 43(2) of the Treaty.

The production regions referred to in paragraph 2 shall be determined in accordance with the same procedure.

4. The Council, acting by a qualified majority on a proposal from the Commission, shall lay down the general rules for the application of this Article and in particular the criteria for determining the qualitative and technical characteristics referred to in paragraph 2.

5. The following shall be adopted in accordance with the procedure laid down in Article 26:

- the detailed rules for the application of this Article,

- the qualitative and technical characteristics required of durum wheat in order to be eligible for aid and, where appropriate, a list of the varieties concerned.

Article 11

1. A production refund may be granted:

(a) for maize and common wheat used in the Community for the manufacture of starch;

(b) for potato starch;

(c) for maize groats and meal used in the Community for the manufacture of glucose by direct hydrolysis;

2. The payment of the production refund for potato starch shall be subject to the condition that the processor has paid a minimum free-at-factory price for the potatoes.

The minimum price to be received by the producer shall consist of the minimum price to be paid by the starch manufacturer plus an amount corresponding to the production refund.

3. The Council, acting by a qualified majority on a proposal from the Commission, shall adopt rules for the application of this Article and fix the amount of the production refund.

TITLE II

Trade with third countries

Article 12

1. Imports into the Community or exports therefrom of any of the products listed in Article 1 shall be subject to the submission of an import or export licence which may be issued by Member States to any applicant irrespective of the place of his establishment in the Community. Where the levy or refund is fixed in advance, the advance fixing shall be noted on the licence which serves as supporting document for such advance fixing.

However, the issue of import licences for wheat and wheat flour shall be suspended in respect of imports from countries which are not parties to the Wheat Trade Convention when compliance with the obligations entered into within the framework of that convention so requires.

The import or export licence shall be valid throughout the Community.

The issue of such licences shall be conditional on the lodging of a deposit guaranteeing that importation or exportation will be effected during the period of validity of the licence; the deposit shall be forfeited in whole or in part if the transaction is not effected, within that period.

2. The period of validity of licences and other detailed rules for the application of this Article shall be adopted in accordance with the procedure laid down in Article 26.

Article 13

1. A levy equal for each product to the threshold price less the cif price shall be charged on imports of the products listed in Article 1(a), (b) and (c).

2. The cif prices shall be calculated for Rotterdam on the basis of the most favourable purchasing opportunities on the world market, determined for each product on the basis of the quotations and prices of that market after adjustment for any differences in quality as compared with the standard quality for which the threshold price is fixed.

Differences in quality shall be expressed in coefficients of equivalence.

3. Where free quotations on the world market are not a determining factor for the offer price and where this price is lower than world market prices, a special cif price calculated on the basis of the offer price shall be substituted for the cif price solely for the imports in question.

4. Detailed rules for the application of this Article, and in particular the coefficients of equivalence, the rules for determining cif prices and the margin within which variations in the factors used for calculating the levy do not require any alteration of the levy, shall be adopted in accordance with the procedure laid down in Article 26.

5. The Commission shall fix the levies mentioned in this Article.

Article 14

1. A levy shall be charged on the importation of products referred to in Article 1(d), consisting of two components:

A. A variable component which may be fixed and revised on a flat-rate basis:

(a) corresponding, in respect of products processed from basic products listed in Article 1(a), to the incidence on their prime cost of the levies on those basic products;

(b) increased, where appropriate, for processed products which contain both basic products listed in Article 1(a) and other products, by the amount of the incidence on their prime cost of the levies or customs duties charged on those other products;

(c) fixed, for products which do not contain any basic products listed in Article 1(a), with reference to market conditions for those Article 1 products which are in competition with them;

B. A fixed component designed to protect the processing industry.

2. Where actual offers from third countries of products referred to in Article 1(d), do not correspond to the price which results from the price of basic products used in their manufacture plus processing costs, an amount fixed in accordance with the procedure laid down in Article 26 may be added to the levy fixed in accordance with paragraph 1.

3. The Council, acting by a qualified majority on a proposal from the Commission, shall adopt rules for the application of this Article.

4. The Commission shall fix the levies specified in paragraph 1.

Article 15

1. The levy to be charged shall be that applicable on the day of importation.

2. However, as regards imports of products listed in Article 1(a) and (b), the levy applicable on the day on which application for a licence is lodged, adjusted on the basis of the threshold price which will be in force during the month of importation, shall be applied to an import to be effected during the period of validity of the licence, if the applicant so requests when applying for the licence. In this case, a premium, fixed at the same time as the levy, shall be added to the levy.

3. A decision may be taken in accordance with the procedure laid down in Article 26 to apply the provisions of paragraph 2, in whole or in part, to any of the products listed in Article 1(c) and (d).

If the carry-over payment envisaged by Article 9 is not granted for malt and if an advanced fixing of the levy has been prescribed for this product, the levy shall be adjusted during the first two months of the marketing year on the basis of the threshold price in force during the last month of the preceeding marketing year.

4. The Council, acting by a qualified majority on a proposal from the Commisison, shall adopt rules for fixing the scale of premiums and adopt measures to be taken in exceptional circumstances.

5. Detailed rules for advanced fixing shall be adopted in accordance with the procedure laid down in Article 26.

6. The scale of premiums shall be fixed by the Commission.

7. Where examination of the market situation shows that the application of the provisions concerning the advance fixing of the levy has given rise or may give rise to difficulties, a decision may be taken, in accordance with the procedure laid down in Article 26, to suspend the application of those provisions for the period strictly necessary.

In cases of extreme urgency, the Commission may, after examination of the situation on the basis of all the information available to it, decide to suspend advance fixing for a maximum of three working days.

Applications for licences accompanied by applications for advance fixing lodged during the period of suspension shall be rejected.

Article 17

To the extent necessary for the proper working of the common organisation of the market in cereals, the Council, acting by a qualified majority on a proposal from the Commission, may prohibit in whole or in part the use of inward processing arrangements:

- in respect of products listed in Article 1 which are intended for the manufacture of products listed in Article 1(c) and (d),

- and, in special cases, in respect of products listed in Article 1
  which are intended for the manufacture of goods listed in Annex B.

Article 18

1. Without prejudice to the provisions of Regulation (EEC) No 2729/75,
the general rules for the interpretation of the Common Customs Tariff
and the special rules for its application shall apply to the tariff
classification of products covered by this Regulation; the tariff nomenclature resulting from application of this Regulation shall be incorporated in the Common Customs Tariff.

2. Save as otherwise provided in this Regulation or where derogation
therefrom is decided by the Council, acting by a qualified majority
on a proposal from the Commission, the following shall be prohibited:

- the levying of any customs duty or charge having equivalent effect,

- the application of any quantitative restriction or measure having
  equivalent effect.

The restriction of import or export licences to a specified category
of those entitled to receive them shall be considered to constitute a
measure having effect equivalent to a quantitative restriction.

Article 19

1. When the quotations or prices on the world market for one or more
of the products mentioned in Article 2 reach the level of Community
prices, and when that situation is likely to continue and to deterio-
rate, thereby disturbing or threatening to disturb the Community market, appropriate measures may be taken.

2. The Council, acting by a qualified majority on a proposal from the
Commission, shall adopt general rules for the application of this Article.

3. The detailed rules for the application of this Article shall be
adopted in accordance with the procedure laid down in Article 26.

Article 20

1. If by reason of imports or exports the Community market in one or
more of the products listed in Article 1 experiences or is threatened
with serious disturbances which may endanger the objectives set out in
Article 39 of the Treaty, appropriate measures may be applied in trade
with third countries until such disturbance or threat of disturbance
has ceased.

The Council, acting by a qualified majority on a proposal from the Commission, shall adopt rules for the application of this paragraph and
define the cases in which and limits within which Member States may
take protective measures.

2. If the situation mentioned in paragraph 1 arises, the Commission shall, at the request of a Member State or on its own initiative, decide upon the necessary measures; the measures shall be communicated to the Member States and shall be immediately applicable. If the Commission receives a request from a Member State, it shall take a decision thereon within 24 hours following receipt of the request.

3. Measures decided upon by the Commission may be referred to the Council by any Member State within three working days following the day on which they were communicated. The Council shall meet without delay. It may, acting by a qualified majority, amend or repeal the measures in question.

TITLE III

General Provisions

Article 21

Goods listed in Article 1 which are manufactured or obtained from products to which Article 9(2) and 10(1) of the Treaty do not apply shall not be admitted to free circulation within the Community.

Article 22

Save as otherwise provided in this Regulation, Articles 92 to 94 of the Treaty shall apply to the production of and trade in the products listed in Article 1.

Article 23

1. When barley, oats, maize, grain sorghum or millet are imported by sea into the Italian Republic, that Member States may reduce the levy.

The amount of reduction in the levy shall be fixed by the Council, acting by a qualified majority on a proposal from the Commission, at the same time as the prices for each marketing year.

This reduction may be made only if an equal subsidy is granted for deliveries of the same cereals by sea from Member States unless this subsidy has, at the request of the sender of the cereals, been paid to him by the Member State of origin which shall inform the Italian Republic forthwith. The Italian Republic shall keep all Member States informed at all times of the amount of subsidy in force.

2. If Italy makes use of the power conferred by paragraph 1, the Council, acting by a qualified majority on a proposal from the Commission, shall take the measures necessary to prevent discrimination between Community producers and distortions of competition intrade between denatured common wheat, on the one hand, and the cereals referred to in paragraph 1, in particular barley, on the other.

3. Detailed rules for the application of this Article shall be adopted in accordance with the procedure laid down in Article 26.

425

Article 24

Member States and the Commission shall communicate to each other the information necessary for implementing this Regulation and for complying with the international obligations concerning cereals. Rules for the communication and distribution of such information shall be adopted in accordance with the procedure laid down in Article 26.

Article 25

1. A Management Committee for Cereals (hereinafter called the 'Committee') shall be established consisting of representatives of the Member States and presided over by a representative of the Commission.

2. Within the Committee the votes of Member States shall be weighted in accordance with Article 148(2) of the Treaty. The Chairman shall not vote.

Article 26

1. Where the procedure laid down in this Article is to be followed, the Chairman shall refer the matter to the Committee, either on his own initiative or at the request of the representative of a Member State.

2. The representative of the Commission shall submit a draft of the measures to be adopted. The Committee shall deliver its Opinion on the draft within a time limit set by the Chairman according to the urgency of the matter. An Opinion shall be delivered by a majority of 41 votes.

3. The Commission shall adopt measures which shall apply immediately. However, if these measures are not in accordance with the Opinion of the Committee, they shall forthwith be communicated by the Commission to the Council. In that event the Commission may defer application of the measures which it has adopted for not more than one month from the date of such communication.

The Council, acting by a qualified majority, may take a different decision within one month.

Article 27

The Committee may consider any other question referred to it by its Chairman either on his own initiative or at the request of the representative of a Member State.

Article 28

1. Obligations arising under the food-aid conventions shall be met by the purchase on the Community market of the products specified in Article 1 or by the use of cereals held by intervention agencies.

2. The criteria for mobilising the products, in particular those governing purchase on the Community market or the use of cereals held by
intervention agencies, shall be adopted by the Council, acting by a
qualified majority on a proposal from the Commission.

3. In exceptional circumstances products specified in Article 1 may
be mobilised by purchases on the world market. Detailed rules for the
application of this paragraph shall be adopted in accordance with the
procedure laid down in Article 26.

Article 29

This Regulation shall be so applied that appropriate account is taken,
at the same time, of the objectives set out in Articles 39 and 110 of
the Treaty.

Article 30

1. Council Regulation No 120/67/EEC of 13 June 1967 on the common organisation of the market in cereals, as last amended by Council Regulation (EEC) No 665/75, is hereby repealed.

2. References to the Regulation repealed by paragraph 1 shall be construed as references to this Regulation.

A table is provided in Annex C for the purposes of correlating cita-
tions of and references to the Articles of that Regulation with those
of this Regulation.

Article 31

This Regulation shall enter into force on 1 November 1975.

This Regulation shall be binding in its entirety and directly applicable in all Member States.

Done at Luxembourg, 29 October 1975.

For the Council

The President

G. MARCORA

Chapter Six

EXTERNAL RELATIONS

1. ARRANGEMENT REGARDING INTERNATIONAL
TRADE IN TEXTILES

(O.J. No L118, 30 April 1974)

COUNCIL DECISION

of 21 March 1974

concluding the Arrangement regarding International
Trade in Textiles

(74/214/EEC)

THE COUNCIL OF THE EUROPEAN COMMUNITIES,

Having regard to the Treaty establishing the European Economic Community and in particular Article 113 thereof;

Having regard to the recommendation from the Commission;

Whereas the Commission has participated, on behalf of the Community,
in the negotiations within the framework of a Negotiating Group on
Textiles established by the GATT Council which have led to the drawing
up of the Arrangement regarding International Trade in Textiles;

Whereas it is desirable that the Community conclude the Arrangement,

HAS DECIDED AS FOLLOWS:

Article 1

The Arrangement regarding International Trade in Textiles, the text
of which is annexed hereto, is concluded on behalf of the European
Economic Community.

Article 2

The President of the Council shall be authorised to designate the
person empowered to accept the Arrangement in accordance with Article
13 thereof and to confer upon him the powers he requires to bind the
Community.

Done at Brussels, 21 March 1974.

For the Council
The President
J. ERTL

2. INTERNATIONAL CONVENTION ON THE
SIMPLIFICATION AND HARMONISATION OF
CUSTOMS PROCEDURES

(O.J. No L100, 21 April 1975)

COUNCIL DECISION

of 18 March 1975

concluding an international convention on the simplification and
harmonisation of customs procedures and accepting the Annex
thereto concerning customs warehouses

(75/199/EEC)

THE COUNCIL OF THE EUROPEAN COMMUNITIES,

Having regard to the Treaty establishing the European Economic Community;

Having regard to the recommendation from the Commission;

Whereas the international convention on the simplification and harmonisation of customs procedures negotiated within the Customs Cooperation Council can effectively contribute to the development of international trade;

Whereas, in accordance with Article 11 of that convention, each Contracting Party must, when concluding the convention, also accept one
of the Annexes thereto; whereas the Community should therefore accept
the Annex concerning customs warehouses;

Whereas that convention should therefore be concluded and that Annex
thereto accepted,

HAS DECIDED AS FOLLOWS:

Article 1

The international convention on the simplification and harmonisation
of customs procedures and the Annex thereto concerning customs warehouses are hereby respectively concluded and accepted on behalf of the
Community.

The texts of the convention and of the Annex are contained in the
Annex to this Decision.

Article 2

The President of the Council is hereby authorised to designate the persons empowered to sign the convention referred to in Article 1 and to accept the Annex also referred to in Article 1 and to confer on them the powers required to bind the Community.

These persons shall also inform the Secretary-General of the Customs Cooperation Council that, for the application of the aforesaid Annex, the customs territories of the Member States of the European Economic Community are to be considered as a single territory.

Done at Brussels, 18 March 1975.

For the Council
The President
R. RYAN

3. AGREEMENT
ON THE ESTABLISHMENT OF A
EUROPEAN INFORMATICS NETWORK

(Brussels, 21 November 1971, not published in the O.J.)

The Governments of the French Republic,

the Italian Republic,

the Socialist Federal Republic of Yugoslavia,

the Kingdom of Norway,

the Republic of Portugal,

the Swiss Confederation,

Sweden,

the United Kingdom of Great Britain and Northern Ireland and

the European Atomic Energy Community (Euratom),

hereinafter referred to as the 'Signatories',

Have accepted participation in the project described below, hereinafter referred to as 'the project', and have agreed as follows:

Article 1

The Signatories shall coordinate their efforts in the project which

is being undertaken in order to establish an informatics network
linking certain European data-processing centres, in order to facilitate research into methods of exchanging information and to share
data processing facilities among such centres. An outline description
of the work envisaged for the project is contained in the Annex.

. . . . .

4. COUNCIL DECISION

of 19 July 1982

on the conclusion of the Agreement between the European
Economic Community and the Government of the Republic
of Senegal amending the Agreement on fishing off the
coast of Senegal, signed on 15 June 1979, and of the
Protocol referring thereto

(82/531/EEC)

(O.J. No L234, 9 August 1982, p. 8)

THE COUNCIL OF THE EUROPEAN COMMUMITIES,

Having regard to the Treaty establishing the European Economic Community, and in particular Article 43 thereof,

Having regard to the proposal from the Commission,

Having regard to the opinion of the European Parliament,

Whereas the Community and Senegal have conducted negotiations in
accordance with the second subparagraph of Article 17 of the Agreement between the Government of the Republic of Senegal and the European Economic Community on fishing off the coast of Senegal, in order
to determine the amendments or additions to be made to the Annexes
or to the Protocol referred to in Article 9 thereof;

Whereas, following these negotiations, an agreement amending the abovementioned fisheries agreement and a protocol were signed on 21 January
1982;

Whereas it is in the Community's interest to approve the Agreement;

Whereas the conclusion of the Agreement renders nugatory Council
Decision 81/1055/EEC of 21 December 1981 on the conclusion of an Agreement in the form of an exchange of letters providing for provisional
application of the Agreement between the Government of the Republic
of Senegal and the European Economic Community amending the Agreement
on fishing off the coast of Senegal, and of the Protocol thereto,

HAS DECIDED AS FOLLOWS:

Article 1

The Agreement between the European Economic Community and the Government of the Republic of Senegal amending the Agreement on fishing off the coast of Senegal, signed on 15 June 1979, the Protocol, referring thereto, are hereby approved on behalf of the Community.

The texts referred to in the first subparagraph are attached to this Decision.

Article 2

The President of the Council shall give the notification provided for in Article 2 of the Agreement.

Article 3

Decision 81/1055/EEC is hereby repealed with effect from the date of entry into force of the Agreement.

Done at Brussels, 19 July 1982.

For the Council
The President
B. WESTH

5. COUNCIL DECISION

of 12 July 1982

concluding the Agreement on the International Carriage of Passengers by Road by means of Occasional Coach and Bus Services (ASOR)

(82/505/EEC)

(O.J. No L230, 5 August 1982, p. 38)

THE COUNCIL OF THE EUROPEAN COMMUNITIES,

Having regard to the Treaty establishing the European Economic Community, and in particular Article 75 thereof,

Having regard to the proposal from the Commission,

Having regard to the opinion of the European Parliament,

Having regard to the opinion of the Economic and Social Committee,

Whereas the Agreement on the International Carriage of Passengers by

Road by means of Occasional Coach and Bus Services (ASOR) was negotiated between the Commission on behalf of the European Economic Community and Austria, Spain, Finland, Norway, Portugal, Sweden, Switzerland and Turkey in accordance with the negotiating directives adopted by the Council;

Whereas the ASOR will help to facilitate the operation of occasional services and will promote tourism in Western Europe,

HAS DECIDED AS FOLLOWS:

Article 1

The Agreement on the International Carriage of Passengers by Road by means of Occasional Coach and Bus Services (ASOR) together with the declarations annexed to the Final Act are hereby approved on behalf of the European Economic Community.

The texts referred to in the first paragraph are attached to this Decision.

Article 2

The President of the Council shall deposit the acts provided for in Article 18 of the Agreement.

Done at Brussels, 12 July 1982.

For the Council
The President
J. NORGAARD

AGREEMENT

on the International Carriage of Passengers by Road by means of Occasional Coach and Bus Services (ASOR)

THE COUNCIL OF THE EUROPEAN COMMUNITIES,

THE FEDERAL PRESIDENT OF THE REPUBLIC OF AUSTRIA,

THE GOVERNMENT OF SPAIN,

THE PRESIDENT OF THE REPUBLIC OF FINLAND,

THE GOVERNMENT OF THE KINGDOM OF NORWAY,

THE GOVERNMENT OF THE PORTUGUESE REPUBLIC,

THE GOVERNMENT OF SWEDEN,

THE SWISS FEDERAL COUNCIL,

THE PRESIDENT OF THE REPUBLIC OF TURKEY,

DESIRING to promote the development of international transport and especially to facilitate the organisation and operation thereof;

WHEREAS some international carriage of passengers by road by means of occasional coach and bus services are liberalised as far as the European Economic Community is concerned by Council Regulation No 117/66/EEC of 28 July 1966 on the introduction of common rules for the international carriage of passengers by coach and bus and by Regulation (EEC) No 1016/68 of the Commission of 9 July 1968 prescribing the model control documents referred to in Articles 6 and 9 of Council Regulation No 117/66/EEC;

WHEREAS, in addition, the European Conference of Ministers of Transport (ECMT) adopted on 16 December 1969 resolution No 20 concerning the formulation of general rules for international coach and bus transport which also concerns the liberalisation of some international carriage of passengers by road by means of occasional coach and bus services;

WHEREAS it is desirable to provide for harmonised liberalisation measures for occasional international services for passengers by road and to simplify inspection procedures by introducing a single document;

WHEREAS it is desirable to assign some administrative tasks concerned with the Agreement to the Secretariat of the European Conference of Ministers of Transport;

HAVE DECIDED to establish uniform rules for the international carriage of passengers by road by means of occasional coach and bus services,

AND TO THIS END have designated as their Plenipotentiaries:

THE COUNCIL OF THE EUROPEAN COMMUNITIES:

M. Herman DE CROO,

Ministre des Communications du Royaume de Belgique,

Président en exercice du Conseil des Communautés européennes;

M.G. CONTOGEORGIS

Membre de la Commission des Communautés européennes;

. . . . .

6. COUNCIL REGULATION (EEC) No 954/79

of 15 May 1979

concerning the ratification by Member States of, or their accession
to, the United Nations Convention on a Code of Conduct for
Liner Conferences

(O.J. No L121, 17 May 1979, p. 1)

THE COUNCIL OF THE EUROPEAN COMMUNITIES,

Having regard to the Treaty establishing the European Economic Community, and in particular Article 84(2) thereof,

Having regard to the draft Regulation submitted by the Commission,

Having regard to the opinion of the European Parliament,

Having regard to the opinion of the Economic and Social Committee,

Whereas a Convention on a Code of Conduct for Liner Conferences has
been drawn up by a Conference convened under the auspices of the
United Nations Conference on Trade and Development and is open for
ratification or accession;

Whereas the questions covered by the Code of Conduct are of importance
not only to the Member States but also to the Community, in particular
from the shipping and trading viewpoints, and it is therefore important that a common position should be adopted in relation to this
Code;

Whereas this common position should respect the principles and objectives of the Treaty and make a major contribution to meeting the
aspirations of developing countries in the field of shipping while at
the same time pursuing the objective of the continuing application in
this field of the commercial principles applied by shipping lines of
the OECD countries and in trades between these countries;

Whereas to secure observance of these principles and objectives, since
the Code of Conduct contains no provision allowing the accession of
the Community as such, it is important that Member States ratify or
accede to the Code of Conduct subject to certain arrangements provided for in this Regulation;

Whereas the stabilising role of conferences in ensuring reliable services to shippers is recognised, but it is nevertheless necessary to
avoid possible breaches by conferences of the rules of competition
laid down in the Treaty; whereas the Commission will accordingly
forward to the Council a proposal for a Regulation concerning the
application of those rules to sea transport,

435

HAS ADOPTED THIS REGULATION:

Article 1

1. When ratifying the United Nations Convention on a Code of Conduct for Liner Conferences, or when acceding thereto, Member States shall inform the Secretary-General of the United Nations in writing that such ratification or accession has taken place in accordance with this Regulation.

2. The instrument of ratification or accession shall be accompanied by the reservations set out in Annex 1.

Article 2

1. In the case of an existing conference, each group of shipping lines of the same nationality which are members thereof shall determine by commercial negotiations with another shipping line of that nationality whether the latter may participate as a national shipping line in the said conference.

If a new conference is created, the shipping lines of the same nationality shall determine by commercial negotiations which of them may participate as a national shipping line in the future conference.

2. Where the negotiations referred to in paragraph 1 fail to result in agreement, each Member State may, at the request of one of the lines concerned and after hearing all of them, take the necessary steps to settle the dispute.

3. Each Member State shall ensure that all vessel-operating shipping lines established on its territory under the Treaty establishing the European Economic Community are treated in the same way as lines which have their management head office on its territory and the effective control of which is exercised there.

Article 3

1. Where a liner conference operates a pool or a berthing, sailing and/or any other form of cargo allocation agreement in accordance with Article 2 of the Code of Conduct, the volume of cargo to which the group of national shipping lines of each Member State participating in that trade or the shipping lines of the Member States participating in that trade as third-country shipping lines are entitled under the code shall be redistributed, unless a decision is taken to the contrary by all the lines which are members of the Conference and parties to the present redistribution rules. This redistribution of cargo shares shall be carried out on the basis of a unanimous decision by those shipping lines which are members of the conference and participate in the redistribution, with a view to all these lines carrying a fair share of the conference trade.

2. The share finally allocated to each participant shall be determined

436

by the application of commercial principles, taking account in particular of:

(a) the volume of cargo carried by the conference and generated by the Member States whose trade is served by it;

(b) past performance of the shipping lines in the trade covered by the pool;

(c) the volume of cargo carried by the conference and shipped through the ports of the Member States;

(d) the needs of the shippers whose cargoes are carried by the conference.

3. If no agreement is reached on the redistribution of cargoes referred to in paragraph 1, the matter shall, at the request of one of the parties, be referred to conciliation in accordance with the procedure set out in Annex II. Any dispute not settled by the conciliation procedure may, with the agreement of the parties, be referred to arbitration. In that event, the award of the arbitrator shall be binding.

4. At intervals to be laid down in advance, shares allocated in accordance with paragraphs 1, 2 and 3 shall be regularly reviewed, taking into account the criteria set out in paragraph 2 and in particular from the viewpoint of providing adequate and efficient service to shippers.

Article 4

1. In a conference trade between a Member State of the Community and a State which is a party to the Code of Conduct and not an OECD country, a shipping line of another Member State of the OECD wishing to participate in the redistribution provided for in Article 3 of this Regulation may do so subject to reciprocity defined at governmental or ship-owners' level.

2. Without prejudice to paragraph 3 of this Article, Article 2 of the Code of Conduct shall not be applied in conference trades between Member States or, on a reciprocal basis, between such States and the other OECD countries which are parties to the Code.

3. Paragraph 2 of this Article shall not affect the opportunities for participation as third-country shipping lines in such trades, in accordance with the principles reflected in Article 2 of the Code of Conduct, of the shipping lines of a developing country which are recognised as national shipping lines under the Code and which are:

(a) already members of a conference serving these trades; or

(b) admitted to such a conference under Article 1(3) of the Code.

4. Articles 3 and 14(9) of the Code of Conduct shall not be applied in conference trades between Member States or, on a reciprocal basis, between such States and other OECD countries which are parties to the code.

5. In conference trades between Member States and between these States and other OECD countries which are parties to the Code of Conduct, the shippers and ship-owners of Member States shall not insist on applying the procedures for settling disputes provided for in Chapter VI of the Code in their mutual relationships or, on a reciprocal basis, in relation to shippers and ship-owners of other OECD countries where other procedures for settling disputes have been agreed between them. They shall in particular take full advantage of the possibilities provided by Article 25(1) and (2) of the Code for resolving disputes by means of procedures other than those laid down in Chapter VI of the Code.

Article 5

For the adoption of decisions relating to matters defined in the conference agreement concerning the trade of a Member State, other than those referred to in Article 3 of this Regulation, the national shipping lines of such State shall consult all other Community lines which are members of the conference before giving or withholding their assent.

Article 6

Member States shall, in due course and after consulting the Commission, adopt the laws, regulations or administrative provisions necessary for the implementation of this Regulation.

This Regulation shall be binding in its entirety and directly applicable in all Member States.

Done at Brussels, 15 May 1979.

> For the Council
> The President
> R. BOULIN

7. COUNCIL REGULATION (EEC) No 877/82

of 16 April 1982

suspending imports of all products originating in Argentina

(O.J. No L102, 16 April 1982, p. 1)

THE COUNCIL OF THE EUROPEAN COMMUNITIES,

Whereas the serious situation resulting from the invasion of the Falkland Islands by Argentina, which was the subject of Resolution 502 of the Security Council of the United Nations has given rise to discussions in the context of European political cooperation which have led in particular to the decision that economic measures will be taken with regard to Argentina in accordance with the relevant provisions of the Community Treaties;

Whereas, following the measures already taken by the United Kingdom, the Member States have consulted one another pursuant to Article 224 of the Treaty establishing the European Economic Community;

Whereas in the context of these consultations it has proved important to take urgent and uniform measures; whereas the Member States have therefore decided to adopt a Council Regulation pursuant to the Treaty;

Whereas, in these circumstances, the interests of the Community and the Member States demand the temporary suspension of imports of all products originating in Argentina;

Whereas import documents issued and contracts concluded before the entry into force of this Regulation should not be affected by it; whereas, however, transitional provisions should not be applied to imports into the United Kingdom which were the subject of United Kingdom measures with effect from 7 April;

Having regard to the Treaty establishing the European Economic Community, and in particular Article 113 thereof,

Having regard to the proposal from the Commission,

HAS ADOPTED THIS REGULATION:

Article 1

Imports of all products originating in Argentina for the purpose of putting them into free circulation in the Community are hereby suspended.

Article 2

1. This Regulation shall not preclude the putting into free circulation of products originating in Argentina:

- accompanied by import documents issued before the date of its entry into force which mention Argentina as the country of origin, or

- to be imported in execution of contracts concluded before that date, or

- in course of shipment to the Community at that date.

439

2. The provisions of paragraph 1 shall not apply to imports into the United Kingdom of products covered by this Regulation which were the subject of measures adopted by the United Kingdom with effect from 7 April.

Article 3

This Regulation shall enter into force on the day of its publication in the *Official Journal of the European Communities*.

It shall apply until 17 May 1982.

Before that date, the Council, acting on a proposal from the Commission, shall examine whether it is appropriate to extend, amend, or, if necessary, repeal this Regulation.

This Regulation shall be binding in its entirety and directly applicable in all Member States.

Done at Brussels, 16 April 1982.

For the Council
The President
L. TINDEMANS

----

8. DECISION

OF THE REPRESENTATIVES OF THE GOVERNMENTS OF THE MEMBER STATES OF THE EUROPEAN COAL AND STEEL COMMUNITY, MEETING WITHIN THE COUNCIL

of 16 April 1982

suspending imports of all products originating in Argentina

(82/221/ECSC)

(O.J. No L102, 16 April 1982, p. 3)

THE REPRESENTATIVES OF THE GOVERNMENTS OF THE MEMBER STATES OF THE EUROPEAN COAL AND STEEL COMMUNITY, MEETING WITHIN THE COUNCIL, in agreement with the Commission,

HAVE DECIDED AS FOLLOWS:

Article 1

Imports of all products covered by the ECSC Treaty and originating in Argentina for the purpose of putting them into free circulation in a Member State of the Community are hereby suspended.

Article 2

1. This Decision shall not preclude the putting into free circulation of products originating in Argentina:

- accompanied by import documents issued before the date of its entry into force which mention Argentina as the country of origin, or

- to be imported in execution of contracts concluded before that date, or

- in course of shipment to the Community at that date.

2. Paragraph 1 shall not apply to imports into the United Kingdom of products covered by this Decision which were the subject of measures adopted by the United Kingdom with effect from 7 April.

Article 3

This Decision shall enter into force on the day of its publication in the *Official Journal of the European Communities*.

It shall apply until 17 May 1982.

Before that date, the desirability of extending, amending, or, if necessary, repealing this Decision shall be examined.

Done at Brussels, 16 April 1982.

The President
L. TINDEMANS

9. COUNCIL DECISION

of 12 August 1982

authorising extension or tacit renewal of certain trade agreements
concluded between the Member States and third countries

(82/591/EEC)

(O.J. No L244, 19 August 1982, p. 24)

THE COUNCIL OF THE EUROPEAN COMMUNITIES,

Having regard to the Treaty establishing the European Economic Community, and in particular Article 113 thereof,

Having regard to Council Decision 69/494/EEC of 16 December 1969 on the progressive standardisation of agreements concerning commercial relations between Member States and third countries and on the negotiation of Community agreements, and in particular Article 3 thereof,

Having regard to the proposal from the Commission,

Whereas extension or tacit renewal beyond the end of the transitional period was last authorised in the case of the Agreements and Protocols listed in the Annex by Council Decision 81/590/EEC;

Whereas the Member States concerned have with a view to avoiding disruption of their commercial relations with the third countries concerned based on agreement, requested authorisation to extend or renew the abovementioned Agreements;

Whereas, however, most of the areas covered by these national agreements are henceforth the subject of Community agreements; whereas in this situation there should be authorisation for the maintenance of national agreements only for those areas not covered by Community agreements; whereas, in addition, such authorisation should not, therefore, adversely affect the obligation incumbent upon the Member States to avoid and, where appropriate, to eliminate any incompatibility between such agreements and the provisions of Community law;

Whereas the provisions of the instruments to be either extended or tacitly renewed should not, furthermore, during the period under consideration, constitute an obstacle to the implementation of the common commercial policy;

Whereas the Member States concerned have declared that the extension or tacit renewal of these agreements would neither constitute an

442

obstacle to the opening of Community negotiations with the third
countries concerned and the transfer of the commercial substance
thereof to Community agreements nor, during the period under consideration, hinder the adoption of the measures necessary to complete the
standardisation of the import arrangements applied by the Member
States;

Whereas at the conclusion of the consultations provided for in Article
2 of Decision 69/494/EEC it was established, as the aforesaid declarations by the Member States concerned confirm, that the provisions
of the agreements to be extended or tacitly renewed would not, during
the period under consideration, constitute an obstacle to the implementation of the common commercial policy;

Whereas, in these circumstances, the agreements concerned may be
either extended or tacitly renewed for a limited period,

HAS ADOPTED THIS DECISION:

Article 1

The Trade Agreements and Protocols between Member States and third
countries listed in the Annex hereto may be extended or tacitly renewed up to the dates indicated for each of them for those areas not
covered by agreements between the Community and the third countries
concerned and in so far as their provisions are not contrary to
existing common policies.

Article 2

This Decision is addressed to the Member States.

Done at Brussels, 12 August 1982.

For the Council
The President
O. MOLLER

Member State	Third Country	Type and date of Agreement		Extended until
BENELUX	Japon / Japan	Accord commercial/ Handelsakkoord	8.10.1960	
		Protocoles et agreed minutes / Protocollen en Agreed minutes	13. 4.1963	31.12.1982
		Echange de lettres/ Briefwisseling	30. 4.1963	
DANMARK	Argentina	Handels- og betalings- aftale	25.11.1957	31.12.1983
	Elfenbens- kysten	Handelsaftale	23.11.1966	9. 1.1984
	Irak	Handelsaftale	13. 1.1960	13. 1.1984
	Israel	Handelsaftale	14.11.1952	14.11.1983
	Ostrig	Vareudvekslings- aftale	29.11.1948	28.11.1983
	Portugal	Vareudvekslings- aftale	2. 6.1950	31.12.1983
DEUTSCHLAND	Arabische Republik Ägypten	Abkommen über den Warenverkehr	18. 2.1956	31.12.1983
	Argentinien	Handels- und Zahl- ungsabkommen	25.11.1957	31.12.1983
	Äthiopien	Wirtschafts- und Handelsabkommen	21. 4.1964	31.12.1983
	Brasilien	Handelsabkommen	1. 7.1955	31.12.1983
	Chile	Protokoll über Hand- els- und Zahlungs- verkehr	2.11.1956	31.12.1983
	Dahome	Wirtschaftsabkommen	19. 6.1961	31.12.1983
	Elfenbeinküste	Wirtschaftsabkommen	18.12.1961	31.12.1983
	Finnland	Notenwechsel	3.12.1969	2.12.1983
	Gabun	Wirtschaftsabkommen	11. 7.1962	31.12.1983
	Guinea	Wirtschaftsabkommen	19. 4.1962	31.12.1983
	Irak	Handelsabkommen	7.10.1951	31. 1.1984
	Japan	Handelsabkommen	1. 7.1960	31.12.1983
	Kamerun	Handelsabkommen	8. 3.1962	31.12.1983
	Kenia	Wirtschafts- und Handelsabkommen	4.12.1964	31.12.1983
	Kongo	Wirtschaftsabkommen	30.10.1962	31.12.1983
	Madagaskar	Wirtschaftsabkommen	6. 6.1962	31.12.1983
	Marokko	Handelsabkommen und Briefwechsel Protokoll	15. 4.1961 20. 1.1964	31.12.1983
	Neuseeland	Handelsabkommen	20. 4.1959	31.12.1983
	Niger	Wirtschaftsabkommen	14. 6.1961	31.12.1983
	Nigeria	Handelsabkommen	25. 3.1963	31.12.1983

DEUTSCHLAND (Fort-setzung)	Österreich	Handelsabkommen Briefwechsel und Protokoll	13. 5.1954 21. 1.1963	31.12.1983
	Obervolta	Wirtschaftsabkommen	8. 6.1961	31.12.1983
	Pakistan	Handelsabkommen und Protokoll	9. 3.1957	31.12.1983
	Paraguay	Handelsabkommen	25. 7.1955	31.12.1983
	Schweiz	21. Zusatzprotokoll zum (aufgehobenen) deutsch-schweizer- ischen Handelsabkom- men	13. 9.1977	31.12.1983
	Sambia	Wirtschaftsabkommen	10.12.1966	31.12.1983
	Sierra Leone	Wirtschaftsabkommen	13. 9.1963	31.12.1983
	Somalia	Handelsabkommen	19. 1.1962	31.12.1983
	Sri Lanka	Handelsabkommen	1. 4.1955	31.12.1983
	Südafrika	Liste der Einfuhr- kontingente		31. 8.1983
	Tansania	Handels- und Wirtschaftsabkommen	6. 9.1962	31.12.1983
	Tschad	Wirtschaftsabkommen	31. 5.1963	31.12.1983
	Tunesien	Handelsabkommen und Zusatzprotokoll	29. 1.1960 22.12.1963	31.12.1983
	Uganda	Handelsabkommen	17. 3.1964	31.12.1983
	Zentralafri- kanische Republik	Wirtschaftsabkommen	29.12.1962	31.12.1983
	Zypern	Handelsabkommen	30.10.1961	31.12.1983
HELLAS	Canada	Trade Agreement	28. 8.1947	25. 8.1983
	Soudan	Trade Agreement	10.10.1978	10.10.1983
	Zaïre	Trade Agreement	3.10.1968	3.10.1983
	Korea	Trade Agreement	4.10.1974	4.10.1983
	Cyprus	Trade Agreement	23. 8.1962	23. 8.1983
FRANCE	Argentine	Accord commercial et de paiement	25.11.1957	31.12.1983
	Autriche	Accord commercial et protocole	26. 7.1963	31.12.1983
	Espagne	Accord commercial	27.11.1963	31.10.1983
	Islande	Accord économique	6.12.1951	31.12.1983
	Israël	Accord commercial Protocole Echange de lettres	10. 7.1953 16. 1.1967 24.12.1968	31.12.1983
	Japon	Accord commercial et protocole Protocole	14. 5.1963 26. 7.1966	10. 1.1984
	Mexique	Accord commercial	11. 7.1950	28.11.1983
	Norvège	Accord commercial Protocole Echange de lettres	3. 7.1951 2. 4.1960 6. 2.1964	31.12.1983
	Portugal	Agreement commercial	25. 3.1961	31.12.1983
	Suède	Accord commercial	3. 3.1949	31.12.1983
	Suisse	Accord commercial	21.11.1967	31.12.1983
	Turquie	Accord commercial	31. 8.1946	31.12.1983

FRANCE	Yougoslavie	Accord commercial Protocole	25. 1.1964 6. 5.1970	31.12.1983
IRELAND	Norway	Trade Agreement	2. 7.1951	31.12.1983
ITALIA	Argentina	Accordo commerciale e scambio di note	25.11.1957	31.12.1983
	Canada	Modus vivendi commerciale	28. 4.1948	31.12.1983
	Costa Rica	Modus vivendi commerciale e scambio di note	20. 2.1953 23. 6.1953	12.11.1983
	Giappone	Agreed minutes	31.12.1969	30. 9.1983
	Guatemala	Modus vivendi commerciale	6. 6.1936	31.12.1983
	Irak	Accordo commerciale	30. 9.1963	30.11.1983
	Malta	Accordo commerciale	28. 7.1967	31.12.1983
	Marocco	Accordo commerciale Protocollo	28. 1.1961 24. 2.1963	31.12.1983
	Messico	Accordo commerciale Protocollo Scambio di note	15. 9.1949 28.10.1963 20. 7.1963	31.12.1983
	Pakistan	Accordo commerciale	10. 1.1961	10. 1.1984
	Paraguay	Accordo commerciale	8. 7.1959	23. 1.1984
	Portogallo	Accordo commerciale e scambio di note Scambio di lettere	4. 3.1961 30.12.1961	31.12.1983
	Repubblica araba d'Egitto	Protocollo commerciale	29. 4.1959	31.12.1983
	Siria	Accordo commerciale	10.11.1955	31.12.1983
	Tunisia	Accordo commerciale e protocollo addizionale	23.11.1961 2. 8.1963	31.12.1983
NEDERLAND	Arabische Republiek Egypte	Handelsovereenkomst	21. 3.1953	31.12.1983
	Argentinië	Handels- en betalingsovereenkomst	25.11.1957	31.12.1983
	Turkije	Handelsakkoord	6. 9.1949	31.12.1983
UNITED KINGDOM	Spain	Trade and Payments Agreement and subsequent Exchanges of Notes	23. 6.1948	31.12.1983
UEBL/BLEU	Argentine/ Argentinië	Accord commercial et de paiement/ Handels- en Betalingsakkoord	25.11.1957	31.12.1983

UEBL/BLEU	Finlande/			
	Finland	Accord commercial/		
		Handelsakkoord	8.11.1955	30. 9.1983
	Pakistan	Accord commercial/		
		Handelsakkoord	15. 3.1952	31.12.1983

10. WRITTEN QUESTION No 1621/79

by Mr Cohen

to the Commission of the European Communities

(5 February 1980)

(O.J. No C 160, 30 June 1980, p. 15)

Subject: Application of Article 115 of the EEC Treaty (commercial
policy)

1. Article 115 of the EEC Treaty, according to its accepted interpretation, is considered as a transitional article. If a common commercial policy were established, after the transitional period on the
basis of Article 113, Article 115 would become null and void. Does
not the Commission agree that, for this reason, Article 115 should
be applied as restrictively as possible after the transitional period
has ended? If so, what is the reason for the excessive recourse to
Article 115?

2. Does the Commission consider it right that, if the Community concludes an agreement with a third country on the basis of Article 113,
the Member States may still invoke Article 115?

3. Among the reasons given in the Official Journal for the invocation
of Article 115 was the fact: 'that it is not possible, in the short
term, to apply methods which should enable the other Member States to
achieve the requisite cooperation'. What method does the Commission
think should be used, and is the Commission prepared to present early
proposals on this question to enable the requisite cooperation to be
achieved as soon as possible?

4. Does the Commission share the fear that the common market could
be reduced to a free trade area by the repeated application of Article
115?

Answer given by Mr Jenkins on behalf of the Commission

(2 June 1980)

1. The Commission is committed to the principle of free internal
Community trade and is bound by Community law to respect it. Consequently it applies Article 115 of the Treaty in the most restrictive
manner. As the Honourable Member will be aware, the provisions of
Article 115 are designed to cover acute economic and social difficulties which may occur in Member States and may be invoked beyond the
transition period in respect of products for which fully unified

Community import arrangements have not yet been made.

The increase in requests for protective measures under Article 115 is principally confined to textiles, due firstly to the state of the textile sector, and secondly to the continuing disparities in the terms on which textiles are imported into the Community, in the absence of fully unified import arrangements.

2. When the Community concludes an agreement with a third country this generally has the effect of unifying the commercial policy arrangements applying to that country, and accordingly Article 115 no longer applies.

3. The Commission is investigating ways of achieving statistical and administrative cooperation, whilst thereby also avoiding any increase in import facilities in Member States for products manufactured elsewhere.

4. No.

11. COMMISSION DECISION

of 27 June 1980

authorising Member States to apply intra-Community surveillance to imports of products originating in a third country which have been put into free circulation in the Community and which may be the subject of protective measures under Article 115 of the Treaty

(80/605/EEC)

(O.J. No L164, 30 June 1980, p. 20)

THE COMMISSION OF THE EOROPEAN COMMUNITIES,

Having regard to the Treaty establishing the European Economic Community, and in particular Article 115, first paragraph, thereof,

Having regard to Commission Decision 80/47/EEC of 20 December 1979 on surveillance and protective measures which Member States may be authorised to take in respect of imports of certain products originating in third countries and put into free circulation in another Member State, and in particular Articles 1 and 2 thereof,

Whereas the abovementioned Decision requires Member States to have prior authorisation from the Commission before introducing intra-Community surveillance of the imports concerned;

Whereas the Member States have made 3 066 such applications for authorisation to the Commission, including *inter alia* details of the product in question, the country of origin, the rules governing direct imports from the country of origin and other third countries, the volume and quantity of the imports and the economic difficulties of which there is alleged to be a danger;

Whereas the information given in support of these applications has been subjected to close examination by the Commission;

Whereas the Commission, in view of the differences in the commercial policy measures applied by the Member States, examined first whether the products named in the Member States' applications could legally be made subject to surveillance measures under Article 2 of Decision 80/47/EEC;

Whereas the information received was then examined as regards the economic difficulties alleged, that is in relation to the development of such factors as national production, imports, consumption, the market share held by national production, by imports from third countries and the third country concerned in the application, prices charged by national producers and by importers on the domestic markets, and employment in the sector concerned;

Whereas the Commission also examined, for the reference years set out in Decision 80/47/EEC, whether there had been deflection of trade, or whether intra-Community licence applications had been submitted; whereas the Commission took the view that, in the absence of such elements, there is little risk of a worsening or prolongation of economic difficulties arising out of the circumstances referred to in Article 115, and that consequently the surveillance measures requested in those cases should not be agreed to;

Whereas, however, such measures may be authorised for Group 1 textiles as defined by Council Regulation (EEC) No 3059/78, as last amended by Regulation (EEC) No 3063/79, even if there has been no trade deflection or intra-Community licence applications, in view of the inherent risk of economic difficulties in trade in these products, which are highly sensitive to imports;

Whereas, in cases where there is an important limitation at Community level for a specific product in relation to certain third countries, the risk that economic difficulties will become worse or be prolonged may generally be considered as negligible as regards all those third countries from which the total possible imports to the Community taken together are less than 1 % of the quantitative limit at Community level;

Whereas this examination has shown that there is a risk that the imports set out in the Annexes hereto could worsen or prolong the existing economic difficulties in the different Member States; whereas, therefore, the Member States should be authorised to make them subject to intra-Community surveillance until the end of 1981;

Whereas for those imports not listed in the Annexes, Member States remain entitled to keep account of the imports made and later put forward applications for surveillance;

Whereas, to enable Member States to implement this Decision, the time limit laid down in Article 5(3) of Decision 80/47/EEC should be extended as regards the surveillance of imports not listed in the Annexes,

HAS ADOPTED THIS DECISION:

Article 1

The Member States named in Annexes 1 to 8 are authorised, in so far as each is concerned, to introduce until 31 December 1981 and in accordance with Decision 80/47/EEC, intra-Community surveillance of the products listed in the said Annexes.

Article 2

The time limit laid down in Article 5(3) of Decision 80/47/EEC is hereby extended to 31 July 1980 as regards the surveillance of imports not listed in the Annexes.

Article 3

This Decision is addressed to the Member States.

Done at Brussels, 27 June 1980.

For the Commission
Wilhelm HAFERKAMP
Vice-President

12. COMMISSION DECISION

of 20 December 1979

on surveillance and protective measures which Member States may be authorised to take in respect of imports of certain products originating in third countries and put into free circulation in another Member State

(80/47/EEC)

(O.J. No L16, 22 January 1980, p. 14)

THE COMMISSION OF THE EUROPEAN COMMUNITIES,

Having regard to the Treaty establishing the European Economic Community, and in particular Article 115 thereof,

Whereas Article 30 *et seq.* of the Treaty, concerning the elimination of quantitative restrictions and all measures having equivalent effect, apply without distinction to products originating in the Community and those that have been put into free circulation in any of the Member States irrespective of their origin;

Whereas under these arrangements the requirement, be it purely formal, in intra-Community trade of an import licence or any similar procedure is prohibited;

Whereas, in addition, Article 9(2) of the Treaty precludes any administrative procedure designed to establish different rules for the movement of goods according to whether they originate in the Community or originated in third countries and have been put into free circulation in one of the Member States;

Whereas, however, the full application of these principles presupposes the effective establishment of a common commercial policy; whereas such a policy has been introduced through the establishment of common rules, whether unilaterally or under an Agreement, covering imports into the Community of products not subject to quantitative restrictions and providing for the implementation by the Community of the surveillance and protective measures necessary to safeguard the Community's interests; whereas such measures may be limited to imports into certain regions of the Community;

Whereas the establishment of a common commercial policy is not yet complete as regards the measures relating to liberalisation or quantitative restriction of imports of products from third countries; whereas the measures applied in respect of some of these products by the Member States have not yet been replaced by common rules; whereas the Member States are still empowered to apply these measures, in accordance with the Community procedures and decisions on the progressive coordination and standardisation of the Member States' import arrangements *vis-à-vis* third countries;

Whereas in addition the establishment of common rules for imports of certain textile products originating in third countries has had to be carried out progressively, with the result that the allocation of Community quantitative limits or quotas among the Member States can be adjusted only gradually to the supply requirements in those States;

Whereas the fact that the common commercial policy has not yet been fully established means that there will still be disparities among the Member States' commercial policies which are likely to cause deflections of trade, which Article 115 of the Treaty is designed to prevent where such deflections lead to economic difficulties in one or more of the Member States;

Whereas to this end the Commission is empowered to authorise the Member States, where such economic difficulties so warrant, to take intra-Community surveillance measures or protective measures, by way of derogation from the principle of free movement within the Community of goods originating in third countries and put into free circulation in one of the Member States;

Whereas, in cases where a surveillance measure is authorised, import documents must be issued automatically, free of charge, within a given period and for any quantity requested; whereas, in view of past experience and the need to cause the least possible disturbance to the functioning of the common market, the application of surveillance measures should be restricted to cases where there is a danger that imports may lead in the Member States to economic difficulties within the meaning of Article 115 of the Treaty;

Whereas the information and grounds supplied by the Member States in support of their requests for authorisation to introduce the measures in question must be such as to enable the Commission to assess the need for such authorisation;

Whereas, should a Member State request authorisation to apply protective measures, the time limit for the issue of import documents must be extended if the volume covered by the applications for documents pending reaches a certain level;

Whereas, in order to ensure that checks on origin do not hamper intra-Community trade, it should be provided that the Member States, as a general rule, should request from the importer, as part of the completion of formalities connected with the importation of a product from another Member State, only a simple statement of the origin of the product as he can be reasonably expected to know it,

HAS ADOPTED THIS DECISION:

Article 1

Scope

This Decision shall apply to imports into a Member State of products originating in a third country which have been put into free circulation in the Community, in cases where they are either subject to quantitative import restrictions in that Member State or to voluntary export restraint measures applied by the third country concerned by virtue of a trade agreement and are likely to be the subject of protective measures under Article 115 of the Treaty.

Article 2

Intra-Community surveillance

1. Where there is a danger that imports into a Member State of a product referred to in Article 1 will give rise to economic difficulties, imports of that product may, following an authorisation given by the Commission for a specific period, be made subject to the issue of an import document.

2. Without prejudice to the provisions of Article 3, this document shall be issued by the Member State concerned, for any quantity requested and free of charge, within a maximum period of five working days from the date of the application by the importer irrespective of where he has his place of business in the Community.

3. For the purpose of obtaining the prior authorisation referred to in paragraph 1, the Member State shall supply the following particulars in its request to the Commission:

(a) a description of the product and details of its trade designation, its heading number in the Common Customs Tariff, the NIMEXE code and its country of origin;

(b) the rules governing direct imports *vis-à-vis* the country of origin and other third countries, including the volume and/or quantity of import opportunities, together with the economic considerations on which such are based;

(c) the volume or quantity of imports of the product in question:

- originating in the third country concerned, broken down between direct imports and imports of products in free circulation,

- originating in all third countries,

- originating in the Community;

(d) the economic difficulties of which there is alleged to be a danger, as indicated by factors such as consumption of the product and the respective market shares held by national production, the third country concerned and all third countries.

The information required under subparagraphs (c) and (d) shall cover the two preceding years and the current year. Where this information cannot be supplied with the accuracy required or cannot be supplied in time, the Member State's request shall contain the information available.

4. The Member State that has received the authorisation referred to in paragraph 1 may require from an applicant for an import document only the following information and data:

(a) name of the importer and of the consignor in the exporting Member State;

(b) the country of origin and the exporting Member State;

(c) a description of the product with details of:

- its trade designation,

- its heading number in the Common Customs Tariff and the NIMEXE code;

(d) the value and the quantity of the product in the units customarily in use in trade;

(e) the scheduled date or dates for delivery;

(f) supporting evidence that the product is in free circulation. Failing such supporting evidence, the validity of the import document shall be limited to a period of one month following the issue of the document.

Article 3

Protective measures

1. Where imports into a Member State of a product referred to in Article 1 give rise to economic difficulties, the Member State in question may take protective measures after obtaining the prior authorisation of the Commission, which shall determine the conditions and details of such measures.

2. For the purpose of obtaining such authorisation the Member State shall supply in its request to the Commission the following particulars and data, in addition to those referred to in Article 2(3) (a) and (b):

(a) the exporting Member State;

(b) the date on which the application for an import document was made;

(c) the volume or quantity of imports of the product in question actually effected or authorised:

  (i) originating in the third country concerned, broken down between direct imports and imports of production in free circulation,

  (ii) originating in other third countries in respect of which the requesting Member State maintains similar import arrangements or arrangements having equivalent effect,

  (iii) originating in all third countries,

  (iv) originating in the Community;

(d) where possible , the volume or quantity of re-exports of the product originating in the third country concerned to other Member States and to third countries;

(e) the alleged economic difficulties as shown by the trend of such factors as: production, utilisation of capacity, consumption, respective market shares held by the third country concerned, all third countries and national production, prices, profits or losses, employment.

The information required under subparagraphs (c), (d) and (e) shall cover the two preceding years and the current year. Where this information cannot be supplied with the accuracy required or cannot be supplied in time, the Member State's request shall contain the information available.

3. The introduction of the request by the Member States may not prevent the issue under the conditions and within the period laid down in Article 2 of import documents for which application was made prior to the Commission's decision.

4. However, where the Member State finds that the volume or total quantity covered by applications pending in respect of the product in question originating in the third country concerned is more than, either 5 % of possible direct imports from the third country concerned or 1 % of the total extra-EEC imports during the latest 12 month period for which statistical information is available:

    (i) the maximum period for the issue of import documents shall be increased to 10 working days from the date of the application by the importer;

    (ii) the Member State may reject the application for import documents if the Commission's decision authorises it to do so.

5. The Member State shall inform applicants for import documents of the introduction of a request for protective measures, a copy of which shall be sent to the other Member States.

6. The Commission shall decide on the request of the Member State within five working days of its receipt.

Article 4

Proof of origin

1. As part of the completion of formalities in connection with the importation of products which are subject to intra-Community surveillance measures or protective measures, the relevant authorities of the importing Member State may ask the importer to state the origin of the products on the customs declaration or on the application for an import document.

2. Additional proof may be requested only in cases where serious and well-founded doubts make such proof essential in order to establish the true origin of the products in question. However, a request for such additional proof may not in itself prevent the import of the goods.

Article 5

Transitional and final provisions

1. This Decision shall apply from 1 April 1980.

2. Commission Decision 71/202/EEC of 12 May 1971, as amended by Decision 73/55/EEC of 9 March 1973, shall be repealed as from that date.

3. Measures taken by the Member States in accordance with Article 1 of Decision 71/202/EEC shall remain valid until the grant of an authorisation by the Commission pursuant to Article 2 of this Decision, or until 30 June 1980, whichever is the earlier.

4. Requests for such authorisations must be lodged with the Commission not later than 30 April 1980.

5. The Commission's decision on the requests will be taken not later than 30 June 1980.

Article 6

This Decision is addressed to the Member States.

Done at Brussels, 20 December 1979.

For the Commission
Wilhelm HAFERKAMP
Vice-President

13. REGULATION (EEC) No 2603/69 OF THE COUNCIL

of 20 December 1969

establishing common rules for exports

(J.O. No 324, 27 December 1969, p. 25; O.J. (Special Edition 1969 II) p. 590)

THE COUNCIL OF THE EUROPEAN COMMUNITIES,

Having regard to the Treaty establishing the European Economic Community, and in particular Articles 111 and 113 thereof;

Having regard to the instruments establishing common organisation of agricultural markets and to the instruments concerning processed agricultural products adopted in pursuance of Article 235 of the Treaty, in particular the provisions of those instruments which allow for derogation from the general principle that quantitative restrictions or measures having equivalent effect may be replaced solely by the measures provided for in those same instruments;

Having regard to the proposal from the Commission;

Whereas after the transitional period has ended, the common commercial policy must be based on uniform principles, *inter alia* as regards exports; and whereas implementation of this policy necessarily involves its progressive standardisation during the transitional period;

Whereas common rules should therefore be established for exports from the EEC;

Whereas exports are almost completely liberalised in all the Member States; whereas it is therefore possible to accept as a Community principle that exports to third countries are not subject to any quantitative restriction, subject to the exceptions provided for in

457

this Regulation and without prejudice to such measures as Member States may take in conformity with the Treaty;

Whereas the Commission must be informed if, as a result of unusual developments on the market, a Member State considers that protective measures might be necessary;

Whereas it is essential that examination should take place at Community level, in particular on the basis of any such information and within an advisory committee, of export terms and conditions, of export trends, of the various aspects of the economic and commercial situation, and of the measures, if any, to be taken;

Whereas it may become apparent from this examination that the Community should exercise surveillance over certain exports, or that interim protective measures should be introduced as a safeguard against unforeseen practices; whereas the need for rapid and effective action makes it justifiable for the Commission to be empowered to decide upon such measures, but without prejudice to the subsequent position of the Council, whose responsibility it is to adopt a policy consistent with the interests of the Community;

Whereas any protective measures necessitated by the interests of the Community should be adopted with due regard for existing international obligations;

Whereas it is desirable that Member States be empowered, in certain circumstances and provided that their actions are on an interim basis only, to take protective measures individually;

Whereas it is desirable that while such protective measures are in operation there should be an opportunity for consultation for the purpose of examining the effects of the measures and of ascertaining whether the conditions for their application are still satisfied;

Whereas certain products should be provisionally excluded from Community liberalisation until the Council shall have acted to establish common rules in respect of those products;

Whereas this Regulation is to apply to all products, whether industrial or agricultural; whereas its operation should be complementary to that of the instruments establishing common organisation of agricultural markets, and to that of the special instruments adopted under Article 235 of the Treaty for processed agricultural products; whereas any overlap between the provisions of this Regulation and the provisions of those instruments, particularly the protective clauses thereof, must however be avoided;

HAS ADOPTED THIS REGULATION:

TITLE I

Basic principle

Article 1

The exportation of products from the European Economic Community to third countries shall be free, that is to say, they shall not be subject to any quantitative restriction, with the exception of those restrictions which are applied in conformity with the provisions of this Regulation.

TITLE II

Community information and consultation procedure

Article 2

If, as a result of any unusual developments on the market, a Member State considers that protective measures within the meaning of Title III might be necessary, it shall so notify the Commission, which shall advise the other Member States.

Article 3

1. Consultations may be held at any time, either at the request of a Member State or on the initiative of the Commission.

2. Consultations shall take place within four working days following receipt by the Commission of the notification provided for in Article 2, and in all cases before the introduction of any measure pursuant to Articles 5 to 7.

Article 4

1. Consultation shall take place within an advisory committee (hereinafter called 'the Committee'), which shall consist of representatives of each Member State with a representative of the Commission as Chairman.

2. The Committee shall meet when convened by its Chairman. He shall provide all the Member States, as promptly as possible, with all relevant information.

3. Consultation shall in particular cover:

(a) terms and conditions of export, export trends, and the various aspects of the economic and commercial situation as regards the product in question;

(b) the measures, if any, to be adopted.

Article 5

For the purpose of assessing the economic and commercial situation as regards a particular product, the Commission may request Member States to supply statistical data on market trends in that product and, to this end, acting in accordance with their national legislation and with a procedure to be specified by the Commission, to exercise surveillance over exports of such product. Member States shall take whatever steps are necessary in order to give effect to requests from the Commission and shall forward to the Commission the data requested. The Commission shall inform the other Member States.

TITLE III

Protective measures

Article 6

1. In order to prevent a critical situation from arising on account of a shortage of essential products, or to remedy such a situation, and where Community interests call for immediate intervention, the Commission, acting at the request of a Member State or on its own initiative, and taking account of the nature of the products and of the other particular features of the transactions in question, may make the export of a product subject to the production of an export authorisation, the granting of which shall be governed by such provisions and subject to such limits as the Commission shall lay down pending subsequent action by the Council under Article 7.

2. The Council and the Member States shall be notified of the measures taken. Such measures shall take effect immediately.

3. The measures may be limited to exports to certain countries or to exports from certain regions of the Community. They shall not affect products already on their way to the Community frontier.

4. Where intervention by the Commission has been requested by a Member State, the Commission shall take a decision within a maximum of five working days of receipt of such request. Should the Commission refuse to give effect to the request, it shall forthwith communicate its decision to the Council, which may, acting by a qualified majority, decide differently.

5. Any Member State may, within twelve working days of the day of their communication to the Member States, refer the measures taken to the Council. The Council may, acting by a qualified majority, decide that different action be taken.

6. Where the Commission has acted pursuant to paragraph 1, it shall, not later than twelve working days following the entry into force of the measure which it has taken, make a proposal to the Council on appropriate measures as provided for in Article 7. If, at the end of six weeks following the entry into force of the measure, taken by the Commission, the Council has taken no decision on this proposal, the measure in question shall be deemed revoked.

Article 7

1. Where the interests of the Community so require, the Council may, acting by a qualified majority on a proposal from the Commission, adopt appropriate measures:

- to prevent a critical situation from arising owing to a shortage of essential products, or to remedy such a situation;

- to allow international undertakings entered into by the Community or all the Member States to be fulfilled, in particular those relating to trade in primary products.

2. Such measures may be limited to exports to certain countries or to exports from certain regions of the Community. They shall not affect products already on their way to the Community frontier.

3. When quantitative restrictions on exports are introduced, account shall be taken in particular of:

- the volume of goods exported under contracts concluded on normal terms and conditions before the entry into force of a protective measure within the meaning of this Title and notified by the Member State concerned to the Commission in conformity with its national laws; and

- the need to avoid jeopardising achievement of the aim pursued in introducing quantitative restrictions.

Article 8

1. Where a Member State considers that there exists in its territory a situation such as that defined as regards the Community in Article 6(1), it may, as an interim protective measure, make the export of a product subject to the production of an export authorisation, the granting of which shall be governed by such provisions and subject to such limits as that Member State shall lay down.

2. The Member State shall take such a measure after hearing the opinions expressed in the Committee or, where urgency precludes such a procedure, after notifying the Commission. The latter shall advise the other Member States.

3. The Commission shall be notified by telex of the measure immediately following its adoption; such notification shall be equivalent to a request within the meaning of Article 6(4). The measure shall operate only until the coming into operation of the decision taken by the Commission.

4. The provisions of this Article shall apply until 31 December 1972. Before that date the Council shall, by a qualified majority on a proposal from the Commission, decide on the adjustments to be made thereto.

Article 9

1. While any measure referred to in Articles 6 to 8 is in operation, consultations within the Committee shall be held, either at the request of a Member State or on the initiative of the Commission. The purpose of such consultations shall be:

461

(a) to examine the effects of the measures;

(b) to ascertain whether the conditions for its application are still satisfied.

2. Where the Commission considers that any measure provided for in Article 6 or in Article 7 should be revoked or amended, it shall proceed as follows:

(a) where the Council has taken no decision on a measure taken by the Commission, the latter shall amend or revoke such measure forthwith and shall immediately deliver a report to the Council;

(b) in all other cases, the Commission shall propose to the Council that the measures adopted by the Council be revoked or amended. The Council shall act by a qualified majority.

TITLE IV

Transitional and final provisions

Article 10

Until such time as the Council, acting by a qualified majority on a proposal from the Commission, shall have introduced common rules in respect of the products listed in the Annex to this Regulation, the principle of freedom of export from the Community as laid down in Article 1 shall not apply to those products.

Article 11

Without prejudice to other Community provisions, this Regulation shall not preclude the adoption or application by a Member State of quantitative restrictions on exports on grounds of public morality, public policy or public security; the protection of health and life of humans, animals or plants; the protection of national treasures possessing artistic, historic or archaeological value, or the protection of industrial and commercial property.

Article 12

1. This Regulation shall be without prejudice to the operation of the instruments establishing common organisation of agricultural markets, or of the special instruments adopted under Article 235 of the Treaty for processed agricultural products; it shall operate by way of complement to those instruments.

2. However, in the case of products covered by such instruments, the provisions of Articles 6 and 8 shall not apply to those in respect of which the Community rules on trade with third countries make provision for the application of quantitative export restrictions. The provisions of Article 5 shall not apply to those products in respect of which such rules require the production of a licence or other export document.

462

This Regulation shall enter into force on 31 December 1969.

This Regulation shall be binding in its entirety and directly applicable in all Member States.

Done at Brussels, 20 December 1969.

For the Council
The President
H.J. DE KOSTER

14. COUNCIL REGULATION (EEC) No 288/82

of 5 February 1982

on common rules for imports

(O.J. No L35, 9 February 1982, p. 1)

THE COUNCIL OF THE EUROPEAN COMMUNITIES,

Having regard to the Treaty establishing the European Economic Community, and in particular Article 113 thereof,

Having regard to the instruments establishing common organisation of agricultural markets and to the instruments concerning processed agricultural products adopted in pursuance of Article 235 of the Treaty, in particular the provisions of those instruments which allow for derogation from the general principle that all quantitative restrictions or measures having equivalent effect may be replaced solely by the measures provided for in those same instruments,

Having regard to the proposal from the Commission,

Whereas the common commercial policy must be based on uniform principles; whereas the import rules established by Regulation (EEC) No 926/79 are an important aspect of that policy;

Whereas the liberalisation of imports, that is to say the absence of any quantitative restrictions subject to exceptions and derogations provided for in Community rules, is the starting point for common rules in this field;

Whereas the Commission must be informed by the Member States of any danger created by trends in imports which might call for protective measures;

Whereas, in such a case, the Commission must examine import terms and conditions, import trends, the various aspects of the economic and commercial situation, and the measures, if any, to be taken;

Whereas it may become apparent that there should be either Community surveillance or surveillance at national level over certain of these imports;

Whereas in this case the putting into free citculation of the products concerned should be made subject to production of an import document satisfying uniform criteria; whereas that document must, on declaration or on simple application by the importer, be issued or endorsed by the authorities of the Member States within a certain period but without the importer thereby acquiring any right to import; whereas the document must therefore be valid only during such period as the import rules remain unchanged;

Whereas it is in the interest of the Community that the Member States and the Commission should make as full an exchange as possible of information resulting from either Community surveillance or surveillance at national level;

Whereas it is for the Commission and the Council to adopt the protective measures called for by the interests of the Community with due regard for existing international obligations; whereas, therefore, protective measures against a country which is a contracting party to GATT may be considered only if the product in question is imported into the Community in such greatly increased quantities and on such terms or conditions as to cause, or threaten to cause, substantial injury to Community producers of like or directly competing products, unless international obligations permit derogation from this rule;

Whereas Member States should be empowered, in certain circumstances and provided that their actions are on an interim basis only, to take protective measures individually;

Whereas Articles 14(6) and 16(1) of Regulation (EEC) No 926/79 provide that the Council shall decide on the adjustments to be made to that Regulation;

Whereas a review of the Regulation, in the light of experience gained in applying it, has shown that it is necessary to adopt more precise criteria for assessing possible injury and to produce an investigation procedure while still allowing the Commission and the Member States to introduce appropriate measures in urgent cases;

Whereas to this end more detailed provisions should be introduced on the opening of investigations, on the checks and inspections required, on the hearing of those concerned, the treatment of information obtained and the criteria for assessing injury;

Whereas the provisions on the investigations introduced by this Regulation do not prejudice Community or national rules concerning professional secrecy;

Whereas, furthermore, in a desire for simplicity and greater transparency of import arrangements, it seemed preferable to draw up a list of quantitative restrictions still applicable at national level rather than a common liberalisation list;

Whereas a procedure should be available for application where import restrictions maintained by certain Member States are amended; whereas in order to prevent these autonomous amendments from constituting obstacles to the implementation of the common commercial policy and from injuring the interests of the Community or one of its Member States, these amendments should be subject to prior consultation and, where necessary, to an authorisation procedure;

Whereas, in addition, the provisions of the Agreement on import licencing procedures signed within the framework of GATT should be transposed into Community law, in particular so as to ensure a greater transparency of the systems of restrictions applied by the Member States;

Whereas the Regulation thus amended should be published in its entirety,

HAS ADOPTED THIS REGULATION:

TITLE I

General principles

Article 1

1. This Regulation shall apply to imports of products covered by the Treaty originating in third countries, except for

- textile products subject to specific common import rules for the duration of those rules, subject to measures which may be taken regarding these products in accordance with Title IV,

- the products originating in State-trading countries listed in Regulation (EEC) No 925/79,

- the products originating in the People's Republic of China listed in Regulation (EEC) No 2532/78,

- products originating in Cuba.

2. Importation into the Community of the products referred to in paragraph 1 shall be free, and therefore not subject to any quantitative restriction, without prejudice to

- measures which may be taken under Title V,

- measures maintained under Title VI,

- quantitative restrictions for the products listed in Annex 1 and maintained in the Member States indicated opposite these products in that Annex.

Article 2

The Council may, acting by a qualified majority on a proposal from the Commission, decide to delete certain products from Annex 1, if it considers that such action is not liable to create a situation where the reintroduction of protective measures would be justified.

TITLE II

Community information and consultation procedure

Article 3

The Commission shall be informed by the Member States should trends in imports appear to call for surveillance or protective measures. This information shall contain the available evidence on the basis of the criteria laid down in Article 9. The Commission shall pass on this information to all the Member States forthwith.

Article 4

Consultations may be held, either at the request of a Member State or on the initiative of the Commission. They shall take place within eight working days following receipt by the Commission of the information provided for in Article 3 and, in any event, before the introduction of any measure of surveillance or protective measure by the Community.

Article 5

1. Consultation shall take place within an advisory committee (hereinafter called 'the Committee') which shall consist of representatives of each Member State with a representative of the Commission as chairman.

2. The Committee shall meet when convened by its chairman. He shall provide the Member States, as promptly as possible, with all relevant information.

3. Consultation shall cover in particular:

(a) terms and conditions of importation, import trends, and the various aspects of the economic and commercial situation as regards the product in question;

(b) the measures, if any, to be taken.

4. Consultations may be in writing if necessary. The Commission shall in this event inform the Member States, which may express their opinion or request oral consultations within a period of five to eight working days to be decided by the Commission.

TITLE III

Community investigation procedure

Article 6

1. Where, after consultation it is apparent to the Commission that there is sufficient evidence to justify an investigation, the Commission shall:

(a) announce the opening of an investigation in the *Official Journal of the European Communities;* such announcements shall give a summary of the information received, and stipulate that all relevant information is to be communicated to the Commission; it shall state the period within which interested parties may make known their views in writing;

(b) commence the investigation, acting in cooperation with the Member States.

2. The Commission shall seek all information it deems to be necessary and, where it considers it appropriate, after consulting the Committee, endeavour to check this information with importers, traders, agents, producers, trade associations and organisations.

The Commission shall be assisted in this task by staff of the Member State on whose territory these checks are being carried out, provided this Member State so wishes.

3. The Member States shall supply the Commission, at its request and following procedures laid down by it, with all information at their disposal on developments in the market of the product being investigated.

4. The Commission may hear the interested natural and legal persons. Such parties must be heard where they have applied in writing within the period laid down in the notice published in the *Official Journal of the European Communities*, showing that they are actually likely to be affected by the outcome of the investigations and that there are special reasons for them to be heard orally.

5. Where the information requested by the Commission is not supplied within a reasonable period, or the investigation is significantly impeded, findings may be made on the basis of the facts available.

Article 7

1. At the end of the investigation, the Commission shall submit a report on the results to the Committee.

2. If the Commission considers that no Community surveillance or protective measures are necessary, it shall publish in the *Official Journal of the European Communities*, after consulting the Committee, a notice that the investigations are closed, stating the main conclusions of the investigations.

3. If the Commission considers that Community surveillance or protective measures are necessary, it shall take the necessary decisions in accordance with Titles IV and V.

4. The provisions of this Title shall not preclude the taking, at any

467

time, of surveillance measures in accordance with Articles 10 to 14 or, in an emergency, protective measures in accordance with Articles 15 to 17.

In the latter case, the Commission shall immediately take the investigation measures it considers to be still necessary. The results of the investigation shall be used to re-examine the measures taken.

Article 8

1. Information received in pursuance of this Regulation shall be used only for the purpose for which it was requested.

2. (a) Neither the Council, nor the Commission, nor Member States, nor the officials of any of these, shall reveal any information of a confidential nature received in pursuance of this Regulation, or any information provided on a confidential basis, without specific permission from the supplier of this information.

(b) Each request for confidentiality shall state the reasons why the information is confidential.

However, if it appears that a request for confidentiality is unjustified and if the supplier of the information wishes neither to make it public nor to authorise its disclosure in general terms or in the form of a summary, the information concerned may be disregarded.

3. Information will in any case be considered to be confidential if its disclosure is likely to have a significantly adverse effect upon the supplier or the source of such information.

4. The above paragraphs shall not preclude reference by the Community authorities to general information and in particular to reasons on which decisions taken in pursuance of this Regulation are based. These authorities must, however, take into account the legitimate interest of the legal and natural persons concerned that their business secrets should not be divulged.

Article 9

1. The examination of the trend of imports, of the conditions in which they take place and of the substantial injury or threat of substantial injury to Community producers resulting from such imports, shall cover in particular the following factors:

(a) the volume of imports, in particular where there has been a significant increase, either in absolute terms or relative to production or consumption in the Community;

(b) the prices of the imports, in particular where there has been a significant price undercutting as compared with the price of a like product in the Community;

(c) the consequent impact on the Community producers of similar or directly competitive products as indicated by trends in certain economic factors such as:

- production,

- utilisation of capacity,

- stocks,

- sales,

- market share,

- prices (i.e. depression of prices or prevention of price increases which would normally have occurred),

- profits,

- return on capital employed,

- cash flow,

- employment.

2. Where a threat of serious injury is alleged the Commission shall also examine whether it is clearly foreseeable that a particular situation is likely to develop into actual injury. In this regard account may be taken of factors such as:

(a) rate of increase of the exports to the Community;

(b) export capacity in the country of origin or export, already in existence or which will be operational in the foreseeable future, and the likelihood that the resulting exports will be to the Community.

TITLE IV

Surveillance

Article 10

1. Where developments on the market in respect of a product originating in a third country covered by this Regulation threaten to cause injury to Community producers of like or directly competing products and where the interests of the Community so require, importation of that product may be made subject, as the case may be, to:

(a) retrospective Community surveillance carried out according to the procedures laid down in the Decision referred to in paragraph 2, or

(b) prior Community surveillance carried out according to the procedures laid down in Article 11.

In these cases the product together with the indication 'EUR' shall be entered in Annex II.

2. Where the decision to impose surveillance is taken simultaneously with the liberalisation of importation of the product in question, that decision shall be taken by the Council, acting by a qualified majority on a proposal from the Commission. In all other cases it shall be taken by the Commission and Article 15(5) shall apply.

3. The surveillance measures shall be of limited duration. Unless otherwise provided, they shall cease to be valid at the end of the second half calendar year following that in which they were introduced.

Article 11

1. Products under prior Community surveillance may be put into free circulation only on production of an import document. Such document shall be issued or endorsed by Member States, free of charge, for any quantity requested and within a maximum of five working days following submission, in accordance with the national laws in force, either of a declaration or simply of an application by any Community importer, regardless of his place of business in the Community, without prejudice to the observance of the other conditions required by the regulations in force.

2. Subject to any provision to the contrary made when surveillance was imposed and under the procedure there followed, the declaration or application by the importer must give:

(a) the name and address of the importer;

(b) a description of the product with the following particulars:

  - commercial description,

  - tariff heading, or reference number, of the product in the goods nomenclature used for foreign trade purposes by the country concerned,

  - country of origin,

  - exporting country;

(c) the cif price free-at-frontier and the quantity of the product in units customarily used in the trade in question;

(d) the proposed date or dates as well as the place or places of importation.

Member States may request further particulars.

3. Paragraph 2 shall not preclude the putting into free circulation of the product in question if the unit price at which the transaction is effected exceeds that indicated in the import document, or if the total value or quantity of the products to be imported exceeds the value or quantity given in the import document by less than 5 %. The Commission, having heard the opinions expressed in the Committee and

taking account of the nature of the products and other special features of the transactions concerned, may fix a different percentage, which, however, should not normally exceed 10 %.

4. Import documents may be used only for such time as arrangements for the liberalisation of imports remain in force in respect of the transactions concerned and in any event not beyond the expiry of a period laid down, with regard to the nature of the products and other special features of the transactions, at the same time and by means of the same procedure as the imposition of surveillance.

5. Where the decision taken under Article 10 so requires, the origin of products under Community surveillance must be proved by a certificate of origin. This paragraph shall not prejudice other provisions concerning the production of any such certificate.

6. Where the product under prior Community surveillance is not liberalised in a Member State, the import authorisation granted by that Member State may replace the import document.

Article 12

1. Where importation of a product has not been made subject to prior Community surveillance within a period of eight working days following the end of consultations, the Member State, having informed the Commission under Article 3 may carry out surveillance over such importation at national level.

2. In cases of extreme urgency the Member State may carry out surveillance at national level after informing the Commission in accordance with Article 3. The latter shall inform the other Member States.

3. The Commission shall be informed, upon the entry into force of the surveillance, of the detailed rules for its application and shall amend Annex II by means of a notice published in the *Official Journal of the European Communities,* by entering the name of the Member State applying the surveillance opposite the product in question.

Article 13

Products under national surveillance may be put into free circulation only on production of an import document. Such document shall be issued or endorsed by the Member State, free of charge, for any quantity requested and within a maximum of five working days following submission of a declaration or simply of an application by any Community importer, regardless of his place of business in the Community, without prejudice to the observance of the other conditions required by the regulations in force. Import documents may be used only for such time as arrangements for the liberalisation of imports remain in force in respect of the transactions concerned.

Article 14

1. Member States shall communicate to the Commission within the

first 10 days of each month in the case of Community surveillance
and within the first 20 days of each quarter in the case of national
surveillance:

(a) in the case of prior surveillance, details of the sums of money
    (calculated on the basis of cif prices) and quantities of goods
    in respect of which import documents were issued or endorsed
    during the preceding period;

(b) in every case, details of imports during the period preceding the
    period referred to in subparagraph (a).

The information supplied by Member States shall be broken down by
product and by countries.

Different provisions may be laid down at the same time and by the
same procedure as the surveillance arrangements.

2. Where the nature of the products or special circumstances so
require, the Commission may, at the request of a Member State or on
its own initiative, amend the timetables for submitting this information.

3. The Commission shall inform the Member State.

TITLE V

Protective measures

Article 13

1. Where a product is imported into the Community in such greatly
increased quantities and/or on such terms or conditions as to cause,
or threaten to cause, substantial injury to Community producers of
like or directly competing products, and where a critical situation,
in which any delay would cause injury which it would be difficult to
remedy, calls for immediate intervention in order to safeguard the
interests of the Community, the Commission may, acting at the request
of a Member State or on its own initiative:

(a) limit the period of validity of import documents within the mean-
    ing of Article 11 to be issued or endorsed after the entry into
    force of this measure;

(b) alter the import rules for the product in question by providing
    that it may be put into free circulation only on production of
    an import authorisation, the granting of which shall be governed
    by such provisions and subject to such limits as the Commission
    shall lay down pending action, if any, by the Council under Art-
    icle 16.

The measures referred to in (a) and (b) shall take effect immediately.

2. Where the establishment of a quota constitutes a withdrawal of liberalisation, account shall be taken in particular of:

- the desirability of maintaining, as far as possible, traditional trade flows,

- the volume of goods exported under contracts concluded on normal terms and conditions before the entry into force of a protective measure within the meaning of this Title, where such contracts have been notified to the Commission by the Member State concerned,

- the need to avoid jeopardising achievement of the aim pursued in establishing the quota.

3. (a) The measures referred to in this Article shall apply to every product which is put into free circulation after their entry into force. They may be limited to imports intended for certain regions of the Community.

   (b) However, such measures shall not prevent the putting into free circulation of products already on their way to the Community provided that the destination of such products cannot be changed and that those products which, under Articles 10 and 11 may be put into free circulation only on production of an import document are in fact accompanied by such a document.

4. Where intervention by the Commission has been requested by a Member State, the Commission shall take a decision within a maximum of five working days of receipt of such request.

5. Any decision taken by the Commission under this Article shall be communicated to the Council and to the Member States. Any Member State may, within one month following the day of communication, refer such decision to the Council.

6. If a Member State refers the decision taken by the Commission to the Council, the Council shall, by a qualified majority, confirm, amend or revoke the decision of the Commission.

If within three months of the referral of the matter to the Council, the latter has not given a decision, the measure taken by the Commission shall be deemed revoked.

Article 16

1. Where the interests of the Community so require, the Council may, acting by a qualified majority on a proposal from the Commission, adopt appropriate measures:

(a) to prevent a product being imported into the Community in such greatly increased quantities and/or on such terms or conditions as to cause, or threaten to cause, substantial injury to Community producers of like or directly competing products;

(b) to allow the rights and obligations of the Community or of all its Member States to be exercised and fulfilled at international level, in particular those relating to trade in primary products.

2. Article 15(2) and (3) shall apply.

1. In the following cases a Member State may, as an interim protective measure, alter the import rules for a particular product by providing that it may be put into free circulation only on production of an import authorisation, the granting of which shall be governed by such provisions and subject to such limits as that Member State shall lay down:

(a) where there exists in its territory a situation such as that defined as regards the Community in Article 15(1);

(b) where such measure is justified by a protective clause contained in a bilateral agreement between the Member State and a third country.

2. (a) The Member State shall inform the Commission and the other Member States by telex of the reasons for and the details of the proposed measures. The Commission and the other Member States shall treat this information in strictest confidence. The Commission shall forthwith convene the Committee. The Member State may take these measures after having heard the opinions expressed by the Committee.

   (b) Where a Member State claims that the matter is especially urgent, consultations shall take place within a period of five working days following information transmitted to the Commission: at the end of this period, the Member State may take these measures. During this period the Member State may make imports of the product in question subject to production of an import authorisation to be granted under the procedure and within the limits to be laid down at the end of the said period.

3. The Commission shall be notified by telex of the measures immediately following their adoption.

4. The notification shall be equivalent to a request within the meaning of Article 15(4). The measures shall operate only until the coming into operation of the decision taken by the Commission. However, where the Commission decides not to introduce any measure or adopts measures pursuant to Article 15, different from those taken by the Member State, its decision shall apply as from the sixth day following its entry into force, unless the Member State which has taken the measures refers the decision to the Council; in that case, the national measures shall continue to operate until the entry into force of the decision taken by the Council and for the maximum of one month following referral of the matter to the latter. The Council shall take a decision before the expiry of that period. The Council may under the same conditions decide in certain cases to extend this period, which may, in no fashion, exceed a total of three months.

The preceding subparagraph does not affect the Member States' right of recourse under Article 15(5) and (6).

5. This Article shall apply until 31 December 1984. Before 31 December 1983, the Commission shall propose to the Council amendments to

be made to it. The Council shall act, before 31 December 1984 by a qualified majority, upon the Commission proposal. However, the provisions relating to protective measures:

- justified by a safeguard clause contained in a bilateral agreement shall not be effected by that time limit,

- concerning imports of products which have been liberalised in certain Member States but subject to quota in others shall apply until 31 December 1987.

Article 18

1. While any measure of surveillance or protective measure applied in accordance with Titles IV and V is in operation, consultations within the Committee shall be held, either at the request of a Member State or on the initiative of the Commission. The purpose of such consultations shall be:

(a) to examine the effects of the measure;

(b) to ascertain whether its application is still necessary.

2. Where, as a result of the consultations referred to in paragraph 1, the Commission considers that any measure referred to in Article 10, 12, 15 or 16 should be revoked or amended it shall proceed as follows:

(a) where the Council has acted on a measure, the Commission shall propose that it be revoked or amended; the Council shall act by a qualified majority;

(b) in all other cases, the Commission shall amend or revoke Community protective measures and measures of surveillance. Where this decision concerns national measures of surveillance, it shall apply as from the sixth day following its publication in the *Official Journal of the European Communities*, unless the Member State which has taken the measure refers it to the Council; in that case the national measure shall continue to operate until the entry into force of the decision taken by the Council, but in no event after the expiry of a period of three months following referral of the matter to the latter. The Council shall act before the expiry of that period.

TITLE IV

Transitional and final provisions

Article 19

1. By 31 December 1984 at the latest, the Council shall decide on the adjustments to be made to this Regulation for the purpose of greater uniformity of rules for imports. The Council shall act by a qualified majority on a proposal from the Commission and with due regard to the progress of the common commercial policy.

2. Pending these adjustments:

(a) in so far as standardisation between the areas of liberalisation has not been wholly realised, Member States may subject imports of products not included in the Annex to Regulation (EEC) No 925/79 to the requirement that not only the country of origin but also the country of purchase or the country of export shall be among the countries covered by this Regulation; for the Federal Republic of Germany, this shall apply also to those products included in the Annex to the abovementioned Regulation whose importation is not yet exempted in respect of all third countries, under German import arrangements, from the requirement of an import authorisation;

(b) the Italian Republic may subject imports of products originating in Egypt, Yugoslavia and Japan to the requirement that the country of origin shall be the same as the country of export;

(c) import documents required for Community surveillance under Article 11 shall be valid only in the Member State which issued or endorsed them;

(d) the Benelux countries and the Italian Republic may retain the automatic-licence or import-declaration formalities currently applied by them to imports originating in Japan and Hong Kong;

(e) the Member States listed in Annex II opposite the products marked with an asterisk may retain national surveillance over imports of such products, including imports under automatic licences; Article 12, Article 13, last sentence, Article 14 and Article 18 shall not be applicable.

(f) this Regulation shall not preclude the continuance of measures taken by the Italian Republic - pursuant to the Ministerial Decree of 6 May 1976, including the list annexed thereto and the subsequent amendments to it - making subject to special authorisation the importation of articles, machinery and equipment, whether used or new but in poorly maintained condition, falling within heading No 73.24, Chapters 84 to 87 and 93 or subheading 97.04 B of the Common Customs Tariff.

3. Member States shall forward to the Commission details of any measures taken in conformity with the Agreement on import licensing procedures concluded by the Community by Decision 80/271/EEC. In particular they shall make available to the Commission the rules and all information concerning the procedures for the submission of requests for licences, including the conditions relating to admissibility of persons, enterprises or institutions who submit such requests. All changes of these rules shall also be sent to the Commission.

Article 20

1. Where a Member State which applies an import restriction referred to in the last indent of Article 1(2) intends to change it, it shall inform the Commission and the other Member States thereof.

476

2. (a) At the request of the Commission or a Member State, the measures referred to in paragraph 1 shall be the subject of prior consultation within the Committee.

(b) If the Commission does not request on its own initiative consultations within five working days after receiving the information referred to in paragraph 1, nor at the request of a Member State made sufficiently early before the end of the said period,the Member State concerned may then put the proposed measure into effect.

(c) In other cases, the consultation procedure shall commence within five working days after the expiry of the period provided for in (b).

3. (a) If after consultation no objection has been raised by the other Member States or by the Commission, the Commission shall forthwith inform the Member State concerned, which may put the measure into effect immediately.

(b) In other cases, the Member State concerned may not put the proposed measure into effect until three weeks after the opening of the consultation.

(c) If, within this period, the Commission submits to the Council, under Article 113 of the Treaty, a proposal meeting the objections raised, the proposed measure may not be put into effect until the Council has acted.

4. In cases of extreme urgency, the following provisions shall apply:

(a) a quota may be reduced or any possibility of importation may be taken away without prior consultation but after the transmission of information referred to in paragraph 1;

(b) when a quota has been exhausted and the economic requirements of a Member State call for additional imports from the non-member country or countries benefiting from the quota the Member State concerned may, without prior notification, open additional import facilities up to a maximum of 20 % of the quantity or value of the exhausted quota; it shall forthwith inform the Commission and the other Member States thereof. The emergency procedure laid down in this paragraph shall not apply once the opening of negotiations with the non-member country concerned has been authorised;

(c) at the request of any Member State or of the Commission, subsequent consultation under the terms of paragrah 3 shall be held on measures taken by a Member State under this paragraph.

5. Where a Member State intends to make a unilateral change to its import arrangements for a petroleum product which is entered in Annex 1 and referred to in Article 3 of Council Regulation (EEC) No 802/68 of 27 June 1968 on the common definition of the concept of the origin of goods, it shall inform the Commission and the other Member States thereof. The procedure laid down in paragraphs 2, 3 and 4 shall be applicable in this case; the other provisions of this Regulation shall not apply.

6. The Benelux countries may, where they are mentioned in Annex II opposite a product listed in that Annex and marked with an asterisk, retain the automatic licence formality as currently applied by them; such licences shall be issued, free of charge, for any quantity requested and simply on submission of an application by the Community importer, regardless of his place of business in the Community; Article 13 shall not apply to these products.

Article 21

Without prejudice to other Community provisions, this Regulation shall not preclude the adoption or application by Member States:

(a) of prohibitions, quantitative restrictions or measures of surveillance on grounds of public morality, public policy or public security; the protection of health and life of humans, animals or plants, the protection of national treasures possessing artistic, historic or archaeological value, or the protection of industrial and commercial property;

(b) of special formalities concerning foreign exchange;

(c) of formalities introduced pursuant to international agreements in accordance with the Treaty.

Article 22

1. This Regulation shall be without prejudice to the operation of the instruments establishing the common organisation of agricultural markets or of Community or national administrative provisions derived therefrom or of the specific instruments adopted under Article 235 of the Treaty applicable to goods resulting from the processing of agricultural products; it shall operate by way of complement to those instruments.

2. However, in the case of products covered by the instruments referred to in paragraph 1, Articles 10 to 14 and 18 shall not apply to those in respect of which the Community rules on trade with third countries require the production of a licence or other import document.

Articles 15, 17 and 18 shall not apply to those products in respect of which such rules make provision for the application of quantitative import restrictions.

Article 23

The Commission shall publish at regular intervals an updated text of Annexes I and II which will take account of Acts adopted in accordance with this Regulation both by the Community and by Member States. The Commission shall be informed of the introduction, amendment or repeal of all national measures.

Article 24

Regulation (EEC) No 926/79 is hereby repealed.

References to the repealed Regulation shall be understood as referring to this Regulation.

Article 25

This Regulation shall enter into force on the day of its publication in the *Official Journal of the European Communities*.

This Regulation shall be binding in its entirety and directly applicable in all Member States.

Done at Brussels, 5 February 1982.

> *For the Council*
> *The President*
> L. TINDEMANS

15. COUNCIL REGULATION (EEC) No 3286/80

of 4 December 1980

on import arrangements in respect of State-trading countries

(O.J. No L353, 29 December 1980, p. 1)

THE COUNCIL OF THE EUROPEAN COMMUNITIES,

Having regard to the Treaty establishing the European Economic Community, and in particular Article 113 thereof,

Having regard to the proposal from the Commission,

Whereas, in the context of the common commercial policy, the common arrangements for imports into the Community of products from State-trading countries should be completed; whereas provisions should accordingly be adopted concerning the import arrangements in the Member States in respect of these countries;

Whereas Council Decision 75/210/EEC of 27 March 1975 on unilateral import arrangements in respect of State-trading countries, as last amended by Decision 80/158/EEC, provided for certain provisions relating to the establishment of quantitative import quotas and to the amendment of the import arrangements in the Member States;

Whereas the relevant Decisions should be brought together in a single

instrument and at the same time the improvements suggested by experience should be effected, with a view to rendering the import arrangements in question more transparent and simplifying the procedure for
their amendment;

Whereas provision should be made for Community consultations on the
completion of the common import arrangements in respect of State-
trading countries and on the administration of trade Agreements between the Community and these countries,

HAS ADOPTED THIS REGULATION:

TITLE I

Products covered

Article 1

1. This Regulation shall apply to imports of products originating in
the State-trading countries listed in Annex 1, with the exception of:

- products covered by Council Regulation (EEC) No 925/79 of 8 May 1979
  establishing common rules for imports from State-trading countries,

- products covered by Council Regulation (EEC) No 2532/78 of 16 October 1978 on common rules for imports from the People's Republic of
  China,

- textile products subject to specific common rules for imports, as
  regards the State-trading countries to which those rules apply, and
  during the period of application of the said rules,

- products intended for display or use at exhibitions, fairs, meetings
  or similar events.

2. This Regulation shall apply subject to any special measures taken,
as the case may be, for the application of agreements with State-trading countries.

3. This Regulation shall apply, by way of a complement, to products
which are subject to rules on the common organisation of agricultural
markets or to specific rules adopted pursuant to Article 235 of the
Treaty applicable to goods obtained by processing agricultural
products, in so far as such rules still allow Member States to impose
quantitative import restrictions.

4. For the purposes of this Regulation, the Benelux countries shall
be regarded as constituting a single Member State.

TITLE II

Products subject to quantitative
import restrictions

Article 2

1. The putting into free circulation of the products listed in Annex III originating in State-trading countries shall be subject to quantitative restrictions in the Member States as indicated in that Annex against these products.

2. The putting into free circulation of the products referred to in paragraph 1 shall be subject to production of an import authorisation or equivalent document issued by the competent authorities in the Member States concerned, within limits to be defined in accordance with Article 3 or as laid down in Article 4.

Article 3

1. Before 1 December of each year the Council shall, in accordance with Article 113 of the Treaty, lay down the import quotas to be opened by the Member States for the following year in respect of the various State-trading countries for the products referred to in Article 2(1).

This provision shall not affect the rules governing, in the Member States, the opening and administration of quotas.

2. However, if no Council decision has been adopted by that date, the existing import quotas shall be extended on a provisional basis for the following year. Any amendments made exceptionally during the year and expressly valid for that year only shall not be covered by such extension.

In such case, the Council shall adopt, before 1 March of the new year, pursuant to Article 113 of the Treaty, any necessary amendments to the import quotas thus extended.

3. The Member States shall notify the Commission by any appropriate means of the laws, regulations or administrative provisions whereby they are to open at national level the import quotas fixed in accordance with this Regulation.

Article 4

1. In administering the import arrangements resulting from Articles 2 and 3, Member States may, subject to paragraphs 2 and 3 of this Article, adopt the following measures without having to initiate the amendment procedure provided for in Article 7:

(a) *Products subject to quantitative import restrictions in a single Member State*

   In the light of the economic requirements of the market, the Member State concerned may:

   (i) for products subject to quotas, exceed the amount of the quotas;

(ii) for products for which no quota has been laid down, open import facilities;

(b) ~~Products subject to quantitative restrictions in more than one~~ *Member State*

In an emergency, and if the economic requirements of the market make this necessary, the Member States concerned may, for products subject to quantitative restrictions whether or not subject to quotas, open further import facilities within the following annual limits:

(i) for textile products in Annex II, other than those in Group I, which are subject to quantitative restrictions in seven or more Member States: 5 % of any quota if it has been used up, with the possibility of attaining a value of 50 000 European units of account in any event;

(ii) for the textile products listed above which are subject to quantitative restrictions in six or fewer Member States and for products other than those listed in Annex II: 20 % of any quota if it has been used up, with the possibility of attaining a value of 100 000 European units of account in any event.

2. When a Member State which is alone in maintaining a quantitative import restriction proposes to abolish or suspend such a restriction, it shall inform the Commission and the other Member States in accordance with Article 7(1). The proposed measure shall not be subject to prior consultation and shall be adopted by the Commission within 10 working days.

3. Paragraphs 1 and 2 shall cease to apply in respect of a State-trading country from the time when the opening of trade negotiations between the Community and that country has been authorised until the signature of the agreement negotiated; only Article 7 shall apply in such a case.

4. The Member States shall, every six months, inform the Commission, which will in turn inform the Consultation Committee provided for in Article 12, of the measures adopted in accordance with paragraph 1. Such information shall be supplied concerning the measures provided for in paragraph 1(b) if the limits of 5 % and 20 % are reached.

5. At the request of a Member State or of the Commission, consultations shall be held retrospectively, in accordance with Article 8, on measures adopted by the Member States pursuant to paragraphs 1 and 2.

Article 5

Products imported into the customs territory of the Community and subject to processing or other temporary import arrangements and declared as being intended for re-export from that territory either with or without further processing shall not be charged against the quotas or other import facilities opened in accordance with Article

4, provided the products in question are actually re-exported.

TITLE III

Liberalised products

Article 6

The importation into the Member States of products not subject to the import arrangements provided for in Article 2 shall not be liable to any quantitative restrictions.

Imports of these products may be subject to an automatic licensing system.

TITLE IV

Amendment of the import arrangements

Article 7

1. Where a Member State considers that the import arrangements laid down in accordance with this Regulation should be amended, it shall inform the other Member States and the Commission thereof, specifying *inter alia* whether the proposed measure is to be of an exceptional nature.

2. Amendments to the import arrangements shall be adopted in accordance with the procedure laid down in Articles 8 and 9.

Article 8

1. At the request of a Member State or of the Commission, the proposed measure shall be the subject of prior consultation within the Committee provided for in Article 12.

2. The purpose of the consultation shall be to ascertain the effects of the proposed measure with regard to completion of common import arrangements and to ensure that the proposed measure does not affect the proper functioning of the common market. If necessary, the consultation shall deal with other approaches in the light both of these aims and of the particular situation which prompted the request by the Member State.

3. The Committee shall take into account in particular the situation in the relevant sector of the economy and, where appropriate, the volume of traditional imports.

Article 9

1. If the Commission does not request consultation within five working days of receiving the information provided for in Article 7 and has received no request for consultation from any of the Member

States by the end of that period, it shall forthwith adopt the proposed measure.

2. In other cases, consultation shall commence within 10 working days following receipt of the information referred to in Article 7(1).

3. If after consultation no objection has been raised by a Member State or by the Commission, the latter shall forthwith adopt the proposed measure.

4. In other cases, the Commission shall, within 20 working days of the opening of consultation, either adopt the proposed measure or, in accordance with Article 113 of the Treaty, submit a proposal to the Council concerning the measures to be taken.

In the latter case, until such time as the Council has acted in accordance with paragraph 6, the Member State concerned shall suspend implementation of the proposed measure, except where it makes use of the possibility provided for in Article 10.

5. The decision taken by the Commission pursuant to this Article shall be communicated forthwith to the Council and the Member States.

The decision shall apply at once, subject to paragraph 8.

6. If the Commission refers the matter to the Council, the latter shall act by a qualified majority.

7. Subject to paragraph 8, any Member State which has raised an objection to the proposed measure during consultation may refer the Commission's decision to the Council within one month following the date on which that decision was communicated.

Within a period of two months following the date on which the matter was referred to it, the Council shall decide by a qualified majority whether to amend or revoke the Commission's decision.

8. Where the Commission's decision comprises measures designed to make the import arrangements more flexible, it shall apply as from the sixth working day following the date of its communication, unless a Member State which objected to the proposed measure during consultation refers the decision to the Council. In this case, the Council shall take a decision in accordance with the second subparagraph of paragraph 7. If the Council has not taken a decision at the end of the stipulated period, the Commission's decision shall apply.

9. Amendments made to the import arrangements in accordance with paragraphs 1, 3 and 4 shall be published in the *Official Journal of the European Communities*.

Article 10

In a particularly urgent case, measures to restrict import facilities by:

- withdrawing liberalisation of one or more products,

- abolishing or reducing a quota,

may be applied by the Member States, following the submission of the request for amendment provided for in Article 7, but without awaiting any consultation which might be requested under Article 8.

These measures shall apply until the entry into force of the decision of the Commission or of the Council, if the matter has been referred to the latter in accordance with Article 9(4).

Article 11

Without prejudice to other Community provisions, this Regulation shall not preclude the adoption or application by a Member State of prohibitions or quantitative restrictions on imports on grounds of public morality, public policy or public security, the protection of health and life of humans, animals or plants, the protection of national treasures possessing artistic, historic or archaeological value, or the protection of industrial and commercial property.

TITLE V

Consultation Committee

Article 12

1. A consultation Committee, hereinafter referred to as 'the Committee', is hereby set up, consisting of representatives of the Member States and chaired by a representative of the Commission.

2. Matter shall be put before the Committee by its chairman at his own initiative or at the request of a representative of a Member State.

Article 13

Without prejudice to the consultations provided for in Articles 8 and 9, the Committee may:

- examine questions connected with the application of this Regulation and relating to the administration of import arrangements in respect of State-trading countries,

- deal with questions relating to the administration of trade agreements concluded between the Community and such third countries.

TITLE IV

Final provisions

Article 14

Decisions 75/210/EEC and 79/252/EEC shall be repealed as from 1 January 1981, with the exception of Article 8 of Decision 75/210/EEC which is hereby repealed as from the date on which this Regulation comes into force.

Article 15

This Regulation shall enter into force on the third day following its publication in the *Official Journal of the European Communities*.

It shall apply as from 1 January 1981, except for Article 3 which shall apply as from the date of entry into force.

This Regulation shall be binding in its entirety and directly applicable in all Member States.

Done at Brussels, 4 December 1980.

For the Council
The President
J. BARTHEL

16. COUNCIL REGULATION (EEC) No 1765/82

of 30 June 1982

on common rules for imports from State-trading countries

(O.J. No L195, 5 July 1982, p. 1)

THE COUNCIL OF THE EUROPEAN COMMUNITIES,

Having regard to the Treaty establishing the European Economic Community, and in particular Article 113 thereof,

Having regard to the instruments establishing common organisation of agricultural markets and to the instruments concerning processed agricultural products adopted in pursuance of Article 235 of the Treaty, in particular the provisions of those instruments which allow for derogation from the general principle that all quantitative restrictions or measures having equivalent effect may be replaced solely by the measures provided for in those same instruments,

Having regard to the proposal from the Commission,

Whereas the common commercial policy must be based on uniform principles; whereas the import rules established by Regulation (EEC) No 925/79 are an important aspect of that policy;

Whereas, provided that they are listed in the Annex to this Regulation, products shall be imported into any part of the Community without quantitative restriction, subject to the exceptions and derogations provided for by Community instruments and in particular to Regulation (EEC) No 596/82;

Whereas, however, by reason of the economic system of State-trading countries, it is necessary that Member States should notify the Commission when the trend in imports, or the conditions in which imports are made, appear to call for protective measures and that they should in particular advise it of any application for documents for the importation of a product in notably increased quantities or on exceptional terms or conditions, and that they should do so before such documents are issued;

Whereas it is essential that examination should take place at Community level, in particular on the basis of any such information and within an advisory committee, of the terms and conditions of importation, of import trends, of the various aspects of the economic and commercial situation, and of the measures, if any, to be taken;

Whereas it may become necessary for certain of these imports to be made subject to Community surveillance;

Whereas in this case the putting into free circulation of the products concerned should be made subject to production of an import document satisfying uniform criteria; whereas that document must, on declaration or on simple application by the importer, be issued or endorsed by the authorities of the Member States within a certain period but without the importer thereby acquiring any right to import; whereas the document may not therefore be used until the import rules have been changed;

Whereas it is in the interest of the Community that the Member States and the Commission should make as full an exchange as possible of information resulting from either Community surveillance or surveillance at national level;

Whereas it is for the Commission and the Council to adopt the protective measures called for by the interests of the Community with due regard for existing international obligations;

Whereas Member States should be empowered, in certain circumstances and on an interim basis, to take protective measures individually;

Whereas Articles 9(5) and 11(1) of Regulation (EEC) No 925/79 provide that the Council shall decide on the adjustments to be made to that Regulation;

Whereas a review of the Regulation, in the light of experience gained in applying it, has shown that it is necessary to adopt more precise criteria for assessing possible injury and to introduce an investigation while still allowing the Commission and the Member States to introduce appropriate measures in urgent cases;

Whereas, to this end, more detailed provisions should be introduced on the opening of investigations, on the checks and inspections required, on the hearing of those concerned, the treatment of information obtained and the criteria for assessing injury;

Whereas the provisions on the investigations introduced by this Regulation do not prejudice Community or national rules concerning professional secrecy;

Whereas the Regulation thus amended should be published in its entirety,

HAS ADOPTED THIS REGULATION:

TITLE I

General principles

Article 1

Without prejudice to Articles 11, 12 and 13, imports into the Community covered by the Annex to this Regulation shall not be subject to any quantitative restriction.

Article 2

1. The Council may, acting by a qualified majority on a proposal from the Commission, resolve that the Annex to this Regulation be extended to include other products, provided that such action is not liable to create a situation where the application of protective measures within the meaning of Title V would be justified.

2. Where the Commission finds that, by virtue of the revocation of a quantitative restriction by a Member State, a product is liberalised throughout the Community, it may decide to include that product in the common liberalisation list, unless a Member State, in the course of consultation to be carried out beforehand in accordance with Article 5(4), requests that a proposal within the meaning of paragraph 1 of this Article be submitted to the Council.

TITLE II

Community information and consultation procedure

Article 3

1. Member States shall notify the Commission:

(a) where trends in imports appear to call for protective measures;

(b) where, following their usual administrative procedures and in the light of experience, they find that the granting of an import authorisation applied for might prejudice the success of any subsequent application of protective measures within the meaning of Title V. Notification must be given in all cases where applications are made for documents for the importation of a product in unusually increased quantities or on exceptional terms or conditions.

2. The information referred to in paragraph 1 shall contain the available evidence on the basis of the criteria laid down in Article 9.

3. The Commission shall inform the other Member States forthwith.

Article 4

1. Consultations may be held at any time, either at the request of a Member State or on the initiative of the Commission. Such consultations shall in any event take place before the introduction of any measure pursuant to Articles 10, 11 or 12.

2. In the case referred to in Article 3(1) (a), consultations shall take place within eight working days following receipt by the Commission of the notification provided for in that Article.

3. In the case of notifications to be made under Article 3(1) (b) concerning import authorisations, if within four working days following receipt by the Commission of notifications of the application made to a Member State no consultation has been initiated, the authorisation applied for may be granted. If, however, consultations are held, a further period of four working days from the expiry of the above period must be allowed to elapse, unless neither any Member State nor the Commission raised any objections at the time of the consultations to the authorisation being granted sooner.

Article 5

1. Consultation shall take place within an Advisory Committee (hereinafter called 'the Committee', which shall consist of representatives of each Member State with a representative of the Commission as chairman.

2. The Committee shall meet when convened by its chairman; he shall provide the Member States, as promptly as possible, with all relevant information.

3. Consultation shall in particular cover:

(a) the terms and conditions of importation, import trends, and the various aspects of the economic and commercial situation as regards the product in question;

(b) the measures to be adopted.

4. The above paragraphs shall not preclude reference by the Community authorities to general information and in particular to reasons on which decisions taken in pursuance of this Regulation are based. These authorities must, however, take into account the legitimate interest of the legal and natural persons concerned that their business secrets should not be divulged.

Article 9

1. The examination of the trend of imports, of the conditions in which they take place and of the substantial injury or threat of substantial injury to Community producers resulting from such imports, shall cover in particular the following factors:

(a) the volume of imports, in particular where there has been a significant increase, either in absolute terms or relative to production or consumption in the Community;

(b) the prices of the imports, in particular where there has been a significant price undercutting as compared with the price of a like product in the Community;

(c) the consequent impact on the Community producers of similar or directly competitive products as indicated by trends in certain economic factors such as:

- production,

- utilisation of capacity,

- stocks,

- sales,

- market share,

- prices (i.e. depression of prices or prevention of price increases which would normally have occurred)

- profits,

- return on capital employed,

- cash flow,

- employment.

2. In conducting the investigation, the Commission shall take into account the economic system peculiar to State-trading countries.

3. Where a threat of serious injury is alleged, the Commission shall also examine whether it is clearly foreseeable that a particular situation is likely to develop into actual injury. In this regard account may be taken of factors such as:

(a) rate of increase of the exports to the Community;

(b) export capacity in the country of origin or export, already in existence or which will be operational in the foreseeable future, and the likelihood that the resulting exports will be to the Community.

TITLE IV

Surveillance

Article 10

1. Where Community interests so require, the Commission, at the request
of a Member State or on its own initiative, may:

(a) decide that retrospective surveillance should be exercised over
certain imports, such surveillance to be conducted in accordance
with a procedure to be laid down by the Commission;

(b) decide that, in order to keep a check on trends in certain imports,
such imports should be made subject to the production of an import document, which, subject to provision to the contrary, must
give:

- the name and address of the importer,

- a description of the product with the following particulars:

  - commercial description,

  - tariff heading, or reference number, of the product in the
  goods nomenclature used for foreign trade purposes by the
  country concerned,

  - country of origin,

  - exporting country,

- the cif price, both per unit and total, free-at-frontier, and
the quantity of the product in units customarily used in the
trade in question,

- the expected date of importation.

This document shall be issued or endorsed by Member States;

(c) in cases where the situation referred to in Article 11(1) is likely to arise:

- limit the period of validity of any import documents required
under external trade regulations,

- make the granting of such documents subject to certain conditions and, as an exceptional measure, make the granting of import authorisations subject to the insertion of a revocation
clause or to the prior notification and prior consultation procedure provided for in Article 4(3).

2. Within the first 10 days of each month, Member States shall communicate to the Commission:

(a) details of the sums of money (calculated on the basis of cif prices) and quantities of products in respect of which import documents within the meaning of paragraph 1(b) were issued during the
preceding month;

491

(b) where paragraph 1(a) or (b) has been applied, details of imports during the month preceding the month referred to in subparagraph (a) of this paragraph.

The information supplied by Member States shall be broken down by product and by exporting country. The Commission shall inform the other Member States forthwith.

Arrangements other than those laid down in the first and second subparagraphs may be laid down at the same time and by the same procedure as the surveillance arrangements.

3. The surveillance measures shall be of limited duration. Unless otherwise provided, they shall cease to be valid at the end of the second half-calendar-year following that in which they are introduced.

4. Where the product under prior Community surveillance is not liberalised in a Member State, the import authorisation granted by that Member State may replace the aforementioned import document.

TITLE V

Protective measures

Article 11

1. Where a product is imported into the Community in such greatly increased quantities or on such terms or conditions as to cause or threaten to cause substantial injury to Community producers of like or competing products, and where the interests of the Community require immediate intervention, the Commission may, acting at the request of a Member State or on its own initiative, alter the import rules for that product by providing that it may be put into free circulation only on production of an import authorisation, the granting of which shall be governed by such provisions and subject to such limits as the Commission shall lay down pending any subsequent action by the Council under Article 12.

2. The Council and the Member States shall be notified forthwith of the measures taken; such measures shall take effect immediately.

3. The measures taken shall apply to any product which is put into free circulation after their entry into force. They may be limited to imports intended for certain regions of the Community.

However, such measures shall not prevent the putting into free circulation of products already on their way to the Community, provided that the destination of such products cannot be changed and that those products which under Article 10 may be put into free circulation only on production of an import document are accompanied by such document.

4. Where intervention by the Commission has been requested by a Member State, the Commission shall take a decision within a maximum of five working days of receipt of such a request.

5. Any decision taken by the Commission under this Article shall be communicated to the Council and to the Member States. Any Member State may, within one month following the day of communication, refer such decision to the Council.

6. If a Member State refers the Commission's decision to the Council, the Council shall, acting by a qualified majority, confirm, amend or revoke the decision of the Commission.

If on expiry of three months following referral of the matter to the Council the latter has not taken a decision, the measure taken by the Commission shall be deemed revoked.

Article 12

1. The Council may, in particular in the situation referred to in Article 11(1), adopt appropriate measures. It shall act by a qualified majority on a proposal from the Commission.

2. The measures taken shall apply to every product which is put into free circulation after their entry into force. They may be limited to imports intended for certain regions of the Community.

3. Article 11(3) shall apply.

Article 13

1. A Member State may, as an interim protective measure, alter the import rules for a particular product by providing that it may be put into free circulation only on production of an import authorisation, the granting of which shall be governed by such provisions and subject to such limits as that Member State shall lay down, in particular where the Member State considers that there exists in its territory a situation such as that defined as regards the Community in Article 11(1).

2. The Member State shall inform the Commission and the other Member States by telex of the reasons for and the details of the proposed measures. The Commission and the other Member States shall treat this information in strictest confidence. The Commission shall forthwith convene the Committee. The Member State may take the measures after having heard the opinions expressed by the Committee.

Where a Member State claims that the matter is especially urgent, consultations shall take place within five working days following notification of the Commission. At the end of this five-day period, the Member State may take the said measures. During this period the Member State may make imports of the product in question subject to production of an import authorisation to be granted under the conditions and within the limits to be laid down at the end of the said period.

3. The Commission shall be notified by telex of the measure immediately following its adoption.

4. The notification shall be equivalent to a request within the meaning of Article 11(4). The measures shall operate only until the coming
into operation of the decision taken by the Commission. However,
where the Commission decides not to introduce any measures or adopts
measures pursuant to Article 11, different from those taken by the
Member State, its decision shall apply as from the sixth day following its entry into force, unless the Member State which has taken the
measures refers the decision to the Council; in that case, the national measures shall continue to operate until the entry into force of
the decision taken by the Council and for the maximum of one month
following referral of the matter to the latter. The Council shall take
a decision before the expiry of that period. The Council may under
the same conditions decide in certain cases to extend this period,
which may, in no fashion, exceed a total of three months.

The preceding subparagraph does not affect the Member States' right
of recourse under Article 11(5) and (6).

5. This Article shall apply until 31 December 1984. Before 31 December
1983, the Commission shall propose to the Council amendments to be
made to it. The Council shall act, before 31 December 1984 by a qualified majority, upon the Commission proposal.

Article 14

1. While any measure referred to in Articles 10 to 13 is in operation,
consultations within the Committeee shall be held either at the request of a Member State or on the initiative of the Commission. The
purpose of such consultations shall be:

(a) to examine the effects of such measure;

(b) to ascertain whether the conditions for its application are still
    satisfied.

2. Where the Commission considers that the measure should be revoked
or amended, it shall proceed as follows:

(a) where the Council has taken no decision on a measure taken by
    the Commission, the latter shall amend or revoke such measure
    forthwith and shall immediately deliver a report to the Council;

(b) in all other cases, the Commission shall propose to the Council
    that the measures adopted by the Council be revoked or amended.
    The Council shall act by a qualified majority.

TITLE VI

Transitional and final provisions

Article 15

1. By 31 December 1984 at the latest, the Council shall, acting by
a qualified majority on a proposal from the Commission, decide on the
adjustments to be made to this Regulation for the purpose in partic-

ular of introducing a Community import document valid throughout the Community.

2. Until such time:

- any Member State may refuse to issue or endorse import documents within the meaning of Article 10(1) (b) in respect of persons not established in its territory. This provision shall be without prejudice to obligations arising under the Directives concerning freedom of establishment and freedom to provide services;

- import documents within the meaning of Article 10(1) (b) shall be valid only in the Member State which issued or endorsed them.

Article 16

Without prejudice to other Community provisions, this Regulation shall not preclude the adoption or application by a Member State of prohibitions or quantitative restrictions on imports on grounds of public morality, public policy or public security, the protection of health and life of humans, animals or plants, the protection of national treasures possessing artistic, historic or archaeological value, or the protection of industrial and commercial property.

Article 17

1. This Regulation shall be without prejudice to the operation of the instruments establishing common organisation of agricultural markets, or of the special instruments adopted under Article 235 of the Treaty for processed agricultural products. It shall operate by way of complement to those instruments.

2. However, in the case of products covered by such instruments, Articles 3(1) (b), 4(3) and 10 shall not apply to those in respect of which the Community rules on trade with third countries require the production of a licence or other import document. Articles 11 and 13 shall not apply to those in respect of which such rules make provision for the application of quantitative import restrictions.

Article 18

Regulation (EEC) No 925/79 is hereby repealed. References made to the Regulation thus repealed shall be understood as being made to the present Regulation.

Article 19

This Regulation shall enter into force on the third day following its publication in the *Official Journal of the European Communities*.

This Regulation shall be binding in its entirety and directly applicable in all Member States.

Done at Luxembourg, 30 June 1982.

For the Council
The President
Ph. MAYSTADT

17. COUNCIL REGULATION (EEC) No 1766/82

of 30 June 1982

on common rules for imports from the People's Republic of China

(O.J. No L195, 5 July 1982, p. 21)

THE COUNCIL OF THE EUROPEAN COMMUNITIES,

Having regard to the Treaty establishing the European Economic Community, and in particular Article 113 thereof,

Having regard to the instruments establishing common organisation of agricultural markets and to the instruments concerning processed agricultural products adopted in pursuance of Article 235 of the Treaty, in particular the provisions of those instruments which allow for derogation from the general principle that all quantitative restrictions or measures having equivalent effect may be replaced solely by the measures provided for in those same instruments,

Having regard to the proposal from the Commission,

Whereas the common commercial policy must be based on uniform principles; whereas the import rules established by Regulation (EEC) No 2532/78, as amended by Regulation (EEC) No 799/82, are an important aspect of that policy;

Whereas, provided that they are listed in the Annex to this Regulation, products shall be imported into any part of the Community without quantitative restriction, subject to the exceptions and derogations provided for by Community instruments;

Whereas, however, by reason of the economic system of the People's Republic of China, it is necessary that Member States should notify the Commission when the trend in imports, or the conditions in which imports are made, appear to call for protective measures and that they should in particular advise it of any application for documents for the importation of a product in notably increased quantities or on exceptional terms or conditions, and that they should do so before such documents are issued;

Whereas it is essential that examination should take place at Community level, in particular on the basis of any such information and within an advisory committee, of the terms and conditions of

importation, of import trends; of the various aspects of the economic
and commercial situation, and of the measures, if any, to be taken;

Whereas it may become necessary for certain of these imports to be
made subject to Community surveillance;

Whereas in this case the putting into free circulation of the products
concerned should be made subject to production of an import document
satifying uniform criteria; whereas that document must, on declaration or on simple application by the importer, be issued or endorsed
by the authorities of the Member States within a certain period but
without the importer thereby acquiring any right to import; whereas
the document may not therefore be used until the import rules have
been changed;

Whereas it is in the interest of the Community that the Member States
and the Commission should make as full an exchange as possible of
information resulting from either Community surveillance or surveillance at national level;

Whereas it is for the Commission and the Council to adopt the protective measures called for by the interests of the Community with due
regard for existing international obligations;

Whereas Member States should be empowered, in certain circumstances
and on an interim basis, to take protective measures individually;

Whereas Articles 9(5) and 11(1) of Regulation (EEC) No 2532/78 provide that the Council shall decide on the adjustments to be made to
that Regulation;

Whereas a review of the Regulation, in the light of experience gained
in applying it, has shown that it is necessary to adopt more precise
criteria for assessing possible injury and to introduce an investigation while still allowing the Commission and the Member States to introduce appropriate measures in urgent cases;

Whereas, to this end, more detailed provisions should be introduced
on the opening of investigations, on the checks and inspections
required, on the hearing of those concerned, the treatment of information obtained and the criteria for assessing injury;

Whereas the provisions on the investigations introduced by this Regulation do not prejudice Community or national rules concerning prof-
fessional secrecy;

Whereas the Regulation thus amended should be published in its entirety,

HAS ADOPTED THIS REGULATION:

TITLE I

General principles

Article 1

Without prejudice to Articles 11, 12 and 13, imports from the People's Republic of China into the Community covered by the Annex to this Regulation shall not be subject to any quantitative restriction.

Article 2

1. The Council may, acting by a qualified majority on a proposal from the Commission, resolve that the Annex to this Regulation be extended to include other products, provided that such action is not liable to create a situation where the application of protective measures within the meaning of Title V would be justified.

2. Where the Commission finds that by virtue of the revocation of a quantitative restriction by a Member State a product is liberalised throughout the Community, it may decide to include that product in the common liberalisation list, unless a Member State, in the course of consumation to be carried out beforehand in accordance with Article 5(4), requests that a proposal within the meaning of paragraph 1 of this Article be submitted to the Council.

TITLE II

Community information and consultation procedure

Article 3

1. Member States shall notify the Commission:

(a) where trends in imports appear to call for protective measures;

(b) where, following their usual administrative procedures and in the light of experience, they find that the granting of an import authorisation applied for might prejudice the success of any subsequent application of protective measures within the meaning of Title V. Notification must be given in all cases where applications are made for documents for the importation of a product in unusually increased quantities or on exceptional terms or conditions.

2. The information referred to in paragraph 1 shall contain the available evidence on the basis of the criteria laid down in Article 9.

3. The Commission shall inform the other Member States forthwith.

Article 4

1. Consultations may be held at any time, either at the request of a Member State or on the initiative of the Commission. Such consultations shall in any event take place before the introduction of any measure pursuant to Articles 10, 11 or 12.

2. In the case referred to in Article 3(1) (a), consultations shall

498

take place within eight working days following receipt by the Commission of the notification provided for in that Article.

3. In the case of notifications to be made under Article 3(1) (b) concerning import authorisations, if within four working days following receipt by the Commission of notification of the application made to a Member State no consultation has been initiated, the authorisation applied for may be granted. If, however, consultations are held, a further period of four working days from the expiry of the above period must be allowed to elapse unless neither any Member State nor the Commission raised any objection at the time of the consultation to the authorisation being granted sooner.

Article 5

1. Consultation shall take place within an Advisory Committee (hereinafter called 'the Committee'), which shall consist of representatives of each Member State with a representative of the Commission as chairman.

2. The Committee shall meet when convened by its chairman; he shall provide the Member States, as promptly as possible, with all relevant information.

3. Consultation shall in particular cover:

(a) the terms and conditions of importation, import trends, and the various aspects of the economic and commercial situation as regards the product in question;

(b) the measures to be adopted.

4. Consultations may be in writing, if necessary. The Commission shall in this event inform the Member States, which may express their opinion or request oral consultations within a period of five to eight working days to be decided by the Commission.

TITLE III

Community investigation procedure

Article 6

1. Where, after consultation, it is apparent to the Commission that there is sufficient evidence to justify an investigation, the Commission shall:

(a) announce the opening of an investigation in the *Official Journal of the European Communities*; such announcements shall give a summary of the information received, and stipulate that all relevant information is to be communicated to the Commission; it shall state the period within which interested parties may make known their views in writing;

(b) commence the investigation, acting in cooperation with the Member

States.

2. The Commission shall seek all information it deems to be necessary and, where it considers it appropriate, after consulting the Committee, endeavour to check this information with importers, traders, agents, producers, trade associations and organisations.

The Commission shall be assisted in this task by staff of the Member State on whose territory these checks are being carried out, provided this Member State so wishes.

3. The Member States shall supply the Commission, at its request and following procedures laid down by it, with all information at their disposal on developments in the market of the product being investigated.

4. The Commission may hear the interested natural and legal persons. Such parties must be heard where they have applied in writing within the period laid down in the notice published in the *Official Journal of the European Communities*, showing that they are actually likely to be affected by the outcome of the investigations and that there are special reasons for them to be heard orally.

5. Where the information requested by the Commission is not supplied within a reasonable period, or the investigation is significantly impeded, findings may be made on the basis of the facts available.

Article 7

1. At the end of the investigation, the Commission shall submit a report on the results to the Committee.

2. If the Commission considers that no Community surveillance or protective measures are necessary, it shall publish in the *Official Journal of the European Communities*, after consulting the Committee, a notice that the investigations are closed, stating the main conclusions of the investigations.

3. If the Commission considers that Community surveillance or protective measures are necessary, it shall take the necessary decisions in accordance with Titles IV and V.

4. Notwithstanding the provisions of this Title, surveillance measures and, in an emergency, protective measures may be taken at any time, in accordance with Articles 11 to 13.

In the latter case, the Commission shall immediately take the investigation measures it considers to be still necessary. The results of the investigation shall be used to re-examine the measures taken.

Article 8

1. Information received in pursuance of this Regulation shall be used only for the purpose for which it was requested.

2. (a) Neither the Council, nor the Commission, nor Member States, nor the officials of any of these, shall reveal any information of a confidential nature received in pursuance of this Regulation, or any information provided on a confidential basis, without specific permission from the supplier of such information.

(b) Each request for confidentiality shall state the reasons why the information is confidential.

However, if it appears that a request for confidentiality is not justified and that the supplier of the information wishes neither to make it public nor to authorise its disclosure in general terms or in the form of a summary, the information concerned may be disregarded.

3. Information will in any case be considered to be confidential if its disclosure is likely to have a significantly adverse effect upon the supplier or the source of such information.

4. The above paragraphs shall not preclude reference by the Community authorities to general information and in particular to reasons on which decisions taken in pursuance of this Regulation are based. These authorities must,however, take into account the legitimate interest of the legal and natural persons concerned that their business secrets should not be divulged.

Article 9

1. The examination of the trend of imports, of the conditions in which they take place and of the substantial injury or threat of substantial injury to Community producers resulting from such imports, shall cover in particular the following factors:

(a) the volume of imports, in particular where there has been a significant increase, either in absolute terms or relative to production or consumption in the Community;

(b) the prices of the imports, in particular where there has been a significant price undercutting as compared with the price of a like product in the Community;

(c) the consequent impact on the Community producers of similar or directly competitive products as indicated by trends in certain economic factors such as:

- production,

- utilisation of capacity,

- stocks,

- sales,

- market share,

- prices (i.e. depression of prices or prevention of price increases which would normally have occurred),

- profits,

- return on capital employed,

- cash flow,

- employment.

2. In conducting the investigation, the Commission shall take into account the economic system peculiar to the People's Republic of China.

3. Where a threat of serious injury is alleged, the Commission shall also examine whether it is clearly foreseeable that a particular situation is likely to develop into actual injury. In this regard account may be taken of factors such as:

(a) the rate of increase of the exports to the Community;

(b) export capacity of China, already in existence or which will be operational in the foreseeable future, and the likelihood that the resulting exports will be to the Community.

TITLE IV

Surveillance

Article 10

1. Where Community interests so require, the Commission, at the request of a Member State or on its own initiative, may:

(a) decide that retrospective surveillance should be exercised over certain imports, such surveillance to be conducted in accordance with a procedure to be laid down by the Commission;

(b) decide that, in order to keep a check on trends in certain imports, such imports should be made subject to the production of an import document, which, subject to provision to the contrary, must give:

- the name and address of the importer,

- a description of the product with the following particulars:

  - commercial description,

  - tariff heading, or reference number, of the product in the goods nomenclature used for foreign trade purposes by the country concerned,

  - country of origin,

502

- exporting country,

- the cif price, both per unit and total, free-at-frontier, and the quantity of the product in units customarily used in the trade in question,

- the expected date of importation.

This document shall be issued or endorsed by Member States, free of charge, for any quantity requested and as quickly as possible following submission, in accordance with the national laws in force, either of a declaration or of an application by any Community importer, regardless of his place of business in the Community, without prejudice to the observance of the other conditions required by the regulations in force;

(c) in cases where the situation referred to in Article 11(1) is likely to arise:

- limit the period of validity of any import documents required under external trade regulations,

- make the granting of such documents subject to certain conditions and, as an exceptional measure, make the granting of import authorisations subject to the insertion of a revocation clause or to the prior notification and prior consultation procedure provided for in Article 4(3).

2. Paragraph 1 shall not preclude the putting into free circulation of the product in question if the unit price at which the transaction is effected exceeds that indicated in the import document, or if the total value or quantity of the products to be imported exceeds the value or quantity given in the import document by less than 5 %. The Commission, having heard the opinions expressed in the Committee and taking account of the nature of the products and other special features of the transactions concerned, may fix a different percentage, which, however, should not normally exceed 10 %.

3. Within the first ten days of each month, Member States shall communicate to the Commission:

(a) details of the sums of money (calculated on the basis of cif prices) and quantities of products in respect of which import documents within the meaning of paragraph 1(b) were issued during the preceding month;

(b) where paragraph 1(a) or (b) has been applied, details of imports during the month preceding the month referred to in subparagraph (a) of this paragraph.

The information supplied by Member States shall be broken down by product. The Commission shall inform the other Member States forthwith.

Arrangements other than those laid down in the first and second subparagraphs may be laid down at the same time and by the same procedure as the surveillance arrangements.

503

4. The surveillance measures shall be of limited duration. Unless otherwise provided, they shall cease to be valid at the end of the second half-calendar-year following that in which they are introduced.

5. Where the product under prior Community surveillance is not liberalised in a Member State, the import authorisation granted by that Member State may replace the aforementioned import document.

TITLE V

Protective measures

Article 11

1. Where a product is imported into the Community in such greatly increased quantities or on such terms or conditions as to cause or threaten to cause substantial injury to Community producers of like or competing products, and where the interests of the Community require immediate intervention, the Commission may, acting at the request of a Member State or on its own initiative, alter the import rules for that product by providing that it may be put into free circulation only on production of an import authorisation, the granting of which shall be governed by such provisions and subject to such limits as the Commission shall lay down pending any subsequent action by the Council under Article 12.

2. The Council and the Member States shall be notified forthwith of the measures taken; such measures shall take effect immediately.

3. The measures taken shall apply to any product which is put into free circulation after their entry into force. They may be limited to imports intended for certain regions of the Community.

However such measures shall not prevent the putting into free circulation of products already on their way to the Community, provided that the destination of such products cannot be changed and that those products which under Article 10 may be put into free circulation only on production of an import document are accompanied by such document.

4. Where intervention by the Commission has been requested by a Member State, the Commission shall take a decision within a maximum of five working days of receipt of such request.

5. Any decision taken by the Commission under this Article shall be communicated to the Council and to the Member States. Any Member State may, within one month following the day of communication, refer such decision to the Council.

6. If a Member State refers the Commission's decision to the Council, the Council shall, acting by a qualified majority, confirm, amend or revoke the decision of the Commission.

If on expiry of three months following referral of the matter to the Council the latter has not taken a decision, the measure taken by the Commission shall be deemed revoked.

Article 12

1. The Council may, in particular in the situation referred to in Article 11(1), adopt appropriate measures. It shall act by a qualified majority on a proposal from the Commission.

2. The measures taken shall apply to every product which is put into free circulation after their entry into force. They may be limited to imports intended for certain regions of the Community.

3. Article 11(3) shall apply.

Article 13

1. A Member State may, as an interim protective measure, alter the import rules for a particular product by providing that it may be put into free circulation only on production of an import authorisation, the granting of which shall be governed by such provisions and subject to such limits as that Member State shall lay down, in particular where the Member State considers that there exists in its territory a situation such as that defined as regards the Community in Article 11 (1).

2. The Member State shall inform the Commission and the other Member States by telex of the reasons for and the details of the proposed measures. The Commission and the other Member States shall treat this information in strictest confidence. The Commission shall forthwith convene the Committee.

The Member State may take the measures after having heard the opinions expressed by the Committee.

Where a Member State claims that the matter is especially urgent, consultations shall take place within five working days following notification of the Commission, at the end of this five-day period, the Member State may take the said measures. During this period the Member State may make imports of the product in question subject to production of an import authorisation to be granted under the conditions and within the limits to be laid down at the end of the said period.

3. The Commission shall be notified by telex of the measure immediately following its adoption.

4. The notification shall be equivalent to a request within the meaning of Article 11(4). The measures shall operate only until the coming into operation of the decision taken by the Commission. However, where the Commission decides not to introduce any measure or adopts measures pursuant to Article 11, different from those taken by the Member State, its decision shall apply as from the sixth day following its entry into force, unless the Member State which has taken the measures refers the decision to the Council; in that case, the national measures shall continue to operate until the entry into force of the decision taken by the Council and for the maximum of one month following referral of the matter to the latter. The Council shall take a decision before the expiry of that period. The Council may under the same conditions decide in certain cases to extend this period, which may, in

no fashion, exceed a total of three months.

The preceding subparagraph does not affect the Member States' right of recourse under Article 11(5) and (6).

5. This Article shall apply until 31 December 1984. Before 31 December 1983, the Commission shall propose to the Council amendments to be made to it. The Council shall act, before 31 December 1984 by a qualified majority, upon the Commission proposal.

Article 14

1. While any measure referred to in Articles 10 to 13 is in operation, consultations within the Committee shall be held either at the request of a Member State or on the initiative of the Commission. The purpose of such consultations shall be:

(a) to examine the effects of such measure;

(b) to ascertain whether the conditions for its application are still satisfied.

2. Where the Commission considers that the measure should be revoked or amended it shall proceed as follows:

(a) where the Council has taken no decision on a measure taken by the Commission, the latter shall amend or revoke such measures forthwith and shall immediately deliver a report to the Council;

(b) in all other cases the Commission shall propose to the Council that the measures adopted by the Council be revoked or amended. The Council shall act by a qualified majority.

TITLE VI

Transitional and final provisions

Article 15

1. By 31 December 1984 at the latest, the Council shall, acting by a qualified majority on a proposal from the Commission, decide on the adjustments to be made to this Regulation for the purpose in particular of introducing a Community import document valid throughout the Community.

2. Until such time:

- any Member State may refuse to issue or endorse import documents within the meaning of Article 10(1) (b) in respect of persons not established in its territory. This provision shall be without prejudice to obligations arising under the Directives concerning freedom of establishment and freedom to provide services;

- import documents within the meaning of Article 10(1) (b) shall be valid only in the Member State which issued or endorsed them.

Article 16

Without prejudice to other Community provisions, this Regulation shall not preclude the adoption or application by a Member State of prohibitions or quantitative restrictions on imports on grounds of public morality, public policy or public security, the protection of health and life of humans, animals or plants, the protection of national treasures possessing artistic, historic or archaeological value, or the protection of industrial and commercial property.

Article 17

1. This Regulation shall be without prejudice to the operation of the instruments establishing common organisation of agricultural markets, or of the special instruments adopted under Article 235 of the Treaty for processed agricultural products. It shall operate by way of complement to those instruments.

2. However, in the case of products covered by such instruments, Articles 3(1) (b), 4(3) and 10 shall not apply to those in respect of which the Community rules on trade with third countries require the production of a licence or other import document. Articles 11 and 13 shall not apply to those in respect of which such rules make provision for the application of quantitative import restrictions.

Article 18

Regulation (EEC) No 2532/78 is hereby repealed.

References made to the Regulation thus repealed shall be understood as being made to the present Regulation.

Article 19

This Regulation shall enter into force on the third day following its publication in the *Official Journal of the European Communities*.

This Regulation shall be binding in its entirety and directly applicable in all Member States.

Done at Luxembourg, 30 June 1982.

For the Council
The President
Ph. MAYSTAD

18. COUNCIL REGULATION (EEC) No 3017/79

of 20 December 1979

on protection against dumped or subsidised imports from countries
not members of the European Economic Community
(O.J. No L339, 31 December 1979, p. 1)

THE COUNCIL OF THE EUROPEAN COMMUNITIES,

Having regard to the Treaty establishing the European Economic Community, and in particular Article 113 thereof,

Having regard to the Regulations establishing the common organisation
of agricultural markets and the Regulations adopted under Article 235 of
the Treaty, applicable to goods manufactured from agricultural products, and in particular the provisions of those Regulations which
allow for derogation from the general principle that protective measures
at frontiers may be replaced solely by the measures provided for in
those Regulations,

Having regard to the proposal from the Commission,

Whereas by Regulation (EEC) No 459/68, as last amended by Regulation
(EEC) No 1681/79, the Council adopted common rules for protection
against dumped or subsidised imports from countries which are not
members of the European Economic Community;

Whereas these rules were adopted in accordance with existing international obligations, in particular those arising from Article VI of the
General Agreement on tariffs and trade (hereinafter referred to as
GATT) and from the first Agreement on Implementation of Article VI
of the GATT (1968 Anti-Dumping Code);

Whereas the multilateral trade negotiations concluded in 1979 have led
to a new Agreement on Implementation of Article VI of the GATT (1979
Anti-Dumping Code) and an Agreement on Interpretation and Application
of Articles VI, XVI and XXIII of the GATT, which concern subsidies
and countervailing measures;

Whereas it is therefore appropriate to amend the Community rules in
the light of the 1979 Agreements, in particular of their provisions
relating to subsidies and possible countermeasures, to the determination of injury, especially the criteria to be applied and the new
rules on causality and regional protection, to undertakings and
their monitoring, to the period of validity of provisional duties and
to the possible retroactive application of anti-dumping and countervailing duties;

508

Whereas in implementing these rules it is essential, in order to maintain the balance of rights and obligations which these Agreements
sought to establish, that the Community take account of their interpretation by the Community's major trading partners, as reflected in
legislation or established practice;

Whereas it is therefore desirable that the rules for determining normal
value should be presented clearly and in sufficient detail; whereas
it should be specifically provided that where sales on the domestic
market of the country of export or origin do not for any reason form
a proper basis for determining the existence of dumping, recourse may
be had to a constructed normal value; whereas it is appropriate to
give examples of situations which may be considered as not representing the ordinary course of trade, in particular where a product is
sold at prices which are less than the costs of production, or where
transactions take place between parties which are associated or which
have a compensatory arrangement; whereas it is appropriate to list
the possible methods of determining normal value in such circumstances;

Whereas it is expedient to define the export price and to enumerate
the necessary adjustments to be made in those cases where reconstruction of this price from the first open-market price is deemed appropriate;

Whereas for the purpose of ensuring a fair comparison between export
price and normal value, it is advisable to establish guidelines for
determining the adjustments to be made in respect of differences in
physical characteristics, in quantities, in conditions and terms of
sale, and in the level of trade and to draw attention to the fact
that the burden of proof falls on any person claiming such adjustments;

Whereas the term 'dumping margin' should be clearly defined and the
Community's established practice for methods of calculation where
prices or margins vary codified;

Whereas it seems advisable to lay down in adequate detail the manner
in which the amount of any subsidy is to be determined;

Whereas it seems appropriate to set out certain factors which may be
relevant for the determination of injury;

Whereas it is necessary to lay down the procedures for anyone acting
on behalf of a Community industry which considers itself injured or
threatened by dumped or subsidised imports to lodge a complaint;
whereas it seems appropriate to make it clear that in the case of
withdrawal of a complaint, proceedings may, but need not necessarily,
be terminated;

Whereas there should be cooperation between the Member States and the
Commission both as regards information about the existence of dumping or subsidisation and injury resulting therefrom, and as regards
the subsequent examination of the matter at Community level; whereas,
to this end, consultations should take place within an advisory committee;

Whereas it is appropriate to lay down clearly the rules of procedure to be followed during the investigation, in particular the rights and obligations of the Community authorities and the parties involved, and the conditions under which interested parties may have access to information and may ask to be informed of the essential facts and considerations on the basis of which it is intended to recommend definitive measures;

Whereas it is necessary that the Community's decision-making process permit rapid and efficient action, in particular through measures taken by the Commission, as for instance the imposition of provisional duties;

Whereas, in order to discourage dumping, it is appropriate to provide, in cases where the facts as finally established show that there is dumping and injury, for the possibility of definitive collection of provisional duties even if the imposition of a definitive anti-dumping duty is not decided on, on particular grounds;

Whereas it is essential, in order to ensure that anti-dumping and countervailing duties are levied in a correct and uniform manner, that common rules for the application of such duties be laid down; whereas, by reason of the nature of the said duties, such rules may differ from the rules for the levying of normal import duties;

Whereas it is appropriate to provide for open and fair procedures for the review of measures taken, and for the investigation to be reopened when the circumstances so require;

Whereas appropriate procedures should be established for examining applications for refunds of anti-dumping duties;

Whereas this Regulation should not prevent the adoption of special measures where this does not run counter to the Community's obligations under the GATT;

Whereas agricultural products and products derived therefrom might also be dumped or subsidised; whereas it is, therefore, necessary to supplement the import rules generally applicable to these products by making provision for protective measures against such practices;

Whereas it is appropriate to take advantage of this occasion to proceed to a general streamlining, linguistic simplification and consolidation of the rules in question,

HAS ADOPTED THIS REGULATION:

Article 1

Applicability

This Regulation lays down provisions for protection against dumped or subsidised imports from countries not members of the European Economic Community.

Article 2

Dumping

A. PRINCIPLE

1. An anti-dumping duty may be applied to any dumped product whose
entry for consumption in the Community causes injury.

2. A product shall be considered to have been dumped if its export
price to the Community is less than the normal value of the like product.

B. NORMAL VALUE

3. For the purposes of this Regulation, the normal value shall be:

(a) the comparable price actually paid or payable in the ordinary
course of trade for the like product intended for consumption in
the exporting country or country of origin; or

(b) when there are no sales of the like product in the ordinary course
of trade on the domestic market of the exporting country or country of origin, or when such sales do not permit a proper comparison:

   (i) the comparable price of the like product when exported to any
   third country, which may be the highest such export price but
   should be a representative price, or

   (ii) the constructed value, i.e. the costs in the ordinary course
   of trade, of materials and manufacture, in the country of origin, plus a reasonable margin for overheads and profit; as a
   general rule and provided that a profit is normally realised
   on sales of products of the same general category on the domestic market of the country of origin, the addition for profit
   shall not exceed such normal profit. In other cases, the addition shall be determined on any reasonable basis, using available information.

4. Whenever there are reasonable grounds for believing or suspecting
that the price at which a product is actually sold for consumption in
the country of origin is less than all costs, both fixed and variable,
ordinarily incurred in its production, sales at such prices may be
considered as not having been made in the ordinary course of trade if
they:

(a) have been made over an extended period of time and in substantial
quantities; and

(b) are not at prices which permit recovery of all costs within a
reasonable period of time in the normal course of trade.

In such circumstances, the normal value may be determined on the basis
of the remaining sales on the domestic market made at a price which

is not less than the cost of production or on the basis of export sales to third countries, on the basis of the constructed value or by adjusting the sub-production-cost price referred to above in order to eliminate loss and provide for a reasonable profit. Such normal-value calculations shall be based on available information.

5. In the case of imports from non-market economy countries and, in particular, those to which Regulations (EEC) No 2532/78[1] and (EEC) No 925/79[2] apply, normal value shall be determined in an appropriate and not unreasonable manner on the basis of one of the following criteria:

(a) the price at which the like product of a market economy third country is actually sold:

    (i) for consumption on the domestic market of that country, or

    (ii) to other countries, including the Community; or

(b) the constructed value of the like product in a market economy third country; or

(c) if neither price nor constructed value as established under (a) or (b) above provides an adequate basis, the price actually paid or payable in the Community for the like product, duly adjusted, if necessary, to include a reasonable profit margin.

6. Where a product is not imported directly from the country of origin but is exported to the Community from an intermediate country, the normal value shall be the comparable price actually paid or payable for the like product on the domestic market of either the country of export or the country of origin. The latter basis might be appropriate *inter alia*, where the product is merely trans-shipped through the country of export, where such products are not produced in the country of export or where no comparable price for it exists in the country of export.

7. For the purpose of determining normal value, transactions between parties which are associated or which have a compensatory arrangement may be considered as not being in the ordinary course of trade unless the Community authorities are satisfied that the prices and costs involved are comparable to those involved in transactions between parties which have no such link.

C. EXPORT PRICE

8. (a) The export price shall be the price actually paid or payable for the product sold for export to the Community.

    (b) In cases where there is no export price or where it appears that there is an association or a compensatory arrangement between the exporter and the importer or a third party, or that for other reasons the price actually paid or payable for the product sold for export to the Community is unreliable, the export price may be constructed on the basis of the price at which the imported product is first resold to an independent buyer, or if the product is not resold to an independent buyer, or not resold in the condition imported, on any reasonable basis. In such cases, allowance shall be made for all costs incurred between importation and resale, including all duties and taxes, and for a reasonable profit margin.

Such allowances shall include, in particular, the following:

(i) usual transport, insurance, handling, loading and ancillary costs;

(ii) customs duties, any anti-dumping duties and other taxes payable in the importing country by reason of the importation or sale of the goods;

(iii) a reasonable margin for overheads and profit and/or any commission usually paid or agreed.

D. COMPARISON

9. For the purposes of a fair comparison, the export price and the normal value shall be on a comparable basis as regards physical characteristics of the product, quantities, and conditions and terms of sale. They shall normally be compared at the same level of trade, preferably at the ex-factory level, and as nearly as possible at the same time.

10. If the export price and the normal value are not on a comparable basis in respect of the factors mentioned in paragraph 9, due allowance shall be made in each case, on its merits, for differences affecting price comparability. Where an interested party claims such an allowance, it must prove that its claim is justified. The following guidelines shall apply in determining these allowances:

(a) differences in physical characteristics of the product: allowance for such differences shall normally be based on the effect on the market value in the country of origin or export; however, where domestic pricing data in that country are not available or do not permit a fair comparison, the calculation shall be based on those production costs accounting for such differences;

(b) differences in quantities: allowances shall be made when the amount of any price differential is wholly or partly due to either:

(i) price discounts for quantity sales which have been made freely available in the normal course of trade over a representative preceding period of time, usually not less than six months, and in respect of a substantial proportion, usually not less than 20 %, of the total sales of the product under consideration made on the domestic market or, where applicable, on a third-country market; deferred discounts may be recognised if they are based on consistent pracice in prior periods, or on an undertaking to comply with the conditions required to qualify for the deferred discount, or

(ii) to savings in the cost of producing different quantities.

513

However, when the export price is based on quantities which are
less than the smallest quantity sold on the domestic market, or,
if applicable, to third countries, then the allowance shall be
determined in such a manner as to reflect the higher price for
the smaller quantity would be sold on the domestic market, or, if
applicable, on a third-country market;

(c) differences in conditions and terms of sale: allowances shall be
limited, in general, to those differences which bear a direct relationship to the sales under consideration and include, for example, differences in duties and indirect taxation, credit terms,
guarantees, warranties, technical assistance, servicing, commissions
or salaries paid to salesmen, packing, transport, insurance, handling, loading and ancillary costs; allowances generally will not
be made for differences in overheads and general expenses, including research and development costs, or advertising; the amount
of these allowances shall normally be determined by the cost of
such differences to the seller, though consideration may also be
given to their effect on the value of the product;

(d) differences in the level of trade: where sales at the same level
of trade do not exist or are insufficient to be regarded as representative, the allowance to be made on sales at a different
level of trade shall be based on the costs directly attributable
to that difference;

(e) allocation of costs: in general, all cost calculations shall be
based on available accounting data, normally allocated, where
necessary, in proportion to the turnover for each product and market under consideration.

11. No product shall be considered to have been dumped by reason of
the exemption of such product from duties or taxes borne by the like
product when destined for consumption in the country of origin or
export, or by reason of the refund of such duties or taxes.

E. LIKE PRODUCT

12. For the purpose of this Regulation, 'like product' means a product
which is identical, i.e., alike in all respects, to the product under
consideration, or, in the absence of such a product, another product
which has characteristics closely resembling those of the product
under consideration.

F. DUMPING MARGIN

13. (a) 'Dumping margin' means the amount by which the normal value
exceeds the export price.

(b) Where prices vary, the dumping margin may be established on a
transaction-by-transaction basis or by reference to the most
frequently occurring, representative or weighted average
prices.

(c) Where dumping margins vary, weighted averages may be established.

Article 3

Subsidies

1. A countervailing duty may be imposed for the purpose of offsetting any subsidy bestowed, directly or indirectly, in the country of origin or export, upon the manufacture, production, export or transport of any product whose entry for consumption in the Community causes injury.

2. Subsidies bestowed on exports include, but are not limited to, the practices listed in the Annex.

3. The exemption of a product from import charges or indirect taxes, as defined in the notes to the Annex, effectively borne by the like product when destined for consumption in the country of origin or export, or the refund of such charges or taxes, shall not be considered as a subsidy for the purposes of this Regulation.

4. (a) The amount of the subsidy shall be determined per unit of the subsidised product exported to the Community.

   (b) In establishing the amount of any subsidy the following elements shall be deducted from the total subsidy:

      (i) any application fee, or other costs necessarily incurred in order to qualify for, or receive benefit of, the subsidy;

      (ii) export taxes, duties or other charges levied on the export of the product to the Community specifically intended to offset the subsidy.

   Where an interested party claims a deduction, it must prove that the claim is justified.

   (c) Where the subsidy is not granted by reference to the quantities manufactured, produced, exported or transported, the amount shall be determined by allocating the value of the subsidy as appropriate over the level of production or exports of the product concerned during a suitable period. Normally this period shall be the accounting year of the beneficiary. However, where the subsidy is based upon the acquisition or future acquisition of fixed assets the period shall correspond to a reasonable period for depreciation, except where the assets are non-depreciating, in which case the subsidy shall be valued as an interest free loan.

   (d) The value of loan or guarantee subsidies shall generally be considered as the difference between interest rates paid or payable by the beneficiary and normal commercial rates effectively payable on comparable loans or guarantees.

   (e) In the case of imports from non-market economy countries and in particular those to which Regulations (EEC) No 2532/78 and

(EEC) No 925/79 apply, the amount of any subsidy may be determined in an appropriate and not unreasonable manner, by comparing the export price as calculated in accordance with Article 2(8) with the normal value as determined in accordance with Article 2(5). Article 2(10) shall apply to such a comparison.

(f) Where the amount of subsidisation varies, weighted averages may be established.

Article 4

Injury

1. A determination of injury shall be made only if the dumped or subsidised imports are, through the effects of dumping or subsidisation, causing injury i.e., causing or threatening to cause material injury to an established Community industry or materially retarding the establishment of such an industry. Injuries caused by other factors, such as volume and prices of imports which are not dumped or subsidised, or contraction in demand, which, individually or in combination, also adversely affect the Community industry must not be attributed to the dumped or subsidised imports.

2. An examination of injury shall involve the following factors, no one or several of which can necessarily give decisive guidance:

(a) volume of dumped or subsidised imports, in particular whether there has been a significant increase, either in absolute terms or relative to production or consumption in the Community;

(b) the prices of dumped or subsidised imports, in particular whether there has been a significant price undercutting as compared with a like product in the Community;

(c) the consequent impact on the industry concerned as indicated by actual or potential trends in the relevant economic factors such as:

- production,

- utilisation of capacity,

- stocks,

- sales,

- market share,

- prices (i.e., depression of prices or prevention of price increases which otherwise would have occurred),

- profits,

- return on investment,

- cash flow,

– employment.

3. A determination of threat of injury may only be made where a particular situation is likely to develop into actual injury. In this regard account may be taken of factors such as:

(a) rate of increase of the dumped or subsidised exports to the Community;

(b) export capacity in the country of origin or export, already in existence or which will be operational in the foreseeable future, and the likelihood that the resulting exports will be to the Community;

(c) the nature of any subsidy and the trade effects likely to arise therefrom.

4. The effect of the dumped or subsidised imports shall be assessed in relation to the Community production of the like product when available data permit its separate identification. When the Community production of the like product has no separate identity, the effect of the dumped or subsidised imports shall be assessed in relation to the production of the narrowest group or range of production which includes the like product for which the necessary information can be found.

5. The term 'Community industry' shall be interpreted as referring to the Community producers as a whole of the like product or to those of them whose collective output of the products constitutes a major proportion of the total Community production of those products except that:

– when producers are related to the exporters or importers or are themselves importers of the allegedly dumped or subsidised product the term 'Community industry' may be interpreted as referring to the rest of the producers;

– in exceptional circumstances the Community may, for the production in question, be divided into two or more competitive markets and the producers within each market regarded as a Community industry if,

   (a) the producers within such market sell all or almost all their production of the product in question in that market, and

   (b) the demand in that market is not to any substantial degree supplied by producers of the product in question located elsewhere in the Community.

In such circumstances injury may be found to exist even where a major proportion of the total Community industry is not injured, provided there is a concentration of dumped or subsidised imports into such an isolated market and provided further that the dumped or subsidised imports are causing injury to the producers of all or almost all of the production within such markets.

Article 5

517

Complaint

1. Any natural or legal person, or any association not having legal personality, acting on behalf of a Community industry which considers itself injured or threatened by dumped or subsidised imports may lodge a written complaint.

2. The complaint shall contain sufficient evidence of the existence of dumping or subsidisation and the injury resulting therefrom.

3. The complaint may be submitted to the Commission, or a Member State, which shall forward it to the Commission. The Commission shall send Member States a copy of any complaint it receives.

4. The complaint may be withdrawn, in which case proceedings may be terminated unless such termination would not be in the interest of the Community.

5. Where it becomes apparent after consultation that the complaint does not provide sufficient evidence to justify initiating an investigation, then the complainant shall be so informed.

6. Where, in the absence of any complaint, a Member State is in possession of sufficient evidence both of dumping or subsidisation and of injury resulting therefrom for a Community industry, it shall immediately communicate such evidence to the Commission.

Article 6

Consultations

1. Any consultations provided for in this Regulation shall take place within an Advisory Committee, which shall consist of representatives of each Member State, with a representative of the Commission as chairman. Consultations shall be held immediately on request by a Member State or on the initiative of the Commission.

2. The Committee shall meet when convened by its chairman. He shall provide the Member States, as promptly as possible, with all relevant information.

3. Where necessary, consultation may be inwriting only; in such case the Commission shall notify the Member States and shall specify a period within which they shall be entitled to express their opinions or to request an oral consultation.

4. Consultation shall in particular cover:

(a) the existence of dumping or of a subsidy and the margin or amount thereof;

(b) the existence and extent of injury;

(c) the causal link between the dumped or subsidised imports and injury;

(d) the measures which, in the circumstances, are appropriate to prevent or remedy the injury caused by dumping or the subsidy and
the ways and means for putting such measures into effect.

Article 7

Initiation and subsequent investigation

1. Where, after consultation it is apparent that there is sufficient
evidence to justify initiating a proceeding the Commission shall immediately:

(a) announce the initiation of a proceeding in the *Official Journal
of the European Communities;* such announcements shall indicate
the product and countries concerned, give a summary of the information received, and provide that all relevant information is to
be communicated to the Commisison; it shall state the period within
which interested parties may make known their views in writing
and may apply to be heard orally by the Commission in accordance
with paragraph 5;

(b) so advise the exporters and importers known to the Commission to
be concerned as well as representatives of the exporting country
and the complainants;

(c) commence the investigation at Community level, acting in cooperation with the Member States; such investigation shall cover both
dumping or subsidisation and injury resulting therefrom and shall
be carried out in accordance with paragraphs 2 to 8.

2. (a) The Commission shall seek all information it deems to be necessary and, where it considers it appropriate, examine and verify the records of importers, exporters, traders, agents, producers, trade associations and organisations.

(b) Where necessary the Commission shall, after consultation, carry
out investigations in third countries, provided that the firms
concerned give their consent and the government of the country
has been officially notified and raises no objection. The Commission shall be assisted by officials of those Member States
who so request.

3. (a) The Commission may request Member States:

– to supply information,

– to carry out all necessary checks and inspections, particularly amongst importers, traders and Community producers,

– to carry out investigations in third countries, provided the
firms concerned give their consent and the government of the
country in question has been officially notified and raises
no objection.

(b) Member States shall take whatever steps are necessary in order
to give effect to requests from the Commission. They shall

519

send to the Commission the information requested together with the results of all inspections, checks or investigations carried out.

(c) The Commission shall forward this information to the other Member States forthwith.

(d) Officials of the Commission shall be authorised, if the Commission or a Member State so requests, to assist the officials of Member States in carrying out their duties.

4. (a) The complainant and the importers and exporters known to be concerned, as well as the representatives of the exporting country, may inspect all information made available to the Commission by any party to an investigation as distinct from internal documents prepared by the authorities of the Community or its Member States, provided that it is relevant to the defence of their interests and not confidential within the meaning of Article 8 and that it is used by the Commission in the investigation. To this end, they shall address a written request to the Commission, indicating the information required.

(b) Exporters and importers of the product subject to investigation and, in the case of subsidisation, the representatives of the country of origin, may request to be informed of the essential facts and considerations on the basis of which it is intended to recommend the imposition of definitive duties or the definitive collection of amounts secured by way of a provisional duty.

(c) (i) requests for information pursuant to (b) shall:

(aa) be addressed to the Commission in writing,

(bb) specify the particular issues on which information is sought,

(cc) be received, in cases where a provisional duty has been applied, not later than one month after publication of the imposition of that duty;

(ii) the information may be given either orally or in writing, as considered appropriate by the Commission. It shall not prejudice any subsequent decision which may be taken by the Commission or the Council. Confidential information shall be treated in accordance with Article 8;

(iii) information shall normally be given no later than 15 days prior to the submission by the Commission of any proposal for final action pursuant to Article 12. Representations made after the information is given shall be taken into consideration only if received within a period to be set by the Commission in each case, which shall be at least 10 days, due consideration being given to the urgency of the matter.

5. The Commisison may hear the interested parties. It shall so hear them if they have, within the period prescribed in the notice published

in the *Official Journal of the European Communities*, made a written
request for a hearing showing that they are an interested party likely
to be affected by the result of the proceeding and that there are particular reasons why they should be heard orally.

6. Furthermore, the Commission shall, on request, give the parties
directly concerned an opportunity to meet, so that opposing views may
be presented and any rebuttal, argument put forward. In providing this
opportunity the Commission shall take account of the need to preserve
confidentiality and of the convenience of the parties. There shall be
no obligation on any party to attend a meeting and failure to do so
shall not be prejudicial to that party's case.

7. (a) This Article shall not preclude the Community authorities from
reaching preliminary determinations or from applying provisional measures expeditiously.

(b) In cases in which any interested party or third country refuses
access to, or otherwise does not provide, necessary information
within a reasonable period, or significantly impedes the investigation, preliminary or final findings, affirmative or negative, may be made on the basis of the facts available.

8. Anti-dumping or countervailing proceedings shall not constitute a
bar to customs clearance of the product concerned.

9. A proceeding is concluded either by its termination or by definitive
action. Conclusion should normally take place within one year of initiation of the proceeding.

Article 8

Confidentiality

1. Information received in pursuance of this Regulation shall be used
only for the purpose for which it was requested.

2. (a) Neither the Council, nor the Commission, nor Member States,
nor the officials for any of these, shall reveal any information of a confidential nature received in pursuance of this
Regulation, or any information provided on a confidential basis
by a party to an anti-dumping or countervailing investigation,
without specific permission from the party submitting such information.

(b) Each request for confidential treatment shall indicate why the
information is confidential and shall be accompanied by a non-
confidential summary of the information, or a statement of the
reasons why the information is not susceptible of such summary.

3. Information will ordinarily be considered to be confidential if its
diclosure is likely to have a significantly adverse effect upon the
supplier or the source of such information.

4. However, if it appears that a request for confidentiality is not
warranted and if the supplier is either unwilling to make the informa-

tion public or to authorise its disclosure in generalised or summary form, the information in question may be disregarded.

5. This Article shall not preclude the disclosure of general information by the Community authorities and in particular of the reasons on which decisions taken in pursuance of this Regulation are based. Such disclosure must take into account the legitimate interest of the parties concerned that their business secrets should not be divulged.

Article 9

Termination of proceedings where protective measures are unnecessary

1. If it becomes apparent after consultation that protective measures are unnecessary, then where no objection is raised within the Committee the proceeding shall be terminated. In all other cases the Commission shall submit to the Council forthwith a report on the results of the consultation, together with a proposal that the proceeding be terminated. The proceeding shall stand terminated if, within one month, the Council, acting by a qualified majority, has not decided otherwise.

2. The Commission shall inform any representatives of the country of origin or export and the parties known to be concerned and shall announce the termination in the *Official Journal of the European Communities* setting forth its basic conclusions and a summary of the reasons therefor.

Article 10

Undertakings

1. Where, during the course of a proceeding, undertakings are offered which the Commission after consultation considers acceptable, anti-dumping/anti-subsidy proceedings may be terminated without the imposition of provisional or definitive duties. Such termination shall be decided in conformity with the procedure laid down in Article 9(1) and information shall be given and notice published in accordance with Article 9(2). Such termination does not preclude the definitive collection of amounts secured by way of provisional duties pursuant to Article 12(2).

2. The undertakings referred to under paragraph 1 are those under which:

(a) the subsidy is eliminated or limited, or other measures concerning its injurious effects taken, by the government of the country of origin or export; or

(b) prices are revised or exports cease to the extent that the Commission is satisfied that either the dumping margin or the amount of the subsidy, or the injurious effects thereof, are eliminated. In case of subsidisation the consent of the country of origin or export shall be obtained.

3. Undertakings may be suggested by the Commission, but the fact that such undertakings are not offered or an invitation to do so is not accepted, shall not prejudice consideration of the case. However, the continuation of dumped or subsidised imports may be taken as evidence that a threat of injury is more likely to be realised.

4. If the undertakings are accepted, the investigation of injury shall nevertheless be completed if the Commission, after consultation so decides or if request is made, in the case of dumping, by exporters representing a significant percentage of the trade involved or, in the case of subsidisation, by the country of origin or export. In such a case, if the Commission, after consultation makes a determination of no injury, the undertaking shall automatically lapse. However, where a determination of no threat of injury is due mainly to the existence of an undertaking, the Commission may require that undertaking be maintained.

5. The Commission may require any party from whom an undertaking has been accepted to provide periodically information relevant to the fulfilment of such undertakings, and to permit verification of pertinent data. Non-compliance with such requirements shall be construed as a violation of the undertaking.

6. Where an undertaking has been withdrawn or where the Commission has reason to believe that it has been violated and that further investigation is warranted, it shall forthwith inform the Member States and reopen the proceeding. Furthermore, where the Community interests call for such intervention, it shall immediately apply provisional measures where warranted using the information available.

Article 11

Provisional duties

1. Where preliminary examination shows that dumping or a subsidy exists and that there is sufficient evidence of injury caused thereby and the interests of the Community call for intervention to prevent injury being caused during the proceeding, the Commission acting at the request of a Member State or on its own initiative, shall impose a provisional anti-dumping or countervailing duty. In such cases entry of the products concerned for Community consumption shall be conditional upon the provision of security for the amount of the provisional duty, definitive collection of which shall be determined by the subsequent decision of the Council under Article 12(2).

2. The Commission shall take such provisional action after consultation or, in cases of extreme urgency, after informing the Member States. In the latter case, consultations shall take place 10 days at the latest after notification to the Member States of the action taken by the Commission.

3. Where a Member State requests immediate intervention by the Commission, the Commission shall within a maximum of five working days of receipt of the request, decide whether a provisional anti-dumping or countervailing duty should be imposed.

4. The Commission shall forthwith inform the Council and the Member States of any decision taken under this Article. The Council, acting by a qualified majority, may decide differently. A decision by the Commission not to impose a provisional duty shall not preclude the imposition of such duty at a later date, either at the request of a Member State, if new factors arise, or on the initiative of the Commission.

5. Provisional duties shall have a maximum period of validity of four months. However, where exporters representing a significant percentage of the trade involved so request or, pursuant to a notice of intention from the Commission, do not object, provisional anti-dumping duties may be extended for a further period of two months.

6. Any proposal for definitive action, or for extension of provisional measures, shall be submitted to the Council by the Commission not later than one month before expiry of the period of validity of provisional duties. The Council shall act by a qualified majority.

7. After expiration of the period of validity of provisional duties, the security shall be released as promptly as possible to the extent that the Council has not decided to collect it definitively.

Article 12

Definitive action

1. Where the facts as finally established show that there is dumping or subsidisation and injury caused thereby, and the interests of the Community call for Community intervention, a definitive anti-dumping or countervailing duty shall be imposed by the Council, acting by qualified majority on a proposal submitted by the Commission after consultation.

2. (a) Where a provisional duty has been applied, the Council shall decide, irrespective of whether a definitive anti-dumping or countervailing duty is to be imposed, what proportion of the provisional duty is to be definitively collected. The Council shall act by a qualified majority on a proposal from the Commission.

   (b) The definitive collection of such amount shall not be decided upon unless the facts as finally established show that there has been dumping or subsidisation, and injury. For this purpose, 'injury' shall not include material retardation of the establishment of a Community industry, nor threat of material injury, except where it is found that this would, in the absence of provisional measures, have developed into material injury.

Article 13

General provisions on duties

1. Anti-dumping or countervailing duties, whether provisional or definitive, shall be imposed by Regulation.

2. Such Regulation shall indicate in particular the amount and type of duty imposed, the product covered, the country of origin or export, the name of the supplier, if practicable, and the reasons on which the Regulation is based.

3. The amount of such duties shall not exceed the dumping margin provisionally estimated or finally established or the amount of the subsidy provisionally estimated or finally established; it should be less if such lesser duty would be adequate to remove injury.

4. (a) Anti-dumping and countervailing duties shall be neither imposed nor increased with retroactive effect and shall apply to the products which, after entry into force of such duties, are entered for Community consumption. For this purpose, the date of acceptance by the customs authorities of the declarant's statement of his intention to enter the goods for consumption shall be determinant.

(b) However, where the Council determines:

(i) for dumped products:

- that there is a history of dumping which caused injury or that the importer was, or should have been, aware that the exporter practices dumping and that such dumping would cause injury, and

- that the injury is caused by sporadic dumping i.e., massive dumped imports of a product in a relatively short period, to such an extent that, in order to preclude it recurring, it appears necessary to impose an anti-dumping duty retroactively on those imports; or

(ii) for subsidised products:

- in critical circumstances that injury which is difficult to repair is caused by massive imports in a relatively short period of a product benefiting from export subsidies paid or bestowed inconsistently with the provisions of the GATT and of the Agreement on interpretation and application of Articles VI, XVI and XXIII of the GATT, and

- that it is necessary, in order to preclude the recurrence of such injury, to assess countervailing duties retroactively on these imports; or

(iii) for dumped or subsidised products:

- that an undertaking has been violated,

the definitive anti-dumping or countervailing duties may be imposed on products which were entered for Community consumption not more than 90 days prior to the date of application of provisional duties, except that in the case of violation of an undertaking such retroactive assessment shall not apply to imports entered before the violation.

5. Where a product is imported into the Community from more than one country, duty shall be levied at an appropriate amount on a non-discriminatory basis on all imports of such product found to be dumped or subsidised and causing injury, other than imports from those sources in respect of which undertakings have been accepted.

6. Where the Community industry has been interpreted as referring to the producers in a certain region, the Commission shall give exporters an opportunity to offer undertakings pursuant to Article 10 in respect of the region concerned. If an adequate undertaking is not given promptly or is not fulfilled, a provisional or definitive duty may be imposed in respect of the Community as a whole.

7. In the absence of any special provisions to the contrary adopted when a definitive or provisional anti-dumping or countervailing duty was imposed, the rules on the common definition of the concept of origin and relevant common implementing provisions shall apply.

8. Anti-dumping or countervailing duties shall be collected by Member States in the form, at the rate and according to the other criteria laid down when the duties were imposed, and independently of the cusoms duties, taxes and other charges normally imposed on imports.

9. No product shall be subject to both anti-dumping and countervailing duties for the purpose of dealing with one and the same situation arising from dumping or from the granting of any subsidy.

Article 14

Review

1. The Regulations imposing provisional or definitive anti-dumping or countervailing duties and the decisions to accept undertakings shall be subject to review where warranted. Such review may be held either at the request of a Member State or on the initiative of the Commission or if any interested party so requests and submits positive information substantiating the need for review. Such requests shall be addressed either to a Member State or to the Commission. A Member State receiving any such request shall inform the Commission, which shall notify the other Member States. Where the Commission receives the request, it shall inform the Member States.

2. Where, after consultation, it becomes apparent that review is warranted, the proceedings shall be re-opened in accordance with Article 7, where the circumstances so require. Such re-opening shall not *per se* affect the measures in operation.

3. Where warranted by the review, carried out either with or without reopening of the proceeding, the measures shall be amended, repealed or annulled by the Community institution competent for their introduction. However, where measures have been taken under the transitional provisions of an Act of Accession the Commission shall itself amend, repeal or annul them and shall report this to the Council; the latter may, acting by a qualified majority, decide that different action be taken.

Refund

1. Where an importer can show that the duty collected exceeds the actual dumping margin or the amount of the subsidy, consideration being given to any application of weighted averages, the excess amount shall be reimbursed; where provisional measures were taken, the same shall apply in respect of release of securities.

2. For this purpose, the importer may within three months of the date on which the products were entered for consumption, submit an application to the Member State in the territory of which they were so entered. That Member State shall forward the application to the Commission as soon as possible, either with or without an opinion as to its merits. The Commission shall inform the other Member States forthwith and give its opinion on the matter. If the Member States agree with the opinion given by the Commission or do not object to it within one month of being informed, the Member State in question may decide in accordance with the said opinion. In all other cases, the Commission shall, after consultation, decide whether and to what extent the Member State should grant the application.

Article 16

Final provisions

This Regulation shall not preclude the application of:

1. any special rules laid down in agreements concluded between the Community and third countries;

2. the Community Regulations in the agricultural sector and of Regulations (EEC) No 1059/69[3], (EEC) No 2730/75[4], and (EEC) No 2783/75[5]; this Regulation shall operate by way of complement to those Regulations and in derogation from any provisions thereof which preclude the application of anti-dumping or countervailing duties;

3. special measures, provided that such action does not run counter to obligations under the GATT.

Article 17

Repeal of existing legislation

Regulation (EEC) No 459/68 is hereby repealed.

References to the repealed Regulation shall be construed as references to this Regulation.

Article 18

Entry into force

This Regulation shall enter into force on 1 January 1980.

This Regulation shall be binding in its entirety and directly applicable in all Member States.

Done at Brussels, 20 December 1979.

For the Council
The President
J. TUNNEY

1. O.J. No L 306, 31.10.1978, p. 1.
2. O.J. No L 131, 29.5.1979, p. 1.
3. O.J. No L 141, 12.6.1969, p. 1.
4. O.J. No L 281, 1.11.1975, p. 20.
5. O.J. No L 282, 1.11.1975, p. 104.

ANNEX

ILLUSTRATIVE LIST OF EXPORT SUBSIDIES

(a) The provision by governments of direct subsidies to a firm or an industry contingent upon export performance.

(b) Currency retention schemes or any similar practices which involve a bonus on exports.

(c) Internal transport and freight charges on export shipments, provided or mandated by governments, on terms more favourable than for domestic shipments.

(d) The delivery by governments or their agencies of imported or domestic products or services for use in the production of exported goods, on terms or conditions more favourable than for delivery of like or directly competitive products or services for use on the production of goods for domestic consumption, if (in the case of products) such terms or conditions are more favourable than those commercially available on world markets to their exporters.

(e) The full or partial exemption, remission or deferral specifically related to exports, of direct taxes or social welfare charges paid or payable by industrial or commercial enterprises. Notwithstanding the foregoing, deferral of taxes and charges referred to above need not amount to an export subsidy where, for example, appropriate interest charges are collected.

(f) The allowance of special deductions directly related to exports
or export performance, over and above those granted in respect of
production for domestic consumption, in the calculation of the
base on which direct taxes are charged.

(g) The exemption or remission in respect of the production and distribution of exported products, of indirect taxes in excess of
those levied in respect of the production and distribution of like
products when sold for domestic consumption. The problem of the
excessive remission of value added tax is exclusively covered by
this paragraph.

(h) The exemption, remission or deferral of prior stage cumulative
indirect taxes on goods or services used in the production of exported products in excess of the exemption, remission or deferral
of like prior stage cumulative indirect taxes on goods or services
used in the production of like products when sold for domestic
consumption; provided, however, that prior stage cumulative indirect taxes may be exempted, remitted or deferred on exported products even when not exempted, remitted or deferred on like products when sold for domestic consumption, if the prior stage cumulative indirect taxes are levied on goods that are physically incorporated (making normal allowance for waste) in the exported
product. This paragraph does not apply to value added tax systems
and border tax adjustments related thereto.

(i) The remission or drawback of import charges in excess of those
levied on imported goods that are physically incorporated (making
normal allowance for waste) in the exported product; provided,
however, that in particular cases a firm may use a quantity of
home market goods equal to, and having the same quality and characteristics as, the imported goods as a substitute for them in order
to benefit from this provision if the import and the corresponding
export operations both occur within a reasonable time period,
normally not to exceed two years. This paragraph does not apply
to value added tax systems and border tax adjustments related
thereto.

(j) The provision by governments (or special institutions controlled
by governments) of export credit guarantee or insurance programmes, of insurance or guarantee programmes against increases in
the costs of exported products or of exchange risk programmes,
at premium rates, which are manifestly inadequate to cover the
long-term operating costs and losses of the programmes.

(k) The grant by governments (or special institutions controlled by
and/or acting under the authority of goverments) of export credits
at rates below those which they actually have to pay for the
funds so employed (or would have to pay if they borrowed on international capital markets in order to obtain funds of the same
maturity and denominated in the same currency as the export credit), or the payment by them of all or part of the costs incurred
by exporters or financial institutions in obtaining credits, in
so far as they are used to secure a material advantage in the
field of export credit terms.

Provided, however, that if the country of origin or export is a party to an international undertaking on official export credits to which at least 12 original signatories to the Agreement on Interpretation and Application of Articles VI, XVI and XXIII of the GATT are parties as of 1 January 1979 (or a successor undertaking which has been adopted by those original signatories), or if in practice the country of origin or export applies the interest rate provisions of the relevant undertaking, an export credit practice which is in conformity with those provisions shall not be considered an export subsidy.

(1) Any other charge on the public account constituting an export subsidy in the sense of Article XVI of the GATT.

Notes:

For the purposes of this Annex the following definitions apply:

1. The term 'direct taxes' shall mean taxes on wages, profits, interest, rents, royalties, and all other forms of income, and taxes on the ownership of real property.

2. The term 'import charges' shall mean tariffs, duties and other fiscal charges not elsewhere enumerated in these notes that are levied on imports.

3. The term 'indirect taxes' shall mean sales, excise, turnover, value added, franchise, stamp, transfer, inventory and equipment taxes, border taxes and all taxes other than direct taxes and import charges.

4. 'Prior stage' indirect taxes are those levied on goods or services used directly or indirectly in making the product.

5. 'Cumulative' indirect taxes are multi-staged taxes levied where there is no mechanisn for subsequent crediting of the tax if the goods or services subject to tax at one stage of production are used in a succeeding stage of production.

6. 'Remission' of taxes includes the refund or rebate of taxes.